SUVA STORIES
A HISTORY OF THE CAPITAL OF FIJI

SUVA STORIES
A HISTORY OF THE CAPITAL OF FIJI

EDITED BY NICHOLAS HALTER

ANU PRESS

PACIFIC SERIES

ANU PRESS

Published by ANU Press
The Australian National University
Canberra ACT 2600, Australia
Email: anupress@anu.edu.au

Available to download for free at press.anu.edu.au

ISBN (print): 9781760465339
ISBN (online): 9781760465346

WorldCat (print): 1342093549
WorldCat (online): 1342093576

DOI: 10.22459/SS.2022

This title is published under a Creative Commons Attribution-NonCommercial-NoDerivatives 4.0 International (CC BY-NC-ND 4.0) licence.

The full licence terms are available at creativecommons.org/licenses/by-nc-nd/4.0/legalcode

Cover design and layout by ANU Press. Cover photograph reproduced courtesy of the Fiji Museum ('Street scene in Suva', n.d., Record no. P32.5/8).

This book is published under the aegis of the Pacific Editorial Board of ANU Press.

This edition © 2022 ANU Press

Contents

Acknowledgements	vii
Language Note	ix
Glossary	xi
Chronology	xv
List of Maps and Figures	xxix
List of Authors	xxxiii
Maps	xxxix
Introduction: Reclaiming Suva Nicholas Halter	1

Part 1. Foundations

1.	The Prehistory of Suva Paul Geraghty	25
2.	Suva and the Fate of the Polynesia Company Max Quanchi	55
3.	The Making of a Capital: A Social History of Suva, 1870–1882 Robert Nicole	85
4.	The Making of a Capital: A Social History of Suva, 1882–1890 Robert Nicole	123
5.	Early Suva Fijians – A View Through *Sere Makawa* Simione Sevudredre	153
6.	The Grand Old Man and the Prince of Thieves Anurag Subramani	167

Part 2. Creations

7.	Piecing Together a History of Suva Prison Nicholas Halter	187
8.	Visibly Hidden in Suva: St Giles Jacqueline Leckie	207

9.	Supreme Court Stories: Narrating Violence in Suva Streets and Homes Kate Stevens	229
10.	Race Relations in Colonial Suva, 1945–1970 Robert Norton	247
11.	Methodist Schools in Suva in the Colonial Era Christine Weir	277
12.	From Laucala Bay to the Region: The University of the South Pacific Jacqueline Leckie	293

Part 3. Reflections

13.	Swimming under the *Ivi* Tree: Ratu Sukuna Park, Land Reclamation and Family Connections Kaliopate Tavola	315
14.	Suva – Once a Colonial Town Daryl Tarte	339
15.	Where Is My Home and Where Is My Heart? Kantilal Jinna	349
16.	Raiwaqa and the Playhouse Larry Thomas	367
17.	Minority Melanesians in Suva Anawaite Matadradra	385
18.	Suva: Resilient Coup Capital? Vijay Naidu	399
19.	Wailea Brij V Lal	425

Bibliography	443
Appendix 1. Recorded Population of Suva	465
Appendix 2. Classification of Communal Units of Suvavou Recorded by Anthropologist Arthur Hocart, c. 1912	469
Appendix 3. Classification of Communal Units of Suvavou Recorded by the *Veitarogivanua* in 1902	471
Appendix 4. Classification of Communal Units of Suvavou According to Testimony Recorded by the *Veitarogivanua* in 1921	473
Appendix 5. Classification of Communal Units of Suvavou According to the Final Report of the *Veitarogivanua*	475
Appendix 6. Nursery Rhymes of Fiji	477

Acknowledgements

First and foremost, I am grateful to the authors who committed their time and energy to this project. In addition to writing chapters for this collection, they also reviewed each other's work, shared photographs and stories from their personal lives, made recommendations and introductions in Fiji, and cleared a path for me to bring this project to fruition. There are many others who are not listed as authors but made valuable contributions to this research nonetheless by participating in our monthly Fiji history *talanoas* since 2018. A number of promising chapters and conversations were postponed due to the unexpected disruptions caused by the coronavirus pandemic, and I extend my deepest sympathies to all those in Fiji who were affected by COVID-19. This includes the people of Suvavou, whom I acknowledge as the traditional custodians of the land and pay my respects to their elders, past and present.

Four institutions played a pivotal role in this project. I wish to express my gratitude to the Fiji Museum, including the director Sipiriano Nemani, and their archives unit, Ratu Jone Balenaivalu and Jeremaia Veisa, who kindly provided many photographs from their collection. The National Archives of Fiji, led by Acting Principal Archivist Timoci Balenaivalu, facilitated access to their extensive collections, including their photographs, colonial records and the *Fiji Times*, and kindly offered their conference room as a space for one of our team meetings. Archivist staff Jennifer Voka, Asena Dame, Losena Tudreu, Vaciseva Levu, Amelia Baubau, Emily Rasoqosoqo and former director Opeta Alefaio provided generous assistance too. This book would not have been possible without the support of the University of the South Pacific, which includes the Pacific Collection of the Library, and the School of Law and Social Sciences, headed by Sandra Tarte, and my colleagues Morgan Tuimaleali'ifano, Jacqueline Ryle and Litea Meo-Sewabu. From The Australian National University, I received valuable assistance from Stewart Firth of the ANU Press Board and Jenny Sheehan from the CartoGIS team. Thank you all!

I was fortunate to have many knowledgeable advisers who were always willing to help me and provide encouragement and inspiration. These include Robert Nicole and Anurag Subramani with whom I had wonderful discussions over lunch in Suva. Robin Yarrow and Pita Nacuva were enthusiastic and supportive of my ambitions and took particular care to introduce me to Suva residents. Robin, a passionate history enthusiast who has been leading efforts to create a heritage trail through Suva for many years, shared many of his personal documents and memories. Seona Smiles's and Beth Battrick's editing skills were exceptional and I am grateful for their diligent work. I am grateful too to Paul Geraghty who patiently reviewed the manuscript and gave thoughtful advice on linguistic and historical minutiae. Last, but not least, I am indebted to the late Fiji historian Professor Brij V Lal, who encouraged this research and generously answered my many questions. Fijians mourned his sudden passing on 25 December 2021 and during a memorial at Jai Narayan College, Suva residents celebrated his legacy as a patriotic and distinguished son of Fiji. This book would not have been possible without him.

As the title suggests, this book does not pretend to be *the* authoritative history of Suva. It is an eclectic mix that reflects the diversity of our contributors, and of Suva in general, and admittedly there are important gaps that remain to be filled. The stories presented here only scratch the surface of this remarkable and resilient city. By making this book open access, I hope it prompts new conversations about what a history of Suva might contain in the future.

Language Note

In 2010, the Fiji Government decreed that all Fiji citizens would be legally called 'Fijian', a term once reserved for the indigenous people. Now indigenous Fijians are officially identified as 'iTaukei' and descendants of Indian immigrants as 'Fijians of Indian descent'. Indian indentured labourers who came to Fiji initially identified themselves as 'girmitiyas'. They and their descendants, and later Indian settlers and their descendants, have been described variously as 'Indo-Fijians' and 'Fiji Indians' in public and scholarly discourse. This text quotes historical sources that reflect the language use and attitudes of their time, such as 'native' (used as a synonym of 'Fijian'), 'coolie' (a derogatory term for 'girmitiyas') and 'Polynesian' (used to refer to labourers from other Pacific islands, including Micronesia and Melanesia).

The spelling of indigenous names also varies throughout this text, depending on the historical sources used. For example, 'Nubukalou Creek' was more commonly spelt 'Nabukalou Creek' in colonial documents and Ratu Avorosa was also known as Ratu Aporosa/Ambrose. Over time, the names of indigenous places have been spelt differently (such as Coloisuva, Colo i Suva and Colo-i-Suva, or Viti Levu and Vitilevu), and the correct pronunciation of placenames, and also the pronunciation of certain terms, may not be typically reflected in everyday usage (e.g. Rātū is more commonly spelt Ratu).

Glossary

bati	warriors
besi	bass
bhaiya	older brother, brother
bhindi	okra
bilibili	bamboo raft
bose vakaturaga	Council of Chiefs; sometime in the early twentieth century, the name was modified to *bose levu vakaturaga*, meaning Great Council of Chiefs
buli	Fijian district officer, appointed by the Colonial Government
bure	in Fijian, a men's house; in English, a house of traditional materials
butukai	a style of dance resembling the movements of treading for freshwater mussels
buturaki	to beat up
camakau	outrigger canoe
colo	hill country; interior
coolie	a disparaging term used in colonial Fiji to denote an Indian indentured labourer
dakua	large forest tree with useful timber: Pacific kauri, *Agathis macrophylla*
dalo	taro, *Colocasia esculenta*
dānisi	Western-style dance
dogo	mangrove

domotolu	trio where one sings the melody, another high tenor and the third harmonises in a lower pitch
drua	double-hulled, traditional Fijian sailing vessel
ghugri	spicy cooked green peas
gonedau	traditional hereditary fishers
icavuti	title, name by which a person or group is identified, the (usually honorific) name by which a kin-group is known
ikanakana	piece of land belonging to a clan, used for planting food crops
ilālā	portent
isulu	clothing
iTaukei	the original people of the land, indigenous Fijians
ivi	Polynesian chestnut, *Inocarpus fagifer*
izzat	honour, reputation or prestige
kai	inhabitant of
kaiwai or *qalivakawai*	sea people
kalokalo	star
kalokalo vakabuina	comet
kanikani	a dry and scaly skin condition that results from excessive drinking of *yaqona*
katikati	women and children
kena iloloku	sign of mourning
kere tūraga	requesting a chief
kerekere	please, a word that introduces a request
kisikisi	a small sea crab, *Matuta* spp
koro	village
korowaiwai	ring-ditch fortification
kumala	sweet potato, *Ipomoea batatas*
laga/lagalaga	to sing, lead off a song
lairo	land crab, *Cardisoma* spp
lālā	customary obligation to a chief

lali	wooden gong or drum
lila balavu	historic infectious disease that devastated the Fijian population in c. 1800
lotu	religion
lovo	earth oven
madrai	traditionally, fermented food such as breadfruit; in modern use bread
masi	paper mulberry, *Broussonetia papyrifera*, and the bark cloth made from it
mataisau	traditional carpenters
matanibure or *matabure*	extended family, a subdivision of a *mataqali*, hence corresponding to the official term *tokatoka*
matanitū	a political federation of *vanua*; state or kingdom
mataqali	landowning unit or clan
matenisolo	tinea, a skin infection
meke	traditional Fijian dance
mithai	Indian sweets
puja	act of Hindu worship
sagale	tree found in mangrove swamps, *Lumnitzera littorea*
salusalu	garland
saqā	barrel or tankard
sautabu	chiefly burial ground
sere makawa	old song
serenicumu	song sung by men facing each other with heads down in a circle
sōlevu	traditional ceremony involving gift exchange
solomoni or *kai Solomoni*	people of Melanesian descent in Fiji
soro	to surrender or apologise in traditional manner
tabu	taboo, prohibited or restricted by social custom
tabua	whale's tooth
tākia	open outrigger canoe with no sail or deck for short trips on rivers or in coastal waters, now obsolete

tātābani	two people sing a line before the rest of the group joins in
tauratale	dance with a partner, usually in a village
tiri	kinds of mangrove with aerial roots, *Rhizophora* spp
tokatoka	official term for family unit, see *matanibure*
Tukutuku Rāraba	historical report of *yavusa* kept by the Native Lands Commission
turaganikoro	village headman
vadivadi	plucking, strumming
vakabābā	third voice that harmonises at a lower pitch
vakavanua	traditional, customary
vale ni bia	brewery
vanua	territory, land, country, nation, place; people; typically, a *vanua* comprises a number of villages speaking the same communalect
vasu	offspring who can make demands for services or goods from their mother's village, especially from their mother's brothers
vatu ni irevo	earth oven stone
Veitarogivanua	Native Lands Commission
vucu	traditional chanting
vude	social dance that involves a lot of bobbing up and down
vūlagi	visitor, guest
yaqona	kava, *Piper methysticum*
yavusa	tribe, the largest official kinship and social division of Fijian society, consisting of the descendants of one originator
yavutū	ancestral home

Chronology

3000 BP	The Fiji Islands are occupied by the Lapita people. While it is possible they landed on the Suva peninsula, archaeological evidence suggests other areas of Fiji are settled first. Later, iTaukei may have traversed the island of Viti Levu, from Saivou in what is now Ra province, or from Matailobau, close to the junction of the Wainibuka and Wainimala rivers. The people of Suva peninsula speak two languages. The Walu communalect is spoken by the fishers and carpenters who live in or near what is now called Walu Bay, and the Suva communalect is introduced by people from the hill country.
1643 AD	The Fiji Islands are sighted by Dutch explorer Abel Tasman. They were later visited by Captain James Cook and Captain William Bligh, who were followed by traders in the early 1800s.
1800s	European accounts suggest there are at least four habitations on the Suva peninsula: a ring-ditch fortification known as Solia, and three hillforts known as Nauluvatu, Nairairaiwaqa and Vatuwaqa. Solia is a new settlement, and later becomes the combined village of Suva. The title of the chief is Rokotui Suva. Different accounts attribute its founding to one of the sons of Roko Saketa, namely Batilekaleka (also known as Batileka or Tuivuya) or Tabakaucoro (also known as Rō Ravulo or Ravulo).
1835	Methodist missionaries David Cargill and William Cross arrive in the eastern Lau group with the intention of converting Fijians to Christianity.
1839	A mission is set up in Rewa, east of Suva.

1840	Methodist missionary Thomas Jagger records that one Suva man became Christian on 22 February, and Methodist missionary David Cargill records the conversion of the 'King of Suva' (Ravulo) and two of his people on 17 May. That same year, the United States Exploring Expedition surveys Suva Harbour.
1841	The *matanitū* of Rewa and Suva prepare for war.
1842	On 23 June, the Rewa army attack Suva. Englishmen William Diaper and Robert Stevens visit Suva to harvest *dakua*.
1843	On 5 April, the Rewa fleet and its allies land troops at Suva and begin their assault. Over several days Suva is sacked and burnt. On 9 April the people surrender and are massacred shortly after. Ravulo, the Rokotui Suva, and the survivors flee Suva.
1844	In January, Bau and Rewa are at war and the Suva army joins the fight. The war concludes in December when Lomainikoro, the chiefly village of Rewa, is sacked.
c. 1845	Suva is rebuilt with the assistance of its allies. Ravulo sends a delegation to Bau to ask for the hand of Adi Elenoa Mila, and later they will have four children.
1849	On 4 July the store of an American trader, JB Williams, is destroyed by fire on nearby Nukulau Island. The Americans claim a debt is owed by Bauan chief Ratu Seru Cakobau.
c. 1850	Suva wins a battle against Vuna and kills their leader Rō Camaisala.
1852	In the passage on the reef opposite Nukulau, the Sydney whaling ship *Solomon Saltus* drifts ashore and is wrecked.
c. 1854	Suva probably becomes Christian at this time, following the conversion of their overlord Cakobau, Vunivalu of Bau.
1855	Cakobau and his Bauan forces secure victory over Rewa at the Battle of Kaba, aided by Tongan warriors.
c. 1857	Ravulo dies in Bau. His widow and children return to Bau. His son Avorosa Tuivuya (also known as Ratu Aporosa or Ambrose) succeeds him as Rokotui Suva.

1860	The settlement at Levuka grows as white settlers begin to arrive in larger numbers. Colonel WT Smythe recommends to the British Government that if it chooses to annex the islands, the capital should be moved from Levuka to Suva to allow for expansion.
1861	British war ship HMS *Harrier* destroys the towns of Vutia and Kinoya.
1864	The Polynesian labour trade begins, as labourers recruited from the islands of New Hebrides and Solomons are brought to Fiji to work in the cotton plantations. They later become known as *kai Solomoni*.
1868	Cakobau persuades the Rokotui Suva to allow him to sell most of the Suva peninsula to the Melbourne-based Polynesia Company to settle his debts.
1869	The first issue of the *Fiji Times* appears on Saturday, 4 September in Levuka. In May, the *Springbok* carries 18 passengers to Suva. One of the passengers, Frederick Cook, is the Polynesia Company's manager who is sent to investigate the delays in obtaining titles to all 200,000 acres granted by Cakobau. The *Springbok* is followed by the bulk of the new settlers on the *Alhambra* on 4 September the following year. These travellers include shareholders in the Polynesia Company with the intention of planting cotton or sugarcane.
1871	A serious cyclone causes extensive damage to Suva. The first sitting of the House of Representatives of Cakobau's government begins in Levuka on 1 August.
1872	The first cane sugar mill in Fiji is built in Suva and is owned by Paul Joske and William Brewer. Known as Naiqaqi, it is located just off Victoria Parade (near the present-day Fiji Broadcasting Commission building). In November a major disturbance breaks out on the premises of the Suva Sugar Plantation Company.
1872	Suva is designated as a Port of Entry.
1873	Ratu Aporosa is appointed *buli* of Suva. Cakobau's government attempts to control the interior Colo region of Viti Levu who dispute his claim to be 'Tui Viti'.

1874	On 10 October, Fiji formally becomes a colony of Great Britain with the signing of the Deed of Cession in Levuka.
1875	A measles epidemic breaks out in Fiji, killing at least a quarter of the population. In December the first British governor of the colony, Sir Arthur Gordon, travels to Suva on a scoping trip to consider the suitability of the area as the new capital.
1876	Suva's first major infrastructure development, the Waimanu Road, begins.
c. 1877	A new *buli* of Suva, Mosese Rokotalau, is appointed. The British Home Office and Queen give approval for Fiji's capital to move from Levuka to Suva.
1878	The Lands Claim Commission begins investigating European claims in the Suva area and discovers only some blocks claimed by company shareholders are occupied by bona fide settlers.
1879	Five hundred indentured labourers arrive from India on 14 May on board the ship *Leonidas*. Most of the *Leonidas* labourers work on Victoria Parade, Suva's main thoroughfare. Around the same time Ratu Aporosa is reappointed as *buli* of Suva.
1880	Ninety-two Suva allotments are sold at a public auction under an *ivi* tree by Nubukalou Creek on 22 November. This place, later known as the 'ivi triangle', is distinct from another *ivi* tree located just over 100 metres south, next to the ocean.
1881	The first legislation for the control and management of towns is passed – Suva was first proclaimed a town under this Ordinance on 2 July and a Town Board was established. Ordinance No. 4 for Regulating the Alignments of Streets in the Town of Suva is passed. Early reclamation work begins along Thomson Street; the Queens Wharf is constructed and a botanical gardens established near Waimanu Road. George L Griffiths launches the *Suva Times* on 29 October.

1882	On 30 August the governor and his staff move from Levuka and Suva formally becomes the capital. By August or September the iTaukei of Suva village are moved to Narikoso, which became known as Suvavou ('New Suva'). The land they once occupied becomes the grounds of the Governor's Residence, and later the Fiji Museum and botanical gardens.
1883	Suva Town Board is established and Suva Public School is founded.
1884	The Public Lunatic Asylum is established. On the night of 11 May the Indian immigrant ship *Syria* is wrecked on Nasilai reef in 1884. It is one of the worst maritime disasters in Fiji's history – 59 people die in the tragedy.
1885	The Fiji Medical School is founded, training students from around the Pacific region. Pacific Islanders from Wallis and Futuna are brought over to assist with the construction of the Sacred Heart Cathedral (which will be consecrated and completed in 1902), and are then settled in Villa Maria, a piece of Catholic-owned land, located just below Mead Road.
1886	On 3 May several gangs of labourers at the plantation in Koronivia (Lower Rewa) organise a strike, with at least 40 of them walking to the Immigration Office in Suva town. The first telephone line is installed between Government House and the Colonial Secretary's Office in March. Tramways are also constructed on Pier Street, Victoria Parade, Pratt Street, Scott Street, Thomson Street and Renwick Road.
1887	The *Fiji Times* moves its offices from Levuka to Suva and incorporates the *Suva Times* into its publication. One hundred and thirty labourers from Nausori plantation march in protest to the agent-general's residence on 6 April.
1888	The Suva warden (mayor), Simeon Lazarus, and the Suva Town Board attempt to prohibit 'Indians, Natives of Fiji, and Polynesians' from using the Suva Sea Baths.
1890	A market for the sale of produce is finally completed. The road from Vatuwaqa to Nasova (in Nasēsē) is completed.

1891	The Suva Sea Baths are opened to the public near the current site of the Suva Olympic Pool. Later, perhaps in 1927, a smaller pool of inferior quality was constructed for non-Europeans beside the main baths.
1892	A Native Dances Ordinance prohibits all *meke* or ceremonial dancing and singing within town boundaries without a permit. A curfew is also imposed between 11 pm and 5 am for 'Indians' and all Islanders.
1898	Ratu Aporosa leads a group of eight Suvavou elders and presents a written submission to government expressing their dissatisfaction with the £200 that villagers were given as compensation for their move to Suvavou. Miss Hannah Dudley establishes the first Methodist school in Toorak for the education of Indian girls. It later becomes Dudley House School.
1902	The Trans-Pacific cable reaches Fiji, connecting North America with Australia and New Zealand.
1904	The Fiji Museum is founded. It is moved several times over the next few decades, to the Town Hall, Veivueti House and Carnegie Library. The first motor car arrives in Suva on 28 December.
1905	The Queen Victoria Memorial Hall (now Suva Town Hall) is opened. The Australian cricket team plays a game against Fiji at Albert Park on its way to tour England.
1909	The Suva City Carnegie Library is opened on 20 November.
1910	A fierce cyclone damages Suva on 25 March.
1911	Reclamation works to the north of Nubukalou Creek for the new Kings Wharf and the Public Works Department depot. The Queens Wharf is demolished and a new wharf constructed the following year.
1913	The botanical gardens are moved to their current location, at Governor Thurston's request.
1914	The Grand Pacific Hotel is built by the New Zealand–owned Union Steamship Company.
1915	The first Fijian contingent sails for war in Europe aboard the RMS *Makura*.

1916	The Indian indentured labour trade (known as *girmit*) ends. An estimated 60,537 Indian *girmitiya* came to Fiji between 1879 and 1916.
1917	The Fiji Labour Corps departs for the European warfront on 19 May, the day after a farewell at the Grand Pacific Hotel, and a march through the town to the wharf.
1918	Suva Grammar School is officially opened on 9 July. A few months later on 14 November the Spanish Flu is carried to Fiji aboard the New Zealand ship *Talune* from Auckland. Approximately 9,000 people (5 per cent of the population) died between November 1918 and April 1919.
1919	Suva Methodist Boys' School is established for Fijian and Indo-Fijian boys in Toorak.
1920	Indian workers at the Public Works Department and the Suva Municipal Council go on strike. It spreads beyond the capital and leads to imprisonments and violent reprisals.
1921	Government House is struck by lightning that starts a fire. It is rebuilt seven years later.
1923	A fire breaks out in Cumming Street on 11 February, destroying a large number of buildings including the market.
1928	On 5 June, the first aircraft to land in Fiji touches down in Albert Park. The *Southern Cross* is captained by Australian pilot Charles Kingsford Smith. That same year, the Central Medical School (formerly Fiji Medical School) is established.
1934	Ballantine Memorial School is founded in Muanikau for the education of girls. The Bank of New South Wales building (now Westpac) is constructed on the site of the old post office. This site is formally the site of the first market.
1935	The Methodist Centenary Church is established in Steward Street. Broadcasting services begin in Fiji by a local subsidiary of Amalgamated Wireless (Australasia) Ltd.
1936	The Public Lunatic Asylum is renamed the Suva Mental Hospital.
1937	The foundation stone is laid for the Government Buildings opposite Albert Park. It is finished in 1939. A new wing is added in 1967.

1940	Following the outbreak of World War II the previous year, the 18th Army Troops Company arrives in Suva, followed by the 8th New Zealand Infantry Brigade. A number of alterations follow – a main camp is established at Samabula. Nausori Airport is built, Suva Girls' Grammar School is converted into a military hospital and construction begins on air raid shelters, underground tunnels and defensive guns as part of the war preparations. The Native Lands Trust Board is established with its headquarters in Suva to oversee land tenure for the welfare of indigenous Fijians.
1941	Another damaging cyclone hits Suva on 20 February.
1942	On 18 July, the United States army assumes full responsibility for the defence of Fiji. Air raid alarms are tested, night-time blackouts and a curfew are imposed.
1943	The Royal New Zealand Air Force's Catalinas start arriving at the newly constructed air base at Laucala Bay in April. The 164th Infantry Regiment is allocated the role of defending Suva and the coast to the west.
1945	Union Club, Fiji's first multiracial social body, is formed in Suva. A Victory Parade marches to Albert Park on 16 August.
1946	The national census confirms Indo-Fijians outnumber iTaukei for the first time.
1950	The first South Pacific conference is held in Suva.
1951	A commercial flying boat service by Tasman Empire Airways Limited begins operations from Auckland to Suva and then to Apia and Rarotonga. The service to Suva is replaced by DC-6 aircraft flying to Nadi in 1954.
1952	Eight hundred men of the 1st Battalion Fiji Infantry Regiment board the troopship *Asturias* for Malaya on 8 January. Another damaging cyclone wreaks havoc on Suva on 29 January. The town boundary is increased to an area of over 6 square miles.

1953	On 14 September an earthquake destroys houses and creates a tsunami that breaks over the sea wall in town, damaging the wharf and many vessels. Suva is proclaimed a city on 7 October under the Local Government (Town) Ordinance of 1947. On 17 December Queen Elizabeth II and the Duke of Edinburgh make their first visit to Suva during a six-month Commonwealth tour.
1954	On 1 February Queen Elizabeth II arrives in Suva aboard her royal yacht. The Fiji Museum is moved to a permanent building at its present location in Thurston Gardens. The Fiji College of Agriculture is established.
1956	The first Miss Hibiscus Festival beauty pageant is held. It becomes an annual event in Suva. That same year the liquor permit system that regulates the consumption of alcohol by non-whites is relaxed, and Suva Sea Baths are no longer segregated. Residents celebrate the return of soldiers from the Malayan Campaign who march through the city. Albert Park also hosts a cricket match between Fiji and the West Indies, which Fiji wins.
1957	The Fiji Law Society is formed in Suva.
1958	iTaukei statesman Sir Ratu Lala Sukuna's casket is driven through Suva on 9 June. A Housing Authority is established to address the pressures caused by population growth and the first public housing was constructed in the suburb of Raiwaqa a year later.
1959	Between 7 and 12 December the Wholesale and Retail General Workers' Union goes on strike to demand a basic wage of 6 pounds sterling. The stalemate between unionists and the government leads to unprecedented rioting and looting in the city. A curfew is declared and the military is mobilised. In the same year the Derrick Technical Institute is established on a block of land located at the junction of Princes and King's roads, formerly the site of Suva's Public Works Department Depot. The Derrick Institute later became the Fiji Institute of Technology, and then the Fiji National University.

1960	Ratu Sukuna Memorial School is opened in Nabua. The Boys Grammar School and the Girls Grammar School decide to unite and move the combined school to Veiuto, Nasēsē. The Suva Mental Hospital is renamed St Giles Psychiatric Hospital around this time.
1963	Derrick Technical Institute is opened. The first South Pacific Games are held in Suva.
1965	The National Federation Party, the first political party to be formalised in Fiji, establishes its Suva branch. The Pacific Theological College is established.
1968	The University of the South Pacific (USP) is opened at Laucala Bay on 5 February. iTaukei rallies and marches in Suva and other towns protest against the Federation Party regaining all communal Indian seats in Legislative Council by-elections.
1970	Queen Elizabeth II presents a charter to Masiofa Fetauimalemau Mataʻafa of Western Samoa, the first pro-chancellor of USP, at a grand ceremony in the former Royal New Zealand Air Force hangar at Laucala Bay on 5 March. Fiji celebrates its independence from the British Empire at Albert Park on 10 October. Ratu Sir Kamisese Mara is Fiji's first prime minister.
1971	Fiji's first outdoor rock music festival is held at Laucala Bay. In July, the National Archives of Fiji is formally established with an amendment of the Public Records Ordinance. It has been known as the Central Archives of Fiji and the Western Pacific High Commission since 1954.
1972	The first South Pacific Festival of Arts is held at Albert Park and lasts a fortnight. The first general elections under the 1970 constitution are held, and the Alliance Party wins 33 of the 52 seats in the Lower House.
1973	Ratu Sir George Cakobau is appointed governor-general and occupies Government House on Queen Elizabeth Drive.
1976	The botanical gardens are renamed Thurston Gardens.

1977	Suva hosts the British Lions in 1977 at Buckhurst Park in a rugby game that Fiji wins 25–21. In that same year the national soccer team defeats Australia 1–0, also at Buckhurst Park.
1979	The South Pacific Games are held in Suva from 28 August to 8 September.
1984	The Reserve Bank of Fiji is opened.
1987	Following the national election, a coalition government led by Dr Timoci Bavadra comes to power. Lieutenant-Colonel Sitiveni Rabuka executes a military coup d'état on 14 May. Armed troops enter the Parliament buildings in Suva. Rabuka conducts a second coup in September, after which Fiji is declared a republic.
1990	A new constitution is promulgated giving Fijians 37 seats in Parliament, Indians 27, general voters five and Rotumans one.
1992	The first general election under the new 1990 constitution is conducted and Rabuka becomes prime minister. In June a new Parliament complex, built with indigenous Fijian designs, is opened in Veiuto. Suva hosts the World Netball Youth Cup.
1993	Community psychiatric nursing for the Suva area begins.
1997	St Giles Day Care Centre for the rehabilitation of discharged patients is established. For the first time the leader of the Opposition, Jai Ram Reddy, addresses the Great Council of Chiefs in Suva on 6 June.
1997	Following a Constitution Review Commission that was appointed in 1995, the Constitution Amendment Bill becomes law.
1999	The Fijian Labour Party wins the national elections and forms the People's Coalition Government with three other political parties. Mahendra Chaudhry is sworn in as prime minister, and becomes the first Indo-Fijian prime minister of Fiji. Hardline iTaukei nationalists are angered by this outcome.

2000	On 19 May, soldiers of the Counter Revolutionary Warfare Unit led by George Speight enter Parliament buildings and hold the parliamentarians hostage for 56 days. Civil unrest follows with looting and rioting in town. An interim government is appointed on 28 July.
2001	Laisenia Qarase is elected prime minister when his party, the Soqosoqo Duavata ni Lewenivanua, wins the majority of seats in the national election.
2003	The South Pacific Games are held in Suva from 28 June to 12 July.
2006	Commodore Josaia Voreqe (Frank) Bainimarama seizes power in a military coup on 5 December.
2009	The Great Council of Chiefs complex is opened at Draiba.
2012	The Great Council of Chiefs is de-established by military decree.
2013	A new constitution is promulgated by a military-backed interim government. It replaces the Senate and House of Representatives with a 50-member Parliament chamber.
2014	Bainimarama's Fiji First Party wins the national election and Parliament returns to the Government Buildings on Victoria Parade.
2016	On 20 February, the most powerful cyclone to hit Fiji, Cyclone Winston, makes landfall causing massive devastation and killing 42 people. Fiji wins its first gold medal in Sevens Rugby at the 2016 Olympics in Rio de Janeiro. The men's team parades through the city on 12 August.
2019	The central building of the Great Council of Chiefs is destroyed by fire.
2020	The COVID-19 pandemic breaches Fiji's quarantine controls on 19 March when the first case is recorded in Lautoka, and subsequent cases are traced to Suva. Borders are closed to nonresidents, and curfews and lockdowns are imposed. The last instance of community transmission is recorded on 18 April and restrictions are gradually eased. COVID cases are limited to managed quarantine facilities at the border. Fiji celebrates its 50th anniversary of Independence at Albert Park on 10 October. By the end of the year, Fiji records 49 COVID cases in total.

2021	On 19 April a case of COVID community transmission in Nadi is detected and rapidly spreads throughout Viti Levu. The new 'Delta' variant is highly infectious, so containment areas are established in Suva, Nausori and Lami, and Suva is placed under lockdown on 26 April. The World Health Organization threshold for an out-of-control pandemic is a daily test positivity rate of 5 per cent, which Fiji passes in June. By July, COVID-positive cases exceed 1,000 per day and health services are under severe stress. On 22 July the government announces that it will no longer test people with COVID symptoms in the Suva–Nausori containment zone, and advises symptomatic people to self-quarantine at home. As the pace of vaccinations increases, some businesses are permitted to reopen. Fiji's borders re-open to international visitors from 1 December.
2022	The Ministry of Health confirms the presence of a new COVID variant named 'Omicron' in Fiji on 4 January. Suva businesses welcome the decision of the Fijian Government to lift its nationwide curfew on 7 February. As of 15 August, Fiji has recorded 67,969 infections and 875 deaths directly attributed to COVID since March 2020.

List of Maps and Figures

Map 1: The Fiji Islands.	xxxix
Map 2: Provinces of Viti Levu.	xl
Map 3: Suva and surrounds.	xl
Map 4: Early settlements of Suva.	xli
Map 5: Suva City and Lami town and environs.	xlii
Figure 0.1: 'Native village near Suva', n.d.	5
Figure 0.2: Suva Harbour, n.d.	7
Figure 0.3: A view of Suva Harbour and Queen's Wharf, n.d.	7
Figure 0.4: 'Indian at Suva Street, 1970'.	8
Figure 0.5: Nubukalou Creek, n.d.	11
Figure 0.6: Women at a market, Suva, 1939.	11
Figure 0.7: Vegetable market in Suva, 1950.	12
Figure 0.8: Indian women in Suva, 1949.	12
Figure 0.9: A garment shop, Suva, n.d.	13
Figure 0.10: Suva town, n.d.	14
Figure 0.11: Suva town, n.d.	14
Figure 0.12: Tamavua, n.d.	17
Figure 1.1: 'Native church at Suva 1870'.	49
Figure 2.1: Sketch of contested blocks of land between Walu Bay and Tamavua River, 1873.	60
Figure 2.2: Polynesia Company plan of selections at Grove Point, 1871.	62
Figure 2.3: Sketch of blocks claimed by the Polynesia Company on Suva peninsula and the hinterland, c.1870s.	64
Figure 2.4: Brewer and Joske's Sugar Mill, Suva, 1875.	70

Figure 2.5: Company map of selections at Suva peninsula, 4 February 1873. Signed by Frederick Cook and GD McCartney, directors, and Joshua Finner, manager. 72

Figure 2.6: Plan for a township; surveyed by DB Sellars, January 1870. The plan was misnamed. It was the plan for Lami Town, west of Suva. 75

Figure 3.1: Map of Suva with proposed township (shaded) and site for cemetery. 100

Figure 3.2: Sketch of the proposed Suva township, 1879. 101

Figure 3.3: Town of Suva and adjoining lands, Viti Levu, Fiji, 1885. 102

Figure 3.4: Bolton Corney report on the selection of a suitable site for a permanent public burial ground in Suva, 1882. 110

Figure 3.5: Letter from Ratu Aporosa Tuivuya to the Native Commissioner, 20 November 1882. 119

Figure 3.6: Map of Suva showing township lots, 1882. 121

Figure 4.1: 'The business street of Suva, Fiji', n.d. 125

Figure 4.2: Plan of the proposed Vatuwaqa settlement, 1887. 131

Figure 4.3: Map of the town of Suva and adjoining lands, 1889. 133

Figure 4.4: Cumming Street under construction, 1876. 140

Figure 4.5: Queen Victoria Memorial Hall, time of Fiji Agricultural Industrial Show, 1908. 142

Figure 4.6: Proposed site for swimming baths – Suva, 1890. 143

Figure 4.7: Ratu Aporosa and Adi Kelera, n.d. 149

Figure 5.1: 'In native village near Suva – Fiji' (probably Suvavou), 1884. 154

Figure 5.2: 'Early Suva: Fijian market. Vuniivi tree, c. 1892'. 155

Figure 5.3: 'Early Suva: Fijian market, c. 1892'. 155

Figure 7.1: 'View of the jail and depot from the hospital', n.d. 191

Figure 7.2: 'Suva Prison, 1946'. 192

Figure 8.1: Walls of St Giles Hospital, 1965. 209

Figures 8.2 and 8.3: Moala ward, 2018. 215

Figure 8.4: Mock ECT, St Giles Hospital, 1965 with Dr M Vuki, deputy head orderly, Asena Ranadi and head orderly, Charlie Sachs. 220

Figure 8.5: Open day, St Giles, 1981. 226

Figure 9.1: Government Buildings from Fiji Club, n.d. 232

LIST OF MAPS AND FIGURES

Figure 9.2: Government House, Suva, Fiji, 1884. 232

Figure 10.1: 'Swimming Baths Suva, About 1930'. 258

Figure 10.2: AD Patel speaks at a Federation Party election rally in Suva, 1966. 263

Figure 10.3: The Indian polling Centre in Suva during the elections for the Southern division, Suva 1963. 271

Figure 10.4: Indian polling station outside Suva Sea Baths, 1966. 273

Figure 10.5: Fijians go in to vote, in mourning dress after death of Ratu Mara's father, Suva 1966. 273

Figure 10.6: Main figures, from left to right: Ratu Sir Edward Cakobau, Andrew Deoki, Aileen Regan and Douglas Brown, on candidates nomination day in Suva, 1966. 274

Figure 10.7: Fijians assisting at the stall of an Indian candidate contesting in a multiracial ('cross voting') electorate, Suva, 1966. 275

Figure 11.1: Miss Griffen and her students, 1935. 281

Figure 11.2: Ballantine schoolgirls at the original site in Muanikau, 1935. 287

Figure 11.3: Photos of Ballantine School on its original site 1935. 288

Figure 11.4: Ballantine students and staff with Australian visitors, 1935. 289

Figure 12.1: 'The Royal New Zealand Air Force base at Laucala Bay'. Painting by Maurice Conley, 1966, now in the USP Chancellery Board Room. 295

Figure 12.2: Women's Hall, USP, 1968. 307

Figure 12.3: USP students demonstrating in downtown Suva against French nuclear testing in the Pacific, 1972. 308

Figure 12.4: Extension Services, 1977. USP at Suva was a global pioneer in the development of distance education long before digital platforms. 311

Figure 12.5: Graduation at the Lower Campus (that was also the gymnasium), 1979. 312

Figure 13.1: The *ivi* tree (1959). The *ivi* tree in the middle of the picture stands in front of what is Vanua Arcade today. The sea is now part of Ratu Sukuna Park. 316

Figure 13.2: The *ivi* tree, from where McDonalds restaurant is today (1959). Part of the Cable & Wireless Building can be seen to the right of the picture. 316

Figure 13.3: Victoria Parade, n.d. 319

Figure 13.4: Suva wharf, n.d. In the background next to the Union Steamship Company store is the same *ivi* tree. 320

Figure 13.5: Victoria Parade, n.d. 323

Figure 13.6: World War I parade near the Ivi Triangle. 329

Figure 14.1: Corner of Scott Street and Renwick Road, n.d. 340

Figure 14.2: Nabukalou Creek, n.d. 341

Figure 14.3: Carnegie Library, n.d. 342

Figure 14.4: Interior of the Grand Pacific Hotel, n.d. 343

Figure 14.5: Welcoming Charles Kingsford Smith's aeroplane *Southern Cross* at Suva, Fiji, 1928. 344

Figure 14.6: Aerial view of Grand Pacific Hotel, Albert Park and Government Buildings, n.d. 344

Figure 15.1: Borron House, n.d. 351

Figure 15.2: The aftermath of the Cumming Street fire, 1923. 354

Figure 15.3: Morris Hedstrom building next to Nabukalou Creek, n.d. 355

Figure 15.4: Aerial view of Kings Wharf, n.d. 356

Figure 15.5: Indian musical group auditioning at Broadcasting House, 1957. 359

Figure 15.6: Indian ladies at Ruve Park, Samabula, 1968. This was presumably to commemorate the end of Indian indenture in Fiji. 362

Figure 15.7: Indian men at Ruve Park, Samabula, 1968. This was presumably to commemorate the end of Indian indenture in Fiji. 362

Figure 16.1: Elephant house, Raiwaqa, 2022. 369

Figure 16.2: Outdoor market, Suva, 1939. 370

Figure 16.3: One of the original houses left in Raiwaqa, 2022. 375

Figure 16.4: The Playhouse, 2022. 376

Figure 17.1: A Solomon Islander's house in Suva, Fiji, approximately 1890. 387

List of Authors

Paul Geraghty

Paul graduated from Cambridge with an MA in Modern Languages and earned his PhD from the University of Hawai'i, with a dissertation on the history of the Fijian languages. He was director of the Institute of Fijian Language and Culture in Suva from 1986 to 2001, and is currently associate professor in linguistics at the University of the South Pacific (USP). Author and editor of several books (including *The History of the Fijian Languages* [University of Hawai'i Press, 1983] and the Lonely Planet *Fijian Phrasebook*) and numerous articles on Fijian and Pacific languages, culture and history, he is also well known in Fiji as a newspaper columnist and radio and TV presenter.

Nicholas Halter

Nicholas is a lecturer in history at USP. He has been teaching courses on Pacific history and historiography at Laucala campus since 2016, and together with his students developed the Fijian History website and mobile app to document some of the historical sites of Fiji. Nicholas has ongoing interests in the history of Australia's relationship with the Pacific Islands, histories of tourism and travel, and the Micronesian region. His monograph *Australian Travellers in the South Seas* was published by ANU Press in 2021.

Kantilal Jinna

Kanti was born in Kaunikuila, Suva. He completed his tertiary schooling in New Zealand, United Kingdom and Australia. He was the chief librarian of the Library Service of Fiji. Kanti migrated to Australia in 1984 and has since lived in Canberra and worked in librarianship and publishing. He is retired and continues his passion in travelling to and in Fiji, reading, writing, publishing and multicultural and multifaith activities. He lives with his wife Jyoti, two children and four grandchildren. In 2010, he received the Member of the Order of Fiji Award (MF) and in 2018 he received the Medal of the Order of Australia Award (OAM) for service to the community.

Brij Vilash Lal

Born in 1952 in Labasa, the grandson of a *girmitiya*, Brij rose from humble beginnings to become Fiji's most prolific and renowned scholar. He published extensively on Fijian history and politics, as well as the Indian diaspora, over 50 monographs and edited collections. An overview of Brij's writings is best obtained by consulting his three volumes of collected essays: *Chalo Jahaji* (2000), *Intersections* (2011) and *Levelling Wind* (2019). He was a member of the Order of Australia and an Officer of the Order of Fiji. In 2009 Brij and his wife Padma were banned for life from Fiji because the Bainimarama government deemed them a threat to Fiji's peace and security. His chapter, reprinted here, was written shortly before he was deported. Brij was emeritus professor of The Australian National University when he died suddenly on 25 December 2021 at his home in Brisbane.

Jacqueline Leckie

Jacqueline is an adjunct research fellow with the Stout Centre for New Zealand Studies, Victoria University of Wellington, and a conjoint associate professor, University of Newcastle. Her research and publications are on the history and anthropology of the Asia-Pacific. Jacqui has taught in the Department of Anthropology and Archaeology at Otago University, USP and at Kenyatta University. In 2018 she was the J.D. Stout Research Fellow at the Stout Research Centre at Victoria University of Wellington. Her most recent books include *Invisible: New Zealand's History of Excluding Kiwi-Indians* (Massey University Press, 2021) and *Colonizing Madness: Asylum and Community in Fiji* (University of Hawai'i Press, 2020).

Anawaite Matadradra

Anawaite is a PhD candidate in the School of Law and Social Sciences at USP. She holds a Bachelor of Arts degree in history and politics and a Master of Arts in development studies from USP. Her PhD thesis is titled 'Melanesians on the Margins: A comparative study of Melanesian communities in Fiji and Samoa'. Anawaite is from Deuba in Serua Province with maternal links to the Ra province.

Vijay Naidu

Vijay obtained his undergraduate and masters qualifications at USP. He completed his doctoral studies in the sociology of development at the University of Sussex, England. He served USP in various academic and senior administration positions. From 2003 to 2006, he was professor and director of development studies at the Victoria University of Wellington. He is currently adjunct professor in the School of Law and Social Sciences, USP. He has researched and written on a range of areas concerning development of Pacific Island countries, including on poverty, social protection and human security.

Robert Nicole

Robert was educated at Suva Grammar School, USP (BA and MA) and the University of Canterbury (PhD). He has held academic and research positions at USP and the University of Canterbury, and has also worked for the Ministry of Pacific Island Affairs in New Zealand. He currently lectures in politics at USP. Robert's publications span several disciplines including literature, cultural studies, education, history and politics. He is currently working on a study of war and peace in Fiji's pre-Christian era.

Robert Norton

Robert is an honorary senior research fellow in the Department of Anthropology at Macquarie University in Sydney, where he taught from 1969 until 2004. He began researching the politics of race and ethnicity in Fiji in 1966 with the encouragement of anthropologist Rusiate Nayacakalou, and has maintained a strong interest in the subject by field and archival research. His *Race and Politics in Fiji* was first published by University of Queensland Press in 1977, the first book-length study relating the national-level politics of Fiji to its societal context. An extensively revised edition was published in 1990. Robert continues to publish papers on Fiji's historical and contemporary politics in various academic journals and books.

Max Quanchi

Max has had a distinguished career as a historian in Australia, Papua New Guinea and Fiji. Born in rural Victoria in 1945, he studied at Frankston Teachers College, Monash University and the University of Queensland. His research includes studies of the history of photography in the Pacific and developing educational resources for Australia and the Pacific. His recent books include *Postcards from Oceania: Plantations, Pirogues and Port Towns* with Max Shekleton (University of the South Pacific Press, 2015), *An Ideal Colony and Epitome of Progress: Colonial Fiji in Picture Postcards* with Max Shekleton (University of the South Pacific Press, 2019) and *Glorious Company: The Polynesia Company in Melbourne and Fiji* (Pacific Studies Press, 2022).

Simione Sevudredre

Simione has been working extensively in the area of indigenous iTaukei performance customs and protocols for the past 15 years. Because indigenous iTaukei culture is traditionally oral, he extracts a deeper insider understanding through studying iTaukei customs, protocols and the semiotics of signs and symbols. He is currently based at the iTaukei Institute of Language & Culture in the Ministry of iTaukei Affairs in Suva, Fiji.

Kate Stevens

Kate (Pākehā) is a senior lecturer in history at the University of Waikato. Her research focuses on comparative histories of cultural, environmental and economic exchange in the colonial and postcolonial Pacific. Her teaching includes courses on Pacific history, global food and commodity history, and histories of the ocean.

Anurag Subramani

Anurag is an academic, researcher and writer, who currently teaches history at USP. He has also taught English literature and creative writing at USP. He attended Suva Grammar School and Dame Elizabeth Cadbury High School in Birmingham, England. He did his tertiary studies in Hawai'i and Fiji, culminating in his gold medal–winning PhD thesis ('Carnivalizing History'), which consists of an original novel (*Dakuwaku*) with a supporting exegesis. He recently completed a commissioned book on the history of the *Fiji Times* and is currently working on a 'people's history' project that seeks to recover and resuscitate the untold and minor narratives from Fiji's past.

Daryl Tarte

Daryl's family came to Fiji in 1868 and settled on Taveuni where he grew up. His parents sent him to boarding school in Suva in 1944 then to Melbourne in 1946. After school he studied accountancy before returning to help his father operate the family business. In 1968 he left Taveuni to join the sugar industry, where he served in various capacities for the next 30 years. His hobby has always been writing and he has published 11 books in Australia, the United Kingdom, Japan and Fiji. He has been married to Jacque for 63 years: he has a son with a family living in Sydney, and a daughter living in Suva with her son, who is the sixth generation of the family in Fiji.

Kaliopate Tavola

Kaliopate, from Dravuni, Ono, Kadavu, worked for 11 years as a civil servant, 14 years as a diplomat in London and Brussels, six years as a politician, and 10 years as a consultant. For the first seven years as a diplomat, he conjointly held the post of the company representative for Fiji Sugar Marketing (FSM) Co Ltd in the EU. He was deputy general manager of FSM Co Ltd when he resigned in 2000 to join politics. Now, fully retired and living in Suva, he enjoys writing, including for his own website.

Larry Thomas

Larry is a former senior lecturer in literature and language with the then School of Humanities, teaching literature and theatre arts. He later joined the Pacific Community (SPC) as coordinator of the Regional Media Centre. He began his writing career over 30 years ago, writing his first play *Just Another Day*. Since then, he has written several more plays and directed many of them. He was also the director of the Pacific Writing Forum. His documentary films include *Compassionate Exile* (1997) and *Race for Riots* (2001). He is currently the acting director of the Oceania Centre for Arts and Culture at USP in Suva, Fiji.

Christine Weir

Christine studied history at the University of Cambridge in the United Kingdom and then trained as a history teacher. In 1976, she accompanied her husband Tony to USP in Fiji for eight years and during that time she taught in Fiji schools and tutored at USP. Later she returned to study at The Australian National University (ANU), gained a PhD in Pacific History in 2003 and in 2007 she took up the position of lecturer in history at USP, which she held for seven years. Her research focuses on colonial and contemporary Christianity in the Pacific. Since returning to Canberra in 2014, she has continued her research as a Petherick reader at the National Library of Australia.

Maps

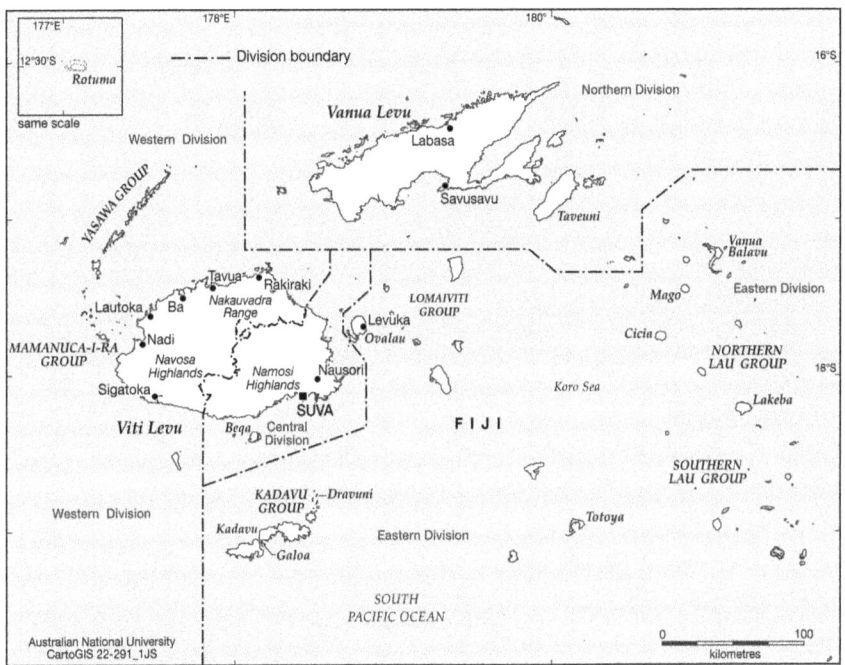

Map 1: The Fiji Islands.
Source: Map provided by CartoGIS Services, Scholarly Information Services, The Australian National University.

SUVA STORIES

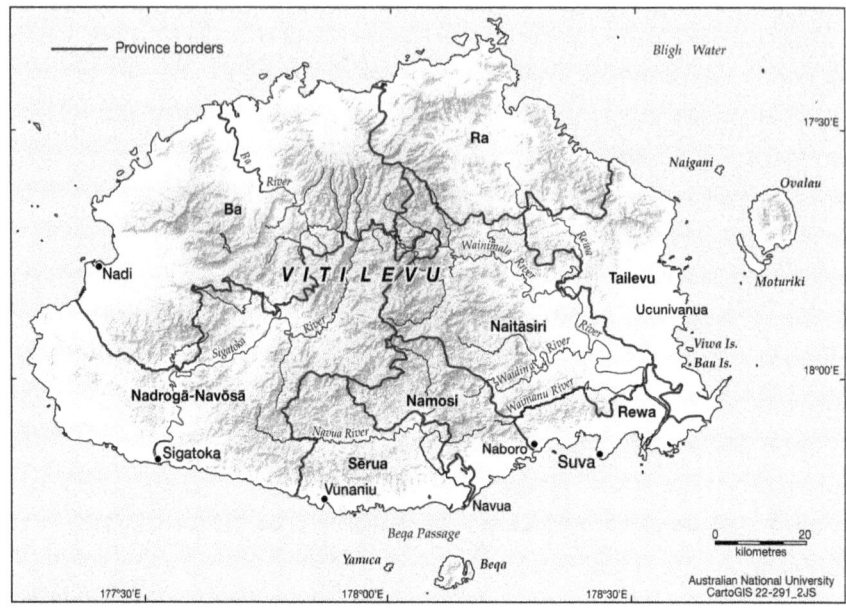

Map 2: Provinces of Viti Levu.
Source: Map provided by CartoGIS Services, Scholarly Information Services, The Australian National University.

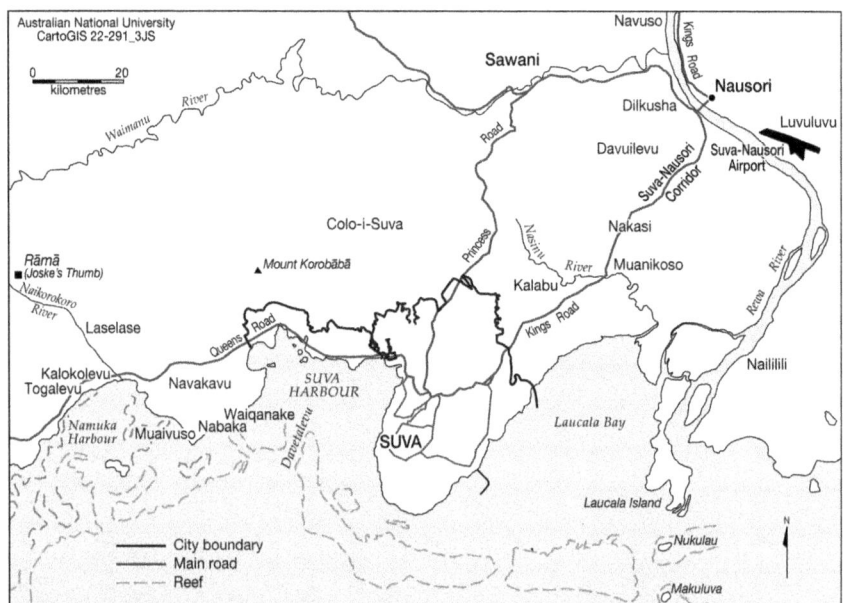

Map 3: Suva and surrounds.
Source: Map provided by CartoGIS Services, Scholarly Information Services, The Australian National University.

MAPS

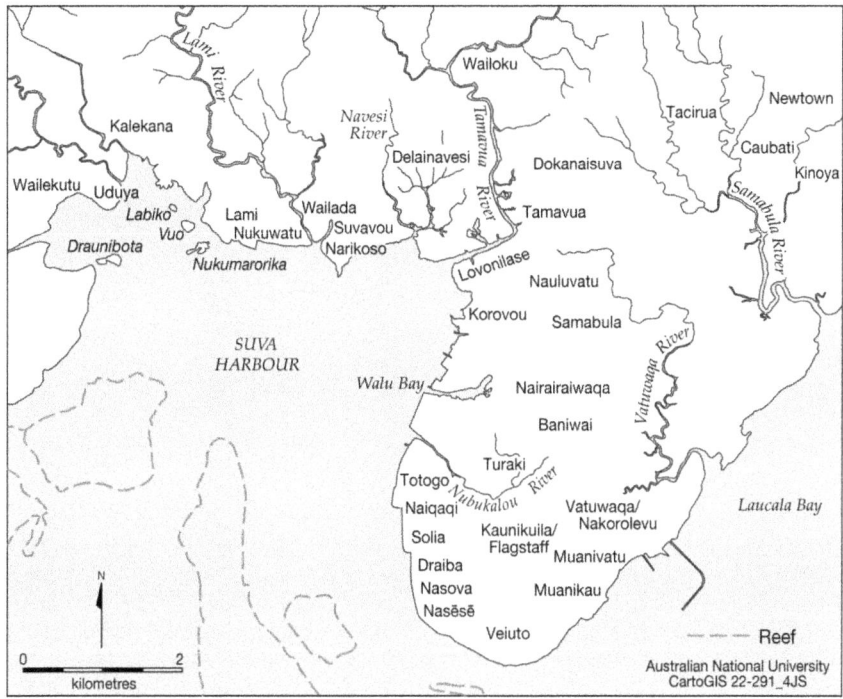

Map 4: Early settlements of Suva.
Source: Map provided by CartoGIS Services, Scholarly Information Services, The Australian National University.

Map 5: Suva City and Lami town and environs.

Note: Readers can enlarge this map digitally by visiting the ANU Press website.

Source: 3rd edition, FMS (Fiji Meteorological Service) 1, Fiji Lands and Surveys Department 2010.

Introduction: Reclaiming Suva

Nicholas Halter

'Welcome to Suva – the capital city of Fiji', reads the banner as you drive into the metropolis. Lautoka advertises itself to the world as the 'Sugar City', Nadi as the 'Jet-Set Town', Sigatoka as the 'Salad Bowl' and Labasa as the 'Friendly North'. But Suva, being Suva, sees no need to advertise its wares and attractions to the world. It is, simply, the 'capital city' of the nation. It has been so since 1882 when the capital of the then British colony moved from Levuka. Home now to over 93,000 people, both longtime residents as well as recently arrived migrants, it is a microcosm of modern Fiji: multicultural, vibrant, resilient, still standing strong despite all the challenges that nature and humans have thrown at it over the decades. Suva remains a special place in a special nation.

It is also a place that defies easy description. How you first 'see' Suva depends on how you enter it. First impressions of Suva are shaped by the mode of arrival. Those privileged enough to fly across the island of Viti Levu will cross the Navōsā and Namosi Highlands before descending to the fertile delta of the Rewa River. To the west of the river mouth, across Laucala Bay, a hilly peninsula juts out from the mainland, a mix of verdant green vegetation, roads that snake like arteries across the land, and tin roofs of all colours, shapes and sizes. Those who approach from the sea enter Suva Harbour from the south, sighting Joske's Thumb protruding from the mountains that silhouette the city and passing the graveyard of shipwrecks at the break in the reef. This deep-water harbour has made Suva a lucrative location for commercial activity – once crowded with the sails of native *drua* and *camakau* watercraft, today populated by fishing trawlers and shipping container vessels. Oil slicks and rubbish decorate the shoreline of concrete walls and mangrove forest. Those who travel by road will see that the settlements increase in number and stature the nearer they approach the city centre. Stuck in crowded buses on congested roads, travellers may gaze at the urban sprawl of the Suva–Nausori corridor, a vast suburbia of makeshift and modern housing encroaching on farmland. Others may travel from the mountains of Namosi or Naitāsiri, descending through the cool climate of the protected Colo-i-Suva rainforest to sell their produce at the bustling waterfront market. Some may gaze across the harbour to nearby Beqa Island as they travel on the Queens Road, crawling through Lami town traffic, past the unsightly industrial areas on the outskirts of the city, passing the old cemetery of Lovonilase and the whitewashed walls of the jail. Older Suva residents will recall the smell of the Suva dump at Naibenubenu that once greeted travellers on this road but has since been relocated to accommodate the growing city.

For those parents bringing their children from the *koro* (village) to Suva for the first time, it is possible to imagine their shock and surprise at the contrast. The hustle and bustle of crowded pavements, the energetic marketplace, the loud noises of shopfront speakers and taxi horns and the unfamiliar fashions and faces. Childhood memories of Suva may recall the pungent smells of the fish market by Nubukalou Creek, the belching smog of buses at the central bus stand, the whiffs of shoe polish from the shoeshine boys, perfumes sold by the ladies on their street stalls, and aromatic hot buns from the tea houses and coffee shops. On rainy days, travellers seek refuge in a bowl of hot meaty bone soup, or an Indian curry or Chinese noodle dish. On sunny days, relief can be found under a flame tree by the water, or on the open expanse of Albert Park, or at the shaded park benches of Thurston Gardens or even on a breezy seaside ride on the bright green Nasēsē bus.

Officially, Suva is the commercial and political centre of Fiji, but for the everyday Fijian, it is a meeting place. A space to welcome families and friends at the docks and the bus stands, a space to gather at the sports grounds to cheer a favourite team, a space to meet for business (or to stand in a queue for a bank statement, a certificate, a licence), a space to meet for pleasure in the clubs and kava bars, or simply a place to *talanoa* (swap stories and chat). A favourite location for this dialogue is under the shade of an aging Tahitian chestnut tree. Others may see Suva as a gateway, the departure point for boats to other islands. Suva is also the arrival point for opportunities that cannot be found in the villages and rural towns – the pursuit of education or employment continues to underscore the rural–

urban migration that grows the city of Suva year after year. This migration encourages new relationships and encounters between different peoples, which results in new lifestyles, new associations and groupings, new attitudes and aspirations, which are then transmitted back to the villages.

This collection is an attempt to document the rapid transformation and expansion of Suva from an indigenous village, to a colonial hub, to bustling metropolis. Such a project has not been attempted for some time – efforts have been made to document pieces of Suva's history by residents, businessmen and government officials. Their names will be familiar to those who have searched the libraries for information about the city – Suva town mayor Len Usher, European educator and historian RA Derrick and linguistics professor Albert Schütz of Hawai'i. Schütz's 1978 history is the last book dedicated solely to the town and it urgently needs updating.[1] With a rich history comparable to the larger urban centres of Honolulu in Hawai'i and Port Moresby in Papua New Guinea,[2] it is surprising that a collection of Suva's histories has yet to be produced.

Shaping the Land

Situated on an undulating peninsula on the east coast of Viti Levu, one of the Fiji group's 300 islands, Suva is a maritime city. Walu Bay was once named for its vibrant fish population, sustaining local villages of fishermen until colonial visitors identified the potential of its deep-water harbour for commercial benefit. In the mid-nineteenth century, settlers of the Polynesia Company began establishing themselves near the mouth of Nubukalou Creek where there was a natural break in the mangroves. The soapstone cliffs and high average rainfall, comparative to other parts of the island, made colonial experiments in agriculture difficult – coffee, cotton and sugarcane were grown, and a crushing mill established at Naiqaqi, but it did not last. Livestock was also farmed on the areas cleared of vegetation, but it was the colonial buildings and roads that would eventually dominate the landscape as the settlement expanded and became a busy entrepot in the British Pacific colonial empire. Nubukalou

---

1   Albert J Schütz, *Suva: A history and guide* (Sydney: Pacific Publications, 1978).
2   Ian Stuart, *Port Moresby: Yesterday and today* (Sydney: Pacific Publications 1970); Gavan Daws and Bennett Hymer (eds), *Honolulu stories: Voices of the town through the years: Two centuries of writing* (Honolulu: Mutual Pub., 2008); N.D. Oram, *Colonial Town to Melanesian City: Port Moresby 1884–1974* (Canberra: Australian National University Press, 1976).

Creek remains at the heart of Suva city centre, one of five wards maintained by Suva City Council today.³ Rural–urban migration since the 1950s has expanded the city well beyond the peninsula. Today the Greater Suva Urban Area comprises 4,000 hectares and includes Lami, Nasinu and Nausori towns.⁴ Once considered the outskirts of Suva town, some of these areas have more residents than Suva itself, which recorded a population of 93,874 in the 2017 Census.⁵

Roughly 3,000 years ago, the first humans occupied the Fiji Islands. While it is possible they landed on the Suva peninsula, archaeological evidence suggests other areas of Fiji were settled first. Some Fijian myths of origin attributed spiritual significance to the Nakauvadra Range, the home of the creator spirit Degei.⁶ Later, people from the hill country of Viti Levu established fortified settlements on top of the Suva peninsula's steep ridges, while fishers settled in or near what is now called Walu Bay. When Europeans arrived in the early nineteenth century, they observed a large human settlement that stretched from present-day Albert Park to the Nasova Police Barracks. This was the combined village of Suva, and Europeans later referred to the central area now occupied by the Fiji Museum and Thurston Gardens as the 'Native Reserve' or Naiqasiqasi. The first curator of the Fiji Museum, Coleman Wall, attributes the name 'Suva' to a mound on which a temple stood – inside the temple was a sacred stone used for chiefly installations.⁷ What happened to the stone is unclear. Much of the village was destroyed during the Bau–Rewa War of 1843, when Christian missionaries recorded the ransacking of the village and massacre of its people. This was a precursor to further marginalisation of the Suva people as European expansion eventually forced the relocation of the villagers to Narikoso, which was named Suvavou (translated as 'New Suva').

---

3   The others being Tamavua, Extension, Samabula and Muanikau: suvacity.org/our-city/.
4   UN-Habitat, *Fiji: Greater Suva urban profile* (Nairobi: UN-Habitat, 2012).
5   Fiji Bureau of Statistics, *2017 Fiji population and housing census: Administration report* (Suva: Fiji Bureau of Statistics 2018), 146. Since 2007, the population of Nasinu has exceeded Suva. See Appendix 1.
6   Aubrey Parke, *Degei's descendants: Spirits, place and people in pre-cession Fiji*, ed. Matthew Spriggs and Deryck Scarr (Canberra: ANU Press, 2014).
7   Colman Wall, 'Sketches in Fijian history', *Transactions of the Fijian Society* (1919); Colman Wall, 'Historical notes on Suva', ed. Paul Geraghty, *Domodomo* 10, no. 2 (1996): 28–39; 11, no. 2 (1997): 15–37; 12, no. 2 (1999): 49–58.

Figure 0.1: 'Native village near Suva', n.d.
Note: This was presumably Suvavou. Archival record notes 'wife of chief on right'.
Source: Burton Brothers, Dunedin, NZ. Andrew, Thomas, 1855–1939: Fijian photographs. Ref: PA7-01-08-2. Alexander Turnbull Library, Wellington, New Zealand. natlib.govt.nz/records/22304049.

The efforts by the Suvavou people to assert their rights to the land of Suva since then has been a consistent attempt to reclaim a history dominated by colonial forces. The arrival of the Polynesia Company in the mid-nineteenth century marked a period in which Suva land was acquired and transformed by white settlers. Like other parts of Fiji, the transfer of land at this time was poorly documented and regulated, and Europeans used this situation to their advantage. The British Colonial Government, which gained control of Fiji in 1874 when a number of chiefs signed a Deed of Cession, saw an opportunity to buy the land from the Polynesia Company to establish a new capital. When the capital was relocated from Levuka to Suva in 1882, the inhabitants of Suva were moved to the Suvavou site and paid compensation of £200 annually. Subsequent government claims that the people were fairly compensated have since been disputed, first by the Roko Tui Suva Ratu Avorosa in 1898 and more recently by the Tui Suva, Ratu Epeli Kanakana in the 1990s. They point to the absence of a formal deed or written agreement as evidence of this dubious arrangement. Kanakana's efforts resulted in a 222-page report titled *Suva State Land: 'Land of My Fathers'*.[8] Anthropologist Hirokazu Miyazaki's ethnographic study of Suvavou in the 1990s argued that apart from monetary gain, the long series of petitions by the Suvavou people 'represent an enduring hope to confirm their self-knowledge, the truth about who they really are'.[9] These claims continue to this day, most recently when the Suvavou village reasserted their rights as traditional custodians of the land to prevent the rezoning of an area near the Fiji Museum for the construction of an embassy.[10]

Suva has been the site of another form of reclamation since Europeans marked it for their capital. As European expansion of the town began, the land was subsequently shaped and remoulded. Forests were felled, mangroves were cleared, rivers were dredged and soil was piled upon the shores to make way for the development of colonial enterprise. Much of the land may now be unrecognisable from its original state. Muanikau, a point named for its thick tree line, was cleared for farmland, and has since become lucrative real estate for suburbs close to the city centre. The shoreline from Nubukalou Creek to Thurston Gardens was slowly reclaimed over time, first at the site of the original markets (present-day Westpac Bank) and then at Ratu Sukuna Park and Suva Grammar School. In the central business district a few lone *ivi* trees are all that remains of the original shoreline, markers of an ancient coast now covered by concrete and rock. Reclamation work continues today in the capital. On the other side of the peninsula in the suburbs of Vatuwaqa, mangroves are cleared to provide space for the expanding urban population. This reclamation has prompted a counter-reclamation, as concerned residents attempt to repossess and restore natural space from the urban sprawl. This includes individual efforts to plant gardens for subsistence, or more coordinated efforts to plant mangroves along the My Suva Park shoreline or clean the polluted waters of Suva Harbour. Some reports indicate that 66 per cent of fish in the area now contain microplastics.[11]

---

8   Anare Matahau and Associates, *Suva state land: 'Land of my fathers'* (Suva: Anare Matahau and Associates, 1991).
9   Hirokazu Miyazaki, *The method of hope: Anthropology, philosophy, and Fijian knowledge* (Stanford: Stanford University Press, 2004), 3.
10 In 2019, the Suva City Council proposed rezoning the vacant area next to the Fiji Museum in order to relocate the Indian High Commission. The people of Suvavou delivered a petition opposing the rezoning, and after much public opposition, the proposal was quietly abandoned. This case is one of a number of rezoning and building regulation reforms since the 2000s that threaten to change the face and character of Suva.
11 Tifa Vataiki, 'Serious concerns raised as research shows microplastic in fish and other seafood sources in Fiji', *Fijivillage*, 2 July 2020, www.fijivillage.com/news/Serious-concerns-raised-as-research-shows-microplastic-in-fish-and-other-seafood-sources-in-Fiji-58f4xr/.

INTRODUCTION

Figure 0.2: Suva Harbour, n.d.
Source: P32.4.141 Fiji Museum.

Figure 0.3: A view of Suva Harbour and Queen's Wharf, n.d.
Source: P32.4.30 Fiji Museum.

Figure 0.4: 'Indian at Suva Street, 1970'.
Source: M6745 National Archives of Fiji.

This edited collection may also be considered a modest form of reclamation, an attempt to redress the imbalances in Fiji's history and expand the breadth of knowledge of Suva beyond a narrow colonial focus. Though the British have played a significant role in shaping the capital from 1882 until formal Independence in 1970, their contribution has been well documented. Suva is replete with reminders of colonial rule, from the streets named after European officials or planters, to the buildings and memorials they left behind. Sir Leonard Usher, a New Zealand–born teacher who later became editor of the *Fiji Times* and mayor of Suva (1966–1976), was one of the members of the Fiji Society who documented the origins of these names.[12] Many of these streets began as simple walkways, and the motor car was a novelty when it arrived in 1904. Foot traffic may explain why the layout of the town's pathways resembles a *koro*, with roads going to and from the centre, but not usually

---

12   Len Usher, *Mainly about Fiji: A collection of writings, broadcasts and speeches* (Suva: Fiji Times, 1987); Len Usher, *50 years in Fiji* (Suva: Shell, 1978); JJ McHugh, 'Recollections of early Suva', *Fiji Society of Science and Industry* (19 July 1943): 210–14; Albert F Ward, 'Old land marks of Suva', *Transactions and Proceedings of the Fiji Society of Science and Industry* 2 (1953): 215–17; Albert Lee, *Historical notes on the city of Suva with particular reference to the central business district* (Suva: National Archives of Fiji, 1974); Albert Lee, *Historical notes on the city of Suva supplement* (Suva: National Archives of Fiji, 1984).

passing through it.¹³ Less well known is the contribution of indentured labourers to the construction of the roads. Melanesian and Indian indentured labourers who were brought to Fiji to make it a profitable sugar colony in the late nineteenth century were also used in Suva's early earthworks and construction. Suva was the first point of arrival for the Indian indentured labourers (*girmitiya*), their boats depositing them on the island of Nukulau to be registered and reallocated across Fiji between 1879 and 1916. They became a valuable and sizable proportion of the population of Suva, with the government creating a new subdivision in the 1930s at Samabula for them.

A focus on Suva's colonial history also risks overlooking the lives of ordinary Fijians in favour of major political players and events. It is tempting to focus on the political implications of Suva's place as the capital of Fiji. It contains the Parliament, the High Court, the headquarters of most ministries. It is the political centre of national decision-making, home to most of the country's public servants, its ministers, the prime minister and president. It is also home to the major educational and training institutions such as the University of the South Pacific and the Fiji National University and the major newspapers, so it is home to influential opinion-makers. Kim Gravelle's volumes of Fiji history based on the *Fiji Times* highlights some of the key political moments in Suva.¹⁴ Ralph Premdas and Jeffrey Stevens observed similar characteristics in the city of Port Moresby, which they observed to be 'the meeting place and melting pot of the best of PNG's [Papua New Guinea's] leadership'.¹⁵ What constitutes the 'best' leadership is a subjective issue considering Suva has been the site of four coups d'état, two in 1987, then in 2000 and in 2006. Yet Suva's character is not defined by its political elite. It is quite the opposite, argues historian Brij V Lal. Though a series of coups reasserted the power of a few over the masses, the historical conditions that led to the coups reflected a changing attitude to traditional chiefly power, as more urban residents questioned the customary authority of Fijian chiefs.¹⁶

---

13   John O'Carroll, 'Multiple cities: Suva and the (post)colonial', *Dreadlocks in Oceania*, 1 (1997): 26–42.
14   Kim Gravelle, *Fiji's times: A history of Fiji*, vols 1–3 (Suva: Fiji Times 1979).
15   Ralph R Premdas and Jeffrey S Stevens, *Electoral politics in a third world city: Port Moresby 1977* (Konedobu: University of Papua New Guinea 1978), 1.
16   Brij V Lal, *Broken waves: A history of the Fiji Islands in the twentieth century* (Honolulu: University of Hawai'i Press, 1992).

Our collective knowledge of the everyday lives of Suva residents is surprisingly limited. Much remains stored in oral traditions or family memorabilia, as well as a rich and vibrant archive of newspapers, in the English language and multiple vernaculars. Anurag Subramani's recent history of the English-language publication the *Fiji Times* is an example of this revisionist turn towards a 'people's history' of Fiji that can provide a more local and personal view of the lives of ordinary Fijians.[17] A vast archive of images also awaits the intrepid researcher seeking a more humane view of Suva. Once hidden within Suva institutions like the *Fiji Times,* the Fiji Museum and the National Archives of Fiji, increasingly images are finding their way into online spaces where they can be shared and scrutinised.[18] They complement a large digital archive of Fijian images stored in Australia and New Zealand, and a number of photographic histories of Fiji.[19] The majority of images reproduced in this volume were chosen from the Fiji Museum and National Archives of Fiji to draw attention to the less visible historical collections available to Suva residents. Admittedly, early photography of Suva reflects the colonial bias of its photographers. Images of city architecture and official portraits are more common than informal settlements or minority ethnic groups, which included Indians, Rotumans, Chinese, Melanesians and Part-Europeans (*kailomas*), the populations of which fluctuated over time in Suva (see Appendix 1). Images of marketplaces are one of the few glimpses we have of the ordinary lives of people in Suva, particularly of women, who are oft overlooked in the archive. Still today, marketplaces play a central role in Suva life bringing people from all walks of life together.

---

17 Anurag Subramani, *The Fiji Times at 150: Imagining the Fijian nation (or, a scrapbook of Fiji's history)* (Suva: Fiji Times, forthcoming).
18 The Fiji Museum created a 'virtual museum' on its website (virtual.fijimuseum.org.fj/), while the National Archives of Fiji has relied on Facebook to share some of its photographic images (Opeta Alefaio, 'Archives Connecting with the Community', paper presented at the International Federation of Library Associations and Institutions, World Library and Information Congress, 'Connections. Collaboration. Community', Session 96: Asia and Oceania, Columbus, Ohio, 9–19 August 2016).
19 The Pacific Virtual Museum pilot project developed a search engine for Pacific archival and library collections in 2020 (digitalpasifik.org/). See also Elsie Stephenson, *Fiji's past on picture postcards* (Suva: Caines Jannif Group, 1997); Ian Thomson, Peter Thomson and Rob Wright, *Fiji in the forties and fifties* (Auckland: Thomson Pacific, 1994); Max Quanchi and Max Shekleton, *An ideal colony and epitome of progress: Colonial Fiji in picture postcards* (Suva: University of the South Pacific Press, 2019).

INTRODUCTION

Figure 0.5: Nubukalou Creek, n.d.
Source: P32.6.25 Fiji Museum.

Figure 0.6: Women at a market, Suva, 1939.
Source: Whites Aviation Ltd: Photographs. Ref: WA-03291-G. Alexander Turnbull Library, Wellington, New Zealand. natlib.govt.nz/records/30663265.

Figure 0.7: Vegetable market in Suva, 1950.
Source: Whites Aviation Ltd: Photographs. Ref: WA-24823-F. Alexander Turnbull Library, Wellington, New Zealand. natlib.govt.nz/records/23226746.

Figure 0.8: Indian women in Suva, 1949.
Source: 2505 National Archives of Fiji.

Figure 0.9: A garment shop, Suva, n.d.
Source: P32.4.91 Fiji Museum.

Shaping the City

What shaped the development of Suva from a colonial town to a multicultural city? Colonial records highlight attempts by British officials to control, shape and mould the growth of the urban area from the early twentieth century. In fact, as the headquarters of the Western Pacific High Commission from 1882 to 1952, Suva was the location where much of the British Pacific Empire was governed. The majority of government buildings were sited close to the wharves and trading houses, reflecting the importance of trade in the colonial entrepot. Over time, the wooden buildings that were constructed by colonial settlers along Nubukalou Creek were gradually replaced by larger, sturdier ones that were more resistant to extreme weather or fire. One notable example was a group of wooden buildings on All-Nations Street (now known as Cumming Street) that once hosted the main market for the town since it moved from behind the old post office on the harbourfront in 1904. Most of the buildings were destroyed in a fire in 1923 that subsequently forced a reorganisation of the fire brigade and prompted new regulations that all new commercial buildings were to be made of stone, brick or concrete.[20]

---

20 Lee, *Historical notes on the city of Suva: Supplement.*

Figure 0.10: Suva town, n.d.
Source: P32.4.94 Fiji Museum.

Figure 0.11: Suva town, n.d.
Source: P32.6.6 Fiji Museum.

As early as the 1910s, cruise ships from Australia, New Zealand and the United States began visiting Suva with regularity. The construction of the iconic Grand Pacific Hotel opposite Albert Park in 1914 was symbolic of the importance tourism would gradually begin to play in Suva, and Fiji more generally. By the 1930s, up to 700 tourists would disembark from a single cruise ship. The Suva they encountered was carefully staged, segregated and regulated. Non-whites needed licences to drink alcohol or to perform dances, and were subject to strict curfews.[21]

Despite these careful controls, Suva's growth was often spontaneous, accidental or indirect – records of Suva's prisons and courts show that people were constantly testing, stretching and breaking the rules that were in place. This is typical of many metropolitan areas of the Global South according to AbdouMaliq Simone's history of Jakarta.[22] Informal networks and processes frequently challenged colonial conformism and planning. Through a process of opportunism that Simone terms 'incrementalism', residents test the water of what is possible to create their own spaces or territories within cities.[23] This involves manoeuvring around authorities and regulations to engage in diverse initiatives, and negotiating relationships with neighbours who have competing claims, skills and aspirations. For example, James Whitelaw noted that in the 1950s 'hawker' licences were issued in a vain attempt to regulate the growth of vendors who walked the city streets to sell their wares for tourists or sell lunches to office workers. Other informal commercial enterprises that emerged were 'barrow boys' who used mobile glass-covered handcarts to sell food and sweets at the fringes of formal markets, office buildings and public events.[24] Simone believes these informal enterprises are responsible for shaping cities:

> Through a continuous process of give-and-take and the interweaving of small and large initiatives that incrementally transformed built and social environments, residents elaborated spaces adept at keeping up with the changes underway in the larger city by generating new opportunities for accumulation, employment, and livelihood.[25]

---

21 See Nicholas Halter, 'Tourists fraternising in Fiji in the 1930s', *Journal of Tourism History* 12, no. 1 (2020): 27–47, doi.org/10.1080/1755182X.2019.1682688.
22 AbdouMaliq Simone, *Jakarta: Drawing the city near* (Minnesota: University of Minnesota Press, 2014), doi.org/10.5749/minnesota/9780816693351.001.0001.
23 Simone, *Jakarta*, 92–101.
24 James Sutherland Whitelaw, 'People, land and government in Suva, Fiji' (PhD thesis, The Australian National University, 1966), 118.
25 Simone, *Jakarta*, 109.

The search for housing in the rapidly growing city was another avenue in which residents and authorities negotiated new spaces and regulations. When Suva was proclaimed a city in 1956, its population had increased to 37,371.[26] This postwar growth and migration concerned town planners and authorities, who observed opportunistic informal settlements emerging on native land, such as Tacirua. They established a Housing Authority two years later to address the pressures caused by population growth. The first public housing was constructed in the suburb of Raiwaqa, and the homes were ready by 1959.[27] As the city expanded, new formal settlements were established in the peri-urban areas. This first began with the subdivision of Samabula for Indians in the 1930s. There were also longstanding *koros* that were formally recognised by the government at Tamavua and Kalabu. These settlements were shaped around the basic outlines of a village, but over time their members grew to include Fijians from different parts of Fiji.[28] Tamavua featured a large *bure* and was visited by organised tours from the city for its traditional Fijian food and dances, while Kalabu was predominantly Indian. Crown land was subdivided by the Lands Department to implement low-income housing projects at settlements along the Kings Road between Suva and Nausori, such as Caubati, Kinoya and Nasole. On the Queens Road, native land in Lami was subdivided from 1951, with people attracted by its views and sea breezes. Nearby were settlements occupied by other Pacific Islanders, including a large number of descendants of the Solomon and New Hebridean labourers at Wailoku and Kalekana. The stories of these emerging settlements and suburbs are largely preserved in the memories of their residents, and only a few have documented their urban lives in writing. Indigenous anthropologist Rusiate Nayacakalou was one of the first to conduct fieldwork in urban iTaukei communities in the early 1960s, and former civil servant and soldier Manu Korovulavula has written about his experiences growing up in Toorak in the 1940s.[29]

---

26   Whitelaw, 'People, land and government in Suva, Fiji'.
27   Joseph Veramu, *Growing up in Fiji* (Suva: Institute of Pacific Studies, 1984); Alexander Mamak, *Colour, culture & conflict: A study of pluralism in Fiji* (Rushcutters Bay: Pergamon Press, 1978).
28   Whitelaw explained that 'official' koros were located on their own land and were recognised by the Fijian Affairs Board.
29   RR Nayacakalou, 'The urban Fijians of Suva', in *Pacific port towns and cities,* ed. Alexander Spoehr (Honolulu: Bishop Museum Press, 1963), 34. Less well known is an unpublished manuscript in the Pacific Collection of USP that contains a survey commissioned by the Colonial Government in the 1950s: Ravuama Vunivalu and WL Verrier, *A social survey of Fijians in Suva* (Suva: 1959); Manunivavalagi Korovulavula, *Gone ni Turaki* (Nasinu: Manu Korovulavula Publisher, 2011).

Figure 0.12: Tamavua, n.d.
Source: P32.5.62 Fiji Museum.

Unexpected natural disasters could also force sudden changes to the urban landscape. On 29 January 1952, Suva was battered by a cyclone with winds recorded at 213 kilometres per hour at Laucala Bay.[30] Many buildings were destroyed and government plans to build the village of Nabua in 1951 were fast-tracked to assist those left homeless – 100 acres of land next to the military camp and 60 dwellings were built over the next four years.[31] The following year, on 14 September 1953 at 12:28 pm, an earthquake resulted in a tsunami that broke across the Suva foreshore. Len Usher recalled the earthquake lasted for half a minute, and water flowed out of Suva Harbour before returning and washing over the sea wall, covering Albert Park. People picked up fish left stranded on the foreshore. In the aftermath, three people were killed, and significant damage was caused to the Kings Wharf, Lami seawall, Nukulau, Makuluva and the Fijian village of Nukui on the Rewa River.[32] Suva has been relatively fortunate

---

30 JR Campbell, *Dealing with disaster: Hurricane response in Fiji* (Honolulu: Pacific Islands Development Program, East-West Center, 1984), 9.
31 Whitelaw, 'People, land and government in Suva, Fiji', 204.
32 Usher, *Mainly about Fiji*. There is reference to another earthquake and tidal wave when Suva's main reef cracked on 15 September 1955: Thomson, Thomson and Wright, *Fiji in the forties and fifties*.

compared to the rest of the country to have avoided major natural disasters, with the exception of the events of 1952/53, and the Category 5 Cyclone Winston in 2016. However, environmental factors have consistently played an understated role in shaping the development of the city. Tropical storms necessitate the regular reconstruction and renovation of buildings and infrastructure in the capital, and residents are constantly adapting to changes in their built and natural environments. This is most clearly visible in the settlements by the ocean, where the effects of climate change cause gradual sea-level rise, or more sudden storm surges, that force residents to be ready to move if required. Global environmental changes will undoubtedly shape the city of Suva in the future.

Government efforts to mitigate the pressures caused by rural–urban migration and respond to the negative effects of urbanisation in Suva have struggled. Unofficial settlements began to emerge in response to restrictive British colonial policies for establishing formal settlements, and their growth was accelerated by the non-renewal of agricultural leases under the Agricultural Landlord and Tenant Act (1977) since the mid-1990s and post-coup economic downturns.[33] Estimates of informal settlements in Fiji vary. In 2016, an estimate of 220 informal settlements argued most of them were in Suva.[34] A more conservative estimate by UN-Habitat identified over 100 settlements in the Greater Suva Urban Area. These were home to 90,000 residents who made up 30 per cent of the area's population.[35] Suva is not yet at the scale of some Melanesian cities, but its growing peri-urban populations and overwhelmingly young demographic resembles Melanesian urbanisation trends. The continued presence of these informal populations reminds us of the power of the masses to shape a city, and the ineffectiveness of the state to effect all the controls and reforms it desires. Suva has been the site of organised protest and resistance in the Pacific, most notably the 1959 oil workers' strike that culminated in rioting in Suva, and the antinuclear activism of the 1970s and 80s. More recently, citizen ratepayer organisations have emerged, in particular in Tamavua and Flagstaff, in response to illegal developments and overdevelopment in areas close to the city centre. They voice concerns

---

[33] Vijay Naidu et al., 'Informal settlements and social inequality in Fiji: Evidence of serious policy gaps', *Journal of Pacific Studies* 35, no. 1 (2015): 27–46.
[34] A Penjueli, '220 squatter settlements across Fiji, majority in Suva', *Newswire Focus*, 10 February 2016, newswire.internet.com.fj/community/220-squatter-settlements-across-fiji-majority-in-suva.
[35] UN-Habitat, *Fiji: Greater Suva urban profile*, 26.

about lack of control over urban development since elected municipal councils were abolished in 2009 and replaced with unelected officials.[36] Willard Miller of Ellis Place, Suva, wrote in the *Fiji Times* in 2020:

> Unelected administrators listen to our complaints and try to placate us if possible but have made promises they don't keep since all local government officials are now first and foremost answerable to their minister, not us.[37]

Suva's population growth also had many positive implications for the future of the city. The multicultural nature of the city has fostered a vibrant and diverse community, evident in the variety of cultural arts, music, food, architecture, dress and lifestyles. Community groups play a vital role in the operation of schools and churches in Suva and have shown great solidarity in times of crisis. Suva has hosted a number of memorable community events and celebrations in the capital. One of the oldest annual urban traditions is the Miss Hibiscus pageants, established in 1956.[38] Another annual celebration is the commemoration of Fiji's independence from Britain, which took place at Albert Park on 10 October 1970. Suva was also the major centre for national and regional sporting fixtures, and was notable for hosting some of the earliest regional events. Len Usher recalled the excitement of the first South Pacific conference in Suva in 1950, when the delegates found shared commonalities 'in the dining rooms and recreation halls, in the dormitories, on the verandahs and lawns … and in the homes of Fijians in Suva'.[39] It was followed by the first South Pacific Games in Suva in 1963 and the first South Pacific Festival of Arts in 1972, which lasted for 15 days at Albert Park. At the South Pacific Games closing ceremony, teams marched as one, not as national groups, as Usher recalled:

> The mixing-up procedure was not a new one in international games, but this was a South Pacific first, with strong and stirring overtones of the rebirth of a regional unity with deep emotional roots.[40]

---

36   Sally Round, 'Motion for local elections defeated in Fiji parliament', *Radio New Zealand*, 3 April 2019, www.rnz.co.nz/international/pacific-news/386256/motion-for-local-elections-defeated-in-fiji-parliament.
37   Willard Miller, 'Taxation without representation', *The Fiji Times*, 14 November 2020, www.pressreader.com/fiji/the-fiji-times/20201114/281676847442554.
38   Claus Bossen, 'Festival mania, tourism and nation building in Fiji: The case of the Hibiscus Festival, 1956—1970', *The Contemporary Pacific* (2000): 123–54, doi.org/10.1353/cp.2000.0006.
39   Usher, *Mainly about Fiji*, 136.
40   Usher, *Mainly about Fiji*, 139-40.

This sentiment would underpin the regional institutions that were created in Suva, namely the University of the South Pacific (established in 1968) and the South Pacific Forum (established in 1971).

Though British colonial authorities regarded Fiji as racially divided, a history of Suva that describes the city according to ethnicity risks reinforcing a colonial assumption. Again, Simone's work on cities is helpful here. He argues that relationships and networks in cities are not based on ethnicity or politics or identity: 'The basis of similarity rests not in people's identities but in what people are trying to do.'[41] This may explain better why different districts or suburbs have specific genealogies that are not necessarily along homogenous ethnic lines. Suva suburbs today are characterised by a mixture of incomes, occupations, residential histories, attitudes and beliefs. For this reason, separating spaces according to class is also problematic. Instead, Simone refers to the 'urban majority' as those who live in the in-between spaces of the rich, poor and middle classes.[42] This is particularly relevant for Suva because it is a place for many who may not fit within a particular group or conform to a conventional lifestyle, and who seek refuge in the urban realm – the elderly, non-indigenous Fijians, religious minorities, the LGBTIQ+ community, informal settlers. For this reason, this collection presents stories of Suva that broaden the history of the city to include the urban majority.

The Authors

Authors were sought from a range of professions and backgrounds, unified by their interest in a shared local past. The chapters presented here are a varied combination of personal reflections and archival research, capturing episodes in Suva's history from its indigenous beginnings to the present. The evolving urban landscape of Suva means that no single book can adequately describe every aspect of its history, but it is hoped this humble collection brings together a number of unique perspectives that add to existing knowledge of the city.

The chapters are grouped into three parts. Part 1 explores the foundation of Suva, beginning with the origins of the indigenous people of Fiji and their displacement to make room for a capital in the late nineteenth century.

---

41   Simone, *Jakarta*, 90.
42   Simone, *Jakarta*, 85.

Paul Geraghty's detailed account of Suva oral traditions highlights the development of the village and the impact of the Bau–Rewa War of 1843. Max Quanchi focuses on the Melbourne-owned Polynesia Company and its efforts to acquire land on the peninsula, examining the lives, successes and failures of the early settlers. Robert Nicole follows with a detailed social history of the capital's early years, with particular focus on the contribution of iTaukei, Indian and Melanesian communities who have been obscured by history. Simione Sevudredre considers the importance of music to iTaukei culture and history, and the ways in which communities have preserved and adapted musical traditions. Anurag Subramani presents glimpses of personal stories from Suva recorded in the *Fiji Times* based on his exhaustive research of Fiji's oldest newspaper. The stories of Dwarka – the so-called 'Prince of Thieves' – and Thomas Le Clair De Francoeur around the turn of the twentieth century highlight the rich archive of the *Fiji Times* and the importance of the 'scraps of history'.

Part 2 explores the development of Suva under British colonial rule in the twentieth century and the creation of new institutions and divisions. Nicholas Halter and Jacqueline Leckie provide histories of Suva's first jail and mental asylum, institutions whose occupants have been stigmatised and overlooked in the past. Kate Stevens explores how women and children responded to violence in Suva's streets and homes, as viewed through the colonial records of the Supreme Court. The division of Fiji's population into races by the British colonial administration had lasting and unintended consequences for the development and segregation of Suva. This is explored by Robert Norton over a 25-year period from the end of World War II to Fiji's Independence. These racial divisions had implications for the education system in Fiji, highlighted by Christine Weir's study of three colonial Suva Methodist schools, namely Dudley House School, Suva Methodist Boys' School and Ballantine School. Another major educational establishment in Suva, the University of the South Pacific, is explored by Jacqueline Leckie who recounts its rich history as the leading tertiary institution in the region for over 50 years.

Part 3 consists of an eclectic mix of reflections and reminiscences by Suva residents who consider aspects of Suva that mean the most to them. In this section uniformity was deliberately avoided and each author was free to write along the lines they wished. Kaliopate Tavola, from the island of Dravuni, reflects on major events in Suva and their implications for his own family members, framing his narrative around the idea of swimming under the *ivi* tree, a geographical marker in the centre of Suva city. Daryl Tarte considers what Suva looked like in the 1940s and 50s when he was a student at Boys Grammar School. Kantilal Jinna recalls the streets, sounds and sights of Suva as a young boy growing up in an Indian family in Flagstaff around the same time. Larry Thomas makes an important contribution to an often overlooked sector of the city – the arts. His account weaves together his memories of Raiwaqa and his experiences in the dramatic arts. Anawaite Matadradra considers the history of the Melanesian minority community that were descended from indentured labourers of the nineteenth century and now have settlements throughout Suva. Her account indicates the challenges and hopes that many minority groups in Fiji have in common. Fijian scholar Vijay Naidu then considers the significance of Suva as a site of turbulence and political violence, recalling his own experiences of coups in 1987, 2000 and 2006. Continuing on the theme of minorities, the late Fijian historian Brij V Lal recalls his personal encounters with informal settlements in Fiji, and a particular encounter with a mother and son from Wailea. This touching reflection speaks to the daily trials and tribulations faced by a growing underclass in Suva society.

So, here it is, this book about Suva, the capital of Fiji. Individual recollections, reflections, perspectives and responses that collectively paint a portrait of a city we call home. There is more, much more, to be said about the dreams, hopes and aspirations of its residents, and one hope for this book will have been amply achieved if it prompts readers to share their own memories of living and working in this lovely place.

Part 1.
Foundations

1

The Prehistory of Suva

Paul Geraghty[1]

Introduction

'Prehistory' refers to the time before written records, but this chapter will cover the history of Suva from earliest times to after written records began, up until the move of the people of Suva across the bay to their present home in Suvavou in 1882, and will also follow briefly the ancient Rokotui Suva line until its demise in 1920.

Archaeology

As is well known, Fiji has been occupied for approximately 3,000 years, since the arrival of its first inhabitants, now known as the 'Lapita people' after their distinctive pottery style.[2] While there are a number of archaeological sites from the Lapita period in places such as Natunuku, Bourewa and Sigatoka in western Fiji and Moturiki, Naigani and Lakeba in eastern Fiji, none has been found in or near Suva. This does not necessarily mean that Suva was not occupied 3,000 years ago – indeed, its extensive harbour and inviting reef passage would have made it attractive

---

1   I would like to acknowledge the assistance of many people of Suvavou and nearby villages in my research, and thank Christina Toren for her transcript of Hocart's 'Heart of Fiji'. Thanks also to Tui Rakuita and Frank Thomas for helpful comments. All translations and mistakes are my own.
2   Frank Thomas, Paul Geraghty and Elizabeth Matisoo-Smith, 'Lapita archaeology in the Southwest Pacific', in *Encyclopedia of global archeology*, ed. Claire Smith (New York: Springer, 2020), doi.org/10.1007/978-3-319-51726-1_3410-1.

to Lapita people – but the explanation for the lack of Lapita sites may lie in sea-level change or topography, or indeed simply that sites may have been built over in Suva's 140-year history as a capital city, before laws on preserving archaeological heritage came into force.

Parry studied aerial photographs and determined that there were many ring-ditch fortifications (*korowaiwai*) on and near the Suva peninsula, dating from the mid-nineteenth century or earlier.[3] Parry gives details for each, such as size, shape, number of ditches and site type, but only one ('Suva', probably Solia) is identified by name. Table 1.1 lists the details from Parry's mapping.

Table 1.1: Ring-ditch fortifications on the Suva peninsula.

Location	Size	Shape	Ditches	Site type
Solia	4	annular	1	beach ridge or strand
Muanikau	2	annular	1	beach ridge or strand
Muanikau	4	annular	1	beach ridge or strand
Vatuwaqa	2	annular	1	knoll
Waidamudamu	2	annular	1	beach ridge or strand
Waidamudamu	2	annular	1	beach ridge or strand
Waidamudamu	2	annular	1	beach ridge or strand

Source: After Parry (1977).

The Solia fort is referred to by Wall: 'Twenty-five years ago [1894] the moat and rampart were practically intact, but now there are no traces of them left.'[4] This is confirmed by the American artist John La Farge who wrote in June 1891 that:

> the [botanical] garden follows a line of moats, once belonging to a fortified town … This is the first recognizable trace that we have yet seen of the fortified place protected by ditches … the laying out of the lines seems to have been determined with some engineering intelligence.[5]

---

3   John T Parry, *Ring-ditch fortifications in the Rewa Delta, Fiji: Air photo interpretation and analysis*, Bulletin of the Fiji Museum 3 (Suva: Fiji Museum, 1977).
4   Colman Wall, 'Sketches in Fijian history', *Transactions of the Fijian Society* (1919), republished as Colman Wall, 'Historical notes on Suva', ed. Paul Geraghty, *Domodomo* 10, no. 2 (1996): 37.
5   John La Farge, *Reminiscences of the South Seas* (London: Grant Richards, 1914), 398–99.

Of Muanikau, he writes:

> Round near the old race-course [now part of University of the South Pacific, or USP] … still stands the old moat and rampart (once surmounted by a war fence) of the town of Muanikau … an old settlement of Fiji carpenters who cut out here the planks, keel-pieces, and steering-oars that were afterwards put together on the white beach inside Quarantine Island.[6]

In addition to these ring-ditch fortifications, there were a number of hillforts on the Suva peninsula, as will be discussed below.

Evidence of Placenames: Suva

Placenames can be important indicators of history, tending to be retained especially when there is continuous occupation and they refer to a relatively large area.[7] So, while we do not know when the placename Suva was coined, if it was used by the earliest settlers – and there are good reasons for believing that they spoke a language ancestral to contemporary Fijian communalects – then their descendants and subsequent immigrants would have most likely preserved that name.

The most popular etymology of the name Suva – and one I consider more plausible than many popular etymologies – is that it originates from the word *suva* meaning 'cairn (pile of stones) or mound marking a boundary'. The earliest evidence for this meaning is from Hazlewood's dictionary:

> Suva, *Suvasuva, n. a mound; sometimes thrown up as a monument, sometimes to intrench behind, as in a siege.[8]

Denicagilaba uses *suvasuva* to mean a mound of earth that mystically grows into an island, while Mokunitulevu Na Rai uses *suva* as a synonym of *buke*, meaning 'yam mound' and *suvasuva* as 'boundary marker'.[9]

---

6   Wall, 'Sketches in Fijian history' ([1919] 1996), 36. 'Quarantine Island' presumably refers to Nukulau.
7   Paul Geraghty, 'Suffixation as a place naming strategy in the Central Pacific and its implications for prehistory', *Names* 65, no. 4 (2017): 235–44, doi.org/10.1080/00277738.2017.1370069.
8   The asterisk indicates that *suvasuva* is 'not properly a word of the Bau dialect … but more extensively known and used throughout the group than the corresponding Bau word'. David Hazlewood, *A Feejeean and English dictionary: With examples of common and peculiar modes of expression* (Viwa: Wesleyan Mission Press, 1850).
9   Denicagilaba [Ilai Motonicocoka], 'A veisisivi talanoa makawa: Ai tukuni ni vanua eda vu maikina', *Na Mata* 1892–1894; Mokunitulevu Na Rai [Epeli Rokowaqa], *Ai tukutuku kei Viti* (Suva: Methodist Church in Fiji, 1928).

Neyret (1935) gives a definition that is more in line with the current understanding:

> SUVA. –n, A mound, a heap of earth, serving as a land-mark.
> SUVASUVA. –n, Dim[inuative]. of above. A smaller mound.[10]

Capell, as was sadly often the case, merely copied Neyret without acknowledgement.[11]

Given this meaning, it is not surprising that there are a number of other places in Fiji with related names. For example, there are places called Suva or Nasuva in Matailobau (Wainimala), Nakorotubu (Ra), Sēqāqā (Macuata) and Udu (north-east Vanualevu) and a village named Suva or Suvalailai (literally 'small Suva') in Rewa. This does not mean that the people of Suva are necessarily related to these places, rather that the placenames have the same origin. However the village name Colo-i-Suva, north of the Suva peninsula, is related, meaning simply 'the hills of Suva', as is Dokanaisuva, 'the ridge of Suva'.

As to why the peninsula was given this name, some say that the ancestor god Rokomautu of Verata placed a *suva* there to mark the boundary of his lands with those of his brother Rō Melāsiga, the Rokotui Dreketi, high chief of Rewa.[12] Another explanation, also with a connection to Verata and not altogether incompatible with the former, is offered by Wall:

> To the old Fijians Suva (a little hill) was the mound on which the temple of Ro Vonu stood, and in which was concealed the sacred stone Vatubulia brought from Vatuwaqa, on which their chiefs were seated at their inauguration, and this mound gave its name to the town – originally the stone was supposed to have been carried by genii from Ucunivanua in Verata. But the name of Suva was never applied by them to any other place.[13]

---

10   J Neyret, 'Fijian dictionary', MS, Fiji Government Archives, 1935.
11   Arthur Capell, *A new Fijian dictionary* (Sydney: Australasian Medical Publishing Co., 1941).
12   Kitione Vesikula, *Tawavanua: Transcription of a series of talks on Radio Fiji One* (Suva: Fiji Broadcasting Commission, 1974), 6.
13   Wall, 'Sketches in Fijian history' ([1919] 1996), 38.

Other Early Placenames

The earliest approximation to a 'gazetteer' of the Suva area was that compiled by French explorer Dumont d'Urville in 1827 from information supplied by the King of Nadrogā.[14] In the following table, arranged approximately from west to east, the first column is the original, and the second is the probable pronunciation using contemporary Fijian spelling, taking into account French spelling conventions. Additional information is given in notes below the table. Note that in the first placename, the article *o* has been recorded incorrectly as part of the name, as commonly occurred around that time.[15]

Table 1.2: Inhabited places[16] in the vicinity of Suva according to the King of Nadrogā.

Olan-Hani	Lagani
Oucilan-Houa	Gusuilagwa
Lacé-Lacé	Laselase
Tama-Boua	Tamavua
Lami	Lami
Souba	Suva
Nakoro-lébou	Nakorolevu
Néréré-Ouanga	Nairairaiwaqa
Solia	Solia
Kalambou	Kalabu
Réken-Réké	Drekedreke

Source: Recorded by Dumont d'Urville (1827).

Notes to Table 1.2:

- Lagani was the old village of the *yavusa* Bativudi, now living in Kalokolevu,[17] described as a hilltop from which the sea is visible.
- Gusuilagwa (also recorded as Gusuinalaga and Gusunilaga) is another former village of the *yavusa* Bativudi,[18] which was also occupied by the people of Navatuvula, now on the Waimanu, and of Burenivalu, now in Nadoi, Rewa.

---

14   Jules SC Dumont d'Urville, *Voyage de Découvertes de l'Astrolabe exécuté par ordre du Roi pendant les années 1826–1827–1828–1829* (Paris: Minstère de la Marine, 1834), 715.
15   Paul Geraghty, 'Maps and the understanding of Fiji's toponymy 1643–1840', *The Globe* 88, no. 43 (2020): 45.
16   Dumont d'Urville states that this was a list of islands, but clearly it is of inhabited places, mostly on the island of Vitilevu.
17   Seveci Naisilisili, *Tukutuku Rāraba* (henceforth *TR*) *Bativudi* (Suva: Native Lands Commission, n.d. [1921?]), 3.
18   Ibid., 4.

- Laselase was the village of Tuisolia on the Naikorokoro river, between Naqara and Suva, burnt along with Namulo by men from the American sloop of war *John Adams* in 1855[19] as reprisal for an attack on Americans living on the offshore island of Namuka. Lady Gordon (wife of the first governor, Sir Arthur Gordon) visited it in January, 1876, and wrote that it was 'the nicest and cleanest [native town] I have seen yet'.[20] The people of Laselase are now classified as the fishers of the *yavusa* Navakavu.[21]
- Suva probably refers to Nauluvatu, see below.
- Nakorolevu is cited, as Korolevu, by Wall as the name of the main part of Vatuwaqa, the hilltop fort near Flagstaff/Kaunikuila marked on some maps as Nacovu.[22]
- Nairairaiwaqa is where Borron House now stands, close to Samabula, the second highest point on the Suva peninsula, after Nauluvatu.
- Solia is said by Hocart and the people of Suvavou to be now the grounds of Government House and the adjacent botanical gardens.[23] The connection with Tuisolia of Laselase and *mataqali* Solia in Maū (Namosi) and Sawani and Navatuvula (Naitāsiri) is unclear.
- Drekedreke is a former village of the Lami people on the Waimanu River;[24] it was still occupied in early colonial times.

This table indicates that, in 1827, there were at least four habitations on the Suva peninsula: Solia, probably a ring-ditch fortification on the west coast, and three hillforts, Nauluvatu (referred to as Suva), Nairairaiwaqa and Vatuwaqa (referred to as Nakorolevu).

In parts of eastern Fiji, names of landings, usually beginning with Matai-, can also be suggestive of relative political importance. The fact that there is a place on the western coast of Rewa called Mataisuva 'Suva landing' suggests that Suva was independent of Rewa, and relatively important.[25] Wall was told that the beach where canoes from Bau landed, near what is now the Government Buildings, was called Ucukobau, based on *ucu* 'headland'.[26]

---

19 Franklin Pierce, *Sloop of War 'John Adams' at Fejee Islands: Message from the President of the United States communicating the report of Captain Boutwell, relative to the operations of the sloop of war 'John Adams' at the Fejee Islands* ([Washington]: House of Representatives Ex Doc No 115, 34th Congress, 1st Session, 1856), 73,75–76; Berthold Seemann, *Viti: An account of a government mission to the Vitian or Fijian Islands in the years 1860-61* (Cambridge: Macmillan, 1862), 107–8, doi.org/10.5962/bhl.title.54719.
20 Lord (Sir Arthur Gordon) Stanmore, *Fiji: Records of private and of public life 1875–1880*, 4 vols (Edinburgh: self-pub., 1897–1912) 392.
21 Samu Toge, *TR Navakavu* (Suva: Native Lands Commission, 1927).
22 Wall, 'Sketches in Fijian history' ([1919] 1996), 33.
23 Arthur Hocart, 'The heart of Fiji', MS, Turnbull Library, Wellington, 3774c, n.d.
24 Vetaia Seni, *TR Nakurukuru* (Suva: Native Lands Commission, 1927).
25 Other named landings in Rewa include Mataibau 'Bau landing' and Mataikalabu 'Kalabu landing'.
26 Wall, 'Sketches in Fijian history' ([1919] 1996), 37.

Language

Suva is, unusually, a *vanua* of one village with two communalects.[27] Typically, a *vanua* comprises a number of villages speaking the same communalect, but in Suva, nowadays the village of Suvavou, there are two communalects – Suva and Walu – neither of which is spoken anywhere else and one of which (Walu) is now extinct.

Walu was spoken by the *kaiwai* (fishers) and *mataisau* (carpenters) who lived in or near what is now the industrial area called Walu Bay, of whom more below. From what little is known, the language of Walu appears to be similar to Rewa, the communalect group to the east of Suva. The Suva communalect is closest to Lami, and they (Suva–Lami) in turn are roughly equidistant from Navakavu (Waiqanake, Muaivusu) and Tamavua-Kalabu. All these communalects belong to the Southeast Vitilevu communalect group,[28] characterised by the transitive suffix *-e* (e.g. *cakave* 'do it', contrast Standard Fijian *cakava*) and a set of labiovelar stops (e.g. *gwalo* 'evening') that are, however, in the case of Suva, obsolescent.

So, in general, the language of Suva is considerably closer to communalects to the west and north – all of which are in or came from the *colo* (hill country) – than to those of Rewa to the east, whereas for Walu the reverse is true. A possible historical inference is that most of the current inhabitants of Suva are relative newcomers from the *colo*, while the Walu people comprised fishers who had been there for longer and carpenters who came from Rewa after the *vanua* of Suva had been established in fairly recent prehistory, over 200 years ago.

A lexical curiosity of the communalect of Suva (and its neighbour to the west, Navakavu) is that the word for reef heron (*Egretta sacra*) is not *belō*, as everywhere else in Fiji, but *sakō*. This word features in the name of a small island to the west of the Navakavu peninsula, Koronisakō 'village (or mountain) of herons'.

---

27   A communalect is a variety of language spoken by people who claim to speak the same.
28   Paul A Geraghty, *The history of the Fijian languages,* Oceanic Linguistics Special Publication 19 (Honolulu: University of Hawai'i Press, 1983), 317–20.

Incidentally, the roadside sign welcoming travellers on the Queens Road to Suvavou 'Ni bula maleka' (for Standard Fijian 'Nī bula vinaka') is a mixture: *maleka* is indeed Suva for 'good', Standard *vinaka*, but the Suva second-person respectful subject pronoun is not *nī* but *nū*, so the sign should read: 'Nū bula maleka'.

The Legends of Di Vivilitabua

Two similar legends relating to Suva were recorded by Pritchard and Brewster.[29] Both feature the beautiful princess of Davetalevu and her many suitors. Davetalevu is the name of the main passage in the reef into Suva Harbour, but also of a village on its western shore where the princess lives, according to Brewster, while in Pritchard's version she lives in Suva. In Pritchard's version, she is wooed by Tongans from Lakeba and is on her way with them when she is extricated by 'Dadarakai' (probably Dādarikai) the ancestor god of Lami, who pursued her in a canoe made of fruit trees, which diverted the Tongans' attention when the ripe fruit fell on their canoe, with the help of his grandmother 'Levatu' (probably Lewatū). In Brewster's version she is forced by her evil grandmother into marriage with the decrepit Rokotui Dreketi, but manages to escape with her true love to his village under Rāmā (Joske's Thumb), so probably Laselase or thereabouts.

Records of Prehistory

Suva is relatively rich in records of prehistory. The main sources I will be referring to – in chronological order – are missionary journals and publications from the mid-nineteenth century;[30] missionary-inspired histories of Fiji in Fijian by Ilai Motonicocoka,[31] Epeli Rokowaqa[32] and Kitione Vesikula;[33] anthropologist Arthur Hocart's unpublished

---

29   WT Pritchard, *Polynesian reminiscences, or life in the South Pacific islands* (London: Chapman & Hall, 1866), 384–7; AB Brewster, *King of the Cannibal Isles* (London: Robert Hales and Company, 1937), 57–61.
30   For example, James Calvert, *Fiji and the Fijians*, vol. 2, *Mission history* (London: Alexander Heylin, 1858); Thomas James Jaggar, *Unto the perfect day: The journal of Thomas James Jaggar, Feejee 1838–1845*, ed. Esther and William Keesing-Styles (Auckland: Solent, 1988).
31   Denicagilaba, 'A veisisivi talanoa makawa'.
32   Mokunitulevu Na Rai, *Ai tukutuku kei Viti*.
33   Vesikula, *Tawavanua*.

1. THE PREHISTORY OF SUVA

manuscript from 1912 (see Appendix 2); Colman Wall's 1919 article in *Transactions of the Fiji Society*, based on conversations with the people of Suvavou, reprinted and annotated in *Domodomo*;[34] records of the Native Lands Commission in the early twentieth century (see Appendixes 3 and 5)[35] and oral material I collected from Suvavou in the 1980s and 1990s.[36]

Certain facts about the *matanitū* (state) of Suva are consistent in all records, for instance that the ceremonial name (*icavu* or *icavuti*) is Nadonumai and that the title of the chief is, or has been in recent times, Rokotui Suva (also spelt Roko Tui Suva). When it became known to Westerners, Suva was a moderately powerful *matanitū* with links to both major kingdoms of recent prehistory, Rewa and Bau, but closer to the latter, and associated clans of *mataisau* (carpenters) who also served as fishermen. The *vanua* of Navakavu to the west are the *bati* (warriors) of Suva, and appropriate food taboos are observed between the two *vanua*. All records also agree in general that major components of the population are groups called Nauluvatu, Vatuwaqa and Nayavumata (or Navumata).

This leads to a question of importance for the prehistory of Suva: given that the people of Nauluvatu originated from Ra, that Vatuwaqa was either an offshoot of Nauluvatu[37] or also from Ra[38] (see discussion below), and that Nayavumata were relatively late arrivals from Nacokaikwā in Naitāsiri, does that mean that, unlikely as it sounds, Suva was vacant before their arrival? The answer is no, but that, as along much if not all of the coast of Vitilevu, the earlier inhabitants were absorbed into these larger, more recently arrived groups, at least for official purposes. Their distinct origin is usually given away by their designation as *gonedau* 'fishers', or *kaiwai* or *qalivakawai* 'sea people' and/or the fact that they observe food restrictions typical of sea people, such as being allowed pork but prohibited fish when in the presence of 'land people'.

---

34   Colman Wall, 'Sketches in Fijian history', *Transactions of the Fijian Society* (1919) republished and annotated as Colman Wall, 'Historical notes on Suva', ed. Paul Geraghty, *Domodomo* 10, no. 2 (1996): 28–39; 11, no. 2 (1997): 15–37; 12, no. 2 (1999): 49–58.
35   Seruveveli Dakai, *TR Nayavumata* (Suva: Native Lands Commission, 1921); Kaminieli Rogo, *TR Nauluvatu* (Suva: Native Lands Commission, 1921); Seni, *TR Nakurukuru*; A Savenaca Seniloli, letter to the Native Lands Commissioner, 30 January 1919, iTaukei Lands and Fisheries Commission, National Archives of Fiji; Toge, *TR Navakavu*; Amenisitai Waqadau, *TR Vatuwaqa* (Suva: Native Lands Commission, 1921); Native Lands Commission, *Final report by chairman on the provinces of Tailevu (North), Rewa, Naitasiri and Colo East* (Suva: Native Lands Commission, 1959).
36   Waisake Tokaduadua, 'Tukutuku kī Vatuwaqa' (transcript of interview in possession of author, 1984); Apete Rokotuiwai Dumaru, 'Suva makawa' (computer file in possession of the author, 1999).
37   Wall, 'Sketches in Fijian history' ([1919] 1996), 31.
38   Tokaduadua, 'Tukutuku kī Vatuwaqa'.

There are numerous parallels around the coast of Vitilevu, but I will point out just one in the neighbouring *vanua* of Navakavu (currently the villages Waiqanake, Nabaka and Muaivuso), immediately to the west of Suva and Lami. According to the official report,[39] all the people belong to the *yavusa* Navakavu, of which one *mataqali*, Laselase, are stated to be *gonedau* 'fishers'. Recalling that the list of places in the vicinity of Suva recorded by Dumont d'Urville in 1827 included Laselase, but not any of the current coastal villages, it is reasonable to infer that at that time the people of Laselase were coastal villagers, who were joined afterwards by Navakavu people descending from the Waidina river valley. So, while they are officially of the one *yavusa*, and now speak the same language and have the same customs, they have separate origins.

Walu

It appears, then, that the earliest occupied site we have secure knowledge of is Walu, the stretch of coast at the foot of Nauluvatu where the Walu Bay industrial area now is. Hocart was told that the original people of Walu, the *kai* Walu, were the fishers of Suva, their leader holding the title of Daunisuva.[40] Wall was told:

> [a]ll the land lying between the Waimanu Road and Walu Bay was in olden days called Waluwalu, from the kai Walu, or fisher clan, who used it constantly, though they dwelt in the town above.[41]

Presumably they lived in Nauluvatu during times of peril, but had a settlement by the beach at other times.

The *kai* Walu however became extinct, but not before teaching the arts of fishing to the carpenters (*mataisau*) who had come to live near them, presumably from Rewa, as an offshoot of the Rewa carpenters now resident in Nukutubu.[42] So in addition to canoe-builders, the carpenters became turtle-fishers. Whether the now extinct communalect of Walu, discussed previously, was the original language of Walu or introduced by the carpenters from Rewa, is now difficult to determine.

---

39 Toge, *TR Navakavu*.
40 Hocart, 'The heart of Fiji', 374D.
41 Wall, 'Sketches in Fijian history' ([1919] 1996), 32.
42 Recall that the carpenters also had a settlement at Muanikau, as noted above.

In a further intriguing parallel with Verata, Walu is also the name of a coastal area to the west of the chiefly village of Ucunivanua formerly inhabited by the *kaiwai* (fisher clan) of Verata, the *kai* Macoi.

Nauluvatu

Nauluvatu is the name of the massive rock that rises above Walu Bay, near the present settlement of the same name. Its name means something like 'rocky summit', and there is no necessary connection to the many other places of the same name such as in Waidina, Tawava (Kadavu), or Vanuavatu, Cicia and Totoya (Lau).

While the *Tukutuku Rāraba* (historical report for the Native Lands Commission[43]) of the Nauluvatu people states that Nauluvatu was their *yavutū* (ancestral home), Wall states that the first people to settle there came from Saivou in what is now Ra province, led by a man called Tabanimakoveve who was the son of a descendant of Degei, the most revered ancestor god of eastern Fiji, residing in the Nakauvadra mountains, and a princess of the *veli* (short people living in the forest).[44] On the other hand, Suva people told Hocart that they originated from Matailobau, close to the junction of the Wainibuka and Wainimala, which may indeed have been a stop on the way from Saivou, but may also have been an inference they drew based on the presence there of a *yavusa* named Suva.[45]

Hocart further recorded that they disembarked at Naivisere in what is now Vuna in Naitāsiri, though there were no Vuna men there at the time.[46] Eventually, according to Wall, they came under pressure from the hostile Vuna tribe arriving from the north, so moved south to Nauluvatu.[47] There, they sent a man to survey the area, and he stopped at a place called Nairairai (the looking-place) because he could see all the canoes from there.[48] This is a plausible etymology, appearing to be an abbreviation of the name Nairairaiwaqa ('the place for looking out for canoes'), as recorded by Dumont d'Urville in 1827 and still used today, referring to the site of Borron House.

---

43   Rogo, *TR Nauluvatu*.
44   Wall, 'Sketches in Fijian history' ([1919] 1996), 28.
45   Hocart, 'The heart of Fiji', 374B.
46   Ibid.
47   Wall, 'Sketches in Fijian history' ([1919] 1997), 16.
48   Hocart, 'The heart of Fiji', 374B.

Wall provides many fascinating details of the hilltop citadel of Nauluvatu, including the fact that the house-mounds were circular, indicating that the buildings were of the 'old conical design'[49] – see Freeman for a discussion of house types in Vitilevu.[50] Their chief was titled 'Vunivalu' ('expert in war'), as were originally the chiefs of all three main components of Suva, and they were served by and lived with a group of *mataisau* (carpenters) called Vuaniwī.[51]

Eventually, most of the people of Nauluvatu moved to Vatuwaqa, but the Naqiōmila remained there for a while before joining the rest in the coastal settlement of Solia.[52]

Vatuwaqa

Wall states that Vatuwaqa was an overflow town of Nauluvatu, and that the 'king' of Suva resided in Nauluvatu while his son and heir lived in Vatuwaqa.[53] However, the report of the Native Lands Commission[54] states that the *yavusa* Vatuwaqa never lived anywhere other than Vatuwaqa. Tokaduadua paints a more interesting, and largely more plausible, picture. Recalling the account given him by his father, he relates that they came on a canoe from Nakauvadra in Ra and anchored at Muanivatu (current site of USP).[55] Wall was told:

> at the mouth of the creek in the pool where the canoes formerly anchored, is a large flat rock … and having some fanciful resemblance to a boat it was termed Vatuwaqa; it gave its name to the creek and to the great town above.[56]

After spending some time in a cave near the shore, they climbed up to Nacovu and settled there. Here they installed a young chief (Roko Saketa) as Tui Vatuwaqa and went to Bau to ask for the hand of Di Elenoa (also known as Adi Lewatū, Elenoa being presumably the name she, or her namesake, adopted on becoming Christian). They were married, and the

---

49 Wall, 'Sketches in Fijian history' ([1919] 1996), 28–29.
50 Susan Freeman, 'The centre-poled houses of western Vitilevu', *Domodomo* 4, no. 1 (1986): 2–19.
51 Rogo, *TR Nauluvatu*, 1.
52 Wall, 'Sketches in Fijian history' ([1919] 1996), 32.
53 Wall, 'Sketches in Fijian history' ([1919] 1996), 33; ([1919] 1997), 18.
54 Waqadau, *TR Vatuwaqa*.
55 Tokaduadua, 'Tukutuku kī Vatuwaqa'.
56 Wall, 'Sketches in Fijian history' ([1919] 1996), 35.

Bau lady asked to move closer to the shore so she and her retinue could fish and collect shellfish, so they moved to a site on the western shore of the peninsula, which other sources name as Solia.

Hocart was told that there is a *vatu ni irevo* (oven stone) in Vatuwaqa, the god of the Vatuwaqa clan.[57] It was forbidden to chip it else the crops would perish. Hocart was unable to obtain the name of the god, but was told that his animal is the *kisikisi*, a small sea crab (PG: *Matuta* sp.) known as the 'turtle' of Vatuwaqa. This is presumably the same 'coronation stone', named Vatubulia, that was mentioned by Wall as having been moved to the mound of the temple of Rō Vonu in Suva. Given that 'Vonu' means turtle, it is likely that this Rō Vonu was the name of the god of Vatuwaqa that Hocart was unable to discover.

Nairairaiwaqa

Some of the population of Nauluvatu spilled over to the two other hillforts, Nairairaiwaqa and Vatuwaqa. When they were joined by the Nayavumata people originally from Nacokaikwā, a village in Naitāsiri on the banks of the Wailevu (Rewa River), but more immediately from Tamavua, they were told to live in Nairairaiwaqa.[58] They had with them two groups of *mataisau* (carpenters), the *matanibure* Beranabuka and Daunivuwai.[59]

The name of this place was clearly Nairairaiwaqa, which was recorded by Dumont d'Urville in 1827 and is also etymologically plausible, meaning 'place for seeing ships/canoes', or shortened to Rairaiwaqa. Inexplicably, Wall consistently referred to it as Rairainawaqa and other versions include Narairainiwaqa and Nairairainiwaqa.[60]

Roko Saketa

Wall was told that the earliest 'King of Suva' recalled in oral traditions at the time was Batileka:

---

57 Hocart, 'The heart of Fiji', 374G.
58 Rogo, *TR Nauluvatu*, 1; Dakai, *TR Nayavumata*, 1.
59 *Matanibure* or *matabure* is an extended family, a subdivision of a *mataqali*, hence corresponding to the official term *tokatoka*. Dakai, *TR Nayavumata*, 1.
60 Wall, 'Sketches in Fijian history' ([1919] 1997); ([1919] 1999).

who married Radi Savasava [perhaps Radi Savusavu], and had by her two children, Ro Kesa, who died childless, and Ro Tanoa, or Tuivuya, who married Ro Limawaqa of Rewa, by whom he had a son called Ro Saketa.[61]

No other accounts mention these people, though a later Rokotui Suva bore the name Tuivuya, so was presumably named after the one mentioned here, and the name Batileka or Batilekaleka also reappears.

The first Vunivalu (chief) of Nauluvatu of whom anything is related in the reports of the Veitarogivanua was this Roko Saketa (also written as one word, and as Rō Saketa), who was married to a Bau lady by the name of Lewatū[62] or Adi Moave,[63] or Adi Kainona according to Bauan traditions, a daughter of Tānoa the Vunivalu with a lady of Vusaradave, hence half-sister of Cakobau. Dumont d'Urville mentions her as one of Tānoa's two daughters, giving her title as Dini Suva, thus indicating that in 1827 she was alive and reigning as the Queen of Suva.[64] Previously, Suva had intermarried mostly with Rewa.[65] This lady brought with her a god of Bau, Cagawalu, who had one temple in Bau, Vatanitawake, and another in (or close to) Solia, the site of the combined village of Suva on the coast near the present botanical gardens.

The *mataqali* Naceva of the *yavusa* Vatuwaqa, on the other hand,[66] believe that Roko Saketa was a Bauan, the son of Raiwālui[67] of the Vusarātū, and Adi Salauca of Somosomo, Taveuni. While this is a minority view, it is not without merit. Requesting a chief (*kere tūraga*) from Bau has parallels in places such as Nairai (Mokunitulevu Na Rai 1928), and a closer relationship than *vasu* may be indicated by the particular affection that both Tānoa and Cakobau had for Suva[68] as well as the fact that Roko Saketa's son, Ravulo, was buried not in Suva but in the temple of

---

61 Wall, 'Sketches in Fijian history' ([1919] 1997), 18.
62 Waqadau, *TR Vatuwaqa*, 1.
63 Wall, 'Sketches in Fijian history' ([1919] 1997), 18.
64 Dumont d'Urville, *Voyage de Découvertes de l'Astrolabe*, 700.
65 Hocart, 'The heart of Fiji', 374C.
66 Epeli Qerea Koroitamudu, letter to Paula Qereti [Paul Geraghty], in possession of the author (2007).
67 A Raiwālui, of the *mataqali* Vuaniivi, was the last to be installed as Rokotui Bau, when Naulivou was Vunivalu; whether this is the same one is unclear.
68 Jaggar MMS Letters 5/7/1845, cited in Marshall Sahlins, *The return of the event, again: With reflections on the beginnings of the great Fijian war of 1843 to 1855 between the kingdoms of Bau and Rewa* (Washington DC: Biersack, 1991), 57; Mary Wallis, *Life in Feejee: Five years among the cannibals. By a lady* (Boston: William Heath, 1851), 163, doi.org/10.4324/9781003113485-5.

Navatanitawake in Bau and his widow and children moved there after his death. The missionary John Hunt also reported that Cakobau had promised to make the younger brother of the Rokotui Dreketi, Cokānauto (also known as Phillips and Komai Namanā), his Rewa *vasu* and ally, the king of rebuilt Suva after the war.[69]

Roko Saketa had at least two sons, Batilekaleka, also known as Tuivuya[70] and Tabakaucoro, also known as Rō Ravulo or simply Ravulo. While Batileka and Tuivuya are not Bauan names, both Tabakaucoro and Ravulo are, Tabakaucoro being his great-grandfather Bānuve's oldest son and Ravulo a son of his grandfather's older brother Naulivou by Bābokola. When they were still young, their father became attached to a lady of Tamavua, named by Wall as Adi Savasava,[71] upon which their mother fled to Vatuwaqa with the boys, and after a while there they went to Rewa to complain to Rokotui Dreketi about Roko Saketa's behaviour. He followed his wife and sons to Rewa, where he was 'clubbed to death on his canoe at the present landing place at Naililili, and his body is said to have drifted down to Nukulau', rendering vacant the position of Vunivalu of Nauluvatu.[72]

Adi Lewatū took Batilekaleka to Bau, leaving Ravulo in Rewa. She then married into Lakeba and after a short while Batilekaleka asked to go back to Vatuwaqa (Suva). Waqadau states that Batilekaleka returned from Lakeba to Vatuwaqa and that it was he who founded the new village of Suva on the west coast of the peninsula, but before long he was killed by the Rewa people.[73] Wall gives a different account of the fate of Batilekaleka, stating that his mother married in Nayau, as did he. He then settled in Kinoya and sailed to the Ra coast on a bêche-de-mer ship, where he was killed.[74]

However Batilekaleka met his fate, it is agreed that Ravulo was his successor as Rokotui Suva, evidently at a very young age. Cargill estimated his age at 18 when he met him in 1840.[75]

---

69 Alan R Tippett, *Aspects of Pacific ethnohistory* (South Pasadena: William Carey Library, 1973), 46.
70 Wall, 'Sketches in Fijian history' ([1919] 1997), 18.
71 Ibid.
72 Wall, 'Sketches in Fijian history' ([1919] 1999), 54, mentions a 'brother' of Ravulo named Vakalailaibula who claimed to be the true chief of Suva, and Ravulo had murdered in Kaukalou on the Tamavua River.
73 Waqadau, *TR Vatuwaqa*, 2.
74 Wall, 'Sketches in Fijian history' ([1919] 1997), 19.
75 Albert J Schütz (ed.), *The diaries and correspondence of David Cargill, 1832–1843* (Canberra: Australian National University, 1977), 178.

Consolidation in Suva/Solia

All accounts agree that Solia was a new settlement and a ring-ditch fort, and that it was inhabited by all, or most, of the people from Nauluvatu, Vatuwaqa and Nairairaiwaqa. While its founding is usually attributed to Ravulo, at least one account states that it was his older brother Batilekaleka. Reasons for its founding vary. Persistent rumours of attack by the army of Vuna is one, and it was indeed well enough fortified to repel an attack from a large Rewa army (see below).[76] Another reason given is that when Roko Saketa's wife was brought from Bau to Vatuwaqa, she asked to move closer to the shore so she could fish and collect shellfish more easily.[77]

Wall gives a detailed description of the village of Suva/Solia as remembered by the people of Suvavou, while some details are to be found in the account of Englishman William Diaper who visited it briefly in 1842.[78]

Arrival of Christianity

Methodist missionaries arrived in Fiji in 1835, and a mission was set up in Rewa, east of Suva, in 1839. One of the missionaries there, Thomas Jaggar, recorded that a Suva man became Christian on 22 February 1840, and his colleague David Cargill recorded the conversion of the 'King of Suva' (Ravulo) and two of his people on 17 May, followed soon by 'a few' of his people.[79] Ravulo arranged for some very good houseposts to be sent to the missionaries,[80] then on 13 June he visited the mission premises in Rewa and was presented with a coat, a hymnbook and other gifts; Jaggar remarked that he had been threatened by Bau chiefs because of his becoming Christian, but remained steadfast. In September, Tepola, the Tongan catechist's wife, reported that one man had reverted to heathenism. On 2 February 1841 Jaggar lamented that the king did not encourage his people to convert, and was lax in his observance of religion, but attributed this to his youth – the king being about 19 years of age.[81]

---

76 Rogo, *TR Nauluvatu*, 1.
77 Waqadau, *TR Vatuwaqa*; Wall, 'Sketches in Fijian history' ([1919] 1997), 19.
78 Wall, 'Sketches in Fijian history' ([1919] 1996), 37–38; [William Diaper] 'Jackson's narrative', in John Elphinstone Erskine, *Journal of a cruise among the islands of the Western Pacific* (London: John Murray, 1853), 475–77.
79 Schütz, *The diaries and correspondence of David Cargill*, 178, 182.
80 Calvert, *Fiji and the Fijians*, 161.
81 Jaggar, *Unto the perfect day*.

Suva's First Resident European – and His Visitor

The same fine *dakua* (*Agathis macrophylla*, similar to *kauri*) timber that Ravulo gave to the missionaries in Rewa as houseposts attracted the interest of an Englishman from Suffolk, Robert Stevens. Fellow Englishman William Diaper, who arrived in Fiji in 1840 and was much involved in local wars, related that he accompanied Stevens to Suva to saw *dakua*, and that they lived in Ravulo's house until they had one built for them, obtaining 16,000 feet of plank for an old musket.[82]

Diaper also recounts in some detail how one afternoon he was wandering around the town on his own and happened upon a tall young man, about 20 years old, who was preparing to be buried alive. He said his god was a shark, which identifies him as a member of the *mataqali* Naqiōmila. Diaper attempted to dissuade him, to no avail, and soon his relatives arrived and they proceeded to the cemetery, where he picked the spot for his grave, was dressed in his finest, then stepped into the shallow grave and lay on the mat with a *tabua* in his hands, clasped across his belly, as his father shovelled in the earth.

We are grateful to the missionary Thomas Jaggar for providing more details and a date for this incident: Monday, 19 September 1842. He also mentions a 'foreigner' who tried to intervene to prevent the burial.[83]

How long Stevens remained in Suva is not known, but he eventually ended up in Vava'u, Tonga, where he was flogged mercilessly by an overzealous missionary for violating the Sabbath.[84]

Prelude to Disaster: A Pig Too Far and a Long-Tailed Star

Jaggar also recorded succinctly the beginning of Fiji's greatest war in his entry for 12 January 1841: 'Sailed to Suva. Q driven away & other chiefs'. Q referred to Qaraniqiō, also known as Rātū Qara, Rō Qaraniqiō and

---

82   [William Diaper] 'Jackson's narrative', 475–76; William Diapea [Diaper], *Cannibal Jack: The true autobiography of a white man in the South Seas* (Oxford: Faber & Gwyer, 1928), 240.
83   Jaggar, *Unto the perfect day*, entry for 24 September 1842.
84   Diaper, *Cannibal Jack*, 240.

Rō Dakuwaqa, the elder of two younger brothers of the Rokotui Dreketi (chief of Rewa), Rō Kania, also known as Bānuve. According to Wiliame Lolowalu of Nakauwaru in Noco, writing in Fijian in 1866, the incident unfolded as follows:

> I will tell of something that happened in the time of Dakuwaqa. He sailed to the west in a canoe named the Uluilakeba. They visited Beqa and many places on Vitilevu, then returned to Rewa. They were close to Suva when night fell so they beached there to spend the night, and killed a pig, which angered the people of Suva, and they had a heated exchange. When they arrived in Rewa, Dakuwaqa immediately prepared for war, sending envoys to all the villages to tell them to prepare to attack Suva.[85]

Wall's account states that they did not kill the pig (which was named 'Tamavua') but attempted to take it, and adds that they then camped at Dakuniwai, on the east side of the peninsula, where one of them was killed the next morning by Suva scouts, before returning to Rewa.[86]

Rewa and Suva both prepared for war. The next month, Jaggar reported:

> they [Suva] are very busy fencing in their town: - also carrying their riches away & burying them as well as leaving the town by night (ie the women & children) and sleeping in the bush.[87]

By April 1842 the situation had become so tense that the wife and daughter of the Tongan catechist were removed. The next month, Jaggar visited Suva and was told that war was expected daily, and that Ravulo and most of his people had withdrawn for defence to 'a town near them' – presumably Nauluvatu. Finally, over a year after the plundered pig affair, on 23 June 1842, the Rewa army attacked Suva. As Jaggar reported:

> Warriors gone today to attack Suva perhaps 2000. The Suva people set fire last night to the house of the Teacher and that of an Englishman [presumably Stevens] which were built outside the fence of the Town in order to prevent the concealment or approach of the enemy.[88]

---

85   Jesse Carey (compiler), n.d. MSS in Fijian. Methodist Church of Australasia, Department of Overseas Missions, Item 164, Mitchell Library, Sydney.
86   Wall, 'Sketches in Fijian history' ([1919] 1997), 20.
87   Jaggar, *Unto the perfect day*, 90.
88   Jaggar, *Unto the perfect day*, entry for 23 June 1842.

Two days later, Jaggar wrote:

> The warriors retd last night without being able to carry out their designs, they found the town too strongly fortified and too well supplied with ammunition for them. 2 Suva men were slain & others wounded. 5 of the enemy also fell and some wounded. Some of the latter were obtained by the Suva people. One Noco man was killed at the attack on S. he was carried to his town & buried: his wife first being strangled and her young infant thus left without a mother. The Teacher reports that they are very busy at S. preparing their town by night & day by planting an innumerable quantity of sokis [sharp bamboo stakes set in foot-traps] that the enemy may not approach. They are dressed & ornamented for the war: the women & children remaining concealed in the bush. It seems that the Rewa people deceived them saying they were going to verikarati [meaning unclear] only: that had the S. people been aware of this they wd have killed more than they did. The R people warriors however destroyed all their plantations and took away such food as they thot useful wh is never done but in a regular war. This conduct incensed the Suva people much. The Suva people seem more inclined to die in their town than Soro [surrender] to Q. The Rewa Chief is very much chagrined at not being able to destroy Suva. He is for going again to try, but he does not seem to be seconded or encouraged by any. Suva can it seems defend itself – it is well fenced. The root of the present attack was a disturbance about some pigs between some of Q's men and the Suva people … (The Suva people said to the chief, we shall not run away or be driven for where shall we turn to – to the reef, – we are not fish but men – this is our land, & if we die we will die in our town – we have but one burial ground and it is this our own town.)

Before Qaraniqiō launched the next attack, a portent appeared in the skies over Fiji. The first to report it was Methodist missionary Thomas Williams, who wrote from Lakeba on 4 March, 1843:

> Observed something bright in the west about two hours after sunset, and was delighted to find upon closer inspection that I was looking upon a comet … its tail … was of great length and very bright, inclined a little towards the south.[89]

---

89   GC Henderson, *The journal of Thomas Williams, missionary in Fiji, 1840–1853* (Sydney: Angus & Robertson, 1, 1931), 151–52.

Williams's colleague Richard Lyth reported seeing the same phenomenon from Somosomo in Taveuni.[90] The Fijian for 'comet' is *kalokalo vakabuina*, literally 'star with a tail'.

Some 20 years later, around 1865, students (all mature) at the Methodist Training Institution in Rijimodi, Kadavu, were asked by their teacher, Jesse Carey, to write accounts of various traditional beliefs, such as ancestor gods and portents (*ilālā*), which he collected and which were eventually deposited in the Mitchell Library in Sydney.[91] No less than nine students, all from Rewa or one of its allies such as Noco or Tokatoka, described the comet and stated that it was a portent of the destruction of Suva (*ilālā kei Suva*), some adding the information that the comet had a name: *lavileca* (for which I can currently offer no etymology).

The Massacre, 6 April 1843

Seeing that direct attack had failed, Rewa turned to more devious means. It gained the support of most of Suva's allies by bribery and the promise of spoils. In particular, a *tabua* was presented to Rō Camaisala, head of the Vuna[92] people then resident in Koroi on the Waimanu, requesting them to visit Suva in a seemingly friendly manner, which they did towards the end of March 1843.[93]

On the morning of 5 April, the Rewa fleet sailed and landed its troops on the eastern shore of the peninsula, whence they marched along the coast to take up positions at the southern end of the town. They had with them a brass cannon from the *L'Aimable Joséphine*, the French brig that had been seized by Bau rebels near Viwa in 1834, in the charge of Charlie Pickering, Qaraniqiō's devoted right-hand man. At the same time troops from Kalabu, Tamavua and various *vanua* to the north and west as far as Maū, most former allies of Suva, assembled around what is now Albert Park.[94]

Cannon fire started around 3 pm, but did little damage. However, the Vuna men who were being hosted in the town rose, following their instructions from Rewa, and set fire to the houses and temples. A group of Suva men defended the northern gate of the town, enabling Ravulo

---

90   Ibid., 152n23.
91   Jesse Carey (compiler), n.d. MSS in Fijian. Methodist Church of Australasia, Department of Overseas Missions, Item 164, Mitchell Library, Sydney.
92   Wall states it was the Lomaivuna people, but other evidence suggests it was Vuna.
93   Wall, 'Sketches in Fijian history' ([1919] 1997), 22.
94   Ibid., 23.

and others to make their escape towards the south, reaching what is now the playing field at Nasova police barracks, and along with the *katikati* (women and children), numbering over 500, they sought refuge in the densely wooded hills to the east. Towards dawn they followed the familiar path to their mountain stronghold of Nauluvatu, where the men set about repairing the defences and the women went out looking for food.[95]

That night they slept in caves near Nauluvatu. They were surrounded by the enemy: Rewa canoes in Walu Bay, canoes of Rewa allies in the mouth of the Tamavua River, while detachments of the armies of Vuna and Tamavua and other Rewa allies such as Noco camped in and around Nairairaiwaqa.[96]

The next morning, the missionary John Hunt sailed past on his way to the west and later wrote:

> Friday April 7th 1843 We had full view of poor Suva this morning, where we once had a few Christians. Yesterday the town was reduced to ashes, and many of its inhabitants killed and eaten by the Rewa people. We saw several canoes which had gone in search of the miserable remnant. The Christian chief is still alive.[97]

Meanwhile the invaders had sent word to Bau that the burning of Suva was sufficient punishment. Nevertheless, most of them left the town the next morning to join their allies besieging Nauluvatu. Realising their impossible situation, the people of Suva decided to *soro* (surrender), and on the morning of the 9th Korotatibi, the envoy to Vuna, set out with a large *tabua* and a fine young lady of chiefly rank and their *isoro* was accepted by Rō Camaisala.[98]

However, while the remnants of the Suva people were making their way from Nauluvatu, a Rewa warrior manhandled a Beqa lady married to a Suva man and clubbed her dead.[99] This led to a general massacre of the Suva people, mostly women, with estimates of casualties ranging from 100 to 400, and ultimately to the most terrible war in Fiji history, indeed probably in the history of the Pacific Islands:[100] that between Bau and Rewa from 1844 to 1855.

---

95   Ibid., 23–25.
96   Ibid., 25–26.
97   Jaggar MMS Letters, Hunt 12/6/1843, cited in Sahlins, *The return of the event, again*, 56.
98   Wall, 'Sketches in Fijian history' ([1919] 1997), 26–28.
99   Ibid., 28–29.
100 Sahlins, *The return of the event, again*, 51.

For more details on the sacking of Suva and its consequences, see Wall and Sahlins.[101]

Wanderings and Return

After the massacre, most of the remnants fled to Lami, and sent a messenger to Leweivunibua,[102] the chief of Soloirā, the main chiefdom on the middle Waidina, requesting to stay in his village of Vunibua (now Nabukāluka).[103] This was approved and they moved there. When Cakobau, the Vunivalu of Bau, heard that they had fled to Vunibua, he sent a message to a certain Nalikuyameyame of Navuso, the chiefly village of Naitāsiri, instructing him to bring the Suva people to Navuso. After a period of residence at nearby Nacokaikwā, the home of the Nayavumata people of Suva, they moved to Navuso, and Ravulo the Rokotui Suva went to stay with his uncle Cakobau on Bau.[104] An anonymous source states that they arrived in Navuso while Cakobau was in Lakeba, which would mean in mid or late 1843.[105]

When in January 1844 war erupted between Bau and Rewa – largely as reprisal for Rewa's attack on Suva – the Suva army joined that of Naitāsiri to attack the Rewa villages from Nakasi to Lokia, along the west bank of the Wailevu (Rewa River), while the Bau armies attacked along the other side of the river, beginning with Verata (Wailevu), until eventually Lomanikoro, the chiefly village of Rewa, was sacked and burned to ashes, and the Rokotui Dreketi clubbed to death, in December 1845.[106] His brother, Qaraniqiō, fled to Colo-i-Suva and returned to continue the war.

The people of Suva remained for a while in Navuso while their hosts, under instructions from Bau, built houses and planted crops for them in Suva in preparation for their return.[107] Another account has it that people of Viwa and Vugalei were ordered to take the *kai* Suva to Nukui in Rewa, which was held by Qaraniqiō's younger brother Rō Cokānauto, a Bau

---

101 Wall, 'Sketches in Fijian history' ([1919] 1997), 22–31; Sahlins, *The return of the event, again*.
102 This is probably a title, meaning 'Lord of Vunibua', rather than a proper name.
103 Rogo, *TR Nauluvatu*, 2; Waqadau, *TR Vatuwaqa*, 2.
104 Wall, 'Sketches in Fijian history' ([1919] 1999), 50; Rogo, *TR Nauluvatu*, 2.
105 Anonymous, 'Ai tukutuku kei Ratu Radomodomo Ramatenikutu na Vunivalu mai Bau', *Na Mata*, May 1891, 8.
106 Rogo, *TR Nauluvatu*, 2.
107 Ibid.

ally, and they all went and rebuilt Suva.¹⁰⁸ Wallis gives 3 March 1845 – so while the war was still in progress – as the date when the Viwa people were ordered to assist in the rebuilding of Suva.¹⁰⁹ An anonymous source states that the Suva men went first and the women remained in Navuso, joining their menfolk only after the war in 1846.¹¹⁰

Upon returning to Suva, a delegation was sent to Bau to ask for the hand of Adi Elenoa Mila, the daughter of Wainiu the Komai Naua, whose grandfather was half-brother to the Vunivalu Naulivou. She came to Suva and they had a boy, Rusieta (probably Rusiate), who was lost at sea as a baby,¹¹¹ then Avorosa Tuivuya (also known as Aporosa and Ambrose, born about 1851), then two girls, Adi Loaloakubou (also known as Vilawasa) and Adi Sālote Lewatū (born about 1853).

Around 1850, a party of Vuna men ventured into Suva territory one morning, searching for shellfish at the mouth of the Vatuwaqa River, and were surprised by a patrol of Suva scouts. In the ensuing melee, one Vuna man was killed and the rest fled. Camaisala again raised an army and set out to attack Suva, the two forces meeting at the present junction of Denison and Duncan Roads. Rō Camaisala was fatally speared, the army fled and a cannibal feast ensued. For more details of this battle, see Wall.¹¹²

Suva probably became Christian around 1854, following the conversion of their overlord Cakobau the Vunivalu of Bau. By 1856 it was reported that there were:

> two Teachers, one chapel, two other preaching-places, and congregations averaging from one to two hundred. … The King and Queen here have been very decided; and having great influence with their people, the work has spread and deepened all the year. About thirty have begun to read the Scriptures; a few are under concern for their souls; and instruction classes have been formed. We entertain great hope of good in this branch.¹¹³

Around 1857 Ravulo passed away in Bau – when he would have been only about 35 years of age – and was buried in Vatanitawake, the temple of the god Cagawalu, the worship of whom his mother was said to have

---

108 Wall, 'Sketches in Fijian history' ([1919] 1999), 50.
109 Wallis, *Life in Feejee*, 76.
110 Anonymous, 'Ai tukutuku kei Ratu Radomodomo Ramatenikutu na Vunivalu mai Bau', 11.
111 Wall, 'Sketches in Fijian history' ([1919] 1999), 55.
112 Ibid., 52–54.
113 Calvert, *Fiji and the Fijians*, 204.

brought from Bau to Suva. Cakobau brought his widow and children to Bau, where they were brought up, and Adi Mila was subsequently married to Golea, the Tui Cakau (high chief of Cakaudrove).[114]

With peace upon the land, something of a golden age set in. There was plenty of food to be had on land and in the sea, with the annual migration of land crabs (*lairo*, Suva *tubā*, *Cardisoma* sp.) an additional bounty.[115] But already by 1860, there were distant rumblings of an uncertain future. Unbeknownst to the people of Suva, Colonel WT Smythe, who had been commissioned by the British Government to consider the suitability of annexing Fiji as a colony, recommended in his report that the capital be moved from Levuka to Suva. As pointed out by Schütz, only slightly tongue-in-cheek, Smythe had been in the vicinity of Suva in the month of August, so knew nothing of the hot or rainy weather for which it has since become famous, which might have caused him to change his recommendation.[116]

Arrival of the Polynesia Company

Cakobau, the Vunivalu of Bau, had incurred debts to the United States and persuaded the Rokotui Suva, Rātū Avorosa, his *vasu* (sister's son), to allow him to sell most of the Suva peninsula to the Polynesia Company of Melbourne for £10,000, which would settle his debts.[117] Negotiations began in 1868, followed by surveying of lots. A sole colonist, Armstrong, arrived in 1869 and occupied land at Suva Point. The ship bearing the bulk of the new settlers, including Brewster himself, then aged 16 and bearing the surname Joske, arrived on Sunday 4 September 1870.[118] Admiring the neatness of the village of Suva and its little white church (approximately where the botanical gardens are now), they were met by Rātū Avorosa and his sister Adi Sālote, both 'young and good-looking'. Rātū Avorosa spoke English fluently, having spent some time on a visiting American ship, the USS *Kearsarge*, the previous year.

---

114 Wall, 'Sketches in Fijian history' ([1919] 1999), 55.
115 Brewster, *King of the Cannibal Isles,* 138–39.
116 Albert J Schütz, *Suva: A history and guide* (Sydney: Pacific Publications, 1978), 8.
117 Brewster, *King of the Cannibal Isles,* 56, 62.
118 Ibid., 80–82.

1. THE PREHISTORY OF SUVA

Figure 1.1: 'Native church at Suva 1870'.
The caption reads: 'the little pond in the right foregrounds was part of the moat which surrounded the old native village … The moat was filled up in 1882, and the Government House gates and sentry-box now stand on the site of the old Church'.
Source: Sketch by Mrs J. Francis Jones (Brewster's sister) in Brewster, 1937: n. p.

Brewster reports that the settlers got on well with the Suva people, who were happy to have a new source of money and European goods. But as he got older he began to wonder about the propriety of the arrangement:

> We did not then recognize the honour and rectitude of the people of Suva, whose lands we seized upon like a lot of cuckoos. Ratu Thakombau, their feudal lord, had begged their fair heritage to get him out of trouble with the overbearing and unjust *kai Merike*, or people of the United States. His dutiful vassals granted his request and loyally they kept their word, although it was the severest of trials having to part with their patrimonies. I was young and thoughtless in those days and took everything as a matter of course, but when in after years I lived alone in the interior, in charge of a large native province, I came to understand the Fijians' attachment to their ancestral soil, and what a wrench it was for the Suva people to part with theirs, but they had accepted the sacred *tambua* of their overlord, the *Vunivalu* of Mbau, which kept them steady and loyal to their promise to him.[119]

---

119 Ibid., 114–15.

For more details of the Polynesia Company and the founding of the town of Suva, see Brewster's *King of the Cannibal Isles* (1937) and the article in this volume by Max Quanchi.

Move to Narikoso (Suvavou)

Rātū Avorosa appears to have led a carefree life as a young bachelor, flitting between Suva, Bau and Levuka. Melbourne journalist Britton met him on Bau in 1870, when he was about 18, and commented on his 'very engaging manners … boiling over with irrepressible mirth and devilry'.[120] He married Adi Kelerayani, a lady of rank from Rewa – niece to Rō Cokānauto the Rokotui Dreketi – and their first-born was named Adi Rejieli, after Lady Gordon, wife of the first governor, Sir Arthur Gordon, with whom Adi Kelerayani had become very friendly.[121] The minister who baptised her at around six months, in September 1876, wrote that she was 'the prettiest little Fijian child I have ever seen'.[122] A second child was born about a year later.[123] As he grew older, Rātū Avorosa lost little of his endearing charm and zest for life; the Chilean mining entrepreneur Charles Lambert, on whose ultra-modern steam yacht he sailed from Levuka to Suva, described him in 1881 as 'a great swell, in clean white shirt with silver studs, black neck-tie, flannel girdle secured with a black scarf, and white turban, with glossy legs and feet'.[124]

Rātū Avorosa was called to Levuka by Cakobau and told that the Colonial Government wished to move its capital from Levuka to Suva. Cakobau had arranged for the Suva people to move to Kiuva, but the elders of Suva preferred Samabula. This was not agreed to by the government, and John Bates Thurston, the then colonial secretary, came to survey Narikoso, a small peninsula belonging to Lami,[125] to which they moved, allowing the capital to move from Levuka in 1882. Narikoso means 'the peninsula', and there is at least one other village with the same name and

---

120 H Britton, *Fiji in 1870: Being the letters of 'The Argus' special correspondent …* (Melbourne: Samuel Mullen, 1870), 52–53.
121 Stanmore, 'Fiji: Records of private and of public life', 149–52.
122 Ibid., 171.
123 CF Gordon Cumming, *At home in Fiji* (Edinburgh: William Blackwood, 2, 1881), 234.
124 CJ Lambert and S Lambert, *Voyage of the 'Wanderer' from the journals and letters of C. & S. Lambert*, ed. Gerald Young (London: Macmillan, 1883), 201–8.
125 Rogo, *TR Nauluvatu*, 3.

etymology, in the south of the island of Ono in Kadavu. The last person born in old Suva was Sarāvina Drōtini, who was still 'hale and hearty' in her late seventies.[126]

End of an Era

By middle age, Rātū Avorosa Tuivuya (known to most Europeans as Rātū Ambrose, or simply Old Ambrose) had acquired a reputation as an embezzler, bad debtor, drunkard, womaniser and wife-beater, and had lost his job as a civil servant and spent time in prison, according to a history of the Seventh Day Adventist church in Fiji.[127] Feeling perhaps it was time to reform, he was receptive to advances by missionaries of this newly arrived church, although nominally a Methodist. In 1898 he invited the Seventh Day Adventist church to set up their headquarters in Suvavou (where they are to this day), and was baptised with his wife the following year in the Lami River.[128]

A more nuanced picture emerges from other, more secular, sources. According to Nicole, he was what would now be called an activist, instigating a Suva dockers' strike in 1890, and being one of two leaders of a movement opposed to excessive taxes and supporting federation with New Zealand, which led to his arrest and imprisonment in 1901.[129] Seen in this light, his conversion to Seventh Day Adventism could have been also a rejection of the Methodist Church he had been raised in and its association with what he considered an oppressive colonial regime, in the same way that other parts of Fiji, such as Namosi, had switched to Catholicism.[130]

Rātū Avorosa and Rō Kelerayani (also known as Adi Kelera) had three children, including Yaca Ravulo (named after his grandfather), who succeeded Rātū Avorosa after his passing away in Rewa in 1912. He was married to a lady from Nukuwatu (see below) but they had no children.

---

126 *Fiji Times,* 21 March 1959.
127 Eric B Hare, *Fulton's footsteps in Fiji* (Washington DC: Review and Herald Publishing Association, 1969), 81–82, 99–100.
128 Ibid., 100.
129 Robert Nicole, *Disturbing history: Resistance in early colonial Fiji* (Suva: University of the South Pacific Press, 2018), 75–76, 120. Also see chapters by Nicole in this volume.
130 Ibid., 78, 152.

Efforts were made to persuade either Rātū Avorosa's sister Sālote, who was married to the Kwālevu of Nadrogā, or her son Rātū Orisi to succeed to the title of Rokotui Suva, but were not successful.[131]

According to Suvavou oral tradition, Rātū Yaca Ravulo, the last Rokotui Suva, died of *matenisolo* (tinea, a skin infection) and was buried in the *sautabu* (chiefly burial ground) of Suvavou, the only Rokotui Suva buried there. Three men of Walu, the *mataisau* (traditional carpenters) of Suva, caught the same disease in mourning (*kena iloloku*). They then threw all their carpentry tools into the sea.

Postscript: Historical Migrants: Nukuwatu and Vunaniu

As recounted in detail by Clunie, Manila men were men of Spanish and Philippine descent who were frequently employed on trading vessels that visited Fiji around the 1820s. Many jumped ship in Fiji and they became probably the most populous immigrant ethnic group in Fiji at the time. A large number of them served in the Bau army. The Bau historian Etuate Sokiveta related:

> following the trouble brought on by their greed at Bau, the Manila-men were banished to Navitiviti on the Cautata coast, and later to Nukuatu, where some of their descendants live to this day.[132]

Nukuatu – usually spelt Nukuwatu – is the long beach to the west of Suvavou and the Lami River, including where Lami town is today. Its name means 'long beach' in the Navakavu communalect, and some nineteenth-century records refer to it as Nukubalavu, the standardised, and perhaps earlier, form of its name.

This settlement is inhabited mostly by descendants of Manila men (many bearing the surnames Rogers, Roden and Shaw) who settled there from Mokani due to a *vasu* connection. An alternative or complementary story told to me in Suvavou is that the Nukuwatu Manila men were from a whaler that was wrecked at Namuka, just west of Lami, while the founder of the Rogers family, Paul Rogers, was a Manila man shipwrecked

---

131 Dumaru, 'Suva makawa'.
132 Fergus Clunie, 'The Manila Brig', *Domodomo* 2, no. 2 (1984): 84.

in Naceva, Beqa, who married a Makerina Vakalutusau and their daughter, Yana Waqabilibili Rogers, married Ravulo, the last Rokotui Suva of the original line.[133]

There were connections far to the west as well. No doubt there are many descendants of Suva men who, contrary to the usual custom, moved to their wife's village and raised a family there, but one in particular is still remembered, though he must have made the move in the 1880s, probably with a young family, shortly after the move to Suvavou. His name was Atunaisa Mocelutu, of the *mataqali* Nayavumata, and his wife was Vani Suranamasi of the *yavusa* Nauabale of Vunaniu, Serua. His descendants constitute a *mataqali* named Nayavumata within the *yavusa* of Nauabale, and the story of their distinct origin is well known in Vunaniu. They now comprise 10 households and have all taken to speaking the Vunaniu communalect but, like all 10 *mataqali* in Vunaniu, retain their distinctiveness by using unique vocatives for 'mother' and 'father', in this case the Suva terms *lei* and *nau*. Incidentally, a great-great-grandson of Atunaisa Mocelutu bears the same name, Seruveveli Dakai, as the man who gave the *Tukutuku Rāraba* of the *yavusa* Nayavumata to the Native Lands Commission in Suvavou in 1921.

The reason for the move to Vunaniu is not known, but it may not be insignificant that the chief of Vunaniu is descended from two men of the Vusarātū clan of Bau who moved there in the early nineteenth century.

---

133 Dumaru, 'Suva makawa'.

2

Suva and the Fate of the Polynesia Company

Max Quanchi

In October 1870, the missionary Lorimor Fison visited Suva peninsula looking for a site for a church and wrote:

> at present things are in a very unsettled state. The weather has been sadly against the newcomers for it has been raining since they came down, and during the last three weeks have had most dismal weather – not one fine day in 21. Settlers living in tents or in hastily built makeshift huts, men to be pitied but worst hardship falls on women and children.

The *Alhambra* had arrived from Melbourne a month previously, carrying the first shipload of Polynesia Company shareholders keen to begin a new life as planters on the Suva peninsula. Henry Armstrong, from the Upper Murray district in Victoria, had been the first shareholder to arrive, in May 1869, joined by his brother in early 1870. Henry had travelled out to Fiji on the *Springbok*, the first vessel to sail direct from Melbourne to Fiji with a group of intending settlers, in what was called the 'Fiji Rush'. They were the only shareholders on the peninsula until the arrival of the *Alhambra* in September 1870.[1]

---

1 This chapter is a compilation of stories about Suva taken from my recent monograph (Max Quanchi, *This glorious company* (Suva: USP Press, 2020)), my MA thesis on Victoria–Fiji links (Max Quanchi, 'This glorious company: The Polynesia Company in Melbourne and Fiji' (master's thesis, Monash University, 1977)) and several unpublished conference presentations. For further reference details, please see the Source Note at the end of the chapter.

The opportunity to establish cotton plantations on Suva peninsula had arisen because of events in Fiji on 4 July 1849 when the store of an American trader, JB Williams, was destroyed by fire on nearby Nukulau Island; caused, it was later said, by his own carelessness in setting off fireworks to celebrate US Independence Day. During the melee, Fijians dashed into the store and, as Fiji custom allowed, claimed the goods saved from the inferno. Williams declared that a local chief, Ratu Seru Cakobau, was responsible for his losses, claiming that Nukulau Island was within the nominal suzerainty of Cakobau's chiefly domain, centred on nearby Bau Island. Other Americans in Fiji then claimed compensation for incidents involving damage or theft and after a series of visits by American gunboats, Cakobau was deemed liable for US$45,000 (around £6,500 in 1849) – an enormous figure and certainly one that Cakobau lacked the cash to pay. Eighteen years passed and each visiting US gunboat added more claims and adjusted the interest due. When USS *Tuscarora* arrived in 1867, Cakobau was courting European favour to support his claim to be the paramount chief of all of Fiji, the Tui Viti. Land under his direct control or over which he had a call due to alliances, marriages or wars, was all he had to pay off the debt. By 1867, he had paid between £1,368 and £1,435, with different figures cited in US consular reports.

Fiji's plantation prospects were being touted due to the collapse in cotton exports caused by the US Civil War (1861–1865). In the colony of Victoria, where there had been a decade of unbounded expansion driven by the wealth of the 1850s gold rushes, Fiji seemed to be an attractive investment opportunity as Cakobau was a likely protector, and cotton prospects were reported to be good. Although the British consul in Fiji lamented that lack of a civilised form of European-style government and a regular labour supply was holding back Fiji's growth,[2] these warnings were overlooked in Melbourne in a climate of unbridled press optimism and Fiji's alleged bountiful prospects. In 1870, the governor of Victoria reported to the Colonial Office in London that:

> Your Lordship is well aware that for some time past the interest felt in the Australasian colonies in the development of the resources and in the civilization and security of the Fiji islands has been considerable and rapidly increasing.

---

2   Her Britannic Majesty's Council (hereafter HBMC) to Colonial Office, 30 June 1864, HBMC Records, Fiji; HBMC, 'Report on Trade and Navigation', 31 December 1868, HBMC Records, Fiji.

2. SUVA AND THE FATE OF THE POLYNESIA COMPANY

The governor was reporting on the excitement in Melbourne as the *Alhambra*, with the first boatload of Polynesia Company shareholders, headed for Suva peninsula.

Two years earlier, after the Polynesia Company promoters, WHO Brewer and JL Evans, returned to Melbourne with a controversial charter signed by Cakobau (allegedly gained under the influence of champagne), it had been a slow process to get the company incorporated, to obtain land title deeds from Cakobau, to have Suva peninsula surveyed and maps drawn up for the selection of blocks and to arrange the transfer of shares into land warrants for those shareholders in Melbourne wanting to settle on a block or to profit by on-selling shares to latecomers joining the Polynesia Company bandwagon. A Melbourne office had been established, a Fiji agent employed and, finally, after two years, the *Alhambra* chartered to carry the first party of eager settlers to Suva peninsula. The story of Suva, the city of today, begins when those aspiring settlers stepped ashore in September 1870. It was with a degree of wariness that they headed ashore after the *Alhambra* anchored in the sheltered anchorage, facing the darkened and forested, low ridges that ran down the core of the Suva peninsula. There were Fijian villages at Suva, near today's Thurston Gardens, and at Nasēsē, a kilometre down the coast.

Suva peninsula was undulating, heavily vegetated and cut with ravines, and Colonel Pratt of the Royal Engineers later noted in his preliminary survey of Suva's suitability as the seat of government, that it was far easier to row around the point than to try and traverse the peninsula west to east from Nabukalou Creek to Laucala Bay.

Adolph Brewster Joske, a young boy under the guardianship of GD McCartney, a company official, gave an account of this first day ashore in his book, *King of the Cannibal Isles,* in which he recalled that only a roughly drawn sketch map pinned to a post in a Ratu Ambrose's *bure* greeted the new arrivals.[3] JS Butters, the company's Fiji agent, was in Levuka and did not visit until November. Those with company lands warrants pencilled their names in on blocks and set about clearing the ground, erecting a house, hiring local Fijians as labour and planning where crops would be planted. Settlers chose blocks laid out across the peninsula,

---

3   Adolphe Joske changed his name to AB Brewster after a family feud with his father, and published the book in 1937, under his new name. See AB Brewster, *King of the Cannibal Islands* (London: Robert Hales and Company, 1937), 74–81.

or along the Tamavua River, which also took advantage of a well-worn Fijian track running from the original Suva village near Naiqoro Creek to Tamavua village and further north to the Waimanu River.[4]

The Melbourne press reported favourably on the Polynesia Company's decision to dispatch a 'local committee' to Suva to watch over the allocation of blocks and to report back, confidentially, on the efforts of the Polynesia Company's agent in Fiji, JS Butters, a former lord mayor of Melbourne; the four on the committee were GD McCartney, William Henry O'Halloran Brewer, BR Henry and PJ Williams. After Williams moved over to Laucala Bay to establish a plantation and McCartney moved to Levuka after a few months, Brewer was left in authority, backed by his friend BR Henry.

The overall authority on allocation of blocks was retained in Melbourne, and this was the cause of confusion, anger and considerable underhanded behaviour in the coming months. David Sellars, a surveyor and company shareholder on the *Alhambra*, was temporarily hired by the company to carry out a survey but he immediately sent a complaint to the board in Melbourne claiming that the Local Committee, primarily Brewer, had monopolised the selection of blocks, so much that when ex-Richmond bootmaker John Henderson arrived in November 1870, the only company land he could select was an isolated, un-surveyed block inland along the Lami River to the west of the Suva peninsula. WH Surplice, from Ballarat, was then retained as the company's new surveyor.

The process seemed simple enough – settlers armed with company land warrants selected blocks according to the number of shares they held, either Surplice or the Local Committee registered their selection and then forwarded the list to Melbourne for approval. It seemed that with three levels of oversight – Butters, Surplice and the Local Committee – the taking up of blocks would proceed smoothly. However, the company began to allow shareholders in Melbourne to make selections, so unbeknown to each other, company shareholders in Melbourne and Suva were selecting the same block. This created a clear distinction between the bona fide settlers establishing plantations and claiming title by occupation, and speculators in Melbourne who claimed, sold and resold the same blocks

---

4 The contested claims for Suva blocks can be followed in the wonderfully fulsome files of the Land Claims Commission, National Archives of Fiji (henceforth referred to as LCC).

while remaining in Victoria. When the Land Claims Commission (LCC) came to judge the 92 applications for Suva blocks, they found it impossible to unravel the competing claims.

Plantation blocks had 400-metre frontages to either Suva Harbour in the west or Laucala Bay in the east. The blocks stretched inland from Suva Point to the Waimanu River, and west along the coast as far as Grove Point (Uduya Point) and Lami. WH Surplice added 14 more blocks to the original plan when he realised additional selections had been made further inland. The company then added 39 more numbered blocks and six unspecified blocks to the maps prepared by Surplice. In April 1874, under the instructions of the directors in Melbourne, several boundaries were changed, and more selections approved west of the Tamavua River and north of the township reserve, and some blocks were reduced in size and a new number allotted to the smaller portions.

Walter Eyre, a land claims commissioner appointed by the first British governor, Sir Arthur Gordon, attempted a block-by-block investigation but gave up due to conflicting claims and a lack of clear evidence of ownership, placing blame firstly on the Local Committee for not immediately sending selections and associated land warrants back to Melbourne, and secondly on the company itself for issuing land warrants for more blocks than it had surveyed.[5]

Eyre was critical of the indiscriminate issuing of conveyances of title to shareholders who never occupied the land or who claimed unspecified acreages in unspecified locations. He criticised the practice of the directors in Melbourne refusing to convey the amount selected, claiming it was over the entitlement allowed, and then issuing conveyances to other shareholders in Melbourne for the lands they had just sheared off an unsuspecting settler in Suva, or conveying them to 'different people in nearly all cases to themselves or their relatives'. Put bluntly, said Eyre, a single block in Suva was being claimed by several shareholders in Melbourne, and often by two or three subsequent purchasers, who thought or were tricked into believing they held land warrants and undisputed title. Eyre drew a hypothetical case demonstrating how one 200-acre block could be subdivided, renumbered, and resold and claimed by four claimants now totalling 500 acres. Eyre declared that:

---

5   Eyre's report on Suva's claims is contained in LCC: P115 ('Rehearing Suva blocks'). Much of this evidence was not produced until petitions against the LCC's initial decisions were heard in 1879–1881.

it is impossible to say if my surmises set out above are correct ... (but) from a perusal of the deeds it is apparent that great laxity has been shown in the management.

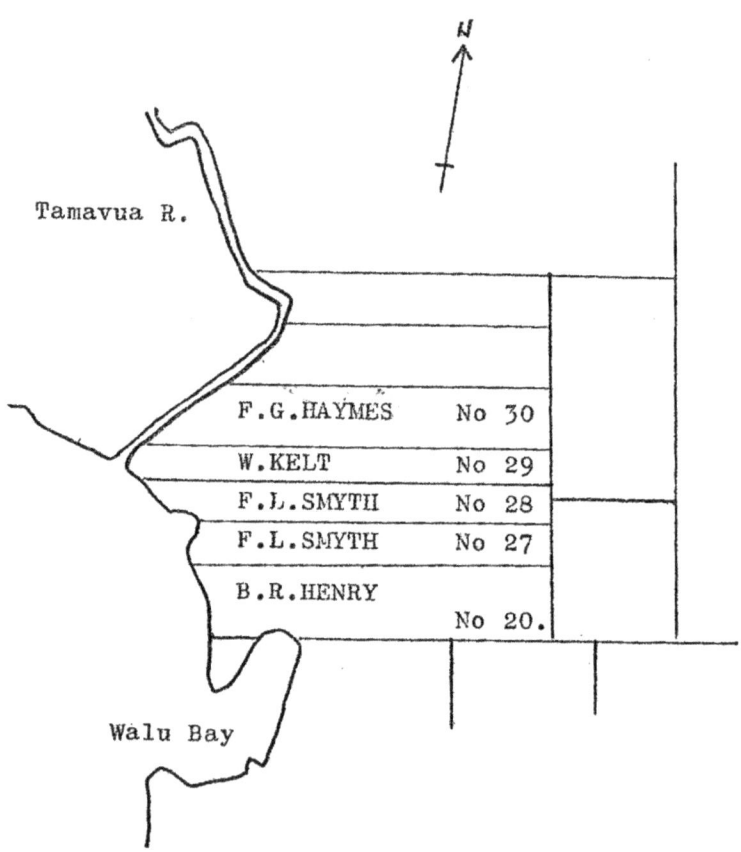

PLAN OF SELECTIONS AT SUVA
    Based on plan of selections issued by the Polynesia Company, 4 Feb 1873. Fiji:LCC., R412.,R428 and P293

(Drawn by author)

Figure 2.1: Sketch of contested blocks of land between Walu Bay and Tamavua River, 1873.
Source: Sketch by the author, 1970s. Held in private collection.

We can test Eyre's summary against the claims before the LCC by bona fide settlers, absentees and blatantly fraudulent claimants for blocks 20, 27, 28, 29 and 30 running along the shore from Walu Bay, north to the Tamavua River. In 1875, these blocks were claimed by BR Henry, TA Copeland, FL Smyth, W Kelt and FG Haymes.[6] Copeland, an American, was a friend of BR Henry's and they made an agreement in Melbourne with Jacob Brache, a company shareholder, in which he loaned them a considerable sum in return for which they would go to Suva, select land and then purchase Brache's land warrants, after which all three would go into a coffee and sugar plantation partnership. Copeland and Henry sailed to Fiji in August 1870 but neither became planters. Gilbert McClymont, who had arrived in Suva in 1870 with Henry, told the LCC that Henry 'never took up land' and that Copeland was a land-jobber and worked as a manager at Brewer and Joske's store in Suva and later went to Levuka as a store clerk and set up his own business. Henry was a foreman at Brewer and Joske's cotton store and ginning sheds and engaged in land-jobbing. In 1874, Jacob Brache was able to convince the Board of Directors that the selections authorised in 1873 for blocks 20, 27, 28, 29 and 30 between Walu Bay and the Tamavua River were incorrect. The directors acquiesced and changed the boundaries and issued new conveyances. Meanwhile, Jacob Brache passed over the titles to his brother CA Brache, manager of the Murray and Ovens Vineyard Wine Cellars in Melbourne and secretary of the Murray and Ovens Vineyard Proprietors Association. When the matter went before the LCC, CA Brache's claim was rejected, noting that Jacob Brache had conveniently forgotten to mention the series of partnerships, renumbering and subsequent transfers of title. This example of just a small parcel of blocks at Suva peninsula demonstrates, as Eyre had succinctly noted, the haphazard and in some cases fraudulent role played by directors in Melbourne.

In 1875, both Copeland and Henry left Fiji in a hurry heading for the United States, Copeland just ahead of his creditors. WHO Brewer had just died. With consular and church approval, Henry, claiming gallant and Christian motives, stepped in and married Brewer's teenage daughter, Ada, in a hastily arranged Church of England ceremony. The girl, listed as Brewer's 16-year-old daughter on the shipping register, was later found not to be Brewer's daughter, but a teenager, Ada Lily Smith, his lover.

---

6   For claims see: LCC, Claims R412, R427, R428, R431, R449 and R1321; Applications 1320, 1434, 1497 and 1630; and Files P293 and P294.

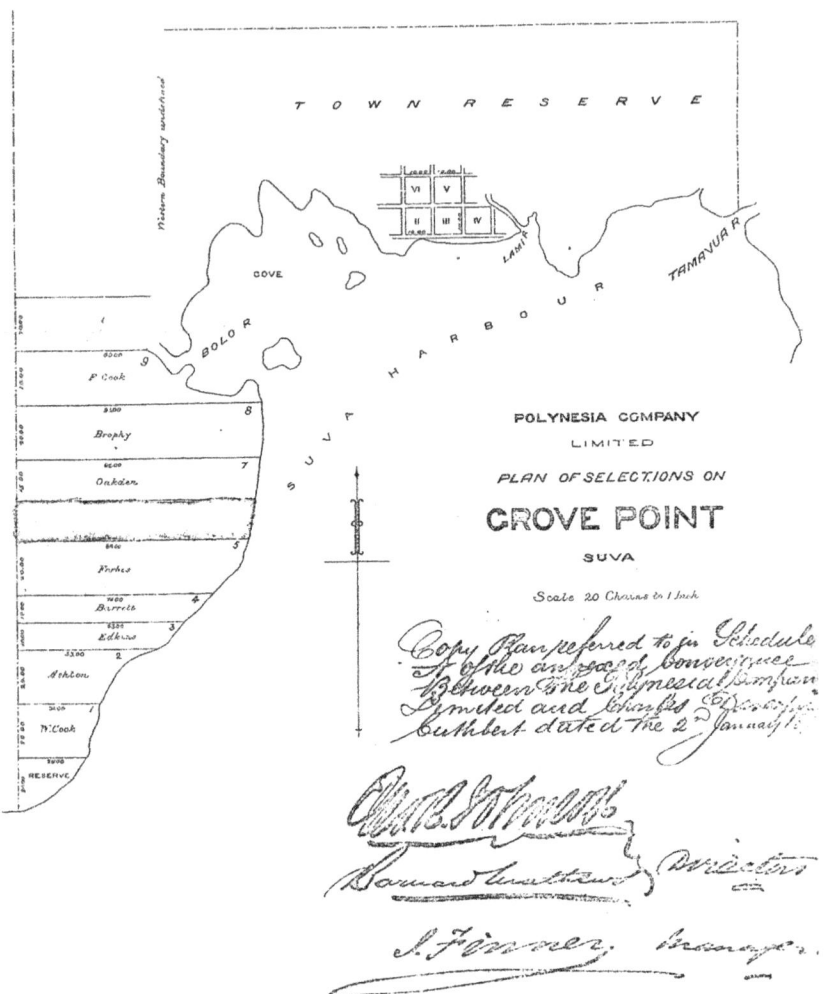

Figure 2.2: Polynesia Company plan of selections at Grove Point, 1871.
Source: LCC: Claim R427.

In Melbourne, the sale of land warrants for blocks in Suva was profitable. The price asked for actual blocks, and often for ones that did not exist, were extraordinarily high as land in Fiji ranged from 1 to 10 shillings an acre, well below the going price in Melbourne of £1 an acre. These sales also highlight the speculative atmosphere of Melbourne and the willingness to buy land in the Pacific in the hope of making a quick sale to an unsuspecting investor or intending planter.[7]

---

7   The trail of warrants and sales can be followed in evidence tended to the LCC.

WB Sellers, a Suva settler originally from Warrnambool in Victoria, had written to the company from Suva criticising Brewer for picking all the best land and this became a public spat when Seller's letter was published in the *Age* in Melbourne. Paul Joske, a Melbourne wine and spirit merchant who arrived in Suva to join his teenage son, called the selection process an outright swindle and, later, Charles Cuthbert presented several maps and lists of contested selections when he was giving evidence at the LCC.[8] The Armstrong brothers also gave evidence that they attempted to select blocks on Polynesia Company land but had to make unspecified selections outside the company's boundaries because there was insufficient acreage for them to take up land that their land warrants entitled them. Cuthbert estimated there had been 26 selections made for Suva blocks prior to December 1870, covering 7,750 acres of the 27,000 acres conveyed by Cakobau to the company. Many were by proxy and did not involve actual occupation or expenditure on establishing a plantation.

An Inefficient Happy-Go-Lucky Crowd

The settlement of Suva peninsula was part of the Fiji Rush or as John Young called the settlers, an 'evanescent ascendency'.[9] The youngster, Adolph Joske, described the settlers on the *Alhambra* whom he travelled down to Fiji with as:

> mostly men of small capital who were leaving openly for their new homes with their wives, children, goods and chattels … taken all round we were an inefficient, happy-go-lucky crowd with inadequate capital who had not sat down and counted properly the cost of the venture but had been caught up with the glamour of the islands and like the immortal Mr Micawber always trusted that something would turn up which would lead us to fortune.

---

8   LCC R1321, see also R1322/P292.
9   JMR Young, 'Evanescent ascendency: The planter community in Fiji', in *Pacific Island portraits*, ed. James Wightman Davidson and Deryck Scarr (Canberra: ANU Press, 1970); see also JMR Young, 'Australia's Pacific frontier', *Australian Historical Studies* 12, no. 47 (1966): 373–88, doi.org/10.1080/10314616608595336; L Cleland et al., 'From the archives', *The Journal of Pacific History* 1, no. 1 (1966): 183–203, doi.org/10.1080/00223346608572089; JMR Young, ed., *Australia's Pacific frontier: Economic and cultural expansion into the Pacific 1795–1885* (Melbourne: Cassell Australia, 1967); JMR Young, *Adventurous spirits: Australian migrant society in pre-cession Fiji* (St Lucia: University of Queensland Press, 1984).

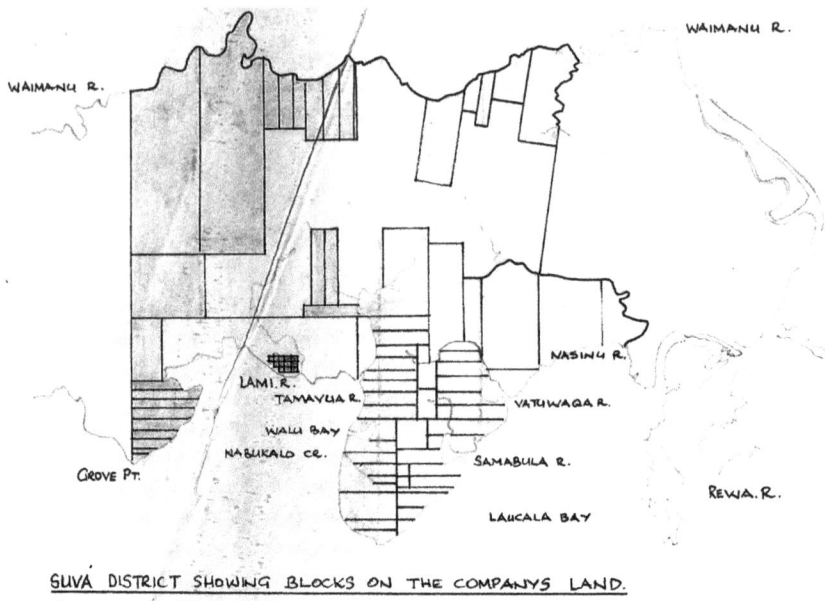

Figure 2.3: Sketch of blocks claimed by the Polynesia Company on Suva peninsula and the hinterland, c.1870s.
Source: Sketch by the author, 1970s. Contained in private collection.

Henry Britton, an *Age* journalist, mistakenly called the passengers ex-gold seekers frustrated in their hopes of easy fortunes of the Australian goldfields. The *Fiji Times* thought they were 'Hawkesbury farmers, squatters, Victorian wine growers, diggers, New Zealand flax dressers and merchants looking for less competition and higher profits'. Litton Forbes, who visited Fiji during the rush, referred to the settlers as 'with scarcely an exception, men of respectability'.[10]

The 122 passengers on the *Alhambra* demonstrate this diversity of background. In the fore cabin were 10 married men with their wives, 38 single men and one boy, all designated as 'labourers'. In salon class, there were 52 adult men and women and 11 children; six men were accompanied by their wives and children, and four women were travelling out to join their husbands.

---

10   Brewster, *King of the Cannibal Islands*, 72, 74; Henry Britton, *Fiji in 1870: Being the letters of 'The Argus' special correspondent ...* (Melbourne: Samuel Mullen, 1870), 6; *Fiji Times* 7 May 1970; Litton Forbes, *Two years in Fiji* (London: Longmans, Green, 1875), 277.

2. SUVA AND THE FATE OF THE POLYNESIA COMPANY

The previous vessels sailing to Fiji had much the same mix of passengers. In May 1869, the *Springbok*, via Sydney, carried 18 passengers, including two women going out to join husbands, six married men, 10 single men all under 30 years of age, and one governess. This group included SG Watson, the Polynesia Company's largest shareholder, 50 years of age, a wealthy pastoralist from the Upper Murray; Henry Armstrong, a 23-year-old also from the Upper Murray; and Frederick Cook, the company's manager who was going out to investigate the delays in obtaining titles to all 200,000 acres granted by Cakobau. In April 1870, the *Springbok* again made passage for Fiji, carrying 23 adults and one child. Eighteen men were single, five were married and included Dr Thomas McGrath and Dr James Roche, both from Castlemaine; Dr Thomas Serrell from Fitzroy; John Bloomfield, a building contractor for Ascot Vale; and Alfred D'este, an ex-French military officer. All were shareholders in the company. The other passengers listed their occupations as 'farmer' or more ambitiously as 'Planter'. When the *Kohinoor* sailed for Fiji in June 1870 the passengers included the indefatigable JS Butters, former lord mayor of Melbourne, and now the company's new agent in Fiji. These were not vessels charted by the company, but 25 per cent of the men on board were shareholders. On the *Alhambra*, 30 per cent of the male passengers were shareholders.[11] The Polynesia Company had chartered the *Alhambra* and the *Albion* but was otherwise not involved in shipping despite press reports of promised shipping lines and new steamer routes.[12]

These shipping figures were a dramatic increase on just a few years earlier when ships carried only two or three passengers bound for Fiji, with Victorians having to travel to Sydney to start the voyage. The Fiji Rush also included hopeful planters from Auckland and Otago.

It was a muddy and disorganised arrival when shareholders landed on the shore near the mouth of Nabukalou Creek and then moved out to their selected blocks. At the head of Laucala Bay, Thomas B Matthews took up 400 acres running south from the Nasinu River to the shoreline. Matthews had purchased 100 shares in the initial float and migrated out to Levuka on the *Kohinoor* in 1870. He immediately hired local Fijians to

---

11 On the *Alhambra*, 31 of the 100 male passengers were Polynesia Company shareholders. Joske (AB Brewster) refers to 'about 40' being shareholders (Brewster, *King of the Cannibal Islands*, 72). A few other shareholders had sailed to Fiji earlier in the year.
12 John Young and Ruth Moses both mistakenly claim the company had a 'remunerative sideline' running ships to Fiji. See Ruth Moses, 'The Polynesia Company Limited of Melbourne and Fiji 1868–1883: A social history', (BA (Hons) thesis, University of Adelaide, 1971), 34, 60.

clear 60 acres and planted cotton. In 1871, he returned to Victoria and married the daughter of Charles Cuthbert, a fellow settler, but when the 25 acres of sugar had to be left to rot when Brewer and Joske's sugar mill broke down, he turned to growing bananas and finally cattle and goat grazing. His proudest achievement was a road, 6 metres wide, 2 kilometres long, with planted trees along both sides. The planned mansion at the end of the avenue never eventuated. He had selected the adjoining block as a proxy for this brother and an unspecified selection east of the Lami River for a Melbourne friend, George Ticknell. He also selected a 40-acre block for himself at Lami and four half-acre Lami town blocks. By 1873, Matthews had expended £1,500 and was forced to mortgage his land to WK Thompson, the managing director of James McEwan and Company of Melbourne, who was then engaged in several pursuits in Suva. In May 1875, Matthews was unable to meet his payments and the mortgage passed wholly to Thompson. Mathews remained on the land on a lease for £84 per annum and attempted to lease what he considered better land along the Waimanu River. Finally in 1880, Matthews moved away to the Lower Rewa River district and took over the Waimanu Hotel and a cane growing block on the richer river plains.[13] Under the settler-led Cakobau Government, Mathews served as warden for Rewa and under the Crown Colony Government as customs and health officer for the port of Suva.

South of Matthews's block, between the Vatuwaqa and Samabula rivers, was the selection of Pierce J Williams. He had been active in the formation of the company and had travelled down on the *Alhambra* with Brewer, McCartney and Henry as part of the company's Local Committee. He had married in Warrnambool and had purchased 150 acres in Polynesia Company land warrants from the member of the Legislative Assembly for Warrnambool, William Plummer. Williams was a dour, resolute clerk of only moderate means when he left Richmond, where he was then living, and headed to Suva to make a success out of cotton planting. He hired 12 men from Tokelau, eight Fijians on long-term contracts and 400 others on casual rates and immediately cleared 100 acres and planted 80 acres in cotton. The company land warrants had cost £375 and both Cuthbert and the Armstrong brothers estimated before the LCC that at last £400 had been spent on improvements and £600 on labour. A year later his wife, Sophie, recalled how 'bright and prosperous the plantation was

---

13 Matthew's story can be followed in the LCC files; see R428, R434 and P1250. See also correspondence in LCC: Miscellaneous Papers and in FIJI: CSO Correspondence 1877–1878, both in Fiji Archives.

then looking'. His neighbours to the south, Fred and Henry Armstrong, testified to his efforts, stating before the LCC that 'he was one who went in heavily for planting witness the rapidity with which he had such a large quantity of cotton planted'.

Williams had dug wells and erected a timber frame house and labourer's quarters. The cotton matured splendidly. Sadly, exactly a year after arriving, Williams died, probably of dysentery, and Sophie could only manage to harvest a few bags of cotton. Williams was buried in the soil he had tilled.

Sophie was forced to admit she knew little of her husband's business matters as 'unfortunately he did not communicate much of his affairs to me'. Sophie's intention was to keep going but as she recalled later, 'all the men ran away the night he died, if they stayed with Mr Surplice as manager we could have survived'. To add to her wretched state, she was confronted the next day by several Fijians who had on occasion worked on the plantation. They demanded money and when Sophie refused, they returned several times, menaced her and threatened to burn down the house. When news of this confrontation reached the settlement at Nabukalou Creek on the other side of the peninsula, a public meeting was called, and rescue mission arranged. A boat was rowed around Suva Point and brought Sophie and her children back to safety. She recalled how she had been saved 'only by the kindness of Mathews, Ryan and others and a meeting of the Suva people who fetched us away'. Cuthbert wrote to the company's agent in Levuka, CR Forwood, that the Toka Toka and Samabula people were responsible for the outrage, and that:

> all the yams and potatoes planted have been stolen and knives, calico and other trade forcibly removed from the house … knives and clubs were held over Mrs W and the servant women who were at home.[14]

Sophie Williams stayed with the Cuthberts at Walu Bay for three months, then after her brother sent money for a passage Sophie and her two young girls, Annie and Eliza, returned to Victoria. Surplice briefly lived on the block, on one occasion uprooting crops planted by local Fijians,

---

14 Cuthbert to Forwood, 12 Dec 1972, Fiji Archives, File T/20. A meeting of the association on 3 February 1972 resolved that one or all of the villages should be removed, especially Suva, in order to enhance the prospects of the company's occupation.

and Matthews kept the house in good repair. Eight years later, destitute, a widow with a sick child and her own health failing, she wrote to Cuthbert from Warrnambool:

> I feel an attraction to Suva. My husband is buried there, and I was befriended when really needed. I am sure you will think this a most melancholy letter ... believe me I cannot endure the thought of losing that land.

In 1881, Sophie received a Crown Grant for 750 acres at Vatuwaqa. After she died in Richmond in 1884, the block was subdivided and sold at auction.

To the south of PJ Williams's block was the large selection of Percy Oakden. A director of the Polynesia Company, Oakden had been instrumental in July 1870 in launching the offshoot Ballarat scheme, the Fiji Planting and Trading Company, to which he had sold all his Polynesia Company landholdings for £500. Although the *Ballarat Star* declared capital was being called up and 'large returns are anticipated', it went into liquidation in 1874 and Percy Oakden purchased its holdings outright for £1,100. Charles Cuthbert, the plantation manager for the first and second versions of the Fiji Planting and Trading Company, had selected two blocks adjoining Oakden's western boundary and together they formed an impressive holding stretching right across the peninsula. Cuthbert had travelled down on the *Alhambra* but when he erected a tent on the shore at Walu Bay he was confronted by Caroline Fitzgibbon, who argued vigorously and successfully to the Local Committee that she had selected the block. She quickly sold it to WHO Brewer and Cuthbert was forced to move to a block further along the coast that he had leased for the Fiji Planting and Trading Company. Cuthbert built a Fiji-style *bure* for £7 and later replaced it with a wooden frame house. A large workshop was built on the Walu Bay block of the Fiji Planting and Trading Company, where many of the small cutters that plied the harbour were later built. Cuthbert weathered the lean years and became a respected 'old hand', a commissioner of peace under the Cakobau Government and secretary of the Planter's Association, and he later sat in the post-annexation Legislative Council. Cuthbert built a fine house at Walu Bay, and despite the long walk uphill, it was a popular meeting place for the Suva community. Aerial survey maps in 1945 showed the long hedge Cuthbert had planted along the road to his house.

In 1872, following several incidents between Europeans and Fijians, Cuthbert wrote on behalf of the Suva settlers to CR Forwood, now the Polynesia Company's Fiji agent, asking for help. Forwood spoke to JB Thurston, the most influential member of the Cakobau Government Executive and well versed in local matters, but the government was in disarray by this time and relations between the Polynesia Company and the government were strained. Forwood appealed to Thurston on personal grounds, writing:

> I shall feel it a personal favour if some action be taken at once taken to set the natives right with the settlers at Suva, even outside our question with the Polynesia Company.

Behind Cuthbert's block at Walu Bay, Charles and Louisa Edkins established a plantation. Charles had arrived alone on the *Alhambra*. After his wife, children and brother arrived he purchased 228 acres from Brewer and put 20 acres under cotton. Edkins then tried maize, sugarcane and vegetables but within two years was bankrupt. In 1872, he gave up planting and took jobs as a store clerk and overseer before leaving Fiji in 1875. Later he wrote to TB Mathews, who was keeping his house in good repair, that once his capital was healthier, he would like to make a second try. He did not return to Fiji.

On Suva Point, the Armstrong brothers managed to survive the failure of cotton. Henry Armstrong had selected land on the peninsula when he arrived and when his brother Fred joined him in a partnership, the company's Local Committee approved this block and a further 100-acre extension by allocating land originally set aside as a 'Native Reserve'. As cotton prices fell the Armstrongs uprooted their cotton and, on Brewer's advice, planted sugarcane. In 1873, Brewer had just formed a partnership with Paul Joske and, in addition to a store and several other commercial ventures, they imported a small sugarcane crushing mill.[15] After crushing an experimental crop of 7 acres, the Armstrong brothers netted £65 profit, a good return. After the success of the first crushing, Brewer and Joske imported a full-scale crushing mill and they contracted the Armstrong brothers for an additional 35 acres of cane and the Armstrongs hired 25 imported labourers. Other settlers at Suva quickly switched to cane.

---

15   Brewer and Joske's sugar enterprise is briefly told in PS Allen, *Cyclopedia of Fiji* (Sydney: McCarron, Stewart & Co., 1907), 168–69.

Figure 2.4: Brewer and Joske's Sugar Mill, Suva, 1875.
Source: ANU Open Research Library, openresearch-repository.anu.edu.au/handle/1885/49155.

The *Fiji Argus* later recalled:

> upon the successful results of Brewer and Joske's offer everyone relied, long before annexation, for the return of the good times King Cotton had so ruthlessly and inexorably banished. As the ships of the firm landed the massive machinery, great promise was made for the future.[16]

The machinery had comprised the sole cargo for two voyages of the brig *Nil Desperandum* and the extent of the venture was such that Brewer and Joske had 175 acres of their own land under cane and a further 30 acres set aside for food crops for their 165 Fijian labourers. Unfortunately, the mill broke down after three months of successful operation and could not be repaired. Several hundred acres of cane across the Suva peninsula were left to rot, uncut and Suva settlers faced yet another setback. The Armstrong brothers were able to supply 14 acres of cane but lost 20 acres when it could not be processed. They then sued Brewer and Joske for breach of contract and were awarded £210 in damages, but this was well below the £1,000 they testified they had invested. After the failure

---

16   *Fiji Argus*, 8 August 1875; *The Argus* (Melbourne) 22 April 1875. In 1998 and 2006, a plea for compensation was lodged by the Suvavou people for the loss of their lands.

of their cane experiment, they moved away briefly and took jobs with the Cakobau Government or as overseers with more successful planters. Henry and his wife later returned to their Suva Point block and grazed cattle. The brothers had also selected an unspecified 750-acre block in the hinterland but as they admitted to the LCC, they did not have funds to 'run one place let alone two'. In 1945, a few hedges and fence lines remained at Suva Point as evidence of their planting adventures.

Paul Joske was a central character in Suva's early development. He travelled out from Melbourne and joined his son, Adolphe, in 1871 and selected several blocks on the peninsula. He then joined WHO Brewer in a partnership involving a store, hotel, various small vessels, several plantations and, later, a sugar crushing mill. Brewer, due to his role on the Local Committee, had been able to dominate the selection of blocks and, after joining up with Joske, they claimed a large share of the company's lands, and made a profit leasing and selling land to late arrivals and newcomers like Edkins. Brewer profitably wearing two coats, for himself and for the company, held title to 1,196 acres not including his half-share in 'Charlie and Bob's'. Joske held a further 746 acres in his own name and the other half of 'Charlie and Bob's'. This large block from Nabukalou to Nasēsē was originally purchased from local chiefs by RS 'Bob' Swanston and Charles Pickering, divided into two then three parts, and eventually passed to Brewer and Joske, then to Renwick and Thompson and then to McEwans and finally to WK Thompson. Part of this block was set aside as a 'Native Reserve'. Joske and Brewer's Nabukalou blocks were the first to be extensively cultivated with cotton and later cane. When the block was later mortgaged to McEwan's it came with 'all the ginning equipment … free and bonded stores, hotel and other buildings thereon'. It was this area around the hotel, store and cane mill that a small township began to grow and where the little community gathered to discuss the weather, crops, labour and prices. The partnership was dissolved upon the death of Brewer in February 1874 and most of the lands they had claimed passed to McEwan's and then to WK Thompson.

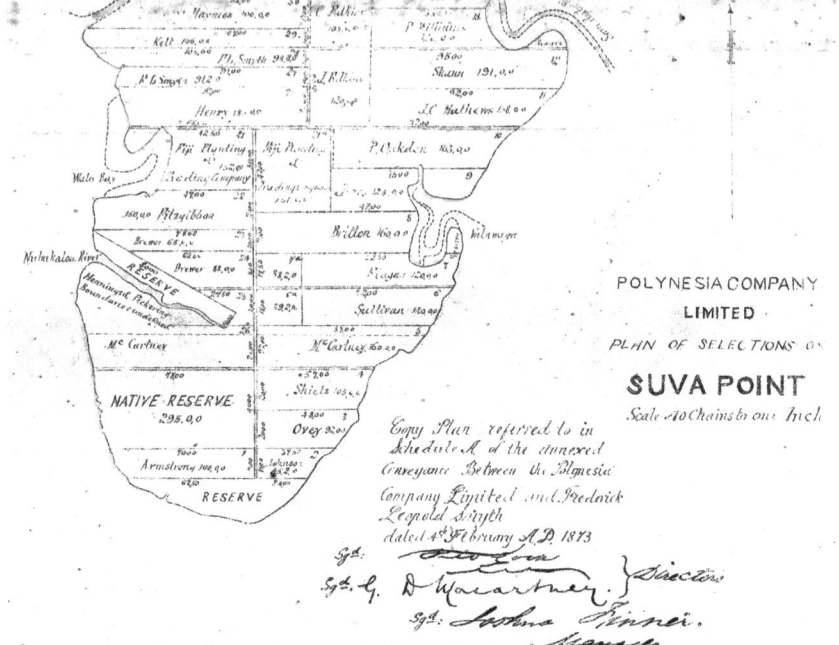

Figure 2.5: Company map of selections at Suva peninsula, 4 February 1873. Signed by Frederick Cook and GD McCartney, directors, and Joshua Finner, manager.
Source: Reproduced courtesy of National Archives of Fiji.

Joske had also selected the block adjoining Davies and McClymont along the Tamavua River. It was here that the most impressive attempt was made to return a profit. Joske eventually obtained all three adjoining blocks in his own name and that of his son Adolphe and daughter Victoria. He treated the three blocks as one entity. No expense was spared, and the two southern blocks were cleared. As Joske was wealthy, he could meet the outlay less well-funded settlers could not afford. He employed a series of European managers and overseers and, although he reckoned on losing £1,000 on the cane, he later made a profit by grazing cattle. He claimed to have spent £1,200 on Victoria's block and £400 on Adolphe's block. Joske later lamented that the dividends promised when hopes were high for cotton, then cane, never eventuated and his three blocks were valued at about a tenth of their value when he purchased them. In 1875, he received only £1,000 for the three blocks when they were sold to Thompson and Renwick. Joske had spent £800 building a fine house on his Tamavua block. It was Suva's most impressive residence and was used by Governor Gordon, a friend of the Joskes, during his visits to Suva prior to the switch of the capital from Levuka to Suva.

Augustus Bartch, a shareholder, had to lease land on the peninsula after he arrived quite late in May 1972, despite having land warrants from the company for 50 acres. As all the available blocks had been selected, he leased a 40-acre block at the back of Nabukalou Creek from Brewer for £10 per annum. He cultivated this block and lived there for five years but by the time he harvested his first crop of cotton, the price had dropped and he received only £13.3.6 in payment. On Brewer's advice he switched to sugarcane, but the 36 acres he had ready to cut had to be left to rot in the field when the mill broke down. The maize he tried next also failed, as the underlying soapstone was too porous and would not retain moisture. He wrote to Governor Gordon in 1880 that:

> having expended all my money on cotton and sugar and having a large family depending on me for sustenance, I rented fifty acres of ground from Mr Joske near Laucala Bay in September 1875, for £12 per year.

Bartsch continued to live and run poultry on his new lease, grow maize and graze cattle. He repeatedly approached Brewer and Joske with efforts to purchase the block he was leasing and after 1876 made determined efforts at the LCC to obtain a Crown Grant based on long occupation. After receiving a 5-acre Crown Grant at Nabukalou from the LCC, he sold it and purchased 100 acres from the estate of the deceased PJ Williams.

Behind Nabukalou Creek, two late arrivals, Aime Augustus Huon and his 15-year-old son, Charles Augustus, purchased 80 acres from Brewer for £2 an acre in 1872. The father formed a partnership with WB Evans, but lacking capital, Evans mortgaged his half of a 32-acre block to Houn, and with this £400 he built a *bure* and planted 16 acres of cane. Huon cleared his half of the block but did not plant. The father also purchased a 1-acre block from WH Surplice, and this later became the centre of a long, acrimonious dispute between Surplice, Joske and Huon. Early in 1875 the father disappeared, and it was later revealed he had sailed to San Francisco leaving no details of when he might return. When Evans decided to return to Melbourne, he sold his half in the block to Aime Huon's son, Charles. Shortly after, Ellen Joske, Paul Joske's wife, obtained the title by redeeming a store debt of Charles Huon and making him a gift of £10.

Paul Joske knew of his wife's land deals but paid little attention, admitting later 'Mrs Joske has a fortune of her own which she spends herself'. Governor Gordon, in an unusually lengthy, 17-page memorandum on this disputed block, noted that from Mrs Joske's point of view it was a shrewd deal. For a store debt at her own store and £10, she gained 40 acres of prime land worth £2,000 to £3,000 when the government shifted the capital to Suva. Huon senior, when he unexpectedly returned to Suva, denied that his son had the right to dispose of the block in his absence. After a long deliberation the LCC decided in the father's favour and he received a Crown Grant for the block.[17] The version of events published in *The Cyclopedia of Fiji* in 1907 was that the Houns, father and son, had 'acquired considerable landed property in the vicinity of Suva' but had been forced to relinquish it due to failure of their plantation enterprises.[18]

Lami was claimed by the company to be the depot for westward expansion, and a grid of streets and a 500-acre reserve was marked on a map prepared for the company. The surveyor, DB Sellars, allocated names to Queen, King, Victoria, Marama, High and Beach streets on the west bank of the Lami River. This was the Fijian *Tikina* lands of the Veisari, Vusi Maoloa and Waibolo people. This map circulated in Melbourne in early 1871 but was misleading, as company shareholders were still clustered around Nabukalou Creek or along the peninsula and immediate hinterland. The directors in Melbourne tried to instil renewed enthusiasm in the company's prospects by holding a ballot for 391 half-acre Lami blocks. The company's Articles of Association allowed one town block for every 10 shares. SG Watson, the company's biggest shareholder, took 36 town blocks at Lami, most of the directors in Melbourne took 12 blocks each and WHO Brewer, heading the Local Committee in Suva, took 24. In a second ballot, more land warrants for Lami were issued. Hoping to stimulate public interest, the company offered a free choice of blocks to the first 20 businesses to occupy and start operating. The company reserved the right to every alternative block. No one took up the offer. It escaped notice at the time that there were only 100 blocks, not 391, delineated on Sellar's map.

---

17 Huon stayed on in Fiji. Huon Street in Suva is named after the father, Aime.
18 Allen, *Cyclopedia of Fiji*, 201–2.

2. SUVA AND THE FATE OF THE POLYNESIA COMPANY

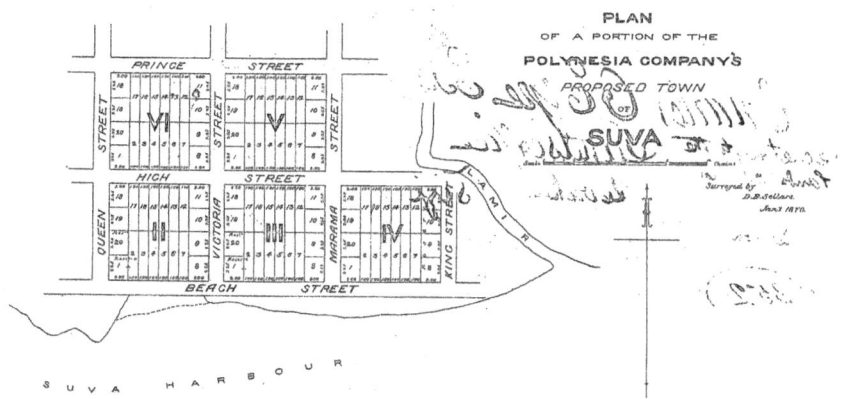

Figure 2.6: Plan for a township; surveyed by DB Sellars, January 1870. The plan was misnamed. It was the plan for Lami Town, west of Suva.
Source: Reproduced courtesy of National Archives of Fiji.

Lami was an illustration of the promotional tactics, speculative posturing and perhaps criminal misrepresentation typical of companies being promoted in Melbourne at the time. The proposed Lami town was separated from Nabukalou Creek by two rivers and no roads or bridges were planned, and the area was low-lying and swampy. The harbourfront was tidal mudflats and unsuited for deep-draught vessels, or even small cutters, and there was no mention of a long deep-water jetty being constructed. In a move to boost support, the company purchased four small islets or islands just offshore in anticipation of Lami becoming a 'bustling harbor'. These four small islets had been astutely purchased from the iTaukei titleholders prior to the company's arrival by William Marshall Moore, the son of a Wesleyan Missionary, in October 1869 for £2, and then sold on to the Polynesia Company four months later for £25.

Two attempts were made to settle in the Lami area. John Henderson, who arrived too late to select a block on the peninsula, had to settle for a 100-acre block at Lami with river frontage that ran 2 kilometres inland from the coast. This selection was approved by Brewer and the Local Committee and the selection was recorded in Melbourne. In December, he moved on to the block with his wife and children. In a testimony to the Cakobau Government's Royal Commission into Quieting Titles, he gave an account of his troubles:

> Soon afterwards certain tribes belonging to the tribe, as your petitioner believes of which Chief Ambrose is the local leader, drove your petitioner and family off the land, beating his servants with clubs, threatening your petitioner's life and plundering his goods so that he was obliged to remove his family into the township of Suva.

Henderson returned several times to the block but could not convince the Lami people of his right to occupy. He offered his opinion to the Royal Commission that 'it will only lead to bloodshed and to the ruin of individuals for the said Company to permit further settlement on this block'. He stayed in Suva and operated a boat hire business until he left Fiji in September 1873.

The Land Claims Commission

When the LCC began investigating European claims in the Suva area in 1878, there were 50 blocks claimed by company shareholders but only 16 of these blocks were occupied by bona fide settlers. For two months the commissioners waded through thick piles of documents submitted by claimants in Fiji and Melbourne and took oral evidence from Fijians and Europeans. Many claims were lodged without nominating an attorney and as they were unrepresented, the commissioners relied solely on the claimant's documentation and opposing depositions, submitted in support of or against a claim. In March 1878, the LCC forwarded its recommendations to the executive-in-council. All claims at Grove Point were rejected on grounds of no occupation. Along the Lami River, Bartsch's claim was disallowed on grounds of adverse Fijian occupation. The claims of Thomas and McGrath in the hinterland already had been granted during investigations in the Lower Rewa district. All other claims for unspecified tracts in the hinterland along the Waibolo, Lami and Tamavua rivers were rejected. The commissioners noted, for example, that a claim had been lodged in the name of Frederick Cook's wife, Alice Cook, for land 'somewhere along the Waimanu'. These claims were summarily dismissed. Individuals such as absentee landlords and Melbourne speculators who never went to Fiji and who claimed land on Suva peninsula using land warrants issued by the Polynesia Company were dismissed under a blanket disavowal of claims based on the company's 1868 charter with Cakobau. On the peninsula, Davies and Edkins, who had since returned to Victoria, and Sophie Williams, the widow of PJ Williams, were allowed Crown

Grants due to prior occupation and expenditure. Cuthbert, Matthews, McClymont, the Joskes and the Armstrong brothers were successful because of their current occupation.

There were inconsistencies in the LCC's deliberations, and complaints were voiced about rejections, the reduction of acreages and bias towards the interests of 'natives' over British subjects. In the case of Sophie Williams, the commission granted her 10 more acres than she had applied for, with no explanation given for the increase, despite her only being in occupation for one year and having cleared only 100 acres of the 700-acre block. The most glaring example of inconsistency in the LCC deliberations concerned Edward Charlwood, a Melbourne bookseller, printer and stationer, a late entry into the Polynesia Company scheme and a speculator who never visited Fiji. He had sent Richard Eaton out to Fiji as his agent. Charlwood had purchased for £5 in Melbourne a dubious title deed for two Suva blocks from the insolvent and disgraced GD McCartney, totalling 160 acres at Nabukalou. These town blocks were now plum in the centre of the planned Suva township site. The Polynesia Company had wrongly granted land warrants and titles for land that was originally known as 'Charlie and Bob's' and the LCC's finding was that Charlwood's purchase was 'as pure a speculation as could be conceived' and that he must have known McCartney had no right to offer it for sale. This block had been subdivided in anticipation of the move of the capital to Suva and several individuals 'squatted' there during the debates over the rightful owners. It was not until 1882, in the second last case considered, that the LCC finally judged Charlwood's claim to be invalid, but then four years later, Charlwood petitioned for reconsideration. In a strange and unexplained reversal, in lieu of his original claim for a 160-acre block, Charlwood was awarded 25 town allotments, now worth several thousand pounds after the shift of the capital to Suva. Charlwood was the most undeserving claimant associated with the Polynesia Company. In an ironic twist, his Crown Grants were all taken up by the Bank of New Zealand in lieu of unpaid mortgages.

The fate of the Polynesia Company is starkly illustrated in the case of the four small islets deep in Suva Harbour. The company had legally purchased these four islets in 1869, anticipating that they would increase the value of the proposed Grove Point blocks and planned Lami town, but did not claim them before the LCC and this was an error as they would certainly have been successful claimants and could have made a small profit from their sale. Instead the four islets were included in a broad claim for 200,000 acres under the 1868 charter signed by Cakobau, and therefore attracted a blanket rejection by the LCC.

Suva, as a township, gradually took shape. In February 1870, the Polynesia Company's manager, Joshua Finner, had declared in Melbourne that Suva would become the 'great central entrepot of all Polynesia' and announced that the laying out of streets and town sites had commenced. This was not true, and the *Fiji Times*, following the company's progress through reports in the colonial press, questioned the tardiness in dispatching settlers to Fiji, but did note that a preliminary survey had been completed. At this stage the company's directors were focusing entirely on large plantation blocks, not creating a town where none existed. But they knew that talk of a town being developed would attract new investors for the second release of shares, so they directed surveyors to set aside a broad area for a town on the shores of Suva Harbour.

The directors lamented, in a letter to the company's agent, JS Butters, still in Levuka, that:

> it is unfortunate that we have not got our town established. You will not overlook the fact that the reserve for the same extends from the Tamavua to the Waibolo, Would natives acclaim settlement there now? It is very desirable that the township should be balloted for at an early date.

That query was the end of the company's involvement in town-building. Fijian *bure* and then later permanent timber frame houses were randomly erected on the small blocks around Nabukalou Creek near Brewer and Joske's ill-fated sugar mill and the mill employed a manager, five overseers, three engineers, four carpenters and two bricklayers, adding significantly to the non-planter European population.

By the early 1870s, Brewer was addressing his letters 'Suva City east', and in the late 1870s, Henderson referred to a 'Suva township' in his testimony to the Land Claims Commission. When Governor Gordon arrived as the new colony's first governor in 1875, the term Suva was in common usage, but rather than being used for the whole peninsula and hinterland it was now being used only to refer to the small settlement along Nabukalou Creek. It was this cluster that became the embryonic town and then city of Suva.[19] By 1880, Suva was declared a 'port of entry' and the Royal Engineers began building a track from Suva to the Waimanu River, and schemes were underway to reclaim parts of the foreshore.

So Multifarious Are the Designs

The settlers on the peninsula were lauded as proof of the company's success but the press in Melbourne and Suva were sceptical once the initial excitement of the *Alhambra*'s departure had worn off. In Melbourne in August 1870, the *Age* announced:

> The Alhambra carries with her divines, doctors, lawyers, legislators, speculators and settlers. The fact that Victoria while yet a colony itself, is undertaking colonization proves the indomitable perseverance of our race, the enterprise and industry of the British people.[20]

This was a grand gesture typical of a colony itself only 30 years after its founding, but the press was also alert to rumblings of disquiet. Two weeks later another editorial warned:

> so multifarious are the designs of the Polynesia Company and intrinsically small are its means of carrying them into effect that we fear some dire catastrophe will happen before long.[21]

The danger alluded to was not falling cotton prices or tropical cyclones. The *Age* told readers that relationships between Fijians and Europeans in Fiji were on a knife's edge. This was an exaggeration and sensationalist reporting, as the period known as the Fiji Rush had been marked not by widespread violence but by Fijian accommodation, tolerance and restraint. In early 1872, Cuthbert wrote to CR Forwood, now the company's agent, on behalf of the Suva Planters Association, complaining that Suva 'natives' would not work, were preventing other Fijians from working and that settlers without imported labour were in dire straits. A meeting of the association in February 1872 resolved that one or all the villages on the

---

19   For Suva see RA Derrick, 'The removal of the capital to Suva', *Transactions and Proceedings of the Fiji Society of Science and Industry* (1953): 203–9; Henry Scott, 'The development of Suva', *Transactions and Proceedings of Fiji Society of Science and Industry* 2, no. 1 (1940): 15–20; McHugh, 'Recollections of early Suva', *Fiji Society of Science and Industry* (19 July 1943): 210–14. The almanac published in 1907, *Cyclopedia of Fiji*, contains details of early settlers, traders and colonial officials.
20   *The Age* (Melbourne), 24 August 1870.
21   *The Age* (Melbourne), 1 September 1870.

peninsula should be removed to enhance the prospects of the company. Later, the Suva people were indeed moved out and resettled at Suvavou ('New Suva') near Lami.[22]

Generally, the situation was tense, but peaceful. In May 1871, Melbourne *Punch* turned to verse to parody the company's affairs:

> We judge of men according to facts
> And everyone will I'm sure agree
> That business runs in a demented groove
> Around the Isles of Fiji.[23]

Early in 1871 a serious cyclone at Suva caused extensive damage, but a Suva Planters Association had been formed and the Cakobau Government in Levuka had empowered Cuthbert, Brewer and Matthews with minor judicial powers over the community. By 1874, the cotton and sugar plantation impetus at Suva had passed and the remaining settlers had diversified into grazing, poultry and vegetable growing or had moved into commercial roles or boat-building or found jobs as plantation managers. When Colonel Pratt arrived on an official survey tour looking for future sites for a capital it sparked a wordy debate over the relative virtues of Levuka and Suva and sites on the west coast of Viti Levu. He noted that the small township at Nabukalou was servicing settlers further along the coast at Navua and Nadroga, and along the lower Rewa River, but the most significant event had been the takeover of Brewer and Joske's extensive holdings and operations by the Melbourne firm of James McEwan and Company and subsequently by William Kerr Thompson and Samuel Renwick. Brewer and Joske's store then became known as Thompson and Renwick, in the style of naming stores after their owners. Thompson and Renwick are remembered today in the names of two Suva streets.

William Kerr Thompson did not purchase shares in the Polynesia Company, probably because he already planned to migrate to Suva and pursue his own investments. Michael Cannon, in *Land Boom and Bust*, wrongly suggests Thompson had invested heavily in a Fiji trading company, and that when its sugar plantations failed he lost £5,000.[24] This may have

---

22 K Vuataki, *Softly Fiji* (Bloomington: West Bow Press, 2013); Ken Chambers, 'Ratu Epeli Kanakana versus A-G for Fiji (the Suvavou case): Blending equitable relief with judicial review', *Journal of South Pacific Law* 12, no. 1 (2008): 111–19.
23 *Punch* (Melbourne), 4 May 1871.
24 For Thompson, see Michael Cannon, *Land boom and bust* (Melbourne: Heritage Publications, 1972), 112–18.

been from confusion over Thompson's many holdings through purchase and mortgages of blocks originally listed by the Polynesia Company, or his takeover of Brewer and Joske's stores and other businesses in Suva initially in partnership with Renwick.

Thompson approached the first governor of Fiji, Sir Arthur Gordon, with an offer of two-thirds to one-third partition of the Suva lands he held. When he later entertained JB Thurston at 'Kamesburg', his mansion in Brighton in Melbourne, they arranged the allocation of town lots between the Crown Colony and Thompson. This deal is wrongly reported in most histories as a sale by the Polynesia Company to the Crown Colony Government. The Polynesia Company attempted to have the auction cancelled on the grounds that its own unsettled land claims needed to be settled first by the Crown Colony Government. The new company agent, GA Woods, protested in Levuka in August 1877 about the new capital being set up on 'Company lands', but the company admitted it had no claim over land being proposed for the new capital, and Governor Gordon reported this admission to the Colonial Office. The Colonial Government already held a 300-acre block that had been set aside by the Polynesia Company as a reserve and the government had acquired a further 600 acres north of Walu Bay after the Land Claims Commission dismissed spurious claims to land. On the first Suva town plan drawn up by Crown Colony Government Surveyor John Berry, Thompson held 177 town blocks and 61 acres at the back of the area now known as the Domain.

In 1880, Thompson travelled to Suva for the first public auction of town blocks. The journalist Henry Britton travelled with Thompson and wrote a report, 'The Suva Land Quest' for the Melbourne *Argus*, which was subsequently published as a small pamphlet with the same title. Correspondence from the Victorian and Fiji governments was still being addressed to John McEwan and Company although by this time WK Thompson had taken over McEwan's extensive Suva interests and holdings. Britton declared:

> it was a curious and historic scene this sale. The table and chairs of the auctioneer and clerks were placed under the shade of a fine umbrageous tree (pronounced 'eevee') in front of the hotel. The bidders were under the verandah. Black men, Fijians, Solomon Islanders and Coolies were all about, wondering and gabbing.

A young friend of Thompson, Vernon Lee Walker, reported over-enthusiastically that 'the whole of Suva belongs to Mr Thompson' and that Thompson had made a 'killing' (sic) selling blocks privately after the public auction of blocks had concluded. The auction was reported in the Levuka press to have been a failure because Levuka merchants had boycotted it, hoping to prevent the capital moving from Levuka to Suva. Later, Thompson donated land at Suva for the Anglican and Presbyterian churches and in 1887 was active in support of a Suva-based proposal for a Victorian annexation movement led by TH Pritchard.[25]

Of the shareholders who had migrated on the *Alhambra* only 13 remained beyond Cession. The remainder returned to Victoria. Some company men became local identities and played significant roles in the emerging settler society. Butters, the 'lion' of Levuka society, was as popular in Levuka as he had been in Melbourne and Paul Joske was Suva's most prominent citizen, patron and friend of the governor. Surplice, Forwood, Glenny, McCartney, Bardwell and Brewer served in the Cakobau Government and after Cession, Cuthbert, Mathews, D'Este, Paul Joske and his son, Adolphe, took positions with the Crown Colony Government. The company played only a minor role in the politics of pre-Cession Levuka, being listed in deputations, tacitly supporting a call for British annexation, denying it was involved in the US annexation movement, and, as late as 1882, GA Woods was listing himself as 'Attorney for the Polynesia Company' and signing petitions of the Land Claimants Protection Society in Levuka. The connections with Melbourne faded as Fiji became a Crown colony and Suva became capital. The so-called 'Fiji Rush' was mostly ignored in the almanac of European achievement published in 1907 as *The Cyclopedia of Fiji*. A suburb called Toorak, a few street names (Amy, Huon, Marks, Renwick and Thompson), and Joske's Thumb, a prominent volcanic neck on the Namosi skyline, are the only reminders of the Polynesia Company days.

By the end of the century, Suva had become the major Pacific entrepot and port city that the Polynesia Company had predicted, but that was not due to funds, plans or involvement by the company. On the shield of the city of Suva, a planter is prominent, and this is appropriate given the first European settlers had been hopeful Polynesia Company shareholders

---

25   Thompson's 40-room, two-storey Italianate mansion in Brighton, built in 1874, later became 'ANZAC House', caring for incapacitated World War I veterans. Weston Bate, *A history of Brighton* (Carlton: Melbourne University Press, 1983).

on the *Alhambra*. The Polynesia Company's speculative banner as the new East India Company and a trading and commercial giant was a ruse perhaps, but at least the *Alhambra* settlers did give birth to a new port town and, indeed, a hub in the South Pacific. The rugged peninsula that the young Adolphe Joske had noted and the missionary Fison described as being in an 'unsettled state' did eventually, for other reasons, become a bustling, national capital and the centre of a regional network for trade, communications, commerce, finance and education.

Source Note

The first brief historical account of the Polynesia Company appeared in *The Cyclopedia of Fiji*, a settler-dominated almanac in 1907. A brief narrative of events was provided in 1937 by AB Brewster in *King of the Cannibal Islands*. The version of events in the *Cyclopedia* and in Brewster was expanded in 1946 by RA Derrick in *The history of Fiji* and this remained the standard account until Deryck Scarr's *I, the very bayonet*, a 1973 biography of JB Thurston which offered a view of the affair seen through the career and ambitions of the former British consul, planter and member of the failed settler-led, pre-annexation Cakobau Government.[26] An extensive record of correspondence between the company, the Victorian Government and the Colonial Office in London, and correspondence with the pre-1874 and post-1874 governments of Fiji, is fortunately preserved in two lengthy documents; a *Remonstrance* from the company to the secretary of state for colonies in London, published by the company in 1877, and an equally long *Refutation* by JB Thurston, by this time colonial secretary for the newly proclaimed colony in Fiji, published in Levuka in 1878.[27] The verbose, pithy, scathing and very detailed argument in these two documents includes letters back and forth; press releases; official correspondence; arguments for compensation; and opinions on the role of Cakobau, the validity of the company's charter

---

26 RA Derrick, *A history of Fiji: Volume one* (Suva: Printing and Stationery Department, 1946); Deryck Scarr, *The majesty of colour: A life of Sir John Bates Thurston*, vol. 1: *I, the very bayonet* (Canberra: ANU Press, 1973).

27 CJ Perry, *Copy of a dispatch to the Right Honorable Earl of Carnarvon, Secretary of State for Colonies from the Polynesia Company, being a remonstrance against the unlawful withholding of the Company's lands at Fiji by his Excellency the Governor, Sir Arthur Hamilton Gordon* (Melbourne: Polynesia Company, 1877); JB Thurston in Frank Spence and Central Archives of Fiji and the Western Pacific High Commission, *The claims and remonstrance of the Polynesia Company of Melbourne, examined and refuted*. Microform, National Library of Australia (Levuka: 1878).

signed with Cakobau in Levuka in 1868 and the bona fides of claimants to Polynesia Company land in Fiji. For full citations of the relevant Suva LCC files, see my MA thesis and monograph (copies held in the University of the South Pacific Library's Pacific Collection, item number HF 491.P6 Q83 1977).

3

The Making of a Capital: A Social History of Suva, 1870–1882[1]

Robert Nicole

As Paul Geraghty has shown in this collection, Suva has a long history that goes back beyond the nineteenth century into the times of pre-European contact. Max Quanchi's chapter examines the manner by which Suva lands were acquired by the Polynesian Company. In the next two (twin) chapters, the baton is passed onwards to explore the process by which the capital of Fiji was transferred from Levuka to Suva over a period of roughly 20 years between 1870 and 1890. These dates are necessarily approximate because it is impossible to identify clear starting and end points for this transition.

This period is packed with almost countless stories. In selecting those that need telling, two criteria were applied. The first was to identify stories that reflected the imperial and colonial nature of the project. The second was to identify stories that those of us who call Suva 'home' might find most compelling – the stories that might give us the best sense of 'when', 'how', and 'why' this city became our capital.

---

1   Acknowledgement: I thank the former director of the National Archives of Fiji (Opeta Alefaio) and his staff for allowing me the use of the documents necessary to produce this chapter. I am also grateful to Olivier, Jacques and Eugenia Nicole, and to Aaron and Cilla Hegarty for opening their homes to me while I worked on it.

Special emphasis is also given to the stories of the numerous, though often anonymous, people who participated in the formation of the new capital. Their actions and voices help to frame the central argument of this study: that the transfer of the capital to Suva was not merely an administrative enterprise conducted by those in power,[2] but one that was layered upon the land, resources, labour and bodies of many others.

I. Early British Interest

When the British Colonel William Smythe visited Fiji in 1860, he judged that Suva was the 'best adapted in Fiji for a white settlement'. From the outset therefore, it seems that the eyes of the empire were set on Suva. In his report, Smythe added that the area was:

> … rich, level, and well-watered. The harbour is, perhaps, the best in the group; it is easy of access, can be entered and quitted with all the prevailing winds, and has communication within the reef with a great extent of coast.[3]

He had been sent by the Queen to lead a special commission of inquiry into an offer of cession that Ratu Cakobau and some Fijian chiefs had made in 1858. His brief was to assess the desirability and viability of the archipelago as a potential colony.

In contrast to Suva, Smythe reported that Levuka, then the principal town of European settlement, was disgraced by constant scenes of drunkenness and rioting. The town had begun as a humble settlement for bêche-de-mer traders in the early 1840s. These traders lived under the protection of Ratu Cakobau and his vassal chief on the island of Ovalau, the Tui Levuka. Levuka had a reasonably good harbour. However, as transport technology changed and larger trans-continental steamships came into operation to service the route between Australia and North America, the shoals and reefs of the Lomaiviti Group in the centre of archipelago became too dangerous to navigate.

---

2   Readers who are interested in the early business and administrative histories of Suva can consult Henry Scott, 'The development of Suva', *Transactions and Proceedings of Fiji Society of Science and Industry* 2, no. 1 (1940): 15–20; RA Derrick, 'The removal of the capital to Suva', *Transactions and Proceedings of the Fiji Society of Science and Industry* (1953): 203–9; and Albert J Schütz, *Suva: A history and guide* (Sydney: Pacific Publications, 1978).
3   See Smythe Report in Berthold Seemann, *Viti: An account of a government mission to the Vitian or Fijian Islands* (London: Dawsons of Pall Mall, 1973), 430.

The captains of these large vessels preferred to anchor off Galoa on the southernmost island of Kadavu before sailing onwards to their distant destinations. Disembarking passengers would then endure the long and uncomfortable voyage from Kadavu to Levuka in the small sailing boats that plied the group. The other problem, as Smythe noted, was that the hills rose so abruptly from the beach that all settlement was 'shut in', and the livelihood of its residents was thus overly dependent on other places in the group.[4]

Smythe's positive opinion of Suva was enthusiastically endorsed by the British/German naturalist Berthold Seemann. While his primary role was to report on botanical matters, Seemann was expected, like most other such travelling scientists, to record everything that could be of value and strategic advantage to the British Empire. Seemann noted that everyone in Fiji was convinced that Suva would become the capital. This conviction had seen the value of land around the harbour rise considerably so that lots not 'worth more than a few pence' a few years before were now selling at £20 an acre.[5] He considered that the peninsula, then known as 'Suva Point', was a land speculator's dream with numerous favourable conditions:

> There is a good harbour, with mud bottom, deep water right alongside of the shore, sheltered by a reef, and having a wide passage for the largest vessels to beat out. When once inside the passage there is clear sea-room, no outlying shoals or reefs. Suva commands the most extensive agricultural district in Fiji, through which run fine rivers (the Navua and Wai Levu or Rewa) navigable for boats for many miles inland … Suva Point is a gently undulated country, free from swamps, and about three miles wide or thereabout at the base … The point itself is open to the prevailing winds; it is thinly timbered with bread-fruit, cocoa-nut, dawa, and other trees of no great growth, and thus requires but little clearing.[6]

Like many imperialists of the time, Seemann was confident in the inevitability of British annexation. However, to his great disappointment Smythe recommended against it and Cakobau's offer was declined. Smythe contended that the offer did not represent the wishes of the

---

4   Smythe Report in Seemann, *Viti*, 430.
5   Seemann, *Viti*, 70.
6   Seemann, *Viti*, 70–71.

people of Fiji and that the potential of the group for British interests was insufficient. As the excitement of a British takeover waned, interest in Suva lost momentum.

II. The *Kai* Suva and the Sale of Their Land

One of the constraints for large-scale settlement in Suva was that the land was owned and occupied by the indigenous population. The history of Suva took an unexpected turn in 1868 when almost all the land was sold by Cakobau to the Polynesian Company to pay the American debt.[7] A crucial factor in the sale is that the people of Suva were then leaderless and the transaction took place without input from the Roko Tui Suva, the traditional head of the people of Suva. Ratu Ravulo, the previous Tui Suva, had died a few years earlier and his son, Ratu Aporosa Tuivuya (also spelt Ratu Ambrose, Abrosa or Avorosa), was still a child. He was brought up in Bau and was in his late teens when he returned to Suva in the late 1860s.

When he was installed as Roko Tui Suva, Ratu Aporosa combined in his one person both temporal and spiritual power. This gave him considerable mana among his people. His mother Adi Elenoa Mila was a sister of Cakobau and his father was a grandson of Ratu Tānoa – Cakobau's father. Hence, from his maternal and paternal side Ratu Aporosa had strong genealogical connections to Fiji's most powerful chiefdom – Bau. He was thus considered by European observers as 'a thorough aristocrat'.[8] His credentials as a chief of the highest order were further enhanced when he married Adi Kelera, a daughter of the Vunivalu of Rewa, another one of Fiji's most powerful kingdoms. As such, he was destined to become a central figure in the process by which Suva became the capital.

In spite of his eminent pedigree, Ratu Aporosa was, in 1870, chief to a people who had just been dispossessed of their land. All that remained were about 300 acres of native reserve around the existing villages of Suva (also known as Naiqasiqasi) and Samabula. The Suva reserve encompassed roughly what is now known as the Domain, an area that included the land between the current Cakobau Road, Queen Elizabeth Drive and Ratu Sukuna Road.

---

7   See Max Quanchi's chapter in this volume for more detail.
8   AB Brewster, *King of the Cannibal Isles* (London: Robert Hales and Company, 1937), 56.

When they arrived to take possession of their lands in 1870, the settlers of the *Alhambra* were largely oblivious to the great sacrifice that the people of Suva had made. As Brewster later attested:

> we did not then recognize the honour and rectitude of the people of Suva, whose lands we seized upon like a lot of cuckoos … [I]n after years … I came to understand the Fijians' attachment to their ancestral soil, and what a wrench it was for the Suva people to part with theirs, but they had accepted the sacred tambua of their overlord, the Vunivalu of Bau, which kept them steady and loyal to their promise to him.[9]

In spite of the loss of their patrimonies, the people of Suva were generally welcoming of the new settlers. Both Ratu Aporosa and his sister Adi Sālote were on hand on 4 September 1870 to help carry the passengers of the *Alhambra* and their belongings to the shore even at the risk of breaking the Sunday tabu. Both were deemed 'good-looking' and thought to be 19 and 14 years old, respectively.[10] Ratu Aporosa spoke fluent English, courtesy of an extended period he had spent on board the visiting American ship *Kearsage* whose name he had tattooed on his arm. Adi Sālote was described as 'a very fine specimen of a pretty Fijian belle'.[11]

Their house was built almost on the beach in front of what is now Thurston Gardens.[12] A few metres away was the bright structure of the 'native church', which in those days was the only building visible to travellers as they entered the harbour. By 1860, most of the inhabitants of Suva had converted to Christianity, including those scattered in outlying villages who had come to settle at Draiba, on the periphery of the Suva village.[13] All around the church stood the houses of the village, tucked away in groves of coconut, breadfruit and *ivi* trees.[14] As there were no roads, it was peaceful and quiet, the sheltered waters between the shore and the protecting reefs being the only highways.[15] Yet, all was not well in Suva, and Brewster noted that the village community was 'small and feeble', having not yet fully recovered from the devastating consequences of the 1843 war.[16]

---

9   Brewster, *King of the Cannibal Isles*, 114.
10 Brewster, *King of the Cannibal Isles*, 82.
11 Brewster, *King of the Cannibal Isles*, 82.
12 Brewster, *King of the Cannibal Isles*, 38.
13 Colman Wall, 'Historical notes on Suva', ed. Paul Geraghty, *Domodomo* 10, no. 2 (1996): 38.
14 Brewster, *King of the Cannibal Isles*, 81.
15 Brewster, *King of the Cannibal Isles*, 25, 74.
16 Brewster, *King of the Cannibal Isles*, 57.

III. Violence on the Plantations: The Death of Ratu Se

Initially, relations between the *Alhambra* immigrants and Suva villagers were friendly. The large European families caused some astonishment among indigenous onlookers. Fijians tended to have small families and after the birth of a child, women expected to be left alone for up to four years. Few husbands dared to interfere with this custom as the wrath of his wife's relatives could be quite unforgiving.[17] The new immigrants lived in rather rough conditions. They all resided in Fijian *bure* made of bamboo, reeds and thatch. These were normally cool, clean and comfortable though some resembled 'disembowelled haystacks'.[18] The men walked around in bare feet and wore little more than a shirt, a pair of duck trousers and a Tokelau hat. Wasting little time to establish their farms, they began raising horses, cattle, pigs, poultry and goats.[19] It was when they began clearing the land for cotton and then sugar that the first tensions emerged.

Converting land into large profitable plantations required labour and a management team to oversee the labourers and administer punishment when misbehaviour or unsatisfactory work were deemed to have occurred. Planters rarely administered violence directly. They normally delegated this task to managers and overseers, some of whom were recruited from as far as the West Indies.[20] Labourers were initially recruited in small gangs from various parts of Fiji. Their immediate tasks were to clear hundreds of acres of bush needed for planting. Their terms usually lasted a month, after which they returned home.

The commercialisation of land was accompanied by a quick deterioration of relations between management and labour. Tensions were first manifested by the numerous labourers who absconded. Planters were greatly inconvenienced by these absences. Each runaway meant lost revenue and additional costs to find a replacement. They responded by tightening security and escalating coercion. Numerous 'petty disputes' soon broke out.[21] The Suva planters organised themselves into an association and began pressing the government for measures that would ensure the more

---

17 Brewster, *King of the Cannibal Isles*, 127.
18 Brewster, *King of the Cannibal Isles*, 36.
19 Brewster, *King of the Cannibal Isles*, 74.
20 Cakobau Government Records (CGR), 854/10/1873, National Archives of Fiji (NAF).
21 CGR 240/10/1872.

effective control and punishment of disobedient workers. In May 1872, they petitioned the chief secretary of the Cakobau Government to erect a police court in Suva and by September they also wanted a constable and a lock-up.[22]

The desertions were often interpreted as symptoms of a natural laziness among indigenous Fijians. However, this stereotype is misplaced. Fijian labourers were widely recruited through the 1860s because they were keen to experience the novelty of working on European-owned plantations. Their reluctance to work coincides with the larger and more exploitative commercial plantations of the 1870s. Moreover, the new labour laws of the Cakobau Government created a framework that allowed planters to legally compel their labourers to work under oppressive conditions. When Fijian labourers walked off their jobs therefore, it was not because they were indolent. They were rejecting an economic and legal system that exploited their labour and no longer fulfilled their curiosity to experience plantation life. To make up for the shortfall of labour, planters began to source labourers from Kiribati (then known as Tokalau or Line Islanders), Vanuatu (then New Hebrides) and Solomon Islands. These labourers were easier to control, having no means of escaping to their home villages and little hope of surviving on their own if they fled into the hills outside Suva.

The deteriorating relations on Suva plantations came to a head in early November 1872 when a major disturbance broke out on the premises of the Suva Sugar Plantation Company owned by Joske and Brewer. The thousand-acre plantation had a southern boundary adjacent to the Suva village native reserve, frontage onto the Suva Harbour (now central Suva) and boundaries eastwards all the way to Laucala Bay. About a third of the land had been purchased from the local traders (Swanston and Hennings), while the rest had been bought from the Polynesian Company. Brewer and Joske had recently switched from cotton to sugar and were employing labour mainly from the Macuata coast and from Santo Island, Vanuatu.[23]

The overseers had been in conflict for some time with a group of about 60 labourers from Macuata. As tensions escalated, the plantation management started carrying firearms and resorted to extreme violence to discipline the workers. Although unarmed, the labourers responded

---

22 CGR 240/10/1872 and 634/10/1872.
23 CGR 854/10/1873.

with their own threats of violence and on the morning of 10 November, they resolved to stop work altogether and refused to come out of their *bure*. The manager, Lester Smith, went in with the whip at which point the labourers all ran outside in what seemed like a premeditated move. When Smith followed them out, they pounced on him. He attempted to shoot them in the resulting scuffle but missed. He was rescued when the overseers and other armed reinforcements came to his aid and surrounded the area. Being in a precarious position the unarmed Macuata labourers ran back into the *bure*. However, in a moment of panic a few of them, including their chief Ratu Se, attempted an escape. They were shot in the act. Ratu Se was shot twice in the back and left unattended to bleed to death. He died the next day. At least one other Macuata man was seriously wounded. The affray ended a few minutes later when the ringleaders of the strike were handcuffed and taken away.[24]

The death by shooting of Ratu Se caused quite a stir. Four of the men involved were charged and put on trial in February 1873 on various charges including manslaughter and shooting with intent to cause grievous bodily harm. The trial was held in one of Brewer's houses, there being no court building in Suva yet, and was presided over by the chief justice. In its case against Smith, the prosecution accused him of aggravated assault against Maiyaca, one of the Macuata labourers. They contended that he had been 'driving natives about like a herd of cattle' and that his use of force had been excessive.[25] When his banned 'cat o' nine' whip with its 10 double-knotted lashes was exhibited in court for all to see, it caused quite a sensation and much indignation that such an implement was used on a Fiji plantation. The prosecution also alleged that Smith had attempted to shoot Maiyaca and that he had inflicted a severe wound to his head with the butt of his revolver. However, in spite of all the evidence, the jury returned a not guilty verdict.[26]

The other four men deliberately conspired to conceal the identity of those who had shot and killed Ratu Se. Expressing his frustration with the case, the prosecutor decried the behaviour of these men for while they claimed to be 'people of Christian parentage and boasting of civilization' they were all guilty of the inhuman neglect of a wounded man. They had all seen him, ignored him and gone home without attending to him. One of the

---

24   *Fiji Times*, 23 November 1872.
25   *Fiji Times*, 17 February 1873.
26   *Fiji Times*, 17 February 1873.

accused, Constable Edward Hicks, was singled out for special criticism because as an officer of the peace he had been quick to arrest a Macuata labourer even as Ratu Se lay dying on the ground. Charles Augustus Huon was also berated:

> … strange to say, when put upon oath, [he] knew nothing, saw nobody, and seemed to hear nothing, although actually joining in the fray. He saw nothing, he heard nothing, he knew nothing, although the most intelligent of the lot.[27]

In spite of being the only arms-bearing persons present during the clash, none of the men were found guilty. By contrast, Maiyaca and a fellow labourer (Tabuaciri) were found guilty of aggravated assault and common assault for which they respectively received sentences of six and three months imprisonment with hard labour. The chief justice concluded that an attempt had been made to conceal the truth and he regretted the effects of the case on the reputation of Suva.[28] Yet, his complicity in letting the conspirators go free while punishing the labourers signalled that the justice system worked more favourably for white men than for others and that different rules applied to employers and employees on plantations in the use and abuse of violence.

IV. Ratu Aporosa Tuivuya

Interestingly, the planters and some officials identified the Tui Suva, Ratu Aporosa, as one of the main instigators of the trouble. In a letter to the chief secretary, the deputy warden (mayor) of Suva pleaded that if Ratu Aporosa was not removed from the district at once, it would be 'utterly impossible to prevent further disturbances'.[29] Ratu Aporosa knew Ratu Se and was one of the witnesses called to identify the body when it was exhumed for a post-mortem. Being domiciled next door to the plantation, Ratu Aporosa had extensive contact with the gangs of labourers who came to work in Suva and could exercise significant influence over them.

This was not lost on the planters, 30 of whom signed a petition in which he was accused not only of causing labourers to be discontented but also of actively encouraging villagers in Suva, Lami and Samabula to disrupt

---

27 *Fiji Times*, 17 February 1873.
28 *Fiji Times*, 17 February 1873.
29 CGR 756/10/1872.

and boycott plantations.[30] The petition suggests that while he and his people may have lost their lands, Ratu Aporosa retained considerable influence over the chiefs, people and resources west of Suva including Lami, Veisari and Naikorokoro up to the boundary with the province of Namosi. He also exerted power over labourers from other parts of Fiji who came to work in Suva.

His motives for inciting labourers to rebel and for disrupting the smooth functioning of plantation operations are difficult to establish. Was he resentful of the manner by which the Suva lands had been alienated? Did he hope to regain ownership of Suva lands if the plantations failed and their owners left? Was he an early champion of the proletariat, capable of discerning worker exploitation and engineering and organising protests?

Upon investigation, government officials found that, unlike other major chiefs around the country, Ratu Aporosa was not employed by the government. The 'Roko Tui' title he held by descent was a customary one and therefore different from that which was held by the Roko Tui (or lieutenant-governors) on the government's payroll. He therefore had little incentive to participate in the implementation of the new order that Cakobau and his European allies were putting in place. Indeed, he had refused to contribute to the *soli vakavanua*, one of the means by which the government raised taxes from the indigenous population. He was not afraid to use 'a good deal of rebellious and insolent talk' against government officials and planters, and thought that as chief of Suva 'he should do as he chose in the district'.[31]

The government was divided about how to handle the renegade chief. Robert Swanston, the minister of native affairs, did not consider him worthy to hold any appointment of trust or honour. He accused Ratu Aporosa of taking money from his people to spend it on gin. In any case, he wrote, there was no money to pay him.[32] Other officials thought that if Ratu Aporosa was appointed to a government position, it might help to neutralise his antagonistic behaviour. Ratu Napolioni, the Roko Tui of the Rewa province – of which Suva was an important district – advised that it was 'absolutely necessary' that the young chief be appointed *buli* (district administrator) of Suva. It should be a trial and if he misbehaved

30   CGR 952/41-42/1872.
31   CGR 1140/41-42/1873.
32   CGR 1140/41-42/1873.

he could then easily be *sivoed* or dismissed.³³ Walter Carew, the secretary of the Rewa province, agreed and advised Swanston that Europeans in the district were much more to blame than the young chief. He favoured Ratu Aporosa's appointment as *buli* and proposed that he be given a stern warning that any further rebellion or bad behaviour would meet with instant dismissal.³⁴ When approached, Ratu Aporosa responded that he was *malumalumu e na cakacaka*, or not contracted to work for the government but that he would make his best efforts if he was appointed and paid.³⁵ Swanston begrudgingly approved the appointment and, from the early months of 1873, Ratu Aporosa was integrated into the government as the *buli* of Suva.

V. The Demise of the Cakobau Government

Ratu Aporosa's tenure of the buliship was short-lived. Through 1872 and 1873 the viability of the Cakobau Government had become increasingly precarious. It could not collect sufficient revenue to fund itself and its attempts at raising a loan in Australia failed because of its poor reputation among Sydney capitalists.³⁶ The government's lack of legitimacy was also visible in large parts of the country, not the least among the tribes of Colo in the interior of Viti Levu, who resented Cakobau and his government's claims over them for he had never conquered them. They also held him responsible for the manner by which they were being gradually dispossessed of their best lands by planters. To bring about the submission of these tribes, Cakobau embarked on the Nadawarau campaign. Although he was victorious, the campaign was an additional cost the government could ill afford. The expense was partly offset by the money the government recuperated from planters in the fees they paid to hire the thousands of Colo prisoners but other problems threatened the complete collapse of the government.

Among them was the riotous behaviour of many European settlers who had become disgruntled by the failure of the cotton industry. With their dreams shattered and their fortunes in tatters, they became

---

33   CGR 1140/41-42/1873. See Arthur Capell's *A new Fijian dictionary* (Sydney: Australasian Medical Publishing Co., 1941) for the translation of 'sivo'.
34   CGR 1185/41-42/1873.
35   CGR 1140/41-42/1873.
36   David Routledge, 'Pre-Cession government in Fiji' (PhD thesis, The Australian National University, 1965), 104.

'vociferous oppositionists',[37] formed a Ku Klux Klan, and vowed to bring the government down by any means necessary. In September of 1873, the situation in Levuka was so dire and the government's regime of law and order so seriously eroded that the country seemed on the brink of civil war.

In Suva, large numbers of labourers continued to abscond. Planters sent renewed requests for the government to establish a police post to deter desertion. They also asked for a proper building to incarcerate those absconders who were recaptured.[38] Some settlers no longer respected the law nor the magistrates who were supposed to administer it, or even the Fijian police whose role was to enforce it. To make matters worse for the government, even the older and more supportive settlers now believed that the only viable option to regain 'a properly ordered society' was British annexation.

The question of ceding Fiji to Great Britain was also on the minds of Cakobau and his chief secretary, JB Thurston. On 13 January of 1873, Thurston sent a cable to London to gauge whether Her Majesty's Government would consider a new offer of cession. The wording of the question did not formally offer cession but it encouraged the British Government to dispatch the Goodenough and Layard Commission to Fiji to assess the desirability of acquiring Fiji as a colony. British appetite for colonies in the early 1870s was vastly different from that which had prevailed when Smythe had visited. Fiji was now part of a world in which European competition for territories and resources was more aggressive. Goodenough and Layard were both enthusiastic imperialists and Goodenough was particularly forceful in pressing the Cakobau Government and the chiefs to sign a formal and unconditional offer of cession. The chiefs assented and, on 10 October 1874, Fiji formally became a colony of Great Britain.[39] The ultimate decision to move Fiji's capital was now removed from one government and placed in the hands of another.

---

37   Routledge, 'Pre-Cession government in Fiji', vii.
38   See CGR 69/10/1873 and 868/10/1873.
39   Annexation occurred for a variety of complex internal and external reasons all of which cannot be discussed in detail here. (See RA Derrick, *A history of Fiji: Volume one* (Suva: Printing and Stationery Department, 1946); Routledge, 'Pre-Cession government in Fiji'; David Routledge, *Matanitu: The struggle for power in early Fiji* (Suva: Institute of Pacific Studies, University of the South Pacific, 1985); Deryck Scarr, *Fiji: A short history* (Sydney: Allen & Unwin, 1984); William Sutherland, *Beyond the politics of race: An alternative history of Fiji to 1992* (Canberra: The Australian National University, 1992); Jane Samson, *Imperial benevolence: Making British authority in the Pacific Islands* (Honolulu: University of Hawai'i Press, 1998), doi.org/10.1515/9780824862947.

VI. The Search for a New Capital

Through this period, Levuka was a hive of activity and retained centre stage in the political and economic life of the country. Since the days of general drunkenness and rioting of the early 1870s, its thriving community of about 700 residents had developed a new pride in what were deemed 'symbols of respectability' such as the performances of the Levuka Repertory, the debating circles, the minstrel choirs, the secluded bathing pool for ladies, the annual regatta to celebrate the new year, cricket matches and billiard matches with visiting champions from the colonies.[40] However, the town continued to suffer from the absence of a proper supply of water, unacceptable sanitary arrangements, an unflattering beach and the absence of a proper bridge to cross Totogo Creek. Levuka was also expensive for business. For instance, the cost of Melanesian labourers in Levuka was estimated to be 65 per cent greater than in Suva.[41]

These lingering issues reignited discussions about moving the capital. In early 1875, Sir Hercules Robinson, the acting governor of Fiji, received a letter from Lord Carnarvon, the secretary of state for colonies, specifying that the capital should not be moved except if 'very strong reasons' such as an unfavourable medical assessment, recommended it.[42] There were many strong reasons to move the capital and Carnarvon's letter acted as a cue for the official process of inquiry to begin.

Signs that Suva was being prepared for a substantial transformation were soon visible. The port of Suva was surveyed and beacons and lights were placed at the entrance of the harbour. Nukulau Island was earmarked as a possible quarantine station.[43] The magistrate for the southern region of Viti Levu was removed from Rewa and brought to Suva.[44] More ominously, a few days after arriving to take up his new role as governor of the colony, Sir Arthur Gordon sent a dispatch to Carnarvon in which he wrote that he could not recommend Levuka as the site of the future capital.[45] In December 1875 he travelled to Suva on a scoping trip to establish for himself the suitability of the area as the new capital. Back then, the

---

40 Routledge, 'Pre-Cession government in Fiji', 58.
41 Colonial Secretary's Office (CSO) 74/1877: all CSO records are found in the National Archives of Fiji (NAF).
42 See CSO 1627/1876.
43 CSO 580/1875.
44 Fiji Provisional Government Records (PGR), 302/1875, NAF.
45 Despatch 34, Gordon to Carnarvon, 22 July 1875, CO 83/6, Public Records Office (PRO).

proposed site around Nabukalou Creek was home to just four or five houses including a wooden church and the defunct Joske and Brewer's sugar mill, whose operational lifespan had been less than three years.[46]

As Gordon scaled up to the top of the hills behind the small settlement, a full view of the peninsula and its back country would have appeared before his eyes. Facing east, he would have discerned the contours of the Rewa Basin, the agricultural heartland of Viti Levu. Hidden from his gaze behind the hills to the north were the large plantations of the Upper Rewa and Waimanu rivers and the alluvial flats of Naitāsiri. For all their value to the Fijian economy, these agricultural districts lacked one key ingredient: a port. Most of the produce farmed up river for export had to be transported at great cost down the length of the river and then across the seas to Levuka where it was loaded onto sailing ships and exported. As he turned to face west, Gordon would have contemplated the key to this problem: Suva Harbour, in all its magnificence.

In his plans to make the colony profitable, Gordon was interested in developing Fiji's fruit trade, particularly banana. However, the sailing ships that docked in Levuka could not deliver this produce fast enough to the Australasian markets to avoid rotting. Steamships were the key. He approached the Australian Steam Navigation Company with a subsidy if it would send one of its steamers to Suva. The scheme was an instant success and within months the Union Steamship Company of New Zealand began to ferry bananas and other fruits to Auckland.[47]

Suva had been designated as a Port of Entry in 1872 but now, as a colonial port, it played a key role in consolidating British domination of maritime traffic in this part of the world. While Suva offered much in settlement and plantation potential, its prospects as a port for all the agricultural products of the Rewa Basin were more important. And yet for this port to become useful Gordon knew that one last obstacle remained: getting the produce from the Rewa Basin to Suva. A road would need to be built.

Gordon saw enough to satisfy him. Within a month he sent Colonel FE Pratt and Dr William MacGregor to investigate the viability of making Suva the new capital of Fiji. Pratt was the surveyor-general and became one of the principal architects of the new town. MacGregor was the colony's

---

46 CF Gordon Cumming, *At home in Fiji* (Edinburgh: William Blackwood and Sons, 1882), 71, 308.
47 John Gorrie, 'Fiji as it is', *Proceedings of the Royal Colonial Institute* 14 (1882–3): 162–63.

3. THE MAKING OF A CAPITAL

chief medical officer and was required to ascertain the sanitary condition of the proposed site. The two men walked the width and breadth of the peninsula, venturing as far inland as the waterfall at the base of Tamavua River and as far west as Veisari. They reported on everything including geology, hydrology, topography, vegetation, timber supply, waterways and drainage, shoreline, anchorage, potential for reclamation, potential road construction to Rewa and the best location to lay the streets of the new town.[48] The report on Suva was sent to London alongside a companion report also authored by Pratt that dismissed the suitability of Levuka. A minute by Carnarvon summed up official attitude in the following terms: 'Levuka is condemned already …'[49]

Gordon now had the unenviable task of notifying the Levuka residents. When he revealed that Suva, Savusavu and Nadi were being considered as potential sites for a new capital,[50] the Levuka residents responded instantly with a petition pleading that the capital not be moved. They argued that the central location of Levuka in the group, its flourishing businesses and the high cost of relocation should be sufficient to retain the status quo.[51]

Not to be outdone, the residents of Rewa and Suva responded with a counter-petition. Led by Paul Joske, they outlined several reasons why Levuka must no longer be the capital. Draining water after high tide was a daily problem and the constant humidity was not good for the health of residents. Further, Levuka did not have enough space to cater for the expanding needs of a colonial capital. Sites to build businesses were 'practically' unobtainable. This had pushed prices so high that property and land were now unaffordable. The unsheltered harbour was vulnerable to winds and therefore unsafe for the large trans-Pacific steamers. To make matters worse, Ovalau was poor in soil quality and could not grow sufficient food for a developing and thriving capital.[52]

---

48 Despatch 12, Gordon to Carnarvon, 25 January 1876, CO 83/9, PRO.
49 Despatch 78, Gordon to Carnarvon, 12 April 1876, CO 83/9, PRO.
50 *New Zealand Times*, 11 January 1877; see paperspast.natlib.govt.nz.
51 CSO 1627/1876.
52 CSO 942/1877.

VII. The Queen Approves: Suva on the Drawing Board

The Suva and Rewa petitioners need not have worried. In a dispatch on 3 April 1877, Lord Carnarvon informed Gordon that the Queen was 'pleased to approve the selection of Suva' as the new capital. Gordon notified the Legislative Council on 26 April, paving the way for the official process of relocating the courts and government offices to begin.[53] The decision was greeted with a great 'howl of dismay' by the householders in Levuka[54] and, one can imagine, much joy and jubilation among the few landowners in Suva.

The decision compelled the government to focus on two immediate priority areas: water supply and land acquisition. The first imperative was resolved when Royal Engineers under the command of Colonel Pratt sunk a well in the centre of the proposed township and found good drinking water.[55]

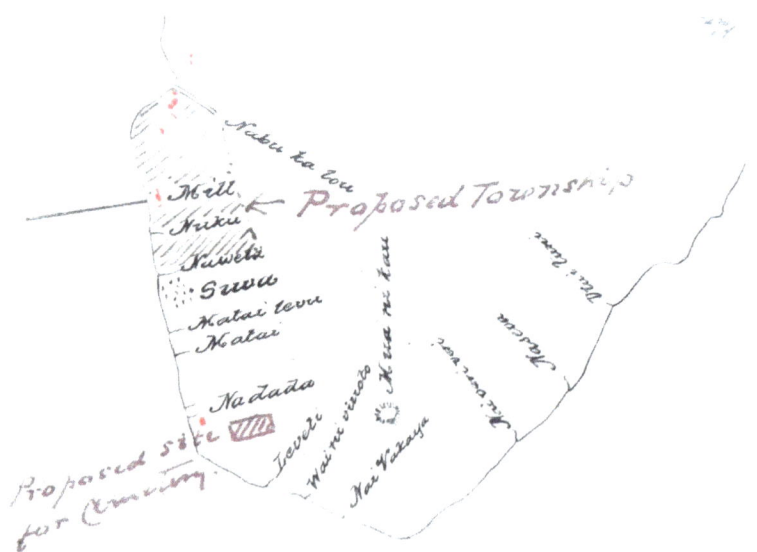

Figure 3.1: Map of Suva with proposed township (shaded) and site for cemetery.
Source: Bolton Corney to Colonial Secretary, 7 August 1878, Colonial Secretary's Office (CSO) 1562/1878, National Archives of Fiji (NAF).

---

53 See CSO 1968/1882; *The Australasian*, 16 June 1877, see trove.nla.gov.au.
54 Gordon Cumming, *At home in Fiji*, 308.
55 *New Zealand Herald*, 8 November 1877; see paperspast.govt.nz. His proposed plan of Suva is kept at the Public Records Office in London (Ref: MPHH 1/74).

3. THE MAKING OF A CAPITAL

Figure 3.2: Sketch of the proposed Suva township, 1879.
Source: John Gorrie to Colonial Secretary, CSO 2190/1879, Miscellaneous Papers, NAF.

The acquisition of land was more complicated. Early maps of the proposed township indicate that it was planned to span the area from the southern bank of the Nabukalou Creek to the boundary with the Native Reserve, now Cakobau Road.[56]

This block (larger shaded area on the map) had recently fallen into the hands of the two Melbourne merchants, William Thomson and Samuel Renwick. They had shrewdly speculated that Suva was bound to become the capital and, consequently, that the value of its lands would rise considerably. They were now in possession of the most valuable piece of real estate in the colony and destined to make handsome profits. They approached Gordon with an offer to surrender a block of land within the area now bordered by Gordon, MacArthur, Carnarvon and Kimberly streets where the new Government Buildings could be erected. They also gifted the government a title to every alternate lot in the rest of the area.[57]

---

56 See CSO 1562/1878 and 278/1879.
57 Schütz, *Suva: A history and guide*, 14.

A sketch drawn in 1879 by John Gorrie, the chief justice of Fiji, suggests how the administrators envisaged the development of the new capital. It shows the planned roads to the Upper and Lower Rewa regions, the site for the government offices, the Supreme Court and Governor's Residence, areas reserved for the outward growth of the town, women's baths, a road to the proposed pier and areas reserved for the 'humbler class of residents'.

Figure 3.3: Town of Suva and adjoining lands, Viti Levu, Fiji, 1885.
Source: Commissioner of Lands to Colonial Secretary, 14 April 1885, CSO 1030/1885, NAF.

Beyond the proposed township area lay large tracts of land owned by a handful of planters. Among the largest were the Irish brothers Thomas and Frederick Armstrong of the Hill Plantation whose land encompassed so much of Nasēsē and Muanikau that the peninsula was often referred to as Armstrong Point.[58] The Joskes owned the land east of the Tamavua River and ran Bayview Plantation. Huon owned most parts of Toorak and sections of Veiuto. Meanwhile large areas in Muanikau, Lacuala Bay, Raiwai, Flagstaff and Walu Bay belonged to Renwick and Thompson. Cuthbert and Richards owned parts of Raiwaqa and Vatuawaqa, and Williams owned most of Vatuwaqa and parts of Samabula. While some of these lands were used for farming, many of them lay idle, their proprietors waiting for profitable opportunities to sell them.

All property owners were wealthy Europeans, the only ones who had sufficient purchasing power to buy land and build on it. Yet, it would be erroneous to assume that Suva was a European town. Indigenous Fijians, Melanesians and Part-Europeans were a vital part of the fledgling township for they possessed a valuable commodity that Suva and its European residents desperately needed: the capacity to work.

The governing ideas about race at this time dictated that no self-respecting colonist would engage in manual labour. Colonised 'coloured' labour was therefore much sought after, though very poorly paid. These workers needed places to stay. From the outset therefore, and regardless of how much some of its residents desired it to be, Suva could never be a homogenous 'white' town. This paradox is well captured in the following passage, loaded as it is with the prejudices of the time:

> As for the blacks, they are numerous enough – almost too muchly so; although if they would but work, we couldn't have too many of them. In fact, we have to go recruiting labor from the Solomons and the New Hebrides …[59]

Labourers were put to work on a variety of public works projects. An impression of the range of these projects can be gauged from a report compiled by Gorrie after visiting Suva in 1879. His opening remarks related to the mangrove swamp that lay along both sides of Nabukalou Creek and in proximity of the hotel he was staying at. The odour rising from the swamp, he wrote, 'was enough to kill a horse'.[60] He recommended it filled.

---

58 Brewster, *King of the Cannibal Isles*, 127.
59 *Evening Star*, 23 September 1881; see paperspast.natlib.govt.nz.
60 CSO 2190/1879.

Several other matters were concerning. The hotels were dirty, objectionable and a concern for public health. Also, Suva did not have a proper landing place for boats, and arriving passengers had to walk on mud flats before reaching the shore. He suggested that part of the shallow offshore area on the southern side of Nabukalou Creek (now Dominion House and Fiji Visitors Bureau) be reclaimed and a pier built that would extend up to the deep sea.[61] He also noted that in the area between the recently removed mill[62] and the native reserve lay a space that was unhealthy for habitation because it was too damp and suggested it be set aside as a public park (now Albert Park).

On the matter of the native reserves, Gorrie proposed that a commission be convened to look into it. Once this was done, he thought the government should advertise in Australia and the United Kingdom to invite prospective settlers. It is difficult to establish whether this commission ever came into existence but we know that Gordon and his administration wanted the villagers living on Suva's native reserves to be evacuated and relocated elsewhere (see below). The large yellow shaded areas on the map (Figure 3.3) indicate that, aside from the Suva village, additional reserves existed for the people of Samabula and one possibly for villagers at Vatuwaqa. Clearly though, Gorrie was one of many officials who believed that while indigenous people and their lands ought to be protected, the long-term welfare of Suva and the rest of the colony lay in the hands of European settlers and should be prioritised.

A year after his report, 92 Suva allotments were sold at a public auction under an *ivi* tree by Nabukalou Creek.[63] The auction was advertised in all the major Australian and New Zealand cities and when it took place on 22 November 1880, the *Fiji Argus* described it as 'spirited throughout'.[64] The government earned approximately £4,000 from the auction, well short of the £12,000 it might have anticipated.[65]

---

61   CSO 2190/1879.
62   It appears that the sugar mill was removed by the Royal Engineers to an area in the Waimanu region in Upper Rewa in 1877. (See *New Zealand Herald*, 8 November 1877, paperspast.govt.nz.)
63   This was not, as is often erroneously believed, the same tree that stood on the corner of Renwick and Scott Streets before it was destroyed by Cyclone Winston in 2016 (see Brewster, *King of the Cannibal Isles*, 129). The tree was cut down soon after the 1880 auction to make way for a hotel.
64   6 December 1880; see paperspast.natlib.govt.nz.
65   *New Zealand Herald*, 25 September 1880; see paperspast.natlib.govt.nz.

But undeniably, as the *Argus* report pointed out, the big winners were 'local capitalists' whose purchasing power allowed them to instantly secure for themselves the best and most valuable real estate in Fiji.[66] Needless to say, the interests of communities and individuals further down the social and economic ladder were never considered in these transactions and the rules of the game were thus, from the very beginning, skewed in favour of wealthy individuals and their families.

VIII. The First Road: Suva to Waimanu

The last major item in Gorrie's report was about roads. Foremost among them was the road that should link the large agricultural districts of the Rewa Basin with the port of Suva. This road had long been in the making. As early as April 1873, the Rewa planters had approached the Cakobau Government with a request to build a road between the Upper Rewa and Suva.[67] As plausible as their argument was, the money to build the road back then was simply non-existent.

In 1876, Suva's first major infrastructure development, the road to Waimanu and the Upper Rewa – the Waimanu Road – was ready to begin. Progress was slow because labour was exceedingly difficult to obtain. Thanks to its defeat of the chiefs and people of Navosa in that same year, the government had a large pool of prisoners at its disposal, many of whom were put to work on the Waimanu Road. Several ni-Vanuatu labourers were also recruited to work on the project.

As there were no motorised vehicles yet (the first cars were imported into Fiji in the 1910s), the road was built for horse-drawn carts carrying people and cargo to and from the Upper Rewa. In the first instance, the labourers cleared the timber and bush over a width of 30 feet for a distance of one and a half miles towards Tacirua. They then worked with pick handles to make the road on the cleared stretch. Some of the labourers also helped with surveying and road marking, or as messengers, cooks and carriers.[68]

---

66 6 December 1880.
67 CGR 246/33/1873.
68 See CSO 607/1876, 629/1876 and 1657/1876.

From 1876, the building of the road sputtered along so that two years later, about two and a half miles of the stretch had been completed. The Colo prisoners worked under the supervision of armed Royal Engineers and Fijian sentries. The mountaineers often complained about the oppressive nature of the work. Their desire to free themselves from bondage can be gauged from a serious incident that took place in the first few days of 1877. In a premediated plan, a group of 30 Colo prisoners suddenly threw down their tools and ran into the bushes. Four were immediately shot and killed while two or three others were recaptured soon after. Most, however, fled into the mountains where, one would assume, they sought to evade the long arm of the Colonial Government for as long as they could.[69]

Plagued by the shortage of labour and yet determined to link Suva to Rewa, the government faced a dilemma. Should it prioritise the Waimanu Road or develop the main streets of the new capital? This dilemma is well reflected in a letter from John Berry, the surveyor-general, to the colonial secretary:

> If it is intended that the streets and roads in and around the site for the proposed township should be commenced at once, and it is desired that the prisoners should be quartered there, I should propose that a gaol large enough to contain about 50 prisoners should be built in the neighbourhood of one of the wells which have been sunk on the old sugar plantation. If the works on the capital are not ready to start, then the gaol should be built at Tamavua, so that the prisoners confined there may continue to build the Waimanu Road.[70]

In 1878, four miles of the middle stretch of the Waimanu Road remained untouched. In most of the completed sections the roadway was at least 16 feet wide making it possible for wheeled traffic to travel through. However, because the middle part was unfinished and impracticable, as Berry explained, it destroyed 'the utility of the whole'.[71] In November of that year, the government received yet another petition from the European residents of Rewa and Suva to improve communication links

---

69   *Auckland Star*, 25 January 1877 and *New Zealand Herald*, 26 January 1877; see paperspast.natlib.govt.nz.
70   CSO 168/1878.
71   CSO 1569/1878.

between the port and the agricultural districts. Berry proposed that, with little expense, a bridle track could be completed to cover that distance so that both horses and footmen could get through.

Without sufficient labour, however, there was little that the surveyor-general or the government could do. Most available prisoners were assigned to other pressing public works projects around the colony, mostly in Taveuni and Levuka. Bringing them to Suva would hamper the completion of those projects. Other prisoners stationed in the Suva area were tied up cutting large trees. This had been instructed by the government for the government buildings and other infrastructural developments in and around the township. To work around the shortage of labour, Berry recommended that the chiefs of Suva, Rewa and Waimanu be approached and urged to contribute men from their villages to build the road.[72]

Gorrie agreed that Fijian villagers should be assigned to work on the roads. For the Waimanu Road, he proposed that the mountaineers of Naitāsiri and Wainimala, as well as villagers from Namosi, Serua and from Sawani and Colo-i-Suva should make the roads as part of *lala* – the non-remunerated tax that all villagers traditionally owed their chiefs.[73] Gorrie proposed further that the new Lower Rewa Road should be completed by the people of Rewa, Bau and Tailevu.[74]

Clearly, the government was availing itself of the cheap labour and resources of people in districts that surrounded Suva to finance the development of the township. This 'free' labour represented a massive saving for the cash-strapped government. However, these villagers had little if any connection with the road and would have been perplexed about why they were to build it when it was clearly intended to meet the interests of European planters.

IX. The *Leonidas* Labourers

The extent to which these villagers actually participated in the construction of the roads is difficult to establish. However, in one of the turning points of Suva and Fiji's history, almost 500 indentured labourers arrived from

---

72   CSO 1569/1878.
73   CSO 2190/1879.
74   CSO 2190/1879.

India on 14 May 1879 on board the ship *Leonidas*. The initial resistance of many planters to employ them meant that the government now had a significant supply of cheap labour to use on its own projects including the development of the Suva township.

By November, many of these labourers could be seen with shovels, picks, hammers and hoes in hand, gradually transforming Suva from a rural outback into an urban grid. They were put to work on the pier, the coastal road from Nabukalou Creek to the native reserve (i.e. Victoria Parade), the Waimanu Road, embanking the sides of the Nabukalou Creek, and filling the swamp on both sides of the creek.[75] The treatment of these indentured labourers was appalling from the beginning. They were accommodated in 'lines' but these buildings were overcrowded and flimsy, and when the hurricane of December 1879 struck, they were completely destroyed. Toilets were scant and no provisions were made for labourers to shelter in the shade when the sun was at its hottest.[76]

Much of the food they ate came in the form of rations of yam and taro. These were grown especially for them by villagers in various parts of the country.[77] This arrangement intimates that while villagers were not directly involved in the construction of the new town, many of them were indirectly implicated in the project because their labour and lands formed an integral part of the production of food and taxes that were necessary for the development of the town.

Most of the *Leonidas* labourers worked on Victoria Parade, Suva's main thoroughfare. At the end of 1881, they had completed approximately 1 kilometre of the road with a width of 16 metres across the whole length. The work was difficult and required the road to be raised more than a metre especially at the northern end near Nabukalou Creek. Some portions of the foreshore also had to be reclaimed. In two places, the workers had to cut through hills. The amount of earth removed in forming the road was estimated at over 20,000 cubic metres, a great part of which had to be transported more than half a mile away.[78]

---

75 CSO 1707/1879.
76 CSO 2167/1879.
77 CSO 855/1882.
78 CSO 2228/1881.

3. THE MAKING OF A CAPITAL

When the photographer and travel writer Gerard Ansdell visited in 1881, Suva had already been systematically laid out in blocks and streets. He commented that Victoria Parade extended:

> … along the sea beach for upwards of a mile, and can be carried along almost *ad infinitum*; here the large stores are being built, and, as the roadway is well 'metalled' with coral, and planted with fine foliage and flowering trees throughout its entire length, it is no doubt, in a few years' time, it is destined to become the fashionable promenade of Fiji.[79]

And yet, this favourable description masks a more unpleasant reality. Progress had in fact been slow partly because of the nature of the work, but also because of the frequency of sickness among the labourers, and the many disputes that arose from their discontent with the conditions of employment.[80]

X. The Shaping of the Town

Other projects were also underway, including the search for a suitable location for a cemetery. Finding a good burial ground was more difficult than anticipated. Dr Bolton Corney, the colony's chief medical officer, complained that he could not find even half a dozen acres of land with a sufficient depth of arable soil, except within the native reserve or at too great a distance from the township. An area on the abandoned Armstrong plantation at Nasēsē looked promising but the idea was abandoned when soapstone was found 5 feet below the soil. It would have required excessive labour to dig the graves.[81]

It took three more years of searching before an appropriate site was found. They settled on an 8-acre area at Nabuli near the Tamavua River, a short distance from the Melanesian Immigrant Depot and the newly built Suva prison. The site was deemed close enough to the township and was conveniently free of excess water and land crabs. The recently completed jetty by the labour depot made it possible for the public to access the burial grounds by road and by sea.[82]

---

79 Gerrard Ansdell, *A trip to the highlands of Viti Levu: Being a description of a series of photographic views taken in the Fiji Islands during the dry season of 1881* (London: H. Blair Ansdell, 1882), 6–7.
80 CSO 2228/1881.
81 CSO 1562/1878.
82 CSO 984/1882 and 1287/1882; see map in Figure 3.4.

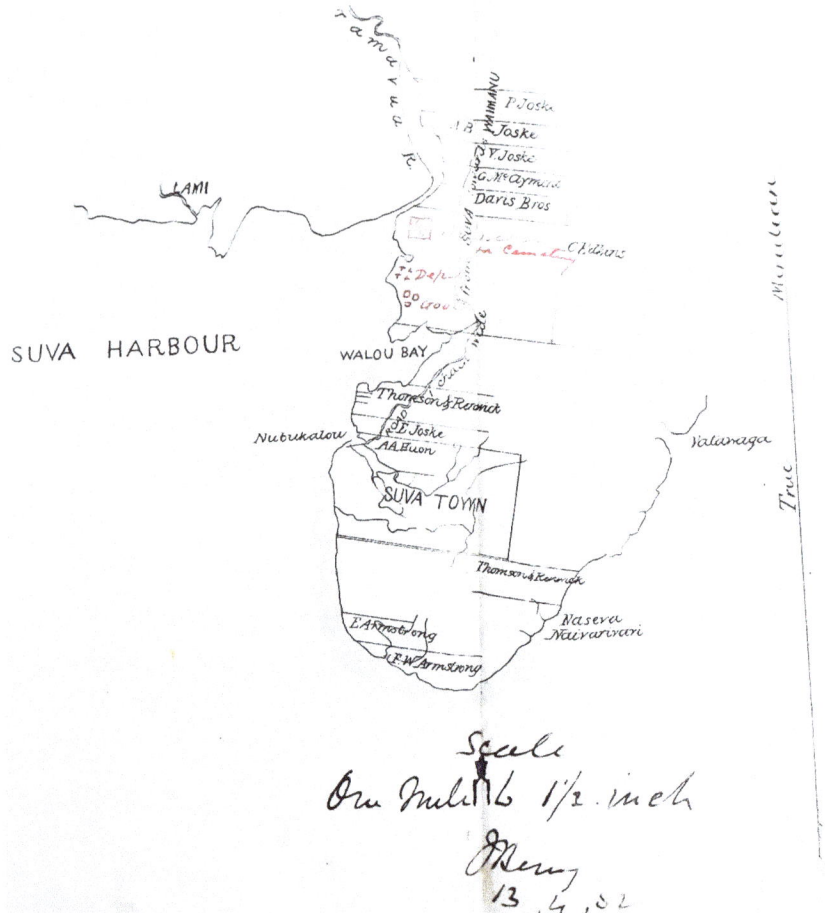

Figure 3.4: Bolton Corney report on the selection of a suitable site for a permanent public burial ground in Suva, 1882.
Source: Chief Medical Officer to Colonial Secretary, 9 April 1882, CSO 1287/1882, NAF.

In the early 1880s, correspondents aptly wrote that Suva was still 'very much in embryo as a town'. There were four hotels and half a dozen stores, a tobacconist, a chemist and a hairdresser, but neither a tailor nor a shoemaker. Some of them were owned by leading Levuka businessmen who had transitioned to Suva. New houses were springing up everywhere and the town was thought to be sprouting like 'a digging township did in the good old days'.[83]

---

83 *Evening Star*, 23 September 1881 and *New Zealand Herald*, 19 September 1881; see paperspast. natlib.govt.nz.

3. THE MAKING OF A CAPITAL

The new settlement also attracted the interest of the church and preparations were made to have missionaries stationed in the town in anticipation of 'a considerable migration of the white population' to Suva.[84] The mission boards of the main Christian denominations of Australasia were quick to respond and worshippers soon flocked to the Saint Andrews Presbyterian Church (1883), the Wesleyan Jubilee Church (1885) and the Holy Trinity Anglican Church (1886).

Several public buildings were also in various stages of completion.[85] These included the hospital with its segregated wards on the heights behind Walu Bay (now St Giles Hospital), the prison (see Figure 3.4) with its segregated cell blocks, the government buildings and court house, the police quarters with separate barracks for European and Fijian policemen, a bank and the first frames on Nukulau Island where a quarantine station was being prepared specifically for indentured labourers from India. At Gordon's direction, his official residence had been built in 1878 of 'native and European materials', but he never occupied it. In 1881, however, plans were made to build a new Government House on the native reserve.[86]

On the educational front, a school was under consideration. Numbering close to 300 at the end of 1881, the European population lobbied the government to open a school to educate their children.[87] It took a further two years and more petitions before the government called for tenders to build the Suva Public school.[88] It was finally constructed on the site of the old Suva village cemetery. Whether the people of Suva were consulted about this use of their former burial grounds is yet to be determined.

Meanwhile, the residents had established a mechanics institute similar to that which thrived in Levuka.[89] This was a business-funded adult educational organisation that hosted a library and held seminars and lectures for European men. Aside from its educational benefits, it gave these men an air of respectability and helped avoid the temptations of disruptive diversions such as gambling and drinking, which might create

---

84 Methodist Mission in Fiji, Minutes of the Fiji District for 1881, F4 A. NAF.
85 CSO 2209/1881.
86 See CSO 142/1882, and *New Zealand Herald*, 16 July 1881; paperspast.natlib.govt.nz.
87 CSO 979/1881.
88 See CSO 582/1883, 1136/1883 and 1207/1883.
89 *New Zealand Herald*, 19 September 1881.

disorder or worse, intimate interaction with other ethnicities. Regattas and cricket matches were other forms of entertainment that residents could look forward to.[90]

As Suva's European residents organised their town in their image, their Levuka counterparts looked on with dismay as the prospects of their own town declined. They made a last-gasp attempt to petition the Queen, again pleading that the government could ill afford the relocation. The British Government had approved a substantial loan of £130,000 to Fiji, £80,000 of which would pay for the Cakobau Government's liabilities and the remainder for development purposes within the colony. Half (£25,000) was earmarked for public works in Suva including roads, quays, drainage and water supply.[91] The administration was also considering further loans from private banks.[92] The consensus in Levuka was that these loans were unnecessary and would 'cause the Colony to retrograde from its present hopeful position'.[93] They calculated the cost to Levuka at £50,000 in lost revenue. As had happened in 1876, this petition was immediately followed by a counter-petition from Suva residents in which they again pointed to Levuka's numerous shortcomings and Suva's many advantages.[94]

Early in 1881, amid 'much wailing and gnashing of teeth', the residents of Levuka received the news from the new governor, William Des Voeux (1880–1885), that their petition had been declined. Efforts were immediately made to send a delegation of 'prominent colonists' to London and again 'forcibly represent to the Imperial Government the injustice and injury which will be done to Levuka and the colony by the removal of the capital to Suva'.[95] In its columns, the *Fiji Times* was particularly damning of the decision. It accused Gordon of discourtesy and railed that his decision would cause a very dire fiscal situation and allow his successor almost no room to manoeuvre.[96]

---

90 See *New Zealand Herald*, 28 February 1882 and 7 December 1882; paperspast.natlib.govt.nz.
91 *Otago Daily Times*, 6 March 1878; see paperspast.natlib.govt.nz.
92 See CSO 1113/1882 for a £15,000 loan for public works from the Bank of New Zealand.
93 See CSO 1287/1880 and 1674/1880.
94 CSO 1287/1880, 1446/1880, and 1309/1880.
95 *Samoa Times and South Sea Gazette*, 16 April 1881; see paperspast.natlib.govt.nz.
96 Among others, see the editorials in the *Fiji Times* of 5 February 1881, 12 February 1881, 19 March 1881 and 27 April 1881.

Amid all the uproar in Levuka was a chorus of enthusiastic support from voices that sung Suva's praises. Its port as well as its rich and ample back country were especially complimented as in this letter from a Mr James Duncan:

> The town has a gentle rise, and room for hundreds of houses, and will make a grand city. Government House, when finished, will have a splendid view seaward, embracing many islands, besides a full sweep of the bay. It has been said that the late Governor (Sir Arthur Gordon) did wrong in making Suva the capital. I know both places well, and can truthfully say that Suva is the best for shipping property, and will make by far the finest city. The buildings are going up fast …[97]

For all their natural beauty, Suva and its surroundings were about to suffer a most brutal assault on their natural environment. In a warning about the enormous stress that the environment was put under, Major Harding wrote in February 1881 that large numbers of logs of all sizes were being felled by villagers in the neighbourhood of Suva for sale to private persons. The *sagali*, a species of mangrove, was particularly sought after because its wood was hard and durable and ideal for all structures including roads and bridges. Harding could see that stocks in the margins of the streams were being severely depleted and ecosystems were coming under severe strain, and he called for regulations.[98]

One major contributor to the depletion of trees was the Colonial Sugar Refinery (CSR) Company whose new mill at Nausori required vast quantities of wood to fuel its crushing and other machines. This wood was sourced from large swathes of *dogo*, *tiri* and mountain timber in the Rewa and Naitāsiri regions.[99] But the government was an even larger and hungrier consumer of wood. It needed timber for all infrastructural developments including the wharf, roads and all buildings. To meet this need, it instructed the chiefs and villagers in the greater Suva district and beyond to cut logs as their tax requirement.[100] The shortfall in local supply was met by fleets of timber vessels from Australia, New Zealand and America.[101]

---

97 *Evening Star*, 28 July 1882; paperspast.natlib.govt.nz.
98 CSO 397/1881.
99 CSO 1683/1880.
100 CSO 2011/1881.
101 See *New Zealand Herald*, 16 July 1881; paperspast.natlib.govt.nz.

XI. The Removal of Suva Village

While colonial officials, businessmen and labourers busied themselves with the structure and form of the township, the villagers of Suva continued to live a relatively confined existence on their reserve. In 1875 they had fought a monumental battle to survive the measles pandemic, which killed a third of indigenous Fijians. As *buli* of Suva, Ratu Aporosa played a leading role in the management of that crisis, ensuring that proper sanitation was observed and that the bodies of the dead were buried well outside village boundaries.[102]

As the pandemic subsided, life slowly returned to normal. The new 'normal' of colonial life required villagers to plant and weed their village plantations. Some were meant to feed the villagers while others were intended to produce tax in kind, mainly taro, yam and cotton, to pay for the expenses of the colonial administration. Chiefs in the wider Suva district were instructed to supervise these plantations and ensure that tax targets were met. The early experiments were disastrous. The stipendiary magistrate for Suva, PS Friend, wrote that these tax plantations were 'a complete failure'. He punished the chiefs of Veisari, Muaivuso and the new *buli* of Suva, Mosese Rokotalau, with one week imprisonment for neglecting their duties.[103] Ratu Aporosa had been replaced, presumably for disciplinary reasons.

One of the principal objections that Friend raised in his report was that so much of the physical work on the plantations was left to women and girls. Overburdened with their own work, he decried that wives weeded all their husbands' taro, via and yam gardens. On the larger cotton plantations, men also left their share of the work almost entirely to their wives. He recommended that women of all ages be prohibited from weeding the plantations.[104]

After his dismissal from government, Ratu Aporosa turned to the timber trade. His operation went as far as the border of the Namosi province where, in January 1881, he became embroiled in a dispute with the Tui Namosi over who owned the forest reserves at Naqara. Commenting on

---

102 CGR 329/43/1875.
103 CSO 576/1877.
104 CSO 144/1877.

the dispute, Friend warned that if the title to the land was not resolved quickly, 'a serious quarrel if nothing worse will be the result between the two chiefs'.[105]

He operated as a private contractor supplying wood both to private individuals and to the government. Because he was directing villagers to cut wood for him, he was in direct competition with the new *buli* whose instructions were to ensure that villagers were cutting logs to fulfil their tax quota. The two men had been at loggerheads before, mainly because Ratu Aporosa thought Rokotalau was inferior in rank and ability. In customary terms, Rokotalau was one of Ratu Aporosa's subordinates but he held the senior government position. As an old hand on Fijian politics, David Wilkinson explained: 'The relative positions of Avorosa and the Buli Suva are very anomalous and has often been the cause of a great deal of heart-burning and trouble.'[106]

Ratu Aporosa was not bound by government directives in the way that Rokotalau was. His spirit of independence must have surprised colonial officials, accustomed as they were to the normal acquiescence of iTaukei chiefs. This independent spirit won the Tui Suva much favour among the town's most powerful businessmen. Indeed, in April 1879, he travelled to Melbourne and visited the city at the invitation of McEwen and Co., the company representing the interests of Thomson and Renwick.[107] The precise nature of Ratu Aporosa's relationship with the two businessmen is yet to be established.

He was certainly well known among Suva's European community. Several men rented from him at Suva village and fed his craving for alcohol. Bringing this matter to the colonial secretary's attention, Friend wrote:

> I would again bring under your notice the undesirability of Europeans living in native towns. The effect cannot possibly be good but cause a great deal of harm. Suva has now several tenants some of whom I am afraid are not very good characters. If this be permitted natives will be allowed to get as much spirits as they like. In fact the policeman reported to me that an English lodger of Ambrose's was seen to take a bottle of gin to the house and next morning several persons remarked that Ambrose and Ratu Joni were under the influence of drink.[108]

---

105 CSO 375/1881.
106 CSO 787/1879.
107 *The Western Star*, 3 May 1879; see trove.nla.gov.au.
108 CSO 858/1881.

Wilkinson also pointed out that Ratu Aporosa had become disenchanted with the government ostensibly because of the way its officials treated him. He had been overlooked for government appointment and even done time in prison as punishment for a disturbance he had caused during the annual meeting of the Council of Chiefs in Rewa in December 1877.[109] Wilkinson suggested that because Rokotalau had repeatedly begged to be allowed to resign, the government ought to appoint Ratu Aporosa as the *buli* and give him one more trial. In spite of resistance from some senior officials who continued to regard Ratu Aporosa as 'a confirmed drunk',[110] Wilkinson's recommendation was adopted.

The government needed Ratu Aporosa on its side because it wanted Suva's native reserve. Hirokazu Miyazaki's anthropological work on Suvavou (2004) contains a valuable section that examines the move from Suva to Suvavou. He points out that, according to Gordon's land policy, no Fijian land could be lawfully alienated. Furthermore, land that had been sold but not occupied by European buyers was deemed to be native land and was returned to the original owners. In Suva, several lots that the Polynesian Company and Renwick and Thomson had sold to Australian clients fell in the category of lands that were never formally occupied. Under the existing policy, they should have been returned to the people of Suva. However, the Gordon and Des Voeux administrations did not return the Suva lands to their original owners and kept them instead for the Crown.[111]

How then, did the government convince the people of Suva to leave their village and move to Suvavou? Clearly, without the Tui Suva's consent the village could not have been moved. The precise nature of the agreement between him and Gordon remains a mystery. A dispatch from William Des Voeux suggests that the arrangement involved an annual rent of £200, an amount that:

---

109 See CSO 215/1878 and 223/1878.
110 CSO 787/1879.
111 See Hirokazu Miyazaki, *The method of hope: Anthropology, philosophy, and Fijian knowledge* (Stanford: Stanford University Press, 2004), 40, and Frances Steel, *Oceania under steam: Sea transport and the cultures of colonialism, c. 1870–1914* (Manchester: Manchester University Press, 2011), 173.

in the opinion of the Commissioner of Native Affairs is the least that will satisfy the Natives of the Suva peninsula, who in accordance with an arrangement made by Sir Arthur Gordon are to vacate these lands and to move the site of their original town.[112]

Writing in 1907 about the absence of any formal documents, Governor im Thurn noted that no report on the arrangement had been sent to the secretary of state for colonies. He lamented that:

> Somewhere about 1882, we by arrangement with the then native occupants took over the land on which Government House stands and a good deal else – but, as I have said, I don't know what else … no title to the land or agreement with the Natives is in existence; … Government has therefore still no title beyond what it may have acquired by the acquiescence of the natives in our possession of the land and by their acceptance of rent since 1882.[113]

With the absence of any formal deed, the government's view of its right to the land has most often rested on the fact that the people of Suva accepted the annual sum of £200 since 1882. This has been taken to mean that they agreed to the arrangement. This was the position taken by Arthur Mahaffy, the acting colonial secretary in 1907, when confronted with another petition from the people of Suvavou for evidence that they had 'surrendered' their right to Suva land to the government. However, his minute indicated his own frustration that the government did not have any documentary proof to substantiate its claims to the land.[114]

By April 1881, the government had taken possession of the land with the intention of building the new Government House on it.[115] Six years later, the Crown and Native Lands Ordinance of 1888 was enacted to plug any outstanding loopholes that might have remained in the Crown's acquisition of Suva lands in the area between the Tamavua and Samabula rivers.[116] With this ordinance the attorney-general, Francis Winter, thought the government had attained absolute proprietorship of Suva lands and that the annual £200 should be regarded as an 'annuity' and not as 'quit rent'.[117]

---

112 Despatch 2, 6 January 1882, cited in Thurn to Colonial Secretary, 16 September 1907, CSO 4469/1907; also cited in Miyazaki, *The method of hope*, 48.
113 CSO 4469/1907; also cited in Miyazaki, *The method of hope*, 47–48.
114 CSO 4469/1907; also cited in Miyazaki, *The method of hope*, 48.
115 CSO 858/1881.
116 CSO 2908/1887.
117 CSO 2908/1887.

As per the agreement, the villagers moved across the bay to Suvavou ('New Suva') by the coast next to Lami village. In the absence of formal documents, one can assume that Lami was chosen because they were the *bati* (warriors) of Suva, and had a traditional obligation to provide for the Tui Suva.[118] Nevertheless, the relocation was not as smooth as might be expected. A mere 10 years later, Suvavou was used as a prime example about the dangers of taking people off their lands. 'Look at Suvavou,' one critic wrote, 'they were taken off their lands and now are quarrelling with their neighbours.'[119]

No sooner had the Suva villagers packed their belongings to move across the bay than *vulagi* or wanderers mainly from Kadavu, Ba and Nadi moved into the deserted village and reoccupied it. They were joined by a few more from Rewa, Tailevu and Naitāsiri who were in Suva to sell their produce.[120] The superintendent of police, Frederick Craigie Halkett, suggested that the government find land in the town centre to accommodate these people but, fearing an influx of other 'vagabonds', the government declined the proposition. The *vulagi* were cast out and the area kept under surveillance day and night by the police to avoid any further such squatting.[121]

Asked to comment on the matter, Ratu Aporosa confirmed that the people of Suva had completed their move to Suvavou around August and September 1882 and that since then, their plantations on the native reserve had been raided and the produce stolen. They did not know any of the *vulagi* who had moved into the village since it had been vacated. He verified that 21 houses had been built and occupied in Suvavou. However, he urged the government to expedite the erection of the remaining 19 houses that had been promised, as several homes in the new village were heavily overcrowded.[122]

---

118 CSO 3221/1893.
119 *Report of the commission appointed to inquire into the decrease of the native population* (Suva: Government Printer, 1893), 91.
120 CSO 1495/1882.
121 CSO 1406/1882 and 1495/1882.
122 CSO 1336/1882, 1406/1882 and 1495/1882.

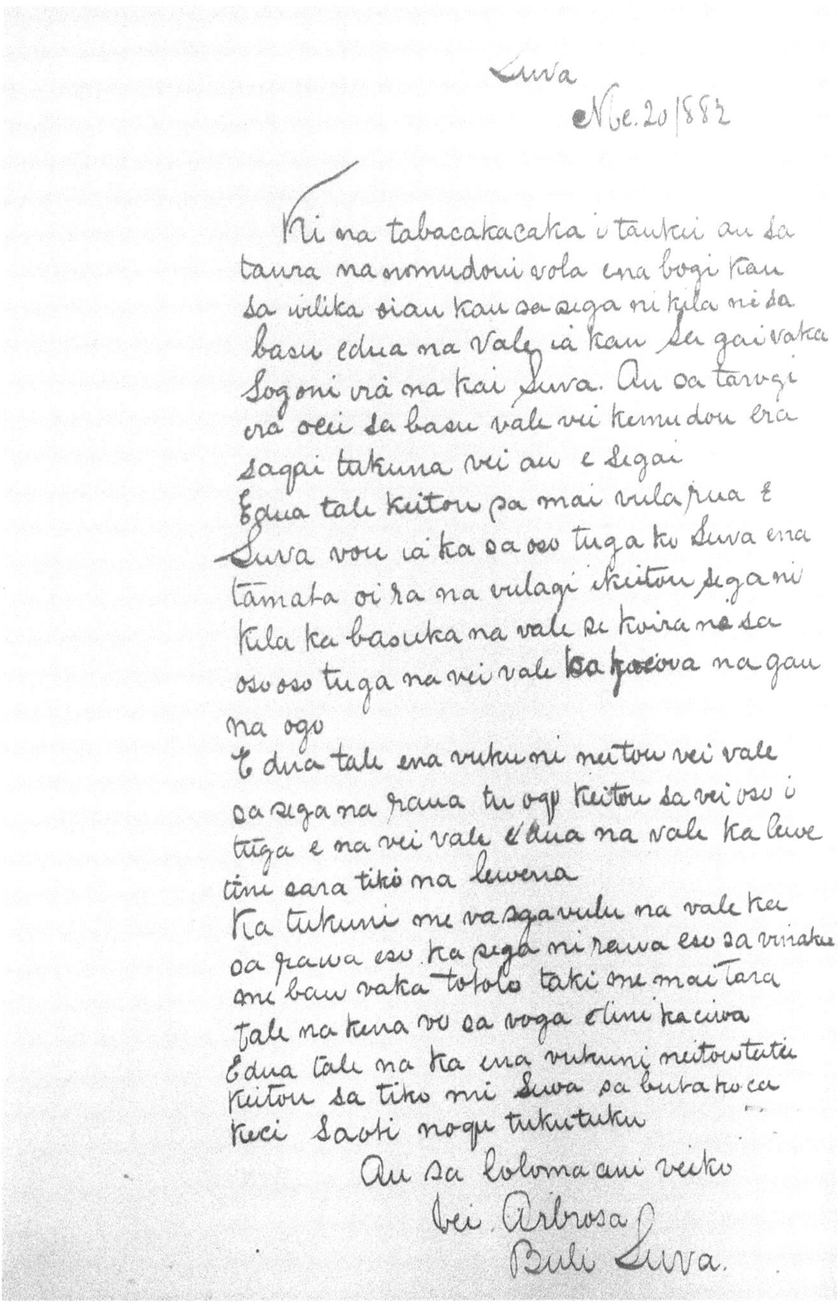

3. THE MAKING OF A CAPITAL

> Suva
> Nov. 20/1882
>
> Ni na tabacakacaka i taukei au sa
> taura na nomudoni vola ena bogi kau
> sa wilika oiau kau sa sega ni kila ni da
> basu edua na vale ia kau sa gai vaka
> sogoni ira na kai Suva. Au sa tarogi
> ira oeii sa basu vale vei kemudou era
> sagai takuna vei au e sigai
> E dua tale kuitou sa mai vulaprua e
> Suva vou ia ka sa oso tuga ko Suva ena
> tamata oi ra na vulagi ikuitou sega ni
> kila ka basuka na vale se kuira na sa
> oso oso tuga na vei vale sa poeova na gau
> na ogo
> E dua tale ena vuku ni neitou vei vale
> sa sega na rawa tu ogo keitou sa vei oso i
> tuga e na vei vale e dua na vale ka lewe
> tini sara tiko na lewena
> Ka tukuni one vasagavulu na vale ka
> sa rawa esu ka sega ni rawa esu sa vinaka
> oni bau vaka tololo taki one mai tara
> tale na kena vo sa voga olini kaciva
> E dua tale na ka ena vukuni neitou tutu
> keitou sa tiko mi Suva sa buta ko ca
> keci saoti nogu tukutuku
> Au sa loloma ani veiko
> bei Arbrosa
> Buli Suva.

Figure 3.5: Letter from Ratu Aporosa Tuivuya to the Native Commissioner, 20 November 1882.
Source: CSO 1406/1882, NAF.

Turning the *vulagi* back to the streets of Suva only worsened the housing crisis. Most of the hundreds of causal labourers who flocked into Suva to meet the labour demand earned between £4 and £6 per annum and could ill afford to rent a place.[123] By 1883, conditions of squalor were appearing on the sea side of Victoria Parade.[124] Several complaints were lodged with the government about the 'inconvenience and annoyance' caused by the great number of people without shelter who each night sought refuge in doorways and verandahs of the stores and banks on the beach.[125] On any given night, their kits of vegetables, boxes, mats, tins, bottles, bundles, cooking utensils and other paraphernalia endlessly encumbered the walkways.

In its response, the government was most preoccupied by questions of security. Because *vulagi* used tobacco and firesticks (matches) so freely, they were thought to be 'a grave source of danger to the security of the town'.[126] Criminal activity also seemed on the rise:

> There can be no doubt that much of the petty crime complained of and which remains undetected is committed by these strangers, who must often be driven to severe straits for food and shelter, and who in their independent search for these, fall into the way of temptation.[127]

Yet, the government also knew that the trade carried on by this floating population was quite considerable and growing quickly. The police continued to be critical of the 'most comfortless and pitiable' existence of these people, especially in stormy weather, and advocated that a piece of land with a few good sheds and a secure fence be set aside for them.[128] However, other officials warned that such provisions would encourage 'vagabondage' and give them false hopes.[129] Public money being in such short supply, they argued that 'the natives themselves should put up houses for their own accommodation'.[130]

---

123 *Evening Star*, 23 Sept 1881; paperspast.natlib.govt.nz.
124 CSO 3297/1883.
125 CSO 3297/1883; see also 2903/1884 and 2174/1886.
126 CSO 3297/1883.
127 CSO 3297/1883.
128 See CSO 866/1880 and 2903/1884.
129 CSO 3297/1883.
130 See CSO 2174/1886.

3. THE MAKING OF A CAPITAL

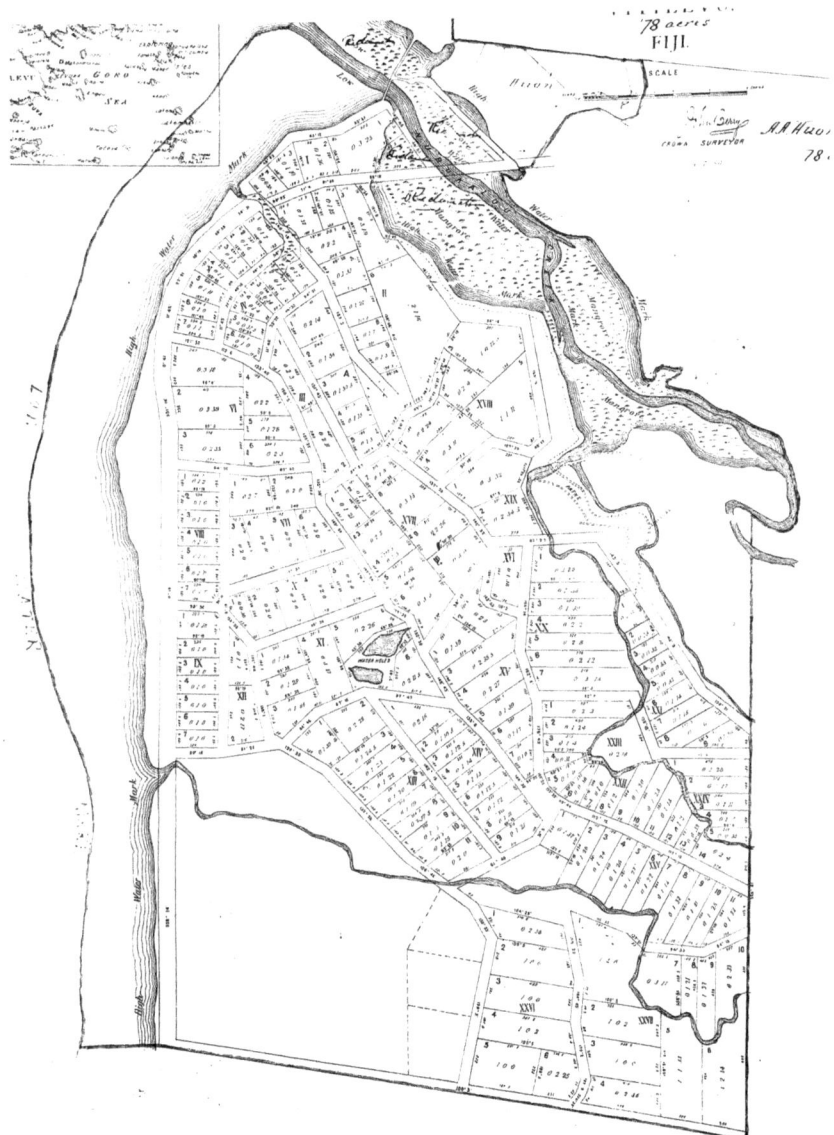

Figure 3.6: Map of Suva showing township lots, 1882.
Source CSO 2123/1882, 2259/1882, NAF.

In the midst of this housing crisis, the government released more town lots for sale. After an initial release of 160 lots in 1881[131] another set was released in 1882.[132] The extent to which these lots had been surveyed can be gauged from the map in Figure 3.6 from 1882. While they appear plentiful, none were affordable to ordinary Fijians, whether indigenous or other. From the perspective of the colonised, therefore, the housing crisis persisted.

The next chapter is a companion chapter in the sense that it discusses the evolution of the issues and challenges that Suva and its people encountered in the decade after 1882 when the last remaining government officials left Levuka to move to Suva, completing the final act in the transfer of the capital. It also provides some concluding remarks of the broader significance of this 20-year period for late nineteenth-century Fijian history.

---

131 See *Royal Fiji Gazette*, 6 June 1881.
132 See *Daily Telegraph*, 4 October 1882; see paperspast.natlib.govt.nz.

4

The Making of a Capital: A Social History of Suva, 1882–1890

Robert Nicole

The previous chapter examined the background and emerging issues relating to the move of the capital from Levuka to Suva. In this companion chapter, we explore how the capital fared in the next decade as Suva and its people responded to the challenge of being the new administrative and commercial centre of Fiji.

XII. The Urban Drift Begins: Toorak and Vatuwaqa

From an official point of view, the big story of 1882 was the final physical move of the government from Levuka to Suva. As the previous chapter shows, the move had been gradual and varying in intensity. In mid-1882, Suva was finally ready to receive the last remaining civil servants from Levuka. The final journey to their new homes in Suva was documented by the *Fiji Times* as follows:

> Just before midnight on August 30, 1882, the Governor, the Colonial Secretary, and numerous other department heads boarded the 'Ocean Queen' in Levuka for the trip to their new capital.[1]

---

1   Kim Gravelle, *Fiji's heritage: A history of Fiji* (Nadi: Tiara Enterprises, 2000), 163.

While this move was important from a symbolic and administrative point of view, changes in Suva continued at a steady pace, fuelled by a growing flow of migrants. An indicator of the increase in population was the proliferation of waste. The authorities responded by employing 'scavengers' to collect rubbish around the town each day, and dump it by Ellery Street, which was then adjacent to the Nabukalou Creek swamp.[2] Refuse was collected in this fashion until 1893 when the Town Board introduced a new system of removing rubbish by horse and cart:

> It will be obligatory on householders to take care that refuse is placed in boxes in readiness for conveyance to the vehicle when the sound of the bell shall announce its arrival.[3]

Another concern about the rise in density was the risk of fire breaking out and spreading from one building to another. Insurance companies stopped their cover for houses built of 'native' materials and a law was soon enacted to prohibit the construction of such houses in the township area.[4] Within a year, the hybrid *bure* that had characterised so many houses disappeared entirely to be replaced by cottages made uniquely of timber. It is tempting to interpret this decision as discriminatory against the vestiges of Fijian culture or as an attempt to regulate who could and could not reside within the confines of the town.[5] In fairness however, house fires were common in Levuka and Suva and often caused several buildings to be burnt at once, inflicting considerable losses on all concerned.

Migrants who flocked to Suva were generally of two types. The first could afford to buy land and build houses. The second came looking for work and needed low-cost accommodation. The former consisted of civil servants, merchants and other businesspeople who relocated from Levuka, as well as migrants from abroad (mostly Australia and New Zealand). They paid rates to the Suva Town Board (first established in 1883) and helped in their own way to shape the colony's capital.

---

2   Colonial Secretary's Office (CSO) 2028/1881; all CSO files are held in National Archives of Fiji (NAF).
3   *Fiji Times*, 17 June 1893. Archived issues of the *Fiji Times* are available at the NAF.
4   CSO 2313/1882 and *Fiji Royal Gazette*, Number 17, Volume VIII, 1882.
5   See Frances Steel, *Oceania under steam: Sea transport and the cultures of colonialism, c. 1870–1914* (Manchester: Manchester University Press, 2011), 181.

Figure 4.1: 'The business street of Suva, Fiji', n.d.
Source: P32.4.14 Fiji Museum.

The latter group, on the other hand, consisted of the verandah-dwelling itinerant labourers from various parts of Fiji, and a growing pool of labourers of Vanuatu, Solomon Islands and Indian origin whose convergence on Suva is now explored in more detail. It is worthy of note that from 1880, Rotumans also began arriving in Suva in significant numbers because their island was integrated in the greater colony of Fiji. Steel points out that many Rotuman women were in Suva waiting for their husbands to return from the Torres Strait where they worked in the pearl shell industry.[6] Their early settlement in Suva deserves greater attention from future research.

iTaukei villagers came to Suva in search of work and to sell their produce but also to evade communal obligations. The government was caught in a bind because, on the one hand, it needed indigenous Fijians to stay in their villages to produce taxes while, on the other, it needed their labour and fresh produce to help build and feed Suva. A regulation had been issued to prevent villagers from being absent from their villages for more than 60 days at any one time. However, villagers circumvented it by travelling and living in Suva (and other urban centres) for 59 days and then returning to their village the day before the deadline, only to head back to Suva the following day.

6   Steel, *Oceania under steam*, 181.

On arrival, they were branded 'strangers'. This word questioned their legitimacy as residents of Suva and implied that they should eventually go back to the places they had come from. The inference was that Suva belonged to residents who could purchase houses and pay rates: white people. 'Coloured' migrants were thus a challenge to those who wanted Suva to be styled a 'white' enclave. A dispatch from Governor Mitchell to the secretary of state for colonies reflects the unease that prevailed among Suva's European population about the large concentration of Fijian males in the town and that this 'idle body' would become 'dangerous to society'.[7] Several attempts to repatriate them were made through the 1880s.[8] Neither Mitchell nor the regulations had much success in stopping this flow. Indeed, many who worked at the wharf openly 'bragged' about being free of communal obligations.[9]

iTaukei women also sought a release from their communal obligations by moving to Suva. Some fled to escape abusive relationships. Others were attracted by the prospects of leading independent lives and finding work to earn a wage, drinking *yaqona*, smoking tobacco more freely, and enjoying the excitement and entertainment that the new town promised. Responding to the complaints of several chiefs on the matter, the native commissioner drew up a list of all these 'unmanageable' women with the intention of returning them to their respective villages.[10] The women were mainly from Rewa but several more were from Bau, Koro, Ba, Ovalau, Lomaloma (in Vanuabalavu) and Macuata – that is, from all over Fiji. Many had previously been sent back to their villages but had stubbornly returned to Suva. The Roko Tui[11] Lomaiviti feared a veritable exodus and exclaimed, 'if the women in our villages hear that other women can defy the law, the evil-disposed of them will flock to Suva'.[12]

In Suva, these women lived in the company of petty storekeepers, medical students, policemen, European men or Melanesian labourers whom they thought treated them better than their own countrymen.[13] Several congregated as a kind of sisterhood and met at a house near Nabukalou

---

7   Despatch 70, 1 June 1887, CO 83/46, Public Records Office (PRO).
8   See CSO 3027/1884, 2715/1885 and 1741/1887.
9   CSO 365/1889; see also Steel, *Oceania under steam*, 177.
10 CSO 2166/1886; see also CSO 1442/1888, and 'Proceedings of a native council or a council of chiefs', 1892, NAF.
11 Provincial governor.
12 CSO 2166/1886.
13 CSO 1442/1888.

Creek they named *vale caviraki*, which a colonial official translated as 'the Kaisi Club'. Their patron was a woman called Sai who welcomed them each night to drink *yaqona* until the early hours of the next day.[14]

As mentioned in the previous chapter, Melanesian labourers were an integral and essential part of the making of the Suva township. By the 1880s, their numbers began to decline mainly because the demand for labour had been met from India. Ships with Melanesian labourers continued to arrive but frequently. Still, by the mid-1880s, the Melanesian labourers in the country consistently totalled between five and six thousand, of which only 7 per cent were women.[15]

They normally worked on the various building and construction sites or on the plantations that bordered the town. On the plantations, they were housed in labour lines and forbidden to venture beyond the borders of the estate. Those who worked within Suva enjoyed a bit more freedom. They were accommodated in the labour depot in Walu Bay or in makeshift lodgings in Toorak. They were generally regarded as hard-working people who endured the harsh working environment and violent treatment often without formal complaints.

They received some protection from the agent-general for immigration. Henry Anson, who occupied the post from 1886 to 1888, was the only official who lived up to this responsibility. He repeatedly denounced planters for maltreating, overtasking and abusing labourers, including those in the vicinity of Suva. He tried to secure land behind the depot so that the labourers who resided there could use it to cultivate crops. However, this was fervently opposed by Thurston who wanted it kept for Suva's new botanical gardens. The disagreement sparked a long feud between Anson and Thurston that culminated in Anson leaving the colony when Thurston was appointed governor in 1888.[16]

Melanesian labourers came from diverse cultures. They were mostly from Tanna, Malekula, Santo, Ambrym (for Vanuatu) and Guadalcanal and Malaita (for Solomon Islands). They worked in 'gangs' according to the islands or tribes they came from. They lived peacefully with one another although tensions occasionally surfaced and caused a few brawls.[17]

---

14   CSO 2166/1886.
15   See the 'Report on Polynesian immigration' for 1885 and 1886 in CSO 3849/1887.
16   See CSO 939/1882, containing minutes and reports up to 1887.
17   *Suva Times*, 11 March 1885.

The most serious of them was a riot on 8 March 1885 between close to 50 Ambrym men and 100 Solomon Islanders on the verandah of the Union Bank building. The seriousness of this altercation can be gauged from the iron bars, stones and bottles that were used in the fight.[18] For the most part however, their favourite pasttime was to assemble on the weekend to hold feasts, play music (with nose and mouth flutes), sing and dance, sometimes without interruption until the early hours of the morning.[19]

A few among them chose to remain in Suva after their contracts expired. However, without land or capital, finding homes was not easy. Government considered some land in Walu Bay, Vatuwaqa (now Suva Point) and Tamavua-i-wai[20] but none were deemed suitable. The permanent settlement of these Melanesians in recognisable neighbourhoods such as Flagstaff, Wailoku, Newtown, Namara, Muanikoso, Matata and Kalekana, thus came much later and was arranged mainly by the Anglican Church.[21]

Labourers from India came in much greater number and were generally more amenable to settle in Fiji after the expiration of their indenture. The first Indian indentured labourers to be 'freed' of their indenture were those who had arrived on the *Leonidas*. While some returned to India, several chose to settle in Suva. They took up various occupations around the town mainly as labourers, but also in laundering clothes and selling vegetables.

Much like the Melanesians, they lacked land and capital and were thus forced into tenancy. They first rented from Huon in Toorak where they quickly congregated in communities.[22] In 1884, they were thought to number about 80 men, women and children, although that number could swell to about 200 on special prayer or carnival nights when the residents were joined by other itinerant labourers.[23]

In November of that year, the colony's chief medical officer, Dr Bolton Corney, visited the hamlets because of concerns about their unsanitary condition. He found nine buildings on half an acre of land, all of them cramped both with lodgers and visitors. Several of the huts had been

---

18   CSO 719/1885 and 754/1885.
19   See CSO 1689/1886.
20   See CSO 1125/1885.
21   See Winston Halapua, *Living on the fringe: Melanesians in Fiji* (Suva: Institute of Pacific Studies, University of the South Pacific, 2001).
22   CSO 2601/1884.
23   CSO 913/1885.

4. THE MAKING OF A CAPITAL

subleased by the original lessee. They were built of palings, biscuit tins, scraps of galvanised iron and reeds. Sawn timber had been used for the frames. Several had no raised floor or bed-places, and only a mat to cover the earthen floor. Ventilation occurred naturally through the numerous holes and crannies by which air could pass. This disease-prone environment was compounded by toilets that were 'very imperfectly constructed' and an irregular disposal of sewage.[24]

His greatest concern was the lack of access to clean water. The labourers had dug wells into the ground but the settlement being in a gully, when rain fell, it collected the impure materials from the surface and drained them into the wells, making the water unfit for drinking or cooking. He condemned the wells as repositories of disease that would cause epidemic outbreaks. His report concluded:

> I have no hesitation in condemning the well system to which the coolies resort, and I beg to submit my very strong opinion that it ought to be entirely prohibited by a special regulation.[25]

Bolton Corney also wanted the new regulation to control the construction of huts, water supply, overcrowding, treatment of infants and rubbish collection. These were noble ideals but they did not address the core problem: poverty. Colonial relations of power had reduced labourers' lives to an experience of permanent abject impoverishment.

These power relations soon manifested themselves again in very concrete terms. On 6 March 1885, just over three months after Bolton Corney's initial visit, a group of 16 European residents of Toorak petitioned the Suva Town Board to have the 'Coolie' hamlets and their occupants removed. The petition made reference to the noise generated by religious ceremonies and 'the unearthly sounds produced by the blowing of horns, ringing of bells beating of drums and general shouting' that took place on such occasions. These, they wrote, were a source of 'perpetual nuisance and annoyance to the European residents' and called on the Town Board to 'take steps to remedy this evil'.[26] They added:

> We would also suggest that the coolie encampments be removed to a distance outside the Town boundaries and we take this opportunity of pointing out that in our opinion this nuisance

---

24 CSO 2601/1884.
25 CSO 2601/1884.
26 CSO 913/1885.

is only in its infancy and as the number of time expired coolies will increase every year they will eventually flock to the centres of population.[27]

Clearly, the European residents of Toorak wanted to keep their neighbourhood 'for whites only' and the petition aptly reflects the prevailing ideas about race among colonists at the end of the nineteenth century. They favoured the compartmentalisation of ethnic groups in separate neighbourhoods. In this case, racist ideas converged with 'good sanitation' to give their request a semblance of moral rectitude.

Within a mere four days of receiving the petition, the Suva Town Board had produced a report on the Toorak hamlets. It gave credence to the petitioners' claims and supported their call to have the occupants removed. Some of its findings were probably exaggerated to shock the government into action. Nevertheless, other observations are useful to us in that they offer a rare insight into the labourers' lives and their struggles to eke out a living after the expiry of their terms of indenture.

The houses were reported to be 'most miserable', overcrowded and unfit for human habitation. In a 10-by-5-feet hut with walls that were just 5 feet high, the officer found huddled together two men, two women, two boys and a 10-day-old baby. The kitchens were more satisfactory. Built adjacent to the main entrance, they ensured that the smoke from the fire could flow into the main living areas and thereby ward off pests and mosquitoes. Goats and fowls roamed freely outside among a few plots used for the cultivation vegetables and root crops. The report concluded that more huts were in the course of being erected.[28]

Responding to the report, Anson did not object to the removal of the Toorak families, but he wanted a guarantee that a suitable long-term alternative was ready to accommodate them. A number of options were presented, including an area near the headwaters of the Nabukalou Creek (the area between Toorak and Flagstaff). This idea was quickly abandoned because of the risk of pollution for the residents living downstream. The back end of Walu Bay was another suggestion, as was an area east of Leveti Creek (between Nasēsē and Veiuto). The latter had a good supply of water and was distant enough 'from the residences of the white population' and yet near enough to the township for labourers to walk to work.[29]

---

27 CSO 913/1885.
28 CSO 913/1885.
29 CSO 1030/1885.

4. THE MAKING OF A CAPITAL

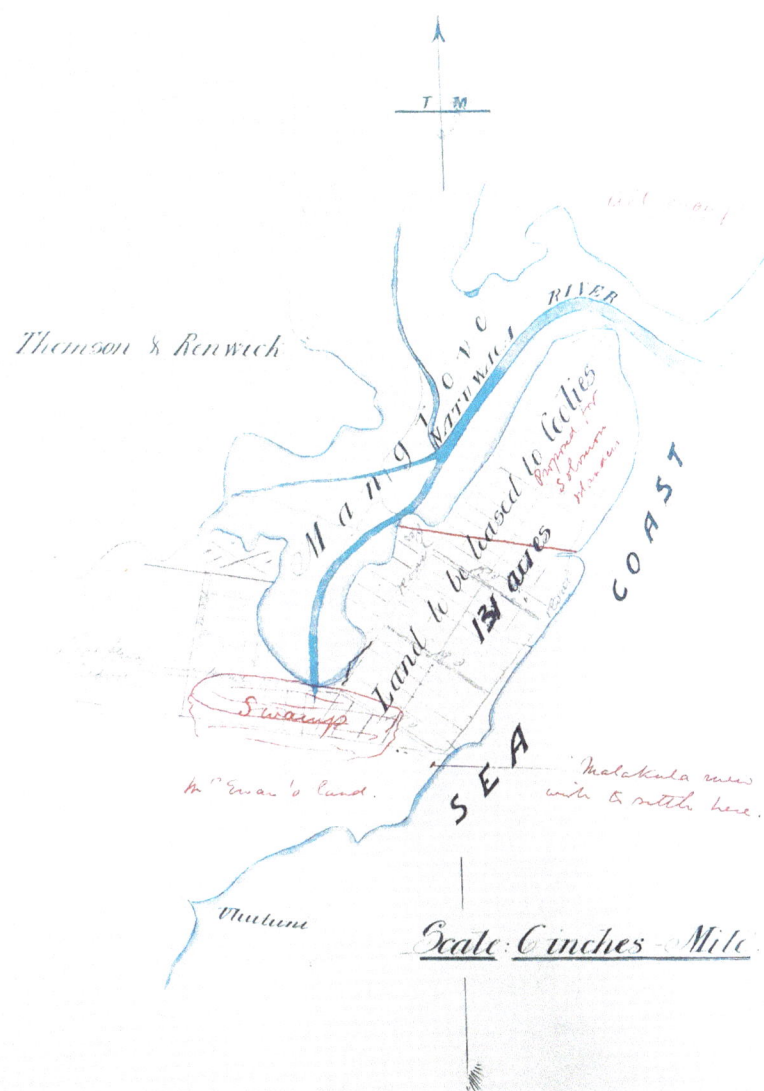

Figure 4.2: Plan of the proposed Vatuwaqa settlement, 1887.
Source: 15 August 1887, CSO 1965/1887.

The preferred site, however, was a government-owned 131-acre stretch of land near the signal station at Vatuwaqa. It was considered 'near enough for a coolie town to be permitted', and 'not too far for the bodies to walk in from'.[30] Several individuals complained that the relocation would be

---

30 CSO 1125/1885.

too expensive and that in any case it was too far from the places where they worked and shopped. The government believed these costs would be more than compensated for by the extent of land to be gained and by improved sanitary conditions.[31] Several families conceded and moved to become the first settlers of what we now call Suva Point. A plan of the area (below) suggests that Melanesians might also be relocated to this area, though no confirmation was found that any of them settled there.

When Anson visited them in mid-1887, the new settlers seemed pleased with the location. 'Their property and resources are scanty,' he reported, 'but they express themselves contented and seem to have no fears as to their prospects.'[32] Of the 24 blocks available, 22 had been cleared of trees and bush and 18 had houses built on them. Most families had planted crops on their sections including corn, yams, kumala, beans, taro, cassava, mustard, Chinese cabbage, potatoes, radish, bananas and pineapples. Some raised goats and chickens and one enterprising man owned a boat while another had purchased a cutter. Wells had been dug to access fresh water, though doubts persisted about the suitability of this water for drinking. On the whole, it appeared as though a climate of 'goodwill and harmony' prevailed in the settlement.[33]

Nevertheless, the new residents requested government action on two matters. The first was a piece of common land they desired to let their goats and cattle feed. This was approved and the community began using the heavily wooded area adjacent to the settlement (the current site of the Vatuwaqa cemetery). The second was the clearance of a path to Suva. As no road to the township existed, those who worked in or carried their produce for sale to Suva were forced to use the shore and walk around the peninsula to reach their destination. Their movements to and from Vatuwaqa were thus regulated by the tide. The commissioner of lands advised that improving the rough track to 'the flagstaff' would cost upwards of £100.[34] In the end the decision was made to build a road from Vatuwaqa to Nasova (in Nasēsē). This road was completed in 1890.[35]

---

31 CSO 1125/1885.
32 CSO 1866/1887.
33 CSO 1866/1887.
34 CSO 1866/1887.
35 See *Fiji Times*, 24 September 1890; see also CSO 108/1890.

Figure 4.3: Map of the town of Suva and adjoining lands, 1889.
Source: 19 February 1889, CSO 466/1889.

While some families moved to Vatuwaqa, several more remained in Toorak. They took on labouring jobs, worked in laundering and tried hawking. A few managed to open stores on the margins of the central business district while a few more made a living from operating gambling dens.[36] These illegal multicultural dens became popular with a great number of iTaukei, Melanesians, Indians and Part-Europeans and suggest

---

36   CSO 2721/1890.

by their existence and popularity that attempts by the government and the Suva Town Board to regulate and discipline the non-European sections of the community were never completely successful. In a kind of subversive disorder, attempts to regulate ethnic relations were often disrupted, impeded or ignored by the people who came to live in the new capital.

Festivals were also popular and brought the neighbourhood to life irrespective of the religion its residents professed. In spite of them fostering a strong sense of community and hope, they were perceived as dangerous by the government and in the late 1880s, it stopped issuing permits for religious processions through the street of Suva, claiming that they endangered public peace and that, as had happened in Trinidad, they might become the source of riots and loss of life.

As more labourers completed their terms of indenture and moved to Suva, they were steered into areas that could be farmed. One such area was the well-watered, low and flat tracts of land to the north of the Vatuwaqa River.[37] Within a decade, Vatuwaqa had grown into a fledgling agricultural community and was considered a town in its own right. The *Fiji Times* described it as a 'beautiful sight' especially when its 'extensive fields of rice' were 'waving to the fresh breeze of Laucala Bay' (6 April 1898). Areas of land were also opened up for farming in parts of Samabula, Nasinu and Wainadoi. The Wainadoi move was one of the first experiments of labourers from India seeking lease agreements with indigenous landowners.[38]

XIII. The Administration of Justice … and Coercion

For those labourers who were under indenture, Suva was the centre for the administration of justice. In Henry Anson they had one of very few colonial officials who listened to their grievances and offered protection and redress from the violence and other injustices they encountered on the plantations. However, to meet and be heard by Anson, the labourers needed to walk the 10-mile path to Suva. On 3 May 1886, for instance, several gangs of labourers at the plantation in Koronivia (Lower Rewa)

---

37 See CSO 758/1890.
38 CSO 3174/1887.

organised a strike, with at least 40 of them deciding to walk to Suva with their spades, hoes, knives and other implements to get real justice from the Immigration Office. Anson being on leave, they met with the acting agent-general, Dr Bolton Corney, and complained to him about being overworked, underfed, abandoned by plantation inspectors and ignored by the magistrate at Rewa.[39] After being promised that their grievances would be looked into, the labourers agreed to be escorted back to Koronivia by the police.

They continued their strike as they waited for an inspector to visit. On the evening of the third day, a group of 70 of them escaped from the plantation and again set off to Suva to seek relief from the acting agent-general. They returned only after further assurances were made that an inspector would shortly be sent. The inspector arrived on 13 May and found the workers 'sullen and unwilling' and their quarters in 'filthy and unhealthy condition'. Many were so poor that they could not earn enough to buy their rations.[40] In spite of being witness to these disturbing scenes, the inspector advised that discipline and punishment should be stepped up to prevent a recurrence of the disorder. Under no circumstances, he advised, should groups of 100 men ever march off their estate in such an unceremonious fashion.[41] Other officials, including Bolton Corney, concurred and warned that 'unruly assemblies' were becoming too common, that the prevailing 'spirit of insubordination' should be quashed immediately, and that 'a law must be drawn up to punish those who engage in such activities'.[42]

Ordinance XIV of 1886 was speedily drafted by Thurston, now acting as governor, and passed into law.[43] In his view, Indian indentured labourers were 'a working population and nothing more'.[44] The ordinance was described as 'Draconian' by the Colonial Office in London[45] and would have probably been fiercely contested by Anson, had he been in Fiji when it was enacted. Its most important clause was the prohibition of more than five immigrants from leaving their plantation in a body for the

---

39 CSO 1107/1886.
40 CSO 987/1886.
41 CSO 987/1886.
42 See CSO 987/1886 and 1107/1886.
43 See CSO 3061/1887.
44 See CSO 1380/1894.
45 See KL Gillion, *Fiji's Indian migrants: A history to the end of indenture in 1920* (New York: Oxford University Press, 1962), 83.

purpose of making a complaint.[46] This was a major victory for employers for it rendered virtually impossible any organised collective action such as labourers' marches to Suva.

Only one other such march to Suva ever took place, when about 130 labourers from Nausori plantation appeared at the agent-general's residence on 6 April 1887. They complained about being overworked, underpaid and frightened by a gun-wielding overseer.[47] After getting assurances from Anson that one of his staff would support them and attend their court hearing, they agreed to return to work. However, on the day of the hearing the officer could not secure a boat to get across to the court house at Naduruloulou. Consequently, six of the marchers' representatives were convicted under the new ordinance and sentenced by the magistrate (Joske) to two months hard labour. Anson was left fuming and described the whole affair as 'a travesty of justice', for he had promised the men a fair hearing.[48] As pointed out by Brij Lal, such examples demonstrate that the colonial state in Fiji seriously absolved its role as trustee of indentured labourers' rights.[49]

Indigenous Fijian and Melanesian labourers also availed themselves of legal avenues in Suva to seek redress. Those employed on smaller islands wrote letters and petitions to complain variously about inhuman treatment, overtasking, unpaid work, insufficient or bad food, work on Sundays, unhygienic lodgings, poor sanitary conditions and insufficient medical care. On Mago Island, 87 petitioners signed a letter of complaint against their manager, Borron, and had it carried by boat by their own representatives all the way to Suva.[50]

In similar fashion, three Solomon Island labourers absconded from an estate in Bureta on Ovalau and sailed to Suva in one of the plantation boats to lay their complaint. This decision was taken in desperation after their grievances were repeatedly ignored by the local magistrate. Like the Mago labourers, they accused the plantation management of forcing them to work on Sundays without pay, feeding them insufficient food and beating them regularly. The sick were forced to work even in the rain and no one was allowed to wander beyond the plantation boundaries even in

---

46   See CSO 3061/1887.
47   CSO 87/921 and *Fiji Times*, 9 April 1887.
48   CSO 921/1887.
49   Brij V Lal, 'Veil of dishonour', in *Chalo Jahaji: On a journey through indenture in Fiji*, ed. Brij V Lal (Suva/Canberra: The Fiji Museum/Australian National University Press, 2000), 174, doi.org/10.22459/CJ.12.2012.
50   CSO 3256/1895.

their own time. Like the Mago representatives above, the three absconders were arrested on arrival in Suva but later released after the conditions of their employment were revealed. The new agent-general for immigration, Arthur Robert Coates, noted that 'had these men not come to Suva, the illegality to which they were subjected would have continued'.[51]

If Suva represented labourers' hopes of obtaining recourse from injustice, the capital was also the centre from which the state operated its coercive apparatus. A large prison had been built in which numerous indentured labourers served sentences for various infractions of the labour ordinances. Many who served sentences 'with hard labour' were quickly sent out to work on public infrastructure projects. Some labourers preferred prison to plantations life and thought they might escape incarceration by paying their fine to the jailer and then earning money in Suva for the rest of their sentence. As the agent-general remarked, labourers knew that Suva did not have an agent for planters, and several stayed on in the town after the completion of their prison term and stayed with free immigrants where they were occasionally joined by deserters fleeing other plantations.[52]

Suva's prison also held indentured women, most of whom were punished for desertion or unlawful absence from work. Records from the superintendent of prisons indicate that in May of 1887, there were 30 women in Suva's jail, only four of whom were Indian indentured women.[53] Two years later, the number of female prisoners had grown to 57, almost all of whom were indentured women.[54] This can be partly explained by a 10 per cent increase in the population of women labourers. It can also indicate that they were particularly targeted because they were the most vulnerable. On the other hand, it may also mean that indentured women became increasingly combative and difficult to manage or that, like some of the menfolk, they thought that enduring a prison term in Suva might be better than the ongoing violence and exploitation of plantation life.

However, some women quickly found that life in prison was not necessarily safer. One such woman, Mahadai, was raped by the chief warden of Suva jail while serving a six-week term for unlawful absence from work. Her case came to light when it was reported by an iTaukei inmate. When asked why she had not lodged the complaint herself she replied 'because I did

---

51   CSO 3490/1894.
52   CSO 1107/1886.
53   CSO 1089/1887.
54   CSO 2042/1892.

not know how to make a complaint' and 'because we get no redress'.[55] Exceptionally, one or two of the female prisoners would be bailed out by 'free' labourers living in the vicinity of the capital and then employed in prostitution.[56] These women may have reasoned that the opportunities for earning income and for safer working conditions were greater in prostitution than in plantation work.

One of the many prisoners who was incarcerated at the Suva jail in the 1880s was Mosese Dukumoi – more popularly known as Navosavakadua. A leading priest from Drauniivi in Ra, he was jailed for his part in leading the Tuka uprising, a mass movement in the Ra province and the interior of Fiji.[57] After his arrest in Vunidawa in December 1885 along with several of his lieutenants, he was brought to Suva and sentenced to 12 months with hard labour for *vakatubuca* or 'conduct calculated to raise evil in the land'.[58] He was kept under constant supervision and allotted a European cell to ensure that he would not communicate with any other prisoner.[59]

A list of offences he committed while serving time impresses the danger with which he was regarded. On 16 May 1886, Navosavakadua was placed in separate confinement with reduced diet for four days 'for singing'. In response to this offence, Thurston ordered the superintendent of prisons to place Navosavakadua in leg irons. On 14 July, he was placed in solitary confinement for 48 hours after being found conversing with another inmate. On 10 September, he was found in possession of half a sheet of foolscap and eight pages of the *Town and Country Journal*. For this offence, he was placed in solitary confinement with reduced diet and without a bed for four days. A week later he was found speaking to another prisoner outside the bathhouse. Both were flogged.[60]

In spite of these draconian measures, Navosavakadua's presence in Suva continued to inspire Tuka. When his prison term ended, the colonial administration was tempted to exclude him permanently from Fiji. This was endorsed by the chiefs at the *Bose Vakaturaga* (Council of Chiefs

---

55 CSO 1842/1887.
56 *Journal of the Fiji Legislative Council* 1885, Paper 25: 13, NAF; and CSO 3061/1887.
57 See Martha Kaplan, *Neither cargo nor cult: Ritual politics and the colonial imagination in Fiji* (Durham: Duke University Press, 1995), doi.org/10.1515/9780822381914, and Robert Nicole, *Disturbing history: Resistance in early colonial Fiji* (Honolulu: University of Hawai'i Press, 2011), doi.org/10.1515/9780824860981.
58 Mitchell to Secretary of State for Colonies, 19 October 1887, Despatch 137, CO 83/46, PRO.
59 CSO 599/1886.
60 CSO 1939/1886.

meeting) of 1887. They resolved that Navosavakadua was a 'monomaniac' and that they were of one mind about the man: 'Let him now be sent far away; to Rotumah if possible.'[61] Ordinance 20 of 1887 providing for 'the deportation and confinement of Disaffected or Dangerous Natives'[62] was immediately drafted and enacted, and the man they called a 'dangerous fanatic'[63] was shipped to the furthest and most isolated island of the colony: Rotuma. He lived there until his death on 13 June 1897, just four months before the expiry of his confining order.[64]

XIV. Socio-Economic Life

Meanwhile, on the commercial side of things, the central business district of the new capital took shape and grew steadily through the 1880s. Filled with the imperial pride of the times, Gorrie declared triumphantly:

> We have seen the green knoll where a small wooden church once stood levelled and rolled out into a pier; a native path along the beach raised to the dignity of Victoria Parade; the tidal swamp at the mouth of the creek reclaimed, and its square yards fought over as choice town sites … Where a few years ago the native canoe alone was seen, or a solitary settler's boat coming up to the solitary store for a few tins of preserved meat and a case of gin, three (if not already four) first-class steamers per month from the Australian Colonies now load and unload their cargoes.[65]

Streets were named after the key figures of the empire (Victoria, Carnarvon, Gladstone, Kimberly, Macarthur), the colony (Gordon, Thurston, Pratt, Goodenough, Gorrie) and the town (Thomson, Renwick, Joske). This is not to say that they were perfectly aligned and clearly defined. An article from the *Suva Times* suggests that they existed nowhere except on the map:

> Indeed on the plan, Suva appears to be a neat and picturesque town, well laid out; with a creek running through the centre of it, and a broad beach extending in front. We see that Gordon Street and MacGregor Road, and others, all so carefully traced out, that we might be forgiven for expecting to find names engraved at the

---

61 Resolution XI, 'Notes of the Proceedings of a Native Council', 1887, NAF.
62 *Fiji Royal Gazette*, 13 October 1887.
63 Mitchell to Secretary of State for Colonies, 4 July 1887. Despatch 97, CO 83/46, PRO.
64 CSO 2550/1897.
65 John Gorrie, 'Fiji as it is', *Proceedings of the Royal Colonial Institute* 14 (1882–3): 160.

corners, and the houses duly numbered. But, as everyone knows, the reality is very different. The unfortunate pedestrian flounders though mud and slips over soapstone; and in many places would have great difficulty in telling whether he were on the street or off it.[66]

Traffic began to proliferate with sulkies and buggies – respectively two and four-wheeled vehicles pulled by horses – keeping Suva's streets busy. From the mid-1880s, parts of the town were laid with rails and in 1886 tramways ran through such streets as Pier Street, Victoria Parade, Pratt Street, Scott Street, Thomson Street and Renwick Road. They delivered cargo from the wharf to the many businesses that had sprung along these streets. The tracks were entirely under the control of indigenous Fijians and Melanesians, but as a new and yet unregulated mode of transportation, it was thought to be 'highly dangerous to foot, horse, and vehicular traffic'.[67]

Figure 4.4: Cumming Street under construction, 1876.
Source: P.32.7.26 Fiji Museum.

---

66   Cited in Albert J Schütz, *Suva: A history and guide* (Sydney: Pacific Publications, 1978), 15.
67   CSO 1843/1888.

4. THE MAKING OF A CAPITAL

Accidents became more numerous but mainly because of the large number of horses that roamed freely in the centre of the city at all hours of the day and night. Reporting on the seriousness of the matter, the *Fiji Times* wrote:

> Attention must be again directed to the nuisance existing in the town by the straying and wandering of horses in all directions … At night, when the lights are not shining very brightly, one is very apt to run or bump against the heels of some fiery untamed heed, and each has really been the case.[68]

Stray dogs and cattle were also problematic. To combat the problem, the government issued a regulation stipulating that all dogs be registered.[69] On poultry, the *Fiji Times* warned that Suva's wild chickens were now under threat from a new predator:

> It behoves the owners of poultry in Suva to look after them with greater care than hereto as the lively mongoose has reached us. These little vampires are spreading rapidly all over this island and won't trouble themselves to hunt rats while chickens can be so easily got at.[70]

In the end, a pound was ordered built and a pound-keeper hired to capture and enclose Suva's stray animals but even this measure had little impact on the problem.

Meanwhile the ownership of horses grew to such an extent that the townsfolk formed a jockey club. The general public was shortly entertained with horse races first at Albert Park in the early 1890s, then at low tide on the Muanikau sands, and finally on a proper racecourse at Veiuto in the late 1890s. The residents also organised other sporting events, such as the Easter program which was held at the Albert Park where a small pavilion had been erected.

According to the *Fiji Times*, these meets were attended by a great number of spectators as well as nearly every vehicle and horse in the community.[71] The athletics events included sprints, long jump, high jump, skipping for girls, obstacle races and other games such as sack races, egg and spoon races, and three-legged races for younger children. A tug of war between

---

68 6 February 1889.
69 *Fiji Times*, 20 February 1889.
70 3 September 1890.
71 *Fiji Times*, 5 June 1889.

the residents of Suva and Rewa often provided the climax of the day.[72] Tennis and cricket tournaments were held each weekend at the same venue, often against the Rewa teams. Competitions between these two districts gave birth to a long sporting rivalry that persists to this day.

Another attraction was the Suva saltwater swimming baths. The process by which they came into existence was highly contentious. An impassioned debate raged through the late 1880s about whether 'coloured people' (as non-Europeans were called) should be allowed to swim in the same area as 'white people'. In 1888 the Suva warden (mayor), Simeon Lazarus, and the Suva Town Board attempted to prohibit 'Indians, Natives of Fiji, and Polynesians from using the baths'.[73] Their draft ordinance also proposed the hours of 10 am and 4 pm were to be reserved for 'ladies' only, and that dogs and the washing of clothes were prohibited.[74]

Figure 4.5: Queen Victoria Memorial Hall, time of Fiji Agricultural Industrial Show, 1908.
Source: Wishart Ryan, P32.4.84 Fiji Museum.

---

72 See for instance the *Fiji Times*, 3 April 1889.
73 CSO 1017/1888. The term 'Polynesians' was commonly used to refer to all Melanesian labourers.
74 CSO 1017/1888.

After due consideration, the government advised that the Town Board had no power to make such ordinances and the proposal was rejected. In 1890, Lazarus and the Town Board amended their request and proposed that 'whites' should bathe on the planned site (see below) while a separate bath should be built 'say near Walu Bay' for the 'coloured races'.[75] His argument was that Suva's European residents contributed more rates and taxes to cover the cost of these baths and they should therefore enjoy the better facilities.

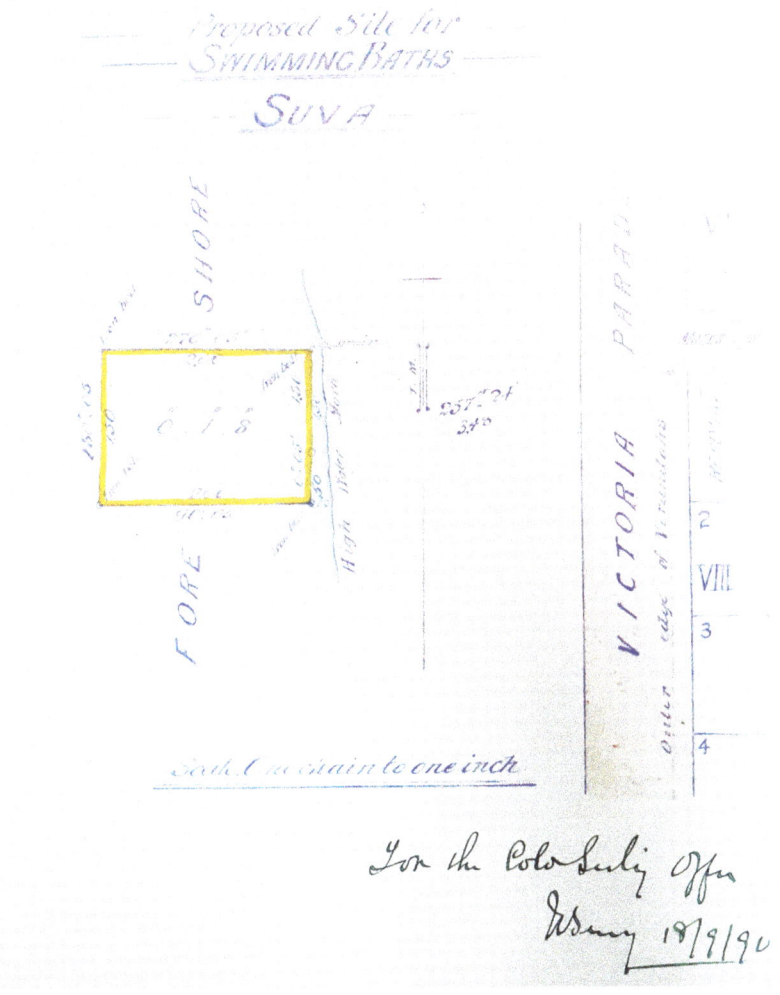

Figure 4.6: Proposed site for swimming baths – Suva, 1890.
Source: 18 September 1890, CSO 2129/1890.

---

75   CSO 1017/1888.

The government again opposed it and advised the Town Board that because the baths were public, they should be 'open to all persons' and that 'Indians, Natives of Fiji, and Polynesians have as much right to use them as anyone else'.[76] The baths were eventually opened to the public in 1891 as a saltwater pool near the current site of the Suva Olympic Pool. This contest reflects the counteracting forces that existed within the larger system of colonial power in the allocation and regulation of space for various ethnic groups. It also shows that the colonial administration did not always make common cause with the narrow interests of certain European settlers.

However, on other matters the government could be more repressive and regimenting. For instance, in 1892 it regulated singing, dancing and other expressions of culture with a Native Dances Ordinance that prohibited all *meke* or ceremonial dancing and singing within town boundaries without a permit. A curfew was also imposed between 11 pm and 5 am for 'Indians' and all Islanders, whatever their origin.[77]

The late 1880s produced several other interesting developments. One of them was the installation of the first telephone line between Government House and the Colonial Secretary's Office in March 1886.[78] A few kerosene lights helped to brighten a handful of streets for a few hours each night. And then, a novelty of a different kind lit up the streets when a wandering barber appeared on the scene. Commenting on this welcome sight, the *Fiji Times* wrote:

> One often hears of a Wandering ministrel [sic] but a wandering barber is a novelty, yet one is to be seen in Suva trampling from house to house, with the usual paraphernalia of looking glass, scissors, razors, etc. This tonsorial artist is an intelligent Indian and carries references as to his qualifications. With such a tradesman in our midst there need not be any more rough chins or unshorn locks and his arrival can be hailed as a great convenience.[79]

Also, a market for the sale of produce was finally completed in 1890. As the *Fiji Times* observed, indigenous vendors could now 'rejoice exceedingly' at the prospect of occupying the new buildings and thus 'escape from roosting under ivi trees and verendahs during the wet cold nights'.[80]

---

76 CSO 1017/1888.
77 Ordinance 3 of 1892; see Steel, *Oceania under steam*, 181, 182.
78 CSO 642/1886.
79 9 February 1889.
80 27 September 1890.

Fiji's first Annual Exhibition also came into existence. Organised by the Agricultural and Industrial Association of Fiji, it brought together products from all over the colony and handed out prizes for the best crops, flowers, animals and other miscellaneous goods. The best products were then selected for exposition at other British imperial exhibitions including the centennial exhibition of 1888–1889 in Melbourne.[81]

Meanwhile, efforts to link Suva to Rewa and other settled areas continued in earnest. In July 1889, between 30 and 50 men began work on a 3-mile long unmetalled road 'for horse and light wheeled traffic' from Samabula to Suva. Lobbied for by prominent Samabula planters, this road replaced a small track that took pedestrians an hour to walk before reaching Suva.[82] It would join the Waimanu Road 'at the bridge on the Walu Creek above the waterfall'.[83] Signs of this waterfall and of another on Nabukalou Creek have all but vanished. The disappearance of these old natural features of Suva remind us of the many other such markers that were erased in the last 150 years in the name of 'development'. Meanwhile segments of the road to the Lower Rewa were also under construction, including the section passing through Kalabu village. To facilitate travel by two-wheeled vehicles across the many rivers that lay between Suva and Rewa, bridges were ordered erected with buabua logs sourced from Kadavu.[84]

XV. The Pebble in the Shoe

Our period of study ends with a return to the enigmatic and controversial figure of the Tui Suva. After supervising the removal of his people to Suvavou in 1882, Ratu Aporosa Tuivuya's relationship with the Colonial Government quickly soured. He found himself in trouble for drinking alcohol and was then punished for *daudara*, when he attempted to molest the wife of a man he was staying with in Rewa. Writing on this matter, one official conceded, 'I feel Ratu Ambrose is almost past praying for'.[85] He was subsequently banished to Fort Carnarvon in Natuatuacoko in the interior of Navosa with his wife, and stripped of his title of *buli*.[86]

---

81 See for instance the *Fiji Times*, 16 October 1889.
82 CSO 107/1890.
83 CSO 108/1890.
84 CSO 1805/1890.
85 CSO 1345/1882.
86 CSO 1675/1883.

However, his incarceration did not have the desired outcome and in 1884 he was arrested for procuring and supplying liquor and for other 'immoralities' with certain Bauan women on the estate of the Rewa Sugar Company at Koronivia. Commenting on the case, Ratu Ilaitia Toroca, an old Bauan high chief, remonstrated that were it not for the protection of the law, 'there would have been bloodshed as in former times', for one of the women was the wife of a chief from Lasakau, the powerful clan of Bauan sea-warriors.[87]

Ratu Aporosa was sentenced to a fine of £50 or six months imprisonment with hard labour. He appealed to the governor about the severity of his sentence but Des Voeux was resolute and instructed the native commissioner to ensure that the people of Suva did not help him pay the fine.[88] After serving his sentence, he faded somewhat from public view before making an ominous return in 1890.

This is not to say that Ratu Aporosa was inactive. He was making good money from the flourishing banana trade. He was also supplying logs to private individuals and to the government for the construction of a substantive wharf. Free to pursue his own interests, he did not hesitate to use his customary title to divert his people from their tax work and to redirect their labour to serve his own business ventures. Hence, as in 1879, this situation made the collection of taxes very difficult. By 1890, in spite of making 'considerable sums of money' as one colonial official put it, the people of Suvavou were behind with the in-kind payment of their taxes.[89] As much as the *buli* tried to get people to meet the tax threshold, his efforts were constantly thwarted by Ratu Aporosa's interference especially in the matter of log cutting. His junior position relative to Ratu Aporosa in the traditional hierarchy dictated that he must not undermine the latter's prestige and authority.

Another matter of concern for the administration was his continued abuse of women. His conduct in this regard was described as 'a perfect nuisance to all' and 'a scandal to the whole community'.[90] One Matelita, a Nacokaika woman, wrote to the colonial secretary to seek government protection against Ratu Aporosa. She complained that he came and took her whenever he wished and kept her against her will. However,

---

87   CSO 1671/1884.
88   CSO 1671/1884.
89   CSO 700/1890.
90   CSO 2182/1890.

4. THE MAKING OF A CAPITAL

she would not lay charges against him because of his rank and neither would his wife. Although the government seemed keen to prosecute him, the two women's refusal to proceed against him allowed Ratu Aporosa to escape punishment.[91]

The government's troubles with Ratu Aporosa continued into the latter months of 1890 when he intervened in the affairs of Suva on a point of economic justice by spearheading the first Suva dockworkers' strike. The strike was linked to industrial action by dockworkers in other parts of the world. In Australia, the shipping companies refused stevedores' demands for better wages and both sides determined to fight to the bitter end. As a result, much of the shipping ground to a halt. Fiji was affected in so far as it was dependent on shipping for its imports and exports. Real fears surfaced that Fijian fruits (especially bananas) would end up rotting on the wharves of Suva and Levuka for want of ships. Many in Suva were also worried that the town might be starved of Australian goods and products.

The battle lines between workers and employers extended to Suva through two brief but dramatic events. The first was when the *Wainui*, a ship sailed by a unionised crew, arrived in Suva in early September 1890 at the same time as the *Pukaki* and its non-unionised labourers. When alongside one another, the *Fiji Times* reported 'there was some ornamental language indulged in by Unionists against non-unionists which culminated in the flinging of such missiles as potatoes and onions'.[92]

A month later, the lead article in the *Fiji Times* began with the words 'strikes are in the air'.[93] The rest of the article reported on an attempted strike by 60 iTaukei dockworkers who had been hired to discharge the trading ship SS *Rockton* that had docked at the Suva Wharf. A man named Timoci Nagusa[94] was said to be at the origin of the strike and had told his fellow workers that Australian stevedores were striking for increased pay and that 'as the ships could not be worked without the men the owners would have to give in'.[95] He encouraged them to strike for an increase of pay from 2 shillings to 4 shillings a day. About 40 of the men followed his advice.

---

91 CSO 2182/1890.
92 10 September 1890.
93 4 October 1890.
94 There are conflicting reports about whether he came from Ra (*Fiji Times*) or from Nadi (CSO 3088/1890).
95 *Fiji Times*, 4 October 1890.

Although colonial officials were certain that Ratu Aporosa was 'the prime mover in the whole affair' and that he was 'at the bottom of the trouble', Nagusa's statement to the police indicates that the dockworkers had been planning the strike for at least two weeks.[96] During that time a number of them, including several from Suvavou, had pledged not to work for any of the steamers for less than 4 shillings a day. When the steamers *Arawata* and *Taupo* left Suva in late September, they met at Suvavou to seek Ratu Aporosa's blessing, as Tui Suva, and resolved that when the next lot of steamers arrived they would stop work or accept work only on their own terms.[97]

Ratu Aporosa was a well-known figure at the wharf. He had developed a close affinity with the dockworkers, notably through his draught-playing skills for which he had acquired the reputation of being unbeatable.[98] With his support it was decided that a group of strikers would go on board the next cargo ships and *tabu* them (prohibit them from working). Regardless of whether the workers were of iTaukei, Melanesian or Indian origin, they were to stop work and get off the ships or be *buturaki-ed* (beaten).[99] Ratu Aporosa's son, Ratu Ravulo (sometimes spelt 'Ravula'), was to represent his father at the wharf and attest of the Tui Suva's approval of the strike.

The plan was executed to the letter. Ratu Aporosa's men arrived at the wharf as the stevedores prepared to unlock the *Rockton* and told them to stop work until Ratu Aporosa had arranged for better wages. Taking leadership for the strike, Nagusa pointed to Ratu Ravulo whose presence was sufficient to persuade the workers. The customs officers tried to get Nagusa arrested but the only constable on duty, Ratu Joshua, seemed to approve of the strike and refused to take him into custody.[100] Nagusa was eventually arrested and the strike was stopped in its tracks, probably because the scheme had been kept secret and failed to get the endorsement and solidarity from all dockworkers. Nagusa was sentenced to six months hard labour in default of a fine of £50.

While Ratu Aporosa was suspected of being the head of the movement, he escaped punishment. He returned to prominence in 1897 when he supported Nakelo villagers in a dispute they had with surveyors of the

---

96   CSO 3088/1890.
97   CSO 3088/1890.
98   Adolph B Brewster, *The hill tribes of Fiji* (London: Seeley, Service & Co. Limited, 1922), 206.
99   Beaten up. See CSO 3088/1890.
100 CSO 3090/1890.

Native Lands Commission.[101] A year later, he embraced the Seventh Day Adventist faith in a further symbol of nonconformity and dissent. That same year (1898) he led a group of eight Suvavou elders and confronted the government with a written submission expressing their dissatisfaction with the £200 that villagers were getting in compensation for their move to Suvavou.[102] In 1900 and 1901, he was one of the main leaders of the Fiji-wide movement that sought constitutional change in Fiji by advocating federation with New Zealand. Described by one colonial official as 'an agitator of the worst type', he was arrested on 20 November 1901 along with the Bauan chief Ratu Savenaca Radomodomo and confined to Oneata for two years.[103] On his return from exile, he was appointed *buli* of Rewa and worked in that capacity for the last six years of his life. He succumbed to typhoid fever in December 1912[104] and thus ended the life of one of the colony's most colourful characters.

Figure 4.7: Ratu Aporosa and Adi Kelera, n.d.
Source: Macmillan Brown Library, University of Canterbury, Christchurch, New Zealand.

---

101 CSO 4573/1897.
102 Hirokazu Miyazaki, *The method of hope: Anthropology, philosophy, and Fijian knowledge* (Stanford: Stanford University Press, 2004), 37.
103 See CSO 1546/1902 and 2678/1902.
104 *Fiji Times*, 10 December 1912.

Conclusion

This and the previous chapter explored the making of Suva as the capital of Fiji by piecing together some of the fragments of that history. A range of components were considered including wealth and poverty; mobility and settlement; capital and labour; race relations; the exercise of power, coercion, violence and brutality; the organisation of resistance and protest; the management of space and infrastructure, of transport and trade, and of justice; and the many expressions of culture, religion, food, sport, leisure and so on. This broad approach reveals the rich and unique texture of Suva's early colonial history.

Amid all the fragments and details raised in the chapter, a few overarching observations can be made. The first is that the spectre of history continues to hover over Suva in the present. For instance, the thorny issue of the original ownership of Suva was back in the news recently when the government announced plans to use a small part of the former native reserve to build the new Indian High Commission.[105]

The second is that a journey into the history of a place throws up old markers and how they were replaced by new ones. For example, Suva village gave way to Government House and the Thurston Gardens. Waterfalls gave way to roads. The beach disappeared when it was reclaimed to build hotels and other high-rise buildings. The mangroves and woodlands were cut. New streets were laid where swamps had previously laid for hundreds of years. Logs were felled all the way to Nausori, Naitāsiri and Namosi by colonised and colonists alike to feed their enormous appetite for cash and for material to build the town and its infrastructure. History marks change across time. In this case, this chapter gives us a sense of some of the things that were given up in the name of progress. Whether these changes are judged useful or detrimental to society is contentious but worth thinking about as we consider how we want the city to develop in the next 20, 50 or 100 years.

The third is the pivotal importance of the port in the choice of capital. To create an economy that was oriented to fulfil the interests of the empire, effective maritime communication was always going to be vital. Viewed in the larger global economic context of expanding trade

---

105 See Parliament of the Republic of Fiji, *Parliamentary debates*, 15 February 2019.

networks to Australia, New Zealand and beyond, the chances of the original inhabitants of Suva holding on to their ancestral lands were quite remote. These chances were eroded further by the involvement of their own chiefs (Ratu Cakobau and Ratu Aporosa Tuivuya) in brokering deals that facilitated their dispossession, even if they (chiefs) negotiated under duress.

The fourth is that the project of building the capital was directed and managed by colonial elites. However, they were always dependent on the labour and skills of thousands of ordinary people of all ethnicities. These people came to Suva, made it their home, and proceeded to give Suva its rich tapestry of cultural diversity. Amid the thousands of people who participated in the making of the capital, a few extraordinary characters emerge. One of them is the Tui Suva. His leadership, independent spirit, flaws and misdemeanours, and his constant defiance of the colonial order, make him one of the more colourful and enduring characters of this period and suggest that drawing a more complete biographical portrait of the man will be a worthwhile endeavour.

Fifth, as they moved into Suva, migrants encountered the regulatory and disciplinary power of the colonial state. However, the state's attempt to impose its colonial order on the bodies, spaces and activities of the colonised was never completely successful and varied greatly over time, place and circumstance. Some weaknesses were internal to the state itself, such as the colossal task of building a capital with very limited funds. Another challenge was the shortage of labour. That the transition was a rather messy affair is also illustrated in the irregular and misaligned streets of Suva and in the many stray animals that roamed the town. The Levuka lobby, the numerous petitions, the many delays caused by the sickness and protests of labourers, the wrangles with the Tui Suva, the housing crisis, all suggest that the making of the capital was often interrupted, disrupted, undermined and contested. That is, ordinary folks often disregarded the various attempts that were made to control and discipline their lives, movements and settlement.

Finally, this chapter suggests that many more stories about Suva lie in the archives. They contain more of the minutiae of life that ordinary folks left in their wake. Their notable and less notable drama, their grand and not so grand accomplishments, their comical and more tragic experiences all call for renewed interest and rediscovery.

5

Early Suva Fijians – A View Through *Sere Makawa*[1]

Simione Sevudredre

Prehistoric Suva

Prehistoric Suva or Suva *makawa* (old Suva) has traditional beginnings at Nakauvadra, mythical home of Fijians in the Ra province in north-eastern Vitilevu. The modern city of Suva takes its name from its original inhabitants who, according to tradition, migrated over the interior headwaters of mainland Vitilevu. This migration eventually settled on the peninsula where modern Suva is located, inhabiting high elevations as fortresses. A folklore predating the settling of Suva holds that when the ancestral god of Verata, Rokomoutu, and his younger brother, the ancestral god of Rewa, Romelasiga, were drawing up boundaries, they named a boundary denoting the end of Verata's jurisdiction and the beginning of Rewa's as *suvasuva*. Whether the name Suva is a derivation of this is unknown but it underscores a meaning in the name.

The original Suva people settled at Nauluvatu, close to where the Australian Chancery is and thence later to where the Thurston Gardens, Fiji Museum and Government House are now located. History tells of the siege and sack of Suva in 1843, which later led to the Bau–Rewa war, the longest battle ever in the annals of Fiji history. By the time the capital was shifted to Suva in 1881, the original Suva dwellers had relocated to a new location – Suvavou meaning 'New Suva'.

---

1   Translated as 'Old Songs' to generically categorise songs from the early colonial period.

Figure 5.1: 'In native village near Suva – Fiji' (probably Suvavou), 1884.
Source: Burton Brothers, P32.4.138 Fiji Museum.

Early Modern Suva

When Suva was established as a town in the late nineteenth century, the bulk of the indigenous Fijian population were still confined to their communal subsistence way of life in the villages. The iTaukei Fijians were restricted from travelling and had to obtain a pass if one wanted to move away from the village in search of opportunities in Suva. The early iTaukei in Suva thronged from nearby provinces of Rewa, Naitāsiri and Tailevu. Using traditional and kinship ties, the early Suva Fijians from Vanualevu, Lomaiviti and Lau connected with villages such as Tamavua and Kalabu (Naitāsiri), creating communities like Tacirua, Nabua, Turaki, Baniwai, Draiba and Nasova. The latter two community names were direct imports from the old capital. These early communities around Suva's periphery were mainly people who had gone to Suva in search of menial paid jobs and possibly to escape from the harsh *lala* system of crop taxation. Suva in the early days was still relatively underdeveloped. Alcohol consumption was still forbidden to the early iTaukei, and schools were not especially established for iTaukei in Suva until the mid-twentieth century.

Figure 5.2: 'Early Suva: Fijian market. Vuniivi tree, c. 1892'.
Source: Basil Thomson Collection c. 1892, P32.7.no1 Fiji Museum.

Figure 5.3: 'Early Suva: Fijian market, c. 1892'.
Source: Basil Thomson Collection c. 1892, P32.7.no2 Fiji Museum.

For the early Suva iTaukei communities, the place where things 'happened' was known as the Naiqaqi (the crusher). This is where Carnarvon Street is in present-day Suva and like iTaukei in the past, places were named according to something perceived to be iconic to that place. Hence Naiqaqi indicated that there had been a sugar mill in the vicinity, which gave rise to its local nomenclature. Naiqaqi then had a few cottages, one of which still stands today as an eatery, and these were known as kava bars or grog saloons. Little is known about who owned them or how many there actually were, but what is known in local folklore is that these grog saloons were venues for kava consumption, the *serenicumu* and for socialisation, as alcohol was expensive and forbidden to locals.

Serenicumu

Serenicumu literally means 'bumping songs', a genre of popular music that is widespread throughout Fiji today and is performed in villages as well as at local resorts and hotels. These songs are covers of, or influenced by, styles from Europe and America, other Pacific Islands or the Caribbean (particularly reggae). They are often performed at informal *yaqona* drinking sessions and are also associated with informal dance types broadly termed *tauratale* or *danisi* (from the English 'dance').

The exact origin of the genre is obscure. *Serenicumu* is said to be associated with the first legally allowed sales of beer to indigenous Fijians in the 1920s in Suva, and suggests it originated at parties where men bumped their drinking glasses together. One particular piece of lore adds that this music was originally *sere ni cumu saqā* (stress on 2nd /a/) (*saqā* meaning barrel or tankard), and that it referred to the practice of Fijian men sitting in a circle at a table and resting their heads against their tankards of beer.

Many *serenicumu* songs still performed today date from World War II – an intense period of creativity for this genre – when soldiers from the US, Aotearoa/New Zealand and Australia interacted extensively with Fijians.[2]

Currently, musicians distinguish two main styles of *serenicumu*: trio and sere bass (also called *sere makawa* or 'old songs', even though they may be 15 or more years old). Sere bass performance features a large group

---

2   See Appendix 6 for rendition of a US nursery rhyme, believed to be heard from US soldiers, into local 'Finglish'.

of bass vocalists (bass/*besi*) in addition to three solo voice parts: *tatabani/ tatabana, domo tolu/vakababa* and *laga/lagalaga* in descending order in terms of their vocal range. Only the three solo parts are heard in trio. The types and roles of the instruments, their tuning and playing techniques have also changed over time. The technique of *vadivadi* (plucking) that characterised sere bass guitar performance in the past has been replaced by various 'scrumming' (strumming) for the rhythm guitar, and a range of left- and right-hand techniques for the lead guitarist. The only chords used in sere bass were *dua* (tonic), *rua* (subdominant) and *tolu* (dominant), whereas trio also featured warning (seventh), minus (minor) and flat (supertonic) chords.

Anyone can participate in sere bass performance, which makes it ideal for use at large social gatherings. Trio performers are expected to perform to a high standard and are usually heard at small social functions such as *yaqona* drinking sessions. The tempo tends to be slower, and the overall pitch lower in sere bass when compared to trio. Sere bass, being closer stylistically to *meke*, tends to be preferred by older people (those in their mid-40s and above) and provides them with a means to connect with and celebrate their cultural roots. Trio, which tends to be popular with those in their 20s and 30s, exhibits a greater degree of Westernisation than sere bass, but is still regarded as being part of the *serenicumu* oral tradition that has been passed down through the generations and that continues to change as new songs are continually added to the repertoire and old ones fall into disuse.

Early Suva iTaukei Seen through Folksongs

The folksong 'Isa ko Suva'[3] is a popular tune from the 1960s. Its composer is unknown but the lyrics of the song mention Naiqaqi, Draiba (the current site of the *Boselevu Vakaturaga* complex) and Turaki (Toorak, one of the first suburbs of Suva). There are places like Nubukalou, which is the waterway that still runs alongside the MHCC shopping mall, but in the song lyrics, it could probably refer to an actual residence close to the waterway. This generic reference to a place using permanent features in nature indicates the indigenous penchant to placenames is always in

---

3   Translation by the author.

reference to a natural land feature even though its equivalent street name may exist. Valenimate and Nuku'alofa too are mentioned but no longer exist. The latter two were probably house names belonging to the early Suva dwellers of that era.

Table 5.1: 'Isa ko Suva' in iTaukei with English translation.

Original iTaukei Lyrics	Translation
I. Isa[a] ko Suva ena gauna sa oti	Isa Suva in the days gone by and by
Kena italanoa dau kena idivi voli	Its lovely stories have never lost their charm
Veivale ni yaqona ena kena dau soqovi	All the kava bars and the people always thronging
O Nubukalou e dua vei ira oqori	At Nubukalou 'twas one endearing place
Tini na kaloko ni dau qiri na lali	Ten o'clock at night when the bells begin chime
So era cabe cake tu ki Turaki	Some begin to travel up to dear old Turaki
So era tube bilikani tu ki Naiqaqi	With their billy cans the remainder to Naiqaqi
Yaco ki vale ra sa baci lose tale	Mixing[b] again when they do arrive at home
itale	chorus
Oiauwe[c] na lasa ga eke	Oiauwe such fun was there to see
Au na sega ni moce, sega ni moce	I would never doze nor slumber
Ke levu na noqu gade	Such adventures oh there were so many
II. Ko Draiba kei Valenimate nodra koro na gone tagane	Now at Draiba and Valenimate the habitation of all young men
Isa Turaki kei Naiqaqai e cake na vanua e taleitaki	Isa Turaki and upwards to Naiqaqi so endearing were these two places
III. Isa na wekaqu Jiupili kei Luisa ko Sanaila, vata kei Titilia	Isa my kinsmen – Jiupili and Luisa, and Sanaila of course dear Titilia
Veivakalasai ena bogi kei na siga	Happiness and fun, by night and by day
Ki Nukualofa mera lai vakasigasiga	At Nukualofa for fun till the break of day

Source: Author's translation.

Notes:
a. *Isa* is a Fijian word whose meaning and emotion is quite difficult to capture in a single English word, but it is uttered aloud denoting deep yearning and nostalgia.
b. 'Mixing' here denotes the mixing of *yaqona* in cloths.
c. *Oiawe* is believed to be a Polynesian derivative with similar meaning to *Isa*.

Another folk song from the same era is titled 'Isa my dear' composed by Nailaga Ba-born Mr Percy Bucknell. The lyrics of the song go:

Table 5.2: 'Isa my dear' in iTaukei with English translation.

Original iTaukei Lyrics	Translation
I. Daumaka dina Adi na cila ni vula	Perfect my dear lady is the shining of the moon
Nida dau yaba ya rua	As we gently tarry along together
Isa lei marama cava tale o nanuma	Please dear lady do tell me of your thoughts
E noda koro levu oqo ko Suva?	about the yonder sight of Suva city?
itale	chorus
Isa my dear moni taura na ligaqu	Isa my dear grab hold of my hand
Dreta noqu vinivo balavu	Tug at my flowing long dress
Au na rai kivita na icavucavu ni yavumu	Your stepping I will follow
Sa iko dear na noqu salusalu	You my dear are my salusalu
II. Daumaka dina nodra roka na marama	A beauty bevy of colours worn by the women
Vulavula kei karakarawa	The shining whites along with the blues
Nida dau raica e boiri na matada	And upon beholding fainting is so easy
Vu ni noqu mai moce tatadra	Falling into sweet fantasies
III. Ono na kaloko ni lutu na yakavi	As twilight falls at six in the evening
Tokara na isulu ni yaviyavi	The evening wear then comes adorning
Na isulu ni cabe cake tu ki Turaki	Clothes for the stroll up to Turaki[a]
Dui tubera nona kabani	Each partner hands clasped together
IV. Ni suka na vude meda veitauriliga	Frivolity now concluded hands held together
Me yaga mada na cila ni vula	The shining moonlight never must be wasted
So e cabe cake tu ki Kaunikuila	Some will continue on to Kaunikuila[b]
So e sisi sobu ki Draiba	Others slither downwards to Draiba[c]

Source: Author's translation.

Notes:
a. Toorak: an early suburb of Suva that was established by the founding fathers of Suva from the Melbourne Polynesian Company.
b. Another early Suva suburb, also known as Flagstaff.
c. This was a community settlement of the early iTaukei who had come into Suva when there were no residential allotments yet. It is the site of the current Ministry iTaukei Affairs and Ministry Foreign Affairs/Ministry of Lands.

Ovini Baleinamau was another composer in the early twentieth century in Suva. Though hailing from Lekutu in Bua, he had settled in Tacirua outside Suva and had formed a string band by the name Caucau ni Delai Seatura.[4] One of his compositions subtly alluded to segregation in Suva's bars, when local iTaukei were not allowed to enter bars and clubs. In the song titled 'Vale ni bia' (Beer brewery), the lyrics sing of indulging in beer when in actuality, home-brewed beer was being served (illegally) but the drinkers nonetheless fantasised that they were actually drinking the beer that was the reserve of the colonial establishment. The lyrics to the first verse go:

Table 5.3: 'Vale ni bia' in iTaukei with English translation.

Original iTaukei Lyrics	Translation
Vale ni bia kamikamica	The beer brewery 'tis so sweet
Vale ni bia kamikamica	The beer brewery 'tis so sweet
Lei vale ni bia kamikamica	Oh the beer brewery 'tis so sweet
Bameti o Vilimaina	The bar maid is Vilimaina
Gone ni Ba ra kasou kina	The guys from Ba get drunk there
Nodra ilavo e sa cagicagina	All their money begins to slowly fly away

Source: Author's translation.

A Brief Socio-Analysis of the Lyrics

A social analysis of the song lyrics reveals the boisterous life of the early iTaukei community in Suva. These were people drawn from all the provinces and villages in Fiji who sought some form of paid employment, or to escape the harsh communal life of the *lala*[5] of the chiefs, or both. The frivolity and excess consumption underscores the rigidity of the cloistered life in the traditional communal village setting. There is hardly anything written in literature about the growing dissention of the common iTaukei in the villages as this was glossed over with the usual clichés of 'paradise, swaying palm trees and the idyllic life'. It was also not the norm for the iTaukei to be seen in open contention with their chieftain or the established status quo. Nor was there any intimation of the class struggle not only between the ordinary iTaukei and their chief, but also

---

4   Translated as Mists atop Seatura Mount, a mythical place in the Bua province, Vanualevu.
5   *Lala* refers to a directive from a chief to his people to carry out an undertaking.

5. EARLY SUVA FIJIANS

between the iTaukei and the ruling colonial class. Access to the towns for the early Fijians was restricted, likewise saloons, bars and alcohol were regulated and only for the British colonisers and their circles. The early Fijians in Suva were unaware that the restrictions they were subjected to was their Pacific version of apartheid. The consumption of *yaqona* or kava in the traditional setting reserved it only for the chieftains and the upper hierarchy of Fijian society. It was not for the common people to indulge in and even if it were a social event in the village, it was not open to frivolity and exuberance. The Fijian chiefs had already become part of the existing colonial structure through membership of the Great Council of Chiefs that, in reality, mirrored the British aristocratic gentlemen's club – all paid for by the Colonial Government and borne by the common iTaukei through a ruthless crop taxation. The iTaukei communities in the rural areas were still reeling under the cumbersome demands of crop taxation from the Colonial Government and development of the iTaukei society was impeded as a consequence. One was the imposed orthodoxy through the sitting of the Native Lands Commission in 1905 and 1947 – an exercise stacked against the local traditions concerning ownership of land and titles. Added to this was the establishment in 1940 of the then Native Lands Trust Board, now iTaukei Lands Trust Board. The backdrop to all this was Governor Gordon's policy for the native Fijian lifestyle not to be disrupted – thereby denying access to commerce and business for the early iTaukei, the effects of which are still discussed today. There were no public primary and secondary schools in Suva for the common iTaukei. The Hindu organisations of the Arya Samaj and the Sanatan Dharm had their own schools, likewise the two mainstream Christian denominations – Roman Catholic[6] and Methodist.[7] Queen Victoria School was still deemed as the *vuli ni turaga* (school for the chiefs) and Adi Cakobau School was initially set up to prepare girls to be wives to Fijian bureaucrats who were schooled at the Queen Victoria School and drawn from the cream of young chiefs whose ancestry was tied to the Deed of Cession and the Great Council of Chiefs.

---

6   For Catholics it was Suva Street, Saint Felix College and Saint Columba, later becoming Marist Brothers High School for boys initially, and Saint Philomena's, Saint Anne's, Saint Joseph Primary and Saint Joseph's Secondary for girls.
7   For Wesleyans it was Suva Methodist Boys, Dudley Primary & Intermediate, Annesley Infant and Ballantine Memorial School or Dudley High School initially.

Further to this backdrop of early Suva, the colonial establishment and the ruling oligarchy of the eastern chiefs stifled, exiled or jailed local iTaukei such as Apolosi Nawai[8] and Mosese Dukumoi,[9] whom the locals saw as their champions. The early iTaukei of Suva managed and dealt with their version of modernist angst with the only tools they had – singing, dancing and the unreserved consumption of kava. The places mentioned in the folksongs – Draiba, Turaki, Kaunikuila, Naiqaqi – were not only saloons for open consumption and exuberance, but also key places of solidarity or empathy – safe places where iTaukei could be themselves, how they wanted to be. These were the people who dared to break out of the norm in their bid to try and create something for themselves, but the entire formal and traditional system was not in their favour.

The frivolity and behaviour extolled in the song lyrics was in subtle defiance to the established status quo. This was not a political backlash but rather an outlet for the preservation of the common collective sanity. Had the powers that be paid attention, these 'cultural outlets' of singing and collective frivolity could have been harnessed and grown to make Suva not only a commercial hub, but also a cultural and artistic hub of Fiji. The early Fijians in Suva were cut from the old traditional cloth of the grand cultural festivals and exchanges or *solevu* that had begun to wane in local history. This was the same period that artistic expressions began to evolve from the traditional chanting or *vucu* to the *sigidrigi* style, then to the quartet or trio style, singing without any formal musical or vocal education. This period of unhindered expression was the rich backdrop from which outstanding composers and poets in Fijian culture emerged. The changing of venues in the songs for continuation of the *vude*[10] indicated the disposition and energy for music composition, singing and dancing using stylised choreography drawn from the traditional *meke* and other activities. In fact, dancing in early Suva to *serenicumu* music was thought to have been adapted from the *butukai*[11] – pacing around on

---

8   Apolosi Nawai (1876–1946), known as the King of Fiji, was a charismatic Fijian leader who challenged British colonial rule. He was held by the Fijian Government.
9   Also known as Mosese Dugumoi and Navosavakadua who was born in Ra in the second half of the nineteenth century. He was considered a rebel by colonial authorities but a prophet by those who followed him.
10 A term denoting a local style of music and dancing.
11 *Butukai* was a style of dance originating in this period. The moves of the *butukai* mirror the actual movements of diving for freshwater mussels where the feet pace around rhythmically on the riverbed feeling for mussels. Freshwater mussels are synonymous with Naitāsiri and Rewa provinces in Vitilevu.

a river bed searching for fresh water mussels (*kai*). The transition from the river to kava saloons with *serenicumu* naturally gave rise to a form of dance expression by the same name.

Running parallel to this backdrop was the localisation of the Methodist Church from its Australian administration. This saw the establishment in 1935 of the Centenary Church in Stewart Street, Suva, named in commemoration of the 100-year anniversary of Wesleyanism or Methodism in Fiji. Prior to the concrete structure that still stands, the building was a simpler wooden house known then as Mission Hall. Singing of hymns and choral songs in the Western major and minor scales were still in their infancy, but groups of iTaukei had banded together in their newly established communities on the peripheries of Suva churning out songs in the *sigidrigi* style. These communities included Nabua (with its Bua ni Lomai Nabua group), Turaki (with its Voqa kei Turaki), Tacirua (with its Caucau ni Delai Seatura group originally from Bua in Vanualevu) and Samabula (with its Seniwaka ni Samabula Noca vocal group). Other groups not confined to Suva's early Fijian communities rallied under a common guild of sorts like the Southern Brothers – a group of Kadavu men returning from World War II with its leader and composer Manu Korovulavula. Caucau ni Waimanu was another *sigidrigi* group whose members had origins in Sawani, Naitāsiri. Another group calling themselves the Phoenix Choir was led by Sir Josua Rabukawaqa. This was a small a cappella choral group adapting *sigidrigi* folksongs into choral arrangements. The group would eventually begin singing Methodist hymnodies under the same name as a precursor or benchmark for the newly established Centenary Church Choir. Thus Fijian society and expression was gradually ushered into choral singing and the Western major and minor scales. The *sigidrigi* style of singing had evolved into quartets, trios and eventually sacred choral singing.

By the turn of the 1970s, Fijian society had settled and grown in and around Suva. The baby boomers from post–World War II had become integrated into contemporary Suva through education becoming more accessible to all. It was this generation that became the new bureaucrats of Suva, serving in education, health and other government ministries. It was also this generation that were subjected to the heavy-handed policies from the New Zealand educators who imposed regulations against the indigenous language and its cultural expressions. It was considered shameful and inferior to promote the indigenous language in schools or to express oral traditions and history openly.[12]

Now as we look back from the twenty-first century, the predominant sources of information for the early Suva Fijians was the *Na Mata* (*The Herald*), a government quarterly published in the iTaukei language but whose content was a mix of history and government notices. Its accessibility was also restricted to those within government circles. The *Fiji Times* had begun printing a weekly Fijian paper, *Na iLalakai*. Radio broadcasts from the (then) Fiji Broadcasting Commission's (FBC) Radio Fiji One were predominately in English with an hour a week devoted to a Fijian program. This did not change until the mid-70s when FBC would broadcast songs, jingles and government programs in the Fijian language from 6 am until 8 pm in the evening, when English programs would resume.

Conclusion

As Suva progresses into the first quarter of the twenty-first century, the world has shrunk with digitisation and globalisation, and in the process, a great bulk of our indigenous collective memory, be it from the early Suva Fijian communities or the overall collective from the villages, has been almost suppressed into oblivion. Attempts to capture slivers of history from these people and communities still presents challenges. Even earlier, the arrival of Christianity in 1835 set the stage for the colonisation of the land and the mind leading up to 1874. What we see today in contemporary iTaukei society is the fruition of colonisation, beginning way before Suva was established, taking us right back to Cession in 1874, a major turning point historically and culturally.

There is an opportunity for folksong lyrics to be used for local ethno-music study in the school curriculum and at tertiary level. The *serenicumu* and *sigidrigi* lyrics are replete with local history, kinships and romances, using poetry and style from a time when formal education and modernisation had yet to make deep imprints on the Fijian psyche. In fact, drawing from the tradition of *vucu* or sung poetry, song lyrics of the *serenicumu* and

---

12   See GB Milner, David George Arms and Paul A Geraghty, *Duivosavosa: Fiji's languages, their use and their future*, Bulletin of the Fiji Museum no. 8 (Suva: Fiji Museum, 1984).

sigidrigi rhyming schemes and verses in themselves provide a window onto early literary forms or poetry in the iTaukei language. Bear in mind that being an oral society, traditional oratory was the height of oral expression and not only was it diplomatic, but also was full of idiomatic expressions and figures of speech. These oral expressions found their way into the *sigidrigi* and *serenicumu* lyrics.

In moving away from the traditional village lifestyle and settling in Suva, the early Suva Fijians had inadvertently created a new music and dance form – the *sigidrigi/serenicumu* and the *butukai*. This is a social reality that the iTaukei today must appreciate and give more respect to. It is Fiji's original musical expression that had its beginnings in the traditional *vucu* and *meke* chants. By interrogating the lyrics, history from the perspective of the locals can emerge as the slivers of history on early Fijian society in Suva, upon which the books are as yet silent.

6

The Grand Old Man and the Prince of Thieves

Anurag Subramani

At the Old Suva Cemetery, overlooking the Tamavua-i-wai bridge, lies grave no. 7193, unadorned and ordinary-looking, without any form of inscription. No flowers are resting on its deck, as there is on the surrounding graves, and the prison officer who located it said that no one, as far as he can remember, has visited the site. However, this unremarkable and forgotten grave does not belong to any ordinary individual. It is that of TL Francoeur, one of the most extraordinary men who lived in Suva in the early 1900s.

Thomas Le Clair De Francoeur was a descendant of a French ducal family. During the French Revolution, his father, Joseph Le Clair De Francoeur, who was Duc de Francoeur of Navarre, fled France and took refuge in England. Being a close friend of the Duke of Kent, Queen Victoria's father, he settled in Kent.[1] Joseph later immigrated to Canada and married Mary Ann Le Clair De Francoeur, née Badwin. Thomas Le Clair De Francoeur was born in La Roche, Quebec, Canada, on 15 January 1829.[2] Francoeur received training as a cabinetmaker at an early age. In his obituary, the *New Zealand Herald* said that he became so skilful that, at the age of 16, his employer sent him to England 'to execute some particularly fine and delicate work in a church in London'.[3] Francoeur impressed everyone

---

1 *Auckland Star*, 1 December 1925.
2 Thomas Le Clair De Francoeur, marriage certificate, District of Auckland, 23 July 1925.
3 *New Zealand Herald*, 1 December 1925.

with the quality of his work, and he was commissioned to undertake more projects around England. Thus began a life of travel and adventure that would take him to many parts of the globe and have him participate in many important events.

On 2 February 1852, Francoeur was in Paris at the invitation of writer Alexandre Dumas to attend the premiere of the stage adaption of his *La Dame aux Camélias* (*The Lady with the Camellias*) at the Théâtre du Vaudeville. Many years later, on Tuesday 5 May 1925, he was invited by Miss Bayly (a sister of JP Bayly) of Universal Pictures (the theatre was located opposite the Old Pier Hotel, the building now occupied by Jack's Handicraft) to be a guest of honour at the screening of *La Camille*. In the *Fiji Times* of Thursday 7 May 1925, he thanked Miss Bayly for the honour and said he thoroughly enjoyed the picture 'which faithfully portrayed the scenes as he saw them four score years ago' in Paris.

Francoeur's thirst for adventure saw him participate in two wars. The first was in the 1879 war between the British Empire and the Zulu Kingdom in South Africa. In 1885, he fought on the government side against the rebellion by Louis Riel. Riel was a Canadian politician and the leader of the Métis people of the Canadian Prairies. He led two uprisings against the Canadian Government to preserve the culture and rights of his people. In 1923, Francoeur also claimed that he had had 'an accident' in the American Civil War in 1862, but nothing further is known about this.

There is an indication that Francoeur spent some time in New York. He was a Freemason and attended several meetings of the Lodge of Fiji when he was in Suva. There is no record of his attendance at Lodge meetings between 1910 and 1918. However, he attended meetings between 1921 and 1924. His last recorded presence was in 1925, on 19 and 24 June. The secretary added the notation 'Acacia 48 NYC' next to his name for the 24 June meeting. Acacia was his 'Mother Lodge', and being a member of that lodge, he probably spent quite a bit of time in New York City. The exact dates of his stay, however, remain unknown. He likely did not become an associate member of the Lodge of Fiji because Acacia was under a jurisdiction not recognised by the governing body, the United Grand Lodge of England.

Francoeur spent several years in Vancouver, Canada, before making the trip to the Pacific. *Henderson's British Columbia Gazetteer and Directory* for 1889 lists a 'Francoeur, T.' as a mill hand for Muirhead & Mann, but it is not clear if it is the same individual.[4] The *Henderson's British Columbia Gazetteer and Directory* for 1890 lists a 'Francoeur, L. T.' as a woodcarver for Cassady and Company.[5] *Williams' Vancouver and New Westminster Cities Directory 1890* also lists 'Francoeur, T. L.' as an artistic woodworker at 317 Pender.[6] The 1890 records are almost certainly of Francoeur. Francoeur also suffixed his name with 'Late of Vancouver, B.C.' in his *Fiji Times* ads in 1910.

Francoeur arrived in Suva from Vancouver on the *Aorangi* on 25 November 1908. He later stated that he had intended to go from North America to Auckland but stayed in Suva because he fell in love with the place. Francoeur also said that he spent time on several other islands but makes no mention of the names.

On arrival, Francoeur established two companies in Suva: the Suva Funeral Parlour, which supplied caskets, coffins and a hearse service, and the Fiji Novelty Works, his furniture business. We learn much about Francoeur during his time at Suva from advertisements, letters to the editor, and the minutes of the Suva Municipal Council meetings in the *Fiji Times* between 1908 and 1925. Francoeur had a penchant for announcing the minor aspects of his life in the papers. Perhaps his most memorable attribute was his great sense of humour. His ads and his encounters with people were never short of fun and drama. The items from the *Fiji Times* provide insight into the man and his life and reveal his rapier wit. Francoeur was also not afraid of verbal jousts with those who offended him in face-to-face encounters and the media.

On Saturday 15 January 1910, Francoeur announced in the *Fiji Times* that he would not be found at his place of business as he was 'taking a day off' to celebrate his 76th birthday. The *Fiji Times* said that Francoeur was a Canadian of French-Scotch descent and combined the volatility of the one race with the stability of the other to a very unusual degree.

---

4   *Henderson's British Columbia gazetteer and directory: Including a complete classified business directory of British Columbia for the year 1889* (Victoria, British Columbia: LG Henderson, 1889), 457.
5   *Henderson's British Columbia gazetteer and directory: Containing complete street and alphabetical directories of the cities Vancouver and Victoria and a complete classified business directory* (Victoria, British Columbia: LG Henderson, 1890), 315.
6   Thomas Draper, *Williams' Vancouver & New Westminster cities directory, 1890, containing general provincial information* (Vancouver: RT Williams, 1890), 105.

The *Fiji Times* issue of Wednesday 27 July 1910 notified the public that Francoeur intended to construct a modern and 'unique' two-storey building at the corner of Murray and Pratt streets, next to his existing premises. The ground floor was to have a 'grand dining area' for around 32 patrons and would be a place where 'a busy man can get an appetising "snack" at any hour'. The upstairs would house the showroom or 'Arcade' stocked with 'groceries, hardware, cutlery, silver, paint and glass and [chinaware]'. Francoeur also planned to have a photographic studio, an 'imposing picture gallery', and '18 airy cool and inviting double [bedrooms]'. The two floors were to be connected by a grand staircase. The staircase entrance was to be called the bazaar room and 'fitted either side with stalls of ornamental and useful articles ranging in value from 1s. to 5s'. Francoeur intended to make his new establishment 'quite the best thing in Suva in all departments'. The *Fiji Times* said that although old in years, Francoeur was in 'excellent health and in energy and [could] give most of our young men long odds and then beat them "hands down"'.

In 1911 Francoeur placed an ad in the *Fiji Times* that first appeared on Tuesday 10 January and that ran for the next few weeks, in which he sought a first-class cabinetmaker for his business, the Fiji Novelty Works. He offered 15/- per day in wages and said that the prospective employee had to be a 'good all around man' and that 'no lazy bone need apply'.

In the *Fiji Times* issue of Tuesday 28 February 1911, Francoeur announced that the Fiji Novelty Works had opened a new showroom in Victoria Parade with 'a very handsome and attractive display'. He also said he had 'useful and ornamental articles in various woods, the specialising being work in Yaka, which should be seen to be appreciated'.

On Thursday 27 April 1911, the *Fiji Times* ran an article that said a vacant plot of land opposite the Cable Office, which weeds had long overrun, had been cleared and the rustic kern removed. It noted that there had been rumours in town that Mr Francoeur had obtained a 10-year lease of a portion of the land, and he intended to erect a two-storey building.

In 1913, Francoeur took out a full-page ad in the *Fiji Times* announcing a 'Grand Exhibition and Discount Sale'. With his usual wit and eccentricity, the ad read: 'Ladies, don't forget to come and see the old man. He is not dead yet; the Town Board has not been able to kill him; he is too tough for them all.' The exhibition opened on Wednesday 5 July and closed on Saturday 5 August.

6. THE GRAND OLD MAN AND THE PRINCE OF THIEVES

Another ad from 18 February 1913 read: 'The Town Council having cut their weeds in Pratt Street, MR DE FRANCOUER has CUT his PRICES at his wonderful Clearance Sale of BEAUTIFUL FURNITURE.'

An item in the *Fiji Times* from 12 July of the same year informed readers that Francoeur '[did] not consider it necessary to do more than to announce in his advertisement that his factory [was] running at high speed all the time'.

Francoeur's most over-the-top advertisement appeared in the Saturday 13 August 1910 issue of the *Fiji Times* as a four-page supplement. In it, 'Professor T. L. de Francoeur' provided a complete catalogue of his services, products and prices. He offered to give a free coffin to all, 'white or coloured', who had lost a family member and were 'too poor to pay for a coffin', as long as they were able to satisfy him that they were 'respectable and worthy people'. Francoeur warned patrons not to trust 'bogus and hypocrite agents', claiming that due to his 'sixty-three years of reverent and careful attention to all the different points of funeral undertaking, and the study of the embalming of the body, from the old Egyptian dates down to the present time', he was 'the only reliable and responsible funeral contractor and conductor in Suva, or in any other place on the Pacific'.

Francoeur took a keen interest in the municipal affairs of Suva. Mr WH Johnson's resignation as a town councillor in 1911 presented him with an opportunity to put his interest to practical action. Francoeur announced his intention to stand as a candidate in the *Fiji Times* (Tuesday 21 March) and said he would address the ratepayers at the Town Hall at 8 pm on Saturday 25 March. On 25 March, the returning officer, WM Good, announced that an extraordinary election of a member for the municipal council of Suva was set to take place on Tuesday 28 March 1911, at the Town Hall between 10 am and 2 pm. He provided a list of the candidates vying for the vacant seat: Joseph Harper, nominated by Robert Crompton and Arthur J Ratford; S Porges, nominated by SL Lazarus and HM Scott; and TL De Francoeur, put forward by Arthur H Ogilvie and Arthur G Griffiths (he was the son of *Fiji Times*' founder, George L Griffiths).

Francoeur's meeting on the evening of 25 March was marked by an overbrimming of laughter, cheers and jeers. The event more resembled a night at a comedy club than a gathering of concerned ratepayers and the *Fiji Times* in their issue of Tuesday 28 March 1911 aptly headlined it, 'Fun Fast and Furious'.

The audience began filling up the hall at an early hour to the accompaniment of music by the Weaver's Orchestra, and soon the place was filled to the rafters. At the appointed time of 8 pm, the deputy mayor, JB Turner, 'in a happy little speech, terse and to the point, introduced Mr Francoeur, who was greeted in most hearty fashion'. Francoeur wasted no time in getting to his election manifesto. He began by saying that his campaign's first pillar 'was independence, void of all partiality and selfishness' and that he would do everything to benefit the ratepayers or resign. This assurance brought cheers and applause from the audience.

Francoeur then went to the heart of his manifesto, which was beautifying Suva. He said that he had come to Suva as a temporary rest stop on his journey to New Zealand but had taken a fancy to the place. He said he had been to other islands but considered Suva the 'Jewel of the Pacific' and felt that it could be made even better through hard work and dedication. He said the main thing to do was to concentrate on sanitation and sewerage. Francoeur explained he would upgrade the roads and footpaths, embark on an electrification project and ensure the upkeep of the public swimming baths.

At the mention of the latter, one of his chief hecklers of the night, one Captain Callaghan, stood up and, despite a chorus of hisses and cries, asked Francoeur if he would take a bath himself once a month. This comment sparked a round of raucous laughter, and Francoeur added to the fray by saying that he would bathe once a week if he had dirty work. It was clear who was the star of the show and had the sympathy of the audience, for every time Mr Green and Captain Callaghan rose to ask questions, they were jeered and heckled and told to 'sit down'. Francoeur's speech continued with more promises and digressions, and there was more cheering with staccato bursts of jeers from the two antagonists, Mr Green and Captain Callaghan. The chairman had to interpose several times to stop Mr Green's mocking and taunting. After his presentation, the orchestra struck up 'Marching through Georgia' as Mr J Harper, another candidate, took to the stage but in more subdued tones, without the same outburst of cheering and celebration from the audience that marked Francoeur's grand entrance.

But despite attempts by his detractors to derail his campaign, Francoeur's address to the ratepayers seems to have done the trick, for on Tuesday 28 March 1911, the *Fiji Times* announced that he had won the election, 170 out of the 389 votes cast. The other candidates, J Harper and S Porges, received 156 votes and 60 votes, respectively.

6. THE GRAND OLD MAN AND THE PRINCE OF THIEVES

After being elected, Francoeur went straight to the business of bringing about change. At a municipal council meeting at the Town Hall on Monday 19 June 1911, Francoeur addressed a large gathering of ratepayers giving what the *Fiji Times* called 'a dissertation on municipal matters'. His tone was very cryptic, and he said that he had called the meeting to reveal some facts of what had taken place since his election to the council but that he would not expose everything. With the usual accompaniment of cheers and heckling and the usual dose of pointless banter and digressions that had become the hallmark of his interventions in these public meetings, Francoeur voiced his disapproval of the performance of the council. He said that the condition of the steps in Suva Street, the general disposition of Amy Street, the lack of progress on the development of the Pratt Street sidewalk, the wholesale granting of building permits to Indians and the want of attention on the part of the Works Committee were an indictment against the council's ineffectiveness.

He also strongly objected to the treatment of his motion to use the Town Hall for board meetings. He gave an ultimatum that he would not remain on the council for too long given the state of affairs. His proposal that he would provide boxes for his fellow councilmen and dump them into the Pacific brought on a round of wild laughter and applause. The *Fiji Times* of Tuesday 20 June 1911 reported that the meeting did not accomplish much, 'but most people agreed that [it] was better fun than the average picture-show – and cost nothing'.

On Monday 30 October 1913, Francoeur was forced to cancel a meeting of ratepayers at the Town Hall due to inclement weather. However, the cancellation caused more trouble than he would have liked. The next day, a ratepayer calling himself 'Fresh Air Meeting' wrote a tongue-in-cheek letter to the editor of the *Fiji Times* designed to rile the 'old man'.

The letter titled 'Alice, Where Art Thou?' described how the writer and his friends hired several cabs and arrived at the venue at 8:05 pm only to find Francoeur absent. He protested that several hundred people waited like 'ducks in the rain' but that the proposed meeting did not occur. He said should it be that he and his friends 'have contracted the "flue"' due to standing outside in the rain and cold, Francoeur should pay for their doctor's bills. He also questioned Francoeur's credibility, asking whether the old man had made an impact as a councillor or if he had been 'giving us more B.S. (I mean brandy and soda)'. He said that the ratepayers had had enough of the 'Canadian bluff'.

On Thursday 16 November 1911, a livid Francoeur wrote a rejoinder to the letter by 'Fresh Air Meeting', calling it a slur against him 'by some person from the Suva Petticoat Lane'. He said the letter contained nothing but lies 'against an old man who has sacrificed his time and money during the last six months against a Town Board Works Committee of experimentalists'. He explained that he was at the venue with three others until 8:10 pm, and no one else was there. He signed off by saying, 'good-bye, Mugwump, alias Mudbound, alias "Fresh Air Meeting," alias Hon. of the Suva Petticoat Lane. From your great grand-dad, Cr. De Francoeur, Suva Town Board (Not ashamed of his name)'.

However, this was not the end of the matter. Over the next few weeks, several individuals wrote letters to the editor of the *Fiji Times*, both criticising and defending Francoeur. A 'Voter' wrote on Saturday 18 November 1911, saying that the 'Old Man' was 'a connoisseur of ignorance'. One of the individuals who came to Francoeur's defence was J Harper, who had stood against him in the Town Board elections. Harper said that the ratepayers had preferred Francoeur in the polls and that he was 'grateful to them for their choice'. He noted that Francoeur had 'done more good by muddling', and he admired the fact that age had not 'made the slightest difference in that gentleman's abilities'.

In March 1923, Francoeur stood as a candidate for the third time in the Suva Municipal Council elections (the second was in 1913 when he lost), styling himself 'The Old Warhorse'. He addressed the electors by saying that he 'was only 49 years, no he meant 94 years old, and he felt well and active'. He was the only candidate who canvassed door to door, but unfortunately, this was not enough to secure victory. After his loss, he thanked all those who voted for him – 'thirteen of you with myself, making fourteen votes' – as well as those who made promises to vote. To the latter, he spoke with his usual searing wit: 'they had turned their coats, while others had put on their double faces, forgetting their promises to me ... my most sincere thanks to them changing their faces, and for the trouble, they took to turn their coat over.'

On Friday 7 November 1913, someone broke into Francoeur's private room between five and six in the morning. The burglar ransacked the cupboards and a chest of drawers and attempted to open his strongbox with a screwdriver. Fortunately, Francoeur had put all his money in his pocket before leaving his residence.

Francoeur directly addressed the intruder in the *Fiji Times* issue of Saturday 8 November 1913, mocking him with his usual caustic wit. He called him a 'donkey' and said that the next time 'he wishes to try his hand at his thieving game', he would give him the key to his box 'or something else that he will probably never forget'. He spoke to 'burglars of all denominations', saying because he wished to spare them the trouble of 'carrying a heavy load to Hospital', he would in future leave the door of his room open and the box unlocked. He did not mind 'so long as they [did] not steal any coffins or the hearse during the smallpox scare'.

Although he attributed his longevity to the fact that he never married, the records show that he got married in Auckland on 23 July 1915, to a widow named Armandine Marc Souron, née Corvisier. She was the daughter of Eugene Corvisier, a farmer, and Marie Corvisier, née Monchot. Her first husband passed away in December 1908. Souron was 37 at the time of her marriage to Francoeur, who was 66. She died in Auckland on 11 November 1918. She left no children to either spouse. Her probate papers show 'Thomas' was her executor.

After Souron's death, Thomas may have returned to Fiji, as there is a note, dated 3 April 1919, in the probate papers that nothing is to be done without reference to Henry Hubert Ostler, solicitor for Thomas De Francoeur of Suva. This caveat was removed on 2 July, and he seems to have returned to New Zealand. However, it appears he went back and forth between Auckland and Suva from 1915 to the 1920s. Francoeur never remarried, and during his final years, his only companions were two fox terriers that 'shared his bed'.

An advertisement for 'Furniture Factory' appeared under the 'Businesses for Sale' column in the *New Zealand Herald* (31 March 1916). The sale was of Francoeur's furniture company, and the ad described it as the 'largest and most up-to-date factory in Suva, Fiji, with the best connections in the islands'. The ad explained that the 'reason for selling is the owner is retiring on account of failing old age'. Interested buyers were asked to contact Messrs Phillippe and Impey Ltd., Queen Street, Auckland, or inquire directly with the proprietor. The company that eventually purchased Francoeur's business thought they were getting a bargain by convincing him to accept an annuity, paid in monthly instalments, until his death. However, according to the *Auckland Star* of 1 December 1925, 'the old man held the best end of the bargain, and drew his annuity with regularity'. By the time Francoeur died in his 90s, he had received a sum that was several times the property's value.

After retiring, Francoeur kept an establishment at 30 Hercules Street, Suva, that he let out to lodgers. The *Fiji Times* frequently published ads for the establishment. One of the ads said the 'grand old house' formerly owned by AH Ogilvie had been renovated and converted into lodging by the new owner, TL Francoeur. Situated between the Fiji Club and the vicarage, the establishment had 'first class furnished rooms' and were available from between 6 shillings to 18 shillings per week. Also, it contained a reading room supplied with 'the best of reading, books, magazines, and papers', and had a parlour, lounge, verandah, swing, flower garden and grove for use by lodgers. Music was also provided 'whenever required'. The lodging was for 'respectable, sober, young and single men or widowers', and Francoeur stressed that any lodger 'coming home intoxicated and disturbing the other lodgers, or the peace of others, [would] be turned out without notice'.

The *Auckland Star* of 2 February 1923, under the headline 'Fiji's Grand Old Man', reported that Francoeur had recently celebrated his 94th birthday. The newspaper said that Francoeur 'entertained a large company of guests and kept them amused all afternoon by telling all sorts of episodes in his long career'. It added that despite his age, Francoeur '[could] read easily without glasses the smallest of print' and took a daily walk downtown 'to have a yarn with old friends'. The newspaper also noted that Francoeur was keenly interested in writing his memoirs as his memory would not be as sharp in the coming years.

The *Fiji Times* also congratulated him on his 94th birthday. It said Francoeur was in 'fine health' and made his way daily downtown 'with considerable vigour'. It said that he received many visitors 'at his pretty home on Gladstone Road', who stopped by to wish him well. The paper noted that like Johnny Walker (whisky), which '[had] a reputation for still going strong', Francoeur was nearly 100 and also 'still going strong'. Two years later, on Thursday 15 January 1925, the *Fiji Times* congratulated him on yet another birthday. The paper explained that although Francoeur was 96, he was sure he was 98.

6. THE GRAND OLD MAN AND THE PRINCE OF THIEVES

Not much was heard from Francoeur in 1924 and early 1925, but on Monday 30 March 1925, he placed an ad in the *Fiji Times* announcing that he was offering for private sale at his residence at 21 Gladstone Road, all his household furniture and a pedestal gramophone with 164 records. This announcement was uncanny because eight months later, he died. However, it seems Francoeur had long prepared for the inevitable.

On Tuesday 6 January 1970, the *Fiji Times* published an article on Herbert Spencer Faddy, a Suva resident in the 1920s, who had spent his last days at the Pearce Home. Faddy told an amusing anecdote about Francoeur – there seemed to be a lapse in his memory, however, as he referred to Francoeur as Le Feveur – 'who used to invite friends and customers into his bedroom to admire a handsome coffin he had prepared for himself'.

Thomas Le Clair De Francoeur, cabinetmaker, undertaker, soldier, auctioneer, town councillor and the son of a Duke, died at the War Memorial Hospital, Suva, on Sunday 22 November 1925, at the grand old age of 96. He had been ill and admitted to the hospital for a week before passing away. The attending physician, Eric Molesworth, declared the cause of death to be heart failure due to old age. Obituaries for Francoeur appeared in the *Fiji Times*, *The Herald* (Melbourne), the *Auckland Star* and the *New Zealand Herald*, the latter running the headline 'Death in exile'. He was buried at the Old Suva Cemetery on Monday 23 November on plot no. 7193. Rev. Hands of the Church of England conducted the funeral service. It is certain that his funeral was attended by hundreds of people, both admirers and wellwishers and even those whom he offended at some point in his life (there were many). There must have been both tears and laughter as the townsfolk remembered the 'grand old man of Suva'.

As a postscript to the account of a remarkable and eccentric individual's life, the author adds the following. Although the *Fiji Times* (Monday 23 November 1925) mentions a photograph of him in full Masonic regalia, the author has been unable to find any extant photos. Francoeur's only description is in CW Whonsbon-Aston's *Pacific Irishman*.[7] Speaking of the beautifully carved high altar placed in the Church of the Holy Redeemer in Levuka by Rev. AE Frost as a memorial to Floyd, he writes:

---

7   Charles W Whonsbon-Aston, *Pacific Irishman*, William Floyd memorial lecture, inaugural lecture (Stanmore: Australian Board of Missions, 1970). Available at: anglicanhistory.org/oceania/whonsbon-aston1970.html.

'The work was done by a French Canadian of Huguenot stock, M. le Francoeur, a tall, very dignified, handsome gentleman with a full set of Habsburg facial fungus, as particular in his work as he was in his person.'[8]

* * *

Between November 1912 and August 1913, an individual named Dwarka, who styled himself the 'Prince of Thieves', committed a series of what the *Fiji Times* of the day called 'daring robberies' in Suva town and its suburbs. Though he managed to evade the law for much of the time, he was arrested and convicted on four occasions.

On the first occasion, on 30 November 1912, he was given 12 strokes of birch for being on the premises of Sturt Ogilvie and Co. for some unlawful purpose. Despite the lashing, he continued his crime spree, breaking into Mr Porges's store on 12 December and making off with a gold wristwatch and 2 pounds, 2 shillings in coin. Dwarka was later arrested and appeared in court on 24 December, charged with larceny. He pleaded guilty to the charge, and this time the authorities punished him with 24 strokes of the birch.

A few days after his conviction, Dwarka entered into the service of one Mrs Lee of Toorak, under the false name of Jimmy. While engaged as a domestic servant, he stole a Kruger sovereign brooch, valued at £2, and two purses, valued at 3 pence, one containing 2 shillings, 6 pence in cash. He appeared before Acting Chief Police Magistrate Henniker Heaton on 6 January 1913, charged with larceny for this latest offence.

The police prosecutor, Inspector Barnett, said that Dwarka had made 'a bold confession of his guilt', but other individuals implicated would be presented later in court charged with receiving stolen property. Although Magistrate Heaton sentenced Dwarka to six months imprisonment, he suggested that the governor might pardon him on the condition that some European would take charge of him, for you see, Dwarka, the Prince of Thieves, the infamous burglar of Suva, was a mere 10 years old and the vulnerability of one so young in years was sufficiently apparent to the police magistrate. One can imagine 10-year-old Dwarka sitting in the box awaiting sentencing, shedding copious tears to win leniency.

---

8   Ibid., Chapter 16.

Despite the editorial opinion of the *Fiji Times* that 'he is not exactly the sort of servant the average person is looking for', it seemed Dwarka's case weighed heavily on Henniker Heaton's conscience. Over the next few weeks, he tried to find ways of disciplining him while keeping him out of prison. A few days after convicting the boy, he interviewed his father, Gangaram, a cook, to see if he could intervene. The father was distraught and informed Heaton that he had tried his utmost to reform his son through whipping and various other equally persuasive means. Unfortunately, he had to concede that he had been unable to mend his son's ways.

On 7 January 1913, Heaton wrote to the colonial secretary,[9] suggesting that something should be done urgently about Dwarka, as he was afraid the boy had all the makings of 'an incorrigible rogue and thief'. He explained that since there was no provision in the colony's laws by which a magistrate could order police supervision, he had no choice but to sentence him to six months imprisonment. However, he would recommend that the governor remit the sentence 'on such terms as he might consider fitting'. He prayed that the governor would pardon Dwarka on the understanding that he be handed over to a European, perhaps a police or prison official as a domestic servant until the completion of his six months sentence. He pointed out that such a course of action was taken previously in the case of another Indian boy convicted by the Supreme Court, who was handed over to the care of Mr Cyril Francis for a year or two.

Records show that between 9 and 14 January, after Dwarka's sentencing, there was a series of high-level exchanges between government officials on the boy's fate.[10] On 9 January, the inspector general constabulary wrote to Magistrate Henniker Heaton suggesting that while Dwarka was in jail, he be under the immediate care and supervision of the keeper of the jail. He also proposed that under no circumstances he be allowed to mix with the more seasoned prisoners, who would impact him negatively. Heaton replied the next day, enquiring whether the keeper of the jail would agree to such an arrangement and, if not, was there a possibility that the Methodist mission could take charge of him. Three days later, on 13 January the inspector general constabulary informed Heaton that the keeper of the jail would not take Dwarka as a servant but agreed to keep him separated from the other adult criminals.

---

9   Colonial Secretary's Office (CSO) correspondence, MP 206/1913; all CSO files held at the National Archives of Fiji (NAF).
10 CSO MP 206/1913.

Later that day, Heaton informed the colonial secretary that Dwarka's father, Gangaram, had expressed the desire to take him to Cicia, Lau, to put him in the service of his former employer, Walter Atkin Hickson. Walter Hickson was the son of the late Captain Robert Atkin Hickson and manager of the island estate. Gangaram explained that Hickson had explicitly asked for Dwarka and felt he was a suitable person to take charge of his son. Heaton told the colonial secretary that, in his view, their primary objective was to get Dwarka out of Suva and all the temptations that came with living in an urban environment. He, however, had reservations about sending him to the Methodist mission station at Davuilevu because he felt that Dwarka was likely to corrupt the other boys, given 'the trouble he has caused in Suva'. He said whatever the case, it was imperative that the boy 'should not be allowed to become familiarised with the Gaol'.

The colonial secretary responded to Heaton on 14 January saying that after their phone conversation the previous evening, he had instructed the inspector general constabulary, Mr Francis, to interview Gangaram further. He noted that Gangaram gave Francis his assurance that he would take his son to Cicia and hand him over to Hickson for a year. He also expressed his intention to return to India with his son after he completed his indenture with Hickson.[11]

After the various negotiations and assurances, Magistrate Heaton presented Dwarka's case before Governor Ernest Sweet-Escott. The latter agreed to extend his pardon upon the condition that Dwarka be transferred to the Cicia Estate as soon as possible and enter into Walter Atkin Hickson's domestic service for a year. So, having been given the governor's pardon, young Dwarka was released from Suva Prison on 16 January at 8 pm and handed over to the care of one Constable Peni. The constable escorted him the next day to the *Amara* bound for Cicia and handed him over to his father, Gangaram.

There is no record of Dwarka's time at Cicia, but Hickson returned to Suva a few months later with the lad for reasons unknown. Unfortunately, upon his return to Suva, Dwarka absconded. An irate Mr Hickson filed papers in court charging him with neglect of duty as a domestic servant. The few months spent in Hickson's company at Cicia did not seem to have fully reformed the boy, and it was not before long he was back to his

---

11   CSO MP 206/1913.

6. THE GRAND OLD MAN AND THE PRINCE OF THIEVES

old ways. The *Fiji Times* of Thursday 7 August 1913, announced the boy's return to Suva and his most recent encounter with the law with a simple, 'Dwarka again'.

On this latest breach of the law, Dwarka appeared in the Police Magistrates Court on 7 August, charged with being in possession of stolen property. The police prosecutor described how the boy went one evening to the residence of one Mr JH Thompson looking for work. Thompson refused him employment and later discovered that someone had ransacked his son's room and stolen many items. He reported the matter to the police, who, from the information given by his son, recognised the culprit to be Dwarka.

The police issued a warrant for his arrest and later found him in Toorak about to enter the service of a European. When arrested, he had many items, including opera glasses, binoculars, a tin of cocoa, a knife, a coat and other objects, presumed to be stolen. Dwarka pleaded guilty to larceny, and Acting Chief Police Magistrate Cyril Francis sentenced him to six months imprisonment with hard labour and 12 strokes with a birch. However, he said that given the boy's tender age, he would communicate with the governor for a pardon.

Later that day, Magistrate Francis wrote to the colonial secretary, Eyre Hutson, furnishing him with the details of Dwarka's case.[12] He explained that he was faced with the same dilemma as his predecessor, Henniker Heaton, whether to condemn a child to prison 'to mix with criminals and undesirables' or find alternative ways to reform him. He explained that a more significant objection existed, which was 'to his being at large in Suva while such an incorrigible thief'.

Magistrate Francis said that despite Dwarka's guilty plea to larceny, he recommended favourable consideration. As a start, he recommended that the authorities cancel Dwarka's service with Mr Hickson as he was no longer living at Cicia. He also suggested that if Dwarka was willing to enter into indenture to the inspector general of constabulary as a domestic servant to the Officer's Quarters Totogo, or elsewhere at a low rate of pay for a term of two or three years, the governor could perhaps grant him a pardon as on the previous occasion. He felt that this was the only efficient method of dealing with him and that supervision at a police

---

12   CSO MP 6493/1913.

station would tend a great deal towards reforming him. He gave the example of an Indian boy named Ramcharan, who had previously been placed in his care for three years after being pardoned for murder.

Meanwhile, a few miles from Suva, at Nausori, an individual had been following Dwarka's misadventures with a great deal of sympathy and concern. Rev. Cyril Bavin, superintendent of the Nausori Circuit of the Methodist Church Indian Mission, wrote to the inspector general of police on 12 August, saying he was disturbed to read in the *Fiji Times* that Dwarka had been before the court again and sentenced to six months imprisonment. He said that the Indian Mission of the Methodist Church had a boarding school for boys at Nausori where several lads 'with equally bad reputations' had been sent but who were now 'well-behaved children'. He offered to take charge of Dwarka for the duration of his six months sentence and report to the authorities at regular intervals regarding the boy's behaviour and welfare.[13]

On 1 September, the governor wrote to the keeper of Suva Prison, informing him of his decision to pardon Dwarka. He said that it appeared desirable to him to extend mercy to Dwarka upon the condition that Rev. Cyril Bavin took charge of him at his Mission School Dilkusha for six months. Following the governor's orders, the inspector of constabulary, Rewa, handed over Dwarka to Rev. Cyril Bavin on 6 September.[14]

During his time at Dilkusha, Dwarka had been under the care and watchful eye of sisters Mabel M Graham and Hester J Clark. On 17 December, Rev. Bavin wrote to the inspector general of constabulary, presenting a report on Dwarka's conduct and progress.[15] He said the sisters-in-charge had been very happy with his progress, seeing nothing of the behaviour that had perpetually landed him in trouble with the authorities. The sisters had also been pleased with his conduct and performance in school, stating that he had made good progress in Roman-Urdu, English and arithmetic. They said that the change in his attitude and character was further apparent from the fact that his peers no longer referred to him as Dwarka but as 'Naya Dil' (New Heart).

---

13   CSO MP 6493/1913.
14   CSO MP 6493/1913.
15   CSO MP 10226/1913.

6. THE GRAND OLD MAN AND THE PRINCE OF THIEVES

Rev. Bavin told the inspector general of constabulary that the lad had given no trouble and was rapidly improving mentally and physically. He hoped that when his appointed term of six months at Dilkusha came to an end, he would choose to remain for a further period. The acting colonial secretary, J Stewart, was so pleased with the boy's reformation that he wrote to Rev. Bavin on 31 December, thanking him for making such an effort. He said that the governor was happy to hear of the positive report.[16]

The correspondence between Stewart and Rev. Bavin was the last documented exchange between the authorities regarding Dwarka. There are also no further records regarding the lad's days at the boarding school at Davuilevu, and nothing is known about whether he continued his positive growth. However, the records show that he remained at Dilkusha beyond the six months he was allocated to stay, leaving in February 1916 after two and a half years. However, what happened to the boy after that, whether he returned to India with his father or stayed in Fiji, whether he reformed his ways for good or went back to a life of crime, is unclear. There is also nothing in the records about his mother.

There exists at Dilkusha today photographs of the children who lived there during Dwarka's brief stay. There are photographs of individuals who must have been his friends – Allah Diya, Chimdagu, Rajah, Daniel Wood, Rasuli, Bharat, Mohan, Ram Gharan, Ram Bharosa, Shamud Din, Jhinku, Masih Prakash and Shubrati Jack – and with whom he must have played, laughed and shared his sorrow and happiness. The author laments, however, that there exists no photograph of Dwarka, New Heart.

---

16 CSO MP 10226/1913.

Part 2.
Creations

7

Piecing Together a History of Suva Prison

Nicholas Halter

Suva Prison has long been an imposing concrete landmark in the capital of Fiji – whereas once its walls and buildings symbolised modernity and the progress of the British colony in Fiji, today they represent the decay and dereliction of incarceration. Constructed to be the main prison in the colony, Suva Prison in 2020 is one of 15 'correction centres' and serves as a receiving and remand centre. Despite its prominent position in the capital, little is known of the lives of its transient inhabitants. Not only have they been physically obscured behind the whitewashed coral walls that line Foster Road, they have also been lost within the colonial archive. What little remains tells a story of a racially divided Fiji under British colonial rule and haphazard efforts to regulate and control a dissident populace.

This chapter pieces together the archival remnants of Fiji's colonial prison system to chart the development of the Suva prison from its establishment in the new capital in the 1880s until the 1960s. It considers the construction of prison buildings, the segregation and classification of prisoners, the system of punishment and discipline that was imposed and the reforms to prison legislation and operations. The 1960s was a significant decade for Fiji's prisons, marked by the implementation of a new Fiji Prisons Act in 1966 that sought to address international standards for imprisonment and rehabilitation. It was also a decade when Suva Prison inmates prepared to move to a new facility at the same time as the country prepared for independence from Britain in 1970. Most of Fiji's colonial prison records from the late nineteenth century onwards were stored at Suva Prison and destroyed in a fire during a prison riot in 1979. What remains is a varied collection of papers from the Colonial Secretary's Office (CSO files), Legislative Council minutes and Annual Colonial Reports to Britain containing correspondence, prisoner records and statistics. As a result, scholars have relied on the account of BM Sellers, superintendent of prisons in 1962, who published the only documented history of Fiji's prison service in the *Proceedings of the Fiji Society*.[1] Piecing together the archival remnants of Fiji's colonial prison system offers an understanding of the institutionalised and racialised colonial hierarchies and assumptions of the twentieth century.

Construction

The first documented prison in Fiji was established in the town of Levuka on Ovalau island in the 1860s. Many of the inmates were Fijians who refused to pay taxes to the self-proclaimed Tui Viti, Ratu Seru Epenisa Cakobau. He was a Bauan chief who had gained ascendancy during a time of colonial contact and commercial enterprise and had attempted to set up a formal government to control his territories, which were mostly confined to the eastern provinces and coastal areas of Fiji. Prior to the prison's establishment, Fijians who were alleged to have committed crimes were arrested and detained aboard visiting warships, and in some cases taken to foreign countries illegally and against their will, such as the well-publicised case of a Rewan man, Rō Veidovi, in the 1840s.[2] Levuka had the largest concentration of European residents in the late 1800s, and so it was chosen as the capital of the British colony and the site of the first colonial prison in Fiji in 1874 when the Deed of Cession was signed. The exact location of the prison is unclear – reports from the *Fiji Times* newspaper suggest the prison was surrounded by an 8-foot wooden fence and was situated across an open square opposite the wooden police station then known as 'Totoga'.[3] Surviving colonial reports suggest the

---

1   BM Sellers, 'Development of Fiji prison service', *Proceedings of the Fiji Society 1955–1963* 6 (1962).
2   Antony Adler, 'The capture and curation of the Cannibal "Vendovi": Reality and representation of a Pacific frontier', *The Journal of Pacific History* 49, no. 3 (2014): 255–82, doi.org/10.1080/00223344.2014.914623.
3   Matilda Simmons, 'First police station', *Fiji Times,* 25 January 2020. 'Totoga' may have been a reference to the Tongan native police who worked there, but this name later changed to 'Totogo'.

prison was small, with only eight cells in 1894.⁴ The British established administrative centres around the country, which included approximately 20 lock-ups supervised by European police officers and district officials. They were usually located wherever a magistrate was. These lock-ups began as simple huts with reed fences and were gradually replaced with stone and crushed coral structures built by the inmates. One of these lock-ups on the mainland of Viti Levu at Namena (now called Naburenivalu Village) in Tailevu province likely held prisoners that could not be accommodated in Levuka. Like many other prisons in the British Empire, Namena kept unwelcome individuals at arm's length from the colonial centre. Interestingly, villagers have since reinterpreted this colonial legacy by claiming Namena village was chosen for a prison because of the might of their warriors who served as prison guards.⁵ Namena prison was closed in 1888.⁶

Prisons played an important part in maintaining British colonial rule. Not all chiefdoms had agreed to the Deed of Cession signed by Cakobau in 1874, and there were many disgruntled Fijians, particularly in the western districts of Viti Levu, that resisted British rule. Robert Nicole has documented indigenous resistance during the so-called 'Little War' of 1875 in the Colo region.⁷ As Nicole has shown, British forces were ill-equipped to fight a protracted war in the rugged highlands of the Colo region and, for a time, were unable to gain superiority in their colonial mission. However one successful tactic for pacifying the population was to imprison key leaders. By removing antagonistic individuals from their villages and placing them in urban prisons some distance away, the British found they could discourage rebellious activities in the rural areas. This trend continued throughout the twentieth century. Notorious Fijian leader Apolosi Nawai was jailed and later exiled to Rotuma in the early 1920s for his critical views of the Colonial Government, for example.

In 1882 the capital was shifted to Suva on the main island of Viti Levu to allow for further expansion of the town, and it quickly became a central hub in the British Pacific empire, and in the Pacific region generally. It is

---

4   Colony of Fiji, *Blue book of Fiji for 1894* (Suva: Government Printer, 1894), 199.
5   'Namena Tailevu – Noda Gauna', YouTube, 16 July 2010, youtu.be/9KeZfVGY8IY (site discontinued).
6   Colonial Secretary's Office (CSO) F88.2241, CSO Secretariat Files, National Archives of Fiji (NAF).
7   Robert Nicole, *Disturbing history: Resistance in early colonial Fiji* (Suva: University of the South Pacific Press, 2018).

not clear when the prison was first built, but it likely began as a series of huts behind a reed fence and was gradually replaced with coral rock buildings in the late nineteenth century.[8] Both the prison and mental hospital were located close to one another on the outskirts of the town, along with the Lovonilase cemetery. As institutions of incarceration, it was important for both spaces to be situated away from the capital. The low-lying land around Walu Bay where the prison was constructed was once occupied by the *kai* Walu or fishermen according to Colman Wall's history of precolonial Suva.[9] Other indigenous settlements were located on the ridge above Walu Bay, most notably the rocky outcrop known as Uluvatu, but were gradually displaced by colonial Australian planters who acquired land. The last major Fijian settlement in Suva, once located at the southern end of the peninsula near the present-day Fiji Museum, was relocated to Suvavou ('New Suva'), not far from the prison and mental hospital. One of the pragmatic justifications for moving prisoners, mental patients and indigenous people to the edge of Suva was the availability of land for gardening.[10] Symbolically, the move kept these groups of people out of sight and out of mind, to be joined in the twentieth century by the town's rubbish dump.

According to a report by the National Trust of Fiji, the prison was initially called Nasēsē, derived from the Fijian word *sese* meaning 'wrong or foolish'. The people who went there were also called *na sese*.[11] Another explanation may be that the prison was originally located at Nasēsē in close proximity to the police compound at Nasova, before it was moved to Korovou sometime in the early 1880s. Nasova, like Totogo and Draiba, was one of a number of placenames that were transferred from Levuka to Suva during the shift of capital.

---

8   According to BM Sellers, 'I am told by old colonists that the gaol was composed of a collection of huts behind a reed fence and that the road stopped at the foot of Old Hospital Hill'. Sellers, 'Development of Fiji prison service', 46. Robert Nicole's chapter in this collection identifies Suva prison on a map of the town dated 1882.
9   Colman Wall, 'Historical notes on Suva', ed. Paul Geraghty, *Domodomo* 10, no. 2 (1996): 28–39.
10   Historian Jacqueline Leckie also noted it was considered beneficial for a hospital to have 'breeze'. Jacqueline Leckie, *Colonizing madness: Asylum and community in Fiji* (Honolulu: University of Hawai'i Press, 2019), doi.org/10.2307/j.ctvgs09bn.
11   Bart van Aller, *Suva gaol* (Suva: National Trust of Fiji, 2015). Other interpretations of *na sese* may exist. 'Sese' can also be translated as 'to wander' or 'to lose one's way'. Colman Wall claims the suburb of Nasēsē at the southern end of the peninsula was named for the waves breaking there.

7. PIECING TOGETHER A HISTORY OF SUVA PRISON

Figure 7.1: 'View of the jail and depot from the hospital', n.d.
Source: P32.6.38 Fiji Museum.

Over the next 30 years, the Suva prison was gradually expanded and strengthened. Coral rock walls replaced reed fences (some of which are still visible from Foster Road in 2020) and by 1894 the prison was comprised of 23 cells and six wards.[12] A fixed execution chamber was constructed in July 1905, and between 1912 and 1913 a two-storey block containing 171 cells was constructed. This building was the first ferro-concrete building in Fiji and was proclaimed by British colonial reports as evidence of a modern and progressive colony. Subsequent correspondence suggests the prison was underfunded and overcrowded in the following decades.[13] Electricity was introduced in the 1920s but there was no sewerage system so prisoners had to empty buckets from their cells on a daily basis. Other buildings were constructed by prison labour with bricks from the Fiji Brick Company under the direction of prison officer William Peter Marr. These included a prison hospital and officer's quarters. Levuka prison

---

12 Colony of Fiji, *Blue book of Fiji for 1894*, 199.
13 Correspondence details that requests to update prison security and construct new buildings like a chapel were denied. There were detailed debates about how best to employ prisoners as labourers and the cost of food rationed for prisoners.

continued to operate throughout the twentieth century but Suva Prison grew to become the largest prison in the country and home to Fiji's most serious criminal cases. From 1900, all prisoners serving sentences greater than three months were sent to Suva, with numbers fluctuating between 300 and over 1,000 in any given year.

Figure 7.2: 'Suva Prison, 1946'.
Source: Bart van Aller, *Suva Gaol* (Suva: National Trust of Fiji, 2015).

There is little evidence available that gives insight into the daily lives of inmates in Suva Prison. A strict regimen was imposed that confined inmates to their cells with the exception of labour, meals, exercise and divine service. Prisoners were allowed to send and receive letters but visits were not permitted without permission or unless a prisoner was on death row. European tourists to Fiji at the beginning of the twentieth century came in increasing numbers to Suva and occasionally commented on the prison. Many of these visitors were curious about the building and its inmates, particularly the apparent lax system of supervision and discipline. Beatrice Grimshaw's well-publicised travelogue in 1907 was one of the most notable accounts of the time and she reacted with shock that prisoners could roam in and out of the grounds as they pleased.[14] Few travellers took a close look within the prison grounds and there is no evidence of dark tourism or a fascination with the inner workings of the prison, as there was with visitors to New Caledonia.[15] Rather, most made observations from a safe distance, noting that prisoners worked in the farms, or in the case of Suva, cleaning the grounds of the cemetery. Their observations and praise of British efforts to discipline the Fijians conformed to a broader British colonial narrative in the Pacific that reinforced the civilised nature of British rule over purportedly 'savage' peoples.

Activities at Suva Prison have remained similar from its establishment until the early twenty-first century. Prisoners still attend to the cemetery as they did in the early 1900s, tending to plots and digging graves. They also provided labour for other government work, such as gardening on Government House grounds, repairing public buildings, working as boat crews or medical staff, and producing items such as mats, brushes, printing and 'tinsmithy'.[16] By the 1940s the prison had been expanded to accommodate a saw mill, taro farm, tailors and canvas workers, blacksmith and tinsmith, sanitary services and a bakery. The prison bakery was 'one of the leading bakeries in the Colony, baking an average of nearly 2000 pounds of bread per day'. Several requests for more funds and equipment were recorded between the 1930s and 50s, with 11 bakers producing hand-made bread for most of the Suva area, including all government departments, schools and the hospital.[17]

Segregation

Within Suva Prison, colonial authorities reinforced the racial division of Fijians, Indians and Europeans with a system of classifications for both inmates and prison staff. This replicated policies outside the prison that provided different rules for different sections of society from the beginning of British colonial rule until the 1960s: Indian indentured labourers

---

14 Beatrice Grimshaw, *From Fiji to the Cannibal Islands* (London: Eveleigh Nash, 1907).
15 Nicholas Halter, '"Cannibals and convicts": Australian travel writing about New Caledonia', in *The Palgrave Handbook of Prison Tourism,* ed. JZ Wilson, S Hodginkson, J Piché and K Walby (New York: Springer Nature 2017), 867–84, doi.org/10.1057/978-1-137-56135-0_41.
16 The latter were introduced in 1911. *Colonial Report – Annual Fiji, 1911*, No. 727 (London: H.M.S.O., 1912).
17 Gaol bakery oven Suva, 1937–1953, CSO F121/39/1, CSO Secretariat Files, NAF. The bakery was eventually transferred to Naboro prison in the 1970s where it continues to operate today.

were governed by Indian Labour Ordinances while Fijians obeyed Fijian Native Regulations. An ordinance 'for the better regulation of prisons', more commonly known as the Prisons Ordinance 1884, established strict rules and procedures underpinned by racial assumptions and prejudices. It appointed a superintendent of prisons to oversee operations of all the prisons of Fiji: usually a European man residing in Suva.[18] Beneath him were jailers, a European man for each prison, who was tasked with living in the compound and maintaining control of the inmates. Jailers were also expected to keep 11 books documenting details such as prison incidents, punishments, rations and visitors. Later, around 1917, another position, the inspector general of prisons, was created. This was another European position modelled after British prison reforms of the 1830s, which appointed inspectors to ensure prisons were uniform and acceptable.[19] Details of the men who ran the prisons and the records they kept are either scattered in the archives or missing, which is surprising considering their influence on the conduct and development of Fiji's prisons. These three men oversaw a number of warders who were responsible for day-to-day operations in the prisons, the majority of whom were Fijian men.

Following World War II, population growth in the colony forced changes to the way prisons were operated and staffed. To accommodate its size and functions, Suva Prison was staffed by two European overseers, one European clerk, one non-European clerk, an Indian medical practitioner, 29 male warders and two female warders, according to 1944 records.[20] Little is known about these prison officers – how they were chosen, and how they related with one another and the inmates. There was a ranking system among the warders, and different uniforms were supplied for Fijians (sulus) and Indians (turbans). A request in 1949 by Fijian warders for sandals and coats similar to the ones policemen were given suggests that prison staff were not regarded as highly by Europeans as the famed Fijian 'native' policeman, a figure much publicised abroad for their distinctive uniforms.[21] Unlike the police forces, prison staff did not receive any formal training until the 1980s.

---

18   According to CSO files, Mr Halkett was the superintendent of prisons in 1884. Leckie, *Colonizing madness*, 1.
19   A British Act of 1835 authorised inspectors in prisons. Eric Stockdale, 'A short history of prison inspection in England', *The British Journal of Criminology* 23, no. 3 (1983): 209–28, doi.org/10.1093/oxfordjournals.bjc.a047376. The first *Annual Colonial Report* on Fiji to mention this post was 1917.
20   Prison department annual report, CSO F121/4/2, CSO Secretariat Files, NAF.
21   Prison warders uniforms, 1949, CSO F121/30, CSO Secretariat Files, NAF.

Rules

The ways in which Fiji colonial officials classified prisoners was inconsistent and changed over time. Eric Stockdale's history of prison reforms in Britain in the 1800s argues that 'classification' became the preferred idea to 'separation'[22] and that this was likely applied to the colonies too. In practice, classifications of prisoners according to crimes and ethnicity had direct implications for their living conditions. The 'Prison Rules' within Fiji's 1884 Prisons Ordinance was the first official document that established four classes of prisoners:

> Prisoners shall be classified as follows:-
>
> First class viz. – Prisoners sentenced to penal servitude or imprisonment with hard labour.
>
> Second class viz. – Prisoners under sentence of imprisonment only.
>
> Third class viz. – Prisoners awaiting trial or under examination.
>
> Fourth class viz. – Debtors comprising persons confined for contempt or upon civil process of for want of sureties to keep the peace.[23]

All classes except first class were allowed privileges such as wearing their own clothes, buying products in the prison, sending and receiving letters more regularly, and not being forced to shave. Third class prisoners were separated from the main population and permitted access to a legal adviser. The *Blue Books* produced by the Fiji colony provided general statistics of the prisoners' sentences. One example from the 1894 *Blue Book* is typical, when Suva Prison hosted 519 prisoners, of which 457 were serving penal servitude (presumably class 1), 62 were there 'for safe custody until trial' (presumably class 3) and none were registered for debt (class 4).[24] These *Blue Books* show that Fiji's prison population varied erratically from 300 to 1,300 between the 1880s and 1920s (on average less than half a per cent of the population when compared to census data). Discernible trends in these statistics are obscured by the absences, inconsistencies and probable inaccuracies within colonial reports.

---

22   Stockdale, 'A short history of prison inspection in England', 214.
23   'Prison rules' in An Ordinance for the Better Regulation of Prisons, No. 12 (14 November 1884), 51.
24   Colony of Fiji, *Blue book of Fiji for 1894*, 198.

Official records of the ethnicity of inmates varied as categories and classifications changed over time. Annual colonial reports published statistics of crimes committed and prisoners interred, usually labelled 'natives' or 'Indians' in the nineteenth century. This evolved as annual reports of the early twentieth century categorised inmates as European, Fijian, Indian and Polynesian, but in some cases other labels such as half-castes, Rotumans, Chinese, Samoans and 'others' were used in prison documents and national censuses. Criminal statistics provide a clearer picture of ethnicity because they followed a more standardised report format in the annual reports, with the majority of cases reported as Indian offences. In 1900 for example, 8,799 offences were reported: 708 were offences against the person, 387 were larceny, 148 were offences against property and 7,556 were 'principally breaches of the Labour Ordinances by Indian Immigrants'.[25] Occasionally the number of breaches of Native Fijian Regulations was reported, but this was a small number compared to Indian Labour Ordinance cases. The over-representation of Indians in Fiji's prisons in the late nineteenth and early twentieth centuries, I argue, reflected dissatisfaction with British colonial policies at the time. Although some Indians did commit serious crimes, there were also those who were subjected unfairly to harsh penal regulations and punishments for minor transgressions because they upset colonial officials, resisted colonial regulations or agitated for greater political recognition. Overseen by iTaukei warders and supervised by European officials, Indian prisoners were likely to be misunderstood or mistreated by the justice system. Brij Lal has shown that British colonial officials often misinterpreted statistics and drew erroneous conclusions based on racialised assumptions. His study of incidents of suicide among Indian indentured labourers pointed to a misconception that Indians were predisposed to crimes of passion and violence because of the limited number of Indian women available.[26]

Europeans were a small minority in the prisons, and the standards for Europeans were very different to those for indigenous peoples, as they were informed by racial prejudices. In 1963 LJ Riddell petitioned to be transferred to Australia to be closer to his family. He wrote, 'I am continually referred to by the other prisoners as being un-natural

---

25 *Colonial Report – Annual Fiji, 1900,* No. 727 (London: H.M.S.O., 1901), 16.
26 Brij V Lal, 'Veil of dishonour: Sexual jealousy and suicide on Fiji plantations', *The Journal of Pacific History* 20, no. 3 (1985): 135–55, doi.org/10.1080/00223348508572516.

European'.²⁷ In 1961 a Suva inmate Thomas C Norman petitioned to be deported to his home in England because he claimed 'the conditions here are for a native not European'. He claimed:

> My work is in the cemetery, where I am a curiousity [sic] piece, being the only white man, to tourists etc. and this adds to my humiliation of being a prisoner.

Norman was one of the few prisoners who described the relationships within the prison, noting:

> I receive the same treatment as a native, and they are quick to take advantage of that and that is not good as there is already enough trouble with racial prejudice here, and the possibility is that the boys will try to treat Europeans outside the same.

The Colonial Secretary's Office regarded his claims as exaggerated and noted that there were also 14 Part-Europeans in the prison, and that he received a full European diet as well as 'the usual European table appointments'.²⁸ Europeans received more quantities of food and more expensive items like potatoes compared to other inmates. When costs were high, fresh meat was replaced with tinned meat, and bread with biscuits.²⁹

Suva Prison remained an overwhelmingly masculine domain, although there were some women imprisoned there. According to annual reports of the country's prisons (from which women were sometimes omitted entirely), the number of women in prisons ranged between zero and 10 until the 1960s, compared to a general prison population that ranged between 300 and 1,300. Initially female prisoners were housed in a female section of Suva Prison, according to Sellers, with a matron assigned to supervise and keep the females apart from the males.³⁰ They were not usually mentioned in great detail and, when mentioned, were not considered a threat: for example, a report of a prisoner charged with larceny in the 1960s described her as 'just a domestic'.³¹ Levuka Prison was converted in 1964 for women prisoners. However, in 1976 it was converted to a male prison and all female prisoners were moved to Suva, where a separate dormitory was constructed.

---

27 CSO F121/5/41, CSO Secretariat Files, NAF.
28 CSO F121/5/25, CSO Secretariat Files, NAF.
29 CSO Minute Paper No. 2619/1899, Department of Prisons, CSO Secretariat Files, NAF.
30 Sellers, 'Development of Fiji prison service'.
31 CSO F121/31/17, CSO Secretariat Files, NAF.

The age of offenders was also not reported in official statistics, though it was likely recorded in individual prisoner files. Juvenile offenders under the age of 16 years were allegedly housed at Suva Prison from 1925, but it is not clear how they were dealt with prior.[32] There were a series of experiments in moving juveniles to alternate locations such as Makuluva Island (in 1929), 9 miles (in 1938) and Naboro (in 1965), until a formal complex for young offenders between 16 and 19 years of age was constructed in Nasinu in 1971.

Punishment

The operation of prisons in Fiji was modelled after British practices of incarceration, like many other colonial prisons in the empire, and involved a highly regulated system of rules and punishments to enforce discipline. Initial reports in 1880 noted that there was little crime in the colony, but it was feared contact with Europeans would 'wear away their respect for authority'.[33] Thus prisons were considered an important institution for teaching the indigenous population about British justice and values. These early experiments in incarceration typically ignored precolonial forms of maintaining law and order in Fijian society.

Missionaries were some of the first to document how iTaukei communities enforced disciplinary measures before colonial contact. In 1860, Thomas Williams and James Calvert published a detailed description of punishments.[34] Chiefs usually determined the type and severity of punishment, which could include fines, the seizure of property (land or a canoe), the destruction of property (the burning of a house or plantation), physical harm (the loss of a finger, ear or nose), beatings (by hand, or with clubs or stones), or death (by clubbing, shooting or strangulation). Williams and Calvert's account should be read within a broader context of colonial mission reports that demonised Melanesians as 'savage' by referring extreme cases, such as strangulation or cannibalism. The term *buturaki* has been used more recently with reference to domestic violence to suggest a traditional culture of beating, but it is not clear whether

---

32   Jone Luvenitoga, 'Fiji correctional service to celebrate 114 years of service', *Mailife*, 22 October 2018.
33   *Colonial Report – Annual Fiji, 1880* (London: H.M.S.O., 1883). Of the 891 reported cases, 194 were for 'common larceny' and 104 for 'drunkenness'.
34   Thomas Williams and James Calvert, *Fiji and the Fijians* (New York: Alexander Heylin, 1860), 22–25.

this was a widespread practice in precolonial times. Imprisonment was not common – captives of war *(bokola)* were often killed and eaten or ceremonially buried beneath house foundations *(yavu)* soon after their capture. Williams and Calvert reported instances when women could be seized and taken to another village as punishment, or when individuals could be tied up for short periods of time (to suffer from physical pain and exposure to the elements).

The nature of traditional Fijian society suggests that the crimes of one individual would likely have required a response from the village to which he/she belonged. Ceremonies of reciprocity and exchange were likely specific to particular regions within the Fiji Islands. Mary Rokonadravu gives an example from the province of Rewa of *Keteniyalewa* ('the woman's womb') to describe the use of land to ensure the protection of women in marriages.[35] In 1908 British colonial administrator Basil Thompson described a process in which land was seized as punishment for adultery:

> As soon as the offence became known, the friends of the injured person planted reeds (sau) on the land of the offender, or of his family as a token of forfeiture. Reeds so planted were called 'ai-wau-tu-i-vuni-vudi' (the club set in the banana patch). The family of the offender knew that they must either abandon the land or fight for it (which they seldom did). When by the lapse of time, the offence was forgotten, the land could be redeemed.[36]

Williams and Calvert recorded five types of *soro* or atonement that were used throughout Fiji, with a whale's tooth, a reed, a spear, a basket of earth or ashes.[37]

In stark contrast to traditional forms of punishment, the colonial justice system identified and removed individuals from communities for punishment or imprisonment. This was a successful method for pacifying the population and isolating dissenting individuals from their communal settings. For example, in 1894 the annual report mentioned an intertribal

---

35 Mary Rokonadravu, 'Open letter to Mr. Kris Prasad (Fiji)', *Medium,* 30 October 2019.
36 Basil Thompson, *The Fijians: A study of the decay of custom* (London: William Heinemann, 1908), 373.
37 Ibid., 24. Five kinds of *soro*: with a whale's tooth *(tabua)*, with a reed *(mata ni gasau)*, with a spear *(mata nimoto)*, with a basket of earth *(kau vanua)* and with ashes *(bisi dravu)*.

disturbance on Vanua Levu that left 10 'natives' dead after a skirmish with the government party. The leaders were tried in Suva, with two being executed and the rest imprisoned.[38]

European prisons were initially a holding place for the transfer of prisoners but sometime in the late eighteenth century prisons became a form of punishment. French philosopher Michel Foucault theorised that the 'technology of discipline' within the prison was an additional punishment to incarceration. Responding to the excessive punishments of public torture by European sovereigns, reformists called for a more generalised and regulated form of punishment from the state. What emerged was a system of rules and regulations that observed, classified and controlled bodies within institutions.[39]

In Fiji, discipline was maintained with a system of 'corporal punishments' that were formalised by the Prisons Ordinance. They resembled similar punishments in other British colonies like Papua New Guinea and included flogging, shot-drill and the death penalty. Floggings were a common punishment at the turn of the century – the Prisons Ordinance permitted 100 lashes with a cat-o-nine tails, with 39 allowed at one time. In an 1888 case, a man convicted of aggravated assault on his wife was sentenced to 20 lashes, which were administered in prison.[40] Floggings continued as late as the 1960s, with a report of '6 strokes' given to one man for 'defilement of a girl' in 1960, though with less frequency.[41] Shot-drill, which involved carrying heavy weights across an open ground, was used as an alternative punishment for breaching prison rules. The Prisons Ordinance allowed no more than two hours per day. Other forms of punishment included solitary confinement, standing for long periods, leg irons and a reduced diet.[42]

The 'technology of discipline' in Fiji was fine-tuned in the 1910s as the colony attempted to standardise the prisons system. When the new 'modern' Suva Prison compound was constructed in 1913, the annual report also announced improvements to the 'discipline of prisons' and 'separate confinement'. This included abolishing shot-drill as a punishment and replacing it with a 'system of marks for good behaviour'.[43]

---

38 *Colonial Report – Annual Fiji, 1894* (London: H.M.S.O., 1895).
39 Michel Foucault, *Discipline and punish: The birth of the prison* (New York: Pantheon Books 1977).
40 CSO 88.2241, CSO Secretariat Files, NAF.
41 CSO F121/31/12, CSO Secretariat Files, NAF.
42 768 punishments were recorded in the 1894 *Blue book* for a prison population of 519.
43 *Colonial Report – Annual Fiji, 1913* (London: H.M.S.O., 1914).

A new position above the superintendent of prisons, called the inspector general of prisons, was also created sometime in this decade. Proforma reports on individual prisoners gradually became more standardised, listing a prisoner's conviction, their mental and physical condition, any particular incidents they had been involved in in the prison, and ranked categories of behaviour, work, relationship with prison officers and outlook (see Table 7.1). This is further evidence of the system of classification imposed by the 'technology of discipline'.

Table 7.1: 'Report on a Prisoner Under Regulation 129 of the Prisons Regulations, 1963'.

Official Comments					
Behaviour	Bad	Fair	Good	Very Good	Excellent
Work	Bad	Fair	Good	Very Good	Excellent
Relationship with prison officers	Antagonistic	Sullen	Fairly Co-operative	Co-operative but reserved	Good
Outlook	Unregenerate	Lethargic	Confused – difficult to assess	Accepts the justice of his punishment	Remorseful – likely to reform

Source: Annual prisoner reports 1961–1965, F121/31/5, CSO Secretariat Files, National Archives of Fiji (NAF).

The most serious case of punishment was the death penalty, which existed in Fiji from 1899 to 1964. At Suva Prison the first hanging occurred on 4 April 1899 at a temporary gallows set up on the hill behind the wall before a fixed chamber was built in 1905.[44] Great care was taken by the inspector general of prisons to ensure the gallows were 'of modern construction' and working order – he reported in 1917 an average of six prisoners per year had been hanged in the last 10 years.[45] That same year colonial officials debated the length of rope required to ensure death. A 'table of drops' used in English prisons specified the length of rope needed according to prisoner's weight, and Fiji officials suggested 'a longer drop for the Indians who are lighter than Europeans'.[46] Such a macabre discussion may have been due to failed executions in the past, as was the case of Antonio Franks who survived a hanging in Levuka in 1872.[47]

---

44 Sellers, 'Development of Fiji prison service'.
45 Minute by Inspector General of Prisons to Colonial Secretary, 7 July 1917, Colonial Office (CO), CO83 No.41409, Public Record Office, London.
46 Executions at Suva, 10 July 1917, CO83 No.41409, Public Record Office, London; Table of Drops, 18 September 1917, CO83 No.46201, Public Record Office, London.
47 Anurag Subramani, 'The execution of Antonio Franks, Part 1 and 2', *The Fiji Times,* 17 and 24 November 2019.

Executions were carefully controlled and orchestrated events. Attended by an executioner, religious minister and prison officers, the *Fiji Times* reported:

> Condemned criminals were told the infamous instruction to take their last look at Beqa Island, known in the iTaukei language as *Rai ki Beqa* before they were led to the gallows, at the back of Suva's Korovou Prison.[48]

Executions were reported to have occurred at night. Prisoners sentenced to death waited in a separate 'condemned cell compound'. It is not specified why this was the practice, but comparison with execution practices in Papuan prisons suggests the death penalty was regarded as a sensitive matter and British colonial officials were reluctant to make corporal punishment public for fear of retribution.[49] Despite such care being taken to orchestrate the death penalty, deaths in custody were inconsistently recorded in official records. Inquiries were required by law upon a death in custody, but these records cannot be found today. Some annual reports did not distinguish between deaths in custody and executions, or whether deaths in custody were by natural causes or suicide. When executions were recorded, numbers ranged between zero and 10, or an average of three per year.

Threats

Apart from those prisoners who were tasked with public works in Suva town, few residents would have known about the inner workings of the prison or its inmates. As the largest prison in Fiji for much of the twentieth century, it was home to some of Fiji's most serious criminals and was likely viewed by the public as an important institution for ensuring dangerous threats were safely behind bars. Newspapers regularly reported criminal cases, but did not usually report on the perpetrators after they were sentenced. Instead, prisons only appeared in the news when there was a riot or an escape. Riots were rare in Suva Prison until severe overcrowding created favourable conditions for disruption in the 1960s onwards. Escapes occurred with greater frequency, particularly in

---

48 John Mitchell, '150th anniversary: Fiji's death penalty', *The Fiji Times*, 30 October 2019.
49 Adam Reed, *Papua New Guinea's last place: Experiences of constraint in a postcolonial prison* (New York: Berghahn Books, 2003), 33.

the early days of Suva Prison when it was still in construction, much to the fascination of newspapers and the public. Punishment for escape could be up to five years imprisonment according to the Prisons Ordinance, but this did not deter three escapees in 1892, four in 1893 and four in 1894.[50] Later, in a 1944 prison department annual report, seven escapes were reported but only one was from Suva.[51] In contrast to official reports of statistics, the *Fiji Times* provided more exciting tales of escape for its readers. In one curious case, a Samoan traveller called Pila Wilkes was sentenced to six months imprisonment in 1936 for illegally landing in Fiji as a crew member aboard the *Aorangi*. It was discovered that he had escaped similar charges in Canada, New Zealand and Australia, and soon after, he managed to escape from Fiji.[52] Such cases show that Pacific Islanders were not static or passive, and that colonial attempts to control and restrict the indigenous population were not always successful.

Other forms of resistance were likely within prison compounds in Fiji but were either underreported or the documents have since been lost. One surviving file referred to a 'sit down strike' of prisoners in relation to the transfer of iTaukei prison staff in 1965.[53] In an earlier case in 1956 a man sentenced to 12 months imprisonment for indecent assault began a hunger strike and refused medical treatment for six days.[54] Other minor forms of resistance can be found in the letters of inmates and their families who would write letters appealing to the prison or the courts.

Though Suva Prison did contain some prisoners who had committed serious crimes, these were a small minority compared to the rest of the prison population. Not all records distinguished between those serving long sentences and those in remand but when they did, the statistics reveal that many of Suva Prison's inmates were temporary. Of the 457 prisoners sentenced to penal servitude at Suva Prison in 1894, 275 were serving sentences less three months, 177 less than one year, 47 less than five years and only 18 over five years.[55] Those prisoners serving short sentences at Suva Prison committed minor crimes such as refusal to pay fines and taxes, or disobedience of laws designed to restrict the indigenous population.

---

50   Colony of Fiji, *Blue book of Fiji for 1894*, 198.
51   Prison department annual report 1944, CSO F121/4/2, CSO Secretariat Files, NAF.
52   *The Fiji Times*, 6 July 1936.
53   Epeli Vuase – petition against transfer of prison staff, 1965, CSO F121/5/60, CSO Secretariat Files, NAF.
54   Prisoner Thomas Lancaster Norman Davis, CSO F121/35, CSO Secretariat Files, NAF.
55   Colony of Fiji, *Blue book of Fiji for 1894*, 198.

Until the 1940s, there was strict control of non-European populations in Suva town. Fijians required a licence to buy or drink alcohol (prescribed by the 1892 ordinance 'to regulate the supply of spirituous liquor to natives and others'), and the *Fiji Times* recorded incidents of fines being given for breaking curfew or dancing without a licence.[56] In Suva town, the most common arrests were for drunkenness, assault and burglary, with reports of Fijian and Indian gangs in the urban centre.[57] According to the minutes of one meeting with the colonial secretary in 1961, the increase in iTaukei inmates was attributed to 'Provincial Tax Defaulters' who discovered a loophole in the Fijian Affairs Regulations by which they could cancel their tax obligations with a stay in prison.[58] In this specific case, prison was not necessarily a deterrent. Contrary to European notions of punishment and incarceration, prisoners in Fiji were often mobile and transient. Adam Reed observed a similar trend in Papua New Guinea's prisons; inmates there referred to it as a 'bus stop' because of the constant movement of inmates in and out of the prison.[59]

Reforms

For the most part, Suva Prison and the incarceration system in Fiji generally remained largely unchanged for the first half of the twentieth century. A major shift was prompted in 1955 when the United Nations Standard Minimum Rules for the Treatment of Prisoners was adopted. It specified rules regarding work, recreation and education for prisoners, and alternative proposals for forestry work, stamp collecting and trade training were considered by Fiji officials.[60] A visiting committee visited Suva Prison in 1961 and noted significant overcrowding.[61] In 1961 the governor reported a 15 per cent rise in the prison population per annum, and an increasing proportion of crimes of violence ('approximately

---

56 In one case in 1936 a Fijian, Samuela Naisoro, was fined £2 for conducting a native dance without a licence inside a building at midnight. *Fiji Times*, 21 July 1936.
57 Minutes of a meeting with Colonial Secretary, 13 March 1961, CSO F121/30 Naboro prison complex, 1960–1965, CSO Secretariat Files, NAF.
58 Minutes of a meeting with Colonial Secretary, 13 March 1961, CSO F121/30 Naboro prison complex, 1960–1965, CSO Secretariat Files, NAF.
59 Reed, *Papua New Guinea's last place*, 77.
60 Several proposals for work details were considered in response to the UN regulations. Prison labour and employment, 1955–1957, CSO F121/32, CSO Secretariat Files, NAF.
61 Gaol Visiting Committee Suva Reports 1961, CSO F121/1/1, CSO Secretariat Files, NAF.

half') across the country.[62] The composition of the prisoners had also changed – the majority of inmates were iTaukei, reflecting the economic disparity between indigenous Fijians and the growing Indian population. Officials were also conscious of external scrutiny and complaints about the treatment of prisoners. The superintendent of prisons suggested to the colonial secretary that Hindu priests be provided because he was worried the prison staff would be accused of trying to convert Indian inmates to Christianity by only providing a Methodist service.[63] The outcome of the UN standard was the development of Fiji's first Prisons Act in 1966. It formally established a Fiji Prisons Service headed by a controller, with new clauses regarding female prisoners, and revisions to prison rules and punishments. The new Act represented a shift in focus towards reform and rehabilitation in the prison system.

Concerns about the rehabilitation of prisoners and overcrowding that decade, combined with a prison riot in 1963, contributed to pressure to establish a new prison at Naboro, 18 kilometres west of Suva. Naboro was initially proposed in 1961 as an experimental 'corrective training centre' where youth with short sentences could be sent for a six-month stay to 'shock' them.[64] The Naboro Prison Farm was completed on 22 July 1965 with capacity for 96 inmates. It was later expanded to include a medium security facility in 1968 and a maximum security facility in 1972. It is now the largest prison facility in Fiji, with a current capacity of 342.

Since Fiji's Independence in 1970, the country's prisons have come under closer scrutiny as the government has worked on decolonising its institutions and meeting international standards for imprisonment and rehabilitation. There is a lack of history of Fiji's prisons, as admitted by Vijay Naidu, Mahendra Reddy and Steven Ratuva in their 2009 report on Fiji prison reforms.[65] According to their report, Fiji's Independence in 1970 marked a shift from the colonial days of 'containment' to 'correction', and was followed by several government inquiries – the Grant Report (1974), a Royal Commission (1975), the Bale Report (1980) and the Buadromo Report (1994) – that attempted to address concerns about the

---

62 Letter from Governor to Secretary of State for the Colonies, 6 March 1961, CSO F121/29 Prisons, rural – expansion of, 1960–1961, CSO Secretariat Files, NAF.
63 Visits by Hindu priests to Suva gaol, 1956, CSO F121/33/1, CSO Secretariat Files, NAF.
64 Minutes of a meeting with Colonial Secretary, 13 March 1961, CSO F121/30 Naboro prison complex, 1960–1965, CSO Secretariat Files, NAF.
65 Vijay Naidu, Mahendra Reddy and Steven Ratuva, *Fiji prison reforms: From containment to correction and beyond* (Suva: Ecumenical Centre for Research, Education and Advocacy, 2009).

corrections system. Isolated incidents within prisons have also prompted government action, such as a 1979 Suva Prison riot, which resulted in the establishment of a staff training centre adjacent to the prison in 1981 and a training college at Naboro in 1983. Significant legal reform was not made until 2006 when a Prisons and Corrections Act replaced the Prisons Act of 1966 after a review by the UN Development Programme and Fiji Law Reform Commission.[66]

Today there are 15 prisons in Fiji, the largest being the facility at Naboro that has a minimum, medium and maximum security centre and a prerelease centre. Suva and Lautoka each have a remand centre and a women's correction centre. There are also prisons in Nasinu, Levuka, Labasa, Ba and Taveuni.[67] Due to disrepair, the central building of the Suva Prison complex has been empty since 1998. Consultations with the National Trust of Fiji to protect the heritage building were unable to prevent its demolition in late 2019.[68] Opposite this site on Foster Road there is another contemporary building, the Tagimoucia Art Gallery. Since 2008, prisoners have promoted their products there as part of the 'Yellow Ribbon' rehabilitation program introduced by Iowane Naivalurua, then commissioner of prisons and correctional services, and supported by local Suva volunteers such as Jane Ricketts, a retired educator who has been teaching art to prisoners for over a decade. A creative writing course by Mary Daya in 2008 highlighted the experiences of Suva's prisoners in their own words and was published as an anthology titled *Shedding Silences*.[69] These unique examples of creative expression and rehabilitation would not be possible without the quiet dedication of many volunteers who regularly visit the prison to provide support, training and inspiration to those behind the walls, and they highlight the vast potential of those prisoners who are given a second chance.

---

66   Shailin Gonelevu, 'From containment to correction and reformation: Exploring punishment and reform in the disciplinary system of Fiji Women's Prison' (master's thesis, University of the South Pacific, 2015).
67   '15 Corrections Centres', Fiji Corrections Service (2017), www.corrections.gov.fj/institutions (accessed 24 March 2022).
68   van Aller, *Suva Gaol*.
69   Mary Daya, ed., *Shedding silences: An anthology of writing from Fiji prisons* (Suva: University of the South Pacific, 2008).

8

Visibly Hidden in Suva: St Giles

Jacqueline Leckie

Since 1884 Suva has had a mental asylum, first known as the Public Lunatic Asylum or the Suva Asylum: a physical site that has conjured fear and mystery, and been pivotal to the stigma associated with mental illness in Fiji. In 1936 the asylum was renamed the Suva Mental Hospital, because the old name was 'too redolent of Bedlam'.[1] During the early 1960s the name St Giles Psychiatric Hospital came into use, but the term 'asylum' has persisted.[2]

One reason mental asylums were so foreboding is because they were physically separated from the rest of the community. St Giles is located on a steep ridge some distance from the main town in Suva. It was surrounded by high concrete walls – impenetrable barriers that screamed incarceration and separation, like the piercing screams and wailing from inside that people could hear from outside the walls. Similar to many asylums, St Giles has vast grounds to accommodate patients and staff, and to supply food for the asylum. By the time St Giles was established,

---

1 Margaret Guthrie, *Misi Utu: Dr D. W. Hoodless and the development of medical education in the South Pacific* (Suva: Institute of Pacific Studies, University of the South Pacific with the South Pacific Social Sciences Association, 1979), 34. Guthrie was the daughter of Medical Superintendent David Hoodless. Much of this chapter is based on Jacqueline Leckie, *Colonizing madness: Asylum and community in Fiji* (Honolulu: University of Hawai'i Press, 2020), doi.org/10.1515/9780824881900, where extensive documentation can be found.
2 For example, Sainimili Lewa, 'Madman attacks asylum staff', *Fiji Times,* 18 January 2002, 12; Irene Manueli, 'Asylum can't cure morphine addict', *Fiji Times,* 5 January 2002.

many European asylums had gardens because these were considered therapeutic for mental patients; but in Fiji, digging and planting cassava and *dalo* was often more exhausting than the genteel tending of flower gardens in more temperate climes. St Giles in Suva occupies a site of physical beauty, amid lush tropical vegetation and breath-taking views of Suva Harbour. The vista also takes in Suva Prison – a reminder that the asylum is located above another institution of incarceration. St Giles is also adjacent to Suva's military and Chinese cemeteries and so the locale embraces key sites of separation, fear and danger, as well as between 1945 to around 2004 being near Suva's rubbish dump: 'The dump, the dead, the mad and the bad.'[3] Asylums throughout the world were associated with prisons, metaphorically as well as by proximity. Before the asylum was built, lunatics in Suva were confined in jail. The links between the jail and the asylum continued – eventually connected by a road – and with many patients sentenced to the prison before certification and transfer to the asylum. Suva's public have tended to regard St Giles as a prison rather than as a hospital. In 1992 Alison Cupit, chair of St Giles's Board of Visitors, condemned St Giles's buildings 'as prison camps without the elaborate fencing'.[4] But the asylum has always occupied an ambiguous space between prison and hospital: a place of incarceration, but equally of treatment, care and possible cure. St Giles is also known in Suva as a *vale ni mate* (place of death) or *bakava* (tin shack) – a reference to the fences that replaced the hospital's foreboding concrete walls during the 1960s. *Bakava* also became an adjective meaning a crazy, silly person.[5]

As the chapter's title reflects, St Giles and its inhabitants are 'visibly hidden'. In one sense, the place is easily recognisable, but in another sense, it is well hidden within Suva's history. It would be a huge injustice to portray St Giles's role in Suva as just a place of fear and incarceration. Although this dominant representation threads throughout this chapter, we will explore: firstly how patients at St Giles are a window into the social history of Suva, secondly St Giles as a community in itself, and finally the relationship between St Giles and Suva.

---

3   Seona Smiles, *Fiji Times,* 2 April 2011.
4   *Friends of St Giles*, newsletter, 1992, St Giles file (STG) 1/3–I. Held at St Giles Hospital.
5   Ronald Gatty, *Fijian–English dictionary: With notes on Fijian culture and natural history* (Suva: Southeast Asia Program, Cornell University, 2010), 11.

Figure 8.1: Walls of St Giles Hospital, 1965.
Source: Courtesy National Archives of Fiji, # G7247.

The Asylum: Suva's Hidden History

The story of Taniela, a villager from Vanua Balavu, encapsulates how the path into the asylum offers insight into a lesser known social history of Suva as well as the asylum and Suva's relationship with other parts of Fiji. In 1895 the *buli* Lomaloma, the iTaukei official in charge of the district, noticed that Taniela 'gave strange wandering answers and looked and wandered about in a dazed fashion'.[6] The *buli* ordered Taniela to Suva for further examination by a European practitioner – not unusual, as Suva was the centre where villagers were sent for specialised medical treatment. On one of the islands where the boat stopped, Taniela killed, boiled and ate a cat, with the skin on it. He briefly moved throughout Suva before incarceration in the prison and the asylum. Things were not quite right with the man and, as planned, Taniela was admitted to the Colonial Hospital. He sneaked away and was reported to the police as 'an insane man' wandering in the bush near Vatuwaqa. After another stint in

---

6 'Assault committed by Taniela mad Tongan on 7th inst', CSO (Colonial Secretary's Office: Outwards correspondence of Colonial Secretary) 1465/95. All documents, unless stated, are from the National Archives of Fiji.

hospital, Taniela stayed in a Fijian's house near the Government Buildings and said he spent a night 'with a devil in the Indian town'. Taniela then stayed overnight with another Fijian near Cumming Street. The following morning he fatally attacked a Malaitan labourer. Sergeant Ulaiasi pursued Taniela up Waimanu Road, only for the sergeant to be seriously wounded. Police came running from the police station and overpowered Taniela. He was charged with murder and detained for 24 hours in the asylum before spending eight days in jail. He was acquitted of murder on the grounds of insanity and sentenced to confinement in the asylum, where he died on Christmas Day, 1896.

Taniela's narrative shows how Suva was a centre for many sick patients from all over Fiji – indeed, from many parts of the Pacific. Colonial authorities did not want Suva to be a dumping ground for sick, let alone mad, people. The colonial secretary advised Sir John Bates Thurston, the governor, that 'Lunatics should not be indiscriminately shipped to Hospital by Native Officers'.[7] According to Dr Bolton Corney, this irregularity could result in a delay in admission to the asylum, which posed a 'possible public danger as they are kept at large'.[8]

Throughout much of Fiji's colonial history, there were few personnel outside Suva who could legally diagnose mentally ill people. Native medical practitioners were not permitted to certify asylum admissions. Taniela's case evidenced considerable ambiguity: despite his strange behaviour, the *buli* had not suspected 'mental disease'. The medical and legal expertise for determining insanity was in Suva. A key reason for establishing the asylum had been to provide a place of observation to determine if someone was really mad.[9] Possibly because Taniela was relatively docile, he was sent to the main hospital for observation. The Colonial Hospital did not like to hold disruptive patients, and if suspected of being mentally ill, they might be sent on to the asylum.

---

7   CSO 1465/95.
8   CSO 317/96 on PN 112. Unless stated, personal information is from admission papers, usually cited as a patient's first admission number (PN), at St Giles Hospital.
9   This points to the complex problems of diagnosis and definitions of insanity that varied between cultures. Medical diagnoses changed throughout St Giles's history. See Leckie, *Colonizing madness*, 116–51. It would have been very difficult to have someone committed to the asylum who did not suffer from a serious mental disorder and such people were also cared for or confined within their communities. Leckie, *Colonizing madness*, 77–85, discusses the controversial issue of some iTaukei political and religious leaders who were committed to St Giles.

For example, a 19-year-old from the Armed Native Constabulary in Suva, first treated in the Colonial Hospital, was admitted to the asylum in 1901 after he:

> ran away several times from [the colonial] hospital; fought violently attempts to bring him back; struck some of the students taking care of him; threatens to kill them as soon as he gets well … noisy, threatening, restless and violent delirium at night while in hospital ward, terrorising other patients and nurses; says possessed by demons whose business is to slay people.[10]

The need for a separate space to confine and treat disruptive patients was yet another impetus behind the establishment of the Suva asylum.

Despite evidence of Taniela's disordered mind, it was not until he had committed a murder that he was finally sent to the asylum. Very few St Giles patients were dangerous. A notable exception was Qaqa, among the first intake of asylum patients in 1884. He had been declared a 'victim of homicidal mania'.[11] Since 1882 he had been an inmate at Suva Prison because he had viciously assaulted a European woman on Ovalau. Prison authorities considered him dangerously insane – proven when he killed another prisoner, John Murray. Mr Halkett, Fiji's superintendent of prisons, despaired that he could not manage prisoners like Qaqa, who 'should be sent to an asylum as soon as it was built'.[12]

Over the years, many patients, like Taniela, originated from outside Suva. Several were overseas migrants: indentured labourers, travellers and settlers from all over the Pacific and beyond, who, by the time they disembarked in or near Suva, were suffering from severe mental illness. When Dr William MacGregor, Fiji's chief medical officer and colonial secretary, who was pivotal in the establishment of the asylum, remarked that Fiji was 'a great sufferer from the arrival here of insane persons', he could have just been referring to Suva.[13] Sukudaia, an indentured immigrant from India was among the asylum's 1884 intake. She was highly visible in Suva where she wandered the streets with her child.

---

10   PN 175.
11   PN 6. Colonial Secretary (CS) to Superintendent of Prisons, CSO 888/84.
12   CSO 1178/84, Outwards Correspondence of CS.
13   CSO MP (Minute Paper) 86/84, 21 April 1886.

Once the asylum had opened, she could be hidden from view.¹⁴ By 1915, Acting Magistrate R Greene described Suva as 'reeking' with vagrants.¹⁵ Among the destitutes admitted to the asylum were some Europeans and indigenous Fijians but the majority were *girmitiyas* who could not endure indenture or lacked support after their bonds ended. Some flowed into Suva and were extremely disorientated, such as an Indian 'found in Suva' in 1902 who would not talk but laughed, shouted, cried and behaved indecently. His condition deteriorated when he was confined to a prison cell, and he was briefly transferred to the asylum.¹⁶

Below St Giles the Indian Depot at Korovou was also known as the Poor House. It was originally established to accommodate new immigrants and those awaiting repatriation to India. Patients admitted to the mental hospital from the depot tended to be in a very weak physical condition, such as a 60-year-old male in 1934, in a 'religious frenzy … helpless and dirty … [who] could not assist himself in any way'.¹⁷ By the 1930s more elderly Indians were admitted to the asylum than before, reflecting both an aging Indo-Fijian demographic and, for some, no family support. For example, a 75-year-old woman was admitted from the Indian Depot in 1941, where she had been abusing others and wandering at night.¹⁸ A Muslim beggar, aged 70, was admitted in 1948 after attempting to hit a Muslim priest over the head with a stone. While in hospital he 'always appeared depressed' and committed suicide in 1950.¹⁹

Not all patients were destitute or immigrants. St Giles was a microcosm of Suva's changing population: an intersection of ethnicities, occupations and classes. Initially Europeans accounted for around 18.6 per cent of total admissions but after 1900 the proportion of Europeans fell in the asylum – a larger proportion than the 2.7 per cent in Fiji as a whole, but smaller than Suva's European population of around 27 per cent in

---

14   See Leckie, *Colonizing madness*, 10, 26, 87–88, 112–114; Sudesh Mishra, '"Bending closer to the ground": Girmit as minor history', *Australian Humanities Review* 52 (2012): n.p., australianhumanities review.org/2012/05/01/bending-closer-to-the-ground-girmit-as-minor-history, doi.org/10.22459/AHR. 52.2012.02.
15   'Island news', *Auckland Star*, 7 September 1915, 9.
16   PN 186.
17   PN 1041; Colony of Fiji, *Blue book of Fiji, 1934* (Suva: Government Printer, 1934). British colonies had to submit annual *Blue books* of statistical and other information to the colonial office.
18   PN 1312.
19   PN 1530.

1911.[20] After World War I, admissions of Europeans and those who were not Fijians nor Indians dropped to approximately 5 per cent of total admissions. In 1921 Fijians made up 17 per cent and Indo-Fijians 64 per cent of Suva's population,[21] which is relatively similar to the figures among first admissions between 1919 and 1923 of 21 per cent Fijians and 66 per cent Indo-Fijians. Indo-Fijians represented the largest ethnic grouping of patients admitted to St Giles during the colonial period, although briefly from around 1889 to 1904, Fijians formed a higher percentage of admissions. As indigenous Fijian migration to Suva increased during the late colonial and postcolonial years,[22] so too did the number and proportion of indigenous Fijian patients in St Giles. The late colonial decades brought intense social and economic change and mobility for Fijians of all ethnicities, increasing permanent migration to Suva. Many were attracted to paid employment and educational opportunities. Change impinged upon villages and settlements on Suva's periphery and beyond, increasing economic vulnerability, social problems and mental stress. As social and economic changes for indigenous Fijians and Indo-Fijians intensified during the decades after World War II, the capacity of communities to care for those with mental disorders became stretched.

The St Giles Community

A distinct community emerged over several decades at St Giles, but nevertheless it was still part of Suva. A cursory view might suggest that St Giles was a 'total institution':

> a place of residence and work where a large number of like-situated individuals, cut off from the wider society for an appreciable period of time, together lead an enclosed, formally administered round of life.[23]

---

20 Fiji Bureau of Statistics, 'Key Statistics: June 2012', Table 1.2A Census population of Fiji by ethnicity. catalog.ihsn.org/index.php/catalog/3602/download/50136, accessed 5 December 2019. Suva figures from James Sutherland Whitelaw, 'People, land and government in Suva, Fiji' (PhD thesis, The Australian National University, 1966), 51. For a detailed discussion of race and ethnicity in the asylum, see Leckie, *Colonizing madness*.
21 Whitelaw, 'People, land and government', 55.
22 See for example, Chris Griffin and Michael Monsell-Davis, *Fijians in town* (Suva: Institute of Pacific Studies, University of the South Pacific, 1986).
23 Erving Goffman, *Asylums: Essays on the social situation of mental patients and other inmates* (New York: Doubleday Anchor, 1961), 1.

As discussed below, the walls were more porous and St Giles was hidden but still visible to the rest of Suva. That community was forged by location, infrastructure, history, legislation, rules, diet, dress codes and therapies, but above all by the social relationships within. These could be short encounters, such as between doctors and patients, or, more commonly, between those who resided and worked within the asylum compound and might form a relationship over several decades: that is, the patients and their keepers, known as warders, attendants and orderlies.

Insanity created a unique community by throwing together groups usually segregated spatially and socially. Suva was a colonial city segmented by racial segregation within workplaces, schools, social clubs, recreational areas and residential areas.[24] However, unlike many colonies where separate asylums for Europeans and 'natives' were established – where 'native' meant all non-Europeans – the Suva Asylum catered to all ethnicities. Instead, from the early twentieth century until the 1960s racial and gendered boundaries operated internally, with separate wards for European men, European women, native men and native women. In 1906 a female 'side', enclosed within a fence, was established and by 1910 there were European wards.[25] The European Women's Ward had a separate entrance (possibly for privacy) from the asylum's main entrance and was located away from the men's wards, with the native female ward between. During the early twentieth century, however, insufficient beds for 'natives' meant that some were accommodated within the European wards.[26]

Part-Europeans were usually accommodated with Europeans, although family connections or class could determine to which ward they were allocated. A Part-European admitted in 1948 was assigned to the European women's ward. But the next day she was sent to the main women's ward after threatening to hang herself and being 'uncontrollable'. She was allowed to return to the European ward but after another escape attempt she was sent to the 'native cells'.[27] Disruptive Europeans might also be punished by being consigned to the native wards. On 27 March 1951, a European male, who voluntarily sought admission, damaged his bed and room. He then jumped over the asylum's wall and was later apprehended by police on a launch in nearby Walu Bay. He was sent to the native ward until 6 April when he was 'moved to European quarters as he had settled'.[28]

---

24 Suva was proclaimed a city in 1953.
25 *Fiji Royal Gazette* 1907; CSO MP 9771/09.
26 CSO 14/8621: CSO 3916/15.
27 Case books (CB) of Suva's asylum, 19 May 1948; PN 1537.
28 CB, 6 April 1951; PN 1673.

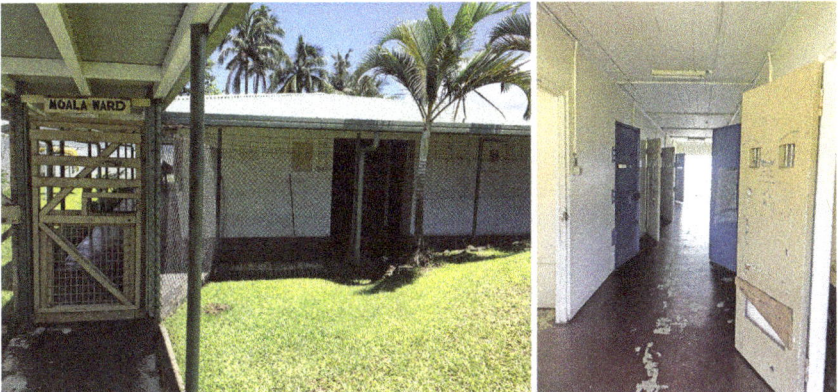

Figures 8.2 and 8.3: Moala ward, 2018.
Source: Courtesy Jacqueline Leckie.

During the late colonial period the wards were named after some of Fiji's islands and localities. The wards, with differing protocols and routine, were designated for different patient groups. The European women's ward, which closed in about 1962, was Levuka ward. The main women's ward (rebuilt in 1962 where the receiving ward had been) became Moala ward. Male patients were housed in Kadavu ward, or if at 'low risk' of escaping, in Vuda ward. Bua ward was a locked ward for patients under seclusion. The rooms in here were grim concrete cells with bars on the windows. Padded cells were installed from 1910 until World War II, but humidity and patients destroyed these. In 1977 St Elizabeth's Home, formerly for leprosy patients, was absorbed into St Giles, mainly for the care of those with severe intellectual and mental impairment.

The physical infrastructure also framed the hospital's culture; within a closed institution, poor sanitation and overcrowding heightened tensions between the residents. Sanitation throughout the compound was appalling during the first half of the twentieth century. In 1927, there were only one bath and two bucket-closets in each of the native wards, with 46 patients in the male native ward and 31 in the female native ward.[29] In the same year, approximately 45 native attendants and their families lived in the asylum's compound sharing only one bucket-closet and one bath. Sarjudei's death in 1927 from septicaemia, caused by dysentery, precipitated Dr Philip Harper, the acting chief medical

---

29 'Head attendant (Anderson) Public Lunatic Asylum to Medical Superintendent: Sanitary arrangements at the asylum', CSO 2216/27.

officer, to highlight the dreadful sanitation for both attendants and patients, 'with a consequent high mortality from dysentery, the Samoan attendants have been grossly overcrowded with a consequent high morbidity and mortality from lung diseases'.[30] Harper blamed structural issues and the government's inadequate expenditure on the asylum for its high death rate: 'the Asylum is in fact starved and we work against great difficulties until something goes wrong'.[31] Chief Medical Officer and Medical Superintendent Dr Aubrey Montague denied these assertions, but admitted that he had 'been willing to pinch, perhaps unduly, the expenditure on the asylum' because of other financial demands.[32]

By the 1920s, the average patient population increased to 61 and by the 1930s to 80. In early 1955, 143 patients resided in the hospital, despite only 80 official bed spaces:

> sixty men and women must sleep on the exposed verandas. In the cold weather or when the verandas are wet with rain these patients lie huddled in their blankets on the cold, wet cement.[33]

After a visit in 1951, the chair of the Board of Visitors, EC Woodward, remarked that these crowded and substandard conditions exacerbated 'quarrelling and annoyance' among patients as they sought out the few dry spots.[34] Overcrowding continued to plague St Giles, peaking at around 235 inpatients by the end of 1960 when the official bed capacity was 98.[35]

The asylum community comprised patients and those staff who had to be onsite for nursing, cooking, cleaning, laundry and security. From the beginning, the primary care and custody of patients at St Giles was entrusted to warders who had a huge responsibility. They assessed, managed, cared for and controlled, with minimal resources, patients from diverse cultures who had wide-ranging mental and neurological disorders. Many patients were admitted as malnourished and destitute, with physical injuries or other signs of bodily neglect such as scabies, lice, fleas or tropical ulcers. Several patients had serious illnesses, such as tuberculosis,

---

30 Harper to CS, 'Issues raised following report of Chief Police Magistrate into death of Sarjudei, 10 August 1927', 19 August 1927, CSO MP 27/3359. See PN 848.
31 Ibid. See PN 848.
32 Montague to CS, 3 January 1928, CSO MP 27/3359.
33 Unpublished annual reports on the mental hospital, 1954, St Giles Hospital.
34 Board of Visitor Reports, 6 March 1951, CSO MP 3359/27, F48/10, part 2.
35 Colony of Fiji, Council Paper (CP) 32/61, *Medical department: Annual report for 1960* (Suva: Government Printer, 1961), 23.

anaemia or tertiary stage syphilis, or contracted life-threatening sickness, especially influenza, in the asylum. A number of female patients suffered from severe mental conditions exacerbated by childbirth or from physical and mental abuse. Regulations governed the asylum but were negotiated between patients and warders. Warders, as much as their charges, forged a community within the asylum. All residents endured substandard conditions, including poor sanitation. In 1947 health authorities condemned the warders' quarters.[36]

Warders also had their own hierarchy, headed by the chief warder, and they were subsumed within medical and administrative hierarchies, having to defer to doctors and the medical superintendent. A permanent medical officer, Dr Isaac Karim, was not appointed at St Giles until 1962. Two years later Dr Duncan Macgregor became the hospital's first psychiatrist and full-time medical superintendent. A psychiatric nurse was only appointed at St Giles in 1970.

St Giles's unique community until the 1960s rested with its Samoan staff, who were also a well-known part of Suva's Samoan community.[37] The growth of a Samoan community at St Giles reflected Suva's diverse cultural heritage from being a centre of trans-Pacific mobility. Fusi, from Samoa via Hawai'i, was one of the first warders appointed at the asylum in 1885.[38] Acting Chief Medical Officer Corney considered that Fusi 'is nearly as competent as a white man'[39] – a sign of the future preferential hiring of Samoans as warders. Racialised stereotypes concerning the abilities of different ethnic groups were entrenched within Suva's colonial networks: 'Samoan warders in many ways do their work very well, better than any other natives could do it, but they are South Sea Islanders and must be treated as such.'[40] Preferential hiring also reflected Suva's racially drawn labour pool, which was constrained by restrictions inhibiting Fijian settlement in town. Samoans and their descendants were landless immigrants in Suva, dependent on paid work. Over the generations at the asylum Samoans acquired a reputation for 'the special aptitude of the people of those islands for the duties of attending to people of

---

36   Board of Visitors report, 24 January 1947.
37   See Morgan Tuimaleali'ifano, *Samoans in Fiji: Migration, identity and communication* (Suva: Institute of Pacific Studies, Fiji, Tonga, and Western Samoa Extension Centres of the University of the South Pacific, 1990).
38   CSO 1645/85, 8 June 1885.
39   CSO 1047/85, 15 April 1885. Corney, Acting Chief Medical Officer (CMO) to CS.
40   MP 1412/14, 6 February 1914, to CMO.

unsound mind'.[41] Samoans were also positioned to work across the two main 'races' of Fijians and Indians, while Europeans cared for their own kind. Ethnic and kinship networks within Suva were important in hiring Samoan employees. The St Giles community of warders and their families became more ethnically diverse as Fijians were hired after World War II and a Kailoma (ethnically mixed) identity developed at St Giles, through intermarriage between Samoans, Fijians, Europeans, Indo-Fijians and others. Many lived onsite, although some orderlies lived just outside the compound in Valenimanumanu, Suva's oldest indigenous Fijian settlement,[42] or elsewhere in Suva.

The institutional stamp was pervasive for both patients and staff, where distinct routines, including the language of the asylum (and later psychiatry), emerged. Culture could be framed by legislation covering clothing and diet.[43] The rules varied according to gender and ethnicity. In 1914, Europeans were provided with considerably more clothing than natives, with separate clothing for day and night wear as well as shoes, socks or stockings. Native women patients were allocated cloth to make jackets and *sulus*, but it is unclear what clothing Indian women were expected to wear in the asylum. Native men were supposed to be issued with *sulus* and jumpers, while in 1914 the Board of Visitors found that Indian men were often provided only with a loincloth, which was 'totally insufficient'.[44] Separate diets were also stipulated for Europeans, Fijians and Polynesians, and Indians. These diets differed with respect to quantity and content. European diets consisted of more variety, meat and dairy products than the other diets. In December 1887 diets were formalised according to two classes, which equated to differential fees levied on patients that usually corresponded to racial categories. In practice these diets varied depending on the availability and cost of food and supplies in Suva, the number of patients and the superintendent's prerogative to approve special diets.

Patients and staff shared highly regimented daily routines that were inevitably disrupted by the unpredictability of mental illness, struggles between patients and between patients and staff, as well as environmental

---

41   Colony of Fiji, CP 40/38, *Medical department: Annual report for 1938* (Suva: Government Printer, 1940), 7.
42   IK Vuetibau, 'Squatting and the California Highway settlement, Suva', in *In Search of a Home*, ed. Leonard Mason and Patricia Hereniko (Suva: Institute of Pacific Studies, University of the South Pacific, 1987), 149.
43   See Leckie *Colonizing madness*, especially 91–93.
44   CSO MP 8621/14, Board of Visitors report, 1914.

vagaries such as tropical cyclones, landslides and even an earthquake in 1953 that destroyed several walls and much of the dispensary.[45] Patients and their keepers closely scrutinised one another, engaged in a dance of control and submission, or patients feigned acquiescence. Just as warders could read the signs of a patient's impending 'episode', so too could patients detect when they could challenge the rules and even escape. In 1914, when two warders fell asleep at 10 am in the male yard, 'a lunatic took the key from above their heads and walked out'.[46] Orderlies were playing cards with patients in 1966 when one was able to walk past unnoticed and escape, much to the patient's amusement.[47] Negligence by staff inverted the usual institutional hierarchies; patients disciplined staff by occasionally reporting staff breaches of security and care. During the 1960s, a patient, Temesi, wrote a letter to Head Attendant Charlie Sachs at 3:30 am, reporting that a warder 'paid no attention to his duty' and 'sleeps when he should be on guard'. This breach enabled Temesi and another patient to escape. In his letter, Temesi wrote, 'Dr—you shouldn't employ this hopeless man', and threatened to contact political and chiefly leader Ratu Kamisese Mara if his complaints were not considered. An Indo-Fijian patient also reported that a warder was asleep while on night duty and the warder was dismissed.[48]

Violence has been part of the St Giles community – embedded within institutional informal rules and a hierarchy that has often, but certainly not always, turned a blind eye to the struggles between patients and staff and between patients. Ideally, and according to asylum regulations, patients were not meant to be controlled through physical force, but staff did resort to physical coercion, including spatial and solitary confinement, to quell patients. The introduction after World War II of long-term drug therapy was supposed to alleviate violence. The true extent of violence and abuse has notoriously been kept within the confines of closed institutions. In Suva, this blanket was briefly lifted when allegations of a culture of violence were headlined in 1970 in the *Pacific Review*: 'Are Mental Patients At Suva Subjected To Cruelty? A CORRESPONDENT SAYS "YES".'[49]

---

45 CB, 15 September 1953.
46 CSO MP 7315/14.
47 MS (Medical Superintendent) to DMS (Director, Medical Services), 30 November 1966, 'MS. 56.2 Incidents' file at St Giles.
48 Confidential files, MS; PN 2471; PN 2783. Temesi is a pseudonym.
49 'Are mental patients at Suva subjected to cruelty?', *Pacific Review*, 29 August 1970; PN 2633.

The letter writer, signed as 'A sick patient' of Suva, claimed that St Giles is 'run like a 12th century Roman slavery camp' and 'virtually run like a prison':

> The inmates are treated very harshly, cruelty and savagery is rampant everywhere ... A common source of fun for SOME ORDERLIES is 'Charlie' and 'Safique'. These two unfortunate patients have been inmates of this institution for some time. These poor unfortunate beings are treated like punching bags. One orderly takes pleasure in punching Charlie everytime he passes him. Poor Charlie simply steps aside trembling. If someone else speaks for Charlie, the orderly tells him to 'shut up' and mind his own business. It is no use complaining to the visiting doctor or anyone else. They simply ignore us and accept the words of the Orderly ... Some orderlies excite other patients to violence and when the patients start fighting among themselves, the orderlies appear to derive sadistic pleasure out of it and simply stand and watch and actually kick some of the patients and provoke them to fight.

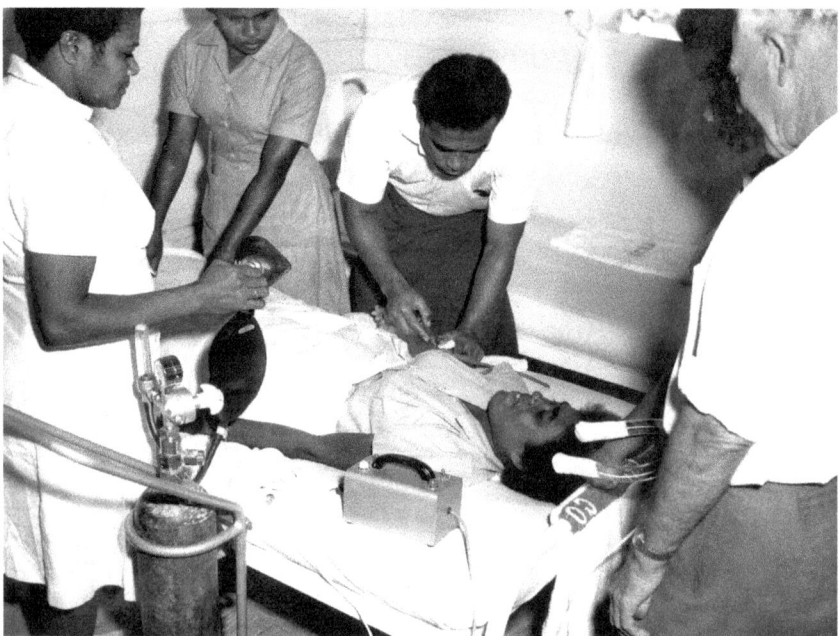

Figure 8.4: Mock ECT, St Giles Hospital, 1965 with Dr M Vuki, deputy head orderly, Asena Ranadi and head orderly, Charlie Sachs.
Source: Courtesy National Archives of Fiji, #G7245.

Routines changed for the St Giles community after World War II, when new drug regimens of antipsychotic and sedative medication and shock therapies of cardiazol, modified insulin coma, but mostly electro-convulsive therapy (ECT), were introduced.[50] A calmer atmosphere enabled patients to be provided with some amenities previously limited to the European ward: curtains, mats, pictures, chairs, dining tables and cutlery.

A large part of the daily routine at St Giles during the colonial era centred on work and occupational therapy. Work has long been regarded as therapeutic and essential in the restoration of moral, mental and physical normalcy for mental patients.[51] In 1887 the asylum's Board of Visitors observed that some patients were 'permitted to amuse themselves in gardening close to the Asylum grounds, under the supervision of a warder'.[52] Work was not simply for pleasure, but patients' labour and food production was necessary to supplement the asylum's meagre budget. The chief warder was denied prison labour in 1888 because 'the work must be done, as opportunity occurs, by the patients who may be physically fit'.[53] Patients produced crops such as *dalo*, cassava, yams, bananas and pawpaw.[54] They maintained the asylum lawns and gardens and at times did heavier labouring.[55] The asylum even had dairy cows in 1915. Many patients enjoyed participating in familiar routines, such as planting, weeding and harvesting crops.

Patients who were able were expected to clean the wards and some patients were selected to clean the staff quarters.[56] Before World War II, a few patients served as messengers for staff. Regulations in 1914 stipulated that the European female attendant was to 'endeavour to find occupation[s] for all the patients, such as reading, gardening, sewing clothes, washing, scrubbing and other suitable occupation[s]'.[57] At various times patients worked in painting, carpentry, the asylum's laundry, a canteen, bookbindery and even making envelopes for government. Suva's weather was often a dampener on outdoor activities and confined patients indoors or

---

50   Leckie, *Colonizing madness*, 174–78.
51   See Waltraud Ernst, *Work, psychiatry and society, c. 1750–2015* (Manchester: Manchester University Press, 2016), doi.org/10.7228/manchester/9780719097690.001.0001.
52   Board of Visitors report, *Annual report*, 16 December 1887, CSO 3847/87.
53   Corney, Acting MS to Chief Warder, 14 January 1888, St Giles Hospital.
54   For example, Montague to DMS, Annual Report, 1932, F48/4/5.
55   Commented on in several annual reports, for example, *Board of Visitors annual report, 1897*, CSO 96/98; *Annual report for 1938*, F48/4/5.
56   Dorothy Sachs, personal communication, 17 January 2002.
57   CP 8621/14.

on verandahs, where they were often bored and in cramped conditions. Only some patients were considered suitable to participate in occupational therapy: art, sewing and craft work such as making doormats and quilts and weaving mats, fans and baskets.

Patients did object to working and in 1924 one wrote a clearly exaggerated letter to the 'Protector of the poor', alleging that the asylum operated with forced labour – 'we are treated as prisoners' – with male patients working between seven and nine hours a day, carrying firewood and stones. He claimed that patients were beaten and held, suffering 'blows on our stomachs', and that patients were almost starved.[58]

Hidden and Visible: St Giles and Suva

The power of all-encompassing and enclosed institutions and the fear of mental institutions has partly been because of the secrecy over their internal functioning. St Giles has moreover unfortunately been not only a hospital for care and treatment but also used as a 'dumping ground' for a small number of people suffering from mental illness. Yet St Giles was never an institution totally cut off from the rest of Suva. Government authorities tried to manage public perceptions. The letter written by a patient to the *Pacific Review* could not have been published at a more sensitive time, with Fiji's looming Independence. The newspaper's editor, Ratu Mosese Varesekele, although a watchdog of the civil service,[59] was circumspect in his response: 'It is well known that the St Giles Mental Hospital in Suva is a humane institution with warm and understanding staff.' Doctors privately regarded the letter writer as 'a delusional' patient who had made allegations that were 'quite untrue' and his 'absurd allegations are lies and fabrications'.[60] Publicly, the acting director of medical services, DW Beckett, denied the 'cruel charge', defended St Giles staff and suggested that such allegations could deter mentally ill people from seeking treatment. He explained that the letter was symptomatic of mental disease where there can be a desire to make complaints and cause trouble out of sheer maliciousness.[61]

---

58   PN 693; PN 737; CSO 24/1059.
59   See Brij V Lal, *A vision for change: A. D. Patel and the politics of Fiji* (Canberra: Australian National University Press, 2011), 121–24, doi.org/10.22459/VC.11.2011.
60   Confidential file seen by author.
61   Letter to the editor, *Pacific Review*, 18 September 1970, 16.

Such media attention to patient conditions at St Giles was unusual before the twenty-first century. Information about the hospital was more likely to be based on rumour or, at best, when a family member or neighbour was taken there. A few Suva residents worked at the hospital either permanently or were brought in, such as Public Works Department workers. Prisoners sometimes worked at the asylum, but, as during St Giles's earlier years, patients were expected to provide much of the labour.[62]

Suva's main hospital was another conduit between the asylum and Suva. The asylum had started in 1884 as an annex to the hospital before asylum patients were moved to new buildings at the present-day site. The asylum's medical superintendent and nurse visited from the Colonial Hospital every few days. Patients could be temporarily transferred to the main hospital for medical treatment that was unavailable at St Giles. People with acute mental episodes, including those who attempted suicide or who had chronic conditions such as alcoholism, might be treated at the main hospital before admission to St Giles. In 1968 medical and nursing students began to be posted at St Giles for short periods.

Medical authorities tried to manage the visibility of asylum patients. Patient confidentiality and patient safety from public ridicule were key considerations, but minimising embarrassing or adverse publicity about St Giles was important. When concern was raised in the Legislative Council in 1929 over patients frequently carrying supplies and wood from the town and prison to the asylum, the official line was:

> that there is nothing degrading or menial in the performance of useful labour in public, by persons who while mentally unsound are capable of performing the service without hardship and whose bodily health in some cases is materially benefited thereby.[63]

The 'aesthetic aspect' of patients working in public was raised by Dr MacPherson, the director of medical services, when he suggested in 1941 that the mental hospital could be developed like a farm colony, where the 'more fit inmates' could undertake market gardening and milk production to supply government departments. MacPherson pointed out that a 'number of patients tend to divest themselves of clothing, etc., and accordingly public scandal may be provoked'.[64]

---

62 Prisoner Labour, 28 February 1885, Memorandum from Corney, Acting CMO, CSO 598/85.
63 Question asked in Legislative Council, 30 October 1929, CSO 5191/29.
64 DMS to CS, 2 June 1941, F48/10 part 1.

MacPherson was also concerned that working in the community might offer patients opportunities for escape, a fear held by many within the Suva public who considered all asylum patients as violent. Mental patients were not allowed to leave asylum premises without legal authority or unless accompanied by hospital staff. Some escapees were quite determined, bending wires or removing iron bars, as a patient did in 1946. He then scaled the concrete walls and got as far as Navua where warders caught him.[65] Pita Turaganivalu, diagnosed as a religious maniac and also arrested for seditious activities on Vanua Levu, escaped during the night of 6 June 1913. Like many escapees he fled towards the prison, where he managed to steal a boat. Pita tried to sail to Beqa before he was rescued and captured.[66] Other fleeing patients headed towards nearby Valenimanumanu, up the hill towards Samabula or Tamavua, or down to Tamavua-i-wai settlement, Walu Bay or central Suva. These were mostly uneventful escapes and captures. Patients might take the opportunity to walk past a sleeping attendant. A patient in 1992 calmly waited at St Giles's gates because he had been granted home leave. No one came to collect him, so he proceeded to his home in Nasinu and yet he became an 'escapee'.[67] As earlier noted, a patient here named Temesi who escaped was found by Head Attendant Sachs in town enjoying a cigarette with a watchman before he was returned to St Giles. By the 1990s some patients quietly sauntered out to purchase cigarettes and sweets in Samabula and returned of their own volition. If caught, they were recorded as escapees and could be punished through confinement to Bua ward, 'behaviour modification' and sometimes ECT.

St Giles had non-medical visitors from Suva and further afield. Most of these were carefully staged formal visits, such as the governor's visit in 1946. He was 'impressed by the cleanliness and generally cheerful atmosphere: almost unique, I imagine, in an institution of its kind. It reflects great credit on the Head Attendant and his staff'.[68] The Board of Visitors, appointed by Fiji's Legislative Council and the colonial secretary, was the legal linchpin between St Giles and the community outside. It comprised the attorney-general, the chief medical officer and three governor's appointees who were usually prominent Suva citizens. The board was expected to visit the hospital at least once every three months to

---

65 CB, 2 December 1946; Board of Visitors report, 24 January 1946.
66 'Reward for the capture of Pita', 20 June 1913, CSO MP 5279/13.
67 File, 'escapes', 15 February 1992–October 1996, St Giles Hospital.
68 CP 1/48 *Annual report 1946*.

report on patients, staffing, management and conditions. Other visitors from Suva were from philanthropic, charitable and religious organisations, who, along with some businesspeople, might donate items to the hospital. Some groups gifted food treats to patients, such as the Indian Ladies Association in 1934 or villagers from Vatoa island who visited St Giles in 1996.[69] In 1977, Grace Deoki, chair of the Board of Visitors, initiated the hospital's first open day. This provided a chance for the curious public to see behind the walls and to purchase items made by patients and plants and produce from the gardens. Proceeds went into a Patients' Comfort Fund, which along with donations collected by the Board of Visitors paid for patients' necessities not provided by families (e.g. soap), recreation equipment, excursions, social evenings (Indian nights, Fijian nights, South Pacific nights), dances, celebrations and feasts such as for Diwali, Christmas and New Year. From the 1970s, selected patients were taken on excursions into town and into the surrounding areas to see movies, attend the Hibiscus Festival, the Diwali lights of Suva, or enjoy bus rides and picnics to, for example, Suva Point, Sawani waterfalls, Deuba beach, Mosquito Island and Orchid Island. Such activities ceased with the 1987 coups. During the 1990s, the open days at St Giles became part of a newly introduced Mental Awareness Week.

The most crucial outside contact for patients was when their families and friends visited them during designated visiting hours. Sadly, many patients never had visitors. Visitors informed others about conditions within St Giles. On 28 February 1940, a visitor complained to politician Vishnu Deo that his son had been hit by a warder. In 1944 another visitor complained that a Samoan warder had 'roughly handled' an elderly male European patient: objections as much about transgressions of race and status.[70] St Giles has also had irregular or unwelcome visitors, some who harassed patients, stole crops or found the compound a convenient space in which to drink alcohol and *yaqona*.[71] St Giles's walls and security have been to keep the public out as much as keep patients in.

---

69   18/12/34 Board of Visitors Report; *Fiji Times*, 14 October 1996.
70   Visitor to CS, 15 February 1944, DMS F48/353.
71   For example, GR Anderson, the head attendant, reported thieving in the asylum's plantations. CSO MP 16/2206.

SUVA STORIES

Figure 8.5: Open day, St Giles, 1981.
From left: Mrs Grace Deoki (chair, St Giles Board of Visitors), Matron Qamrul Nisha Mohammed, Governor-General Ratu Sir George Cakobau and Medical Superintendent Dr Balram Iyer examine a raffia tray made by a patient.
Source: Courtesy National Archives of Fiji, # MB5655.

The first psychiatrist and full-time medical superintendent, Duncan Macgregor, took a decisive step towards breaking down the barriers between patients and outsiders when, in 1966, he ordered the demolition of most of the concrete walls that encircled St Giles.[72] Macgregor hoped that removing the impenetrable walls would offer patients a sense of freedom and that greater visibility might reduce the stigma associated with the place and the patients. His successor, Dr David Sell, reiterated that: 'The mental hospital has stood for too long in isolation with its inhabitants out of sight, out of mind and socially stigmatized.'[73] Those stone walls left standing after 1966 were given new visibility in 2010, when they were painted with vibrant murals by artist John Mausio, staff, patients and members of the Youth Champs for Mental Health.

---

72   Colony of Fiji, CP 12/68, *Medical department: Annual report for 1966* (Suva: Government Press, 1968), 9.
73   Colony of Fiji, CP 39/69, *Medical department: Annual report for 1968* (Suva: Government Press, 1969), 10.

A potent change in the relationship between St Giles and Suva since the 1960s was the introduction of outpatient mental health services and community care for former patients. For many years such inroads into the community had a very slow uptake, impeded by inadequate aftercare and resources and the persistence of stigma and misunderstanding surrounding mental illness. Community psychiatric nursing for the Suva area began in 1993. The goals were impressive – to provide community psychiatric care, support affected families, decrease hospital admission and readmission rates, prevent new admissions, educate the public and health professionals, raise the profile of mental health and promote community mental health – but hampered through minimal resources and the city's social and economic problems.[74] In 1997 the St Giles Day Care Centre for the rehabilitation of discharged patients was established to encourage their integration into and employment in the community.[75] In contrast to the colonial years, when many patients spent most of their lives hidden from the community,[76] many former patients are more likely to still live within the community, care for their children and engage in productive work. A radical overhaul of mental health legislation in 2010 – the Fiji Mental Health Decree – widened the definition of mental health and treatment away from the restrictive legislation dating from 1884, to liberalise patient treatment and review, the prevention of mental disorders, mental health awareness and the development of rehabilitative and community psychiatric services.[77] Stress Management Wards were established within general hospitals in Suva, Labasa and Lautoka. The new discourse of stress aimed to destigmatise the association of mental health with madness and to treat mental disorders such as depression, anxiety and substance abuse.

---

74 Abel Smith, 'Community psychiatric nursing: The Fiji experience', Presentation to Community Health Workshop, 15–19 April 1996, St Giles Hospital.
75 Kevin Gounder and Luciana Brugnoli, 'Mental health education', *Mental Health Nursing Newsletter* (February–March 1998). STG 2/3/9.
76 Before 1961 only 35 to 65 per cent of patients were discharged within two years. Duncan Macgregor, 'Notes of a meeting between three South Pacific psychiatrists', in South Pacific Commission, *Mental health in the South Pacific: Report of a meeting of experts held at Suva (Fiji) from 19 to 22 May, and at Nouméa (New Caledonia) from 23 to 27 May 1967*, Technical Paper no. 154 (Nouméa: South Pacific Commission, 1967), 2.
77 Mental Health Decree 2010 (54/2010), *Republic of Fiji Islands Government Gazette* 11, no. 119 (2010).

In 2018 Rosy Akbar, minister for health and medical services, announced that St Giles Hospital would be relocated to the former Ba Mission Hospital site.[78] Talk of resiting St Giles has surfaced over the years, beginning as early as 1955, when Vishnu Deo suggested that the buildings be used to house the poor and destitutes from Samabula. Government told Deo that there were competing claims on the site.[79] Many years later I heard that developers wanted to build a luxury hotel on this prime site but possible landslips have been one deterrent to these plans.

By 2016 there were only between 60 to 80 patients in St Giles; no indication of the 4,401 outpatients seen at St Giles in 2015 or the 405 patients admitted that year,[80] or the services and training that the hospital provides to Suva, Fiji and the Pacific. Mental health provisions in Suva are now far more community-based than during the colonial years but there remains a serious lack of supported accommodation for former St Giles patients in Suva.[81] St Giles is still a site of fear and mystery for many within Suva, and as long as this persists, the stigma associated with mental health will remain. Meanwhile an increasing number of people in Suva face mental health issues – even if most will never warrant admission to St Giles. Others who are homeless or begging on the streets are visible, but their plight and mental health needs are hidden. This chapter has provided a synopsis of St Giles's history in an attempt to shed light on these dark corners of Suva's history.

---

78   Luke Nacei, 'Health minister reveals plans to relocate St Giles Hospital to Ba', *Fiji Times*, 15 October 2018.
79   'Mental hospital. Complaints regarding treatment of patients raised in Legislative Council', 5 December 1955, F 48/524.
80   Gary Batt, 'St Giles hospital Fiji: A step back in time', *Australian College of Mental Health Nurses* (Winter 2017): 12–13.
81   Ana Ravulo, 'Finding homes for patients is a challenge: Dr Koroivuki', *FBC News*, 8 October 2018, www.fbcnews.com.fj/news/finding-homes-for-patients-is-a-challenge-dr-koroivuki/.

9

Supreme Court Stories: Narrating Violence in Suva Streets and Homes

Kate Stevens

The establishment of British law was a cornerstone of the colonial civilising mission in Fiji. The Supreme Court was a key symbolic and physical presence in the landscape of colonial Suva. It was both a monument to colonial power as well as a space where intimate and personal stories were retold. When the courts adjudicated hearings over criminal cases, many of the accounts recounted violent and painful experiences. The remaining archive is thus a place where the personal and private intersects with practical, quotidian enforcement of colonial rule. The stories told before colonial magistrates thus reveal a darker side of Suva life and how women and children responded to violence that occurred in Suva's streets and homes. However, these stories were also constrained and silenced by the judicial process.

This chapter looks at the establishment and limits of the colonial legal system in the early decades of colonial Suva, focusing on the cases of rape and sexual violence brought before the Supreme Court between 1875 and 1920. Individuals appearing before the courts navigated relationships in the urban environment and negotiated how ideas of race, gender and respectability were overlaid on the changing colonial landscape. Though overall few in number, these cases reveal Suva as a cosmopolitan and culturally mixed settlement in a colony predicated on ideas of racial and economic separation. The evidence presented also highlights aspects of women's experiences within the urban environment. Cases of sexual violence are one of the few places where women appeared before the Supreme Court and one of the few places where their words are recorded in the colonial archive. Such cases therefore suggest some of the challenges that women experienced living in Suva as well as in meeting colonial standards of respectability and credibility. The silences and limits also speak to the challenges in accessing justice through the colonial courts.

This is, in Sally Engle Merry's phrase, 'law at its bottom fringes, where it intersects the social life of ordinary people rather than where legal doctrines are created'.[1] As the chief police magistrate in Fiji and later British judge in the New Hebrides, Gilchrist Alexander stated '[t]he Magistrate finds himself the repository of the domestic secrets not only of the native, but also of the white element of the population'.[2] Focusing specifically on sexual crime thus enables insight into aspects of Suva life that are otherwise largely absent in the archive.[3]

---

1   Sally Engle Merry, *Colonizing Hawai'i: The cultural power of law* (Princeton: Princeton University Press, 2000), 8, doi.org/10.1515/9780691221984.
2   Gilchrist Alexander, *From the Middle Temple to the South Seas* (London: John Murray, Albemarle Street, 1927), 82. See also 84–85 for more comments on the way in which court gave insight into human nature and 'the whole domestic atmosphere which seems inevitably to permeate the discussion of native sayings and doings'.
3   For scholarship on how anxieties around rape or assault of white women framed unequal colonial social and economic relations, and conversely created conditions enabling sexual violence towards indigenous women, see Norman Etherington, 'Natal's black rape scare of the 1870s', *Journal of Southern African Studies* 15, no. 1 (1988): 36–53, doi.org/10.1080/03057078808708190; John Pape, 'Black and white: The "perils of sex" in colonial Zimbabwe', *Journal of Southern African Studies* 16, no. 4 (1990): 699–720, doi.org/10.1080/03057079008708257; Pamela Scully, 'Rape, race and colonial culture: The sexual politics of identity in the nineteenth-century Cape Colony, South Africa', *American Historical Review* 100, no. 2 (1995): 335–59, doi.org/10.2307/2169002; Jonathan Saha, 'The male state: Colonialism, corruption and rape investigations in the Irrawaddy Delta c.1900', *Indian Economic and Social History Review* 48, no. 3 (2010): 343–76, doi.org/10.1177/001946461004700303; and on the history of rape generally, Joanna Bourke, *Rape: A history from 1860 to the present* (London: Virago, 2007); Anna Clark, *Women's silence, men's violence: Sexual assault in England, 1770–1845* (London and New York: Pandora Press, 1987); and Georges Vigarello, *A history of rape: Sexual violence in France from the 16th to 20th century* (Cambridge: Polity Press, 2000).

Colonial Space, Race and Courts

In early colonial Fiji, the evolution of a plurality of courts divided criminal cases, deliberately or otherwise, along the boundaries of race as well as geography, thereby separating indigenous and European subjects (and indentured labourers in Fiji) within the judicial system. The pattern of courts across the colony broadly reflected the attempts to compartmentalise racial groups into different geographic and economic spaces. Fijians were encouraged under Gordon and subsequent governors to maintain a 'traditional' lifestyle and non-monetary economy in villages.[4] Native Regulation No. 5 (1878) restricted Fijians' movements, requiring chiefly permission to leave the village or to take up paid labour.[5] Though restrictions on entering paid labour were relaxed somewhat in 1912, the importance of village life and obedience to chiefs was maintained. Indentured labourers were also subject to restrictions. They were housed in plantation 'lines' (cramped and unsanitary blocks of housing) and labour laws curtailed their freedom to travel. Though Europeans managing plantations lived in relative isolation, traders, officials and settlers mostly congregated in the urban centres. Norman Etherington outlines how different court systems existed in different spaces broadly contiguous with these socio-economic fault lines. He found:

> a system articulated into four separate legal worlds operating side by side. What mattered most was not the race or national origins of persons charged, but the arena in which those persons operated. Town justice was different from plantation justice, and both were in their turn different from justice meted out in the Provincial Courts.[6]

I argue, however, that race did play a large part in determining legal outcomes, as the different arenas of the plantation and the village were frequently demarcated along racial, as well as economic, lines.

---

4   Nicholas Thomas, *Colonialism's culture: Anthropology, travel, and government* (Princeton: Princeton University Press, 1994), 116. Note that this encouragement could be highly interventionalist involving, for example, the relocation of villages considered to be in too remote or unsanitary locations and thus allowing for easier oversight of the village and its inhabitants.
5   See Regulation No. 5 1878 in *Regulations of the Native Regulation Board: 1877–1882* (London: Harrison and Sons, 1883), 38–39.
6   Norman Etherington, 'The gendering of indirect rule: Criminal law and colonial Fiji, 1875–1900', *The Journal of Pacific History* 31, no. 1 (1996): 45–46, doi.org/10.1080/00223349608572805.

Figure 9.1: Government Buildings from Fiji Club, n.d.
Source: RD Fitzgerald, P32.4.150 Fiji Museum.

Figure 9.2: Government House, Suva, Fiji, 1884.
Source: Burton Brothers, P32.4.106 Fiji Museum.

Police courts, which operated in Suva and Levuka, dealt with crimes stemming from the problems of urban settlement (theft, drunkenness and offences to public order and morals) and operated like their equivalents in Britain or British settler colonies. The Supreme Court adjudicated on serious crime, including murder, assault, rape and sexual assault. These cases were forwarded from the lower courts to the criminal sittings held quarterly in Suva or Levuka. Trials could be conducted by jury but only if all parties involved were European, or by assessors, who advised the chief justice but did not have a decisive vote in the outcome of the case. The Criminal Procedure Ordinance of 1875 ensured that any cases involving Fijians or Polynesian immigrants were tried by assessors, as the impartiality of a European jury in judging crimes involving non-Europeans was deemed dubious at best.[7] This was justified on the basis of similar procedures in India, but nevertheless irked settlers who regarded trial-by-jury as a British birthright.[8]

Of the different courts, the most complete records survive for the Supreme Court. Depositions, arrest warrants and some verdicts are preserved and offer insight into the operation of criminal trials. These records are not always complete, as verdicts were not always recorded and the registers were missing at the time of research. I have supplemented where possible with newspaper coverage, though this is limited in other ways. Archives themselves are colonial structures, and this is reflected in the way historians encounter them too. In the court cases for rape and sexual assault, for example, when reading each file the medical evidence is encountered first in the bundle of depositions held together in the file.

The cases that I examine include charges of rape, attempted rape, carnal knowledge, attempted carnal knowledge, and indecent assault. These offer insight into how official and local ideas about sexuality, morality, race and gender intersected and diverged.[9] Rape cases centred on questions of penetration and consent. Indecent assault (sexual assault short of

---

7   See Peter Duff, 'The evolution of trial by judge and assessors in Fiji', *The Journal of Pacific Studies* 21 (1997): 189–213. Trial by assessor was extended to Indian, Chinese and Pacific Islanders in 1883; Bridget Brereton, *Law, justice, empire: The colonial career of John Gorrie, 1829–1892* (Barbados: University of the West Indies Press, 1997), 127. The chief native commissioner was 'to serve *ex officio* as assessor' on any criminal cases involving a Fijian.
8   See Martin Wiener, *An empire on trial: Race, murder, and justice under British Rule, 1870–1935* (Cambridge: Cambridge University Press, 2009), 83, doi.org/10.1017/CBO9780511800665.
9   While sodomy (sexual intercourse between men) and bestiality (sexual relationships with an animal) appear rarely in the Supreme Court, they involved a different gendered dynamic and are not considered here.

penetrative rape) required proof of lack of consent though the physical evidence required was less defined. Carnal knowledge, the charge for rape or indecent assault of (female) children, specified that if the victim was under 16 years or, more commonly, under 12 or 13 years, the question of consent was irrelevant.[10] Only physical proof of the assault was required, though this could be problematic to establish and therefore the subject of speculation. Cases of sexual crime thus offer valuable case studies because they involved both physical evidence and moral judgment, and gendered, racialised hierarchies of knowledge and reliability.[11]

While the Supreme Court in Suva heard cases from across the colony, the examples in this article come primarily from a small number of cases of rape and sexual assault that occurred in the town between 1880 and 1920. The majority of the Supreme Court case files for serious crimes, including murder, rape and serious assault, survive.[12] The paper trail for individual cases is, however, almost always fragmented.[13] Qualitative analysis is difficult for a number of reasons. Colonial *Blue Book* reports for Fiji during this period divided all crime into categories that are overly broad for the purpose of most historical analysis. For example, rape and sexual assault cases were included as 'offences against the person', while other crimes were categorised as 'larceny', 'property offences other than larceny', 'drunkenness' or 'other offences'.[14] Moreover, such figures tell us little about the true extent of sexual crime due to non-reporting, stigma and shame, a problem noted across historical and contemporary settings.[15]

---

10   Supreme Court Ordinance 1875 (No. 14) Criminal Procedure Ordinance 1875 (No. 23), and Summary Offences Ordinance 1876 (No. 17), Fiji Certified Copies of Acts 1875–1880, CO 84/1, National Archives Kew, London (hereafter NAK).
11   Moreover, as Martin Wiener explains, interracial murder – like sexual crime – trials provide 'revealing episodes in the ordinary operation of the criminal law across the Empire, cases in which this underlying conflict [between liberalism and inequality] could not simply be argued in the abstract but had to be resolved by a courtroom decision over the fate of an actual defendant'. Wiener, *An empire on trial*, 5.
12   Each case file generally contains the indictment, arrest warrants and court summons and depositions from the lower court taken from the victim, witnesses and accused (if a statement was made) that were forwarded from the lower courts. They do not contain a record of the testimony heard in the Supreme Court itself, leaving open the possibility that the statements provided were different.
13   At the time of research, the registers of criminal cases were missing from the National Archives of Fiji, making it difficult to draw robust conclusions regarding the relative volume of sexual versus other cases before the court over the 45 years analysed or especially to establish the number of cases dismissed as *nolle prosequi*.
14   Police reports for some years give a detailed breakdown of cases heard in the Police Courts in Suva and Levuka.
15   Bourke, *Rape: A History from 1860*; Susan Estrich, 'Rape', *The Yale Law Journal* 95, no. 6 (1986): 1087–184, doi.org/10.2307/796522.

Magistrates' comments nevertheless reveal that many cases were not pursued beyond the lower courts. For example, European Stipendiary Magistrate Valla requested instruction on this matter from the colonial secretary, noting that:

> Many cases occur from time to time, some of them are actually rape, but I find that so far, the cases sent to the Att Gen. have not sufficient evidence in his option to ensure a <u>conviction</u> for rape and in consequence the accused is dismissed with absolutely no punishment – even for assault …[16]

Officials preferred to pursue certain cases in the lower courts.[17] Of cases tried by the Supreme Court, verdicts and sentences were not always recorded in individual files (particularly after 1889), complicating efforts to assess longer-term patterns and trends in rape and sexual assault cases and the relationship between evidence, testimony and the outcome.[18]

Dangerous Streets: Protesting Colonial Law

Such cases could be a site for political protest in Suva, as elsewhere across empire. Many European residents, alongside officials and lawmakers, conceptualised Suva as a European space. The perceived threats to European women and children in the town are best illustrated by an editorial in the *Fiji Times* in April 1884, which concerned a case of sexual assault that did not make it to the Supreme Court. Mirroring the stirrings of discontent in Papua New Guinea examined by Amirah Inglis and Claudia Knapman's previous work on Fiji, this article decried the 'dastardly attempts upon defenceless white women' by 'colored barbarians' and 'semi-barbarians' in the Fijian capital.[19] While there were a relatively high number of Suva sexual violence cases brought to the Supreme Court in that year (three in total), the editorial focused on a case dealt with in the lower police court. The author asked:

---

16 Memo for the Assistant Colonial Secretary, SM Valia, 13/1/93 CSO 304/1893, in CSO 2320/1985, National Archives of Fiji, Suva (hereafter NAF).
17 Brereton, *Law, justice, empire*, 136–37.
18 This was problematic given that the registers that would enable cross-referencing of case files to trial outcomes were missing.
19 *Fiji Times*, Wednesday 9 April 1884; Amirah Inglis, *Not a white woman safe: Sexual anxiety and politics in Port Moresby, 1920–1934* (Canberra: Australian National University Press, 1974); Claudia Knapman, *White women in Fiji 1835–1930: The ruin of empire?* (Sydney: Allen & Unwin, 1986), Kindle.

> Can anyone read with temperate pulsation and hands unclenched the tale of the miscreant found concealed in a white woman's bedchamber, arrested, brought before a police court, and sentenced to – two months imprisonment! Can any one wonder that the result has been, not the suppression, but the rapid increase of attempts so lightly regarded, and so playfully punished.[20]

They called attention to 'the failure of the law to punish in a befitting manner a crime so heinous [it] has had the natural effect of encouraging the lustful savage to persistence in his attempts'. The piece continues well over a thousand words in this vein. The outcry reflected the claimed 'general sympathy' of the Suva population, at least some of who joined a public meeting in protest of the handling of this case (and another letter to the editor supported the use of physical punishment).[21] The editorial suggested whipping as punishment as a means to prevent further such violence.

The concern over this specific incident, and the perceived threats towards white women, reflected the anxieties over European status in the colony: 'White men were quick to respond to any hint of Fijian interest in white women.'[22] The protection of women and children in Suva – or more specifically the failure to do so – stood for broader settler perspectives that their standing in the capital and colony was undermined by government protectionism towards Fiji's indigenous subjects. This strategy was a common one across the British imperial world.

Claiming that the government was at fault and 'itself directly responsible for the evil now attaining to such alarming proportion', the editorial presented a gendered narrative of white hegemony under threat:

> Ten years ago, before her Majesty's Colonial Government assumed rule in Fiji, Europeans were objects of respect throughout the group. Their womenfolk especially were held in esteem almost in veneration, and enjoyed an absolute immunity from insult or annoyance. From the day the first Governor entered upon his tenure of office until now the constant official effort has been to degrade the European in the eyes of the native, to elevate the native at the expense of the whiteman, to sneer down in the native mind the idea, till then firmly fixed, of a 'superior race,' and to

---

20 *Fiji Times*, Wednesday 9 April 1884.
21 *Fiji Times*, Wednesday 23 April 1884.
22 Knapman, *White women in Fiji*, Location 2806, Kindle.

increase official importance by making it appear to the native that all outside the circle are men of no consequence whatever. This most injudicious policy has been strictly adhered to and has been but too successful. As in the case of all lower orders, the idea of a perfect equality with those above then [sic – them?] was easily instituted, and in the attempt to assert it, self-conscious equality became an affectation of superiority. This feeling has been fostered and nurtured by the systematic petting of natives by prominent officials, generally during the first years of residence in the colony only, but in some notable instances, as a continuing habit. The force of such example has spread widely. It has been further strengthened by the attitude assumed by these same officials towards what both they and their colored associates are accustomed to regard as the white commonality, and the natural result is seen in the disposition which prompts the dregs of colored rascality to attempt the violation of white women.[23]

While I do not have records of the specific incident that lead to this outcry, the piece is revealing of local European perceptions of the city: that it should be a white space and that this was infringed upon by the presence and behaviour of non-European men. However, the voices of women and of non-European residents are absent in this construction of the city.

Suva Lives on Trial

But what of the cases that do make it to the Supreme Court itself? What do the experiences and narratives recorded in this archive reveal of intimacy, violence and colonial rule in Suva? Across the first 40 years of the Supreme Court's operation in Suva, I have identified 13 relevant cases that took place in the town during this period. Elsewhere I look at cases across the colony, and I draw on some of these here for what they reveal about attitudes to justice and race across Fiji more broadly. Where possible, I have matched the Suva cases with coverage in the *Fiji Times*.[24] Of course, as the *Fiji Times* editorial quoted above suggests, many incidents never made it to the level of the Supreme Court.

---

23   *Fiji Times*, Wednesday 9 April 1884.
24   Some microfilm were unavailable or missing during research in July 2019.

Among those cases heard, a high number of complainants were young, indicative of who could be considered a victim. Children, particularly European children, were more often victims in these cases than adult women. In such cases, the home was frequently a space of vulnerability: a site of intimate interaction but also of policing and anxiety. Domestic servants, household visitors and family members were frequently cited as defendants in charges of carnal knowledge.[25] Indeed, cases of interracial sexual crime almost exclusively involved European children and non-European domestic servants. The disquiet of the European parents of young victims echo Stoler's work on anxieties over domestic space in the Dutch East Indies.[26] Overall, the large number of sexual cases involving child victims is striking. This likely reflects their vulnerability, official perceptions of innocence linked to age that were independent of race, and the role that family members played in bringing complaints forward to the police and courts.[27] These cases also tended to result in longer sentences for the accused, regardless of the racial dynamics in a particular case.

Aside from these cases involving children, there were few cases of interracial rape or sexual assault brought to Supreme Court trial in Suva or elsewhere. Given Knapman's scholarship highlighting the powerful and persistent ideologies of virtuous white womanhood held by colonial officials and settlers in Fiji, it is striking that few cases of rape and sexual assault involving European women are recorded before the courts.[28] Rather, many of the cases heard in the highest court involved violence between indentured labourers on plantations, illustrative of the constructed narrative of sexual jealousy explored by Brij Lal.[29] In Suva itself, the most common of those few cases recorded were between indentured Islanders and Fijians, given the city's more cosmopolitan population compared to other parts of the colony. Despite these limits, the cases hint at the diversity of living arrangements and economic participation in the capital, despite government, chiefly and the Colonial Sugar Refinery's attempts to keep individuals in their homes, villages or plantation communities.

---

25 For example in Case 48/1906, the accused allegedly had carnal knowledge of MC, six-year-old daughter of RA while helping move a bedstead into the house. See also Case 10/1882, Case 52/1917, Criminal Sittings, Fiji Supreme Court, NAF.
26 Ann Laura Stoler, *Carnal knowledge and imperial power: Race and the intimate in colonial rule* (Berkeley, Los Angeles and London: University of California Press, 2003).
27 See for example Case 13/1908; and Case 42/1908, Criminal Sittings, Fiji Supreme Court, NAF.
28 Knapman, *White women in Fiji*, Locations 2795, 2806, 2836, Kindle.
29 Brij V Lal, 'Veil of dishonour' in *Chalo Jahaji: On a journey through indenture in Fiji*, ed. Brij V Lal (Suva/Canberra: The Fiji Museum/Australian National University Press, 2000), 215–38.

For example, an 1884 trial involved a Fijian man charged with rape of a woman from Tokelau. The victim was working in Suva, and living with her husband along with other Islanders with a Chinese man in Suva.[30] The defendant appears to have been among the residents of this diverse household. On the night of 6 April, according to the woman's deposition, the accused came and lay naked beside the victim and felt her all over while she was asleep beside her husband. She promptly woke her husband and they sent for the police. Another resident, a 'boy' from the Solomon Islands, supported the woman's statement. The defendant denied the accusations: he stated he had gone to bed at 10 pm and awoke only when the woman was hurling bad language at him. The verdict for this case is not recorded with the depositions. Nevertheless, the case highlights the cosmopolitan nature of household life – something that officials and missionaries were keen to avoid across the colony but struggled to control, above all in the city.

These cases also provide a sense of the ways in which women and children were involved in the economic life and daily rhythms of the city. One such case occurred in 1892, where a 13-year-old Fijian girl, JMK, came from Nukuvatu to Suva with a companion to sell fish on Thursday 26 May. According to the statements from the two girls, the accused enquired what fish they had for sale, and asked them to bring the products to his house. JMK checked with the man if he was married before agreeing.[31] However, when the complainant and her companion arrived at his home, the accused attempted to rape the girl: he grabbed JMK's wrists and asked her to have 'connection' with him. JMK said she was too young. The defendant then 'took hold of my breasts [and] asked What are these?' The man pulled her to the ground and pulled off the victim's sulu as she called out. She then managed to run away, leaving her sulu on the ground behind, and reported the incident to the police.[32]

Another noteworthy case involved the European proprietress of a hotel in Suva, one of the more common occupations for women who sought or needed greater economic independence in the colony.[33] In 1905, the accused man was found not guilty of the attempted rape and indecent assault of AR, proprietress of the Melbourne Hotel. She had been assisting her daughter at the bar on the night of the assault. The medical

---

30   Case 15/1884, Criminal Sittings, Fiji Supreme Court, NAF.
31   The defendant replied that he had two wives.
32   Case 29/1892, Criminal Sittings, Fiji Supreme Court, NAF.
33   Knapman, *White women in Fiji*, Location 1270, Kindle.

practitioner GWA Lynch reported bruises on the victim's face and marks on her jaw, but did not examine the rest of her body. Cook Ghurharan told the court he found the accused's hat and spectacles the next morning.[34] AR was a female business owner and serving alcohol: gendered norms of appropriate occupations for women may have played into the verdict. Moreover, unlike most non-European defendants of the period, the defendant had representation in court and the initial case took place over three days of depositions at the Suva Police Court. This case parallels the gendered and racial narratives that underpinned the 1915 case against Stella Spencer for slapping a Fijian man. James Heartfield convincingly argues that Spencer's conviction in the case 'was not motivated by a desire to protect Fijians, but to punish those Europeans who failed to observe the policy of separation from the natives'.[35] Neither Spencer nor AR upheld the propriety expected of white women in the colony, and this influenced how they were perceived in the courtroom.

Overall, however, as was the case across the colony, there were relatively high numbers of convictions from Suva cases: for those 10 cases where I know the outcome, seven resulted in guilty verdicts, though sometimes of a lesser charge. The proportion of convictions likely reflects the high barriers for cases to proceed to the Supreme Court in the first place, as well as constraints in how these narratives of violence could be told and who could tell them and be believed within the colonial court system. The construction of the appropriate victim highlights some of the ways in which the courtroom was constructed as a male, colonial space in Fiji, as explored below.

Words and Bodies: Constructing Credible Victims

These cases provide one of the few places where women's voices can be heard directly in the colonial archive, yet their stories are structured by the nature of the court process.[36] Their testimony was often overshadowed by

---

34 Case 5/1905, Criminal Sittings, Fiji Supreme Court, NAF.
35 James Heartfield, '"You are not a white woman!"', *The Journal of Pacific History* 38, no. 1 (2003): 69–83, doi.org/10.1080/00223340306076.
36 For more on the voices of the colonised in Fiji's courts, see John Kelly, '"Coolie" as labour commodity: Race, sex, and European dignity in colonial Fiji', *The Journal of Peasant Studies* 19, nos. 3–4 (1992): 262, doi.org/10.1080/03066159208438495.

both colonial politics and the court's focus on the medical evidence, on the victim's body instead of the victim's words. The limits of the archive (and indeed the trial process for those that made it to court) demonstrate the gendered operation of colonial courtrooms, particularly in the assessment of women's testimony and medical evidence in trials of sexual violence in Fiji. The prioritisation of certain types of evidence – male, European and increasingly scientific – demonstrates who was considered suitable to contribute to the production of colonial and legal knowledge and the processes by which non-European voices were devalued. This masculine medicalisation of evidence parallels processes occurring across the British Empire, in ways that continue to shape the perceptions of women's testimony and reliability in sexual violence trials today. In an increasingly cosmopolitan Suva, the courtroom remained a colonial space.

Underpinning these factors, in the minds of European magistrates, was the pervasive influence of influential jurist Matthew Hale's 1778 warning that 'rape is … an accusation easily to be made and hard to prove, and harder to be defended by the party accused, tho never so innocent'.[37] Hale drew attention to his (unsubstantiated) fears of false and pernicious rape accusations, arguing the importance of a fresh complaint and corroborating evidence. As many contemporary commentators and historians on rape acknowledge, such implicit distrust of women's testimony disadvantaged female victims in courtrooms across the British Empire and frequently focused attention on the victim's actions, morality and credibility.[38] The female body had to be proved innocent in cases of sexual crime. More broadly, sexual cases involved complicated assessments of gender-appropriate behaviour and reputation.[39]

---

37   Matthew Hale, 1778, quoted in Estrich, 'Rape', 1094–95.
38   See Estrich, 'Rape', 1087–184; Bourke, *Rape: A History from 1860*; Vigarello, *A history of rape*; Elizabeth Kolsky, '"The body evidencing the crime": Rape on trial in colonial India, 1860–1947', *Gender & History* 22, no. 1 (2010): 109–30, doi.org/10.1111/j.1468-0424.2009.01581.x; Elizabeth Kolsky, 'The rule of colonial indifference: Rape on trial in early colonial India, 1805–1857', *The Journal of Asian Studies* 69, no. 4 (2010): 1093–117, doi.org/10.1017/S0021911810002937; Scully, 'Rape, race and colonial culture', 335–59; Durba Ghosh, 'Household crimes and domestic order: Keeping the peace in colonial Calcutta, c. 1770–c.1840', *Modern Asian Studies* 38 (2004): 599–623, doi.org/10.1017/S0026749X03001124.
39   As Carolyn Strange has illustrated in the case of intimate femicide in colonial and early national Australia, 'masculine characterizations in femicide trials were judged reciprocally in relation to female victims' reputation'. The interdependent nature of gendered assumptions also underpinned trials involving intimate and sexual relationships. Carolyn Strange, 'Masculinities, intimate femicide and the death penalty in Australia, 1890–1920', *British Journal of Criminology* 43 (2003): 335, doi.org/10.1093/bjc/43.2.310; Paula Byrne, *Criminal law and colonial subject: New South Wales, 1810–1830* (Cambridge: Cambridge University Press, 1993), 116, doi.org/10.1017/CBO9780511586101.

Overlaid on the mistrust of female testimony were racialised ascriptions regarding the validity of statements made by Islanders and Indians in court. Non-European women were 'doubly suspect suspects'.[40] The 'native' witness was variously portrayed as either deceitful and untrustworthy, or naïve, confused and therefore unreliable. They were participants in what Elizabeth Kolsky has described as 'scientific inquiries, generating certain and factual knowledge under objective conditions'.[41] She further notes that the 'rationalization and modernization of law' opens further questions regarding 'the gendered consequences of colonial modernity'.[42] In general, non-European or indigenous actors were perceived as unable to contribute to, and excluded from, this increasingly 'scientific' legal project on the basis of empire-wide concepts of racial difference. These perceived differences were themselves the products of an increasingly rigid and scientific discourse of race, further contributing to a damaging cycle that reinforced colonial hierarchies within the courts.[43] Both indigenous Fijians and indentured Indians were the subject of discourse that equated whiteness with credibility and rationality, and non-whiteness with unreliability. This discourse enabled colonial law to 'enunciate equality while fabricating a racial taxonomy through which to operate unequally'.[44] The questions of reliability contributed to the many cases that never made it to the courtroom, especially at the level of the Supreme Court. The legacies of this are ongoing; arguably it is not even an afterlife of imperialism but an ongoing reality for rape and sexual assault victims in courtrooms from Fiji to Britain, despite recent initiatives to deal with these issues and change how policing and justice operates.

Despite these limits, the case files highlight the intersections and contradictions between ideals of morality, race, gender and the female body, from the perspective of both magistrates and trial participants. As John Kelly notes:

---

40   Kolsky, 'The body evidencing the crime', 111.
41   Kolsky, 'The body evidencing the crime', 112.
42   Kolsky, 'The rule of colonial indifference', 1106.
43   Nancy Stepan, *The idea of race in science: Great Britain 1800–1960* (London: Macmillan, 1982), doi.org/10.1007/978-1-349-05452-7.
44   Salesa makes this statement with references to policies of racial amalgamation, but it can equally be applied to law. Damon Salesa, *Racial crossings: Race, intermarriage, and the Victorian British Empire* (Oxford: Oxford University Press, 2011), 42.

> Court records are the one documentary source in Fiji's archives in which the intrusion of white overseers in the sexual and social lives of the indentured labourers is repeatedly and provocatively discussed – almost always by the Indian defendants and their witnesses.[45]

Kelly's assessment equally applies to the intimate lives of Suva residents more generally, offering a glimpse into how Indian, Fijian and European women encountered unwanted intrusions upon their bodies.

One of the aims of my broader research was to recover and make visible women's experiences of sexual violence and intimate relationships more generally, and of their work in navigating colonial legal processes. Individual experiences of intimate life are often absent in colonial records but constituted the lived experience of colonial rule. Disappointingly, I found that insight into women's experiences through trial records was limited: their narratives of rape, sexual assault and domestic relationships were heavily structured by the court process. Apart from the occasional phrase or expression, all the Supreme Court files were translated and transcribed into English by court interpreters, whose ability and accuracy were often questioned. Further, each case was filtered through various levels of the judicial process, from reporting, to depositions before the local court before being dismissed or forwarded to the Supreme Court. Officials preferred to pursue certain cases in the lower courts, with a high bar set for cases to proceed to the Supreme Court sittings in the city.[46]

As a result, many incidents described by the victims are almost formulaic, with limited words expressing their pain and shame. Rather, common elements included the isolated location of the incident (in homes alone, remote gardens, paths or streets), the use of force, and attempts (often stifled) by the victim to cry out or resist the assailant. It appears that, given the reluctance, difficulties and suspicion often associated with such complaints, these were key elements to cases successfully proceeding from initial complaint, through the lower courts to trial in Suva. Similarly, younger victims – where consent was irrelevant to the charge – appear more frequently. This trend resonates with findings of rape and sexual assault trials from colonial India, New Zealand and the Cape Colony as well as nineteenth and twentieth-century England. Moreover, as Wiener argues, in the courtroom arena the leading actors in a trial were often

---

45   Kelly, '"Coolie" as labour commodity', 262.
46   Brereton, *Law, justice, empire*, 136–37.

the offender and the officials.[47] Rather than giving voice to the variety of victims' emotional experiences, trials recorded those incidents that were most representative of the strict legal definition and prevailing cultural perceptions of rape. The victim's bodies had to give evidence of the violence, not just their words.

Nevertheless, through the court process victims provided a brief glimpse of the physical or emotional impact of the violence upon them. Many victims and witnesses mentioned they felt afraid to report the crime, especially if the offender was a chief or an overseer.[48] Others focused on the physicality of the attack. For example, K highlighted the violence of rape, describing to the court in 1917 how the accused 'lifted her bodily', 'fisted' her thighs and shoulders so she was 'rendered weak and he overcame me'.[49] By contrast, in an 1881 case M emphasised her fear of Savanaca, stating: 'When near I saw the expression of his eyes were not good. I was afraid and ran away.'[50] R, an indentured labourer viciously assaulted and raped by a group of men on a plantation one night in 1907, described feeling she was 'silly' and lost her senses after the attack.[51]

Other cases drew attention to the resultant suffering. The sense of shame caused by such assaults was prominent, and drew attention to the emotional as well as the physical violence of the attack. After describing her physical wounds, rape victim TB said simply: 'My mind also is in pain.'[52] In an 1881 rape case, witness S reported that Solomon Islands labourer L told her 'M has forced me and made a fool of me'.[53] Tokelauan woman K said: 'A Fijian has insulted me as if I were a pig.'[54] These accounts go beyond a description of the assault itself to hint at the devastating physical and psychological effect of sexual crime. Other accounts focus on the physical act alone, though it is unclear whether this reflected an inability or unwillingness to articulate emotional suffering in the public courtroom, or that the process of translation and transcription testimony obscured the victim's tone and emotion.

---

47 Wiener, *An empire on trial*, 10.
48 Case 13/1875, Case 27/1879; see also Case 6/1910, where Fijian woman S told the court she had been sent by the accused ER to bring the 15-year-old victim E to him. She said she did this because she 'was afraid as Ralulu is a big chief'. All from Criminal Sittings, Fiji Supreme Court, NAF.
49 Case 89/1917, Criminal Sittings, Fiji Supreme Court, NAF.
50 Case 7/1881, Criminal Sittings, Fiji Supreme Court, NAF.
51 Case 21/1907, Criminal Sittings, Fiji Supreme Court, NAF.
52 Case 16[?]/1879, Criminal Sittings, Fiji Supreme Court, NAF.
53 Case 13/1881, Criminal Sittings, Fiji Supreme Court, NAF.
54 Case 6/1891, Criminal Sittings, Fiji Supreme Court, NAF.

Conclusion

Legislation from both the Colonial Government and from the Bose Vakaturanga (or Great Council of Chiefs – a colonial institution itself) sought to curtail the mobility of non-European individuals in the colonial town, highlighting the attempts to designate urban space as a white one. Of course, the lived experience of residents meant that this was never achieved. Suva quickly became cosmopolitan in ways that officials, missionaries and chiefs felt was problematic, and some of the cases in the Supreme Court reflect this contested urban diversity. Women and children were widely involved in the growing economic and social life of the emerging city. In this context, they also found themselves subject to violence in homes, streets and workplaces, as well as contestations over the policing of violence in Suva.

The adversarial nature of cases before the Supreme Court resulted in the narration of differing versions of the same incident by victims, defendants and witnesses. The job of the judge or investigating magistrate, the assessors advising him, and on rare occasions the jury, was to disentangle the facts of the case, to establish the truth of the matter in order to make judgment.[55] In making judgments, racial and gendered biases were clearly at play in the courtroom. The Supreme Court itself was a settler space, serving as heart of empire in the colonial town, subscribing to colonial hierarchies of truth and reliability and reinforcing power structures.

The establishment of British law was an underpinning justification for colonial rule in Fiji, as elsewhere. Law had the power to help 'civilise' the islands, despite the fact that the British were increasingly drawn into Fiji to control the unruly behaviour of their own subjects in the decades prior to annexation. Once established, the court served as a symbolic and theatrical space, both its physical presence in the urban landscape and the performances within reinforcing the structures of colonialism. However, it is also a place in which these hierarchies could be contested and challenged, where the voices of varied men and women enter the colonial archive and had at least some ability to narrate their own stories of Suva within the context of violence.

---

55 Trial by jury was rare in Fiji, and reserved for capital cases involving Europeans only. It was felt that an all-white jury (as only Europeans were on the list as jurors) would not give non-Europeans a fair trial. The difference between trial by jury versus by assessors is that the court is not bound by the advice of the assessors. See Duff, 'The evolution of trial by judge and assessors in Fiji', 189–213.

10

Race Relations in Colonial Suva, 1945–1970

Robert Norton

The years after the war were a time of immense change. The war had taken its toll and left its mark on the political and psychological landscape of the colony. The practice of unquestioned racial segregation and white supremacy had entered its last throes.
— Brij Lal, pre-eminent historian of Fiji.[1]

Where the prestige of the European is of such importance it is very disconcerting to find our influence undermined by unsavoury and ugly phases of civilisation depicted in American films and reflected in the harmful example set by some members of the European community.
— Acting inspector general for film censorship, 1936.[2]

As to improving interracial relationships … it would not be a bad thing if the European would sometimes pause and consider whether his culture and civilisation are superior in all respects to those of other races.
— Governor Sir Alexander Grantham, 1947.[3]

---

1 Brij V Lal, *Broken waves: A history of the Fiji Islands in the twentieth century* (Honolulu: University of Hawai'i Press, 1992), 163.
2 NAF F113/2 part 1, National Archives of Fiji (hereinafter NAF), Suva.
3 'Farewell radio broadcast', *Fiji Times,* 24 March 1947, 4–5.

> [T]he aim of government must be, in all its actions and policies, to strengthen the sense of unity of the people of this colony, ... to promote all measures that will help people to regard themselves not merely as Indians or as Fijians ... or as Europeans or Chinese, but as citizens of Fiji – Fijians in the wider sense ... [T]he objective should be ever before us of ... emphasising common interests ...
> — Governor Sir Kenneth Maddocks, 1959.[4]

Introduction

The concept of a division of humanity into discrete 'racial' groups distinguished by genetically determined characteristics of ability and behaviour has long been discredited by scientific researchers. Yet until relatively recently this little diminished the idea's potency in social and political discourse and practice. The concept was widely used well into the twentieth century by colonial powers in the justification and organisation of their rule.

'Racial' categorisation was central in policy and law and social relations in colonial Fiji, far more so than in other British colonies with which Fiji is often compared, such as Mauritius, Trinidad and Guyana.[5] Its consequences for rights and inequalities in opportunities of various kinds and for social interactions were ever present. In everyday parlance and in official discourse it was conventional to talk of the people in terms of the 'the races', 'the different races', 'the racial groups' and a simplification into a triad of 'Fijians', 'Indians' and 'Europeans', with stereotyping ideas that disregarded differences within these 'groups' and interests linking them. On the margins in this categorisation were the Chinese, Part-Europeans and 'others' (including indigenes from other South Pacific countries).

This chapter discusses social changes in Suva, in peoples' relationships, attitudes and aspirations, initiated by the impact of the Pacific War and postwar international pressures for the ending of colonial empire. There

---

4   Fiji Legislative Council Debates, 17 June 1959, 146–47.
5   Racial tension did exist in these countries, mainly between descendants of indentured workers or free settlers from India and descendants of African slaves. However, status and rights in political, administrative and school systems were not generally prescribed by an official racial classification, as was the case in colonial Fiji. Gordon Lewis, *The growth of the modern West Indies* (New York: Monthly Review Press, 1969); Thomas Eriksen, *Common denominators: Ethnicity, nation-building, and compromise in Mauritius* (Oxford: Berg, 1998).

were two trends in race relations: a heightening of antagonism of many Europeans and Fijians towards Indians, but also the beginning of a softening of discrimination in both law and social life and new affirmations of shared citizenship. A discussion of interracial social relations in the urban middle class highlights the elevated status often accorded leading Fijians in the life of clubs and service organisations, and the accommodation of moderate Indian political leadership. Notwithstanding the progressive social trends, reciprocal prejudices continued in Fijian–Indian relations. But balancing these was a shared resentment of European privilege and racialist attitudes. By the late 1950s, with rapid growth in urban population and poverty, some animosity towards Europeans was strengthening and marked a strike and riot in Suva. Those events persuaded major Suva-based business companies to widen employment opportunities for non-Europeans in the last decade of British rule. The chapter concludes with discussion of how political party rivalry in the context of decolonisation provoked new racial tension between Fijians and Indians, yet also encouraged further softening of old boundaries in urban social organisations.

Colonial Paternalism and the Impact of War

Before the Pacific War, Fiji's colonial rulers were concerned largely with the Fijians, to the relative neglect of the Indians, for the majority of whom the Colonial Sugar Refining Company (CSR Co) held the major responsibility. Government gave little thought to a prospect of developing Fiji as a unitary society. Europeans, both official and non-official, generally held paternalistic convictions of racial superiority in their attitudes towards both Indians and Fijians, typically with a sentiment of protective affection for the latter and often ambivalence, sometimes disdain, towards the former. 'Fraternisation' between Europeans and non-Europeans was uncommon and generally disapproved by Europeans, official and non-official.[6] Self-government was but a distant future possibility and little thought was given to preparing the colonial subjects for it.

---

6   'There was an effective colour bar and fraternising was regarded askance by the white people': William Geddes, 'Acceleration of social change in a Fijian community', *Oceania* 16, no. 1 (1945): 1–14, 7, doi.org/10.1002/j.1834-4461.1945.tb00428.x; Robert Norton, 'Averting "irresponsible nationalism": Political origins of Ratu Sukuna's Fijian administration', *The Journal of Pacific History* 48, no. 4 (2013): 409–28, doi.org/10.1080/00223344.2013.852706; 'Relations between Europeans and Natives', 1943, NAF CF50/22.

Friendly interactions with New Zealand and US personnel in Fiji and on the battlefield during the war with Japan began the erosion of the old social order, encouraging a questioning of European claims to superiority and privilege and giving rise, especially among Fijians, to new aspirations to share in the good things of the modern economy. The social and economic impacts of the occupying personnel were experienced mainly in Suva and its immediate hinterland, and in the western Viti Levu towns and districts of Nadi and Lautoka. A *Fiji Times* editorial voiced the consternation of many Europeans over the disruption of conventional social mores and economic conditions:

> We see a complete upheaval in which all previous standards of life and morality are discarded … Our problem [will be] … to get the people back to more or less normal standards.[7]

Wartime events and trends also raised tensions between Indians on the one hand and Europeans and Fijians on the other: the general Indian objection to military service because of racial inequality in wages and conditions, the sugar cane farmers' strike at the height of the war, and large profits made by many Indians from transactions with the occupying troops.

The Early Postwar Years: Race Tensions and Initiatives for Change

The postwar years saw the beginnings of a weakened emphasis on racial categorisation and of the growth of a consciousness of shared citizenship. The major push was the redirection of British colonial policy towards preparations for self-government under pressure from the United Nations (UN) and the US. Change was compelled, too, by the new outlooks and aspirations among the subject people stimulated by wartime social experiences with members of the US and New Zealand forces and economic gains from commercial dealings with them.

---

7   Allport Barker, 'Repercussions', *Fiji Times*, 23 January 1943, 4. The occupying European personnel greatly outnumbered the resident Europeans. There were also many Afro-Americans whose seeming equality with their European compatriots contrasted with local race conventions and gave local Europeans some anxiety about the likely unsettling effects in Fijian minds of 'the introduction into the colony of people of a native race who are no longer native' (Barker, 4). Fraternisation with the Americans was often accompanied by their derisory remarks about colonial rule and the British Crown, urging on the locals a subversive way of thinking about the social order. For a review of wartime conditions and social change, see Lal, *Broken waves*, 108–25, 163.

10. RACE RELATIONS IN COLONIAL SUVA, 1945–1970

The widespread condemnation of racialism following the defeat of Nazi Germany had particular implications for discrimination in the colonies. Early in 1947, anticipating interrogation by the UN Human Rights Commission, the UK Government instructed colonial governors to prioritise reviewing and, where feasible, eliminating racially discriminating legislation.[8] Fiji's response, sent three years later by Governor Sir Brian Freeston (1948–1951), reported some legislative changes, described existing racial segregation in various contexts, and gave assurance of continuing 'evolution' away from discrimination. Freeston expressed opposition to change being made under UN pressure that disregarded local conditions:

> I should prefer to see the whole matter left alone … insofar as Fiji is concerned, because such problems as exist in this colony can be solved, if at all, only by natural process of evolution.[9]

But Freeston soon addressed his Legislative Council in the new official anti-racialist spirit. He was pleased to see a 'growing readiness … to sink racial differences in pursuit of the common welfare', and declared that it was 'the supreme duty of each and all of us to foster that growing tendency to unity'.[10]

Fostering unity was impeded by continuing tensions. India's Independence in 1947 strengthened the anticolonial mood in many parts of the world. Fiji's Indians viewed the event as the harbinger of freedom from colonial domination everywhere and expected a Congress Government would soon pressure the British and Fiji governments to make reforms in Fiji. For several years Indians in Fiji celebrated the new India at public rallies with oratory by political leaders, displays of India's flag and photos of its leaders, and the singing of its national anthem.[11] European and Fijian fear that India would, with the UN, press Britain to bring changes especially advantaging Indians was heightened by the 1946 census confirming that they outnumbered Fijians and were reproducing at a far greater rate.[12]

---

8   A Creech Jones, circular despatch, 8 January 1947, NA CO83/257/7, Colonial Office (hereinafter CO), National Archives (NA), London.
9   Freeston's response, 19 January 1950, NA CO83/257/7; also: NAF F6/38. A major reform had been made before the London directive. Late in 1946, salary inequality between local European and non-European civil servants was ended, Governor Sir Alexander Grantham declaring that 'racial discrimination is repugnant to … Government'. Fiji Legislative Council Debates, 1 November 1946, 297.
10 Fiji Legislative Council Debates, 25 November 1949, 156–57.
11 NAF files concerning celebrations in Fiji of India's independence: NAF CF51/47, CF51/51, CF51/54, CF51/64.
12 Indian growth from 1936 to 1946 was 41.7 per cent, the Fijian rate was 21 per cent; growth from 1946 to 1956 was Indians 40.7 per cent, Fijians 25.5 per cent.

Racial tension rose particularly in Suva where the affluence achieved by many Indians during the war was viewed by Europeans as a threat to their status and privilege.[13] In the late 1940s, prosperous Indians were purchasing houses in hitherto *de facto* European areas, adding fuel to European animosity towards Indians as economic competitors and challengers to racial privilege. The minister of St Andrews Church wrote to the governor about 'widespread discontent and alarm … the distress caused to Europeans by the proximity … of Indian homes'. Affluent Indians 'were outbidding Europeans as houses were put up for sale'. He believed it was 'too late now to arrange for any reasonable segregation of the races', but asked the government to set a ceiling on the pricing of houses to 'enable Europeans to buy them'. The sympathetic official response was that the trend could not be stopped.[14]

The mood of many Europeans was expressed by remarks of Amy Ragg, a leading politician from an old settler family, in a letter to a prewar governor: 'You have no idea how things have changed since you were in Fiji. The Indians have acquired wealth and have become arrogant to both Fijians and Europeans'.[15] The European–Fijian political alliance was frequently affirmed, and a suspicion voiced that under pressure from the UK and the UN the government was thinking of compromising its commitment to uphold the 'paramountcy' of indigenous interests by taking control over Fijian land for the sake of economic development that would particularly benefit Indians.[16]

---

13 Suva's population grew by 64 per cent from 1936 to 1946, to 25,395 of whom 50 per cent were Indians, 25 per cent Fijians and 9 per cent Europeans; the remaining 16 per cent included Chinese, Part-Europeans and indigenes from other Pacific islands.

14 Watson to Freeston, 13 April 1948, and minute by the colonial secretary 'Segregation of races in residential areas', 25 May 1948, NAF CF37/16. An article in *Pacific Islands Monthly* in June 1946 (p. 24) illustrates the racialist attitudes of some Europeans: 'Indians overrunning residential areas in Suva'. In his account of racial patterns in Suva's residential areas in the early 1960s, James Whitelaw describes an informal agreement among European houseowners in Lami to sell only to Europeans or Part-Europeans and to this end to avoid public advertising (James Sutherland Whitelaw, 'People, land and government in Suva, Fiji' (PhD thesis, The Australian National University, 1966), 196–97).

15 Ragg to Richards, 4 February 1953, NAF C166/13/1. In a survey of Fijian–Indian relations in 1954, 63 per cent of the Fijian interviewees 'revealed an attitude of complete intolerance of the presence of the Indians in Fiji': A Cato, 'Fijians and Fiji-Indians: A culture-contact problem in the south Pacific', *Oceania* 26, no. 1 (1955): 17, doi.org/10.1002/j.1834-4461.1955.tb00655.x. On European attitudes see Lal, *Broken waves*, 143–49.

16 For example, *Fiji Times* editorials 17 December 1952, 4; 26 June 1953, 4; 4 May 1954, 1. A measure of official concern about racial tensions was the attention given to preparing for possible future civil disturbance by securing agreement for military support from New Zealand. Acting Governor T Stoddart to T Macdonald, Minister of Defence, Wellington, 18 July 1955, NA CO1036/80.

The tension was starkly reflected in the European-owned English daily the *Fiji Times*. Every opportunity was taken to emphasise racial division, particularly the alleged threat from Indian demographic and economic advances and political ambition.[17] At its annual meeting in 1952, the Indian Association in Suva resolved to ask the Colonial Government to 'abate the creation of ill-feeling and hostilities against … particularly the Indian people'.[18] The pre-eminent Indian political leader Vishnu Deo accused the *Fiji Times* of 'continuous propaganda and agitation of seditious character, fostering racial hatred against us'.[19]

In counterpoint to the tensions were initiatives begun in Suva in the early aftermath of war to encourage interracial ties. Fiji's first multiracial social body, the Union Club, was formed in Suva in 1945 with the encouragement of colonial officials.[20] Chief information officer, Harold Cooper, took the lead, stressing the need 'to find a basis for lasting and sincere cooperation between the three races of the colony'. He was especially concerned that the government reform its past often indifferent treatment of the Indians to persuade their full identification with Fiji:

> It is useless to pretend that they have not … had some excuse for suspecting that we regarded them as an inferior race … We have just finished a world war fought largely to decide the ideological issue of whether certain races may claim to have the inherent right to dominate others … [M]any coloured communities in all parts of the world, including the Indians in Fiji, are waiting to see how prompt the victor nations will be to translate into practice the fine precepts they voiced while the guns were still firing …[21]

Governor Grantham had already reported to London his proposal to achieve 'proper administrative contact with the Indian population', explaining that in contrast to the government's close contact with the

---

17 See, for example, *Fiji Times* 25 July and 15, 17, 21, 23 August 1950. Racial identity was frequently emphasised in headlines: for example, 'Indian cost of living shows sharp increase'; 'Ten Fijians charged with liquor offences'; 'Indian woman injured in collision'; 'Indians hurt in fight with Fijians'; 'Six Indians fight in Waimanu road'; 'Five Fijians fined for gambling'; 'Indian charged with arson'; 'Fijian hurt in fall from bus'.
18 NAF F51/113, Indian Association of Fiji.
19 *Fiji Times*, 3 March 1954, 6–7. Ironically, under the heading 'Going forward together', the *Fiji Times* editor had earlier written against emphasising race differences: 'We should think of ourselves as being people of Fiji … We cannot expect any advancement in this country by promoting racial discord' (8 November 1950, 4).
20 NAF F6/12; and Linden Mander, *Some dependent peoples of the South Pacific* (New York: Macmillan, 1954), 446–47.
21 Cooper to Colonial Secretary, 24 February 1946, NAF CF51/47, Mother India Day.

Fijians through the Fijian Administration, it had no such means for contact with the Indians – 'an unsatisfactory state of affairs which must be remedied'.[22] At their annual conferences, administration officials discussed the need to improve relations with Indians who they acknowledged had tended to be neglected in the past. How can government officials 'make the Fiji born Indian feel that Fiji is his home and make out of him a contented and constructive citizen?' There was a need to have 'more intimate contact with the Indians' – 'to discover [their] aspirations'.[23] There were political reasons for these concerns: recognition of a need to strengthen Indian loyalty to Fiji at a time of enthusiasm over India's achievement of Independence.

The Union Club grew from this official concern. Active members were predominantly Indians, from taxi drivers and white-collar workers to businessmen and professionals. There were also many Fijians and Europeans, typically in government posts. With the objective 'to bring the races together', the Suva venture inspired the formation of similar clubs in other towns. They contrasted with bodies such as the Fiji Club and the Defence Club, both dominated by Europeans and admitting a very few elite Fijians but no Indians. Another Suva club, the United Club, also reflected the racial divides with a membership mainly of Part-Europeans.[24]

Initiatives supporting multiracialism were taken in Suva by the British Council: the Viti Club for young Fijians, and the Youth Club, multiracial though predominantly Indian, for 'social and educational activities and to foster harmony between the various races'.[25] Members from these clubs and students from the teachers' college socialised at debating contests and other events organised by the council.[26] In sport, too, there were moves towards interracial competition and cooperation, such as 'triangular'

---

22 Grantham to Secretary of State, 14 July 1945, NA CO83/242/85403, Australian Joint Copying Project (AJCP) microfilm reel 5021.
23 Administrative officers' conferences 1944–1957, NAF F4/3/7 part 1, F4/3/7-5, C4/4/2-2. While several leading Fijian chiefs were appointed as district officers as early as 1950, no Indian held the post until 1961.
24 On the clubs, see Robert Norton, *Race and politics in Fiji*, 2nd ed. (St. Lucia: University of Queensland Press, 1990): 54–58; Alexander Mamak, *Colour, culture and conflict: A study of pluralism in Fiji* (Rushcutters Bay: Pergamon Press, 1978), 108–11. Union Club members in 1948 included 144 Indians, 89 Fijians, 119 Europeans: NAF F6/12.
25 *Fiji Times*, 18 March 1952, 3, 7.
26 *Fiji Times*, 13 March 1951, 6; 5 October 1951, 4; 12 October 1951, 5; 15 November 1951, 5; 18 March 1952, 3, 7.

cricket matches with European, Fijian and Indian teams competing, and sometimes multiracial teams.[27] Though a political alliance between European and Fijian leaders had existed since the 1920s, 'fraternisation' between Europeans and Fijians had been generally discouraged. But in wartime it became commonplace with the occupying servicemen and between Fijian and Fiji European soldiers. A *Fiji Times* editorial in 1950 urging sharing in sport reflected that transformative experience. Sport, especially rugby, the editor declared, 'will help to create personal friendships between Fijians and Europeans, bringing them closer together in a proper understanding of each other and in mutual respect'.[28] A major ending of official racial discrimination at this time was the introduction of jury lists for Fijians and Indians. Until 1950 only Europeans were allowed jury trials and European 'assessors' judged cases brought against non-Europeans.[29]

From the early 1950s, the government-backed radio broadcaster planned reforms declaring that its programs:

> should help to weld the people into a homogeneous unit – the Indians to realise that their first loyalty is to Fiji … and the Fijians to keep alive their native customs and abreast of social progress, and the whole community to develop a national consciousness and pride.[30]

More time was to be allowed for programs in the vernaculars; there was especially a concern to wean Indians away from short-wave broadcasts from India and Pakistan.

The 1950s were also a time of rapid growth in the trade union movement in which Indians, Fijians and others united in disputes with government and private European employers. Unity was sometimes vulnerable, however, as in the case of the Public Works Department Employees Union where racial tension eventually led to a Fijian 'breakaway union'. The commissioner for labour attributed the difficulties to cultural differences in leadership styles and to the tendency for Indians to predominate

---

27   *Fiji Times*, 25 January 1951, 7; 22 March 1951, 5; 5 January 1952, 5; 22 February 1957, 5; 17 April 1957, 5.
28   *Fiji Times*, 28 September 1950, 4.
29   *Fiji Times*, 25 May 1950, 6.
30   Fiji Broadcasting Commission Chair, Robert Munro, 1953, NAF C146/3-1. Munro urged in 1956 that 'the station should continue to "indoctrinate" into good "kai vitis" the Indian population and wean them away from listening to Indian stations': NAF C146/3-2.

among the office-bearers, a trend that would long continue as a source of conflict within some unions.[31] It was sometimes difficult to separate trade union life from tensions in the political arena where Fijian and European anxieties about potential Indian domination were always latent if not overtly expressed.

Governor Garvey and the Promotion of 'Multiracialism'

Reform of race relations in Suva was strengthened from the mid-1950s, thanks especially to a new governor's efforts. Far more than his two postwar predecessors, Sir Ronald Garvey (1952–1958) stressed the need to work for the unity and prosperity of Fiji as a whole. At his swearing-in he talked of challenges facing the colony:

> It must be a time of great endeavour for all … It will entail sacrifices, and it will be necessary for us to abandon some preconceived ideas … as well as bury some old-fashioned prejudices …[32]

In 1955 Garvey had discussions at the Colonial Office where preparations were underway for granting independence to two major colonies, the Gold Coast (Ghana) and Malaya. These decolonisation projects and others anticipated made all the more pressing in the discussions with Garvey a focus on Fiji's social, economic, and political problems, and progress towards self-government. On returning to Fiji, Garvey declared his intention to devote the remainder of his term to promoting economic development and a consciousness of national unity. All in Fiji, he said, must think of themselves as forming a united people and put Fiji ahead of their racial identities and interests: '[W]e must think not as Fijians, Indians, or Europeans, but as one, and join our hands to bring to the colony the prosperity within our grasp.'[33] The rhetoric echoed views expressed several years before by a young Fijian, Ratu Kamisese Mara,

---

31   CS Reay to President of Fiji Industrial Workers Congress, 15 October 1953, NAF C36/2/8-1; Mamak, *Colour, culture and conflict*, 69–71; Jacqueline Leckie, *To labour with the state: The Fiji Public Service Association* (Dunedin: University of Otago Press, 1997), Chapter 6; William Sutherland, *Beyond the politics of race: An alternative history of Fiji to 1992* (Canberra: Australian National University, 1992), 87–88, 98–99.
32   *Fiji Times*, 6 October 1952, 1.
33   *Fiji Times*, 29 September 1955, 4. Sir Robert Sanders, a district officer at that time, told me of how Garvey, in his speeches around Fiji, would hold up one finger to symbolise unity, alluding to Churchill's 'V' for victory.

who would lead Fiji's first multiracial political party and become the first prime minister. In a controversial speech after returning from studies in the UK Mara had declared:

> The future citizen of Fiji should be in a position to be proud ... that he was a Fiji national and not so much that he was a member of any particular race.[34]

Marking the reform of official vision for Fiji was, from 1954, a change in Cession Day celebrations. Hitherto the occasion had concerned mainly the Fijians and the Colonial Government. Garvey now insisted that it should be made the day for celebrating Fiji's growth as a multiracial nation. He encouraged the holding of interracial activities such as sporting events as part of the festivities: 'The day should be a focal point for the spirit of unity which ... should prevail among all the peoples of this Colony.'[35]

An egregious expression of European prejudice was the *de facto* bar against non-Europeans using the Suva Sea Baths. A small pool of inferior quality constructed for them beside the main baths highlighted the racialism and, in protest, was rarely used. In 1956, after three years of intermittent and at times acrimonious argument among the elected Indians and Europeans in the municipal council, it was decided to open the main baths to all.[36] Most European councillors were not enthusiastic in their agreement, the mayor saying that his support should not be taken as criticism of the past discrimination. The strengthening Indian middle class was a pressure for the change, especially as its ratepayers contributed to the baths' maintenance; a ratepayers association had been formed two years before with Europeans and Indians together in its council.[37]

---

34 Address to Marist High School Association, *Fiji Times*, 7 November 1950, 7. The *Fiji Times* editor praised Mara's speech and declared: 'We cannot expect any advancement in this country by promoting racial discord' (8 November 1950, 4). Yet well into the 1950s it was the newspaper's practice to emphasise race differences.
35 Fiji Legislative Council Debates, 6 November 1953, 204; *Fiji Times*, 6 November 1953, 4.
36 *Fiji Times*, 24 June 1956, 5; 30 August 1956, 1, 4; 2 October 1956; also *Fiji Times*, 15 January 1953, 4; 2 February 1953, 4; 24 June 1953, 5; NAF CF45/3; Carl Hughes, 'Racial issues in Fiji' (DPhil thesis, Oxford University, 1965), 259–68. The Town Board (later Council) had not imposed an official ban, but instructed the baths caretaker to exclude non-Europeans (though Chinese were admitted).
37 *Fiji Times*, 24 September 1954, 4; Hughes, 'Racial issues in Fiji', 268.

Figure 10.1: 'Swimming Baths Suva, About 1930'.
Source: P32.4.17 Fiji Museum.

Fijians, then represented on the council by one nominated member, expressed little interest in the issue.[38] Yet during the war it had been a Fijian member, Semesa Sikivou, who protested against the discrimination when the then Town Board debated whether to temporarily allow non-European military personnel to use the baths. While endorsing this, Sikivou hoped:

> that because we are bearing our burden together in this war, we shall enjoy what we are fighting for together when the enemies are crushed and all race differences and barriers [are] removed.[39]

That possibility was tested in 1950, when Fijians, supported by some Europeans, formed a swimming association with a plan to establish links with such groups in New Zealand. A case might have been made for letting them train at the baths. However, 'the fact that such an application might open the door to potential difficulties' led to the abandonment of the project. The *Fiji Times* had praised the Fijians for not having pressed the council and government on the issue, declaring this was 'an excellent indication of the extent to which Fijian patience and consideration

---

38 Fijians contributed tiny proportions of Suva rates. Even by the mid 1960s, their average over the four council wards was only 1.7 per cent in contrast to the Indians' 32 per cent and the Europeans' 40 per cent (Whitelaw, 'People, land and government in Suva, Fiji', 163–65).
39 *Fiji Times,* 12 June 1942, 7; 17 June 1942, 7.

for other races is carried'.[40] Now, in 1956, the newspaper applauded the abolition of discrimination as 'long overdue': 'timely, progressive, and humane'.[41]

The English daily was undergoing a striking transformation, with far less emphasis now on racial division and an alleged Indian threat. There was doubtless a quiet pressure for reform from official quarters. But the change was influenced in part by the realisation that, contrary to European and Fijian fears, the new India would not, after all, be pushing for radical reforms in the colonies. To the disillusionment of some Fiji Indian leaders, India's commissioners urged them to moderation and loyalty to the Fiji Government and the British Crown.[42] Early in 1957 the *Fiji Times* praised India's commissioners for their wise counsel and extended congratulations on India Republic Day. India's representatives, the editor acknowledged, had encouraged Fiji Indians to think of themselves as 'British citizens of Fiji' and 'to seek a happy and profitable association with other races … ':

> It would have been easy for India to interfere in Fiji's affairs, but it hasn't … The overall racial picture in Fiji today is a reasonably happy and reassuring one, and all the other communities … can sincerely join with their Indian friends and associates in greeting Republic Day.[43]

The paper had signalled its change of heart several months before in its editorial for Cession Day. After extolling the Fijians' virtues and the need to safeguard their land rights, the editor recognised the 'equally virile Indian community with the ordinary rights of human beings'. Their land needs must be met too, he said, as the problems of population pressure and land are shared problems.[44] Garvey spoke of Cession Day in 1957 as 'Fiji's national day', when 'we should reflect not upon … the interest of the race to which we belong, but upon the interests of the country of which we are citizens':

---

40   Editorial, *Fiji Times*, 21 January 1953, 4. See also 'Fijian swimmers have no place to swim', *Pacific Islands Monthly*, August 1950, 83.
41   *Fiji Times*, 30 August 1956, 4.
42   For example, India Commissioner SA Waiz's farewell speech, *Fiji Samachar*, 13 October 1950, 11–12 and *Fiji Times*, 6 October 1950, 1, and a speech by a new commissioner in Ba, *Fiji Times*, 20 January 1954, 6; Donald Calman, 'A history of Indians in Fiji' (MA thesis, University of Sydney, 1952), 231–35.
43   'Fiji's greeting to Indian Republic Day', *Fiji Times*, 26 January 1957, 2.
44   *Fiji Times*, 6 October 1956, 2.

> Our responsibilities as citizens should prevail over racial interests when the two conflict ... We should regard others as human beings first and secondly as the members of any particular race.

Garvey even questioned the view that the Deed of Cession was a charter for the paramountcy of Fijian interests: 'The Indians are equally eligible to have their rights respected.'[45]

Other expressions of changing attitudes and relations included the invitation in 1956 by the Suva Chamber of Commerce, a European body, to the Indian Chamber to send delegates to observe its meetings and to perhaps make a reciprocal invitation with a view to the two bodies presenting joint submissions to government: 'The problems of the Indian Chamber of Commerce are our problems.'[46] The *Fiji Times* reported in 1957 the formation in Suva of the Fiji Law Society 'to promote the welfare and integrity of the law profession', with a committee of six Indians and five Europeans.[47] Also established that year was the Fiji Cricket Association with the governor its patron and a committee of 13 Europeans, three Fijians and three Indians.[48] Changing interracial attitudes were evidenced in the launching in Suva of a new teachers' body, the Education Workers' Society, whose Fijian chair declared: 'The teaching profession can no longer remain in its racial camps. The era of racialism is coming to its end.' Though this venture failed to achieve much support, it was a noteworthy attempt to bridge the divide between the two predominantly race-based unions, Fiji Teachers Union and the Fijian Teachers Association.[49]

A year after the sea baths were opened to all a start was made on abolishing racial restrictions on sale of alcohol. The liquor permit system, with graded rights from exclusion through various levels of restriction to unrestricted access, was a humiliating marker of colonial racialist paternalism that affected mainly Fijians and Indians (Europeans, Part-Europeans and Chinese were exempted).[50] Non-exempted persons wishing to purchase liquor were required to keep a permit book, like a passport, where vendors recorded details of every transaction. Garvey declared in 1956 that 'the only real solution to our liquor problem ... is by educating our people

---

45   *Fiji Times*, 15 October 1957, 1.
46   *Fiji Times*, 20 September 1956, 5.
47   *Fiji Times*, 19 June 1957, 5.
48   *Fiji Times*, 18 December 1956, 5.
49   *Fiji Times*, 2 April 1956, 4.
50   The Council of Chiefs and the Fijian Affairs Board, dominated by leading chiefs, supported the restrictions.

to a proper sense of responsibility ... by a gradual lessening of a system of control'. As a start, the drinking of beer was to be 'open to all races without restriction by permit'. The community, Garvey counselled, 'must learn to develop a sense of responsibility to this new found freedom from control'.[51] The change was in force from late 1957 and restrictions on liquor consumption were entirely removed for Indian and Fijian men early in 1963.

The outstanding initiative promoting multiracialism and a consciousness of shared 'national' identity in the 1950s was Suva's Hibiscus Festival, inspired by Hawai'i's Aloha Festival and planned towards the end of 1956 by government officials and leaders in the tourist industry. Its significance, anthropologist Claus Bossen explains, 'was reinforced by the lack in these years of a civil public event that could encompass all ethnic groups'. Though Cession Day was now declared a 'national' day affirming the value of all citizens for Fiji's prosperity and progress, its core meaning continued to be celebration of the sanctified Fijian–British alliance. In the Hibiscus Festival the emphasis was on the prideful affirmation of the cultural identities of all major groups and 'the equality ... and unity of them all'.[52] More than any other social innovation of the 1950s, the festival, Bossen says, expressed the shaping of a new 'urban public sphere' marked by interracial activities affirming shared identity. Yet the festival highlight, the crowning of Miss Hibiscus, did not display a multiracial balance. Of the 15 awards from 1956 to 1970, nine were won by Part-Europeans, four by Fijians, one by a European and one by a Part-Chinese. Although there were 30 Indian contestants during this period, an Indian was not crowned until 1979.[53]

Shortly before the first Hibiscus Festival, in December 1956, a 'carnival' of dance and theatre was presented by children 'of all races' at the Suva Town Hall, attended by Garvey and his wife.[54] On Christmas Eve the vice-regal couple graced 'carols by candlelight' in Suva's Albert Park, organised by the British Council: European, Indian and Fijian choirs sang

---

51 Fiji Legislative Council Debates, 14 September 1956, 77; *Fiji Times*, 11 December 1957, 5, and 12 December 1957, 1.
52 Claus Bossen, 'Festival mania, tourism, and nation building in Fiji: The case of the Hibiscus Festival, 1956–1970', *The Contemporary Pacific* 12, no. 1 (2000): 123–54, 141–42, doi.org/10.1353/cp.2000.0006.
53 Bossen, 'Festival mania, tourism, and nation building in Fiji', 144.
54 *Fiji Times*, 11 December 1956, 5.

the same carols in their respective languages, backed by the army band.[55] Garvey had advised London early that year: 'If one can believe local talk, the different races of which our community is composed have seldom been on more friendly terms.'[56]

Garvey's successor as governor, Sir Phillip Maddocks (1959–1963), continued the policy of encouraging 'multiracialism', stressing to his Legislative Council in 1959 'the need to recognise the goal to which our efforts must be constantly directed – that of a genuine multiracial community':

> [T]he aim of Government must be, in all its actions and policies, to strengthen the sense of unity of the people of this colony, … to promote all measures that will help people to regard themselves not merely as Indians or as Fijians … or as Europeans or Chinese, but as citizens of Fiji – Fijians in the wider sense … [T]he objective should be ever before us of … emphasising common interests.[57]

The Structure of Interracial Relations in Suva's Middle Class[58]

In Suva's middle-class multiracial milieu, developing from the mid-1950s, Fijian and European leaders were often patrons of social status and favours and Indians were their clients. Indian civic and political leaders valued the friendship and support of Fijian and European notables for advancing their status and influence. While Fijians prized friendships with eminent Europeans, they did not take special pride in ties with prominent Indians, nor did Fijian organisations seek their favour. This asymmetry in race relations derived particularly from official values affirming the special position of the Fijians and the long-established Fijian–European bond.

Pressure on Indian politicians to endorse the ideal of 'Fijian paramountcy' had come to a head in 1946 when the census confirmed that Indians outnumbered the Fijians. A European leader proposed in the colonial legislature that:

---

55 *Fiji Times*, 24 December 1956, 2.
56 Garvey to Lloyd, 11 February 1956, NA CO1036/10.
57 Fiji Legislative Council Debates, 17 June 1959, 146–47.
58 This section draws mainly from Robert Norton, *Race and politics in Fiji*, 2nd ed. (St. Lucia: University of Queensland Press, 1990), 53–58, 72–73.

in the opinion of this Council the time has arrived – in view of the great increase in the non-Fijian inhabitants and its consequential political development – to emphasise the terms of the Deed of Cession to assure that the interests of the Fijian race are safeguarded and a guarantee given that Fiji is to be preserved … as a Fijian country for all time.

Figure 10.2: AD Patel speaks at a Federation Party election rally in Suva, 1966.
Source: Robert Norton, PMB Photos 103-069.

In the ensuing debate Europeans and Fijians united in emphasising an alleged threat of Indian domination. The Europeans reaffirmed claims to political privilege as the Fijians' protectors, insisting that the Indians had no such responsibility under the deed. The Indians retorted that protection of the Fijian was the British Government's responsibility and that if Europeans were co-trustees so equally, as British subjects, were the Indians. The principal Indian leaders, AD Patel and Vishnu Deo, reaffirmed their endorsement of the principle of the paramountcy of Fijian interests. The debate, at times acrimonious, ended in an atmosphere of accord with unanimous support for a watered-down amended motion that the government and the non-Fijians 'stand by' the Deed of Cession as a charter of the Fijian people.[59] The debate's initiator, Amy Ragg, believed

---

59 Fiji Legislative Council Debates, 16 July 1946, 163–214.

his motion 'will in the future be a ... milestone in the history of this colony, something for the people to go on'. The *Fiji Times* apparently agreed, describing the debate as an event 'without precedence in the history of the legislative council'.[60]

Indians seeking ties with Fijians and Europeans and official favours, such as appointments to boards and committees, had to disavow political radicalism. The longstanding sources of racial conflict that all wished to contain helped encourage cooperation by providing a focus for dialogue and reciprocal affirmations of goodwill and understanding. Indian leaders continued to call for constitutional change and land reform, but with moderation to preserve harmonious relations with government officials, and Fijian and European leaders. Changes in the Indian Association reflected this. Militants formed it during the original campaign in the 1920s for political equality with Europeans. It declined following the dissolution of that movement. It was revived in Suva after World War II with a membership mainly of well-to-do businessmen and professionals. As well as providing a base for political careers, it cultivated relations with Fijians and Europeans, earning their esteem by building schools that were well-managed and open to all. Social functions and deputations to the colonial governor on public matters also enhanced the Indian Association's respectability in the wider community. Social events welcomed representatives from the government of India and were attended by dignitaries of all races. Subjects of the deputations included, among others, constitutional advancement, franchise for women, education and land problems. Presented against a background of friendly interracial mixing and ritualised in petitions, such calls made Indian political assertiveness acceptable.

The Indian Association had a counterpart in the Fijian Association. Members of each had friendly interactions in multiracial institutions, and high-ranking chiefs in Fijian Association leadership were sometimes president of the predominantly Indian Union Club. The pressures and incentives to moderation in Indian leadership in Suva contrasted with the industrial conflict between the Australian CSR Co. and cane farmers' unions that was conducive to a confrontational leadership in the sugar districts, the foundation of the dominant Indian political leadership during Fiji's decolonisation.

---

60   *Fiji Times*, 17 July 1946, 6.

10. RACE RELATIONS IN COLONIAL SUVA, 1945–1970

Persistence of Racial Prejudice and Division

Though in the 1950s there was progress in breaking or softening racial barriers, this happened mainly in the urban middle class. Racial prejudices and antipathies persisted. Particularly invidious, for its frequent association with status, wealth and power, was the attitude of many Europeans towards non-Europeans. The president of the multiracial Nadi Chamber of Commerce, AJ Foster, highlighted this in his contribution to the *Fiji Times* series of articles in 1957 on 'The Future of Fiji'. Denouncing European prejudice as an obstacle to 'cementing the racial divergencies of Fiji into a harmonious whole', he lamented that 'we have very few Europeans who work for the betterment of human relations' and even maintained that Europeans had created a 'caste' system.[61]

Foster's remarks concurred with those of an Australian journalist reporting on Fiji the previous year. Richard Aspinall was struck by European racial attitudes, especially against Indians: 'The attitude of many of these people towards their Indian fellow citizens is rude and ignorant'. He recounted the experience of a young Sydney woman working for a European firm in Suva who, after visiting relatives of an Indian student she met in Sydney, was warned 'that if she persisted in her friendship with Indians she would lose her job'. Indian leaders, Aspinall said, 'have one explanation' for the racism: 'The Europeans cannot bear to see the sons of indentured labourers becoming their equals'.[62]

In a dispatch to Canberra in 1965, Australia's first commissioner to Fiji mentioned his impression of attitudes of Europeans, especially those in the colony for limited terms who comprised the vast majority. The latter, he said, 'seemed to assume that they were obligated from the moment of arrival … to strike firm pro-Fijian, anti-Indian postures and to sustain these continually'.[63] When researching Fiji's political development in the mid-1960s I sometimes encountered European aversion towards Indians and the implicit view that I was crossing boundaries by meeting with Indian politicians and attending their campaign rallies. A leading Federation

---

61 *Fiji Times,* 2 October 1957, 2; and 3 October 1957, 2.
62 'The Fijis: Our "off-shore" islands have their race problems', *Voice,* April 1956, 21–22.
63 Robert Hamilton to External Affairs, 17 May 1965, NAA A1838 316/1/8 part 2, National Archives of Australia (hereinafter NAA), Canberra.

Party politician at that time,⁶⁴ Irene Jai Narayan, who represented Suva Indians for many years, later told me that few Europeans fraternised then with Indians who they tended to view as 'interlopers'. So, she said, my attendance at rallies and socialising with Indians was seen by the party leaders and their followers as remarkable.

European prejudice was often suffered by Part-Europeans, predominantly people of mixed Fijian and European descent. Many took the major part of their identity, cultural values and customs from the Europeans who tended to view them as the products of racial boundary transgression and to exclude them from their social circles. Though Fijians and especially Indians often experienced European prejudice, their positive sense of identity and status had strong independent social and cultural supports. Few Part-Europeans were fully incorporated into Fijian communities. Colonial officials tended to view Part-Europeans as a problematic anomaly outside the system of racial categorisation, often remarking on their neglect and conflicted identity.⁶⁵

Rodney Acraman, a junior colonial official in the 1960s, recounted his humiliating experience of the 'colour bar' growing up in Suva as a person of mixed European, Fijian and Samoan descent attending the predominantly European Suva Grammar School.⁶⁶ In her account of a childhood in Suva in the 1940s, Patricia Page recalls her mother's gentle counselling against playing with 'half caste' children, children who had 'a touch of the tar brush'.⁶⁷ A complaint of many Part-Europeans was their marginalisation in schooling opportunities. Most were excluded from schools reserved mainly for Europeans; nor were they always welcome in 'Fijian' or 'Indian' schools.

The schooling system was a major contributor to intergenerational perpetuation of prejudices. An official investigation in 1944 by a New Zealand academic was critical of the siloing of most pupils in segregated schools. His report was considered too controversial for debate in the Legislative Council and a new inquiry recommended continued emphasis

---

64   This political party was renamed National Federation Party in the late 1960s.
65   On the Part-Europeans, see Annelise Riles, 'Part-Europeans and Fijians', in *Fiji in Transition,* vol. 1, ed. Brij V Lal and Tomasi Vakatora (Suva: University of the South Pacific, 1997), 105–29; Lucy de Bruce, 'Histories of diversity: Kailoma testimonies and "Part-European" tales from colonial Fiji (1920–1970)', *Journal of Intercultural Studies* 28, no. 1 (2007): 113–28, doi.org/10.1080/07256860601082970.
66   Marsali MacKinnon, interview with Rodney Acraman, 9 March 1999, transcripts, Pacific Manuscripts Bureau (PMB), Audio 26–27.
67   Patricia Page, *Across the magic line: Growing up in Fiji* (Canberra: Pandanus Books, 2004), 66–73.

on maintaining racial boundaries.⁶⁸ Thus in the 1950s and 1960s the majority of children and adolescents continued to receive their education in racially exclusive schools. Voices in favour of interracial school experience to build foundations for mutual understanding and a sense of shared citizenship were outweighed by conservative opinion, mainly of Europeans and Fijians. Garvey himself supported continued separation at primary level, 'in view of the difficulties of language and culture and the geographical distribution of the different races'.⁶⁹

When Garvey's successor Sir Kenneth Maddocks advocated multiracial schools he encountered strong resistance, mainly from Fijian leaders. He reluctantly advised London that ending racial division in the school system, in accordance with a new UNESCO convention, was not feasible: 'It would be politically impracticable … to make any sudden change in the organisation of education in Fiji with a view to making it more interracial in character'.⁷⁰ Initially sanguine about the prospects for promoting multiracialism, Maddocks became pessimistic in his last two years, daunted especially by the Fijian fear 'that any advance towards interracialism in matters of importance is a step towards Indian domination'.⁷¹

Urban Migration, the Labour Movement and a New Racial Tension

In the towns interactions across the race divides were frequent and awareness of European affluence and racialist attitudes was sharp. Towns were also where interracial ties often developed: in workplaces, between

---

68   FB Stephens, 'Report on Education in Fiji', *Journal of the Fiji Legislative Council,* Council Paper no.18 (1944); and Report of Board of Education, Legislative Council Paper 27 of 1946 (debated in Fiji's Legislative Council 19–20 November 1946, 462–553). See also Clive Whitehead, *Education in Fiji: Policy, problems and progress in primary and secondary education 1939–1973* (Canberra: Development Studies Centre, Australian National University, 1981), 31–55.
69   Fiji Legislative Council Debates, 26 November 1954, 179.
70   Maddocks to Secretary of State, 26 March 1962, NAF C28/37. Early in 1965, the Indian politician, AD Patel, then in government as 'member for social services', proposed to primary school managers in Suva that racial division in the school system should end. While the Indian and European managers were in favour, the Fijians unanimously opposed the suggestion as a threat to cultural and social identity: *Fiji Times,* 9 January 1965, 3–4. Only the Catholic Church and some Indian organisations encouraged multiracial enrolment. Many schools excluded from the category of 'mixed race' did have multiracial rolls. The vast majority of their students were of a particular racial category and the others comprised less than 25 per cent of the roll, the minimum for a school to be designated as 'multiracial'. Hughes, 'Racial issues in Fiji', 308; Whitehead, *Education in Fiji,* 148.
71   Maddocks to Secretary of State, 19 June 1962, NA CO1036/775.

neighbours, in trade unions, in clubs and voluntary associations, and in some schools. This was particularly true of postwar Suva as its population rapidly grew, especially with Fijian migration from rural villages.[72]

From the early 1950s there was a growing demographic of young Fijian men deserting their villages to seek opportunities in Suva and other towns, only to soon find themselves in impoverished conditions without regular income. They were viewed by government and self-supporting residents as a major social problem: '*koro*-less' Fijians detached from the social constraints and supports of *koro* (village) life, with frustrated aspirations and disposed to petty crime.

In his contribution to the *Fiji Times* 'Future of Fiji' series, Alan Tippett, a prominent church leader, presciently warned of a looming threat from a discontented young 'proletariat' forming on racial lines: non-Europeans, mainly Fijians, set against Europeans. This development, he said, 'simply oozes with trouble': 'Sooner or later disillusionment must come and then we shall have a major social and labour problem on our hands.'[73]

By the late 1950s, difficulties for urban workers and the unemployed were exacerbated by rising living costs. In December 1959 Suva experienced an unprecedented violent social disturbance after police, attempting to disperse a crowd gathering to hear leaders of striking workers, threw tear gas and made a baton charge. This provoked in many people an outburst of anger and rioting energised also by resentments against European wealth and racialist attitudes.[74] Ratu Mara, who played a prominent role in the official inquiry, recalled in his memoirs 'a hostile anti-European atmosphere' and the stoning of European-owned cars.[75] Governor Maddock advised London that:

---

72   In 1956, Fijians made up 26 per cent of Suva's population, a 46 per cent increase since 1946. From 1956 to 1966, Suva's Fijians increased by 170 per cent to form 33 per cent of the city's population. Suva's Indian population increased over this period by 108 per cent to 50 per cent of the total; the Europeans comprised only 4.3 per cent and Part-Europeans 4.8 per cent. Still the only sociological monograph study of Suva is Alexander Mamak's valuable book, based on field research in the early 1970s (Mamak, *Colour, culture and conflict*, especially chapters 9 and 10 on race relations and attitudes).
73   *Fiji Times*, 12 August 1957, 2.
74   Peter Hempenstall and Noel Rutherford, *Protest and dissent in the Colonial Pacific* (Suva: Institute of Pacific Studies, University of the South Pacific, 1984), 73–86; A Lowe, 'Report of Commission of Inquiry into the disturbances in Suva, December 1959', *Journal of the Fiji Legislative Council*, Council Paper No. 10 of 1960; Francis West, 'Background to the Fijian riots', *Australian Quarterly*, 32 (1960): 46–53, doi.org/10.2307/20633592.
75   Ratu Sir Kamisese Mara, *The Pacific way: A memoir* (Honolulu: University of Hawai'i Press, 1997), 65.

> the anti-European feeling demonstrates … that in industrial matters, where land and political control are not concerned, the racial line-up tends to be an alliance of Fijian and Indian against the European.[76]

The racial aspect of the riot was emphasised in accounts I heard in 1966 as I began my Fiji research. A senior British official described to me how the episode brought a change in non-European attitudes to Europeans 'overnight'. For example, he said, the disposition of many house servants quickly cooled from seemingly friendly relations with their European employers.[77]

Historian James Heartfield maintains that the racial tension in the Suva crisis of December 1959 has been exaggerated, a projection of European fears of a potential for rebellious unity of Fijians and Indians.[78] He is perhaps correct in asserting that emphasis on the anti-European sentiment has distracted attention from the reality of class conflict and the significance of the strike in the development of Fiji's multiracial labour movement. Yet the racial 'edge' in the rioting was strong and jolted officials into recognising the need to address popular discontents and aspirations.

Governor Maddocks soon briefed Australian Government leaders in Canberra, stressing the antagonism towards Australian companies, the 'colour' consciousness and aloofness of many Europeans in commerce and industry, and the continued employment of expatriate staff in posts for which locals could be trained. He reported to London that in this briefing he 'spoke frankly about the changing attitude that has grown up recently towards Europeans … and, since European commerce and industry in Fiji is almost entirely Australian, especially towards Australians'.[79]

The events in Suva, Maddocks later wrote, were marked 'for the first time in the history of the colony' by a 'short-lived alliance between the Indians and the Fijians against the Europeans'. Within a year 'the traditional Fijian–European alliance had been restored', due mainly to the influence of Fijian chiefs. But 'it would be wrong', he cautioned, 'to imagine that

---

76 Maddocks to Secretary of State, 11 December 1959, NA CO1036/333.
77 Carl Hughes, personal communication, Suva, 3 August 1966.
78 James Heartfield, '"The dark races against the light"? Official reaction to the 1959 Fiji riots', *The Journal of Pacific History* 37, no. 1 (2002): 76, doi.org/10.1080/00223340120096242A.
79 Maddocks to Secretary of State, 16 May 1960, NA CO1036/720. Another source of resentment against European privilege was the continuing dominance of expatriate Europeans at senior levels of the civil service, restricting career advancement of locals (Leckie, *To labour with the state,* 38–47; Mamak, *Colour, culture and conflict,* 71–77).

[the Fijians] love the European ... [T]he individual European is judged upon his merits and all too often ... found wanting – largely because of the grasping attitude and the aloofness and colour consciousness of the representatives of Australian big business':

> The traditional alliance has become one of convenience, of mutual support against the Indian ... Beneath the friendly surface there is, particularly in the urban areas, a growing envy of the wealth and security of Europeans and if leading Fijians turned against Britain the spark that showed itself in December 1959 could quickly be fanned into flame.[80]

The Impact of Decolonisation and Party Politics

Whatever potential there might have been for a bonding of Fijians and Indians in a shared resentment against Europeans was dampened by resurgence of tension between them from the early 1960s. This was initially provoked by a cane farmers' harvesting strike against the CSR Co. The Indian strike leaders divided between militants and moderates and the stance of the militants escalated the confrontation, provoking the governor to deploy army reserves to protect farmers who wished to harvest. European and Fijian political leaders accused the militants of damaging the economy and seeking to control the industry.[81] As the British took the first steps to end their colonial rule, the militants launched the Federation Party, based initially on cane farmers' unions.

The prospect of the British leaving Fiji engendered Fijian apprehension, dramatically in evidence at a large rally of the Fijian Association early in 1961, chaired by Ratu Mara, on the roof of Suva's Native Land Trust Board building. Speakers insisted that if British rule was to end, Fijian paramountcy must be preserved and Fijians alone must govern the country. The police special branch observer reported 'a very strong anti-Indian atmosphere

---

80   Maddocks to Secretary of State, 28 February 1961, NA CO1036/774. In 1961–1963, leading Australian companies such as the CSR Co. and the Bank of NSW, responding to the racial tension and official concerns, began to recruit local people to office jobs that had been the preserve of Europeans.
81   On the harvesting strike see Lal, *Broken waves,* 169–80. The Fiji Intelligence Committee noted in its September 1960 report that anti-Indian feeling amongst Fijians 'has grown tremendously, principally because of the cane dispute' as many viewed the militants' actions as indicating ambitions for economic and political power (NA CO1036/700).

throughout the meeting'.[82] Fijian fears were strengthened by the Federation Party's call for a common franchise as the necessary foundation of an integrated democratic Fiji, an electoral reform that would end secure racial group representation. As the Federation Party leaders established branches throughout much of Fiji they focused on Indian political status interests. Fijian leaders encouraged their followers to oppose the party as a threat to Fiji's stability and to their land and political interests.

It was initially in Suva, the centre of decolonisation talks and preparations, that the new political rivalry, with its racial overtones, played out most strongly. The Federation Party established its Suva branch early in 1965 just before talks commenced in the city among political leaders to seek agreements in preparation for the first constitutional conference in London. The Federation Party leaders soon withdrew from the discussions in an atmosphere of tension and mistrust.[83] Their action provoked steps towards the formation of the Alliance Party whose leadership included Fijians, Europeans and Indians, with the Fijians and Europeans dominant and the Fijian Association its strongest popular base.

Figure 10.3: The Indian polling Centre in Suva during the elections for the Southern division, Suva 1963.
Source: M2134, National Archives of Fiji.

---

82 NAF C5/12/1; Hughes, 'Racial issues in Fiji', 359–66.
83 Lal, *Broken waves*, 195–97.

The advent of the Federation Party in Suva tested the political potential in the interracial accommodation nurtured there. Would this middle-class milieu encourage Indian support for the Alliance Party? Urban moderatism was jarred by the new militancy honed in the industrial strife of the cane districts, and many Suva Indians initially viewed the Federation Party with apprehension as a threat to peaceful interracial relations. The party recruited its Suva office-bearers and workers mainly from among people outside multiracial society, of modest occupational status in the lower middle class, offering them new prestige and influence. It was soon attracting large crowds to its rallies by aggressive oratory against the colonial establishment of European officials and business leaders and Fijian chiefs, denouncing them for relegating Indians to the status of second-class citizens.

The Federation Party grew as an embodiment of Indian strength and pride, sometimes denouncing Indian opponents as traitors to their race. No Indian in Suva and its hinterland was willing to contest a communal seat for the Alliance Party in the general elections of 1966 when for the first time parties competed for influence in the legislature. In by-elections for the communal Indian seats in 1968 following a Federation Party boycott of the council, Alliance candidates in southeast Viti Levu received only 10 per cent of the votes against the Federation Party's 88 per cent. The Alliance failure to build substantial Indian support in Suva and its environs reflected the limited social penetration of the ethos of moderatism.

Yet the political rivalry did have some positive effect on race relations. The prominence given by the Federation Party to racial status issues persuaded the Alliance Party's European leaders and backers to relax club membership restrictions. There were invitations to selected prominent Indians to join the hitherto racially exclusive Fiji Club, Defence Club and Suva Golf Club, and fund-raising dinners and parties that were open to all. Though there was little positive effect on voter support for the Alliance Party, the strategy, as part of the discourse of multiracialism, helped further the erosion of old barriers in urban social life.

10. RACE RELATIONS IN COLONIAL SUVA, 1945–1970

Figure 10.4: Indian polling station outside Suva Sea Baths, 1966.
Source: Robert Norton. PMB photos 103-154.

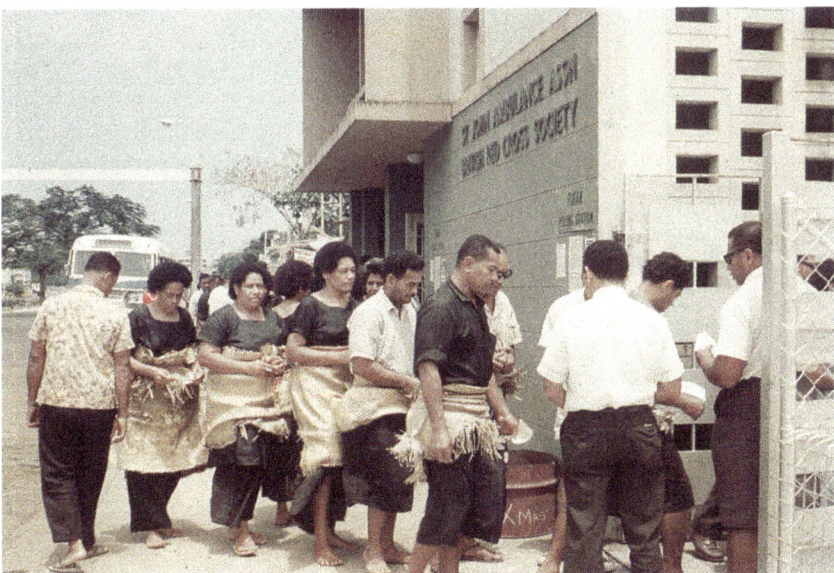

Figure 10.5: Fijians go in to vote, in mourning dress after death of Ratu Mara's father, Suva 1966.
Source: Robert Norton. PMB photos 103-158.

Voluntary service associations such as Rotary and Jaycees, and Suva's municipal council, were also contexts in which interracial ties were nurtured in counterpoint to tensions of the political arena. An instance from my field notes illustrates this: cooperation on the city council between a Fijian deputy mayor and an Indian lawyer to persuade Fijian Methodist Church leaders to end street protests against merchants who wished to open their shops to cruise ship tourists on Sundays. The value the lawyer put on this social tie influenced his decision to resign from the Suva committee of the Federation Party and contest the 1966 Legislative Council elections as an independent candidate, stressing the need for cooperation with Fijian leaders.

Figure 10.6: Main figures, from left to right: Ratu Sir Edward Cakobau, Andrew Deoki, Aileen Regan and Douglas Brown, on candidates nomination day in Suva, 1966.
Source: Robert Norton. PMB photos 103-169.

Figure 10.7: Fijians assisting at the stall of an Indian candidate contesting in a multiracial ('cross voting') electorate, Suva, 1966.
Source: Robert Norton. PMB photos 103-157.

The concern of the new governor, Sir Derek Jakeway (1964–1968), to encourage interracial political cooperation was reflected in the scene Australia's first commissioner encountered on a private visit to Government House a few months before the elections. He found Jakeway immersed in preparing a guest list for the Queen's birthday garden party:

> I was pleased to see … that the governor was revising the list … [In the past] one finds frequently a large preponderance of European guests and a remarkably small number of non-European guests … The governor appears now to be in a mood to improve the balance.[84]

Conclusion

The social changes of the 1950s put in sharp relief the racialist paternalism of the past. They were compelled by the war and its aftermath, particularly the changes in British colonial policy in response to pressures from the US and the UN. The postwar era had begun with a heightening of tension

---

84   Robert Hamilton to External Affairs, Canberra, 24 May 1966, NAA A1838 316/2/1/1 part 2.

opposing Europeans and Fijians to Indians. This eased as the feared push by the new India for radical political reform in Fiji did not eventuate and as the value of 'the races coming together' was affirmed in a variety of social contexts, from social and sports clubs to community service associations, local government councils and town festivals.

Bridging difference, getting happily together despite persisting divides in most of routine social life, began to slowly emerge as a shared middle-class value in urban society during the last two decades of the colonial era, encouraged by the multiracial social milieu of leaders in Suva. It was from the mid-1950s that the concept of a collective identity began to frequently appear in public discourse, especially in statements by the governor and other senior officials and urban festival speakers, and in editorials and articles in the *Fiji Times* – 'the people of Fiji', 'the citizens of Fiji', 'national identity', 'national consciousness'. This hopeful vision of a unified Fiji reflected the UN ideology pressing for transformation of colonies into self-governing nation-states.

The decade ended with a trend to solidarity among many Fijians and Indians in pursuit of shared class and status interests in opposition to European bosses, signalling the possibility of a radical shift in popular dispositions that the colonial establishment, official and non-official, had long feared. It was a social development, driven by urban migration and increasing wage employment, that encouraged a working-class consciousness with an anti-European edge in the trade union movement and industrial strikes. Occurring on the eve of preparations for self-government, a strike and riot in Suva provoked official efforts to persuade European-owned businesses to end longstanding racial discrimination in their recruitment policies.

Pressure from international events and authorities had influenced positive social change during the 1950s. In the 1960s new international political pressure brought both negative and positive trends in race relations. The potential for interracial labour unity, dramatically evident in the Suva strike and riot, was soon outweighed by a resurgence of Fijian–Indian tensions provoked by the advent of decolonisation and party politics. There was a return to conflict and enmity that had marred the early postwar years, but now arising from contending political ambitions and demands amid the uncertainties of radical constitutional change. On the other hand, pressure on leaders, particularly Alliance Party leaders, to build multiracial electoral support reinforced efforts to soften racial barriers in social relations in Suva and other towns.

11

Methodist Schools in Suva in the Colonial Era

Christine Weir

Despite Methodism being the dominant Christian denomination in Fiji, there are not many Methodist schools in Suva, and in colonial times there were fewer still; several of the present schools are fairly recent foundations, like the John Wesley College in Raiwaqa, founded in 1996, with its associated primary school also a post-Independence school.[1] This essay concentrates on three colonial Suva Methodist schools: Dudley House School, Suva Methodist Boys' School and Ballantine School. There are very good reasons for the limited number of Methodist schools in Suva, and they lie in both the history of the way the Methodist mission worked and the history of Suva itself. As other contributors have noted, Suva grew as an administrative and commercial centre and in the first 50 years at least of its history had a relatively low iTaukei population. European administrators and Indo-Fijian merchants made up the bulk of the visible population, with iTaukei Fijians confined mostly to domestic, labouring and other manual tasks.

---

1   'History of John Wesley College', *Fiji Sun*, 9 November 2008, fijisun.com.fj/2008/11/09/history-of-john-wesley-college/. There were also a few short-lived Methodist schools in Suva, including Wesley School 'for children of mixed descent' operating in Butt Street from 1936 for a few years (*Missionary Review*, April 1938,7–8). There does not seem to be direct connection between this school and the present John Wesley College.

The policy of Sir Arthur Gordon, the first British governor of the colony of Fiji, was protectionist. He believed, largely in response to the appalling death rate from measles in the epidemic of 1875,[2] that iTaukei should remain in their villages under their chiefs, and not be employed by Europeans in plantation or other work. As 'Atu Emberson-Bain has demonstrated, there were always more iTaukei employed outside their villages than official policy deemed proper, and many of them were in Suva. Methodists however tended to ignore them. In particular, there were few iTaukei children in Suva. It has been estimated that the population of Suva in 1901 was 4,600, of whom 1,073 were, in the nomenclature of the time, Europeans, 1,728 Indians and 701 Fijians; and that while the population grew to 24,000 by the 1940s, it remained predominantly Indian, though the reclamation work along the sea front from the Kings Wharf to Government House brought in Fijian labourers, as did work on the wharves.[3]

The Methodist mission, the providers of the first Western-style schools in Fiji, was initially based in the rural areas. The first centres set up by the Methodists were in or near the centres of chiefly power: Lakeba, Rewa, Vanuabalavu, Bau, Cuvu. This reflects the fact that, from the earliest days, Methodist missionaries found it essential to negotiate with local chiefs for protection, for permission to preach and to acquire resources for the mission. Chiefs discovered that having a missionary under their protection gave them access to literacy and to Western knowledge. Group conversion, with the chief and his people converting to Christianity together, was the early norm. Over time this interdependence between the Methodist mission and the iTaukei chiefly hierarchy became entrenched, with chiefs frequently taking roles as lay leaders and stewards, and in some cases taking ordination into the Methodist ministry.[4]

The first Christian presence in most iTaukei villages was the Methodist *vakavuvuli*, the teacher/pastor, whose responsibilities covered both evangelism and the promotion of literacy, seen by most missionaries as essential for growth in Christian knowledge and devotion through private reading of the Bible. Trained at a district circuit institution to be an evangelist rather than a schoolteacher, the *vakavuvuli*'s own secular

---

2   RA Derrick, '1875: Fiji's darkest hour – An account of the measles epidemic of 1875', *Transactions and Proceedings of the Fiji Society* 6, no. 1 (1955): 3–16.
3   James Sutherland Whitelaw, 'People, land and government in Suva, Fiji' (PhD thesis, The Australian National University, 1966), 50-60.
4   Andrew Thornley, 'Fijian Methodism 1874–1945: The emergence of a national church' (PhD thesis, The Australian National University, 1979), 72–98.

education was rudimentary: reading, writing, some elementary arithmetic and perhaps some geography or natural history alongside Biblical knowledge – all in Fijian language.[5] Children were taught religion, reading, writing and singing for around two to three hours a day. These schools did mean that almost all iTaukei children, including girls, were literate, but they were strictly limited in the education they offered, with most children only completing Grade 2 or 3.[6]

Since most iTaukei children were living in the rural areas, setting up schools in Suva was not seen as a priority. The brightest boys were encouraged to move after Class 3 or 4 in a village school to one of the district circuit institutions, co-located with the district mission stations (i.e. where the European missionary lived) where the missionary trained evangelists and *vakavuvuli*. After its development from 1913 (when it moved from Navaloa in the Rewa delta), Davuilevu continued the training in theology, and gradually the Davuilevu campus gained a technical training school and a teacher training college (separate from the theological training), as well as a primary school offering schooling beyond Grade 4. Next door was Dilkusha, the educational centre for the Indian mission. While today we may think of Davuilevu and Dilkusha as being on the outskirts of Suva, with an easy journey between them, that has not always been the case. The road was in such poor shape that when John Burton, the general secretary of the Methodist Missionary Society, visited in 1924 he stayed the night at Davuilevu rather than returning to Suva and making the journey again the next day.[7] Certainly the Methodist mission did not think of Davuilevu or Dilkusha as being in Suva, and this essay does not look at their development.

Dudley House School

The first school run by the Methodists in Suva was a small school started in 1898 by Miss Hannah Dudley for the education of Indian girls, as part of her mission to the indentured labourers and their descendants, some

---

5   Thornley, 'Fijian Methodism', 228–30.
6   Clive Whitehead, *Education in Fiji: Policy, problems and progress in primary and secondary education 1939–1973* (Canberra: Development Studies Centre, The Australian National University, 1981), 26.
7   John Burton, 'Fiji 1924', 28–29 August 1924, in John Burton's papers, ML MSS 2899 Add-on 990, Mitchell Library (ML), Sydney. John Burton was missionary to the Indian community, based in Nausori from 1901 to 1911. He was later general secretary of the Methodist Missionary Society of Australia from 1924 to 1945, during which time he visited Fiji several times.

of whom lived in Suva by the 1910s.[8] The first school, with 30 children, was held on the on verandah of the house where Hannah Dudley lodged. It then had a few temporary homes and in 1901 a schoolroom was built in Eden Street, Toorak, near the present Dudley Memorial Church. The school had varying fortunes over the first few years, since it was hard to get parental support from Indian parents for their daughters' education,[9] and after Miss Dudley's departure from Fiji in 1912 there was no regular replacement teacher.[10] Burton reported in 1924 that there was a Methodist girls' school in Suva, catering to a small number of both Indian and Fijian girls, under Miss Edwards and a 'good Indian assistant';[11] this school, a successor to Miss Dudley's school, was developed by Miss Maude Griffen into Dudley House School.

Miss Griffen, a trained New Zealand teacher, had worked for some years at Dilkusha before taking the job of principal at Dudley School in 1926.[12] It was under her leadership that the school developed a boarding hostel (1928) and began to train girls to be teachers, mainly through an apprenticeship scheme where students taught under supervision while undertaking studies under Griffen's tutelage after normal school hours. Writing in 1936, Griffen considered the importance of education for Indian girls, and her concern that they were not staying at school beyond Class 5.[13] One of the reasons was the lack of women teachers to teach at girls' schools; parents were unwilling to let their daughters attend co-educational schools, or be taught by men. But the life of girls at home waiting to be married at around 13 was, Griffen felt, stultifying. Her solution to both problems was to develop a cadre of young female teachers, and she used an interesting argument to encourage parental consent:

---

8   Morven Sidal, *Hannah Dudley Hamari Maa: Honoured mother, educator and missioner to the indentured Indians of Fiji 1864–1931* (Suva: Pacific Theological College, 1997), 34–36. I use the terms 'Indian' and 'Fijian' in the historical sections of this essay as that was the general usage at the time.
9   A Harold Wood, *Overseas missions of the Australian Methodist Church,* vol. 3: *Fiji-Indian and Rotuma* (Melbourne: Aldersgate Press, 1978), 48.
10 Sidal, *Hannah Dudley Hamari Maa*, 103.
11 Burton 'Fiji 1924', 11 August 1924.
12 Wood, *Overseas missions,* vol. 3, 92, 104.
13 Letter from Miss Griffen to Mr Mayhew, September 1936, published as Appendix I to AI Mayhew, 'Report on education in Fiji', *Legislative Council Paper* no. 3 (1937): 21–22. In this publication the name is spelled 'Griffen', but Wood uses 'Griffin', as does the Methodist Centenary souvenir: Methodist Missionary Society of Australasia, *At the gateway of the day* (Suva: Methodist Missionary Society of Australasia, 1935). Here I use Griffen, as this is how it appears at the end of her own letter.

There needs to be encouragement of the parents to send and keep a girl at school. If the girl has at 12, 13 or 14 reached Class 7 she will herself make great efforts to stay. If she can then begin training with the prospect of being soon able to add even a probationer's salary to the family fund her parents will not hurry marriage.[14]

Figure 11.1: Miss Griffen and her students, 1935.
Source: From the Methodist Centenary souvenir *At the Gateway of the Day* (1935), 47.

14 Griffen to Mayhew, September 1936, 21.

Her arguments met with considerable success; by the time she retired in 1945, Griffen had trained 67 girls as teachers, enabling the expansion of schooling more widely for Indian girls.[15] Though successful in its main aims, this rather ad hoc system did not meet with the approval of the more professionally focused Stephens Report,[16] and was replaced by standardised teacher training at the new Nasinu Teachers' College in 1949.

Dudley School and others benefited from two separate but related trends within colonial education in Fiji. The first was the development of government funding for mission schools. Grants-in-aid (grants to mission or church schools without taking over control of them) spread gradually and rather informally to British colonies from around 1900. In 1916 a few of the larger Fiji mission schools began to receive government grants to help with their more advanced classes. These classes had to be inspected by government officials and reach a designated standard of education, including some study of the English language. Some Methodist missionaries had reservations about teaching English, believing that it was unnecessary for Christian development or rural life.[17] But parents persistently demanded English education, so that their children (sons in particular) could access employment in the growing government and commercial sectors, and the Methodist Church had little choice but to provide more advanced education. Government financial support made it possible.[18]

Grants-in-aid were formalised as colonial policy with the 1925 memorandum 'Educational Policy in British Tropical Africa', which became standard practice in Africa and beyond, including the Pacific. The rationale behind this policy was twofold. The first argument was economic; it was recognised that growing colonial economies needed more skilled employees as clerks, technical and health workers, and in business, and that meant more students needed to be educated beyond the Class 3 level of the village schools. But it was cheaper and easier to

---

15   Wood, *Overseas missions*, vol. 3, 104.
16   FB Stephens, 'Report on education in Fiji', *Journal of the Fiji Legislative Council* no. 18 (1944): 25–26.
17   Cecil W Mann, *Education in Fiji* (Melbourne: Melbourne University Press, 1935), 35.
18   Christine Weir, 'Methodist childhoods: The education and formation of the young Methodist in Australia and Fiji, 1900–1950', in *Creating religious childhoods: Children, young people and Christianity in Anglo-world and British colonial contexts, 1800–1950,* ed. Hugh Morrison and Mary Clare Martin (London: Ashgate, 2019), 103–21.

partially fund already existing schools than to set up government schools. Secondly, British Colonial officials were preoccupied with fears of social disintegration on contact with modern 'civilization' and the consequent weakening of 'the sanctions of existing beliefs'. Christianity was seen as a useful way of establishing new religious ideas that might inculcate 'habits of self-discipline and loyalty to the community'.[19] In practice, the policy meant that the Methodists could get government help to run their schools, provided they conformed to certain conditions about employing trained teachers and teaching English. The doubts of some missionaries about the need for English education were overcome. By the 1930s, Dudley House School was receiving the grant, enabling an expansion of the school with three new classrooms in 1938, with half the cost borne by the government.

The grant-in-aid system encouraged and enabled the Methodist mission to concentrate on education beyond the village school level, as village schools usually did not have enough advanced students or sufficiently qualified teachers to qualify for the grants. In 1931, in a move accelerated by the financial stress of the Depression, the Methodist mission handed over the majority of its village schools to village control, and instead concentrated its efforts on more advanced schools and teacher training.[20]

Suva Methodist Boys' School

The Methodist shift to more advanced primary schools can be seen in the development of a new school in Toorak in 1919 for boys, many of whom who had completed Classes 1 to 3 at a village school and whose parents wanted them to continue education with a view to employment in the new jobs requiring English proficiency and more mathematics than the village schools could supply. From the beginning, this school had government assistance, to the tune of half the initial building costs of £1,000. It had an expatriate headmaster, first WM Norton then, from 1934, William Donnelly from New Zealand. This school took both Fijian and Indo-Fijian boys to Grade 8 and the Qualifying Examination. Religious education was incorporated into the regular program, which

---

19 'Educational Policy in British Tropical Africa', 1925, Cmd 2374, 5.
20 A Harold Wood, *Overseas missions of the Australian Methodist church,* vol. 2: *Fiji* (Melbourne: Aldersgate Press, 1978), 272–73.

also included English, mathematics, history, geography and industrial subjects such as woodwork. They also ran school gardens and sold the surplus produce, using the money raised to buy woodworking tools.[21]

Fijian parents, both iTaukei and Indo-Fijian, wanted English-medium education and were prepared to make considerable sacrifices of their children to access it. Suva Methodist Boys' School was a popular school, with an enrolment of 450 in 1938, and 582 in 1956.[22] Tomasi Vakatora was one of those who went from Class 4 (the top class) at a village school in the Rewa delta to the Suva Methodist Boys School in Toorak in 1937. Like many such boys, he boarded with relatives in Suva; the school did not have a boarding house. The fees were 12 shillings a year, often beyond the means of a village family, but Vakatora found that after-school work was available helping to establish the school playing fields (now Furnivall Park), so boys were able to earn money for their own fees.[23] A boy who passed the Qualifying Examination at the end of Class 8 could apply for entry to the Central Medical School for training as a Native Medical Practitioner, go to Davuilevu to train as a teacher or as a minister, or gain employment in the public service or private sector, both small but growing by the 1930s. Suva Methodist Boys' School was seen by the Stephens Report of 1944 as marking a new trend in multiethnic education, which should be followed by other schools.[24]

The Stephens Report, and later the 1956–1960 Educational Development Plan, marked a move in Fiji towards a stronger secondary school system. In postwar Fiji, schools like Suva Methodist Boys' School, which had been the apex of the educational system within Fiji with provision of education to Grade 8, were being supplemented by secondary schools, starting with Marist High School and Lelean Memorial School, which took students for a further two years' education. In 1955 the locally developed Fiji Junior Certificate replaced the Cambridge Junior Certificate, and this became the new qualifying standard for admittance to Nasinu Teachers' College, the medical school and the clerical branch of the civil service.[25] As a result, during the years 1950–1970 many schools were reorganised; a common pattern was to establish intermediate schools for Classes 7 and

---

21   *Missionary Review*, June 1922, 12–13.
22   *Missionary Review*, August 1938, 16; November 1956, 11.
23   Tomasi Vakatora, *From the mangrove swamps* (Suva: Institute of Pacific Studies, University of the South Pacific, 1998), 7.
24   Stephens, 'Report on education in Fiji', 59.
25   Department of Education, 'Report for the year 1960', *Legislative Council Papers* no. 29 (1961), 6.

8, while primary schools finished at Class 6. Secondary schools either started at Form 1 (Class 7) or Form 3 (depending on the local availability of intermediate schools), and offered the Fiji Junior Certificate at the end of Form 4. Increasingly the bigger secondary schools then offered New Zealand School Certificate in Form 5 and New Zealand University Entrance at the end of Form 6, but this was far from universal at the time of Independence.

The Methodist Church reorganised its Toorak schools in 1965. Dudley High School became co-educational and multiracial, incorporating the boys in higher classes from Suva Methodist Boys' School, and older Fijian girls from the neighbouring (newer and smaller) Fijian Girls' School, with a separate intermediate department for Classes 7 and 8. All the younger children from the Methodist schools in Toorak were reorganised into Annesley Infants School (now Classes 1–3) and Suva Methodist Primary School (now Classes 4–6), using many of the old buildings and building new ones.[26] For some years after the reorganisation, and still when I taught there in 1977, Dudley High had a predominance of Indo-Fijian girls in the higher forms, while the demographics were becoming more diverse in the younger forms.

Ballantine Memorial School

The initial purpose behind Ballantine School was to educate iTaukei girls in domestic arts and science so that they could in turn teach other village women, and to train girls as teachers and nurses to serve the iTaukei population. This emphasis was triggered by widespread concern about the 'decline of the race', dating from the devastating loss of life in the measles epidemic throughout Fiji in 1875, when it was estimated that around one-quarter of the population had died, and it continued to drop until the 1920s.[27] The response of the Colonial Government was to appoint a Commission into the Decrease of the Race (1896).[28] Both the Methodist

---

26   Wood, *Overseas missions*, vol. 3, 93.
27   Brij V Lal, *Broken waves: A history of the Fiji Islands in the twentieth century* (Honolulu: University of Hawai'i Press, 1992), 336–37.
28   Victoria Lukere, 'The native mother', in *The Cambridge History of the Pacific Islanders*, ed. Donald Denoon (Cambridge: Cambridge University Press, 1997), 280–83.

and Catholic missions embarked on a variety of schemes to improve hygiene in the villages, including Matavelo School at Ba in northern Viti Levu (founded 1899), which had a domestic focus.

Ballantine Memorial School (founded in Suva in 1934) widened the scope for girls' education a little further; at the opening of the school the Rev. McDonald expounded on the three objectives of the school:

> The training of Fijian female teachers, the preparation of Fijian girls for entrance to the War Memorial Hospital to be trained as nurses, and the general education of Fijian girls that would make them worthy and capable mothers of the next generation.[29]

While the envisaged career options may have been somewhat limited, the subjects taught at Ballantine School included English and arithmetic, history and geography as well as domestic economy and hygiene.[30] According to a memo from the missionary sisters of the Fiji District, the school was to have 200 girls and would be a special school with primary, post-primary and teacher training departments. In order to improve the infant mortality rate and train more Fijian women teachers, two European sisters would be employed. 'The training of Fijian girls has been culpably neglected in the past', the missionary sisters noted, so this new school must be staffed properly.[31]

The first Ballantine School was built at Muanikau, partly funded by a legacy[32] left by Mary Ballantine, who had died in 1918 while a teacher at Matavelo. The time lag between her death and the building of the school was a result of several factors: the Depression and subsequent cost constraints on the mission during the 1920s and early 1930s, the fact that much of the money required needed to be raised from Australian and local sources, and debates within the mission about the location for the new school. The location was the subject of heated argument between those who wanted the school built among the other educational institutions at Davuilevu and those who wanted it built in Suva; in the end those who wanted a new institution in a new place close to the growing population

---

29 *Missionary Review*, January 1934, 7.
30 'Papers concerning the establishment of Ballantine Memorial School 1928–36', File E/9/B, Methodist Missionary Society of Australasia archives (MMSA), National Archives of Fiji (NAF).
31 Memo from the missionary sisters in the Fiji District – Misses Hames, Clark, Weston, Tolley, Brokenshire, Lawrence, Russell, Griffin, Foulcher, n.d., File E/9/B, MMSA, NAF.
32 Mary Ballantine left the Mission 104 pounds, 15 shillings and 10 pence for a new school, but the cost of the school at Muanikau was estimated in 1931 to be £5,660, of which £3,000 was made up of a government grant: File E/9/B, MMSA, NAF.

of Suva won. They included most of the Fijian members of the Methodist Synod and Miss Tolley, who was to be the first headmistress; the defeated included RA Derrick and others from Davuilevu.[33]

The Muanikau site is marked clearly on a map of Suva dated 1934, on the present Vuya Road, more or less the same site as the present Fiji War Memorial. The mission recognised it as a prime site, elevated with a good breeze, close enough to be convenient for Suva girls, but not right in the centre of town. The closest neighbour on the 1934 map is the racecourse, which covers the area now occupied by the Pacific Theological College and Suva Grammar and Veiuto Schools. The school was seen as having model facilities, 13 acres of planting land for crops to feed the boarders,[34] and by 1938 there were three European teachers as well as several local teachers.[35] It operated as an amalgam of primary school, mainly Classes 3–8, and teacher training institute with classes similar to those at Dudley House School, where older girls were taught on an apprenticeship model. Several Australian guests to the Centenary celebrations of the Methodist Church in 1935 visited the school, and from them we have photographs of the building, students and teachers.

Figure 11.2: Ballantine schoolgirls at the original site in Muanikau, 1935.
Source: From an album by J Heaps, a visitor to the Centenary celebrations, in author's possession.

---

33   Letter from R Macdonald to JW Burton, n.d. [?1933], File E/9/B, MMSA, NAF; Wood, *Overseas missions*, vol. 2, 273–76.
34   *Missionary Review*, November 1935, 12.
35   *Missionary Review*, August 1938, 16.

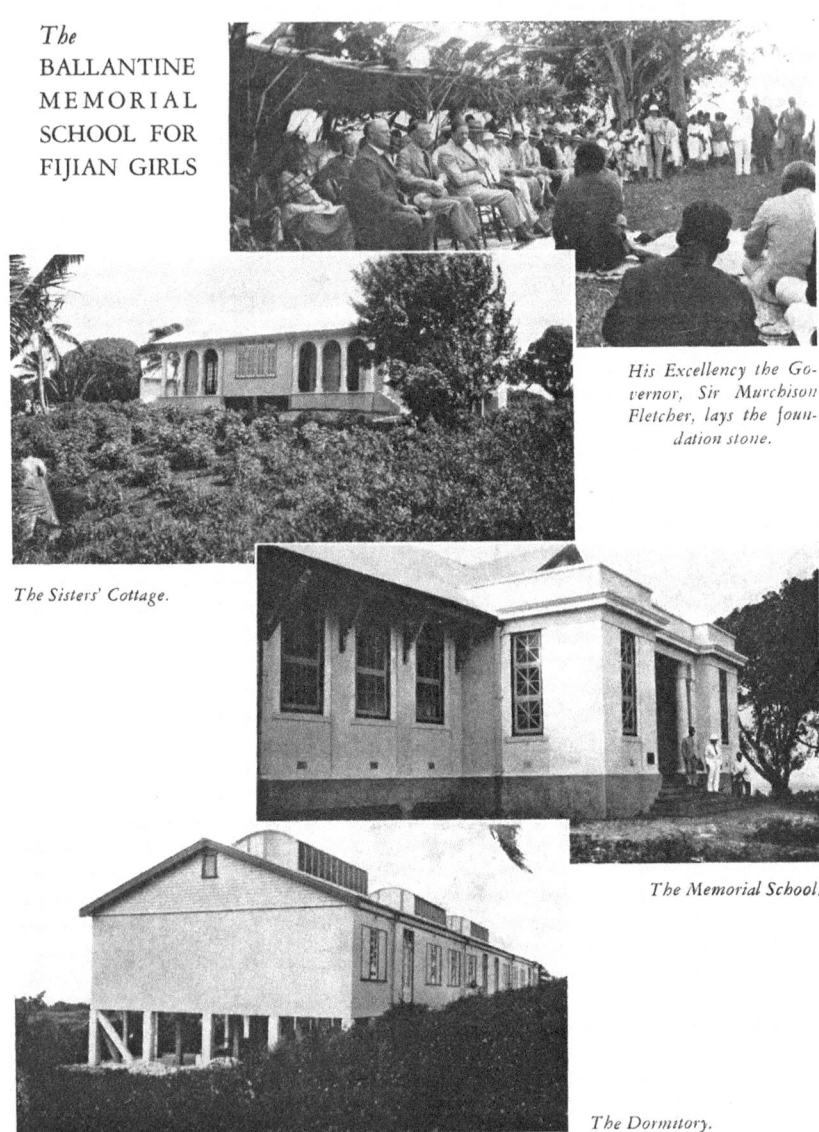

Figure 11.3: Photos of Ballantine School on its original site 1935.
Source: From the Methodist Centenary souvenir *At the Gateway of the Day* (1935), 50.

Figure 11.4: Ballantine students and staff with Australian visitors, 1935.
Source: Photo by J Heaps, in author's possession.

But trouble was brewing in the shape of World War II, and the magnificence of the site overlooking the harbour entrance became a problem for the school. Immediately after war broke out in Europe, the Government of Fiji took over the land. In a letter dated 12 October 1939, the government demanded that the Methodist mission vacate the site within one month, since it would 'take permanent possession of our Muanikau land and buildings for urgent and essential defence purposes', that compensation would be offered and that the girls at Ballantine had to go back home, or to Dudley School.[36] It is notable that the synod (yearly meeting of all the European missionaries and leading Fijian ministers) of the Methodist Church was held during the first week of October. Perhaps it was not accidental the requisition order came only when the synod was over and most of the ministers and missionaries were back home. Within a month, and after some disagreement over the valuation of the Muanikau land, the mission accepted the offer from the government of alternative land at Delainavesi. This, Rev. William Green wrote, was a 'very suitable block of land in an elevated position overlooking the harbour', and the mission managed to negotiate for the government to move most of the buildings

---

36   Letter from W Green to JW Burton in Board Minutes, 3 November 1939, MOM339, MMSA, Mitchell Library, Sydney. There was brief discussion about combining Dudley School and Ballantine School into a multiracial girls' school on the model of Suva Methodist Boys' School, but Rev. Green reported that 'Fijian opinion was unfavourable' and the idea was dropped. Board Minutes, 8 December 1939.

from Muanikau and re-erect them at government expense, as well as build an access road to the new school.[37] In the meantime many of the girls went to Matavelo School, or returned home.

Meanwhile the old school site was being transformed into a gun battery. While the official history of World War II in Fiji says the construction started in September 1939, Ballantine School did not vacate the site until November.[38] In December 1939 guns for the battery were brought into Fiji from Britain on the HMS *Leander;* guns were brought in on the same ship for another gun battery, Nasonini, on the present Pacific Forum site. It seems then that the two batteries were part of a single process of fortification and developed together – two batteries with guns pointing in opposite directions, protecting both the harbour and its approaches. According to Young, '[a] blackout was observed within the Suva vicinity to allow the two guns to be conveyed to the Muanikau hill to avoid the enemy's knowledge of its location',[39] but unless the coconut wireless was a great deal less efficient in 1939 than it is today, most of Suva would have known what was going on. The *Fiji Times* kept silent, however, and it was silent too about the closure and removal of Ballantine School, though moving a school of 200 girls could hardly have been kept a secret. There is nothing in the *Fiji Times* from October to December 1939 about either of these events, such was wartime censorship. The date of the development of the gun batteries also suggests that at this early stage of the war the main enemy was perceived to be German naval raiders.[40]

Ballantine School was reopened in late 1940 on the new site in Delainavesi. Rev. Robert Green, describing the school for Australian supporters, claimed that 'the main building with its four airy, well-lit and verandah-shaded classrooms is a decided improvement on the old school'. There was a waiting list for places and the boarding facilities were to be expanded, and so while the mission had not wanted the disruption of moving the school, all had turned out well.[41] By the 1950s, Ballantine School was, like many Fiji schools, looking to incorporate more senior classes, and under

---

37   Board Minutes, 8 December 1939, MMSA, Mitchell Library, Sydney.
38   Robert Howlett, *The history of the Fiji military forces 1939–1945* (London: Crown Agents for the Colonies on behalf of the Government of Fiji, 1948), 18, cited in Allison Young, 'World War II archaeology in Fiji: Assessing the material record', *Nebraska Anthropologist* 170 (2012): 83–84.
39   Young, 'World War II archaeology in Fiji', 83.
40   Britain did not declare war on Japan until December 1941. Australian fears about Japanese expansion were growing in the late 1930s, but the colonial authorities in Fiji were more concerned about German attacks.
41   *Missionary Review*, December 1940, 7.

Miss Phoebe Mills developed into a secondary school with the younger girls relocated to Navesi Primary School further up Delainavesi Road.[42] It also extended its aims beyond just nursing and teaching to a more general secondary education, though nursing in particular remains the career choice of many of its students.

Conclusion

The history of Suva's Methodist schools in the colonial era is replicated in the histories of the schools of other religious and community bodies. In some cases, Indo-Fijians had to start their own schools to counter the colonial state's indifference in the matter, and there remains a rich history to be explored. There is a move from churches and other voluntary bodies aiming to educate their own children and perhaps convert others, to increasing involvement with government priorities and government money. The Colonial Government, and many parents, wanted more advanced education, and used the grant-in-aid system to subsidise church and other schools rather than build their own schools. Gradually government influence increased, with the development of inspectors, standardised examinations and advice from experts about the way the education system should develop. On occasion, such as the closing of the teacher training schemes at Dudley and Ballantine schools in favour of centralised training, the government effectively forced professional qualification standards on the missions. But in general the Methodist mission was happy to accommodate government demands in return for financial support, provided it could retain the Christian character of its schools, which the Colonial Government had no desire to interfere with. It was an arrangement that served, and continues to serve, Fiji well.

---

42 Wood, *Overseas missions,* vol. 2, 337. For an obituary of Phoebe Mills see 'The woman who changed the lives of many Fijian women', *FijiSun,* 19 September 2016, fijisun.com.fj/2016/09/19/the-woman-who-changed-the-lives-of-many-fijian-women.

12

From Laucala Bay to the Region: The University of the South Pacific

Jacqueline Leckie

One of the most significant institutions, and social and physical spaces in Suva, is the main campus of the University of the South Pacific (USP) at Laucala Bay. The importance is not just for the city and nation but also for the South Pacific region. This chapter, mostly drawn from the anniversary book to mark the 50 years of USP, outlines the foundations.[1]

* * *

The USP opened on 5 February 1968 at Laucala Bay in Suva to little fanfare in a brief ceremony that commenced at 8:45 am. This allowed just enough time for a few words from Sir Norman Alexander, the acting vice-chancellor, and Freda Gwilliam, the women's education adviser of the Overseas Development Mission. Fifteen minutes later staff were administering English tests for the university's first intake of 160 students.

---

1   Jacqueline Leckie (with contributors), *A university for the Pacific: 50 years of USP* (Suva: University of the South Pacific, 2018), 25–51. Much of these pages have been reproduced with the permission of the University of the South Pacific's (USP) 50th Centennial Committee. Due to time constraints, I could hardly research all of the university's records and did not have access to 'active' records. The reflections of some former prominent staff that I wanted to include were vetoed in that publication – but I included memories of some of those staff within the text.

While the few speakers reflected the Pacific's colonial past, the class of '68 represented the culturally diverse future of the region's independent and emergent nations. These first students came from Fiji, American Samoa, Western Samoa, Tonga, British Solomon Islands, Cook Islands, Gilbert and Ellice Islands (subsequently Kiribati and Tuvalu), New Hebrides (later Vanuatu), Niue, Tokelau and the United States Trust Territory, and in later years would be joined by students from Nauru and New Caledonia, and students from outside the Pacific. No wonder former student and chemistry lecturer Ravi Naidu recalled that USP 'acted like a mini United Nations'[2] – a mix that also enhanced Suva's cosmopolitanism and multiculturalism.

The brevity and simplicity of the opening ceremony belied the complexity involved in establishing a university that would serve a widely scattered and sparse population of about 1 million in the world's largest ocean and region – the Pacific. USP was formed shortly after the visit in October 1965 by the Higher Education Mission, appointed by the British and New Zealand governments, with Australia's participation, and led by Sir Charles Morris, vice-chairman of the Inter-University Council for Higher Education Overseas, and former vice-chancellor of the University of Leeds. The 1966 Morris Report urged 'that steps be taken as soon as possible'[3] for:

> the establishment of a fully autonomous University, with headquarters at the Laucala Bay Base in Suva, Fiji, to serve the needs of the English speaking territories of the South Pacific, under the name of the University of the South Pacific.[4]

---

2   Ravi Naidu, 'Reflections of the grandchild of an indentured labourer: USP 1972 to 1989', in Leckie, *A university for the Pacific*, 178.
3   Ministry of Overseas Development, *Report of the Higher Education Mission to the South Pacific: Appointed by agreement between the Governments of Britain and New Zealand with the co-operation of the Government of Australia* (London: H.M.S.O., 1966), 24.
4   Colony of Fiji, Council Paper (CP) 67/3, *Report on the University of the South Pacific* (Suva: Legislative Council of Fiji, 1967), 1.

Figure 12.1: 'The Royal New Zealand Air Force base at Laucala Bay'. Painting by Maurice Conley, 1966, now in the USP Chancellery Board Room.
Source: Courtesy Jacqueline Leckie.

Discussions in Fiji during the 1950s and 1960s had mooted the establishment of a central tertiary training institution in Fiji. In 1956 Fiji politician, AD Patel, poignantly summed up the need for a 'University College of the South Pacific', 'to create a wise and competent indigenous leadership, essential for the solution of the problems facing the territories and the general advancement of their own communities'.[5] No action was taken until a suitable site and buildings at Laucala Bay became available after the New Zealand Government announced in the 1960s that it was closing the Royal New Zealand Air Force (RNZAF) flying boat base established there in World War II.[6] The base's buildings and facilities were offered for much-needed educational purposes in the region. This opportunity was seized by J Box, an Auckland District inspector of schools, who recommended that the Fiji and New Zealand governments be asked

---

5 Cited in Brij V Lal, *A vision for change: A. D. Patel and the politics of Fiji* (Canberra: Australian National University Press, 1997), 121, doi.org/10.22459/VC.11.2011.
6 Bee Dawson, *Laucala Bay: The story of the RNZAF in Fiji 1939 to 1967* (Auckland: Penguin Random House, 2017).

to donate the grounds and buildings of the base for a secondary teachers' training college. Fiji's governor took the proposals further when, on a visit to New Zealand, he conveyed regional interest in adapting the base not just for a teachers' college but also for an institution for higher education in the region. The Fijian Government agreed to provide Crown land and identified adjacent land for the university's future expansion. The Morris Report endorsed the suitability of the 78.8-hectare site, which was divided into upper, middle and lower camps. Quarters, messes and administrative buildings were located in the upper camp, while the airport hangar, the slipway, workshops and transport yard were in the lower camp, an area that extended over 7.7 hectares adjacent to the sea. The lower and middle parts of the base had been well cleared of the former dense vegetation of mangoes, guavas, wild lemon trees and *ivi* trees.[7] The students of 1968 were probably unaware of their campus's origins during the upheaval of World War II when the New Zealand Army Corps set up a tent camp at Laucala Bay in 1941. However, the buildings and infrastructure that students and staff were to work and live in would long be a reminder that the campus was once an air force base.

Local and Global Precedents

These early murmurings for a regional university were set against the colonial context in which formal higher education in the Pacific had slowly emerged.[8] The rich cultural and linguistic diversity of Pacific peoples was overlaid by colonial and Christian educational and administrative structures. Before World War II, tertiary education in the Pacific was generally the preserve of churches that established theological colleges to train ministers and teachers. After the war, colonial governments set up teachers' colleges, which also educated future local civil servants. Many students, usually on scholarships, followed colonial ties when they pursued tertiary education, mostly in New Zealand, Australia and the United Kingdom. Smaller numbers of students studied in North America, India, Pakistan, France and the Caribbean. Educational migration, within and outside islands, or trans-Pacific, was entrenched within the region's

---

7   USP, *A garland of achievement: University of the South Pacific 1968–1993* (Suva: University of the South Pacific, 1993), 69–72.
8   See Ron Crocombe, Tupeni Baba and Malama Meleisea, 'The development of higher education in the Pacific Islands', in *Pacific universities. Achievements, problems and prospects,* ed. Ron Crocombe and Malama Meleisea (Suva: Institute of Pacific Studies, University of the South Pacific, 1988), 20–31.

long and rich history of mobility. Suva was a key destination, because of the concentration of tertiary institutions there. The Fiji School of Medicine, the successor of Suva Medical School founded in 1885, trained medical practitioners from throughout the Pacific, especially after the Central Medical School was established in 1928.[9] It was renamed the Fiji School of Medicine in 1961. After the Fiji College of Agriculture was set up in 1954 it offered a three-year diploma in agriculture. The Derrick Technical Institute, operating from 1963, and its successor the Fiji Institute of Technology, specialised in vocational training. Since 1965 Suva has hosted the regional and ecumenical Pacific Theological College, which offered degree-level theological education for students from Pacific Island churches.

Two other regional universities in former British colonies predated USP.[10] The most comparable model of a transnational university outside the Pacific was the University College of the West Indies, which served several small tropical island states and Belize. Founded in 1948 on Jamaica, it was affiliated with the University of London until 1962 when it attained autonomous degree-granting status. The University of East Africa, which was established as an independent college of the University of London in 1963, was designed to serve Kenya, Tanzania and Uganda. It only lasted until 1970, when the independent nations demanded national universities. The demand for and provision of tertiary education markedly increased during the 1960s, regionally and globally. As new institutions expanded, greatly increased access to education was accompanied by the opening of new areas of academic inquiry. This educational revolution gave rise to, and was a consequence of, vibrant youth cultures that challenged the status quo. The demand for tertiary education also came from colonial territories and newly independent nations as they faced a complex array of developmental, social and political issues. The presence of USP in Suva undoubtedly facilitated the emergence of an urban youth culture in Suva from the late-1960s until the first coup d'état there in May 1987.

---

9   Margaret W Guthrie, *Misi Utu: Dr D. W. Hoodless and the development of medical education in the South Pacific* (Suva: Institute of Pacific Studies, University of the South Pacific with the South Pacific Social Sciences Association, 1979).
10 See V Lynn Meek and David R Jones, 'Particularism, universality, and the university', in Crocombe and Meleisea, *Pacific universities,* 13–17.

SUVA STORIES

The Need for a University in and of the Pacific

Before the decision was made to establish a regional university based in Suva, only a small and largely male elite of indigenous Pacific Islanders gained tertiary and secondary educational qualifications. Developing Pacific countries, whether independent, newly independent, self-governing or still under colonial rule needed local people as educated and skilled workers, professionals and leaders. The demand for teachers to educate growing island populations was greater than ever, as was the need for educational curricula and resources suited to the region's cultures and future. The Morris Report identified that the provision for education and training of non-graduate post-primary teachers was the most serious deficiency within the region's 'scant' post-secondary educational facilities and so recommended the establishment of an Institute of Education as a priority for the new university. At the same time there was an increasing demand for higher education and skilled personnel to staff the expanding public service and replace former colonial administrators. However, sending students overseas for training was costly and it was doubtful whether newly independent nations could sustain this practice. External aid and subsidies for Pacific students were not guaranteed and the willingness or ability of metropolitan counties to admit large numbers of foreign students in the future was in doubt. The relevance of an overseas education to university students from the Pacific Islands and the needs of the region were pressing reasons for establishing the university in Suva. A locally based university was a means to counteract the 'brain drain' of educated personnel from emergent Pacific nations and to address local development issues.

Only a month after the Morris Report, the Inter-University Council for Higher Education Overseas appointed Alexander to draw up a blueprint for the proposed university. He bluntly spelled out the dual dilemma faced by new universities in developing countries:

> It is the function of a university to produce a group with a foot in each camp – rooted in their own society and learned in modern developments and modern ways of thinking.[11]

---

11   CP 67/3, 4.

The distinctive principles that set the planned University of the South Pacific apart from other colonial precedents were to be its regional character and structure, and complete autonomy as a university. The Morris Report recommended that courses should be designed to embrace the interests and aptitudes of local students, as well as the circumstances and needs of participant countries. These regional goals were to be shaped by infrastructure that took learning into the region and did not just bring students to Suva. The university's commitment to extension or distance education was firmly laid down in the Morris Report:

> The University should have an Extra-mural Department to enable it to carry university studies to towns and villages through the Region, and to promote understanding of and affection for the University in the people of distant areas.[12]

Alexander added that the 'the greatest return' for the planned university would come from raising the general standard of village life and changing its pattern. He had been impressed with the success of the Community Training Centre in Suva and the extramural Social Training Centre at the University of the West Indies. Alexander added a third foundational principle to that of regionalism and autonomy: the new university must be prepared to be unorthodox:

> There is perhaps no parallel to the proposed university – one university serving a number of territories under a number of Governments of widely differing pattern; and certainly no single university which caters for such an enormous area. Special problems will require special measures, and precedents from more developed countries simply will not apply.[13]

The founding goal that the university should be an agency for social and economic development, and 'provide services that no other organisation is able to do' was closely followed during the following 50 years. This Pacific university had to work more closely with government departments than was usual in developed countries. In practice, USP's contribution to the region would be to work with non-governmental organisations and international organisations and experts. The planners stressed research in addition to education and training; the Morris Report identified

---

12   Ministry of Overseas Development, *Report of the Higher Education Mission*, 48.
13   CP 67/3, 5.

a 'striking need in the Region for a flourishing centre of Research' that was interdisciplinary and would attract researchers and visitors globally.[14] Suva undoubtedly became a beneficiary of such international collaboration.

On 26 June 1967, Fiji's Legislative Council passed an ordinance 'for the planning, construction and establishment in Fiji of a University of the South Pacific' with the council as the executive governing body. Fiji's governor, Sir Derek Jakeway, opened the Interim Council's first meeting on 18 September 1967 with Morris appointed as chair. Alexander was acting vice-chancellor (designate) until May 1968 when New Zealander Colin Aikman assumed duties as the first vice-chancellor. Aikman held a Master of Laws from Victoria University of Wellington and a PhD from the London School of Economics. Since 1955 he had been professor of jurisprudence and constitutional law at Victoria University, and dean of the Law Faculty. Council was headed by the chancellor, who would be a regional head of state or head of government. King Taufa'ahau Tupou of Tonga was USP's first chancellor. Although based in Suva, USP was nevertheless a regional university of Pacific countries. The regional and multi-country nature of USP posed constitutional complexity in drafting foundational legislation. Following consultation with the British Ministry of Overseas Development, the Privy Council, regional governments and university staff, the Interim Council, chaired by Morris, requested a royal charter. Queen Elizabeth II approved the charter on 4 February 1970. The Queen presented the charter to Masiofa Fetauimalemau Mata'afa of Western Samoa, USP's first pro-chancellor, at a grand ceremony in the former RNZAF hangar at Laucala Bay on 5 March 1970. Mata'afa proudly declared that 'they were standing at the threshold of a new era of educational achievement in the South Pacific'.[15]

Structure

The Morris Report's recommendations had ambitiously included the Fiji School of Medicine, the Pacific Theological College, the Derrick Technical Institute and the Fiji School of Agriculture within the university's Suva reach. Alexander rejected a theology department because the new university would specialise in economic development

---

14 Ministry of Overseas Development, *Report of the Higher Education Mission*, 27.
15 Newspaper clipping, undated, USP Pacific Collection, USP Library.

12. FROM LAUCALA BAY TO THE REGION

and had to recognise the 'special circumstances of Fiji' (presumably the non-Christian population). It was proposed that the medical school and technical institute would be autonomous institutes within the university, along with an Institute of Agriculture that embraced the Fiji School of Agriculture and the Agriculture College at Alafua in Western Samoa, and an Institute of Education and Extra-Mural Studies. Institutes were to focus on development training and applied research. While institutes were initiated during the following decade, the technical institute was not incorporated. Although later reports recommended that the medical school be transferred to USP, this was never fully realised. During the 1980s and 1990s medical and dental students took some science courses at the university and some medical degrees were awarded by USP, but most teaching was done separately at the Fiji School of Medicine.

Four months after the university opened, the British Ministry of Overseas Development and the Carnegie Corporation funded a Programme Planning Seminar, during which regional and international academics thrashed out the guidelines for the university's academic structure. The seminar proposed schools, rather than Morris and Alexander's recommended faculties of arts and sciences, as the university's academic foundation. Schools would expose students to the interdisciplinary studies that were considered the best fit for the needs and context of the South Pacific. Schools lasted until 2006 when they were replaced by faculties.

Morris and Alexander identified one of the most urgent needs in the Pacific as the provision of local facilities for training secondary and intermediate schoolteachers. This goal became the responsibility of the School of Education (SOE), which had a leading role in regional educational development as countries moved towards independence. SOE staff worked closely with education departments and teachers' colleges in the region to set up a Diploma in Education, and a bachelor's degree in arts or science (BA/BSc) with a Graduate Certificate in Teaching. In-service courses for teachers were also important. In 1975 a two-year Bachelor of Education (BEd) was introduced so that university diplomas and qualified primary teachers could gain professional educational tertiary qualifications. Professor Reginald Honeybone, formerly at University College, Dar es Salaam, was SOE's first head of school.[16] Among the 12 academic staff initially appointed in education, English and mathematics

---

16   See Srinivasiah Muralidhar, 'School of Humanities', in USP, *A garland of achievement*, 37–39.

was New Zealander Frank Brosnahan, professor of English language. He served as deputy vice-chancellor (1972–1979) and interim vice-chancellor (1982–1983). Jo Nacola and Satendra Nandan were the only regional academics in the school. Nacola wrote one of USP's first plays, 'I Native No More', while Nandan became a widely acclaimed poet and author. SOE provided many educational and creative roles during the following 50 years. In 1969 with the support of regional governments, through the United Nations Development Programme/UNESCO Regional Project for Curriculum Development, SOE was charged with developing new courses and curricula that would be relevant to the region and its new nations. As a student in 1971 pointed out: 'When I graduated from secondary school I knew more about England than I did about Fiji.'[17] SOE took a leading role in the region with innovative and applied educational research. The creativity and Pacific focus in music, drama and creative writing fostered by SOE spilled over into performances and exhibitions that many of Suva's inhabitants enjoyed over the years.

The Programme Planning Seminar also recommended that a School of Social Development offer programs in politics, history, sociology and geography.[18] Politics was not initially offered but economics was. The first head of geography was Fijian Isireli Lasaqa, who went on to study for a doctorate at The Australian National University and later became a prominent Fijian civil servant. The first head of school was LV Castle, professor of economics, while Dr John Harre ran sociology. Anthony Chapelle taught preliminary history. The school had a strong emphasis on preparing students for careers in teaching and the civil service, so public administration was added to the offerings. Professor Ron Crocombe arrived in 1970 to teach Pacific studies and the discipline of politics was introduced with the appointment of Dr John Chick in 1972. The broad and interdisciplinary nature of the school (renamed the School of Social and Economic Development in 1970 and known as SSED), and the often contentious questions raised by those lecturers passionate about their subject, led to many SSED graduates entering a wide range of careers and taking on challenging leadership roles within and beyond Suva.

---

17 Frank Galland, 'Relevance & the U.S.P.', *NATION Newsmagazine*, September 1971, 7.
18 See Vijay Naidu, 'School of Social and Economic Development', in USP, *A garland of achievement*, 43–45.

12. FROM LAUCALA BAY TO THE REGION

The School of Natural Resources (SNR) started with 12 staff, with Peter Beveridge as head of biology, JWA Strachan as head of chemistry and EJ Brown as head of physics. Distinguished British botanist Professor Roy Clapham was appointed as the first head of school in 1971. Uday Raj was initially the only local science lecturer. After he obtained his doctorate he established and ran the Diploma of Tropical Fisheries Programme for many years, inspiring many students to channel their love of the ocean into postgraduate research. Staff concentrated on training graduates to meet the developing needs of countries in the region, especially the utilisation of natural resources in agriculture, forestry, marine biology and geology, the development of science in secondary schools, and for research and technical positions within the public sector.

The site at Laucala Bay was ideally suited to SNR's emphasis on applied science and marine studies. The former air force hangar was a distinctive feature of USP's early years and is still remembered by former science students and staff. Stephen Willatt, head of the School of Pure and Applied Sciences, has provided a vivid recollection:

> It was a massive structure visible from Kadavu Passage miles to the south. Not surprisingly, the more adventurous SNR anglers used it as a navigational aid during deep-sea fishing expeditions! The hangar was shared by SNR (occupying the northern offices) and two Fiji Government Departments, viz. the Road Transport Control Authority (occupying the southern offices) and Customs. Screeching brakes and loud horns emanating from the non-academic side of the hangar were constant occupational hazards for staff. The Customs Department used the central part of the hangar floor for storing impounded merchandise and holding regular auctions. SNR staff found the auctions a respite from their work. Staff time used to be enlivened at times by various sea-plane services which took off from the ramp nearby. Staff did not mind the noise as it was all very interesting and often lectures stopped and staff and students watched to see if the sea-plane managed to clear the breakwater!

> Lectures used to be held in small dilapidated wooden buildings. The Canadian-funded Diploma in Tropical Fisheries programme was conducted in a poorly ventilated building unfit for human occupation. USP must have been on good terms with the Suva City Council for the building was never condemned! … The biology laboratory was accommodated in reasonably sturdy structures. The physics laboratory, the former RNZAF radar workshop,

had a panoramic view of Laucala Bay. The chemists were rather unfortunate: they had to make do with a derelict RNZAF building as a laboratory. It was a wooden structure with gaping floorboards on piles. Both students and cleaners found the cracks convenient to get rid of broken glassware and instruments. Below the floor was a pond, the shores of which provided the biologists with a guaranteed supply of prothalli for their practical lessons.[19]

In 1996 the hangar was demolished. Two years later USP's world-class marine studies complex opened on the lower campus at Laucala, the same year as the United Nations International Year of the Ocean.

Another former RNZAF building that had several iterations was the officers' mess. Initially it housed USP's library with Mrs Kirwan as the interim university librarian. After the library was relocated to a new purpose-built building in 1972, under USP's first librarian, Harold Holdsworth (lauded by USP Vice-Chancellor Colin Aikman as 'the Doyen of Commonwealth Librarians'),[20] the Institute of Pacific Studies (IPS) was set up in the old wooden building in 1976. IPS was eventually replaced by the Oceania Centre for Arts, Culture and Pacific Studies.[21]

The Students

As USP's pioneering students departed from their homes on an adventure of discovery they were full of trepidation and excitement. Jean Pierre-Nirua (in 2020, minister for education in Vanuatu), who started university studies in 1981, recalled that they were trailblazers; usually the first in their communities to embark upon tertiary, often even secondary education.[22] These students, who were picked to become the region's future teachers, administrators and leaders, carried huge expectations from their families, communities and the new nations they represented. A female student told Frank Galland in 1971 that coming to university in Suva 'is the most important thing that ever happened in my life; my family could never have sent me overseas to college'.[23] Added to such expectations was the bittersweet pain of leaving home and tasting new

---

19 Stephen Willatt, 'School of Pure and Applied Sciences', in USP, *A garland of achievement*, 40–41.
20 Colin M Aikman, 'Establishment: 1968–74', in Crocombe and Meleisea, *Pacific universities*, 50.
21 See Leckie, *A university for the Pacific*, 114–18.
22 Interview with Jacqueline Leckie, 23 August 2017.
23 Galland, 'Relevance & the U.S.P.', 7.

freedoms. Although some students had already separated from their families when they attended boarding school, the huge move to Suva was a decisive break from kin, culture and familiar physical environments. Even for Suva-ites, the change from school to university, and living off-campus with immediate family commitments could be challenging. But Padma Narsey Lal found being a science student at USP had its liberating moments:

> I was doing soil biology. Soil biology meant that we would go out into different field sites and open pits to look at the layers and so on. Anyways, for me to get out, USP gave me a perfect opportunity to defy all the rules where all the Gujaratis were concerned, like wear jeans.

After the fieldtrip Lal would stay in her dirty jeans, be dropped off downtown and walk up the hill to Toorak:

> I would deliberately walk all the way up in my muddy jeans and, oh it was fun. So … there was always this talk talk. It gave the opportunity to perhaps defy some of those things.[24]

But Ethel Sigimanu from Solomon Islands, who arrived at USP over a decade after Lal, recalled feeling shy, embarrassed, awkward and lonely. She was acutely aware of the disparities between students from different economic and cultural backgrounds. Some students wore Western-style clothing and makeup, but many of those who desired to follow this trend lacked the money to do so. Sigimanu was overwhelmed by the consumer choice available in Suva although little was available to her and other students on very limited allowances. She had been schooled in English, but like many students she was conscious of her 'grammar and quite intimidated by the fact that others could speak really fluently'.[25] Her lack of work experience, compared to some students who had been working as civil servants, also alarmed her. 'I moved straight from school and I was green.' Yet like so many students at USP, Sigimanu established new friendships that later merged into regional networks and were significant in her professional career. USP also set her up with the confidence to embark upon an impressive career in the public service. In 2018 she was the permanent secretary of justice and legal affairs in Solomon Islands. As fellow Solomon Islands alumnus Sir Francis Billy Hilly, who came

---

24 Interview with Jacqueline Leckie, 21 August 2017.
25 Interview with Jacqueline Leckie, 31 August 2017.

to Suva in 1968, remarked: 'USP sets you up for life – with a basic foundation trying to understand more of what life is and basically what you need to be doing.'[26] Hilly was the first student from the Solomon Islands to graduate with a BA in 1973 and became a leading civil servant, and politician, including periods as prime minister and leader of the opposition in Solomon Islands.

Living together with peers from different parts of the region could be a big factor in the transition from being shy or 'green' about worldly matters to developing a more confident and wider regional perspective. In 1969 there were two halls of residence, divided according to gender. When the university opened, only 20 per cent of students were female. The women's hall of residence, which could accommodate 60, was located towards the southern end of the campus. Two students shared a room. They were encouraged to discuss personal or study problems with the female tutors who lived at the residence. They could also talk to Merran Harris, mistress of the Women's Hall and one of the only three women among the 40 academic and senior professional staff at USP in 1969. The men's hall of residence was situated on the hill overlooking the main office block and could house 132 students. Male students had more confined conditions than females did, usually with four to a room. When future Pacific historian Brij Lal lived in First Hall in 1971, he shared a cubicle, which was divided by 'curtain walls', with three other students from Rotuma, Solomon Islands and Tonga:

> I came from a very rural isolated family and went to Labasa Secondary and then it was essentially Indo-Fijian. I had never met a Pacific Islander. And one of the great things about USP in that first year was that … students interacted with each other … I think that broadened my cultural horizon.[27]

By 1970 there was an urgent need for accommodation as approximately 300 students, or two-thirds of the student population, were living on campus. The following year British aid financed the building of two, four-storey 'student villages'. The *University News* of March 1970 reported that the architects had consulted with students and staff to 'break new ground in the design, economics and planning of buildings in the South Pacific as befits the first buildings of a new, Regional university'. The building faced directly into the trade winds, with features that allowed cross ventilation.

---

26   Interview with Jacqueline Leckie, 1 September 2017.
27   Interview with Jacqueline Leckie, 21 August 2017.

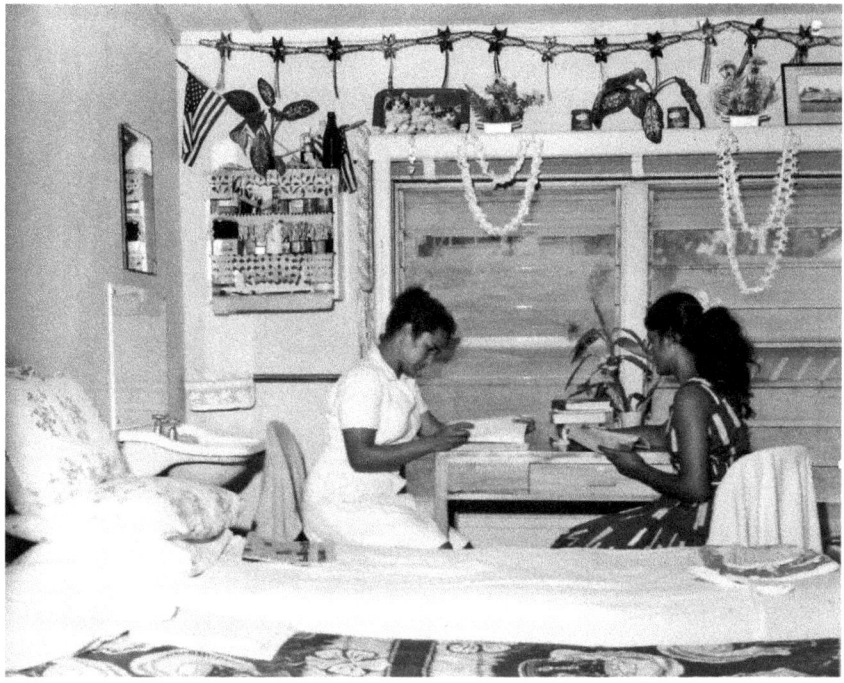

Figure 12.2: Women's Hall, USP, 1968.
Source: Courtesy USP.

Even the dining hall facilitated intermingling between students from different cultures. For many years menus and seating arrangements were divided into the 'Islander' and 'Indian' sections. Island food tended to be *dalo* (taro), cassava, fish, lolo, pork or beef, while Indian selections might comprise dhal, rice, roti, chicken, fish or vegetarian curry. Brij Lal recalls: 'You went straight inside, you went to the Indian side and they went to their side and there was hardly any interaction in the dining hall.' Even more striking was the lack of contact between male and female, especially for those of Indian heritage: 'Boys and girls did not sit together. They would know each other but there would be no social interaction.' These rigid barriers quietly changed and students from later years recall the dining hall as conducive to breaking down cultural barriers, a site where young romance sometimes bloomed, or where heated exchanges about student politics erupted. One issue that did unite students from different backgrounds was the quality of the food. Francis Saemala led a strike in 1969 when students stopped attending class and organised protests, even outside Suva's police station. The complaints were about the quality of food provided to students, a recurring theme at USP.

Figure 12.3: USP students demonstrating in downtown Suva against French nuclear testing in the Pacific, 1972.
Source: Courtesy Fiji National Archives, # M8350.

Suva residents also became aware of and were sometimes drawn into student protests and less vocal forms of activism until this was inhibited by the 1987 coups. During its early decades USP was a hotbed of radicalism. Students and staff were pivotal in the Pacific antinuclear, anticolonialism, environmental and women's rights movements. Even the vice-chancellor, James Maraj, gave support when he opened the first South Pacific International Conference of Students for a Nuclear-Free and Independent Pacific on 14 December 1981 at Laucala campus. Students also protested about issues outside the region. When Sir Denis Blundell and Lady Blundell visited the Laucala campus in August 1976 they were greeted by angry students protesting not only about nuclear testing but also a proposed New Zealand rugby tour of South Africa, and the New Zealand Government's racist attitudes towards visitors from the Pacific.

Former student and chemistry lecturer Anirudh Singh vividly describes how USP and student life was a conduit through which global youth culture and politics was brought to the streets of Suva:

> 1969 was the year of Woodstock, the iconic music event symbolizing the new hippy movement. A wave of flower power and student radicalism was sweeping around the globe. And we were affected as well. We did our best to emulate our overseas

counterparts. We embraced the peace symbol and organized our own student protests. We were amongst the first groups in the Pacific to demonstrate against the French testing in Mururoa. Our group, called the Against Tests On Mururoa (ATOM) Committee, led by biology lecturer Graham Baines, organized a rally in the new Civic Auditorium, and a banner-carrying, placard-waving march to Sukuna Park.[28]

Vijay Naidu, another early student and later professor of development studies at USP, has also outlined the networks between USP students and staff and civil society groups in Suva:

> In Fiji, trade unionists, USP staff and students, civil society organisations such as the YWCA and the Fiji Council of Churches, and concerned citizens formed the Fiji Anti-Nuclear Group (FANG) to continue the fight against the tests and to oppose the shipment of radioactive materials, and the movement of nuclear powered and nuclear weapons carrying ships in Oceania. Several protests were held in Suva when suspected nuclear armed and powered vessels visited the city's port. In 1980, in a significant protest in Suva, USP staff and students and anti-nuclear activists occupied the French Embassy office and held a sit-in. The university was also the site of debates and conferences about Pacific futures, the ending of colonial rule and what kind of development trajectories that emerging independent Pacific states should take.[29]

The influx of students into Suva greatly enriched the city in other ways such as in the growth of the city's popular culture and nightlife. Fiji's first outdoor rock music festival at Laucala Bay in 1971 included gigs by students, Neal Engledow and Ata Mai'a'i, with Mai'a'i's band 'Mode of Existence'.[30] Local sporting bodies in Suva also benefited from new sporting talent. Nirua had been a New Hebrides' volleyball representative but in Suva, like many of his wantoks from there and Solomon Islands, he switched to competitive soccer, and played for the USP, Suva and Nasinu teams. Students also regularly took part in community projects in Fiji, sometimes in structured activities between semesters, other times

---

28 Anirudh Singh, 'Two generations of change', in Leckie, *A university for the Pacific*, 198. See also Steven Ratuva, 'Those naughty student days', in Leckie, *A university for the Pacific*, 193–95.
29 Vijay Naidu, 'USP's Laucala campus as a centre of activism', in Leckie, *A university for the Pacific*, 184.
30 'Ata Mai'a'i leads "Mode of Existence"', *UNISPAC* 4, no. 4 (1971): 27, USP Pacific Collection, USP Library.

as fieldwork within their courses. This work ranged from working with disabled groups in Suva to village rural development such as building sea walls or installing water tanks.

From Air Force Base to a Regional University

This chapter has outlined the origins and some of the features of USP at Laucala Bay in the early years. During the following decades the campus was greatly transformed in terms of the infrastructure, physical landscape, student composition and the number and range of course offerings and degree programs. Student numbers burgeoned from an initial 154 to around 30,000 in 2017 (for all of USP, not just at Laucala Bay). The changing gender patterns among students was also striking; females slowly increased from 20 per cent of students in 1968 to 51 per cent in 2001, to reach 57 per cent in 2018. Although by then a far greater proportion of students lived off-campus (both within and outside Suva) than in USP's earlier years, there were far more student hostels at Laucala Bay than the two halls that had housed many of the first students.

Several of the new buildings established during USP's early years were repurposed. For example, in 1991, University Extension Services relocated to the former library building that was renamed the Communications Building as it also housed Media and Computing Services. The library had moved in 1988 into a striking new building, funded by Australia, that University Librarian Esther Batiri Williams said, 'changed the face of the "old" campus'.[31] Other substantial new buildings included the School of Natural Resources, opened by Pierre Trudeau on 8 October 1981 because Canada funded it. Australian aid also provided for the new SSED building opened in 1981, while British aid enabled a new administration complex to open in 1983. The most imposing building complex on USP's Laucala campus is the Japan Pacific ICT Centre with technical and computer facilities. The centre's large multipurpose theatre was opened by Fijian Prime Minister Frank Bainimarama, and Japanese Ambassador to Fiji Yutaka Yoshizawa, on 22 February 2012.

---

31 Esther Batiri Williams, 'The library', in Leckie, *A university for the Pacific*, 54–55.

Figure 12.4: Extension Services, 1977. USP at Suva was a global pioneer in the development of distance education long before digital platforms.
Source: Courtesy USP.

But perhaps the most visible change at Laucala Bay has been the landscape. While many vestiges of the buildings and roads left by the RNZAF remain – including the popular swimming pool – since the 1980s, the campus has been filled with verdant vegetation and neatly maintained grounds.[32] During the 1980s, Ian Banner, director of buildings and grounds, brought a fresh vision to the look of the campus. He advocated that a tropical campus should reflect the wealth of its floral and cultural biodiversity. Edible fruit trees and plants were planted, many around staff and student housing. Saula Vodonaivalu, the curator of the South Pacific Regional Herbarium, planted several Fijian indigenous trees throughout the campus. On 14 September 1988, Fiji's president, Ratu Sir Penaia Ganilau, opened a magnificent and lush botanical garden in a valley near the entrance to the Laucala campus. Visually striking artworks have also been installed on campus, especially after the opening of the Oceanic Centre of Arts and Culture in 1997. The centre was part of Professor Epeli Hauʻofa's vison to revitalise indigenous and local art. On USP's 25th anniversary in 1993,

---

32 See Randolph R Thaman with Michael P Gregory and Shingo Takeda, *Trees of life: A guide to trees and shrubs of the University of the South Pacific* (Suva: The University of the South Pacific Press, 2012).

he wrote that the Laucala campus had become like a beautiful intellectual cemetery: devoid of creativity and critical thought after the coups and the subsequent encroachment of neoliberalism into the university.[33]

This chapter began with USP's modest opening ceremony at Laucala Bay in 1968. On 2 December 1971 a far grander ceremony, with 2,000 supporters, took place in the former RNZAF hangar. The national anthems of Great Britain and Tonga were played but the stand out music was the university song 'Garland of Achievement', composed by Tiresa Malietoa. Forty-nine graduates received their degrees or diplomas from the chancellor, King Taufa'ahau. The king was resplendent in his specially designed academic robes with tapa facings representing USP's member countries and Pacific identity. This occasion proudly demonstrated that USP had taken root and was there to stay. Although during the following 50 years Laucala Bay remained at the centre of USP's activities, the university expanded elsewhere in Fiji and throughout the region. In 2018 there were 14 campuses in 12 countries with a further 11 centres. This is an astonishing coverage of tertiary educational provision for the Pacific. Suva has played a major role in the growth of national and regional tertiary and secondary education and research and training through the university that took root in Laucala Bay.

Figure 12.5: Graduation at the Lower Campus (that was also the gymnasium), 1979.
Source: Courtesy USP.

---

33   Epeli Hau'ofa, 'A beautiful cemetery', in USP, *A garland of achievement*, 81–82.

Part 3.
Reflections

13

Swimming under the *Ivi* Tree: Ratu Sukuna Park, Land Reclamation and Family Connections

Kaliopate Tavola

> The farther backward you can look
> the farther forward you are likely to see
> — Winston S Churchill

My favourite early memory of Suva was swimming under the *ivi* tree opposite Vanua House, along Victoria Parade, where Ratu Sukuna Park is today (see Figures 13.1 and 13.2). The year was 1955, some seven or eight years before the park was established.[1] The land reclamation that resulted in the park was part of the grand plan to develop the Suva waterfront from the current port area, along Thomson Street and all the way along Victoria Parade. In the 1880s, Thomson Street crossed Nubukalou Creek and was the main waterfront.

---

1   Ratu Sukuna is the affectionate form of the longer version: Ratu Josefa Vanaaliali Lala Sukuna. On being knighted twice, he was popularly referred to as Ratu Sir Lala Sukuna. The school named after him carries the latter as Ratu Sir Lala Sukuna Memorial School (RSMS). This chapter continues to use the affectionate version given to the park.

Figure 13.1: The *ivi* tree (1959). The *ivi* tree in the middle of the picture stands in front of what is Vanua Arcade today. The sea is now part of Ratu Sukuna Park.
Source: National Archives of Fiji.

Figure 13.2: The *ivi* tree, from where McDonalds restaurant is today (1959). Part of the Cable & Wireless Building can be seen to the right of the picture.
Source: National Archives of Fiji.

In retrospect, while the idea of a recreational area for the capital might have been part of the grand civic plan, the naming of the park after the great chief, however, was necessarily an upshot of history. Had not Ratu Sukuna died in 1958, the park may not have been so named.

The reclamation continues today past the Grand Pacific Hotel, the Suva Bowling Club green, the Queen Elizabeth Drive Park and beyond.

In my moments of reverie over the years, I have always looked back at how Suva City has grown and developed. I have pondered particularly about that swim under the *ivi* tree and asked myself whether, apart from my fellow swimmer and myself, how many others have had the opportunity to have swum there before the sea became land and well before the park was first conceived. In retrospect, we were perhaps making history – swimming into Suva's history.

This chapter is similarly predisposed regarding its approach. It is a narrative that focuses essentially on the general historical development of Suva and by way of parallelism, for instance, narrates its corresponding impact on aspects of my own family history including my community. Inevitably, I become both a narrator of history and a consequential participant in some aspects of it as it evolved. But more so, I become selective of issues through circumspect restriction but ensuring coherence and palpability of the story.

The Approach

In *History is a weapon*,[2] the unnamed writer opens with: 'History isn't what happened, but a story of what happened'. They later elaborate and qualify that it is not only about the story that happened but also of 'the lessons these stories include'. The narrative below comprises my story. The lessons that can be drawn would, by necessity, be pivoted around my own experience. This necessitates therefore the use of additional primary sources of information[3] and of the autonomy of my own interpretation.

---

2   See *History is a weapon* (website), accessed July 2019: www.historyisaweapon.com.
3   These include family archives and the internet. See especially my blog: Kaliopate Tavola, *Kaidravuni*, www.kaidravuni.com.

The latter agrees with the conclusions drawn by British historian EH Carr in *What is history?*[4] Further, the approach proffers autoethnography[5] as its mode of disciplined scientific study.

Carr also characterises history in terms of cause and effect and concludes that 'everything has a reason'. In this context, I have introduced two related metaphors to demonstrate the relations between cause and effect and the reasons why these happened. I have used the concept of 'arrow of time' to underline, firstly, the relational aspect between cause and effect, and the direction of the relations. Secondly, I have used 'parallelism', not as a literary device, but as a means of demonstrating cause and effect as corresponding features. Each section of the paper reflects such correspondence.

Carr raises two more conclusions. He sees history as progress, which widens horizons. This story aims to demonstrate the progress and development of Suva being reflected in my own history and that of my community. In terms of widening horizons, the story itself, in the way it is conceived, goes beyond the conventional way of recording history. It proffers the observer himself in the act of observing 'so that man is simultaneously the subject and the object of thought and observation'.

The Chronicle from the Late Nineteenth Century: 1882–1888/1889

In Suva, during this period, Thomson Street was the main waterfront street. What is Victoria Parade today was essentially the coast, lined on the seaside with magnificent raintrees that provided welcome shade for citizens and their horses.

While the official move to make Suva Fiji's capital was made in 1882, the decision relating to that had been done earlier in 1877. In that year, Suva administrators had agreed to a township plan and passed Towns Ordinance No. 16 of 1877, which provided for the establishment of a partially elected Town Board. The work of the board was further assisted by Ordinance No. 4 of 1881: An Ordinance for Regulating the Alignments of Streets in the Town of Suva. This marked the start of civic planning control. The board sat until 1883.

---

4   Edward Hallett Carr, *What is history?* (London: Macmillan, 1961).
5   See Margot Duncan, 'Autoethnography: Critical appreciation of an emerging art', *International Journal of Qualitative Methods* 3, no. 4 (2004): 28–39, doi.org/10.1177/160940690400300403.

Figure 13.3: Victoria Parade, n.d.
Source: P32.6.27 Fiji Museum.

The original plan of the township envisaged the construction of a pier extending out from the mouth of Nubukalou Creek in a north-westerly direction, following the creek's line of flow. However, this was found to be inconvenient, since many of the business houses were situated in the area of Thomson Street and Renwick Road. Ease of access presented a problem.

The subsequent decision to situate the wharf close to the business houses led to early reclamation work in 1881, along Thomson Street, where the General Post Office is situated (site of the old Suva Post Office). The wharf was constructed there. Pier Street was thus named appropriately due to its proximity to the wharf.

Near to the wharf, a local marketplace had developed there and was popular for those sailing in with their produce. Passengers wanting to board ships in the harbour would congregate under the *ivi* tree at the corner of Thomson Street and Renwick Road (the Ivi Triangle today) for their boat transfer services.

Figure 13.4: Suva wharf, n.d. In the background next to the Union Steamship Company store is the same *ivi* tree.
Source: P.32.4.51 Fiji Museum.

Out to sea and beyond Suva Harbour, the volume of ships to and from Suva was definitely on the rise, reflecting the development of Suva as Fiji's capital and trading port. The construction of Solo Lighthouse[6] in 1888 in the middle of the North Astrolabe Reef, at the northern end of the Great Astrolabe Reef, 65 kilometres south of Suva, was a vital navigational aid for mariners.

The land reclamation that led to the construction of the wharf in 1881 along Thomson Street was only the beginning of many reclamation projects to permanently change the Suva shoreline. The reclamation that would give rise to Ratu Sukuna Park, however, was still some 70 years away.

The beaming light from Solo Lighthouse within the Great Astrolabe Reef was a great sensation for the villagers on Dravuni Island, 13 kilometres away. The sensation was one of fascination. In the first place, it reaffirmed their expectation that by making Suva Fiji's capital, there was bound to be unprecedented development taking place there and from which they

---

6   See Sea Reel Productions, *A mariner's guide to Fiji shores & marinas 2019* (Suva: Sea Reel Productions Ltd., 2019) for background including the legend behind the rock on which it sits. See also Tavola, *Kaidravuni*, for other related stories.

would benefit. Dravuni's 'arrow of time', from their perspective, was thus established. The villagers could relate to the lighthouse, a great symbol of development that they could see. Its beaming light promised more. The direction of the benefit flow, totally unprecedented, was from the new capital, the centre, to the periphery.

This heightened the villagers' sense of anticipation as to what else was on offer. In this exalted mood, it was easy for them to imagine the legendary promises of the past from ancestors who lived on Solo and to whom homage is still offered today.

In 1888, the village on Dravuni was situated on the south-eastern part of the island, facing away from the new lighthouse. The villagers could not see the lighthouse nor Solo's light at night directly since the central ridge running the length of the island was in the way. They keenly awaited nightfall when they would climb to the top of the ridge to enjoy the light display from the new lighthouse.

This fascination was not transitory either. It lasted a long time. Further, it planted a seed of enquiry in the minds of the villagers on the practicality and justification of the location of the village. Villagers were aware that with increased traffic from the capital, it was wise to move the village site for convenience and logistical expediency. In any case, such a move in a similar direction was not unprecedented in the context of the village history.

Prior to 1800, the village site had moved from its south-eastern location to the northern end of the island, Muanalailai, facing Viti Levu and Suva of yesteryear. The reasons for that move remain today as an issue for self-reflection and self-discovery. This is particularly so since the move proved disastrous when in 1800 *lila balavu,* Asian cholera, killed many villagers, who had to be buried in mass graves. The villagers lacked natural resistance to the imported scourge. The end result was an immediate return to the previous village site. This lasted more than eight decades before the Solo Lighthouse and Fiji's new capital beckoned for another move.[7] That move came after 1888.

---

7 For details on *lila balavu* and its impact on decision to move village site, see *Kaidravuni.com (blog)* – History: 'The village site changed with time', accessed July 2019.

For the villagers, the move was 'in the wind'. Their rising expectations, elicited by the proximity of the new capital, were yielding dividends. The shift to the new site coincided with the visit of Rev. Eliesa Bula[8] of the Methodist Church of Fiji. He carried out a mass baptism on a plot of land within the demarcated village precinct. He commemorated his visit and his divine work by naming that particular plot of land, Vitiri, after his *tokatoka* in Somosomo Village, Gau, Lomaiviti.

Two village elders, including my great-grandfather, had given up their *kanakana*, family owned land intended for garden plots, for the village site. When his son was born in 1889, my great-grandfather was already on posting as a Methodist catechist in Nabukelevuira, southern Kadavu. Grandfather Livai Veilawa was destined to play a role with Ratu Sukuna (born a year earlier) in the next section of this story.

The Chronicle from a 30-Year Period: 1889–1919

Suva's growth as Fiji's capital was better planned compared to that of Levuka.[9] The city fathers made sure of that. A critical part of that plan was of course land reclamation. Substantial land reclamation took place during this period.

The focus of land reclamation at the time was the seaward side of Thomson Street. By the onset of the current period of study, the focus had shifted along to what is Victoria Parade today, even though the reclamation work along Thomson Street had not been completed.[10]

In the 1900s, land reclamation started on sites to accommodate the Cable & Wireless building and the Suva Town Hall. Any reclamation along the intervening shoreline from the beginning of Victoria Parade (end of Thomson Street) to the new reclamation site that was to accommodate, inter alia, Ratu Sukuna Park, was not part of the civic plan at the time. Two small hills nearby were removed and the soil from them used for the reclamation.

---

8   See Kaliopate Tavola – *Kaidravuni.com* (blog) – History: 'The unstoppable march of Christianity', accessed July 2019.
9   RA Derrick discussed Levuka's haphazard development in Derrick, 'The removal of the capital to Suva', *Transactions and Proceedings of the Fiji Society of Science and Industry* (1953): 203–9.
10 The reclamation seaward from the GPO was still underway in 1959 – see Negative No. M1318, National Archives of Fiji (NAF). Subsequent to that, all old reclamations were encircled by new reclamations to gain more waterfront land and the foreshore line shifted to Stinson Parade.

Figure 13.5: Victoria Parade, n.d.
Source: P.32.7.32, Fiji Museum.

The Suva Town Hall was completed and opened in 1905. Its original name was Queen Victoria Memorial Hall. The town hall remained as Suva's finest building for many years.[11] It served another purpose at the time. It initially housed the Fiji Museum that was founded the year before in 1904, the same year when the first elected and nominated 19-member Legislative Council was established. The museum finally moved to its permanent building in Thurston Gardens in 1954.

The reclamation further progressed southward to accommodate the building of the Suva City Carnegie Library, which was opened on 20 November 1909. Governor Sir Everard im Thurn, who assumed office on 11 October 1904, officiated at the opening. He also donated books to the library. A further donation of books came from Sir Alport Barker, then proprietor and publisher of the Fiji Times and Herald Limited.

The planning of the library had started on 1 September 1908 when Andrew Carnegie, an American iron and steel manufacturer, provided the grant that enabled the completion of the central portion of the library building. But the library did not start on a good footing. Its roof was blown off by a hurricane on 25 March 1910. Other changes to the library were to follow.

Land reclamation continued in the 1910s. However, the approach this time around was different. It took place on both sides of the Nubukalou Creek – northwards to Walu Bay and further southward along Victoria Parade. Between 1911 and 1913, reclamation took place to the north of the creek for the new Kings Wharf and the old Public Works Department depot. This allowed the work on the new wharf to start in 1912. It was a wooden structure that serviced Fiji and the Pacific region for nearly 50 years before major renovations in 1961 and 1982. Major renovations still needed further land reclamation and this was carried out between 1913 and 1916. Apart from accommodating the renovation work on the Kings Wharf, the reclaimed area also accommodated development on the Walu Bay industrial site.

---

11   Other buildings were a close second: e.g. the Sacred Heart Cathedral – consecrated in 1885 and completed in 1902.

The period 1911–1913 also saw reclamation work further along Victoria Parade, the site of the Grand Pacific Hotel (GPH). The soil used for this reclamation came from removal of a hill nearby, 'backing the greensward of Albert Park'.[12] The hotel was built by the Union Steamship Company in 1914 to serve the needs of passengers on its trans-Pacific routes. It can be imagined that, at the time, there was still much unreclaimed foreshore-line to walk or to ride a horse to get to the new hotel from the business end of Suva. Suva citizens from the business end of town used to complain about the hotel's remoteness.[13]

The work of reclamation, however, did not abate. At about the same time, late 1910s, there was reclamation at the beginning of Victoria Parade, along Central Street of today. The site eventually accommodated the Central building – the CMLA building of today.

In 1917, Suva Grammar School for boys, located near Suva City Carnegie Library, was built after the completion of land reclamation, which followed the decision to establish the school. The school officially opened there on 8 July 1918. This historic building has seen many changes over the years. It later became St Stephens Boys Hostel or St Stephens House/Building. Still later it housed the government's Electronic Data Processing Services. At one time, in the first half of 2000, it was planned to accommodate the Ministry of Foreign Affairs and International Cooperation but that came to nought. The plan for the future is to convert this heritage building to Fiji's first National Gallery of Contemporary Arts.

By the onset of World War I, Suva had been Fiji's capital for more than three decades. It was by and large in an adequate state of readiness to respond to the call of duty. Ratu Sukuna in particular, then in his late 20s, played great leadership roles during this time, earning for himself national and international recognition.

---

12 A post from an online forum stated that this hill was higher than those two knolls removed for the reclamation for the Suva Town Hall and Cable & Wireless building: maskedman, 'Savage world', Karate Resource forum, 10 December 2005, karateresource.proboards.com/thread/337.
13 See maskedman, 'Savage world'. These complainants would have felt aggrieved if they had had to walk to nearby Thurston Gardens that opened in 1913, a year before the GPH. There were hardly any motor cars in Suva then. See *Fiji Times,* 7 January 1905 for the story of the first motor car to land in Fiji. On 31 January 1914, the *Fiji Times* reported an observation by Adolf Brewster, a British colonial administrator, who remarked how when he left Fiji in 1911, there were no 'land motors' or cars in the country.

The capital's unifying essence was formed from celebrations of its growth in all aspects – civic, infrastructural, social, economic and political – and was tested by the unprecedented demands of World War I. It responded with remarkable alacrity, carrying the country to glory in the defence of country and king. This was so despite the anxieties of the war, a rumoured attack by a German cruiser (17 September 1914), curfews, news censorship, exodus to safer locale, price inflation, family losses and even the racial selectivity of soldiers to the war fronts.[14]

Altogether, Fiji mobilised three contingents under the Fiji flag.[15] But a large number of personnel, including non-Europeans (indigenous and Indo-Fijians) were mobilised through other country's forces, such as Britain, Australia, New Zealand (including the Māori Battalion), India, South Africa, East African (sic), Canada and America. Fiji soldiers fought in 10 theatres of war, namely France, Turkey (Gallipoli), Mesopotamia, Egypt, Palestine, North Sea, India, Russian Armenia, the African campaign, and even here in the Pacific when 10 Fiji personnel joined the New Zealand Expeditionary Force in August 1914 to invade Samoa, then a German colony.

The team spirit and common bonds that led to this enthused participation were pervasive. Suva and Fiji communities – different tiers of the communities – rushed to play their parts in the war efforts. At first people readily gave financial contributions that were disbursed to London. Later, communities, including provinces, gave cash for specific purchases for

---

14 See 'Life continues as normal', *Fiji News Herald*, 4 August 1916. It did however list the difficulties and losses experienced and 'for those of us who have lived through this war vicariously from these distant shores, life has remained much the same as it was before the war started'. It added: 'Among Fiji's ordinary inhabitants in the villages and on plantations, life goes on. Villagers are still busy producing taxes for the government and servicing the needs of their chiefs and the church. Indentured labourers continued to toil on our sugar plantations to make this colony profitable.'

15 The First Fijian Contingent, 56 personnel, sailed to Europe aboard RMS *Makura* on 1 January 1915. The men were farewelled at a lunch at Suva's Club Hotel and hosted by the Hon. Henry Marks, a member of the Legislative Council. The call for a more active participation in the war effort quickly found voice in the council where advocates called for the raising and equipping of units for service at the Front. The council then passed the relevant resolutions. The men of the First Contingent fought in Flanders and Somme (Belgium and France). Some joined the Kings Royal Rifle Corps. The Second Fijian Contingent left the following July. The Third Fiji Contingent, which departed Suva on 14 August 1918 on board RMS *Niagara*, only got as far as Auckland when the war ended. They were on their way to Egypt. The contingent's enlistment was done in joint arrangement with the NZ Expeditionary Force. The contingent arrived back in Suva on 11 December the same year. The men of this contingent did not qualify for war gratuity.

the war efforts or in kind. Others gave personnel or made other offers that were declined.[16] Citizens readily volunteered for the country's self-defence.[17] And Suva's women did not disappoint.[18]

Of all Fiji's contributions to World War I, those by Ratu Sukuna himself and by his brainchild, the Fiji Labour Corps (FLC), were perhaps the most thought-provoking, giving one a comforting feeling of contentment. Ratu Sukuna's rejection by the British Army after taking leave from his law study at Wadham College, Oxford University, and his subsequent enlisting in the French Foreign Legion[19] is legendary. But more so are his citations for bravery during his short sojourn with the Foreign Legion and being awarded the highest honour, the Médaille militaire.

He returned home wounded but he had already conceived the idea of the FLC for indigenous Fijians in a non-combat World War I role. It was at the FLC the Dravuni's 'arrow of time' was directed this time around. But that was consequential to the initial pull of the capital as a haven for employment opportunities.

By 1914, Livai Veilawa was 25 years old but had not lived on Dravuni since birth. His father had opted to live instead in Naqara, Ono Island, Kadavu, his wife's village, after his posting as a catechist had ended. Like many others, Livai saw World War I and related economic activities in Suva as an opportunity to find work. The freedom to leave one's village for work purposes permitted by the Colonial Government at the time was an incentive as well.[20]

Livai found work at the Suva Wharf as a stevedore. He responded to the national call to enlist for the FLC. He passed the medical test at the Drill Hall in Suva where enlistment took place, as well as the subsequent

---

16 On 15 August 1914, leading Indo-Fijian leaders petitioned the governor to give them training in the defence of Suva.
17 A Fiji Defence Force was formed: members of Fiji's rifle clubs were mobilised as part of the force and were seen performing military drills on the Suva foreshore.
18 *Fiji News Herald* (commemorative edition, date unavailable): 'We also acknowledge the many women who have joined the local force as volunteer nurses. We remember that several of them were on standby when the New Zealand Expeditionary Force invaded Samoa last year.' (They were trained at the Suva Hospital in readiness to treat casualties from the invasion of Samoa).
19 Ratu Sukuna enrolled in the First Battalion of the French Foreign Legion on 8 January 1915.
20 Brij V Lal, for example, discusses the status of the Fijian labour laws relating to the Fijian Labour Ordinances of 1905 and 1912 and the resultant freedom of movement within the colony. Brij V Lal, *Broken waves: A history of the Fiji Islands in the twentieth century* (Honolulu: University of Hawai'i Press, 1992), 27–28.

selection[21] to reduce the number since many had passed the fitness test.[22] His brief experience as a stevedore would have helped his selection, given the task FLC was to carry out in Europe. Despite having not lived in his village, he received the villagers' and provincial blessings when these were sought.

The villagers' acquiescence was unexpected, from the family's perspective. On reflection, however, there was obviously much to credit the underlying factors prompting Dravuni's 'arrow of time'.

Training and drills followed the final selection. In the meantime, the choice of the final destination for the FLC came through. It was to be Calais not Basra. The latter was declined for reasons that it was undesirable due to 'unhealthy conditions and climate'.

When it was time for departure for Calais, there was the farewell on 18 May at the GPH with speeches galore, photo calls and the march through town to the Suva Wharf. The FLC departed for Europe on 19 May 1917 on board a steamer.[23] The travel route was via Honolulu, Vancouver, then overland by train to the Port of Liverpool on the eastern coast of Canada, and thence to Calais, France.

---

21 *Fiji Planters' Journal*, May 1917 (available at the National Archives of Fiji): 'The Contingent consisting of 100 natives which are being sent to France sometime this month to assist in transport work is now being selected. It seems a pity that these fine men should be used as non-combatants only, and there is really no valid reason for supressing that they will not fight as well or endure the climate etc; as well as other coloured races who are at present doing good work in the trenches.'

22 At the Drill Hall, more than 100 Fijians passed the medical test. Only 100 were required. Selection therefore was needed and a committee was formed on 29 March 1917. Sir Henry Marks, who donated £10,000 for the formation of the FLC, was a member of the committee. Selection got underway on 3 April 1917. Those selected were known as the 'Marks Boys' in recognition of this contribution. Sir Henry Marks was a member of the Legislative Council and the managing director of Messrs Henry Marks & Co, and his contribution went towards 'raising, equipping and transporting FLC to and from France and for paying the separation allowances of dependents of men' selected. Other contributions included £50 from Apolosi Nawai of the 'Viti Kabani'. The 100 men selected had to be supported and endorsed by their traditional communities. Since discipline and solidarity were important, Ratu Sukuna selected 15 traditional chiefs to keep the peace. Broken down by provinces, Kadavu provided the majority – 26 per cent altogether. Others were Tailevu – 23 per cent; Cakaudrove – 18 per cent; Lomaiviti – 9 per cent; Naitasiri – 5 per cent; Rewa – 5 per cent; Ba – 4 per cent; Lau – 3 per cent; Ra – 3 per cent; Bua – 2 per cent; Serua – 1 per cent; Nadrogā – 1 per cent. Livai Veilawa, under the FLC list was at No. 62 and recorded as having come 'from the island of Kadavu'. 'Na Mata' printed the list and recorded Livai Veilawa as from Dravuni, Ono, Kadavu. In trying to assist the European officers to pronounce and understand Fijian names, Ratu Sukuna gave each name an English translation. Livai Veilawa was recorded as 'Veilawa – a cross, such as is made by the intersecting the stripes of a pattern (as on a mat)'.

23 The *Fiji Times*, the next day (20 May 1917), wrote: 'They have gone. The officers and men of the Fiji Native Transport Contingent, who have become popularly and almost affectionately known as "Marks Boys" had a send-off worthy of the occasion, except that the rain came down too heavily at times to be comfortable. Still, rain has almost come to be inseparably associated with public and other functions in Suva, so that it can be said there was really nothing wanting to complete the success attending the departure of the boys on their long journey to do their bit for the Empire.'

Figure 13.6: World War I parade near the Ivi Triangle.
Source: P32.7.12 Fiji Museum.

Between 1917 and 1919, the FLC worked the docks in Calais, Marseilles (southern France) and in Taranto (southern Italy). The men of the FLC made an impression wherever they were. England's King George V visited them in France. World War I ended at 5 am (GMT) on 11 November 1918. But the FLC was still needed for postwar demobilisation efforts and did not get back to Suva until October 1919.

Ratu Sukuna was 31 years old then – a war veteran, a national hero – and the glittering acclaim and illustriousness that he amassed and that the country and the people of Fiji have attached to his name were becoming self-evident. The park that was to commemorate this high chief however, was still over four decades away.

Dravuni's 'arrow of time', in relation to Fiji's capital, Suva, in the first part of the story, can be said to have benefited the whole community. This time around, the choice is personalised. The beneficiary was Livai Veilawa, a Dravuni villager, my grandfather. The choice, additionally, is momentous in that Livai was able to make the connection to the great Fijian chief in whose memory one of Suva's favourite parks was named – a naming that is historically significant. Furthermore, it is significant in

SUVA STORIES

the overall context of this story, for example, by being subsequent to 'that swim under the *ivi* tree'; it also plays out that metaphorical 'swimming into Suva's history'.

In the next part of the story, in the three decades following the end of World War I, Dravuni's 'arrow of time' was to involve the whole community once again.

Suva Witnessed Progress, War and Peace: 1920–1953

While new land reclamations continued to shape and configure Suva's physical and civic developments, the sea and shoreline that was to become Ratu Sukuna Park remained unreclaimed. Other infrastructural developments during this period arose from existing reclaimed land. Suva's development proved resilient despite unexpected natural disasters; and the country's engagements in World War II did not seem to hinder civic and national development either. When Suva was proclaimed a city on 7 October 1953, it was ready to greet the newly crowned Her Majesty Queen Elizabeth II during her coronation visit before the year's end.

Progress was marked at the onset of this period by the demolishing of the old Queens Wharf off Pier Street, built in 1881. The demolition was necessitated after the completion of the new Kings Wharf on the north side of Nubukalou Creek in 1912[24] and took two years, 1921–1922.

A form of demolition that also took place in 1921 was due to nature's wrath. Lightning struck Government House, causing extensive destruction. It took seven years to rebuild it (by 1928).[25] Destruction was

---

24   The location of the new Kings Wharf built in 1912 on the northern side of Nubukalou Creek proved to be inconvenient for the bulk of the businesses that were still located in Thomson Street and Renwick Road area. The inconvenience explained why, when the wharf moved north, the old Customs House near the old Post Office remained at its old location well into the 1950s, its location being considered very central by businesses in the town. It took a while for businesses to relocate nearer the new wharf. The first to build near there was Burns Philp in 1930. The Suva Market was delayed also: from near the old Post Office at the old Queens Wharf, the market first moved to Cumming Street for 20 years, then to its present site in 1948/1949. W.R. Carpenters Store soon moved in nearer the new wharf, after Burns Philp.
25   The first Government House was built in 1882. The original building was a simple wooden bungalow. The site was the original village site of Nakorobaba. The new design was a replica of Government House in Colombo, Sri Lanka (Ceylon), a crown colony then.

also wrought by fire in Cumming Street in February 1923.[26] A devastating hurricane struck Suva in 1952[27] and this was followed in September 1953 by an earthquake[28] and tsunami a couple of months or so before the royal (coronation) visit.

Progress also came in other forms. In 1935, drainage work started at the site of the Government Buildings. The site was once the flowing waters of a creek. The foundation stone for the building was laid in 1937 and building finished in 1939. A new wing was added in 1967.

Land reclamations that started from the first part of this story continued during this period. There was still work to be done and more shoreline to be reclaimed. Adjacent to the shoreline that was to be Ratu Sukuna Park, on the side where McDonald's stands today, was the site next to be reclaimed, in the 1920s. The Bhanabhai Building was subsequently built there. This housed Suva's fire station at one time. The sea gap between the reclamation discussed above and that along Central Street and on which the CMLA Building stands today was reclaimed between 1936 and 1939. The Regal Theatre Building stands there today.

In 1923, however, more reclamation was needed next to Suva Grammar School, on the site of the Fiji Development Bank Building today, to accommodate a new playground for the increasing number of students attending that school. Later in the 1930s, the school building itself was extended seaward, taking up more previously reclaimed land in the process. To cater for the increasing school roll in the 1940s, more temporary buildings were needed and these were sited on reclaimed land between the school and the GPH.[29]

---

26 The fire destroyed most of Cumming Street. Since colonial times, the street had been a vibrant shopping area. Early tourism started there. An earlier fire in Suva was recorded in 1891.
27 The hurricane damaged many wooden buildings in the section of Victoria Parade between Pratt Street and Gordon Street. Two hotels were damaged. Others damaged included the Central Building and the Fiji Times Printery. All had to be rebuilt. In quick succession, modern concrete buildings were erected to replace the old wooden ones. They included the Garrick Estate Block, the Queensland Insurance Company's block of shops in Victoria Parade and the new Club Hotel.
28 Redevelopment after the earthquake included the dilapidated *Fiji Times* replaced by the Sabina Building. This contained a shopping block. The Millet and Prasad Buildings filled in the intervening gap as far as the Fiji Trading Company Building (built by *Fiji Times* proprietor Sir Alport Barker in 1948). Further south, the Bhura Building (1950s), Dahia Building (1953) and Central Trading Company (1956) were put up. A building erected by the proprietor of the Golden Dragon and the Housing Authority joined the old Whan's Construction Company Building (Automotive Supplies) erected on the old sugar mill site.
29 Students used to refer to the site where temporary buildings were built as the 'reclamation'. It was the space that was later occupied by the Fiji Travelodge. In the 1950s, Boys Grammar School and Girls Grammar School discussed merging and relocating to a single site. The ideal location suggested by the Board of Education was Veiuto, Nasēsē. The school moved there in 1960.

Development during this period also included building on existing reclamation, even going right back to land reclaimed in the 1880s on the seaward side of Thomson Street. The Westpac Bank Building we see today on 1 Thomson Street and which serves as its Suva branch was built in 1934.[30]

In a space of nine years (1939–1945 and 1952–1955) during this period, Suva and the country were again mobilised for war efforts. In World War II and in post–World War II (the Malayan Campaign), like World War I before them, the response was overwhelming. Fiji mobilised for the Solomon Islands Campaign (1942–1944) and for the Malayan Campaign (1952–1956),[31] not forgetting of course the Territorial Force[32] for national defence.

Apart from the facilitations that Suva ably provided in both the Solomon Islands and the Malayan campaigns, what is of particular note for this chapter is the patriotic role that our central figure, Ratu Sukuna, played in both campaigns.[33] But he was a man of all seasons. When peace returned and Queen Elizabeth II visited at the end of 1953, Ratu Sukuna was again prominent in receiving and welcoming Her Majesty.

Dravuni's 'arrow of time' and its connectedness with events in the capital, this time around, seemed presupposed. However, it was misdirected. An invitation was sent out from Suva to the clan Natusara (comprising Dravuni and Buliya villages) to send a *takia*[34] that would be part of the

---

30 A wooden building existed on the site. The Union Steam Ship Co of NZ Ltd Building next door was built earlier.
31 On 18 June 1948, three years after Japan's surrender, Britain announced its intention to fight against the communist guerrillas known as the Malayan Race Liberation Army. This was after the murder of three rubber planters. This prompted the war in Malaya. On 8 January 1952, more than 800 men of the First Battalion Fiji Infantry Regiment boarded the troopship *Asturias* for Malaya, after the march through Suva.
32 Livai Veilawa (senior)'s son, Maciu Waqanisau, turned 18 in 1942. He joined the Territorial Force.
33 Ratu Sukuna had been assigned a leading role in the Fiji Defence Force on his return from World War I. By World War II, he held the post of lieutenant-colonel. In his role, he told the Fijians why they had to go to war: 'We'll never be recognized, unless our blood is shed first.' When the First Battalion returned from the Solomon Islands Campaign on 4 August 1944 on board *Altnitah*, Ratu Sukuna, along with the governor and Brigadier Dittmer, stood on the wharf to welcome the troops home. After the troops had disembarked, the *Altnitah* was returning to bring back the other troops of the Third Battalion.
34 On the basis of the parallelism format adopted for this chapter, two events on my side could have been considered for the narration of the continuation of Dravuni's 'arrow of time'. I have opted for the *takia* race instead of Dravuni's contribution of two soldiers to the Malayan Campaign, namely: Isimeli Vulatolu and Livai Veilawa (Junior). See the latter in Kaliopate Tavola, 'Dravuni men in Malayan Campaign', *Kaidravuni* (blog), 13 June 2010, kaidravuni.com/2010/06/13/dravuni-men-in-malayan-campaign-1952-56/.

13. SWIMMING UNDER THE *IVI* TREE

armada of small crafts to greet the Queen on her royal yacht *Gothic*. Further, there would also be a *takia* race as part of the commemoration of the visit. The invitation however specified that a *takia* from Buliya Village was to represent the clan. The Roko Tui Kadavu received the message and overruled that Buliya would represent the clan – the *takia* would be crewed by representatives of the clan from both villages.[35]

And so it was. The clan *takia* sailed to Suva with the other *takia* from Kadavu to join others from other maritime provinces. Her Majesty Queen Elizabeth II was greeted suitably by the armada of *takia* and other small craft. Suva citizens witnessed the *takia* race[36] on Suva Harbour. The clan *takia* triumphed. The triumph however had already been foreseen in a dream. Elderly villager Rusiate Qirivabea saw in his sleep the night before the clan *takia* sailing back from Suva with its winner's *masi* banner at the top of the mast, flapping proudly in the wind.

Events Turned Full Circle in 1955

By 1955, when I was to be nine years old, my parents were in search of better educational opportunities for my older brother and I. Suva beckoned, as it had done 67 years earlier in 1888 for the first time and had continued to do so in the intervening years – in 1889–1919 and 1920–1953 as described above. Dravuni's 'arrow of time' was then conceived as a determinant of historicity.

The opportunities, however, that Suva was presenting were different for different periods, as were the beneficiaries, as we have seen above. The beneficiary for the period 1920–1953 was the community. It was the larger community, *yavusa* Natusara that received recognition of their ancient *takia* sailing skills with royal patronage. By 1955, the mode of benefit of Dravuni's 'arrow of time' reverted to personalisation.

---

35   The Roko Tui Kadavu's rationale in overruling the invitation was that the chief of the clan resides on Dravuni and any participation by the clan would best be sanctioned by Dravuni. After consultations, it was agreed that the crew of the *takia* would include the two chiefs from both villages and their respective *matanivanua*. However, on inspecting the size of the *takia*, it was agreed that there would only be three crew members; both chiefs would pull out and be replaced by Marika Koroivui, acknowledged as the best sailor in the clan.
36   See Kaliopate Tavola, 'Dravuni victorious at the canoe race during HM Queen Elizabeth's coronation visit, 1953', *Kaidravuni* (blog), 17 April 2010, kaidravuni.com/2010/04/17/dravuni-victorious-at-the-canoe-race-during-hm-queen-elizabeths-coronation-visit-1953.

My parents' search for educational opportunities led to the family's migration from the comfort of the village with its rural subsistence affluence to an urban existence with its concomitant challenges. In 1955, the family lived on Toorak Road. I had failed to get a place at Nabua Central Fijian School that year due to being placed low in the priority list, as my birthdate falls late in the second half of the year. I had time therefore for my traditional circumcision and that led to my first sanctioned swim in the sea under the *ivi* tree, and, as metaphorised above, my 'swimming into Suva's history'.

The metaphor can be examined critically in two ways. The first is that by residing in Suva with effect from 1955 and participating in its activities therefrom, my family and I were essentially engaged in creating Suva's own history. We were part of history from the time we arrived. I narrate some of these experiences below.

But apart from the collective history, my family and I were making our own history at the same time. This is where the second critical way of examining the metaphor applies. That is, in 'swimming into Suva's history', I find that Suva's history has had the fortuitous habit of casting its influence on the direction my own history has taken: the individualisation of the history of the collective. I also narrate experiences of this below.

In the intervening year of 1954, after the 1953 royal visit and the arrival of my family in Suva to settle at Toorak Road, and for the succeeding period, Suva witnessed and made its own history. My family and I, by association and/or with some degree of participation, were part of that. There were still, for example, some troops that left and were farewelled for the Malayan Campaign that year in 1954. Suva witnessed their embarkation. The move of the Fiji Museum from its temporary accommodation in the Suva Town Hall from when it opened in 1905 to its present site in Thurston Gardens was another example.

In the same year, Suva celebrated the opening of Broadcasting House and the creation of the Fiji Broadcasting Commission.[37]

In 1956, Suva celebrated its first Miss Hibiscus Festival. Miss Liebling Hoeflich (Marlow) was the proud wearer of the splendid crown. The next festival in 1957, however, is firmly etched in my mind as a momentous

---

37 See Lal, *Broken waves*, for background and significance.

one. How could I forget the first ever Soapbox Derby on Cakobau Road? Miss Filimaina Koto, who later married Nelson Delailomaloma, was the Hibiscus Festival Queen. Both worked at Ratu Sukuna Memorial School when I attended in 1961–1964. Nelson was a science teacher and Filimaina was the principal's personal assistant and general office manager.

Also in 1956, Suva witnessed the march through the city of the returning soldiers from the Malayan Campaign – the 1st Battalion Fiji Infantry Regiment. The troops arrived on the troopship SS *Devonshire*. I was in Class 4 at Nabua Central Fijian School. School children from various Suva schools were bussed down to the city to line the streets to greet our national heroes.[38]

The next time school children were bussed to line the streets of Suva was two years later on 9 June 1958. This time around it was a sad occasion to honour and farewell perhaps Fiji's greatest hero.[39] Ratu Sukuna's casket was driven through Suva to the wharf to board the Adi Maopa on its way to Lakeba for the chiefly burial. The funerary procession proceeded silently past the *ivi* tree at the site of the future park, still under water. But the long wait was almost at its end. The passing of the great chief was to create its own history to add to that of the country's capital city.

But before the memorial park was created, Ratu Sukuna Memorial School opened to its first intake of secondary school students in 1960. I was in the second intake in 1961. RSMS was my first choice and for me, the choice was plain. My family by then lived in Nabua Village along Ratu Mara Road, a stone's throw directly opposite the school.

When it came to choosing a school for Form 7 (then called Upper 6th), Suva's history proved a revelation once again. In 1960, both the Boys Grammar School and the Girls Grammar School opted to join up and it was decided to move the combined school to Veiuto, Nasēsē. Six years later, in 1966, I attended that school.

---

38 See Manu Korovulavula for a lively commentary of the parade, its configuration, the reception, the ceremonies at Albert Park, and the celebrations by the public: Manunivavalagi Dalituicama Korovulavula, *Malayan Campaign – 1st Battalion Fiji Infantry Regiment, 1952-1956* (Suva: Max Marketing and Publisher Limited, 2014).
39 Ratu Sukuna retired in 1958. He and Lady Liku were on their way to Oxford. They were aboard the cruise ship *Arcadia*. Ratu Sukuna died when the *Arcadia* was off the coast of Ceylon. See Kim Gravelle for an account of the *Arcadia*'s captain sending the message to Fiji, the return of Ratu Sukuna's body to Nadi and then to Rairaiwaqa. Gravelle captured the sober mood of the funereal gathering, and the ceremonies performed in his account: Kim Gravelle, *Fiji's times: A history of Fiji*, vols 1–3 (Suva: Fiji Times, 1979).

I was a civil servant for 11 years from 1973 to 1984 in the Ministry of Agriculture. The ministry had different names and permutations over the years. It became the Ministry of Agriculture, Fisheries and Forests (MAFF) at one time. The site of its head office remained for a long time on what is referred to loosely by many as the 'MAFF land' adjacent to the Suva Bus Stand. Of the 11 years, I worked at MAFF's head office for eight years. It is certainly not lost to me now the significance of that land adjacent to all the reclamations that were taking place to build, expand and improve Suva's Kings Wharf with effect from 1911–1913, 1913–1916, 1961 and 1982. The land adjacent to the port area took some time to grow as a business enclave after the construction of Kings Wharf in 1912.

In my post-diplomatic career, I had three offices in Suva in buildings that are all on reclaimed land from different decades. In 1998–2000, I had an office in Dominion House, now called BSP Life Centre. That building stands on land reclaimed in the 1880s. Between 2000 and 2013, I had offices in Suvavou House and later in one of the bungalows behind Kadavu House. The land on which the two houses stand today was still in the early stage of reclamation in 1955 when my family migrated from the village and lived on Toorak Road.

The completion of land reclamation between the old Suva Grammar School for Boys and the GPH occurred in the 1960s, after the school moved to Veiuto in 1960. This phase of reclamation provided the impetus to reclaim what ended up as the Ratu Sukuna Park. In that specific context, the wait of over eight decades since the first round of reclamation of the Suva waterfront off Thomson Street had finally come to an end.

Conclusions

The title of my chapter is rather long. However, the story I have woven and the approach I have taken have tried to connect these various facets into a coherent whole. In the process, I have invoked the metaphors of 'arrow of time' and parallelism as means of connectedness and directionality while retaining the historicity and periodicity of events. The connectedness arising from these metaphors implies benefit. My family and others have duly benefited as a result.

'Swimming under the *ivi* tree' was that which triggered off the narrative flow. But it also provided the underlying essence of the narrative – best depicted by the metaphor 'swimming into Suva's history'. I have applied the metaphor as further means of connectedness to additionally bring into play 'family connections' in the narrative. And as the essence itself, the metaphor has a way of reflecting and/or impacting family history chronology. In my case, past historical events have had a way of impacting the directions of my own history. This is noteworthy notwithstanding the restricted nature of history under study.

The swim under the *ivi* tree is central in the narrative. Apart from its historical significance, it was indeed a geographical marker, indicating the locale that was to undergo reclamation from the sea for the establishment of Ratu Sukuna Park in memory of one of Fiji's greatest sons. At the time of the swim, Ratu Sukuna was 67 years old. He passed away three years later.

Suva, of course, has a long history of land reclamation. Its origin dates back to the start of the 1880s, even before Suva became Fiji's capital in 1882. In my narrative, I have discussed the chronology of land reclamation spanning a period of over eight decades.

The reclamation did not proceed unidirectionally. The pattern was clearly dependent on the planned development of Suva once it became Fiji's capital. In retrospect, Suva's waterfront over the years resembled a line with straight-edged indentations in places.

The phase of land reclamation that eventually resulted in the establishment of Ratu Sukuna Park commenced in the early 1960s, a few years after Ratu Sukuna's demise. While the creation and naming of the park have brought closure to one of the facets of this narrative, it has not brought closure to the reclamation of Suva's foreshores. Suva's waterfront will continue to be transformed for a few more years.

# 14

Suva – Once a Colonial Town

Daryl Tarte

My great-grandfather settled on Taveuni in 1868, so my sister and I are the fourth generation. She was born in 1931 and I followed in 1934. Our coconut and cattle plantation was the centre of our world and our only connection with Suva was the inter-island cargo and passenger ship that also brought our mail each month. There was the government-owned telegraph station, by which we could send morse code messages, and of course the radio. I had no concept of Suva as a place, except that I was told it was the capital of Fiji and the centre of our colonial government and business.

In 1944 my parents decided that my sister and I should go to the boarding school in Suva and I clearly remember that as a very daunting prospect. We embarked one day on the 400-ton inter-island ship *Yanawai*. It had six, two-berth cabins, a place for deck passengers and a cargo hold. The journey took one day to Savusavu, another day to Levuka and we cruised into Suva Harbour on the afternoon of the third day, landing at Princes Wharf, which was then a simple wooden decked structure. We boarded a taxi, and my mother said we were going to the Grand Pacific Hotel (GPH).

I remember my first images of that journey through the streets of Suva, which was not then considered a city – simply a large town – but to the boy from rural Taveuni it was an eye-opener. A real colonial town with cars, buses and lorries and dominated by the white elite – predominately British civil servants.

Figure 14.1: Corner of Scott Street and Renwick Road, n.d.
Source: P32.4.16 Fiji Museum.

The first big building I saw was the two-storey Burns Philp head office structure, now owned by the Fiji National Provident Fund retirement scheme. Burns Philp was then the largest trader in Fiji. That was also when I saw my first traffic cop, at the intersection of Thomson and Marks streets. He was a huge ethnic Fijian who stood on a raised platform, wearing a white serrated sulu and red jacket, directing the slow-moving traffic with white-gloved hands.

We crossed a small bridge over what I was told was Nabukalau Creek. The creek was as unimpressive then as it is today. On our left was the largest store in town – Morris Hedstrom. There was a branch on Taveuni so I knew about them. It was a long, wooden, single-storey shop with large plate glass windows. Just past it on the left was the Garrick Hotel, which I was told was one of the best in town. The building is now owned by Gokals. On the right I saw the green-timbered General Post Office, and beside it the very impressive cream, concrete Bank of New South Wales. It looked much the same then as today's Westpac.

Figure 14.2: Nabukalou Creek, n.d.
Morris Hedstrom building is on the right, and *bilibili* (rafts) are on the left making deliveries to the market.
Source: P32.6.25 Fiji Museum.

At the intersection of Thomson and Renwick roads stood the *ivi* tree and another uniformed policeman directing traffic. My mother pointed out Boots the Chemist, Levy's Jewellery store, Caines photography store, McDonalds Hotel, Bank of New Zealand and Melbourne Hotel. As we passed Central Street I could see the waters of the harbour that lapped against the sea wall behind the bank. There was no marketplace nor car park in those days. Also in Central Street, where Bank South Pacific now stands, was a one-storey wooden structure where, my mother said, were the offices of Suva's top lawyers and accountants.

Beside Central Building was the Regal Theatre. More about that later. I was far more impressed with the fire station beside the theatre. Parked in the open doorway was a large red fire engine, the only one in Suva, I was told. A far cry from the McDonalds that is now there.

The sea washed against the wall of the fire station and Victoria Parade, as the whole of the Sukuna Park area was then part of the harbour. We passed the massive bulk of the Carnegie Library and I saw the lattice work on the first floor balcony of what was then the Town Hall.

Figure 14.3: Carnegie Library, n.d.
Source: P32.4.18 Fiji Museum.

Beside it was the bowling green, and then I had my first look at my future home away from home – the cream-coloured walls and arches of Boys Grammar School and the sports field. There were no buildings between the school and the GPH where we were to stay – just a long wall holding back the sea. But on the land side of Victoria Parade were the squat, grey Government Buildings, which seemed to symbolise the power and authority of the Colonial Government.

At the entrance to the GPH we were welcomed by a large Punjabi with a green turban and white jacket with green cummerbund. I was impressed by the architecture of the GPH, which was so different to any structure I had ever seen. As I look at it today, still basically the same, it seems to epitomise as much grandeur as it did then.

I was taken to Boys Grammar School and my sister to Girls Grammar School. On the first floor of BGS there were three dormitories – the junior, middle school and senior. I was put in the junior dorm with nine other boys from Taveuni, Savusavu, Levuka, Vatukoula, Ba and Lautoka. I did not know any of them, but our matron was a lady who had been matron of Taveuni District Hospital, so that was some comfort.

Figure 14.4: Interior of the Grand Pacific Hotel, n.d.
Source: P32.6.28 Fiji Museum.

My sister was taken to a similar style building, which is now part of the education department, situated beside the Fiji Club on the hill.

The strange anomaly of our education was that the primary education was conducted at Girls Grammar while the secondary education was conducted at Boys Grammar. So my sister attended classes at Boys Grammar while I went to Girls Grammar.

The students at BGS were all white. Ethnic Fijians and Indian people were not admitted and only a restricted number of mixed-race students were. Suva was then a very racially divided town.

While there were a number of other schools in and around Suva there were no interschool sports competitions. In fact the main sports were traditional British games like cricket, tennis, bowls, hockey and some rugby. Next to the BGS, where the Development Bank now stands, was the school's playing field. But we junior boys usually played marbles. On the sea side of the school was a shed where the Sea Scouts and Sea Cubs had their various activities. There was also a boat moored by the sea wall where we fished.

Figure 14.5: Welcoming Charles Kingsford Smith's aeroplane *Southern Cross* at Suva, Fiji, 1928.
Source: Milton Vikery (1928), 1467-ALBUM-274-106-5, Auckland Libraries Heritage Collections.

Figure 14.6: Aerial view of Grand Pacific Hotel, Albert Park and Government Buildings, n.d.
Source: P32.4.103 Fiji Museum.

14. SUVA – ONCE A COLONIAL TOWN

The main sports field was Albert Park, where I was told Kingsford Smith landed on his flight across the Pacific. I had never seen a plane so could not assess the suitability of the park as an airfield. The other main sports field was Buckhurst Park out at Suva Point. None of the schools with their large playing fields now situated around the peninsula existed at that time. In fact in the 1920s that area had been a horse racetrack.

At that time, Laucala Bay was the base for the Royal New Zealand Air Force (RNZAF) Catalina and Sunderland flying boats that were moored within the massive stone breakwater, which had been constructed to protect them from the south-easterly winds. The breakwater remains today. When the aircraft were on land they were housed in a huge hanger that has long gone.

Laucala Bay was also the international gateway airport. In 1946, when I went to boarding school in Melbourne, we flew out of Laucala Bay on a Sunderland flying boat owned by Tasman Empire Airways Limited. Nadi was then still a military base and there was no airport at Nausori.

The RNZAF staff were accommodated in green and cream wooden buildings where the University of the South Pacific is now located. Officers were housed in an area that became known as Suva Point, accommodated in well-constructed wooden homes made of good quality imported pine. Many of them remain today.

Another exclusive residential area was the Domain, where British civil servants were housed in large wooden bungalows or in elegant British-style cottages. They were surrounded by manicured lawns and neatly trimmed hedges of tropical plants. Sadly, today most of the Domain is badly neglected.

There were then two movie theatres in Suva – in fact the only ones in Fiji. The Regal Theatre was beside the fire station and the Lilac was on the corner of Waimanu and Toorak roads. Movies were shown by 35 mm projectors and in 1944 I saw my first movie – *The North West Mounted Police*. It was an amazing experience. The rows of seats sloped from the cheaper ones at the front, very near the screen, to the higher-priced ones at the back. White people sat at the back and others at the front. We boys often went to the Lilac on a Saturday afternoon to see cowboy serials, or one about a superhero of the time – *The Green Hornet*.

There was little industrial activity in 1944/45. Along Rodwell Road, past Burns Philp, was a biscuit company, a soap manufacturer, the coconut oil mill and a fuel storage base. Walu Bay was just a mangrove swamp and a gravel road ran through it, past the cemetery and out to Lami, where there were a few homes.

Waimanu road was the main access north. Past the Colonial War Memorial Hospital were a number of homes on the ridge overlooking Suva Harbour where white business and professional people lived. Tamavua was mostly vacant scrub land with just a few palatial homes.

Because Fiji was a British colony, the Church of England was the pre-eminent religion. Its wooden cathedral on Gordon Street was later demolished and a new one built on the present site. The Catholic cathedral was in Pratt Street and the Methodist church in Marks Street. There were also some Hindu temples.

I don't recall then having any sentimental attachment to Suva as I had for my home on Taveuni. But I seem to remember my first pangs of patriotism when we were told in 1945 that the war was over. I vividly remember standing in class singing 'God Save the King'. There were great celebrations in and around the town and people seemed very proud of the part Fijian soldiers had played in the Solomon campaign.

Fast-forward to the year 2000.

By then my family and I were living in our home at Tamavua, a suburb that had developed into one of the main residential areas. Many international organisations had offices and residences in the area. There were new subdivisions, supermarkets and good roads. Many people from rural areas had drifted into the city to find work. Low-cost housing areas had sprung up and there were many more poor people.

Colonial rule was over. Fiji had become independent in 1970; a moving ceremony had been held at Albert Park. Suva had grown tremendously since the 1940s and had become a city. A great deal of land on the foreshore had been reclaimed from the harbour and multistorey buildings constructed along Victoria Parade. Sukuna Park was a place for people to gather and there was a new city hall, new hotels and movie theatres, and the population had exploded. The racial divisions of the 1940s had gone and the population was warm and friendly. Suva had become a tourist city with tourist ships calling regularly at Kings Wharf. This had been rebuilt

14. SUVA – ONCE A COLONIAL TOWN

to cater for the ever-increasing number of container and tourist vessels. The huge market nearby was a centre of attraction and the adjacent bus station was the busiest place in the city. Walu Bay had been fully reclaimed from the mangroves and had become the centre of industrial activity.

One of the important decisions by the government had been to move Parliament out of central Suva to a new parliamentary complex at Draiba. This was an imposing *bure*-style structure with offices for the prime minister and parliament staff.

The area around the peninsula had become the main educational centre of Suva, with a number of schools and training institutions having been established. The University of the South Pacific had grown to become the dominant university of the region and the Laucala Bay area became the sporting centre of Fiji, with good facilities for most sports.

Fiji and Suva were on a progressive path into the new millennium. People were confident. The economy was booming. Then in 2000 it all came crashing down after an Indian was elected to be prime minister. A gang of thugs led by George Speight took control of Parliament and rampaged through the city causing absolute chaos. I sat on the verandah of my home in Tamavua looking down on Suva and watched with horror as flames and smoke billowed into the skies about the city. But the real damage was done to the morale and confidence of Suva's citizens.

Fast-forward to 2018.

Suva is fortunate that following the 2000 upheavals a strong and capable government emerged to restore the faith of the citizens and introduce strategies to grow the economy. Business confidence led to commercial expansion in the city and along Grantham Road, Nasēsē, Samabula, Nasinu, Nabou and all the areas along Ratu Mara road to Nausori. Vast sums have been spent on the roads in and around the city. However prosperity has led to many more vehicle owners and traffic congestion.

One of the significant actions taken by the government was to move Parliament back to the Government Buildings in the city. The whole structure was restored to its former glory and projects an inspiring image of a dynamic nation and city.

There was a time when the city ratepayers voted for a council, which in turn elected a mayor and they managed the city affairs. Now there are no elections, simply an administrator appointed by the government. While the government is voted into power democratically, and while there is a free TV, press and radio to monitor its affairs, the citizens have no control over the management of the city. Yet it is a place where thousands of people of all races have spent most of their lives. A place where they have found peace, security and happiness in an otherwise troubled world.

Despite the passage of years and changes in power and ethnic diversity, Suva has always retained a distinctive character or ethos that makes it different from other towns and cities around the world. When people walk along its streets they invariably eyeball each other, or smile faintly, as if to say ' hello' or ' I hope all is well with you'.

This attitude can be traced back to the unique Fijian concept of *vakaturaga*, which embraces respect, humility, kindness, tolerance and understanding.

As a 10-year-old in 1944, when I walked to the Lilac Theatre to watch movies, I vaguely recall sensing an attitude that was different to that I'd known on Taveuni and that I could not then define, but now understand.

Now, as an elderly man, I am inspired when people I've never seen before smile as we pass in the street, for I know this is not a superficial expression, but is deeply ingrained.

This is what makes Suva different.

15

Where Is My Home and Where Is My Heart?

Kantilal Jinna

I am often asked by friends who have known me for a long time what years I was at Natabua High School. It is difficult, almost disloyal, for me to say that I went to Marist Brothers High School in Flagstaff, Suva. The first 16 years of my life almost to the day were in Flagstaff, then Tavua (just over a year) and Samabula. The following three years were in Auckland, followed by 21 years mostly in Lautoka, including two years in Canberra and a year in Leeds, UK. My wife Jyoti and our children accompanied me in later years to these places. After Leeds, we moved to Suva for a year and then to Canberra, where I spent a year on secondment to the Fiji High Commission. Jyoti and the children settled in to live there and remained. Yes, my life has been one of constant change.

There is no doubt that the most exciting period of my life was spent in Suva. It is almost like saying that we grew up together. My father and previously my grandfather spent very difficult days earning a living as barbers there. Their initial business was in the colonnaded corridor of Morris Hedstrom's store, along Nubukalou Creek.

It was not a shop but a footpath. My father would set up 'shop' at 7:00 am and close at 7:00 pm when he would wrap up his equipment with a sulu cloth and take it with his chair across Renwick Road to Bhulabhai & Sons to leave there overnight, taking the washing home with him. He would go to the room above Wahley's Butchery in Cumming Street where he, my grandfather and four cousins would sleep. It was also a kitchen where my grandfather, an excellent cook, would feed everyone. This continued until my mother arrived from India in January 1938, after a three-night and four-day train ride from Surat, Bombay, to Calcutta. There she boarded her namesake ship *Ganges* (her name was Ganga) for a five-week boat ride, which brought them to Nukulau Island for a month-long quarantine period.

My grandfather had in the meantime taken a small shop next to a laundry in Flagstaff and rented a room for my parents where the current Bhura & Jokhan Service Station is situated, directly opposite the newly constructed Flagstaff Plaza and my future high school, Marist Brothers.

My early recollections are from the age of five in 1944 when I started attending St Columba's High School, now called Marist Suva Street. On the same campus was St Felix, a primary school for Part-European and European Catholics. Later, the first Marist Brothers High School was established on the campus.

Up Spring Street, joining Amy Street on the right-hand side, was the Methodist Boys School and the Dudley House School for girls. If you turned left you would pass High Street and Toorak Road and the Dudley Church, leading to the Anderson Maternity Hospital, where our son Rohit was born, and the Colonial War Memorial (CWM) Hospital at the T-junction. My dear friend Radike and his wife Eta gave Rohit his middle name of Vulivavalagi while we were studying librarianship together in Canberra many years later in 1966.

We used to be scared passing this corner because the first hospital building was the morgue. If you turned right, you went through Brown Street and continued to Rewa Street and Milverton Road towards Raiwaqa and Suva Point, while the left turn at Rewa Street took you to Samabula.

The CWM Hospital was called the 'Vale ni Mate' (House of Death) in my days and I am glad it later changed to 'Vale ni Bula'. Going right from the hospital along Waimanu Road, the area was occupied by elite expatriates with beautiful homes and magnificent views of Walu Bay and Tamavua. After passing the one-mile post you came to Borron House, the residence in those days of the highly respected leader Ratu Sir Lala Sukuna, and continued to Kings Road and Samabula.

15. WHERE IS MY HOME AND WHERE IS MY HEART?

Figure 15.1: Borron House, n.d.
Source: P32.4.9 Fiji Museum.

A left turn on Waimanu Road at the hospital took you down to Robertson Road on your right, but if you maintained the left you went past Dr CMP Gopalan's surgery on your right, Marks Park on your left at the Bidesi Construction corner and then the Lilac Theatre further down, next to Mar Gip's cafe. Lilac Café was a mixture of things. You could always hear the ruffle of mahjong tiles and excited chatter of Chinese players and cooks. There were 1-penny ice blocks and threepence ice creams in shop-made waffle cones. We came to learn as we grew older that what was in the smoking pipes was a bit more than Fiji tobacco and was provided to government-licensed imbibers.

Curry mutton and rice was 1 shilling and 9 pence, including a slice of buttered Fiji long-loaf bread (*madrai*) and a cup of tea, and all came with chillies, salt, sugar, tomato sauce and soy sauce.

If you turned left from there you would end up on Toorak Road, which led to several laundries at the top after passing Kuchappan's corner, which was previously Dr George Hemming's surgery. The right turn took you back to St Columba's, past Gospel Hall, and on the left you walked past my classmate Jack Hanson's home and reached the Madar Baksh settlement complex. Madar Baksh's shop in Cumming Street repaired anything mechanical like primus stoves, benzene lights and knickknacks and sold spare parts. At the Lilac Cinema, Mr John Grant would be at the door in his tie and coat with Mr Dalton or Mr Basil Guruwaiya selling tickets, equally smartly dressed. As you came down you could turn to Marks Street with its greengrocers, shoemakers, bicycle hiring and repairing shop and barbershops and on to Suva Book Shop, then Pacific Transport, which operated nine small passenger buses leaving daily for Lautoka via Queen's Road, and the Century movie theatre.

Just across was a stepped lane past the imported mutton shop, Leyland's butcher and the ice-making shop, selling large blocks of ice for cool storage, fridges and ice cream making. At the end of the lane was a public toilet block leading to Cumming Street. Immediately after the toilet block at the end of the lane was Kwong Tiy & Co Ltd, General Merchants, and Wahley's Butchery, followed by Leong Lee Parshottam, greengrocers and seed merchants catering to the expatriate population. The top end of Marks Street led to the very smelly McGowan's sea shell warehouse for tortoiseshell buttons and jewellery-making, and then Burns Philp (SS) Co Ltd leading to the Suva wharves.

If you continued from the Lilac theatre down Waimanu Road, the first turn left led you to Marks Lane (*Vale Karasini*) now Raojibhai Patel Street, but if you persisted straight, it would take you along Renwick Road to Morris Hedstrom Limited and past Narseys Limited, Boots the Chemist and Caines Janif, photographers and picture framers. A left turn to Pratt Street led you to Vidal Library and Bookshop and the Sacred Heart Cathedral, the Central Police Station and St Anne's Primary School, eventually joining Gordon Street. Moving straight on was Desai Book Depot and the Club Hotel.

At the end of Marks Street, a turn immediately right would have taken you to the Centenary Methodist Church and a left turn would bring you to Thomson Street. About 30 yards further on your left was Cumming Street, arguably the busiest street in Fiji. On the right side were the Suva Markets with their rear on Nubukalou Creek, where putt-putts brought produce from various villages along the coast from as far as Nausori or towards Navua in the other direction. A few yards from the markets were Mouat's Pharmacy and a series of five barbershops and four well-patronised Indian restaurants: Suva Lodge, Ram Garib Lodge, Indian Lodge (Karians) and Fiji Lodge catered for food and provided lodging for single workers and students from all parts of Fiji. The lodging rooms were upstairs and their washing was catered for by laundries on Toorak Road.

The barbershops started with Jinna Bros (my father) at the entrance of Suva Lodge, two more on the right and two across the street.

My father often reminded me that there was a fire in Cumming Street in 1923. Kim Gravelle, in his book *Fiji's Times: A History of Fiji*, writes that the fire on 10 February started in a combined grog shop and boarding house, gutted all the buildings in Cumming Street; and spilled onto the right-hand side into Renwick Road where it was stopped by the two-storeyed building owned by Henry Marks.[1] The inferno swallowed shop after shop until it reached a gap near a building occupied by Kwong Tiy and the Coronation Bakery. The fire crossed the street and destroyed everything on the Nubukalou Creek side, sparing only Jack Kee's furniture factory. According to Gravelle, 'Cumming Street, by Sunday morning, was nothing more than an expanse of flattened sheet metal. 45 shops, including nine tailor shops, 18 refreshment rooms and a number of retailers had been destroyed … to the Indians and Chinese who were the primary tenants of the street, the damage was catastrophic.'[2] After the fire, the kava saloons shifted to Marks Street. Suva Markets moved into the ruins that were Cumming Street and remained there for 20 years until it moved towards the Suva Wharf adjoining the Suva Bus Station.

Along Thomson Street and running parallel to Cumming Street was Nubukalou Creek. From there was a commenced but abandoned plan to build a jetty right up into Suva Harbour to enable shipping, and to develop a sugarcane farm and sugar mill, a project of Suva businessmen Brown and Joske. The project would have stretched along Victoria Parade to the Government Buildings.

---

1   Kim Gravelle, *Fiji's times: A history of Fiji*, vols 1–3 (Suva: Fiji Times 1979). See in particular Volume 3, Chapter 40, 'The Cumming Street fire', 29–32.
2   Ibid., 31.

Figure 15.2: The aftermath of the Cumming Street fire, 1923.
Source: P32.4.33 Fiji Museum.

Morris Hedstrom's entrance displayed their confectionary department that left children drooling, unable to afford the expensive imported chocolates and lollies rolled up in beautiful see-through coloured wrappers. But it was the next shop that bedazzled every curious child. Walter Horne & Company Limited, General Merchants had their shop counter fairly close to their front door and all customers were given a receipt for purchases. What amazed me and aroused my curiosity every time was that the shop attendant put the customer's money and invoice into a small tube, then pulled a handle that sucked it up to a mysterious destination from where the change and a stamped receipt would arrive a few moments later.

My curiosity was even greater across the road at Millers Limited, sited next to Union Taxis at the edge of the hooped Nubukalou Bridge and selling beautiful new cars. I remember the names in metal stating 'Hillman Minx' and 'Vauxhall Velox'. They were so shiny and clean and ready for rich customers. A friend of my father bought one for his taxi business. In fact, it was across from my father's barbershop in Cumming Street in the mid-50s that I had my first job as the telephone boy for Viti Taxis, owned by Mr CP Bidesi. I don't know what I got paid but it went straight to my father. I was 12 years old and could speak English, unlike the drivers, who did not. My parents were really proud I had this job because I had superiority over six much older taxi drivers and could give them orders to go to the customers, mainly European, to take them to various destinations.

Figure 15.3: Morris Hedstrom building next to Nabukalou Creek, n.d.
Source: P32.4.39 Fiji Museum.

The only other regular work was in my father's barbershop on Saturdays, giving children a haircut and older customers a shave. I would also sit outside the shop and sell 'three inch' lengths of Fiji tobacco from a rope-like *bhindi* twisted roll.

Along Marks Street towards the wharf (instead of taking Thomson Street) was the Hotel Metropole and on the right was Burns Philp (SS) Co Ltd known familiarly as BPs. As part of the building on the corner of Nina Street was the small stand-alone shop of Thaw and Weaver, Jewellers.

The BP building had a special interest for me. It had the only customer lift in the city, which was operated by an Indian man who was always dressed in white and white. He would attend to every customer or curious wanderers like me instead of referring them to the wide staircase. My fascination to travel on the lift was insatiable.

To the right of BPs you went towards the Suva Bus Station and two major factories: Union Soaps Limited, manufacturing blue and white bars of washing soap and other soap products smelling of tallow and copra; and the Pacific Biscuit Company, making cabin crackers sold in packets or small and large tins. The biscuits were jawbreakers and the best way to eat them was to soak them in your tea. Fijian people took the biscuit tins, both small and large, to their villages as gifts or for special occasions. Multiple bars of soap were often included in such presentations, together with 4-gallon drums of kerosene, boxes of corned mutton and beef, canned fish and packets of matches and cigarettes. The children received Wrigley's PK and Juicy Fruit chewing gum and other lollies.

The alternate road from BPs led to the wharves. On the left were the wooden or small metal ships like the *Yanawai* connecting passengers, mail and cargo between the main and island ports. Further along was the major wharf handling inter-Pacific Islands and international cargo, and international passenger ships. The wharves were very busy when the Home Boat arrived from England and the *Matua* and *Tofua* arrived from New Zealand and Australia.

A good time to come here was when overseas tourist ships paid a day visit, welcomed or farewelled by the Fiji Military Forces or the Fiji Police bands. Children gathered on the wharves and scrambled for the coins that the tourists threw down as the boats were about to leave.

Figure 15.4: Aerial view of Kings Wharf, n.d.
Source: P32.4.149 Fiji Museum.

15. WHERE IS MY HOME AND WHERE IS MY HEART?

That was in my twelfth year when I was about to finish primary school. It was 1951.

Moving along Victoria Parade was the General Post Office (the GPO, now located across the road), after passing the Pier Hotel in Pier Street owned by Sir Hugh Ragg. Sir Hugh owned and operated a number of hotels near the main towns on Viti Levu. D Gokal and Co. have their duty free shop where the street level of the Pier Hotel used to be. Moving on towards Albert Park, there were three places of interest for me. They were the Union Steamship Company, a travel agent and the Bank of New South Wales. Across the road on a triangle stood the age-old meeting place, the everlasting, still famous '*ivi* tree', these days propped up with a sturdy concrete post in its trunk.

This bank building was of special interest to me because on the top floor, Sir Henry Milne Scott and his son Maurice Scott had their law office. My father had a weekly contract with Sir Henry to cut his hair in his office. The same floor had the office of TEAL (Tasman Empire Airways Limited), later NZ NAC and now Air New Zealand. The counter officer, Mr Indarjeet, was a well-known soccer referee in Suva and would give away beautiful postcard-sized blotting paper with pictures of TEAL aircraft. These were quite a prestigious haul, as we used fountain pens or 1164 nib and ink pens at school. Downstairs in the bank, the staff, all expatriates, were well dressed in ties and coats. Only large businesses had bank accounts. My father had a small wooden money box in which the custodian, my mother, kept the 1 penny, 5 shillings, 10 shillings and the occasional pound note. The coin box was a glass jar with a screw tin top.

No one spoke to Sir Henry except his senior staff and the secretary Miss Underwood, who would tell my father when to go into his office and also pay him. One day, my father gathered enough courage to speak to Miss Underwood and Mr Tazim Raza the law clerk to ask if Sir Henry would give me a job in his office. He said I would be 13 years old in a few days' time and could speak English. I had also been accepted by the Marist Brothers High School to start secondary school at the end of January 1952.

The timing was perfect, as I was finishing my primary school and had 'appeared' for my School Leaving qualifying exam for Marist Brothers High School – and the tea boy and messenger for Sir Henry was going on leave for three weeks. I got the job and started on Monday 7 January 1952. I remember making and serving morning and afternoon tea for Sir Henry Scott every day and going to the post office to collect the mail. I also did the occasional errand.

As fate would have it, a severe cyclone hit Suva on Thursday 24 January 1952 during the day when everyone was at work. The three long sirens and yellow flag went up on the GPO at 10:00 am. Sir Henry told me to collect my belongings, get ready and go with his son to his house in Bau Street. We were all there at the house when a water leak was detected near an external window and Maurice Scott and I nailed a piece of timber to stop it. I was then told by Maurice Scott to accompany him to his house at Suva Point and stay with him till the cyclone passed Fiji. I was given a sumptuous meal by the enormous Mr Pirthipal Singh, Sir Henry's cook.

At around 6:00 pm, when the cyclone calmed down, Mr Maurice Scott took me to my father's barbershop in Cumming Street in his car to find my anxious father was there waiting for me. He had gone there after checking for me at the law office and finding it closed. We were dropped at our home on Kings Road, Samabula, where my mother and rest of my brothers and sisters, all six of them, were relieved to see father and son well and together. The next day was my last day at work and I was told by Mr Raza that 'Saheb' wanted to see me in his office. I went into his room and was given an envelope, which I took to my father. It contained a 1-pound note. My three weeks' pay was 15 shillings and I was given an extra 5 shillings for doing a good job. A few short years later, Sir Henry Maurice Scott was fully qualified, knighted and, like his father, became the Speaker of the Legislative Council of Fiji.

In October 1952, Suva was proclaimed a city.

Behind the Bank of New South Wales, Charles Stinson's Photography Shop, the Regent Theatre and the Suva Fire Brigade was the Suva shoreline as it continued right behind Cable & Wireless Limited, the Suva Town Hall, the Carnegie Library, the Suva Sea Baths, the Suva Grammar School, the Grand Pacific Hotel and the Suva Bowling Club.

Going past the *ivi* tree and continuing on from the Club Hotel was the Fiji Times and Pacific Islands Monthly Fiji office, run by Sir Thomas William Alport Barker CBE. Opposite Sir Alport Barker's office was the imposing white Cable & Wireless building. It was an important place for many people, especially those with overseas connections. This is where you could telephone anyone in the world and send and receive telegrams. My father received his telegrams from relatives in his village of Vesma, Gujarat, stating urgent messages like 'Mother seriously ill, send money' or 'Your sister Bhikhi has "expired" in Nairobi'. Receiving a telegram was never good news for him. On the left side of C&W was the precursor to the Fiji Broadcasting Service, running as Radio ZJV. I remember Mr Niranjan Singh presenting the Hindi program for 15 minutes on Wednesdays and Saturdays. I also liked the English breakfast program and songs like *Jambalaya (On the Bayou)*, a song written and recorded by American country music singer Hank Williams, which was first released in July 1952. My father had a Bush radio that was quite large in size and accompanied by a large battery. The front of our two-room home would be full of Indian friends and relatives and our Fijian neighbours for Hindi and Fijian programs four times a week. My mother was not happy about this because it was our parents' and sisters' bedroom and our sitting room.

Figure 15.5: Indian musical group auditioning at Broadcasting House, 1957.
Source: G4143 National Archives of Fiji.

Would my mother have dreamed that Suva would someday have several radio stations, multiple language presentations 24 hours a day and television stations not only local but in the hundreds, at any given time?

It was difficult enough for me to explain to her that on 20 July 1969, man walked on the moon for the first time ever. 'Chanda Mama' (a respectful name for the moon known to Indian children from a nursery lullaby) cannot be touched, my mother said. I had to remind her of her trip to Fiji, such a long way from a tiny village in India, and how she got to Nukulau, the quarantine island over 7,000 miles away. I may have convinced her by reasoning but not by belief.

Along Victoria Parade , we went past many offices until we came to the corner of the British Council Library and its Fiji headquarters. This institution had a major impact on my life in years to come. Firstly, I was invited to join the British Council Youth Club when I was in Form 4 and was asked to be the treasurer (I have an autograph to prove this) and later I was invited to join the Library Service of Fiji at the Western Regional Library, Lautoka. Neither I nor Radike Qereqeretabua, the two pioneering local librarians, ever applied for our jobs. It was quite true that I could be neither a member of the Carnegie Library nor of the Suva Sea Baths until they were opened to the public. I was, however, an accidental hero when I took a large live centipede in a glass bottle, which had been caught in our bathroom by my mother, and presented it to the curator of the Suva Museum, which in those days was on the floor above the Carnegie Library.

The British Council provided the initial funds for the establishment of the Library Service of Fiji operating from the Western Regional Library in Lautoka, and paid for the first two chief librarians, Robert Pearce (UK) and Dennis Edwards (Australia). They funded the extension to the library and later provided a scholarship for me to complete my master's degree at Leeds.

There were not too many exciting places in between the British Council and the Government Buildings except that you could easily go from the library to Flagstaff along MacGregor Road past Suva Chinese School or Girls Grammar School, depending on which turn you took, and then drive past Scott's residence and onto Marist Brothers High School.

15. WHERE IS MY HOME AND WHERE IS MY HEART?

The other major items of interest on and beyond Victoria Parade were Suva Motors, opposite the Carnegie Library, the Fiji Government Printer (now the National Archives of Fiji) and CC David Café, staffed by three beautiful sisters, and their 'Choc Bums', which were a cone of ice cream with a chocolate topping.

The Government Buildings had a charm of their own. If you were bold enough to go to the Public Relations Office you could get a haul of freebies, such as copies of royal family photographs and Empire Games posters. Inside the Government Buildings were fascinating places like the Legislative Council Chambers and the Supreme Court. Coming out at the Albert Park end, you were treated to a festival of sports.

On weekends, spectators and passers-by could see rugby, men's and women's hockey, cricket, basketball, lawn tennis and soccer matches. There were special occasions too such as the Indian Independence celebration, when everyone received free *mithai* sweets, and Coronation Day, when we all got a beautiful tin box full of lollies with a British Flag cover plus a bonus gift of a Union Jack.

Once you came to this end of town, you had to go to the Botanical Gardens and also see the Fiji soldier standing perfectly still, impeccable in full dress military uniform, at the entrance to the drive of the Governor-General's (President's) Residence and Government House.

On rare occasions we would end up at Suva Point where we could see the jetty where Royal New Zealand Air Force Sunderlands and other passenger seaplanes landed. We came twice to receive relatives arriving by seaplane instead of picking them up from Luvu Luvu airport at Nausori.

Samabula, a dormitory suburb of Suva, was the beginning or the end of a tour around Viti Levu along Kings Road. The Reliance and Sunbeam buses went past our house every day for Raki Raki, Tavua, Ba and Lautoka. Here, unlike in the big town of Suva, although only 2 miles away, we had a world of our own with people of all races and religions living side by side. Our immediate neighbour was Ning Soon and on the floor above lived Eroni and Setaita with children Setariki, Emma and Seremaia. Sharing the same bathrooms and toilets were Ram Din, wife Barki and their three sons and two daughters.

Figure 15.6: Indian ladies at Ruve Park, Samabula, 1968. This was presumably to commemorate the end of Indian indenture in Fiji.
Source: 561-S National Archives of Fiji.

Figure 15.7: Indian men at Ruve Park, Samabula, 1968. This was presumably to commemorate the end of Indian indenture in Fiji.
Source: 562-S National Archives of Fiji.

15. WHERE IS MY HOME AND WHERE IS MY HEART?

The daily 2-mile walk to St Columba's, past Samabula Government Boys School next door, wound by Samabula Police Station and the Public Works Department Depot, later transformed to Derrick Technical School, then the Fiji Institute of Technology and eventually the Fiji National University.

The choice was yours: you could turn right towards Tamavua where the Central Medical School, the Tuberculosis Hospital and the Central Nursing School were located or follow an ocean view bypass road at Walu Bay, where the fork leads to Queen's Road on which Pacific Transport buses take passengers to Lami, Navua, Sigatoka, Nadi and Lautoka. The left fork goes back into the city of Suva, to the soap and biscuit factories, the bus stand and the wharves.

For eight long years, how I longed for rain each weekday as I left home for school in order to get the threepence to catch the Atomic Power Hospital Bus instead of walking.

My commencement at secondary school took me along Baniwai Road, past Howell Road where the annual Hindu firewalking was held. I could not do my homework or studies at home because there was no electricity. The kerosene lamp was inadequate but thankfully the Brothers allowed a couple of dozen students to come to the school each night for a couple of hours to do their homework and swot for tests and Overseas Junior and Senior Cambridge examinations. The road became quite familiar for me as we passed Ritova and Matanitobua streets, learning soon afterwards that they were named after signatories of Fiji's Deed of Session to Britain on 10 October 1874.

Starting secondary school was a new experience for me. Having seven children, my father could not afford my fees and uniform but a timely intervention by Mr SB Desai, another customer of my father, provided me a job in his bookshop, which changed the course of my life. He paid for my fees and uniforms for four years while I worked for him every weekend and school holiday. I often stayed at his home on Waimanu Road, opposite Dr CMP Gopalan.

A interesting aside is that in 1953, on 14 September at 12:29 pm, while at Marist, we were waiting for Rishikesh Prasad, the only person in the class with a wristwatch, to ring the school bell for lunch, when the *Une Une*, an earthquake, shook us all. We were in Form 4 but the first person to beat everyone up to Bau Street away from the danger of a tsunami was James

Vei Makasiale, a descendant of Tongan prince and Fiji chief Ma'afu, and student in Form 3, all 12 stone of him, shooting past the fastest at school. The aftershocks lasted several days.

Desai Book Shop was on Victoria Parade opposite today's Sukuna Park. The tsunami that followed the earthquake brought live fish and debris into the shop, leaving the pure vegetarian Mr Desai and his staff bewildered. The subsequent reclamation has left no sign of the earlier landscape from where one could see Suva Harbour and ships small and large, sailing to or leaving their berth at Suva Wharf.

When I finished Form 4, having completed my Senior Cambridge Examinations at the end of 1955, Brother Anthony and the Principal Brother Cassian at Marist recommended to my father that I should continue my studies. With some financial assistance and further help by Br Cassian to enrol at St Peter's Christian Brothers School, I left for Auckland from the old Nadi Airport on the multi-propeller Pan American World Airways. The flight lasted six hours.

In my first letter to my father I told him that New Zealand was a strange country where Europeans sweep the streets. I was now in a new world from 1956 onwards.

A few years later in Lautoka, a friend named Tony Wilkinson, manager and *Fiji Times* correspondent for the Western Division, shared with me that in 1956 he and some Suva Jaycees friends started the Hibiscus Festival, now a national institution held annually in Suva. At that time we were congratulating ourselves on the success of 1963 Lautoka Sugar Festival. Little credit is given to the Jaycees of Fiji who have been involved with successful equivalents of the Hibiscus and Sugar festivals in many towns and settlements in Fiji.

The Suva of today has a charm of its own. Gone are the days of Somerset Maugham and the Grand Pacific Hotel. My memories are from the beginning of World War II, when spot lamps shone into the skies and alarm sirens summoned us to run to the shelters in a cave nearby during trial exercises. That was 25 years before Independence.

Today Fiji is our own and the postwar growth has brought many changes in Suva, the second capital and the first city of Fiji. The international airport, the magnetic tourist trade and economy-driving sugar belt of the Western Division, and the contributions of the rest of Fiji in Vanua Levu and the Northern, Central and Eastern divisions, have made strong contributions and provide strong challenges to important happenings.

My father would no longer have to wait a week to learn that his mother was seriously ill in India or his sister had passed away in Africa. Today he would know within seconds, and he would not have to go searching around Suva during a cyclone looking for his son. He would know a week before of the likelihood of a cyclone.

I recall the day when the five-floor CMLA Building in Central Suva was pronounced the tallest building in Fiji and the 14-storey Reserve Bank Building was the talk of the Pacific Island countries. Now we talk of 27 floors or more.

This was my Suva for the first 16 years of my life. Not all cities can qualify as the economic, political, cultural capital of their country. Add on history and sheer beauty and it becomes unmatched.

Suva has a magnetic quality that makes you want to come back time and time again after throwing your *salusalu* into the receding waters as your vessel leaves the island, as the touching Fiji farewell song, 'Isa Lei', says:

> Bau nanuma na nodatou lasa mai Suva, nanuma …
>
> Please remember the good times we had in Suva, always remember …

16

Raiwaqa and the Playhouse

Larry Thomas

I still remember quite vividly the first time I was in a play. I was in my second year of primary school. I can't recall the name of the play except that it was based on a nursery rhyme about Humpty Dumpty. I played Humpty Dumpty, 'as I was sitting on a wall wondering whether I might fall, I saw a man with sack in hand …' the only line I can remember! Underneath my shirt was padding to make my (small) stomach look very big. It was the annual school concert and I was chosen to play the part presumably because I could 'project' my voice. It was to come in useful many years later, when a director would say, 'you need to project Larry'. My grandmother sitting in the audience at the Civic Centre was very proud of me, even though she didn't understand a word of the play as she couldn't speak or understand English. Outside the Civic Centre she beamed with pride as wellwishers complimented *her* that I was very good. Years later during my last year of primary school we performed scenes from a couple of plays and one I remember well was a dramatised scene from *Great Expectations*. I played Pip. It was the graveyard scene. Years later I not only read the book, I watched a couple of versions of the film and later taught the book at university. It remains one of my favourite books.

At that time, I lived in Derrick Street, in Raiwaqa. Derrick Street was perhaps one of the most, if not the most, well-known street in Raiwaqa! One evening returning home in the taxi I directed the driver to Derrick Street. At the top of Bryce Street just where the Methodist church is, he stopped: 'I'm not going to Derrick Street.' It's a street notorious for youths who'd 'step' taxis, running away without paying. This was common until drivers wised up to it. What distinguishes Derrick Street is the many alleyways and side paths one could run through, making it easier to disappear in.

I grew up in and around the city, in Raiwaqa, a bus ride away, and for my whole life I have always lived a bus ride away from the city except for now: now I actually live in Suva city, and a short walking distance from the Playhouse and a bus ride away to Raiwaqa. With the establishment of the Housing Authority, Raiwaqa was one of the first, if not the first, low-cost housing estates, developed in the early sixties to cater for low-income families. This model has since been replicated throughout the country. Raiwaqa was unique, and continues to remain so, in that the design of the houses varied in shape and size. In those early years, I am sure, these designs were experimental, working out which ones were the most resilient. Within Raiwaqa, there were the two-storey flats, and depending which place you lived the houses varied. Some had the bathroom and toilet downstairs at the back while others had it upstairs. These were the first designs and remained so for a while. There were a few oddly shaped 'domes' or what we referred to as 'elephant houses'. Why we called it that I don't know, but it was and still is known as that. Maybe because it 'resembled' the body of an elephant? Only one still remains, hidden from view by an extension in front. The single units then began to be constructed and appeared together with newer models of prefab (concrete) two-storey flats.

These houses were affordable and, in the true sense of the word, low cost. That was the premise within which the Housing Authority was established: affordable, low-cost housing. People from the outlying islands flocked in and those who met the criteria bought their houses. Mortgage payments were very low. There was many a time when we defaulted with our payments, but we were always safe; occasionally a notice would come for non-payment and we'd scramble to make the payment.

Figure 16.1: Elephant house, Raiwaqa, 2022.
Source: Photo provided by author, March 2022.

People came from the Maritimes, from Kadavu, Lomaiviti and Lau. The neighbourhood was multiracial, Fijians (iTaukei), Indo-Fijians, mixed race, otherwise known as Part-European(/Fijian), Rotumans, Banabans and Chinese, if you throw in the local shops! Each New Year's Eve the Lauans would walk through the streets singing and beating and banging on empty biscuit tins. The merriment was met with people throwing powder on their hair and dancing. Those celebratory moments usually reserved for village festivities were now transported onto the urban streets of Raiwaqa.

The different religious denominations – the Methodists, Catholics, Assemblies of God, Seventh Day Adventists – lived side by side with the Hindus and Muslims. I attended Methodist services since my maternal grandmother was a Methodist, even though all her children and grandchildren were Catholics. I attended Sunday school classes at the Assemblies of God, and also at the Mormon Church. And all this time I continued going to mass, in fact I was forced to go to mass (by my Methodist grandmother), and I was still okay to attend the services of the other denominations.

I cannot look back at a world I once knew without some memories of regret. I sometimes regret that I have forgotten much of my childhood memories and the years of growing up. I reminisce now and again but much of what I remember is filtered through age. I recall the time and the general period of that time, be it the sixties, seventies or eighties or any other time. I remember certain details. For me it was always falling while running, grazing my knees and running to my grandmother, who was not sympathetic at all, instead would give me a whack, I shouldn't cry when I fall. I feel like Humpty Dumpty!

Growing up in the sixties, my grandmother and my mother were the most important people in my life. What I remember a lot was going to the city in the wooden Raiwaqa bus. There was a driver whom people labelled 'superman' because he drove like crazy. Going to Suva city was always an occasion! I remember the bus fare to Suva was threepence – later 3 cents, after Fiji became independent, with her own currency.

Figure 16.2: Outdoor market, Suva, 1939.
Source: Whites Aviation Ltd, Photographs. Ref: WA-03285-G. Alexander Turnbull Library, Wellington, New Zealand. natlib.govt.nz/records/30654320.

And there was Mrs Rounds. We were all afraid of Mrs Rounds. This strict no-nonsense Samoan woman kept all the schoolchildren in check and in place as we lined up each morning to wait for our respective school buses. She always had a stick in her hand and was never afraid to use it. We were all very orderly, each school in their own section. Now as I think back, I wonder who put her there to supervise us? To berate us and discipline us! With a couple of hundred schoolchildren waiting for their buses on the pavement by the side of the road, it was a wonder no one got run over! I remember her face, never smiling. Much later, I got to know her family and she was nothing like the 'bus mistress'.

10 October 1970. I was in primary school and at the end of the day each student was given a loaf of bread to take home. It was our celebratory gift and I guess if it wasn't for the loaf of bread Fiji's Independence would be just another day. When you're poor, a loaf of bread is a meal in itself.

Fast forward to early 1987. Just before the military coup, I set out to produce a series of short radio programs, simply looking at Fiji from the eyes of men and women over the age of 60 and asking what they thought of the country, before and after Independence. All the interviewees said that it was too early to be independent and we should have waited. They were not happy with the changes and preferred when Europeans ran the country, 'they knew what they were doing'. I disagreed with them, but I kept my opinion to myself. I was pleased though that we had become independent. But now as I approach the age my interviewees were, I can appreciate their point of view.

The country has withstood the upheavals over the years following 1987 and has suffered the economic and social impacts of the political turmoil of the last three decades. But in spite of that we struggle on with resilience. That is what makes the country unique, and Suva is at the heart of that: a small vibrant city, the centre of much of the political upheaval and the centre of most things cultural, artistic and political. It is easily accessible, and I like the limitations and the limited selections of choices of many things. Sometimes we can't help it when we make unfair comparisons of Suva to larger cities (for us the [wannabee] sophisticates) but that often stems from frustrations, because we want this city to be like other big cities in its offerings. But often it is good to remember that sometimes being small is beautiful.

SUVA STORIES

Suva is still my favourite place. In many ways it is a microcosm of the larger cities I have visited around the world, and while these larger cities are quite overwhelming, Suva is underwhelming, limited by its size, yet retaining its unique characteristics, the ethnic diversity, the location – the harbour, mountains across the water and the unmistakeable Joske's Thumb, the (remaining) colonial architecture, and the very vibrant and colourful market.

I have lived my whole life in Suva, and my memories of growing up in this city remain vivid. I have watched the city transform; the open-air wooden buses and the 'half-loaf' buses, the 'traffic' police at the market and bus stand standing on a circular wooden platform directing traffic, people always very well dressed, the old buildings sometimes a reminder of a Western movie set.

Two things were quite significant for me. Growing up in Raiwaqa and being involved in theatre, more specifically, the Fiji Arts Club and the Playhouse. Raiwaqa and the Playhouse were the antithesis of each other, one being the 'real world' the other being in 'another world'. Yet one could say there was a symbiosis. The reality of life in Raiwaqa provided the experience for me to draw from as an actor and eventually as a writer. They were just different spaces: one was more restrained, while the other gave me an opportunity to express myself, to enter and be part of a sometimes different world, albeit for a few hours.

If I lived in a more affluent suburb of Suva, came from a middle-class family and completed high school then it would have been more expected for me to be a member of the Fiji Arts Club. In the mid-seventies the members of the club were predominantly expatriates from the United Kingdom, Australia and New Zealand, with a handful from the United States and Europe. The Fiji Arts Club was established by British expatriates who wanted a place for the arts, theatre and dance and music(als). The Playhouse was built and became the only theatre of its kind in Fiji. So, the membership of the club was predominantly expatriates who catered towards a mainly expatriate audience. Into this milieu I entered, a poor brown kid, from the housing estates.

There are good teachers, very good teachers and there are great teachers. I was fortunate to have a great teacher. Bob Miles opened the door to a life that I would otherwise never have been exposed to and I imagine my life today would be quite different without him. He was an eccentric and that is what distinguished him, and for a young kid from Raiwaqa he was really 'different' and interested in my life, but most importantly he introduced me to literature and classical music. He had lived in Fiji for a very long time, having first taught in Levuka and Savusavu before settling in Suva.

Through him I was introduced to the world of theatre, transitioning from high school to performing at the Playhouse and eventually becoming a member of the Fiji Arts Club. When Bob invited me to join the cast of a play he was directing at the Playhouse, I reluctantly agreed, in part because I was very nervous of being in a new environment, quite alien from what I was used to and outside my comfort zone. But I was also curious and it was a new experience and I was quite honoured to be asked by Bob to be in the play, even though I only had two lines!

Though I was just a teenager, I knew the Playhouse was going to be a fun place to be and for a few hours at a time I escaped the reality of my life in Raiwaqa. I was learning something new, something different. It was opening up a whole new world. I marvelled that a (small) space, the stage, could be transformed into a town, a street, a garden, the interior of living rooms and bedrooms and so on, and in the middle of this, emotions were intense, love was declared, wars were fought and murder was committed! It was 'real' but unreal. But in Raiwaqa it was all real. The declaration of love segued into teenage pregnancy, violent physical and verbal abuses, occasional 'gang' (neighbourhood) wars and school dropouts, but this was punctuated by wonderful games, camaraderie, community, respect and an appreciation of how people lived their lives. It was vibrant and always exciting for me and that was the only life I knew; it was a familiar and relatively safe environment. To be exposed to a new and very different one was daunting and scary to say the least. Sometimes it was like being schizophrenic, being who I am in one and being someone else in another. I wanted to really fit in to this other environment.

Following high school, I continued to be active in theatre and worked full-time. My first cousin and 'big sister' happened to be living with Dr Chris Griffin (they're still happily together), an anthropologist and at that time teaching sociology at the University of the South Pacific. I became an 'unofficial' researcher for Chris as he was always keen to listen and hear stories of what was going on in the neighbourhood. It was through this experience that he encouraged me to write a play, more so because he knew of my interest in theatre.

SUVA STORIES

My first play *Just Another Day* was written in my old house in Derrick Street, in Raiwaqa in 1980. Chris gave me his old 'mini' typewriter to use. It took me exactly a whole year to write the play and as I tapped away on my very own typewriter, which in itself was such an exciting novelty, my mother lay upstairs very ill, and around me the cacophony of diverse sounds filled the two-bedroom, two-storey flat.

Each time I sat down to write, each time at the same spot, the characters in the play came 'alive', not so much in my head or on the page but around me. I could hear people talking and laughing, the shouts of a domestic dispute, children being disciplined and crying, or at my door there would be a knock, someone asking for tea or sugar, or just popping in for a chat.

I couldn't stop and say, please don't disturb me, I'm writing! It wouldn't make any difference and far more complicated to explain. I would just stop. If they enquired what I was doing I would just say, I'm writing something. So, as I wrote, the characters I was writing about were visiting me or I'd hear them not too far away or see them through the window, walking past.

After I wrote the play, I gave it to Chris to read and a few others who were all very encouraging with their comments. But it was a friend of mine visiting from Germany who read the play and her one comment that got me was, 'this play is very depressing, it doesn't go anywhere'. And that's the whole point! She nailed it. The play doesn't go anywhere; it is just a cycle reflecting the lives of people living in a poor area just managing to make ends meet and even that was difficult at the best of times. The cycle that keeps going around with no exit in sight, people repeating their actions and words, over and over, day in day out. To break out of the cycle is a challenge but to exit the cycle takes courage.

Having studied a little drama, been part of the drama group in high school, and, at that time, having been involved with a few productions at the Fiji Arts Club, I felt I had a sense of 'the stage'. So, writing the play and knowing where to move and place the characters wasn't as difficult as I imagined. The play was to 'sit' for another seven years before I gathered the courage to produce it. During that time, I did some more work on it and in 1988 it finally saw the light of day and was staged at the Playhouse.

Post-Independence saw an influx of migration into Suva, evidenced by the increase in the construction of more single and two-storey flats and what was then known as the 'Four Storey' or 'Taba Va' in a newly developed area of Raiwaqa, and Raiwai the neighbouring suburb. The 'four storeys' were built specifically to cater for single or small families, ideally waiting to transition to more substantive single or two-storey units they could purchase. These tenements catered a lot for people coming in from the western parts of the island as well as from Vanua Levu and the Maritimes.

These 'four storey' tenements were for rental only and could not be purchased. It was supposed to accommodate up to four people, a couple and perhaps two children. It was easier said than done and having lived in one of these tenements it was clearly not the case. More often than not they were overcrowded and far exceeded the number of people supposed to be living there.

Because of family circumstances I moved around Raiwaqa and Raiwai and ended up back in Derrick Street in my later years of high school. During that time there was a steady increase in the population. In Derrick Street, new faces appeared. The neighbourhood I had grown up in, in the sixties and seventies, had begun to evolve and the sense of community that comes from living in a small populated area was now no longer small. The area had not grown in size, but the population had increased and overcrowding grew as a result of people coming in from around the country.

Figure 16.3: One of the original houses left in Raiwaqa, 2022.
Source: Photo provided by author, March 2022.

With the exception of a couple of houses, the people in my immediate neighbourhood remained the same and the children I had grown up with were now young men and women, a few had already settled with children. They had begun working and had their own families, though still living with their parents.

For the next five years I became heavily involved in theatre and the Playhouse was almost my second home. I enjoyed the acting roles I was given but also equally enjoyed backstage work and that was where I learnt much of the stagecraft that was to come in useful years later when I ventured more into directing. A decade after Independence, there were fewer expatriates around and even though the Arts Club was still active, productions became fewer. There just weren't enough people around to produce and direct. There were so few locals involved or interested in theatre that it became difficult to fill the void left by expatriates. Like any amateur theatre, people become involved because they have a love for drama, acting, dance and music. Theatre provided that space for creativity and a place to share experiences.

Figure 16.4: The Playhouse, 2022.
Source: Photo provided by author, March 2022.

While my involvement in theatre consumed a large part of my social life, I still had to work to pay the bills and this I did with a few exceptional periods of unemployment, but even then I continued to find the bus fare to attend rehearsals. To be a member of the Arts Club one had to pay to become a member. I couldn't afford the membership fee, minimal as it was. I was fortunate that some kind person offered to pay my membership but on condition of anonymity. Eventually I could afford to pay the small amount but when you have low wages, paying membership fees to a club was, for me, a luxury.

Theatre provided the opportunity for me to view my life and life in Raiwaqa differently. It had become a strong influence on my perspective on life. The change in atmosphere for a few hours each evening at the Playhouse dissipated the noise and aimlessness many young people my age were faced with. It was a different world and though it may be a world of 'make believe', the plays reflected a reality, though different from my own, which still resonated with me, moved and cheered me.

Working in the theatre was not a career, it was a hobby. I enjoyed the excitement and fun of it and the passion I began to develop allowed me to cultivate skills that perhaps would have remained dormant. It exposed me to a very different environment and forced me out of my comfort zone. Manoa Rasigatale had the Dance Theatre of Fiji and they were developing and creating amazing dance, still using the *meke* form but taking it to a whole new level. But it was more than that, it was theatre, onsite at their Pacific Harbour cultural village. It was a new and different experience, 'sailing' the audience through Fiji's past history, authentically told and performed. The arts were just never seen as part of development, there was no revenue that could be derived from it. Traditional dances – *mekes* – mat weaving, tapa and pottery making, were viewed as cultural traditions and not as part of the 'arts' per se despite it being labelled 'arts and culture'. The emphasis was on culture and tradition not the arts. For people like me, this could never be a career but for those artists, especially the visual artists – and there were a few – they were courageous enough to decide that their art was their career and they did it because of their passion. Monetary consideration was secondary even though for many of them survival continued to be a struggle.

It was working in the theatre that kept me going and kept me focused and to the point that I seriously considered working full-time and forming a kind of national theatre. Like most things it came down to finance and sustainability and I had to be realistic that it would not work. There was no drama school and drama wasn't even offered at the university. There was no 'national' interest. Each time I produced and directed a play, more often than not I worked with people with no experience and new to acting. Each play was a crash course in Acting 101.

It seemed a seamless transition to graduate from acting and directing to writing plays. It was just something I wanted to do and I wanted to write about the place where I lived and what went on there. I was simply transferring reality to the page and onto the stage. After I wrote the first play, *Just Another Day*, it still didn't occur to me that I would stage it. Of course, it makes sense that a play needs to and should be performed. Somehow, I didn't believe in my own abilities. For a very long time, I struggled with believing that I did indeed write plays drawing from stories of everyday life and directed these plays that people came to watch and enjoy and appreciated. I lacked the confidence to believe and trust in myself. That lack of self-esteem stems largely from growing up in a place like Raiwaqa. To be poor is not to 'shine'. To blow your own trumpet is to show off and be arrogant. One is not taught to think, for to think is to emancipate yourself and to emancipate yourself is to be different. It's very hard to break out of that cycle, and what worked for me would not necessarily work for another. We all have strengths and weaknesses but some of us just have that added strength not to be afraid to take that leap and dare to be different, without meaning to be. It just happened.

To be an artist in this country then, and to an extent even now, is like walking down a long road, alone. There is no encouragement. This is not because people don't want to encourage you, rather they can't understand what you're doing and why you're doing it simply because it doesn't generate any income. And what's worse, you're spending your own money towards what you're wanting to achieve. This lack of interest is reflected in put-downs and jokes about your 'job' such as 'Your job is not feeding the family'. It's not a job, not a real job. To do and be involved in any of these things is to be different. The last 10 years or so has seen a considerable shift in thinking and attitude towards this.

In the seventies there was an excellent bookshop called the Dateline bookshop. It was in an arcade and just a few metres further along was a record store that belonged to Bob Miles, my former teacher. The record store was called Mainstream records. While I could never afford to buy books, nor did I have a record player to play records, I enjoyed just walking

16. RAIWAQA AND THE PLAYHOUSE

in to these two stores and browsing, reading the blurbs of books and the jackets of record covers. In the record shop I discovered music that was 'alien' to me. Classical music was like another language! But through Bob's guidance and encouragement I began to slowly appreciate it and if he was in the shop, he would play me pieces with commentary on the composer and the different movements and what they meant. I was introduced to Mozart, Beethoven and Bach. That was just the beginning.

Similarly, with the bookstore I discovered new writers. At high school I spent much of my free time in the library. At that time, it was a wonderful library and my love of literature and reading grew from there. So, to then have a bookstore in Suva was wonderful! One day, an aunt of mine gave me $20. That was big money then and I couldn't believe my luck to be given this amount. I headed straight for the Dateline bookshop. I wanted to buy a book. This was the first time I bought a book and it was exhilarating! I began browsing and there were so many choices and at the back of my mind I kept telling myself, 'you have money to buy a book'. And then I came upon *War and Peace* by Leo Tolstoy. It was a massive book, over 1,500 pages and at the age of 19 what did I know about history, even more so of revolutions or Napoleonic wars? I read the blurb and it just fascinated me. I remember thinking if I read this, I will learn something, something new about a country and her history. Russia? What did I know about Russia? What did I know about Napoleon?

I checked the price and it was $9.95. Half my money would be gone. I made the huge decision to purchase the book and happily headed home. When I told my dear mother I had bought the book the first thing she asked was how much was it? When I told her, she was very upset that I would spend so much money on a book! She didn't have to tell me that I should have spent the money on more important things like food. She was very disappointed. I still remember that scene very vividly. Normally I would feel guilty, but somehow, in this case I didn't. The $9.95 didn't fill my belly, it fed my intellect and agitated my interest in the world of literature.

When I began to read the novel I couldn't put it down, and while the world Tolstoy writes about and describes was completely alien to me I still 'understood' the story and I was just so amazed that a writer could do that, tell you a story about a different world, a different culture, a different period in time, yet the story could still resonate with me and as young as I was then, reading the book in my small flat in Derrick Street, Raiwaqa,

I learnt about Russia and the Russian aristocracy and most importantly I became a fan of Leo Tolstoy and later the Russian writers. It was so thrilling and exhilarating. I remember cooking and kept forgetting that the pot was on the stove, getting annoyed that I had to stop reading and attend to the pot!

The Suva city I remember was a picture postcard: clean, few cars, well-dressed people walking around. By the market and bus station, the busiest place in town, a lone policeman in his black and white uniform, stood on a raised platform controlling the traffic. I don't recall any traffic lights then. It is hard to imagine that the bus fare then was under 10 cents! The evolution of the city began to take place with the increase in commerce and commercial activities but also with an increase in the population. Old buildings were taken down and replaced with ugly ones. Whoever was working on the design and planning of Suva was clearly someone who had no sense of aesthetics and lacked any understanding of design or how to maximise the use space of the beautiful peninsula. Having lived and grown up in Suva my whole life, I look back now, and sometimes when I am walking through the city I imagine watching scenes in a black and white movie, in slow motion, seeing the variations of change that have occurred and while I don't want to lament the past, I do miss a certain joie de vivre.

The political turmoil of 1987 was traumatic. 'The way the world should be' was no longer the way it was. The coup had a major economic effect not only on the country but on individuals as well. I was about to land a temporary job when the coup happened. For most of that year I was unemployed. Fortunately, I still lived in Derrick Street where the rent was very low. Despite the political situation I managed to still direct a play, a musical called *Runaways* that was about young people who had run away from home and were living on the streets. The musical was almost a metaphor for was what was going on in the country. No sooner had rehearsals started than the second coup took place and soon after a curfew was imposed. A major decision had to be made.

The cast of predominantly young people were too enthusiastic to not put the show on and we decided to continue and work within the curfew hours. The curfew (if I recall) was from 8 pm. Rehearsals began at 5 and finished at 7, allowing people to get home in time. It was decided that the performances would also be from 5 pm. The day before the show opened the curfew was lifted. It was too late to change the time. The show must go on!

1987 was a transformative year. It was the year I became 'politicised', as I am sure happened to many others in the country, trying to understand and make sense of what happened and why the coup(s) happened. The protest marches and the eventual riots removed the safety of the city. We looked at each other differently, it just wasn't the same anymore and people didn't feel safe. Nothing was as straightforward as before. What I saw and heard around me was not pleasant. Suddenly the political landscape had not only shifted it had changed. A great deal of repressed feelings and anxiety came to the surface. The multiracial and 'smiling' Fiji had 'come of age'.

Our transition to Independence was very smooth and one feature that endeared everyone looking in from the outside was Fiji's multiracialism and she prided herself on that. Sometimes we wear our multiracialism on our sleeves because we need that identity to affirm our distinctiveness, that our way of life is different from the rest of the world. Perhaps we try a little too hard? Perhaps to reflect an ideal that we think exists? But then perhaps the effort becomes a little too much, and in earnest things fall apart. But in spite of the political upheavals, over the last three decades we've proven to be quite resilient and where we are now is a testament to that resilience.

I learnt not to be afraid of the dark. I walked the streets at night, unafraid. This is not bravado, rather confidence that has stood me well anywhere in the country especially in the housing estates, squatter settlements and places that may be less frequented by nonresidents. Any time I go to Raiwaqa or other similar housing estates, it is all familiar territory. I feel at home, undaunted, comfortable and safe.

There was no financial support other than the Fiji Arts Club providing funds to stage a play. Revenue from ticket sales went back to the club. Often the actors were unemployed or worked in jobs with very low pay. I eventually summoned up the courage to produce and direct my play *Just Another Day*. While I had given the play to a few people to read, I really hadn't received any critical comments. It would have been great to get feedback from someone who taught theatre or a dramaturg. However, the comments I had received earlier from my friends were encouraging and I did work on some of the comments. One of them was from Bob Miles, my former English teacher. What I appreciated was that he didn't try and correct the grammar as he could clearly see that this was Fiji English and it fitted the context of the play. He did however mention that I needed to be careful about the excessive swearing and use of the four-letter word in the play. Too much swearing would undermine the essence of the play and take away the seriousness of it. I took heed of his comments and removed the swear words, replacing them with more 'suitable' words.

I realised very early on that I can't just transfer what I hear on the streets straight onto the page. Well, I could but I had to moderate it somehow. I was trying to write realism without fully understanding the genre at that time. I mean I was 19 and hadn't completed high school! Eight years later, at the age of 27, I directed the play. I was excited although very nervous of how it would be received. More so, it was revealing aspects of life in Suva, specifically, a low-cost housing estate. It could be anywhere. But somehow most people, locals at least, knew right away that it was Raiwaqa. An expatriate woman who was helping backstage with the production asked me if this was 'real', if a place such as the one I have depicted really does exist in Suva? I said, yes, very much so. This was the 'scene' that I knew very well. These were experiences that I had lived through, the characters were based on people who were my neighbours and friends. For her it was a revelation, it gave her an insight into a life, a place she had been living in for a few years now, but knew nothing about.

The consequence of writing in 'obscurity' is like walking in the wilderness. I just wrote as I felt, describing what I saw and my feelings about things. I realised around then that I enjoyed this writing but felt I didn't have the qualifications to be a writer. When you live and grow up in a place like Raiwaqa there is often no one around who could be a role model. There is no one around to encourage and support you, no one to give you books to read and while there were other writers around, who were at the University of the South Pacific, I was too daunted to approach them. I worked alone for the most part, teaching myself what I needed and remembering all that I had learnt in the seventies and early eighties when the Playhouse was a hive of activity with people who were struggling (with no support for the arts) yet enjoyed doing theatre, purely out of love and joy!

If success could be measured by positive responses then perhaps, I could say that *Just Another Day* was a success. For those not familiar with life in the housing estates, the play allowed people a glimpse into a life they only heard or read about, it provided scenes into life in a low-cost working-class area. It was a novelty and that revelation appeared unreal. Do people really live like that? For those living in the estates, this was an all too familiar scene, except this time they saw their own lives reflected back at them, mirroring their own reality and sometimes that reality can be uncomfortable.

16. RAIWAQA AND THE PLAYHOUSE

Just past the Raiwaqa post office one enters the very well-known area called 'Jittu Estate'. This was and still is largely a squatter settlement, which at one time was quite overpopulated with a reputation that went with it. I had on a few occasions visited people living there and after *Just Another Day* I knew I had to write about the squatter settlement. I won't go into the details of the genesis of it, suffice to say that my next play *Outcasts* was set in a squatter settlement and most people assumed that it was Jittu Estate. They were right.

The stage at the Playhouse was transformed into a squatter neighbourhood right up to a tap with running water in the middle of the stage. It was, at that time, the biggest production I had ever directed and with a large cast to boot. Writing this play almost 10 years after *Just Another Day* was a new experience in writing. I was much older, I had been abroad, seen quite a bit of theatre, and read much more. There were features I had to consider: structure, plot and character. This time I had a small electric typewriter!

In May 1988, I was invited to be part of a group to perform skits at Sukuna Park. It was to be part of a larger protest group and on Saturday at 10 am on 14 May we assembled at Sukuna Park. We were all dressed in black. This was exactly a year after the military coup of 1987. I think we were all quite nervous but, as the saying goes, there was safety in numbers. No sooner had we congregated than the police came and told us to leave. They said it wasn't safe as the Taukei Movement was marching to Sukuna Park and if we remained there would be trouble. The Taukei Movement was formed in 1987 as a protest against the Labour Party–led coalition that had won the elections that year and were the new government. While the prime minister, Dr Timoci Bavadra, was an indigenous person, there were those that felt he was just a front as the majority of the government were Indo-Fijians. The Taukei Movement was very visible and vocal in the weeks leading up to the coup.

Meanwhile, we decided to remain and the singing began, a crowd had begun to gather to watch. We were encouraged and our confidence boosted as our singing gathered momentum. No sooner did that happen than we were arrested and all I can recall was the senior police officer (I gathered as much since he seemed to be calling the shots) shouted out to arrest all those who were dressed in black. I was wearing black jeans and t-shirt. So, the nearest 18 people dressed in black were hauled into police vans and driven to the Central Police Station. It was the first time in my life to be arrested and the first time to be part of such a protest.

We were kept overnight at the Central Police Station in Suva and released the next day. I won't go into the details of that, as that requires a separate story on its own. But it was quite a life-changing experience and the 18 of us who were arrested have remained lifelong friends – sadly quite a few have passed on, may they rest in peace. I returned home to Raiwaqa, to an empty flat. My sister, who was living with me at the time, was fortunately in Perth, Australia, so there was no one to worry about me. Raiwaqa was quiet and people were either in church or preparing lunch. The reaction from the neighbourhood was mixed. The general response was I should not have participated, it was not good. People didn't really want to talk about it. Not long after that I was prevented from leaving the country when I had to go to Nauru on a work-related mission. The immigration officer at Nadi Airport asked me, 'what have you done?' I said, 'what do you mean?' He looked at me a little embarrassed and said, 'sorry but you can't leave country, you have a mark against your name'.

There comes a time when major decisions have to be made and one of those was having to leave Raiwaqa. I was okay but I had to think of my young teenage sister. Raiwaqa, again at that time, just wasn't safe. In a carrier and in just one trip, we moved our small pile of belongings out of a house that I had grown up in, a house that was a part of me, where I had spent my most formative years, out of a street where I ran up and down, falling and getting up again, a street where we played games and sat under the lamppost telling stories and laughing late into the night, and out of a place, a place that I have loved all my life and that had become an ingrained part of me.

Raiwaqa was seminal in my life. It just wasn't a place where I lived and grew up. Yes, we are influenced by our environment but Raiwaqa was much more than that, more than just a place, it was where I discovered life, where I learnt not to be afraid. It was there that I first went abroad, where I wrote my first play, where I first read *War and Peace,* it was there that I became politicised and arrested, where I discovered acting, it was there where two of the most important people in my life died, my mother and grandmother, it was where I lived with an aunt who removed my bad habits and taught me independence, and it was there where I discovered the Playhouse. And it was in Raiwaqa where I knew what I really wanted to be in life.

17

Minority Melanesians in Suva

Anawaite Matadradra

Votu mai Na Sitima ni meli	**I can hear the steamship**
Lei tei dalo ko tamaqu	My father went to the taro plantation
Lei qoliqoli ko tinaqu	My mother went fishing
Au gade ki serea	I am going to Serea
Votu mai na sitimi ni meli	I can hear the steamship afar
Sa qai voce mai na velovelo	A small punt came ashore
Na velovelo me daru mai lele lele	We sailed and sailed away from home
Tauri au na kai valagi	The white man took hold of my hand
Au sa vesu ena dali	Tied me up with a rope
Sa bi na noqu tagi	I cried as hard as I can
Au sa kau dina ga ki Viti	They are taking me to Fiji
Sa yacaqu dina ko Mili	My name is Mili
Sa qai voce mai na velovelo	A small punt came ashore
Na velovelo me daru mai lele lele	We sailed and sailed away from home

Souce: Fijian folk song: translation provided by the author.

Melanesian descendants in Fiji recall that the song above was written specifically about the labour recruitment process to Fiji, as experienced by their ancestors. Many iTaukei children who grew up in Fiji will likely recognise this song, even if they are unaware of its true significance. The song is still performed at many kindergartens in Fiji today, possibly due to its popularity and ease of recitation for preschoolers, as well as its melody and tempo. A *lali* (drum) is frequently used to accompany the tune. I heard this song for the first time during a kindergarten recital two decades ago and did not really know what it meant until my elderly relatives explained it to me. As a child I was vaguely aware of some distant relatives who had married Melanesian descendants, but everyone spoke the same language as me so I could not really tell the difference until I asked about our familial ties.

My own experience growing up in a low-income, underprivileged neighbourhood on Suva's outskirts inspired me to research the limits that poverty, unemployment, limited education and negative preconceptions can impose on one's wellbeing. It was a social and emotional challenge growing up in substandard housing, with limited access to health services, poor food and nutrition, and being stigmatised by others because of our family circumstances. Despite our financial limitations and personal challenges, I never gave up on my education and I worked hard to make it to university. My experiences growing up in an impoverished environment motivated me at university to explore how people break out of those types of situations.

My research involvement with informal settlements began with a community on the outskirts of Labasa, Vanua Levu. This informal settlement was built on a recovered strip of land along the Labasa River's bank, next to a mangrove swamp. The houses in this informal settlement were carefully spaced along the wetland swamp. Most of the dwellings are built on stilts, and the water reaches beneath most of them during high tide. Through this experience, I was introduced to different ethnic groups in the settlement, including some families of iTaukei-Melanesian ancestry who had migrated to Labasa in the hope of being able to access resources and offer a good education for their children. This piqued my curiosity in Melanesian descendants in Fiji, as I wanted to know why those who have resided in Fiji for over a century are still disadvantaged, destitute and living in impoverished communities.

Melanesian labourers who worked on colonial plantations in Fiji have had many different names over time. For Europeans who orchestrated the 'blackbirding' trade in the nineteenth century, it was common to refer to Pacific Islanders in general as Polynesians. In Fiji, all those of Melanesian origin that came during the labour trade period were categorised as 'Solomoni' regardless of their country of origin. The term is applied to the generation of descendants of Melanesian labourers whose ancestors came from the Solomon Islands (the largest number), Vanuatu (formerly New Hebrides) and New Guinea during the period 1864–1911. Most Fijians believed that all Melanesian descendants came from the Solomon Islands, hence the use of the word 'Solomoni' or 'kai Solomoni'. Though they were previously identified as those of Solomoni ancestry, Melanesian descendants in Fiji today prefer the term 'Fijian' as it is more inclusive.

17. MINORITY MELANESIANS IN SUVA

Figure 17.1: A Solomon Islander's house in Suva, Fiji, approximately 1890.
Source: Charles H Kelly, National Library of Australia, PIC Album 1272 #PIC/19988/47, nla.gov.au/nla.obj-332526286.

This chapter is a reflection on the journeys of Melanesian descendants in Suva and how they have fared in terms of access to land, education and socio-economic opportunities. I focus on three settlements in particular – Wailoku, Caubati and Muanikoso. Melanesian settlements in Suva, like many other informal settlements in Fiji, have struggled with land tenure concerns while striving to retain a sense of security and belonging on the land they now call home. Yet there are also positive stories of community solidarity and prosperity. Their lives serve as a catalyst for change, demonstrating that blackbirding's past was more than simply a tale of survival.

As I embarked on a PhD in 2015 to understand this history, I travelled around Fiji interviewing Melanesian descendants. It was part of a broader research study that looked at Melanesians' descendants in Fiji and Samoa, the historical development of identity formation in their new homes, and the social and economic status and prospects of these minorities. Since Winston Halapua's ground-breaking history in 1993 and 2001,[1] much had changed in Fiji, but had the lives and attitudes of Melanesians changed as well? There were 44 Melanesian settlements across Fiji as of 2017. Of these, 22 Melanesian communities are in the Central Division, six in the Western Division, six in the Eastern Division, and 10 in the Northern Division. The largest concentration of Melanesian descendants in Fiji are in Suva, and so this is where I spent the majority of my time conducting research. There were a range of attitudes and responses from the communities, as people spoke of the negative impacts of their minority status in Suva, and of the positive improvements to their lives as a result of greater political recognition.

Melanesians have been vulnerable and subjected to various social problems as a result of ongoing developments in the Suva City area. These problems were related to ongoing resettlement plans, as well as disputes among landowning units over the renewal or non-renewal of land leases.[2] Some Melanesian descendants were served with eviction notices after their land leases expired and were forced to resettle in other areas around Fiji. This has generated fear and instability within the Melanesian communities.[3] Although many consider themselves Fijian, they are aware that they may be regarded differently by others. A 70-year-old Melanesian descendant who has been a resident of an informal Melanesian settlement in Suva argued that:

---

1   Winston Halapua, 'A study of the evolution of marginalization: The case of the Solomoni community of Wailoku in Fiji' (PhD thesis, University of the South Pacific, 1993); Winston Halapua, *Living on the fringe: Melanesians in Fiji* (Suva: Institute of Pacific Studies, University of the South Pacific, 2001).
2   Aduru Kuva, *The Solomons community in Fiji* (Suva: South Pacific Social Sciences Association, 1974).
3   Eseta Mateiviti-Tulavu, 'Connecting identities and relationships through indigenous epistemology: The Solomoni of Fiji' (PhD thesis, University of Auckland, 2013).

we consider ourselves equal to our Fijian counterparts and we get on well with them. There was never a sense of racial differences or any derogatory attitude towards us but sometimes we can be conscious of the attitude of others towards us.[4]

Some Melanesian descendants believe that their social isolation has kept them from benefiting from the social and economic contributions and developments offered by the British colonial administration, the Anglican Church and various former governments. One Melanesian descendant mentioned that, 'to some extent, the experience my ancestors encountered has somehow shaped our current situation. We have over the past years been victimized and marginalized'.[5]

In Fiji, prejudices towards Melanesian migrants were formed in the nineteenth century when the colonisers imposed their rule through a hierarchical system. To some extent, the dominant ethnic groups in Fiji since then extended an ethnocentric attitude towards those of Melanesian ancestry perhaps because of their skin colour and origins, but also because of the white colonial attitude to them.[6] The negligence of various governments in the past to adequately recognise Melanesians prompted Melanesian elders in 1987 to form an association a year later known as the Fiji Melanesian Community Development Association, which was renamed the Fiji Melanesian Council in 2014. According to Fiji Melanesian Council General Secretary Paterisio Nunu, the formation of the association came about to:

> manage and administer issues about those of Melanesian descendants and act as a vehicle to voice their aspiration to the government and other organizations, reconnect descendants to their roots and to revive their tradition, culture, and languages, and empower descendants to be proud of their identity as descendants of Melanesian labourers in Fiji.[7]

It has representatives from all Melanesian settlements and was first recognised by the government through the then Department of Multi-Ethnic Affairs.[8] The Fiji Melanesian Community Development

---

4 Personal interview with Serai, a 70-year-old Melanesian descendant in Suva, July 2017.
5 Personal interview with Melanesian descendant, July 2015.
6 Vijay Naidu et al., *Fiji: The challenges and opportunities of diversity* (Suva: CCF & Minority Rights Group International, 2013).
7 Personal interview with Paterisio Nunu, July 2017.
8 In 2011, the Multiethnic Affairs ministry was devolved, and its functions shared out to other ministries.

Association was founded at a time when Fiji was undergoing a major political upheaval, the country's first coup d'état in 1987. It hoped to focus solely on the social, political and economic wellbeing of Melanesians in Fiji, who had been neglected for years, and how government policies could be more meaningfully directed towards their needs.

In 2017, I attended the Fiji Melanesian Council meeting in Suva as an observer. Representatives from diverse Melanesian communities from throughout Fiji attended the council meeting at Marata Village in Wailoku, which was themed 'A Prosperous Fiji Melanesian Community'. The gathering was officially opened by the minister for women, children, and poverty alleviation, and government representatives were also in attendance. The council meeting lasted two days and was held mostly in the iTaukei language, with iTaukei culture and traditional protocols observed. The meeting was interesting in that each Melanesian settlement or village delegate spoke on behalf of their community, presented community updates and suggested ways forward for their community. Representatives from government ministries also spoke to them in iTaukei language about self-help programs, which included rural housing assistance, disaster risk reduction support, and social welfare and poverty alleviation programs in place.

Melanesian settlements initially emerged on low-lying areas and cliffs around Suva that were isolated and undesirable. Living among individuals from the same tribal groups was a way of maintaining their identity and a means of survival. To date, tribal groups have continually negotiated their conditions of stay with landowners through verbal agreements, but as the city has expanded, land has become increasingly valuable and these negotiations have become more difficult. The populations of these settlements have also changed too. Halapua reported in 1993 that in most cases the initial negotiations were for two or three extended families. Based on my fieldwork observations, intermarriage between the iTaukei and Melanesians has continued over time, settlements have grown and the number of people living in each area has increased. In 2015 the general secretary of the Melanesian Council noted that the iTaukei had begun to outnumber Melanesians in many of the settlements and were gradually marrying into Melanesian settlements. In some cases, married couples would bring their families to the settlements too because it was too expensive to rent in Suva and because the Melanesian settlements are conveniently located.

Wailoku

Wailoku is approximately 6.7 kilometres from Suva and was established as a central settlement in Suva to address the issues and challenges of Melanesians becoming marginalised in the newly formed capital. The Anglican Church leased some land at Wailoku from Fiji's Colonial Government for 99 years in 1941, and the agreement was made on the understanding the land would be used to build a central Melanesian settlement in Suva to meet the needs of the Melanesian community. Hence by 1942, most Melanesian descendants and their families were resettled on the property.[9] During one of my interviews with Nunu, he stated that St John's School and a hostel were relocated from Levuka to Wailoku around the same time. Melanesians were divided into tribes by the colonial authorities and the Anglican Church when they arrived at the Wailoku settlement, after careful consideration of their history and languages.[10]

The Wailoku settlement extends over 254 acres on a flood plain beneath the Princess Road towards Lami town. Wailoku became a centralised settlement for the urban scattered Solomon Islanders in different informal settlements within the Suva and Navua corridor.[11] Settlement boundaries were established within Wailoku to encompass the different Solomon Island tribal groups in Fiji. They are the Malaita districts of Koio (Kwaio), Vataleka (Fataleka), Marata ('Are 'Are), Balibuka (Toabaita) and Wai (Ngwai), which make up the tribal groups in Wailoku.[12] In 1974 Kuva noted that about 1,100 people were living in Wailoku.[13] The Wailoku settlement's population is now believed to be over 3,000 people, a significant growth over the past 40 years. As it has expanded, Melanesians have also settled on land not leased by the Anglican Church. In these cases, access is based on customary arrangements with the indigenous landowners (*vakavanua*) or negotiated with private landowners.

The Wailoku community has a predominantly male population, with males outnumbering females. This supports Kuva's finding from 1974 that there were more males than females, probably since females were expected

---

9   Halapua, 'A study of the evolution of marginalization', 45.
10 Mateiviti-Tulavu, 'Connecting identities and relationships through indigenous epistemology'.
11 Personal interview with Paterisio Nunu, July 2015.
12 Mateiviti-Tulavu, 'Connecting identities and relationships through indigenous epistemology'.
13 Kuva, *The Solomons community in Fiji*, 24.

to move to their husband's village if they married men from outside the settlement.[14] Cement block flooring is used throughout Wailoku, with corrugated iron, wood or combined wood and corrugated iron walls. The income inequalities among settlement households, as well as the level of their socio-economic wellbeing, are shown by the variances in house structure. The Anglican Church, with the help of the Fiji Melanesian Council, remains the primary authority in Wailoku and other Melanesian settlements in Fiji, supervising the settlement's activities.[15] Melanesians in each settlement, together with the Fiji Melanesian Council, nominate a *turaga-ni-koro* to look after their village affairs. In an iTaukei village, a *turaga-ni-koro*'s roles and responsibilities include coordinating the activities of the village, representing the village in wider community meetings, maintaining law and order, and representing the settlement to the local government.

Most of Fiji's Melanesian descendants see their future as linked to the land, but they remain a minority group with no traditional land rights, leaving them unable to assert themselves politically, socially or economically. Melanesians consider themselves on the margins in terms of accessing services and opportunities. Within Suva, some Melanesians were able to secure leased land, however they still feel insecure as the chances of being evicted are high. Levy M Laka, a Melanesian descendant in Wailoku, conducted a study in 1983 where he stated:

> The insecurity of the land faced by the Wailoku Melanesian community comes because our forefathers came from the Solomon Islands and that does not entitle us to any land rights even though our mothers are Fijians. We have no rights, no say, and no share in whatever land that belongs to our mothers.[16]

Years later this issue was addressed when, according to Father Tomu Asioli:

> The Standing Committee of the Diocese of Polynesia agreed to transfer the land lease title from the church to the people of Wailoku during its meeting in Samoa in February 2000. This step by the church can be viewed as an opportunity for Melanesians to make use of their potential and resources through collaborative projects and initiatives giving them a sense of responsibility and

---

14 Kuva, *The Solomons community in Fiji*, 24.
15 Personal interview with Paterisio Nunu, July 2015.
16 Levy M Laka, *Solomon Islands descendants in Fiji: A case study of Wailoku* (Suva: University of the South Pacific, 1983).

belonging. The church in its response was pushing Melanesian descendants to utilise their natural skills and abilities of leadership and management.[17]

Wailoku's experience demonstrates that land tenure has always been at the centre of the Melanesian community's efforts and struggles for belonging. Though there is extensive intermarriage with iTaukei, the small Melanesian community continues to retain a distinct identity, and because many cannot claim land rights, they focus on improving their livelihoods through education or employment. Most Melanesian descendants in Fiji are conscious that they are a landless class with only a few having acquired long-term lease holdings. Some still think it is acceptable to live on the church properties in perpetuity, while others hang on to the insecure tenure of an annual lease holding and hope not to be evicted. Some Melanesians in Wailoku or in other informal settlements may not have a legal title to the land they live on but are shown favour by the landowners and continue to live there today. A Melanesian descendant who I interviewed mentioned that: 'We are at the mercy of the landowners who have largely turned us into tenants at will'.[18] Vijay Naidu further asserts that some people are unaware of the processes for purchasing a leasehold property or the costs of leasing, and hold the concern that they will not be given a lease in the first place.[19]

Caubati

Caubati is in Nasinu, approximately 4.2 kilometres from Suva within the Naitāsiri province. The Caubati Melanesian settlement is on native land owned by the Kalabu *mataqali* in the Naitāsiri province. The Melanesian descendants established their settlement there through a verbal agreement of reciprocity with landowners.[20] The Caubati village near the settlement is believed to be a portion of one of the Lands Department's low-cost subdivisions. Several of the lessees had secured loans from the Housing Authority to finance their homes. Halapua states that the settlers were first-generation Melanesians who left the Laqere settlement in 1910 because

---

17   Personal interview with Father Tomu Asioli, June 2015.
18   Naidu et al., *Fiji: The challenges and opportunities of diversity*, 27.
19   Naidu et al., *Fiji: The challenges and opportunities of diversity*, 27.
20   Mateiviti-Tulavu, 'Connecting identities and relationships through indigenous epistemology', 134.

of overcrowding.[21] When Wailoku was first settled, the Melanesians of Caubati were asked to move to the village of Marata in Wailoku; however, because of the abundant space and Caubati's proximity to Suva, Melanesian residents in Caubati refused to relocate. The Native Land Trust Board (NLTB) and Native Land Development Corporation alerted Melanesians in Caubati in 1988 that their lease had expired and that they needed to subdivide the land. They also informed Melanesian settlers that they were illegally occupying the land and had to pay rent.[22] However, Melanesian descendants in Caubati maintained that the lease agreement was for 99 years beginning from 1914. A Melanesian descendant from Caubati mentioned that:

> It was NLTB's attempt to separate us from the land that had been granted to our forefathers. TLTB did not want to extend our lease when it expired in 2013, and instead wanted to subdivide the 25 acres. They served us with eviction notices and took us to court to have us vacate the land, but we won the case.[23]

Melanesians in Caubati still live there, keeping their ties with the landowners by attending *vanua* meetings, reinforcing a pre-existing relationship.[24]

In 1993, the original households at Caubati increased from two to 105.[25] Today approximately 500 people are residing in Caubati with approximately 70 residential homes. There are more women than men; however, like other Melanesian settlements it is dominated by a youthful population. Due to intermarriages with the iTaukei, the settlement contains a population of mixed ethnicities now and is not limited to those of Melanesian origin. About 65 per cent of Melanesians in Caubati have gone on to complete higher education and have secured white-collar jobs, while about 35 per cent are engaged in informal employment.[26] Their income is supplemented by subsistence farming. Over the years, there have been housing and living standard improvements in Caubati that can be attributed to better income-earning opportunities. Caubati settlement, like any other Melanesian settlement, has a *turaga-ni-koro* who

---

21 Laqere is about 1 kilometre away from Muanikoso, where Ni-Vanuatu descendants live and is about 3 kilometres to Caubati. Halapua, 'A study of the evolution of marginalization', 46–47.
22 Halapua, 'A study of the evolution of marginalization', 46–47.
23 Personal interview with a Melanesian descendant from Caubati, July 2017.
24 Mateiviti-Tulavu, 'Connecting identities and relationships through indigenous epistemology', 134.
25 Halapua, 'A study of the evolution of marginalization', 52.
26 Personal interview with Paterisio Nunu, July 2015.

coordinates settlement activities, oversees community projects and is the community liaison representative to the Anglican Church and provincial council meetings.

In Fiji, education is free, and schooling is compulsory for children aged five to 18 years; however, most families in Melanesian informal settlements find that sending their children to school is costly. As a result, some children choose to drop out of school because they believe they are putting their families in financial hardship. Children from Melanesian informal settlements in Suva are not the only economically disadvantaged students who receive free education; poor children from neighbouring informal settlements make for 70 per cent of the materially disadvantaged student ratio.[27] Increasing fees and food prices force families to make compromises elsewhere in their budgets to pay for their children's education. Due to physical impairment (health problems), rising food prices and other necessities for the families' survival, some parents in the settlement are unable to afford their children's educational fees. Financial constraints may prohibit some children from attending school in Melanesian informal settlements, although education is still highly valued. 'Life in a Melanesian informal settlement is not especially promising,' one responder said, 'so we push our children to work and study hard in school since their future is at stake.'[28] For their ancestry, Melanesian descendants have also reported being discriminated against, marginalised and mocked at school. One Melanesian descendant in Caubati said: 'We are victimized not only by the iTaukei but also by the Indo-Fijians … we are teased and made fun of for being a Kai Solomoni'.[29] Discrimination against Melanesian descendants may have a psychological impact as well as an obvious influence on their school performance, resulting in many becoming disadvantaged and marginalised in the communities they live in.

Muanikoso

Muanikoso is located approximately 8.6 kilometres away from Suva in the Naitāsiri province. Approximately 700 residents are living in Muanikoso today, comprising of Melanesian descendants from the New Hebrides and the Solomon Islands. It is predominantly populated by

---

27 Personal interview with Paterisio Nunu, July 2015.
28 Personal interview with a Melanesian descendant in Muanikoso, June 2017.
29 Personal Interview with a Melanesian descendant in Muanikoso, July 2017.

people of New Hebridean origins, many of whom were relocated from Kaunikuila (Flagstaff) due to a hurricane in 1952.[30] After the hurricane, the Anglican Church offered to settle them in Marata village at Wailoku, but they preferred a location at Muanikoso because it was separate from the Solomon Islanders.[31] The Anglican Church over the years assisted the Melanesians with their movement from Kaunikuila to Muanikoso and today continues to provide pastoral support. Similar to other Melanesian settlements, Muanikoso residents are unsure about their land tenure status. The whole of Muanikoso is partitioned into two - The land where those originally from the Solomon Islands live was initially under Crown Lease and is now under the administration of the Housing Authority of Fiji. Those of New Hebrides origins who live in Muanikoso are on reserved native land that belongs to the Kalabu mataqali in the Naitasiri province. One resident mentioned, 'there is also a lack of interest in working the land if it is obtained. What if we get evicted again?'[32]

Churches continue to be the leading authorities within the settlement. In 2018, the Saint Gabriel Anglican Church in Muanikoso was completed and continues to be a place of gathering and worship for the majority of Melanesian descendants in Muanikoso. It is visible from the roadside opposite the old cement factory as you travel through the Nasinu–Nausori corridor. A mixture of iTaukei and Indo-Fijian homeowners now live in the settlement, which was originally dominated by the Melanesian descendants of New Hebrides origin. There are approximately 120 households in the Muanikoso Melanesian settlement. Families are generally comprised of five to eight people, consisting of two adults and four to six children. The houses in the Muanikoso settlement are mostly made of wood and corrugated iron, and some are in terribly dilapidated condition. The growing population in the Muanikoso residential area, like in other Suva informal settlements, has resulted in overcrowding, poor waste disposal, substandard living conditions and increasing social and sanitary issues, all of which can have an impact on the residents' overall health. Also, given the high cost of living, households in informal settlements tend to rely on multiple sources of income or livelihoods to meet their basic needs.

---

30   Fiji Colonial Secretary's Office 1940, 50/81, Part 2, National Archives of Fiji.
31   Halapua, *Living on the Fringe*, 75.
32   Personal interview with a Melanesian descendant from Muanikoso, June 2017.

Conclusion

As far as Fiji history is concerned, there is insufficient acknowledgement of Melanesians' contributions to its development, and in Suva too, Melanesian communities have been sidelined or overlooked. Once numerically small, the Melanesian descendants of Suva are growing to become a more prominent and vocal section of the population. While people of Melanesian descent in Suva share cultural similarities with iTaukei (in terms of language, lifestyles and customs), they are not politically represented, and have limited access to land, education opportunities and commercial opportunities, compared with the ethnic Fijians. Their communities in Fiji are referred to as 'settlements' rather than villages because they do not have secure land tenure. Melanesian communities live on land that was once isolated and undesirable but is now highly lucrative and well positioned in an expanding urban landscape. Wailoku, Caubati and Muanikoso residents are aware that their occupation is tenuous, relying on the generosity of the church or the consent of traditional landowners or governments. They are aware of their ancestors' historic displacement, exploitation and marginalisation, and some remain fearful today that they could be deemed illegal occupants and served with eviction notices.

There has been some progress, however, as Melanesian descendants have grown in number and pushed for greater recognition in Fiji. All the Melanesian settlements in Suva that I visited have greater access to some form of housing, health care and transportation, compared to other rural Melanesians. In 2018, the Fijian Government established affordable housing and lease-related incentives for first-time house buyers, which are open to all Fijians (including Melanesians). Yet the cost of developed land in Suva still remains out of reach for many residents of Melanesian informal communities and low-income earners, and their socio-economic status continues to limit their opportunities compared to other Suva residents. As mentioned by one young Melanesian descendant:

> We are already landless and lack the financial means to build a proper home, most of us live in informal settlements and we make do with whatever materials we can get our hands on.[33]

---

33   Personal interview with a Fiji Melanesian Council Executive Member, June 2017.

Despite the challenges Melanesian labourers and their descendants today face, many of their children and grandchildren have gone on to complete higher education and hold senior positions in various institutions within Fiji. A 25-year-old University of the South Pacific graduate and Melanesian descendant from Caubati told me:

> There are Melanesia descendants with PhD and Master's degrees, some hold senior positions in government and non-governmental organisations, some even hold noble professions. We always try to not allow our community's history and that sense of historical exclusion and deprivation limit us from achieving our dreams. We want our life stories and our narratives to be the game changer, to be a source of inspiration to the younger generation.[34]

Generations of Melanesian descendants believe that their aspirations for reform and a better future are rendered futile without targeted government policies. Affirmative action policies and better educational opportunities will allow them to break free from the vicious cycle of poverty, allowing them to improve living conditions in their communities and access better opportunities.

---

34 Personal interview with a 25-year-old Melanesian descendant from Caubati, October 2021.

18

Suva: Resilient Coup Capital?

Vijay Naidu

This chapter is my personal account of the coups in Fiji, which severely disrupted the lives of people in the country, and especially Suva. I was born in the capital's CBD and grew up in the city, living in police barracks in Samabula and Nasēsē. I attended kindergarten in Suva Street, Suva Methodist Boy's (now Primary) School in Toorak and Marist Brothers High School in Flagstaff. My father was a police corporal. It was fortunate that the University of the South Pacific (USP) began in 1968, which made it possible for me to attend the Prelim/Foundation program in 1970.

Like most other children growing up in Suva I have fond memories of the different games and sports we played. Some of these had distinct seasons such as the kite season, marbles season, and 'top' spinning and fighting season. We played improvised games such as 'pani', 'guli danda' and hide and seek. I learnt how to swim in the Nubukalou Creek and at the Olooloo Cruise Jetty behind the post office. It was in this now rather polluted creek that I learnt how to fish for a range of estuarine fishes.[1]

Suva was generally a peaceful city in the 1950s and 1960s. The exception to this was during the 1959 riots that accompanied the Wholesale and Retail General Workers' Union strike, which resulted in damages to mainly European-owned businesses. Otherwise rowdiness in the city related to the Christmas and New Year festivities when buckets of water

---

1   During the *kaikai* (striped pony fish) and *ki* (goat fish) seasons, scores of women, men and children would fish sitting side by side on the banks of the Nubukalou Creek, the local wharf and in the Walu Bay area, and just about everyone would catch enough fish to take home.

were thrown on people, and noisy weekend drunks who spent a night at the Central Police Station in Totogo. Political strife and military coups are postcolonial phenomenon of different order and magnitude.

Like many citizens who left the country to settle abroad following each one of the extra-legal takeovers of democratically elected governments, I took up employment at the Victoria University of Wellington in New Zealand in 2003, only to return in 2007 to experience life under yet another military-sponsored government.[2]

In Fiji's tumultuous post-Independence history of 51 years, Suva, the capital city, has experienced four military coups that usurped political power from democratically elected national governments, replacing them with military dictatorships, new constitutions and novel electoral systems to suit the coup-makers, and reversion to supposedly civilian governments. The capital city, called the 'Hub of the South Pacific', is no stranger to unrest and mayhem.

This chapter is based on my personal recollections of the Suva experience of the 1987, 2000 and 2006 coups. To jog my memory, I have relied on news articles published in the *Fiji Times*, and a number of scholarly publications. The discussion will centre especially on the 2000 putsch, hostage taking, military coup and mutiny, as this period of prolonged turbulence was the most disruptive and violent.

The 1987 Coups

On the morning of Thursday 14 May 1987, I was standing by the counter on the ground floor of the USP Library, then located in the Communications Building,[3] when Basant Swann, one of the Indo-Fijian librarians, whispered to me with fear in her eyes that the military had toppled the government. She feared that there might be a repeat of what happened to Indians in Uganda under Idi Amin. I muttered a few words of reassurance along the lines of, 'it was too early to say', and for her to be mindful of her personal safety, and hurried to my office. Academic

---

2   I applied for the position of associate professor and director of development studies in the School of Geography, Environment and Earth Sciences in the Faculty of Science at Victoria University of Wellington in 2002, and was appointed as professor and chair of the program from February 2003 to December 2007. I left VUW because the late Mr Savenaca Siwatibau, the former vice-chancellor of USP had agreed to my request for leave without pay.

3   In December 2018 this building was severely damaged in a massive fire.

colleagues confirmed that the military had overthrown the month-long Fiji Labour Party (FLP) and National Federation Party (NFP) Coalition Government. I had supported the formation of FLP, and was a founding member of the party.

I hurried home to the USP-owned house that I rented at 16 Telau Street, a block away from the Laucala campus. Close friends and activists in the Fiji Anti-Nuclear Group (FANG) and FLP came by to discuss the evolving situation. I learned on the radio[4] that at 10 am on that day 12 gas-masked and balaclava-clad soldiers of the then Royal Fiji Military Forces (RFMF) led by Colonel Sitiveni Ligamamada Rabuka, with guns drawn, barged into the Parliament of Fiji and detained the democratically elected prime minister, Dr Timoci Uluivuda Bavadra, and the government members of parliament. This treason at 10[5] followed in the wake of orchestrated public protests, road blocks, fire bombing and arson in various towns and cities of the country including the capital. The perpetrators of this violent destabilisation were indigenous Fijians.[6]

In the evening, a number of us visited the deposed prime minister, Dr Timoci Uluivuda Bavadra's Laucala Beach Estate house, to express our empathy for and solidarity with his wife, Kuini Bavadra, and their children. Apparently, a gun had been fired in the vicinity of the house. In the early hours of the morning large stones were thrown at my immediate neighbour's USP-owned house, damaging window louvres and security screens. As Professor Bob Briscoe's home was in the same compound as my USP-owned house, and as he was not directly involved in Fiji politics, we agreed that those who pelted his house had mistakenly thought it was mine!

I knew that I would be a possible target of the extremists and the army as I was among a group of USP academics who participated in the Fiji Trades Union Congress deliberations that led to the formation of the FLP, and I had published a working paper in the party's participation in a by-election.[7]

---

4   FM96's Peter Thompson was perhaps the first journalist to report of the armed takeover of parliament and government.
5   Kenneth Bain, *Treason at ten: Fiji at the crossroads* (London: Hodder and Stoughton Ltd, 1989).
6   Not all iTaukei supported the coup. A number of villages and settlements put up banners and placards in support of the FLP–NFP government. Ethno-nationalist Fijians maintained, 'all true Fijians support the coup'.
7   Vijay Naidu, *The Fiji Labour Party and the by-election of December 1985: A report*, SSED Working Paper no. 2 (Suva: School of Economic and Social Development, University of the South Pacific, 1986). Other FLP-supporting colleagues included William Sutherland, Wadan Narsey, Atu Bain, Claire Slatter, Tupeni Baba, Sitiveni Ratuva, Satendra Prasad, Simione Durutalo and Michael Howard.

Interestingly, in the days that followed the coup, Navitalia Naisoro, Institute of Development Studies Sussex University graduate and a friend – and soon to be permanent secretary – and a man he introduced as Frazer, had turned up at my house to warn me that if 'if I didn't want my legs cut off at the knees' then I should not say anything or do anything to oppose the coup.

Rabuka claimed that the military coup d'état was a pre-emptive action to ensure the 'security of life and property'[8] and prevent bloodshed.[9] The commander of RFMF, Brigadier General Ratu Epeli Nailatikau, and his deputy, Chief of Staff Colonel Jim Sanday, were pushed aside as further acts of disloyalty. Rabuka and the RFMF refused to 'return to their lawful allegiance in accordance with the oath of office and their duty of obedience without delay' as required by the governor-general[10] who then declared a state of emergency. The real reason for the RFMF's unprecedented action lay elsewhere.

In the general election of April 1987, the fifth since Independence, the indigenous Fijian chief-led Alliance Party was defeated at the polls by a multiethnic coalition of the newly formed FLP and the NFP. The coalition obtained 28 seats to the Alliance's 24. Although the leader of this coalition was Dr Timoci Bavadra, a medical doctor and an indigenous Fijian from the 'West', the genuinely multiethnic government (cabinet comprised six Fijians, one general elector and seven Indo-Fijians) that was formed was perceived to be 'Indian'. The Fiji Chamber of Commerce, the Fiji Manufacturers' Association and the Duty-Free Dealers Association, farmers' and workers' organisations, expressed their support for the new government, and the prime minister said that the 'overriding mood of Fiji has been one of orderly and peaceful transition'.[11]

However, defeated indigenous Fijian Alliance Party politicians, some of whom were now in the parliamentary opposition, began agitation and civil unrest. Protest marches were held in urban centres and in the

---

8   'Army seizes power coup', *Fiji Times*, 15 May 1987.
9   Rabuka had been disaffected as the third ranking officer in RFMF. He was also angry that the Alliance Party had lost the general election. When approached by three coup conspirators, he readily agreed to overthrow the duly elected government. See JR Sharpham, *Rabuka of Fiji* (Rockhampton: Central Queensland University Press, 2000).
10 Sharpham, *Rabuka of Fiji*.
11 *Fiji Times*, 16 April 1987.

capital. An ethno-nationalist and racist Taukei Movement mobilised to orchestrate these protests. One of its leaders asserted that the movement had dedication to its people as the Nazis had been to Germans![12]

On Friday 24 April, Suva was tense with 100 uniformed police from the Nubukalou Creek bridge to Albert Park on patrol as thousands of indigenous Fijians marched through the city, carrying placards, singing and chanting. Their petition was submitted to the governor-general, Ratu Sir Penaia Ganilau by Viliame Gonelevu, Ratu Inoke Kubuabola and Ratu Inoke Tavuyava. Protesters' banners included, 'Fiji for the Fijians', 'Stop the Indian Government', 'Noqu Kalou, Noqu Vanua' (my God, my land), 'Reddy Gun, Bavadra Bullet', 'Fiji New Little India. Say No'. The petition rejected the Bavadra Government, called for the paramountcy and rule by indigenous Fijians, and the immediate change of the 1970 Independence constitution. I observed the protest march along Victoria Arcade from near the ANZ Building and was surprised that one of my senior university colleagues and his wife were among the protesters!

The protest march was peaceful. However, Ratu Sir Kamisese Mara, the former prime minister, having graciously conceded defeat[13] in the general election and called for a smooth transition, remained silent during the subsequent episodes of protest and violence that were to follow.[14] Following the armed intrusion in the Parliament, Bavadra and his government members were bundled into a military truck and taken to the Queen Elizabeth Barracks in Nabua in the outskirts of Suva. Late in the night, the prime minister, his ministers and members of parliament (MPs) were transported and held at the prime minister's residence in Veiuto. Crowds of people gathered in the vicinity to express their support for the detained leaders, guarded by heavily armed soldiers. Early on the following Tuesday, the hostage MPs were forcefully divided into two ethnic groups – Indo-Fijians were taken to Borron House in Samabula, and indigenous Fijians, including the prime minister, continued to be held in the prime minister's official residence.

---

12   Robbie Robertson, *The general's goose: Fiji's tale of contemporary misadventure* (Canberra: ANU Press, 2017), 62, doi.org/10.22459/GG.08.2017.
13   It was said that Dr James Maraj, the former vice-chancellor of USP who became an adviser to Ratu Mara, had written the statement.
14   *Fiji Times*, 11 April 1987 and 26 April 1987.

My friend, Amelia Rokotuivuna, led a protest march with FLP supporters, mostly young Indo-Fijians from Veiuto along the Queen Elizabeth Drive towards the Government Buildings. The group was disbanded by the police and Amelia was arrested. Following the stone-throwing incident at Bob Briscoe's house, and after receiving warnings that the military were searching for me, I went into hiding. In fact, one late afternoon I managed to narrowly escape soldiers who had parked across the junction of Varani and Telau Street. I drove past them as they waved for me to stop my vehicle. Once inside my yard, I closed the gate. Shortly thereafter I received a phone call from the Raiwaqa Police Station asking me to attend a meeting with military officer, Tarakinikini. I refused. Colleagues and friends sheltered me. For a week or so George and Diane Greg hosted me at their flat on Williamson Road that overlooks Albert Park. I also stayed with Jacques and Eugenia Nicole at their house in the compound of the Pacific Theological College.

Although the deposed prime minister, government ministers and MPs were released after six days, much to the rejoicing crowds of families, friends and supporters, the situation in Suva remained uncertain, insecure and turbulent. Labour Party supporters and FANG members continued to be targeted.[15] The banks and supermarkets reported heavy pressure on their services as people rushed to withdraw funds, and staple items in the shops ran out. Similar trends were reported in other urban centres.

After the two Suva-based dailies' editorials strongly condemned the coup on 15 May, armed soldiers entered the premises of all media organisations and shut them down for six days, following which there was censorship of the media by the military.[16] The Australian Broadcasting Commission (ABC)'s news broadcasts became the primary source of information about the unfolding events in Fiji. Foreign journalists were taken from the Travel Lodge and Suva streets for questioning by soldiers.[17] The latter also raided the rooms of six other overseas journalists at the Courtesy Inn, confiscating tapes and notebooks.[18] Buses stopped running in the city, and the pressure on the Immigration Department to issue passports

---

15 A number of them eventually left the country as refugees.
16 *Fiji Times*, 21 May 1987.
17 *Fiji Times*, 21 May 1987.
18 *Fiji Times*, 21 May 1987.

increased. By the end of the month 10,000 applications for new passports were received, and visa officials in the Australian and New Zealand High Commissions reported 500 to 700 applications a day.[19]

More widely, there were threats by trade unions of strike action, and farmers refused to harvest sugar cane. Tourists stopped arriving, and hotels and resorts reported widespread cancellations of bookings.[20] There was an attempted hijacking of an Air New Zealand jumbo airliner at the Nadi Airport. Schools in Suva reported low school attendance and early closures. USP brought forward its semester break and study leave to close the institution; Indo-Fijian students left for their homes and overseas students also departed, including in chartered flights to their home countries in the region and elsewhere.[21]

Rabuka sought to name a 'Council of Ministers' that included himself, Ratu Mara and other prominent members of the defeated Alliance Party, while the governor-general named a 19-member Council of Advisors that largely comprised the same Alliance Party people, Dr Bavadra and his deputy, Mr Harish Sharma, as well as two or three independent persons. Bavadra, Sharma and Rev. Daniel Mustapha, a former head of the Methodist Church, declined to be advisers.

Even though the state of emergency proscribed unauthorised public gatherings, a large crowd of indigenous Fijians had gathered in the vicinity of the Suva Civic Centre where the Great Council of Chiefs (GCC) began meeting after the coup. They sang hymns and popular songs, and responded to speakers who addressed them. The governor-general, Ratu Sir Penaia, was subjected to 'an unprecedented show of disrespect for a high chief' when he was booed by the 3,000 strong Fijian crowd gathered at the Civic Centre.[22] Rabuka received roars of approval by the same crowd, as he shouted, 'Sa nodana naqaqa (We have won)'. The hitherto silent Ratu Sir Kamisese also addressed the crowd, and in the evening some chiefs danced with women in the crowd.[23]

---

19 'Passport applicants besiege Immigration Office in Suva', *Fiji Times*, 30 May 1987, 10.
20 'Heavy cancellations hit hotels and resorts in Fiji', *Fiji Times*, 26 May 1987, 8.
21 *Fiji Times*, 22 May 1987.
22 *Fiji Times*, 22 May 1987.
23 *Fiji Times*, 22 May 1987.

SUVA STORIES

Besides this hubbub of activity, Suva had become a ghost town after the riots, rampaging, arson, stoning and looting by indigenous Fijian youths on Wednesday 19 May.[24] Suva lay silent on Thursday. 'Most shops, the post-office, doctors' surgeries, bus services remained shut … '[25] The victims of this violence were Indo-Fijians, men and women, old and young who were in the city at that time,[26] and those who were gathering in Albert Park for a prayer meeting. Sweet sellers and market vendors were attacked, and their produce and stalls destroyed. They were kicked, punched and hit with sticks and iron rods. Cars driven by Indo-Fijians and those who looked Indo-Fijian were stoned.[27] Some indigenous Fijian office workers, a retired boxer, and the police sought to protect Indo-Fijians caught up in the chaos in Suva's main streets extending from Rodwell Road, the Suva market and bus stand, Victoria Arcade and Queen Elizabeth Drive.[28] Houses and business premises were stoned and broken into and looted in many suburbs of Suva, and this lawlessness spread to Nausori, Korovou and Navua.

According to the *Fiji Times*, 'from Lami, Delainavesi to Wainibokasi in Nausori, and in the interior from Tacirua to Sawani' rowdy gangs destroyed property, robbed homes and struck fear among Indo-Fijian residents. Stones, sticks and iron rods were used by these gangs. For much of Wednesday and Thursday, residents battened their property and took steps to defend themselves. In one incident in Samabula, an Indo-Fijian shop keeper fired a gun and wounded an indigenous Fijian youth.[29] A bus company owner relied on men from a neighbouring indigenous Fijian village to protect his buses and property.

Indo-Fijians were fearful of their safety and security while the courts were kept busy adjudicating numerous cases of rioting, arson, looting, assault and damage to property. Led by the chief justice, Timoci Tuivaga, judges and magistrates maintained their firm loyalty to the governor-general.

---

24 *Fiji Times*, 22 May 1987.
25 'Suva lies silent', *Fiji Times*, 22 May 1987, 2.
26 'Mob quelled as violence flares', *Fiji Times*, 21 May 1987, 3.
27 A well-known indigenous Fijian rugby referee's car was stoned by rampaging youths who mistook him for an Indo-Fijian (personal communication).
28 My good friend the late Kisor Chetty was attacked by a group along Carnavon Street, and an iTaukei man stepped out of his office block to pull him indoors to safety.
29 'Rowdy gangs strike homes in Suva area', *Fiji Times*, 22 May 1987, 3.

They were joined by the high chief, Ratu Jone Madraiwiwi, and 59 other members of the legal profession.[30] The chief justice advised the governor-general on constitutional and other matters pertaining to the rule of law.

I found it quite dismaying on how the leading chiefs dealt with the matters at hand. The three-day GCC passed a number of motions including maintaining ties with the British monarchy; amnesty for Rabuka and other RFMF military personnel responsible for the coup; a government backed by the military comprising the Council of Advisers; an appeal to the governor-general that Mohammed Apisai Tora and Senator Jone Qio (on bail for $400 and $10,000 respectively) be given amnesty as their alleged crimes were political in nature; to raise $500 per province to fund their legal defence if the governor-general was not able to grant them amnesty; to request the governments of India, Australia, New Zealand and United States to accept all Indo-Fijians who wished to leave the country, and the Fiji Government to pay for the repatriation; and to replace the 1970 constitution with a constitution that ensured the paramountcy of indigenous Fijian interests.[31] A letter writer responding to John Moses's feature article[32] on the coup and its negative short and long-term aftermath asserted that: 'Democracy is a foreign flower – wrong soil'.[33]

A group of male Indo-Fijian students who lived in a house at the junction of Grantham Road and Telau Street got implicated in a number of bombing incidents.[34] Some of these students were known to me and occasionally visited my house. The police found that a number of the explosive devices were wrapped on computer printing papers that came from a USP lab. The students were interrogated and tortured. One of them, whose soccer team I helped to coach during his high school days at Suva Grammar School, had his arm broken as soldiers assaulted him. Moses Driver, a senior police officer, arrived at my home following the bombing incidents to question me about my possible involvement with the group of students. He and his team thoroughly searched every room of the house and paid close attention to all the containers of oil, kerosene and cleaning materials. They also compared samples of computer printing paper to printed material that I had in my study.

---

30   'Chief Justice's role in the rising crisis', *Fiji Times*, 21 May 1987.
31   *Fiji Times*, 27 May 1987.
32   *Fiji Times*, 22 May 1987.
33   '"Foreign flower" letter by Adi Finau Tabakaucoro', *Fiji Times*, 28 May 1987, 6.
34   An Indo-Fijian technical staff at USP lost his life as a result of sustaining injuries when an explosive device was accidentally triggered in his car.

The Back to Early May Movement

I joined some well-respected Suva people who had begun a petition that was labelled the 'Back to Early May Movement' in support of the governor-general's efforts at returning to constitutionality and negotiated settlement between those who supported the deposed government and those who supported the coup and its objectives. Members of the clergy, professional people, academics, representatives of civil society organisations, business people and former civil servants led the movement. Over a relatively short time, large numbers of people signed the petition, which was presented to the governor-general.

It is unclear what impact the petition had but the governor-general, between May and September, was able to mediate between Dr Timoci Bavadra's deposed government and the defeated Alliance Party leadership led by the interim prime minister, Ratu Mara. An accord that was to be known as Deuba Accord was signed on 23 September. There was optimism of a government of national unity that would take the country forward but this was not to be. Rabuka and his ethno-nationalist supporters became increasingly restive as the governor-general's mediation was underway.

In early September, three weeks before the second RFMF coup d'état, an especially unpleasant incident involved the reggae band, 'Rootstrata', whose members dug up a *lovo* pit across from the Parliament in close proximity to Ratu Sir Lala Sukuna's statue, and threatened to cook my friend Richard Naidu, a prominent local lawyer and adviser to Dr Bavadra. Acts of violence, house breaking and robbery, and random mugging escalated to arson and looting of commercial premises. Brij Lal wrote:

> Shops in central Suva parts of the city were torched with petrol bombs and looted in smash-and-grab raids, and Fiji's only medical laboratory, belonging to a known Coalition supporter (Dr Karam Singh) was razed to the ground … Further violence was prevented only after the military erected roadblocks and installed checkpoints at strategic points in the city.[35]

Lawlessness reached epic proportion on 23 September when prison guards supportive of the Taukei Movement released more than 100 prisoners to march from the Nabora Prison, in Suva's hinterland to the

---

35   Brij V Lal, *In the eye of the storm* (Canberra: ANU E Press, 2010), 402, doi.org/10.22459/ES.11.2010.

Governor-General's Residence. They were hurried through the capital's Victoria Parade by their guards to meet the governor-general to submit their objections regarding the court action brought against Ratu Penaia Ganilau by Dr Timoci Bavadra, and to pay their respect to the high chief. They were hosted in the head of state's compound and provided breakfast. Needless to say, for Suva residents, this event of convicted criminals being paraded through the city to the Government House to make their petition and hosted to breakfast was most shocking.

However, an even more traumatic event was unleased a few days later. Dissatisfied and frustrated at being left out of the negotiation process, Rabuka, supported by the extremist ethno-nationalist Taukei Movement, staged the second coup on 28 September.[36] Once again, the military commander appeared on the television screen and the media to declare that he had taken over the government. Soldiers raided and occupied media buildings and airports, and made excursions on the Laucala Campus of USP to take over the satellite communication hub. The armed military was suddenly seen everywhere in twin-cab Toyota utilities and larger trucks. Ethno-nationalist Fijians freely moved around the city. Shops were shuttered and closed, and the media was censored. The Fijian Broadcasting Commission (FBC) played sombre music as announcements were made by Rabuka and/or the governor-general.

Steven Ratuva and I were at my home in Telau Street when Claire Slatter informed us about the coup and that the military was rounding up FLP supporters. We hurried to her place on Beach Road at Suva Point but as night fell, she received a phone call saying that soldiers were coming to detain her. The nightly curfew had begun. We agreed that it was best that Steven and I left the house via the back door. The two of us walked about 100 metres and Steven suggested that we should take different routes so that we were not apprehended together. It began to drizzle. As I anxiously crossed the little park at the junction of Beach Road and Catalina Drive, I contemplated if I should spend the night in a nearby mango tree! It suddenly occurred to me that my USP colleagues and friends Morgan

---

36   At a Citizens Constitutional Forum public consultation in 2012, Rabuka explained that he 'wasn't a tissue paper to be used and cast aside'!

and Eileen Tuimaleali'ifano lived just nearby. I called out their names, and got an immediate welcoming response from Morgan who said watch out for the dog. My relief at this turn of events was overwhelming![37]

Early the following morning Morgan and Eileen's eldest son, John, and I walked along Queen Elizabeth Drive and the USP fenced compound until we were near the clump of mangroves. He pointed to the hole in fence through which I crawled, saying goodbye and thank you to him. I walked through the bush and crossed the park to get to Epeli and Barbara Hau'ofa's house. I stayed with them for a few days until someone tried to phone me. I was supposed to be incognito. We decided that I should leave. I then spent a few days at Rajesh and Dharma Chandra's place on campus. They too were kind hosts but as I did not want to jeopardise their safety, I travelled to Nakasi and stayed with close friends for two nights. I got frustrated with hiding from the police and military and after close to two weeks, I returned to my USP office and called the police inquiring why they were looking for me.

Senior Superintendent of Police Qalo Bulatiko turned up at my office accompanied by two constables. One of them frisked me in case I carried any weapons. I was asked to accompany them to the police station wagon that had been donated to them by Westpac Bank. Bulatiko got me to sit in the boot of the car! At the main gate of the campus, the then vice-chancellor, Geoffrey Caston, tried unsuccessfully to wave the police vehicle down. Bulatiko declared that 'the white man must be careful, otherwise he'll leave the country in a coffin'.

At the Central Police Station, a policeman took my details and got me to empty my pockets and to give him my trouser belt. I was then put into a cell that smelled of urine and excreta. Later in the day, the renowned comedian John Mohammed joined me in the same cell. As in the first coup, scores of people were detained by the military and police. Those who led the 'Back to Early May Movement' and supporters of FLP and NFP were targeted. Suva stood at a standstill as armed soldiers took control of the streets.

---

37 Steven Ratuva somehow managed to stay in the shadows and eventually found a safe house to stay in for the night. Armed soldiers and police led by Senior Superintendent of Police Qalo Bulatiko arrived in three vehicles at Claire Slatter's house. Having asked whether she was Claire Slatter, he inquired if I had been at the house. He held a pistol in his hand, and used a torch to search the house including under the bed in one of the bedrooms. Claire was driven to the Central Police Stations and put in a cell.

Late at night, the police drove me to the Queen Elizabeth Barracks in Nabua, and handed me to the military. I was put into a cell, and heard voices that sounded familiar. A number of FLP members were in the neighbouring cells. They included Kenneth Zinck and Richard Naidu. Stories were shared in the midst of laughter and much bantering about how each one got arrested and his experience with the police and/or the military. The prisoners tried to make light of their predicament. A day or two later, in the company of armed soldiers, Richard Naidu and I were driven in separate Toyota Hilux twin-cab utilities to the back of the Korovou Gaol. Here we were locked away in separate, rather dusty, cells once used to hold death row inmates. We were kept in these cells for at least two days, and on the morning of the third day each one of us were subject to severe beatings by soldiers, and to psychological torture.

I was told that 'educated Indians like you are the problem', that as an academic 'you are like an underwater reef that harmed boats' and that 'you damaged the country by teaching the wrong things to your students'. I was told that I could be killed and my body could be disposed of in Suva Harbour, and nobody would be the wiser. This caused me a lot of trauma and I was also in great pain from what was diagnosed as a hair line fracture caused either by a boot or the butt of a gun struck on my ribs. During my detention, the university's registrar, on the direction of the vice-chancellor, got USP's lawyers to prepare a habeas corpus petition for me to submit to the courts.

Rabuka, as RFMF commander and head of the military government, imposed the Sunday Observance Decree that prohibited the playing of sports, public transport, 'non-essential work', trading, picnicking and other leisure activities on Sundays.[38] The dominant faction of the Methodist Church and its supporters set up roadblocks in various parts of Suva City including on Queen Elizabeth Drive and the country to stop and question motorists. Soldiers and police apprehended Indo-Fijians playing soccer or found engaged in activities deemed to be proscribed or if they were near picnic spots. Suspected Indo-Fijian offenders were often mistreated – slapped, kicked and tortured.

---

38   Fiji Military Government, 'Sunday Observance Decree 1987', Pacific Islands Legal Information Institute, 11 November 1987, www.paclii.org/fj/promu/promu_dec/sod1987206/.

Suspicions between indigenous Fijians and Indo-Fijians and other minorities increased in Suva and elsewhere in the country. There were rumours of fruits and vegetables being poisoned at the local Suva market, and of indigenous Fijians reporting on Indo-Fijian employers. Snitching by indigenous employees, including domestic workers, gardeners, cleaners (even in hospitals), secretaries and students (at USP) and others, on what their Indo-Fijian employers and staff were doing increased as the police and military hounded those who opposed the coups.

Fiji had been declared a republic in October; its membership of the Commonwealth lapsed and the 1970 Independence constitution was abrogated. It was not long before the coup leader realised that the country had taken a disastrous turn. In December of 1987, paramount chiefs Ratu Penaia Ganilau and Ratu Mara were returned to power as allies of Rabuka. The former transitioned from governor-general to president of the strange new republic, and the latter as prime minister.

A number of protests were made against the coup and Rabuka. These included a well-orchestrated protest, despite the presence of police and the military and roadblocks along Rodwell Road, by a few courageous women at the premiere of *Rabuka – No Other Way* at the Phoenix Theatre. They wore T-shirts that suggested that 'there were other ways'. Seven of these women were arrested. On the anniversary of the coup a number of us, later called the 'Democracy 17' by the Fiji media, were arrested for unlawfully gathering in Sukuna Park with anti-coup and pro-democracy banners. Among those arrested were nine women and two Irish Catholic priests'.

While in the prison in the Central Police Station, we discovered that Father Paul Tierney was a great singer who knew the words of 'Streets of London' by heart. We sang hymns and popular resistance songs. We sang most loudly the Fijian national anthem, especially the verse, 'the land of freedom, hope and glory'. This upset the police who, having failed to silence us by shouting 'shut up', proceeded to reverse a large police truck and rev up its engine so that the cells could fill up with noxious exhaust. Fortunately, for us, the breeze and the elevated angle of the truck blew much of the exhaust fumes away.

A number of constitutional review commissions were convened. These included one chaired by Sir John Falvey, and another by Colonel Paul Manueli. I remember making a submission to the Falvey commission and being interrogated by Apisai Tora on my views on what were the provisions of a fair and just constitution. The 1990 constitution was imposed by the military-backed regime. It paid little regard to the submissions made by FLP, NFP and civil society organisations. It was described as feudalistic and racist and was promulgated by the president, and endorsed by the GCC.

Coup leader Rabuka became the elected prime minister following the 1992 general election under the 1990 constitution and its electoral system of entirely communal representation, with 37 of the 70 seats in parliamentary allocated to indigenous Fijians. The chiefs also endorsed the Soqosoqo Vakavulewa ni Taukei (SVT) Party led by Rabuka.

In the early 1990s with deep divisions between political leaders, I joined a number of concerned people inspired by Martin Ennals of Amnesty International and Professor Yash Ghai to form the Citizens Constitutional Forum (CCF). The founding members were from the university, churches, professions and trade unions who wanted to promote peaceful dialogue among political and community leaders and citizens to find common ground regarding the constitutional crisis and to bridge divisions. The principles of democracy and accountability as the bases of governance guided the discussions. A number of national consultations were held on specific aspects of a broadly acceptable constitution. These included electoral systems, power sharing, communal and indigenous interests, and land. International experts in these areas were invited to share their experience, knowledge and advice participants. According to a 1995 CCF report:

> Religious leaders, politicians, academics, unionists, educators, lawyers, social workers and concerned citizens from different backgrounds met in a spirit of conciliation. Broad agreement was reached on the issues of electoral system, power sharing, ethnic interests, accountability, independence of the judiciary and the military.[39]

Meanwhile, the show of ethnic solidarity among indigenous Fijian political leaders was short-lived because of divisions within SVT. The 1994 Fiji national budget was not passed because of the split. The government was compelled to return to the polls. The SVT party was re-elected but

---

39   Citizens Constitutional Forum, *One nation diverse peoples: Building a just and democratic Fiji* (Suva: Citizens Constitutional Forum, September 1995), 2.

needed Mahendra Chaudry's FLP support to form government, and for Rabuka to remain prime minister. He was to hold this position until the 1999 general election.

In accordance with the review provision in the 1990 constitution, a three-person constitutional review commission (CRC) was appointed by the government in consultation with the opposition. Sir Paul Revees, a former archbishop and governor-general of New Zealand was the chair and Tomasi Vakatora, a former parliamentary speaker, and Professor Brij Lal were the two members. Led by Ratu Joni Madraiwiwi, a number of CCF members and I made the CCF submission to the CRC based on the booklet, 'One Nation Diverse Peoples' subtitled, 'Building a Just and Democratic Fiji'. The CCF presentation was one of 852 submissions made to the CRC. The commission made numerous recommendations that significantly changed the 1990 constitution.

The 2000 Putsch, Hostage Taking and Coup

Following the review of the 1990 constitution and the introduction of a relatively complicated electoral system with a preferential alternative vote arrangement in the 1997 constitution, the FLP won a resounding victory in the 1999 general election. It allied with a minority ethnic Fijian political party to form government. In deciding not to follow the power-sharing provision of the 1997 constitution, FLP antagonised the SVT party. Its new leader, Ratu Inoke Kubuabola, promised to prevent the government from completing its term in office. However, unlike the 1987 military coup d'état that replaced the Bavadra Government in a month, the FLP-led government remained in power for a year.

Mahendra Pal Chaudhary became Fiji's very first Indo-Fijian prime minister. This in itself caused some initial controversy but the president, Ratu Mara, was able to persuade minority party Taukei MPs to work with Chaudhary. The government managed the economy well, and increased the allocation of poverty alleviation funds and initiated taxation review, as well as other pro-poor polices. However, in removing certain individuals from statutory boards, and in trying to establish a land use commission as well as appointing his own son as his private secretary, Chaudhary increased the number of people opposed to him. He appeared to have alienated some wealthy Indo-Fijian businessmen over taxation matters. He also antagonised the media, which portrayed him as arrogant.

These provided fuel to his political opponents and especially ethno-nationalists to destabilise the country. Against the advice of his minister for home affairs, and later on the commissioner of police, he allowed the SVT opposition, the Taukei Movement and other ethno-nationalists to hold protest marches in the capital. Three such anti-government ethno-nationalist protests were held with increasing numbers of demonstrators. The last on 19 May was said to have 10,000, protesters making it the largest in the history of protest marches in the city. The protest leaders were supposed to submit their petition to the president at the entrance of the presidential compound.

While attention was focused on the protest, nine Revolutionary Warfare Unit (CRW) soldiers of the RFMF entered Parliament and took the prime minister and the government MPs hostage. The former head of the Fiji Hardwood Corporation, described subsequently as a failed businessman, George Speight, became their spokesman and leader. I can recall a period of confusion as it was not at all clear if those who had seized the prime minister and his government had the support of the military as a whole. Like other people I was aghast that during the first two weeks of the forceful takeover of the legislature, large quantities of arms and ammunitions were transferred from the military armoury to the parliamentary complex. The haul was exhibited to local and overseas journalists by a former British Army special forces retiree who claimed to have trained the CRW soldiers and hostage takers.[40]

Groups of youth who had been part of the protest march entered the parliamentary complex and formed a human shield for the hostage takers. Other groups of youth rampaged through central Suva smashing shop windows, looting, burning and trashing a number of shops. Indo-Fijian men, women and children were attacked, punched and kicked. The police and some indigenous Fijians attempted to protect some of them. There was mayhem in the capital and the police largely failed to deal with the situation. For reasons that were never revealed, the police mobile force, together with its gear and transport, were not used to quell

---

40 Ex-British SAS Major Ilisoni Ligairi had been approached by Rabuka to help establish and train the First Meridian Squadron or Counter Revolutionary Warfare Unit following the 1987 coup.

the rioting. In the wake of the violence, throngs of indigenous Fijians helped themselves to clothing, electrical goods, kitchen wares, alcohol and foodstuff from shops and supermarkets. Supermarket trolleys were used to cart some of the stolen items to various residential areas as far away as Delainavesi, and to informal settlements.

The *Fiji Times* reported that by midday on Friday 19 May, schools in the Suva area had closed. Parents rushed to pick up their children to take them to the safety of their homes. The fire brigade sped to the CBD and to Toorak to put out burning shops that had been looted and trashed. Shops were barricaded and/or cordoned off, and banks shut their doors. Supermarkets in the suburbs of Samabula, Nabua and along the way to Nausori, and in Nausori, did brisk business. Traffic queued on either side of the Suva peninsula as scores of people drove out of the city. On Saturday morning, city council workers and shop owners and their employees cleared away shattered shop display window glass and other debris while having to put up with the stench of rotting food.

Another sight to behold at this time was the hundreds of indigenous Fijians from the provinces of Rewa, Tailevu and Ra (some of whom were related to George Speight) arriving at the parliamentary complex bearing gifts of foodstuff, kava and clothes. They too became part of the human shield in the complex.

In the ensuing 56 days of holding the elected prime minister, his cabinet and backbenchers hostage, mob violence, looting and trashing of shops and residential premises continued. The national TV station, TV One, was attacked by an angry mob of George Speight supporters following a candid interview with my friend and CCF member Jone Dakuvula, a prominent political analyst whose very clear message was that Speight was not genuine in his declaration of being an ethnic Fijian nationalist leader as he had no record whatsoever of being one. The mob smashed windows and doors and destroyed equipment as TV journalists and staff hurriedly escaped through the back door.

There were frequent rumours of mobs of iTaukei youth heading to the president's compound, to central Suva, to USP etc. – with each one of these rumours, schools closed. Parents rushed to pick up their children. Parents also stopped sending children to schools. USP had several periods of stops and starts. In the midst of the civil unrest and political crisis there were power cuts and water supply problems. Lawlessness, looting, burning of homes and assaults, sexual abuse and rapes spread to some neighbouring rural hinterland. In one rather surprisingly blatant case that was televised, a police truck was loaded with the carcass of a bull and bundles of taro and driven back to the parliamentary complex. All these items were forcefully stolen from Indo-Fijian farmers in Muaniweni, Naitāsiri.

These farmers had their houses stoned, looted and trashed by gangs of youths from neighbouring villages. They and their families took shelter in the homes of indigenous Fijians and a white missionary, as well as in nearby bushes. Concerned non-governmental organisations (NGOs) and individuals from Suva provided groceries and other support to them in the following days. I went with Father Kevin Barr and other close friends to Muaniweni, Baulevu and other nearby places to speak to affected families and to share food and grocery items. They were eventually transported to Lautoka as displaced people and took refuge at the Girmit Centre where they were cared for by Shaista Shameem, Sashi Kiran and Anit Singh.

Over the nearly two months of the occupation of the parliamentary complex by the renegade CRW soldiers, scores of young iTaukei men and women gathered in a celebration while the elected prime minister and his government side were held hostage at gunpoint. Kava and alcohol appeared to be shared and consumed, and cooking of food in *lovos* and over open fires took place. Euphoria and bonhomie extended to having sex as well. Some youths acted the part of warriors dressing up in traditional leaf skirts, blackening their faces and raising what appeared to be a *tapa* flag symbolising the *vanua*'s ascendance over Western-style democracy. Several homes in the area had been previously invaded, looted and trashed by gangs of youth who continued to occupy the Parliament. Armed renegade soldiers shot dead Police Corporal Seavula on the evening of Sunday 28 May as he drove a police vehicle along Sukuna Road close to the Parliament.[41]

The number of military personnel within the parliamentary complex increased, to the horror of Suva residents and the nation as a whole, when retired soldiers in uniform were shown on television marching into the parliamentary complex in support of George Speight and his group of armed interlopers. Besides these 100 odd 'Dad's army' types, on 7 July rebel RFMF soldiers mutinied at the Sukunaivalu Barracks. The mutiny

---

41 Arieta Vakasukawaqa Suva, 'Father's death inspired sons to join RFMF', *Fiji Sun*, 25 December 2016, fijisun.com.fj/2016/12/25/fathers-death-inspired-sons-to-join-rfmf/.

was supported by some chiefs in the area. Prominent chiefs also attended meetings in the parliamentary complex and separately, as GCC members. They were not able to end the crisis.

Nor were a number of international attempts able to bring a peaceful resolution. Both the Commonwealth Ministerial Action Group led by Don McKinnon of New Zealand and UN Secretary General Kofi Annan's personal emissary, Mr Sergio D Mello, were unsuccessful in their efforts to negotiate the release of the hostages, and help to end the national crisis.

The president appointed the minister of labour in the Labour Party–led People's Coalition Government as prime minister for a day so that he could then formally resign, and Parliament could be prorogued. Following unsuccessful attempts by the president to calm the situation, and to negotiate with an increasingly belligerent George Speight to release the hostages, the so-called civilian coup made possible by special forces soldiers, the military coup d'état took place on 29 May.

President Ratu Sir Kamisese Mara was approached by Josaia Voreqe Bainimarama, commander of the Republic of Fiji Military Forces, Ratu Mara's son-in-law Ratu Epeli Ganilau, the former RFMF commander, and Sitiveni Rabuka to relinquish his position and leave the city. Overnight he was compelled to leave the capital for 'his own safety' on a naval ship that sailed him to Lakeba, Lau.

The Interim Military Government with Bainimarama as head took control of the state under emergency regulation and established the Military Exclusion Zone around the parliamentary complex. It was not until 9 July that the 'Muanikau Accord' was signed by the military commander, Bainimarama, and George Speight, which facilitated the release of the remaining 27 hostages including the deposed prime minister four days later.

The accord, among other things, appeared to fulfil the wishes of George Speight and to address the grievances of 'the indigenous Fijians': it included abrogation of the 1997 constitution, acknowledgement of the removal of Ratu Sir Kamisese Mara as president, ascendance of Ratu Josefa Iloilo as acting president, appointment of exclusively ethnic Fijian ministers, immunity for all those who committed 'political offences', and the reinstatement of military personnel 'involved in the political takeover … before 19th May'.[42]

The parliamentary complex was cleared of the supporters of the hostage takers, and arms and munitions were returned to the Queen Elizabeth Barracks. Scores of Speight supporters took over a school in Naulu, Nasinu. Having run out of food, they began raiding vegetable gardens in the neighbourhood, and demanding produce from vendors in the nearby roadside market. On Wednesday 26 July at a checkpoint in Nasinu, George Speight was apprehended by the military with two of his advisers and armed bodyguards. They were deemed to be carrying firearms and failing to surrender all the guns and ammunitions that were taken from the military armoury. On the following day RFMF soldiers cracked down on Speight supporters using tear gas. One person died and 56 others were injured with 24 being hospitalised.[43] Rebel soldiers took to the bush with other extremists, and on 8 August Police Corporal Raj Kumar and RFMF's Private Joela Weleilakeba lost their lives in an ambush in the Naitāsiri hills.[44]

For Suva residents and all of Fiji, the ethno-nationalist CRW and George Speight saga had another twist before the year's end. On 2 November at a little after midday, people in Samabula, Vatuwaqa, Nabua, Tamavua, Caubati, Namadi Heights, Bay View Heights and Laucala Beach Estate heard sounds of gunfire coming from the Queen Elizabeth Barracks. Gun noises continued for a few hours. At least one person in Samabula North had a ricocheting bullet shrapnel enter his stomach. Confusion reigned. It was later in the evening, and on the following day that it was clarified that there had been a mutiny at the barracks with CRW and other rebel soldiers taking control of the armoury and overrunning the camp. During the mutiny three unarmed loyal soldiers were killed and the military commander, Voreqe Bainimarama, narrowly escaped an attempt on his life. The mutiny was quelled by the RFMF's 3rd Infantry Regiment led by Colonel Viliame Seruvakula whose troops had returned from training at the Sigatoka Sand Dunes. During the weeks that followed, four CRW soldiers were brutality killed by loyal soldiers.

---

42   'Free at last after 56 days in captivity', *Fiji Times*, 18 August 2015.
43   The Associated Press, 'Coup leader in Fiji is arrested by the military', *New York Times*, 27 July 2000, www.nytimes.com/2000/07/27/world/coup-leader-in-fiji-is-arrested-by-the-military.html.
44   Suva, 'Father's death inspired sons to join RFMF'.

Captain Shane Stevens and 42 other soldiers were subsequently convicted and sentenced to life imprisonment and long prison terms. Implicated in the machinations relating to the mutiny, Ratu Inoke Takiveikata, the Qaranivalu (paramount chief) of Naitāsiri Province was also convicted and sentenced to life imprisonment.[45]

In fact, the Suva courts were kept busy over a number of years adjudicating cases of some 2,500 people charged by police for offences relating to the mayhem of 2000. These trials proceeded following the appointment of an almost exclusive ethnic Fijian civilian government led by Laisenia Qarase. The military commander also appointed Ratu Josefa Iloilo as president of the Republic. Both the appointment of government ministers and the head of state appear to reflect the wishes of George Speight who contested the 2001 general election while in prison.

CCF, and especially Jone Dakavula, worked closely with the lawyers for Chandrika Prasad, a farmer and one of the victims of the Muaniweni disorder to uphold the 1997 constitution against Bainimarama's bid to abrogate it. CCF collected affidavits and evidence to substantiate the argument that the citizens of Fiji had not consented to the new order established by the military, and that the constitution remained valid. CCF was appointed *amicus curiae* during the court proceeding. Much to our delight, the Supreme Court ruled that the constitution had not been abrogated.

In the 2001 general election, Speight, held as a prisoner on Nukulau Island, was a candidate of the Conservative Alliance, the right-wing ethno-nationalist party that advocated indigenous Fijian paramountcy, abolition of the 1997 constitution, the declaration of a Christian State and Sunday Sabbath. He won the Fijian communal seat in his home province of Tailevu. However, Qarase's Soqosoqo Duavata Lewenivanua (SDL) Party won 32 seats to FLP's 27 and formed government. Although his government sought national reconciliation, Prime Minister Qarase was seen to be sympathetic to the standpoint of indigenous Fijian ethno-nationalists. Over time he antagonised the military commander Voreqe Bainimarama, who overthrew his democratically elected government in December 2006.[46]

---

45 Thakur Ranjit Singh, 'Fiji's failed military mutiny: The day Frank Bainimarama was supposed to die – a dark history of modern Fiji', *Fiji Pundit* (blog), 1 November 2014, fijipundit.blogspot.com/2014/11/fijis-failed-military-mutiny-day-frank.html.
46 Vijay Naidu, 'Coups in Fiji seesawing democratic multiracialism and ethno-nationalist extremism', *Devforum* no. 26 (2007): 24–33.

The 2006 coup

I began working at the Victoria University of Wellington (VUW) in early 2003 and made the occasional visit to Fiji to, among other things, participate in conferences and seminars and visit family and friends. A year after I left, Robbie Robertson was appointed as professor and director of development studies at USP. In 2006, I advised Professor Philip Morrison, the head of the School of Geography, Environment and Earth Sciences at VUW, that I would be returning to Fiji at the end of year. He asked me if I was sure about this decision, and he was especially sympathetic when the coup was executed in the first week of December.

This coup appeared to be unusual as it deposed an ethnic Fijian Government that had been elected by 80 per cent of indigenous Fijian voters and had complied with the power-sharing provisions of the 1997 constitution by appointing FLP members into its cabinet. The military also challenged and eventually undermined the influence and authority of Fijian chiefs, and the predominantly ethnic Fijian Methodist Church of Fiji and Rotuma. The military phased out the GCC, which had stood at the apex of the Fijian Administration for over one and a half centuries. Quite surprisingly, even though deposed Prime Minister Laisenia Qarase strongly condemned the coup, apart from a number of small pro-democracy protests in Suva and Lami neighbourhoods, there was no major disruption in the city. The military acted swiftly and firmly against those who protested the coup. Many civil society leaders were detained and tortured, and a number of civilians were killed.

Unlike the clandestine coups of 1987 and the putsch of 2000 followed by the actual military takeover, the 2006 coup followed weeks and months of a public 'arm wrestle' covered by the media between the elected prime minister and the military commander. Qarase had unsuccessfully tried to replace Bainimarama, and to have the killing of four rebel soldiers in 2000 investigated. He also had spoken about downsizing the military. Bainimarama justified the overthrow of the democratically elected government as a 'clean up coup' to address perceived governmental corruption and racism. Suva residents, fearful of further strife, had begun to batten down but were assured by the military commander that the security forces were in control, and they were safe.

My family and I returned in early February 2007 to find the capital in its usual bustle. However, it was not long before I found that there were deep divisions between those who supported the coup and those who opposed it. It was apparent that a majority of Indo-Fijians and other minorities supported Bainimarama while indigenous Fijians were dismayed by what the military had done. Among academic colleagues, some argued that the 2006 coup was a 'good coup'. Trade unionists and FLP were divided because Mahendra Chaudry joined the military-backed interim government. The Christian clergy was divided, with non-Catholic denominations perceiving the Catholic Church as supporting the coup. Among civil society organisations including NGOs a rift emerged between those who advocated human rights and those who upheld social justice.

The 2006 coup continues to divide people today. There are those who recognise Bainimarama as a legitimate leader after his electoral victories in 2014 and 2018, and there are others who question if Fiji is truly democratic.[47] Since 2009, Suva, like other municipalities in Fiji, ceased having an elected city council and mayor accountable to local residents; instead it is governed by a central city administrator appointed by the minister of local government. There is a groundswell of antagonism towards the imposed 2013 constitution that, among other things, reinstated immunity to military personnel involved in coups, and the provision that gives the military primary responsibility to ensure the security and wellbeing of all Fijians. This ascendancy of the military as the final arbiter of civilian social, economic and political dynamics does not provide any guarantee that Suva and Fiji will be free of military intrusion in civil politics in the future. Whether the 2006 coup is the 'coup to end all coups' remains to be seen.

Over the last 30 years, I have witnessed Suva becoming the epicentre of political instability and military coups. The capital has experienced peaceful and not so peaceful demonstrations as well as outright interethnic violence, arson, looting and damage of business premises and private homes. Mobs roamed its streets. The city's daily weekday business routine of the opening of banks, supermarkets, cafes and restaurants, retail and wholesale outlets, factories and garages, the Suva market and bus station were disrupted. Media outlets were compelled to close their doors as soldiers took over. Like other residents I have been alarmed and outraged

---

47   Mary Chapman and Graham Leung, 'Is Fiji still a democracy?', *Fiji Times*, 9 October 2021.

on seeing armed soldiers patrolling the streets with the police force becoming an unarmed appendage of the military. The city was silenced. Residents lived fearful lives behind closed doors.

However, the capital city has remained the social, economic and political hub of the nation where the big-wigs from government, corporations and international agencies rub shoulders in board rooms and cocktail circuits. Social inequality and the presence of the poor is also evident in the homeless street dwellers as well as in the mushrooming informal settlements where 20 per cent of Suva residents live. There are certain things that do not change!

I have been a member of a number of NGOs including FANG and CCF, and after my return from Wellington, I have worked closely with the Ecumenical Centre for Education, Research and Advocacy and the Peoples Community Network and have seen firsthand how people have coped with the difficulties that followed each one of the coups. Suva has experienced natural disasters such as cyclones and, in the post-Independence era, man-made disasters in the form of military coups. The city residents have picked themselves up and rebuilt their lives after each disastrous coup. And in doing so have ensured that Suva regained its vibrant resilience as the central hub of social, economic and political dynamics of Fiji.

19

Wailea[1]

Brij V Lal

Kaali Raaton ke Aage Savera Bhi Haye.
There is always a dawn at the end of the darkest night.

Wailea, Veidogo, Nanuku, Komave, Namadai, Kalokolevu. Nakorova, Lovonilase. Lovely, evocative Fijian names but they are completely unknown to me. I drive past many of them every day in the air-conditioned comfort of my car, unaware of their existence and the lives lived within them. I am not alone. Many people I know can't place the names either. They are, of course, names of some of Fiji's mushrooming squatter settlements around the greater Suva area. Squatter settlements, also known euphemistically as informal settlements, are on the rise on Fiji's main island, Viti Levu, especially in capital city Suva's swampy state-owned land, from Nasēsē through Vatuwaqa onwards towards Nasinu and beyond. That is where between 15 and 20 per cent of Fiji's total population now lives, in the clogged Suva–Nausori corridor. Informal settlements are not new. The Jittu Estate in Samabula, for instance, has been around for decades and some others have acquired the semi-permanent character of an established settlement. But the numbers are now growing rapidly for a variety of reasons: housing shortage in urban areas, unemployment, shrinkage in job opportunities, rural–urban migration, the movement of displaced farmers from non-renewed leases. For the desperately poor

---

1   Originally published in *Road from Mr Tulsi's store* (Suva: University of the South Pacific Press, 2019) under the title 'Bula Dredre', 139–60. This essay is a 'faction piece', that is, an actual observed experience rendered in the fictional mode. The aim in this exercise is to capture the inner truth of an experience rather than its factual accuracy.

with nowhere to go, the informal settlements beckon as respite on what many hope will be a much longer journey, hopefully beyond Fiji's shores. So, these settlements are for most a temporary refuge for shattered hopes and truncated ambitions.

A kilometre from where I live on Beach Road in Suva Point are informal settlements hidden at the edge of mangrove swamps on either side of a major arterial road named after one of Fiji's less illustrious governors, Sir Murchison Fletcher. I know of squatter settlements in the abstract, as an idea, a construct for the purposes of academic research or lectures, but nothing beyond that. Occasionally there might be a snippet on the evening television news if there is flooding or some other outrage – a fire, a murder, rape, violent burglary – but that's about it, a minor tragedy among so many. After a brief moment, the camera moves on. The reality hit me one hot afternoon when I stopped at a roadside store not far from Vatuwaqa Bridge to buy a soft drink. In front of me was a little boy, dark, noticeably thin, about 10 or 12, counting coins to buy ice cream. He did not have enough and was turning around to go back. I tapped him gently on the soldier and said, '*Beta*, let me buy you an ice cream'. He tensed up, looking straight at me as if to say, 'What do you want from me?' When I smiled, he simply said, 'Thank you Uncle', and left. His name was Yogesh.

I could not get Yogesh out of my mind even though our meeting was fleeting. There was something about him, his fine face, the sad, haunted, look in his eyes, the gentle expression of gratitude, or perhaps a mixture of all of these. Over the weeks and months, I saw many children Yogesh's age returning from school along the Fletcher Road and then turning into a narrow muddy path into the mangrove jungle. One day, I parked my car on the road and decided to take a walk on the muddy path myself to see where it led. It is narrow, wet, slippery, with household rubbish strewn on both sides, a few stray, dirt-covered mangy dogs idling about looking for food, grass overgrown. At the end, the evening tide is rising, the water black and thick with rotting leaves, raw sewerage and floating plastic. Above all is the overpowering stench of raw sewerage mixed with the aroma of spicy food being prepared for the evening meal. A few cheerful '*Bula*' shouts come from rusted corrugated structures on stilts as I hurry back to my car. I can still feel that gross smell in my nostrils years later.

The number of squatter settlements in Fiji comes as a huge surprise: over 200, varying in size from a dozen or so residents to well over a hundred. The largest numbers of squatter settlements, by far, are in the greater Suva region. Suva offers the best chance for employment and education for children, and medical facilities are accessible. Some older ones have well-developed community structures for support and sustenance. The newer ones in the mangrove swamps have sprouted overnight while no one was watching, people say. They lack basic amenities of piped water supply and electricity and are wracked by water-borne diseases carried by mosquitoes. In some places there is resigned acceptance of the 'reality' while in others there is determination to make this a temporary stopover on a much longer journey. As a man says to me, 'Life will go on. *Inshallah*, the future will be better.' Another reminds me that there is always a dawn at the end of the darkest night. '*Kaali raat ke baad hamesha sabera aaway haye.*'

I spend most weekends hanging around squatter settlements as unobtrusively as possible. I park my car a discreet distance away and walk. Often I buy a couple of packets of kava to start a conversation with the locals, as much to get information as to establish my credentials. There is understandable suspicion of outsiders, and there is plenty about me. They know about me from my work on the Reeves Commission in the mid-1990s, they have seen me on television, heard me on radio, and some have read my columns in the newspapers. Often the talk begins with politics and my take on things before we get to my quest. 'You standing for elections or something, Doctor?' one person asks me. Was this a way of me introducing myself to the people? 'You doing this for the government?' 'How much they paying you to do this?' This might appear intrusive but it is often nothing more than honest curiosity, a conversation opener. They are jaded by previous encounters with researchers. I realise it will take a long time to establish my bona fides among people who are innocent about the purpose and protocols of academic work. Many have not gone beyond primary school. There is genuine cynicism about surveys. They have answered many intrusive questions about their lives and living conditions, about earnings and expenditure, about government assistance or the lack of it, over the years, with no result. There is also genuine puzzlement about my interest in squatters when I could do so many other things more 'uplifting'. They are nonplussed when I tell them that my next research project will be on female suicides in Fiji. 'Big problem, that one', people tell me.

Squatters come in all shapes and sizes. This realisation came to me slowly as I travelled and talked over several weeks. There is an internal hierarchy and shades of difference that all residents acknowledge but which are invisible to outsiders. Where you live places you in the eyes of the residents. There are at least three different types of informal settlements: those that are on state land, those on private freehold land and those on traditional land. State land is favoured because evicting people from state land is time-consuming. Governments are reluctant to act harshly for fear of adverse public reaction. And there are prospective political costs as well. Squatters vote. 'The voter owns the vote', a man says, grinning. He is on to an increasingly powerful truth. Freehold land is slightly more problematic. Residents of Bhindi Estate do not know who Mr Bhindi is, where he is, whether he is in Fiji at all. There is greater uncertainty about the future. The fear of eviction at any moment haunts the residents. As one resident told me: 'We don't know when the notice (to vacate) will come.' The most vulnerable are the residents of traditional Fijian-owned land. Because it is private property, the courts cannot intervene and the government is reluctant to act. And landlords can do whatever they want, *manmaani*. They may be degrees of difference, but fear is constant everywhere. There can be no planning for the future. Still, there have been no large-scale evictions in recent years. Government is planning alternative sites away from the city which will provide some respite, but people are reluctant to uproot again, to move further away from the city, away from jobs and schools. The comforts of familiarity and certitude even in conditions of harsh adversity should not be underestimated.

One day, I drive to meet a distant niece in Cunningham Estate on the slopes of Khalsa Road. My niece asks me to park the car a safe distance away from their dwelling. Questions will be asked later about the car, its driver, the purpose of the visit, she tells me. The estate has been in the news recently for violent burglary so there is heightened concern and vigilance. The landlord's spies are everywhere. My niece's residence is a corrugated iron structure with a bed at one end and kitchen at the other. Her two boys sleep on the mattress in the middle. The family is from Labasa, so these folks endure the usual taunts against *Labasians*, as cheapskates. I ask my niece – let us call her Sashi – about life in the area. 'It is better here than it was in Labasa', Sashi says. Their 10-acre farm had been reserved and there was nothing left to live on. They had to move. Here at least there is regular income. Both boys are working. One is a hairdresser in a neighbouring settlement, the other is a mechanic, and the husband does odd labouring jobs around the place. Sashi makes Indian sweets – *gulab jamun, lakdi ke mithai, ghugri* – and sells them directly to market vendors and owners of roadside stalls. The money is not much, but they get by.

In settlements on state land, there is more stability and security and, as a result, a more cohesive sense of community. One settlement in Nasinu looks fairly well established from outside. The footpath leading to it is clean, and inside there are hibiscus, bougainvillea, marigold and other plants neatly planted as hedge. It is predominantly Indo-Fijian. When I enquire, I am asked to talk to the *mukhiya*, the community leader, Mr Ram Singh. He is the settlement's shopkeeper, perhaps in his forties, educated and well-spoken. *Bhai saheb, kaise yahaan aanaa hua*? How did you happen to end up here? It is the reason I would hear over and over again, especially among Indo-Fijian squatters. His cane lease in Tavua was not renewed, and so he had to leave. He had a contact in the settlement who invited him to come, and he did. The non-renewal had a story behind it as I discovered later when I got to know him better. His lease was expiring and the landlord was willing to extend it for a substantial goodwill payment. He agreed to offer a certain amount, but his neighbour, keen to add 10 acres of rich cane land to his own, offered more and got the land. Nothing in a village is ever as simple as it appears.

'This place is home now', the *mukhiya* says with some feeling, and he wants to make something of his time here. There are about 30 residents in the area, many with school-age children. Many work in Suva as shop attendants, municipal workers, house cleaners, grass cutters, general handymen. There is an active *Ramayana mandali* in the settlement, with each family hosting a recital every month or so. All the major ceremonial occasions and festivals are observed. Holi is a very popular festival with people from rural backgrounds. People organise themselves in groups and patrol the settlement to guard against burglaries and violence. Safety of women and children is paramount in everyone's mind. As we talk over the weeks, I realise that children's education is the top priority. The residents have suffered disruption and desperation and they are determined that their children will be spared their fate. All this is an integral part of our history and heritage. I am told of some students from the settlements doing high school, and one or two are at Fiji Institute of Technology. This brings back memories of our own predicaments more than a half century ago, the same desperation, the same yearning for a more secure, stable life. I suspect the way we escaped that life, children here will too. But the fact that children have to endure them in the early years of the twenty-first century is a severe indictment of us as a society.

Hidden partly in the mangroves of Vatuwaqa by the river, Wailea is another informal settlement that shows the same mixture of hope and despair I have seen elsewhere. It is a mixed settlement of Fijians and Indo-Fijians. That brings its own challenges caused by the inevitable collision of cultural norms and expectations though overall relations are cordial. 'Too much *kerekere vinaka, Bahini*', a woman says to me. Too much request for simple things such as sugar, salt, rice, kerosene. 'But they are such a generous people,' another says, 'always ready to share whatever little they have. And they look out for each other.' I recognise this is an old Fijian communal custom from the villages. 'No matter what religion or race, *Bhaiya*, we all in the same boat. *Sab jahajibhai baitho.*' It is an apt analogy from our distant past. Thrown together by fate, they struggle, bound by the same concerns: the future of their children. 'We swim together, we sink together', the man says.

Sakiusa, a resident, talks about some particular problems faced by the iTaukei. 'There are too many new denominations here, brother. Too much *katchkatch*', squabbling. 'Whatever the church says must be done, right or wrong. Whatever the *vanua* says must be done, right or wrong.' But the hold of tradition and custom is slowly diminishing due to the levelling pressures of urban living. Survival, not subservience to custom, is the order of the day here. This may be liberating to some but the absence of constraints and established leadership spawns its own problems. Sakiusa talks about wayward young men who have fallen into 'wrong company'. One or two are doing jail time. 'They give us bad name.' And there are murmurs about minor internal friction among the iTaukei from different provinces with their own ways of doing things and particular codes of acceptable conduct invisible to outsiders. I hear muted words about 'Lauans' in the settlement and about frictions in church leadership accused of 'not listening to us'. But for all that, *lotu*, religion, retains a firm hold on people. Everyone goes to church in their Sunday finest, clutching a well-thumbed Bible in their hands. The *talatala*, preacher, is still a figure of authority commanding respect in the community. But for how much longer?

There are idlers here, too, as they are everywhere, but also people with unexpected entrepreneurial skills and ambitions. I meet a man from Kadavu, Vili, who had moved to Viti Levu and eventually to Wailea for the sake of his children. For a while he worked as a casual labourer, but then began to retail kava from his island in Suva. Kadavu kava is considered top of the range, and he makes a living from it. Some mothers tell me about the bulk of their partners' earnings going to kava, and I see many stunted men in the settlement with leathery skin cracked by excessive consumption, *kanikani*. This is a Fiji-wide plague in the Indo-Fijian community, particularly where kava is often consumed without decorum or dignity. But I am more tolerant of 'grog-swipers' now than I once was. There is only so much reality mankind can bear, says TS Eliot, and there is so much grim reality to endure here. But I also feel deeply for mothers who have to feed their families somehow or face abuse and violence.

I meet another man, Harry (Hari), who sells marijuana he is sent from the highlands of Rakiraki. He speaks with a slight hissing sound because of two front teeth missing from a fight some years ago. Does he realise he is in a dangerous business? If caught, he could end up in jail.

> *Babu*, come here after dark and see all the cars parked on the street. They come to buy this stuff. Big business people, police, politicians, everyone. Police are in it up to here. They provide protection for a little freebie on the side.

When I ask a policeman at a *Ramayana* recital in Wailea one evening, he smiles: 'Doc, we have much bigger fish to catch. This is small, *chota mota rojgari*, business. We have to live and let live.' He was not the only man of flexible sense of duty or morality I have met. A young man says to me that 'morality we cannot afford. That is for you rich people, Boss'. *Koi hisaab se aapan kaam chalao.* We have to make ends meet somehow. I ask Harry about high school kids doing drugs. 'No, *Babuji*,' he says looking straight at me, 'I never give them this stuff. Never. That will end their life, *jindagi barbaad.*' I discover that each settlement has its Harry or bootlegger. Drug abuse, once unheard-of or very carefully hidden, is widespread and on the rise. A man who was a regular marijuana user defends his habit because 'I can afford it. I like it. Nothing wrong with that. Better than booze. It's those buggers who can't: that's the problem.' A coin always has two sides.

The policeman I had talked to is a resident of Wailea. In his early forties, he is from Rakiraki and moved to Wailea about 10 years ago for the same reason that so many others have: better opportunities for his family, and especially the education of his two daughters, both now in high school. But why the squatter settlement and not anywhere else? 'Shortage of affordable housing and very high rents,' he says. He is saving for the future of his daughters. So it is a temporary stopover? 'Definitely yes.' But then he hesitates. He has developed an affection for the place. It gives him a sense of community he has not had before. 'People look up to me and

I look after them,' he says. Some of his fellow officers know his address and visit him occasionally for a bowl of grog, but he keeps his life private. He risks derision and ridicule if people come to know where he lives. I meet others, a Suva City Council staff and a primary schoolteacher with similar experience and expectation. They are unaware or are reluctant to admit that it is people like them who give squatters a bad name as freeloaders and spongers who don't belong there.

I have the overall picture of informal settlements. People gravitate to them for a variety of reasons, but mostly for a better future for their families. The public face of the settlements is scarred by cruel comments about being havens for criminals and crooks and spongers on the public purse, places of filth and disease, altogether unfit for human habitation. There are grains of truth in these perceptions, heartless as they might be, but they are grains only. I see despair but also much determination and pride. The squatter settlement is their temporary destination, not their destiny. I see a glimmer of hope in some of the younger men working in town. There is anger building up. One man says over grog:

> They laugh at us, they take us for granted, call us names. How would you feel being unable to send your children to school or buy medicine when they are sick? Who wants to feel humiliated, depressed, worthless? Why don't they do something about the lease problem. *Bolo kutch karo.* We are kicked out but no one wants to know where we will go.

'Give us lease on state land which is lying idle,' another man says. 'We will vote for a party which gives us ninety-nine year leases.' These angry words make me realise how uninformed outsiders are about people in squatter settlements. There is anger and frustration and a willingness to take action. It is only a matter of time before politics comes to this place. This, after all, is where very large numbers of poor, restless people live. The fate of future governments will be determined by the voters of squatter settlements.

My conversations have mostly been with adults but my interest has also been sparked in the experience and perceptions of the children of squatters, their hopes and ambitions, their perceptions of the world around them. I approach Dinesh, the headmaster of Vatuwaqa Primary, an old acquaintance, to seek his advice. He is eager to help and gives me contacts at other schools in Samabula, Nabua and Nasinu that children of squatters attend. At morning tea in his office, he sends for a boy who is from Wailea. It is Yogesh, the boy I had met at the local shop some months before. He avoids eye contact as if to say we have never met. Dinesh asks him to gather some other children like him to meet me after school. I suddenly realise that this breaches the research guidelines of my university. Ethical questions and sensitivities are involved. I have not sought the consent of the students I am about to meet. But it is too late; the die has already been cast. Yogesh is quiet. Perhaps he might be wondering why someone like me would be interested in people like him. Do I have an ulterior motive? It is a reaction I have encountered elsewhere as well. He says nothing and leaves the office head bowed. 'Why him,' I ask Dinesh? 'I will let you find that out for yourself.'

Much later, as I am about to return to Australia, I ask Yogesh about his reaction on our meeting in the headmaster's office. 'Sir, you are only called to the headmaster's office if there is some problem.' 'Such as?' 'If you haven't paid your fees, haven't completed your homework, got into a fight or are to be told not to come back to school.' 'What happens then?' Seems a rather harsh punishment. 'Sir, then you look for work like cutting grass, collecting bottles, sweeping shops, cleaning toilets.' 'You hesitated taking money I was giving you. Why?' 'Sir, ten dollars is a lot of money. People will ask questions. Did I get the money for doing something bad?' This took a second to sink in. So sexual abuse of children is not such an uncommon thing, after all. 'Have you been given big money before?' Yogesh does not answer, his eyes fixed on the ground. Instinctively, I put my arms around him. There are few things more disturbing than seeing innocent children preyed upon.

Yogesh and a group of about seven children gather in a classroom after school. Looking at the students, you could not distinguish them in their dress and demeanour from children not from squatter settlements. They are so polite and respectful. 'How do people react when they find out where you live,' I ask. 'I don't volunteer that information,' a student says. Another: 'They think we are a dirty poor people to keep away from.' 'Some of my friends don't mind, but they sort of just stay away.' One boy sums up what I sense is a general feeling. 'I wish people will see us as normal human beings. It is not our fault that we live in a squatter settlement.' It is clear that this will be a temporary stopover in a very long journey. 'So, what would you like to become when you grow up?' I ask. The professions of choice are medicine, accountancy, engineering, nursing. Why? Invariably, the answer is: 'So we can help people.' A girl, perhaps 13 or 14, who wants to become a nurse, says: 'I will always live here. I will never leave.' I look at her for elaboration. 'Because, there will always be people in need here. They are my people.'

I ask Yogesh about his plans. 'I don't know, Sir.' He hesitates, looking at the ground. 'I don't know whether I will complete school.' He is always late with fees and has been warned several times. Expulsion will come if there are further delays. 'I will take care of that,' I assure him. Suddenly, he looks up at me wondering why, why this stranger is being kind to me. I say nothing. There are other problems at home. There is no electricity and often homework does not get done. There is house flooding in the rainy season. Mosquitoes from the mangrove swamps plague the area. There is dysentery and diarrhea, smallpox and a variety of skin diseases. There is no privacy. Yogesh says his mother will need him. Unprompted, he says: 'She is the only person I have got. She is my everything. I will never leave her.' This is a story I have heard elsewhere as well, the protective feeling children have for their parents, especially single mothers.

I want to meet Yogesh's mother. I suddenly realise that something about Yogesh has touched me, opened my eyes. He is so polite, attentive, bright. He will go places if only he has the opportunity. I am troubled and angry that through no fault of their own, children like Yogesh have to endure this, facing a future that seems so bleak; and the world seems not to care. I have paid his fees and will contribute to his schooling expenses. This is instinctive. I think of the many helping hands I had along my own journey. Ours, too, was a precarious life more than a half century ago. I have thought of starting night and weekend classes for children from squatter settlements to help with their assignments and homework. It is still a dream I have.

I return to Yogesh's mother. 'Sir, my mother is not well,' Yogesh says. 'Anything serious?' 'Woman problem, Sir.' 'Next week or week after will be fine.' Yogesh hesitates. 'Sir?' Perhaps Yogesh does not want me to see his 'house,' the surroundings from where he comes, perhaps out of embarrassment. It is a reaction I have received before. Perhaps there is fear that I might be turned off and leave as so many other researchers have done in the past. 'Sir, I will ask my mother.' Some people I meet at the local shop have seen me with Yogesh. 'Nice boy. You after something, Boss? I can arrange, I know lots of good boys, and girls, too,' a man says to me, winking. 'Fuck you,' I feel like saying but hold my tongue. 'No, I am not looking for cheap sex. I am trying to understand the squatter

19. WAILEA

problem around here.' The man smiles, unrelenting. 'Yes, Boss, that's what they all say. I know what they want.' I explain that I would like to meet Yogesh's parents. 'The father dead long time,' the man says. 'Too much homebrew. Waste time *falla*.' 'And the mother?' The man gives a knowing smile. 'Suzie? Very nice. Good for you. You want?' I do not like the drift of this conversation. 'Where, how, can I meet her?' 'I arrange for you. One packet of cigarette, *bas*.' When I don't reply, he says, 'Go at six to the back of the Air Pacific building near the carpark and ask for Suzie.'

I hesitate. This is unfamiliar territory for me, and I am a little concerned about the public reaction to seeing me in strange places at night. I can visualise the newspaper headline: 'Dr Lal on the Prowl?' But there is something about all I have been told or heard that makes me determined to proceed. I park the car in the carpark behind Westpac and walk tentatively towards the Air Pacific building. I see the glow of cigarettes in the dim light. About four or five women in tight dresses and heavy makeup are loitering around. I ask for Suzie. 'She is "on duty" right now. Back in half an hour', a woman says. 'Can I help, honey? I give you good time, sweetie. Yes?' I thank her and drive back home. The following night, I return, and this time Suzie is around. A woman in her late thirties, perhaps early forties, shortish, heavily perfumed and powdered, cigarette in hand. 'You want? Yes?' I am taken aback by the business-like, transactional directness of her words. Before I can say anything, she says: 'Forty dollars. Behind the Civic Centre. Yes?' 'Thanks, but no.' I hand her $20 along with my telephone number. 'Please call me when you can,' and then leave hurriedly, avoiding notice. Suddenly, I understand Yogesh's hesitation in introducing me to his mother and the man's remarks at the shop. Suzie is a sex worker.

Mid-afternoon a few days later the phone rings. Suzie is on the line. 'You from the police, yes?' 'No, ma'am.' 'From Social Welfare?' 'No.' 'Why you come looking for me then?' 'To talk.' 'About what? I don't talk to strangers.' I suggest I pick her up discreetly at Vatuwaqa Bridge and go to Suva Point for an hour or so. Suzie hesitates, uncertain about me and my motives. Men don't go to people like Suzie to talk, but she agrees for reasons I still cannot fathom. We meet midday Sunday, pick up a couple of cans of soft drinks at the local BP gas station and go to Suva Point. Suzie is in the back seat. It is an awkward drive. We avoid direct eye contact. Suzie looks 'normal' now without her makeup, cheap red lipstick and tight black dress. She is wearing a light blue T-shirt and floral knee-length dress. We sit on a park bench in the shade of an acacia tree facing Suva Point as I explain the purpose of my talking to her. Yogesh had told her about a man who had been kind to him and she asked if it was me. When I say yes, she becomes less tense. *Hamaar jindagi kuchh nahi haye. Bas ek toota khilauna haye.* My life is nothing. I am just a broken toy. Her brutal candour shook me momentarily, as did the embittered hurt in Suzie's voice. 'I will think about it', Suzie says, meaning talking to me, as I drop her off.

Over the next few months, we meet several times at different places around Suva: Bulachino Cafe in Raiwaqa, Colo-i-Suva Coffee Shop, Laucala Bay Teahouse. Suzie will not have any conversation taped. I can only write down notes. I will not use her real name nor the place she lives or comes from. There will be no photos taken. I will pay a small something every time we meet. I will not mention anything she says to Yogesh. Protecting her son is her top priority. 'He is innocent,' she says emphatically, looking directly into my eyes, 'and he must remain that way. Forever, you understand?' And I will never again go to the back of the Air Pacific building either because her co-workers will disown her. 'They don't know what you want.' I agree with all her conditions, grateful for her willingness to cooperate.

Suzie (Sushila Devi) is from the region of Tavua, the second of five children. Her father, Gajadhar, was a prominent cane farmer and community leader in the Bulabula village. A bright student, Sushila dropped out of school after Form 5 (Grade 11). Why, I wondered. 'Because I became pregnant.' A neighbour's son was the culprit. Teenage pregnancy is rare in Indo-Fijian families (or carefully hidden) and the cause of great shame. The 'good name' of the family has to be protected at all cost, especially for her two younger sisters. Abortion was considered, but the news would leak out, causing irreparable damage to the family's reputation. Once or twice Gajadhar thought of dispatching Sushila to remove the stain on the family's name, but the consequences could be disastrous for everyone. A long jail sentence would ruin the family. The best option, the family agreed, would be to dispatch her to an uncle's place in remote village in Ba where she would be unknown. They would give the family food and money in compensation.

But it was an arrangement for the duration of the pregnancy only, and Sushila was expected to find her own way in the world after Yogesh was born. Once or twice Sushila's mother came to visit and wanted to adopt Yogesh without revealing his identity, but Sushila would have none of it. He was her flesh and blood and she would bring him up herself. Gajadhar had vowed never to allow Sushila to set foot on the family property. For him she was as good as dead. Such unforgiving spirit is common among our people. Family *izzat*, honour, counts for a great deal. A way was found. Ram Jattan, a casual labourer from a neighbouring village, had gone to Suva and was living in a squatter settlement there. The uncle arranged for Sushila to live with him, more to get rid of her from his home. There was no paperwork, no documentation, not even a small *puja* to farewell her. It is a very brutal village way of dealing with women who breach patriarchal social boundaries. Men get away scot-free, as the man who impregnated Sushila did. Women bear the burden of abuse for the rest of their lives.

That was how Sushila came to Suva. They moved from one squatter settlement to another every two or three years. Ram Jattan was a casual labourer, cleaning drains, mowing other people's lawns, doing ordinary repair jobs here and there. Sushila took up domestic duties in Suva by turns cooking cleaning, ironing and minding children and doing any other odd job that she came by. As a single woman, young and attractive, she was vulnerable to sexual advances from men in the house and their friends in the neighbourhood . 'Practice sessions', younger men called it. It is a common enough occurrence often excused as 'what boys do'. Refusal to oblige could mean immediate termination. And, so, Sushila 'obliged', week after week, month after month, to forgettable men of nondescript backgrounds. It was part of her 'job', Suzie convinced herself. She never told anybody. Her private grief remained private.

Ram Jattan was no better than other men. Sex was not his thing, drink was. He began making small amounts of homebrew (rice whisky) at the back of his shack among mangrove trees. This after a while became his main preoccupation. All of Sushila's earnings went into buying the ingredients, leaving hardly anything for herself and Yogesh. Police officers demanded free booze for turning a blind eye to illegal activity. Bootlegging was very popular, which led to the emergence of many bootleggers. Each settlement had at least two. Ram Jattan himself drank heavily every night almost to the point of unconsciousness. He demanded hot meals at odd hours of the night. Enraged swear words would fly across the room if Sushila did not jump to her feet immediately: *kutia, chinaar, bajaaru*. More than the hurt the abuse caused Sushila, she was distressed beyond words to see the effect it was having on Yogesh. He would avoid Ram Jattan whenever he could. When he was wild and dangerous with booze, Yogesh would go to his Fijian neighbour's shack to do his homework or just to have a momentary peace of mind. Ram Jattan's violent and abusive ways, now becoming more regular, were well known to the neighbours. One night, Sushila reached the end of her tether when Ram Jattan slapped Yogesh hard when he was late returning from the shop with a packet of cigarettes. '*Bajaaru ke baccha*', he called him, son of a prostitute. That, as the cliché has it, broke the camel's back. As Ram Jattan lay in drunken sleep, Sushila smothered him to death with a pillow. Word spread the next day that a very drunk Ram Jattan had died peacefully in his sleep. A few residents came to his cremation at the Vatuwaqa crematorium.

Ram Jattan's death opened a new chapter in Sushila's life. A few women from the settlement came to offer comfort to a fellow woman facing the world alone. Rambha told Sushila about women she called *Raat ke Rani*, Ladies of the Night, around Suva. There was good money to be made for a few hours' work, she said. Sushila hesitated. It was one thing to submit to her bosses and their friends but quite another to be on the open market to complete strangers from unknown backgrounds. One night she accompanied Rambha to observe the scene for herself. Rambha made close to a hundred dollars that night. A week or two later Suzie joined and has been a 'Lady of the Night' for several years now. The details of her nightly life remained private.

> They call us names, think we are low-lifes, *malicch*, *achoot*, dirty untouchables, *phuta pataka*, spent firecracker, useless. They call us prostitutes, but what do they call men who pay for our services?

A very fair question. I had no idea, still don't. I can still feel the disgust in Suzie's voice. 'You should see who the men are: rich people, leaders, business people, police officers. *Bada bada admi log.* They all the same, these men, married with families, *rakshas.*' She continues: 'Let people accept that this sort of thing happens right under their noses and make it legal. We will all be safer then.' There is some muted discussion about legalising prostitution, but it will not go anywhere. The moral police of society will make sure of that even as they themselves partake of this sordid trade in flesh.

'What would you say are some of the more difficult things about living in a squatter settlement?' I ask. (What a ponderous, academic way of asking a simple question, I now realise.) Suzie misses the freedom she had in the village to visit family and friends whenever she liked. Here she feels imprisoned. 'We are completely cut off from home. No one wants to know us. It is as if we are dead.' One of her sisters got married but she was not invited, did not even know about it. 'I have lost all my family and friends.' No one has ever come to visit her, and she hasn't been back even for a visit for fear of the family's reaction, especially her father's. Of far greater sadness is her concern for Yogesh. 'He will never know his father. He will never know his grandparents. He will have no cousins to grow up with. I will never be able to give him one thing he deserves most, his *bachpana*,' an innocent, carefree childhood. She talks about the squalid living conditions in the settlement. 'Sometimes, you have to go outside to relieve yourself, and you don't know who is watching, lurking in the jungle', she says. Some videos have been circulating in the settlement. The worst for Suzie, though, is the complete lack of privacy at home.

> You cook and sleep in the same tiny room covered with soot and smoke and dust, full of cockroaches and mosquitoes, unbearably damp in the rainy season.

Then: 'Can you imagine how a mother feels having a stranger on top of you while your son lies awake next to you?'

One Sunday at Suva Point, at my request Suzie introduces me to a group of her friends, all women but not all of them 'Ladies of the Night': Rosie, Jasmine, Jema, Rambha (Rambo) and a couple of others. The leader is a lady in her mid-30s who works at the local garment factory. 'We all speak as one', she says. I get the hint. 'United we stand, divided we fall', she says, repeating a trade union slogan pasted of the outside wall of the union office. She is politically engaged. 'We are Labour', she says with the conviction of a true believer. I ask about life on the factory floor. 'You have to seek permission to go to the toilet, your time at lunch is closely monitored. You are thoroughly checked, sometimes body-searched, before you clock-off.' All this is common knowledge around Suva apparently, but nothing ever happens because the lawmakers are in their pockets. 'But they don't always win', the lady says.

I am intrigued. One of them tells a story about a factory owner who was a sexual predator, asking a woman of his choice to stay back after work. When she told her friends what happened, they hatched up a plot. Next time, one of them will bring a camera along and hide in the back room while the man had his way in his office. She captured him in the act and shared the photos with the others. Instead of confronting the man with it, they decided to ask the office boy to take the photos to the owner's wife. 'Hand delivered', they chuckled. He just 'shrivelled up' after that, they said amid uproarious laughter. Another story does the rounds of a manager who constantly made sexually suggestive remarks and stroked his crotch in full view of his female workers. A lesson had to be taught, the women agree. One day at closing time, they closed the door and waited for the man to come out. They jumped on him as soon as he did, pinned him to the floor and took turns urinating on him, using the choicest Hindi swear words they could think of: *bhonsra* (cunt), *maichod* (motherfucker), *gandu* (arsehole). How they came up with this idea I did not have the courage to ask, but I recalled some *girmitiya* women in Labasa punishing a predatory European overseer in this way. Another example I recall old timers recounting was of some *girmitiya* women splashing a bucketful of water on an offending overseer's face, then wrestling the shaken fellow to the ground in the middle of a cane field and roughly rubbing pounded raw hot chilli –*rockete* – on his penis and anus, *puddu* and *chuttar*, causing unimaginable pain and discomfort, not to say acute embarrassment. This apparently is an old, well-understood peasant Indian women's way of protesting and punishing sexual predators. Such moments of triumph are rare, but they are cherished and I applauded the women for their audacity and courage. The manager's humiliation was complete. The next day, he transferred to the company's Lautoka factory, and nothing further was heard from or about him.

These stories and others I hear complicate an otherwise simplistic picture we get of women as submissive, servile people, under the firm foot of their husbands. There is violence and abuse, to be sure, but what I also see are numerous cases of resilience and enterprise that are surprising to find in a place like this. My niece in Cunningham makes Indian sweets to sell. I meet another woman who sews and repairs dresses. In Nanuku a woman runs a small curry catering business for wealthy Suva homes while another makes fried peanuts and *ghugri* (spicy cooked green peas). In Wailea, I meet a woman who weaves baskets from pandanus leaves she collects from neighbouring mangrove swamps. They go about their business with quiet dignity. They are the pillars of their families, and many children I have spoken to over the months talk affectionately about their mothers. They remind me powerfully of mothers of my own generation in rural Vanua Levu, simple peasant women of enormous dignity and pride who understood the meaning of pain and suffering and wanted to spare their children of that fate. And you had Colonial Sugar Refining Company overseers and colonial officials accusing Indian indentured women of lacking the 'motherly instinct'. If only they could witness this – and their rustic wisdom. I recall my mother telling us when the chips were really down, 'Remember, you cannot see stars without darkness'; that is, some hardship can stiffen your spine, nourish your soul. And cautioning against rushed judgments: 'No matter how thin I make it, a *roti* always has two sides.'

'Sir, you met my mother?' Yogesh asks when I see him after a week or so. 'Yes, and she's a very nice person, too. She wants to give you the best future any mother can.' Yogesh looked straight at me and said, 'So you know all about us now.' I couldn't quite read his mind. Was he relieved that I knew the truth without him having to tell me? Or did he think that now that I knew that I would leave. 'Nothing changes, Yogesh. I will still be your friend if you will have me.' Yogesh shook my hand firmly. 'Yes, Sir.' 'Remember, young man, don't dwell on things that went wrong,' I said, 'think about what to do next. You can't change the past, but you can do something about the future. You will never find your future in a rear view mirror.' Homilies like that. Yogesh sensed that the end was coming, that it was time for me to return to Australia. He turned away from me and looked vacantly into the distance. I will miss him too. I promised to keep in touch. And we did. Yogesh had completed his primary school and was preparing to go to Vatuwaqa High. Had he thought of a career, I wondered in one of my letters. 'I want to be a teacher, Sir. I want to help my people. I want to make a difference.' 'All your friends I have met want to make a fast buck. Good onya, son.' There is something deeply moving about such idealism in such fetid, wretched place. We wrote to each other for a while, but it did not last long, not out of fatigue or boredom but because of our, or rather my, pressing preoccupations, the call of duty.

A couple of years later I return to Fiji to cover the general elections of 1999, keen to assess the reaction of the angry squatters. I meet some of them again. They are energised, feel empowered that big politicians are visiting them and listening to their concerns. No one talks about principles here; that is empty talk; they all talk about *pet*, livelihood, issues: water, electricity, high cost of living, minimum wages, social security. 'Bread and butter issues', politicians call it. The Labour Party understands the mood of these people better than its rivals. There is another change that I suspect will be the sign of things to come. The people of the squatter settlements want the leaders to come to them in their settlements if they want their vote. Gone, I suspect, are the big, rousing rallies of the past. 'Pocket meetings' are the order of the day. 'Mohammed must come to the mountain, not the other way around', a man says to me with evident satisfaction. 'We have been on television', a man grins, as if to say, who would have thought. 'Our time is coming.' The election results would bear that out.

I go to Vatuwaqa to look up Yogesh. I asked after him at the local shop. 'We haven't seen the boy for a long time', the shopkeeper says. 'These people don't stay in the same place for very long.' I go to Vatuwaqa High, but Yogesh has not been a student there, nor at other neighbouring schools, such as Muslim High. He has not been seen at the usual haunts around the area. And no one among the 'Ladies of the Night' seems to have heard of Suzie or did not want to speak about her to me. The wall of self-imposed silence is impenetrable. I later hear that a woman had been brutally bashed and died from injuries she suffered during one of the nights behind the Suva Civic Centre. Could it have been Suzie, I wonder? It is difficult to say. The hospital records are silent, and the police are no help. I felt cheated. Somewhere along the way, Suzie had begun to call me *bhaiya*, older brother, and I felt vaguely protective about her, angry at the fate visited upon her through no fault of her own by her own people. She paid the ultimate price, but what about men who abused her to their hearts' content? Suzie had opened for me a window onto a world that I had not previously known. I had in mind to engage her on my next project on female suicides in Fiji. That might never be. For now, there will be no closure, I fear, no final ending. I am more disturbed about Yogesh, this bright boy of promise who could have gone places and might still if he is not damaged beyond repair. Yogesh is somewhere in Suva, alive, I hope. It's a desperate hope, forlorn. I have placed a notice in the papers and mentioned him in an interview on the radio. I hope to hear from him one of these days soon.

Bibliography

Primary Sources

Allen, P.S., ed. *Cyclopedia of Fiji*. Sydney: McCarron, Stewart & Co., 1907.

Anonymous. 'Ai tukutuku kei Ratu Radomodomo Ramatenikutu na Vunivalu mai Bau'. *Na Mata* 1891 (May): 8–11.

Ansdell, Gerrard. *A trip to the highlands of Viti Levu: Being a description of a series of photographic views taken in the Fiji Islands during the dry season of 1881*. London: H. Blair Ansdell, 1882.

'Are mental patients at Suva subjected to cruelty?' *Pacific Review*, 29 August 1970.

'Army seizes power coup'. *Fiji Times,* 15 May 1987.

Associated Press. 'Coup leader is arrested by the military'. *New York Times*, 27 July 2000, www.nytimes.com/2000/07/27/world/coup-leader-in-fiji-is-arrested-by-the-military.html.

Auckland Star. Available at paperspast.natlib.govt.nz.

Australasian. Available at trove.nla.gov.au.

Barker, Allport. 'Repercussions'. *Fiji Times*, 23 January 1943, 4.

Batt, Gary. 'St Giles hospital Fiji: A step back in time'. *Australian College of Mental Health Nurses* (2017, Winter): 12–13.

Board of Education. 'Report of Board of Education'. *Legislative Council Paper* no. 27, 1946.

Brewster, Adolph B. *The hill tribes of Fiji*. London: Seeley, Service & Co. Limited, 1922.

Brewster, Adolph B. *King of the Cannibal Isles*. London: Robert Hales and Company, 1937.

Britton, H. *Fiji in 1870: Being the letters of 'The Argus' special correspondent ...* Melbourne: Samuel Mullen, 1870.

Burton, John. Papers. ML MSS 2899 Add-on 990, Mitchell Library, Sydney.

Cakobau Government Records: Inwards – General – Set 33. National Archives of Fiji.

Calvert, James. *Fiji and the Fijians.* Vol. 2, *Mission History.* Alexander Heylin, 1858.

Capell, Arthur. *A new Fijian dictionary.* Sydney: Australasian Medical Publishing Co., 1941.

Carey, Jesse (compiler). n.d. MSS (in Fijian). Methodist Church of Australasia, Department of Overseas Missions, Item 164, Mitchell Library, Sydney.

Chapman, Mary and Leung, Graham. 'Is Fiji still a democracy?' *Fiji Times*, 9 October 2021.

'Chief Justice's role in the rising crisis'. *Fiji Times,* 21 May 1987.

Colonial Office, Fiji: original correspondence. Public Records Office, National Archives, London.

Colonial Office, Great Britain. *Fiji: Annual general report for the year 1888.* London: H.M.S.O., 1888.

Colonial Report – Annual Fiji, 1880. London: H.M.S.O., 1883.

Colonial Report – Annual Fiji, 1894. London: H.M.S.O., 1895.

Colonial Report – Annual Fiji, 1900. No. 727. London: H.M.S.O., 1901. National Archives of Fiji, Suva.

Colonial Report – Annual Fiji, 1911. No. 727. London: H.M.S.O., 1912.

Colonial Report – Annual Fiji, 1913. London: H.M.S.O., 1914.

Colonial Secretary's Office (CSO): despatches. National Archives of Fiji, Suva.

Colonial Secretary's Office (CSO): inward correspondence. National Archives of Fiji, Suva.

Colony of Fiji. *Blue Book of Fiji for 1894.* Suva: Government Printer, 1894.

Colony of Fiji. *Blue Book of Fiji, 1934.* Suva: Government Printer, 1934.

Colony of Fiji. *Medical department: Annual report for 1938*. Suva: Government Printer, 1940.

Colony of Fiji. *Medical department: Annual report for 1960*. Council paper 32/61. Suva: Government Printer, 1961.

Colony of Fiji. *Medical department: Annual report for 1966*. Council paper 12/68. Suva: Government Press 1968.

Colony of Fiji. *Medical department: Annual report for 1968*. Council paper 39/69. Suva: Government Press, 1969.

Colony of Fiji. *Report on the University of the South Pacific*. Council paper 3/67. Suva: Legislative Council of Fiji, 1967.

Criminal Sittings, Supreme Court of Fiji. National Archives of Fiji, Suva.

Daily Telegraph (Sydney). Available at trove.nla.gov.au.

Dakai, Seruveveli. 1921. *Tukutuku Raraba Nayavumata*. Suva: Native Lands Commission.

Denicagilaba [Ilai Motonicocoka]. 'A veisisivi talanoa makawa: Ai tukuni ni vanua eda vu maikina'. *Na Mata* 1892–1894.

Department of Education. 'Report for the year 1960'. *Legislative Council Papers* no. 29 (1961).

Diapea [Diaper], William. *Cannibal Jack: The true autobiography of a white man in the South Seas*. Oxford: Faber & Gwyer, 1928.

Draper, Thomas. *Williams' Vancouver & New Westminster cities directory, 1890, containing general provincial information*. Vancouver: RT Williams, 1890.

Dumont d'Urville, Jules SC. *Voyage de Découvertes de l'Astrolabe exécuté par ordre du Roi pendant les années 1826–1827–1828–1829*. Paris: Minstère de la Marine, 1834.

Erskine, John Elphinstone. *Journal of a cruise among the islands of the Western Pacific*. London: John Murray, 1853.

Evening Star (Dunedin). Available at paperspast.natlib.govt.nz.

Fiji Bureau of Statistics. *2017 Fiji population and housing census: Administration report*. Suva: Fiji Bureau of Statistics, 2018.

Fiji Bureau of Statistics. 'Key statistics: June 2012'. Table 1.2A census population of Fiji by ethnicity. catalog.ihsn.org/index.php/catalog/3602/download/50136, accessed 5 December 2019.

Fiji Colonial Secretary's Office (FCSO). Files (1940), 50/81, Part 2. National Archives of Fiji, Suva.

Fiji News Herald, National Archives of Fiji, Suva.

Fiji Planters' Journal, National Archives of Fiji, Suva.

Fiji Provisional Government Records. National Archives of Fiji, Suva.

Fiji Royal Gazette. National Archives of Fiji, Suva.

Fiji Times. National Archives of Fiji.

'Fijian swimmers have no place to swim'. *Pacific Islands Monthly,* August 1950, 83.

'Fiji's greeting to Indian Republic Day'. *Fiji Times*, 26 January 1957, 2.

'The Fijis: Our "off-shore" islands have their race problems'. *Voice*, April 1956, 21–22.

Forbes, Litton. *Two years in Fiji.* London: Longmans, Green, 1875.

'"Foreign flower" letter by Adi Finau Tabakaucoro'. *Fiji Times,* 28 May 1987, 6.

'Free at last after 56 days in captivity'. *Fiji Times*, 18 August 2015.

Galland, Frank. 'Relevance & the U.S.P.'. *NATION Newsmagazine.* September 1971.

Gordon Cumming, C.F. *At home in Fiji.* 2 vols. Edinburgh: William Blackwood and Sons, 1881.

Gordon Cumming, C.F. *At home in Fiji.* Edinburgh: William Blackwood and Sons, 1882.

Gorrie, John. 'Fiji as it is'. *Proceedings of the Royal Colonial Institute* 14 (1882–3): 160–85.

Hazlewood, David. *A Feejeean and English dictionary: With examples of common and peculiar modes of expression.* Viwa: Wesleyan Mission Press, 1850.

'Heavy cancellations hit hotels and resorts in Fiji'. *Fiji Times,* 26 May 1987, 8.

Henderson, G.C. *The journal of Thomas Williams, missionary in Fiji, 1840–1853.* Sydney: Angus & Robertson, 1931.

Henderson's British Columbia gazetteer and directory: Containing complete street and alphabetical directories of the cities Vancouver and Victoria and a complete classified business directory. Victoria, British Columbia: LG Henderson, 1890.

Henderson's British Columbia gazetteer and directory: Including a complete classified business directory of British Columbia for the year 1889. Victoria, British Columbia: LG Henderson, 1889.

Heritage Collections. Auckland Libraries.

'History of John Wesley College'. *Fiji Sun,* 9 November 2008, fijisun.com.fj/2008/11/09/history-of-john-wesley-college/.

Hocart, Arthur. *The heart of Fiji.* MS n.d. Turnbull Library, Wellington.

'India Commissioner SA Waiz's farewell speech'. *Fiji Samachar,* 13 October 1950.

'Indians overrunning residential areas in Suva'. *Pacific Islands Monthly,* June 1946.

Jaggar, Thomas James. *Unto the perfect day: The journal of Thomas James Jaggar, Feejee 1838–1845.* Edited by Esther and William Keesing-Styles. Auckland: Solent, 1988.

Journal of the Fiji Legislative Council. National Archives of Fiji.

La Farge, John. *Reminiscences of the South Seas.* Grant Richards, 1914.

Lambert, C.J. and S Lambert. *Voyage of the 'Wanderer' from the journals and letters of C. & S. Lambert.* Edited by Gerald Young. London: Macmillan. 1883.

Lewa, Sainimili. 'Madman attacks asylum staff'. *Fiji Times,* 18 January 2002, 12.

Lowe, A. 'Report of commission of inquiry into the disturbances in Suva, December 1959'. *Journal of the Fiji Legislative Council* no. 10 (1960).

Luvenitoga, Jone. 'Fiji correctional service to celebrate 114 years of service'. *Mailife,* 22 October 2018.

Macgregor, Duncan. 'Notes of a meeting between three South Pacific psychiatrists'. In South Pacific Commission, *Mental health in the South Pacific: Report of a meeting of experts held at Suva (Fiji) from 19 to 22 May, and at Nouméa (New Caledonia) from 23 to 27 May 1967.* Technical Paper no. 154. Nouméa: South Pacific Commission, 1967.

MacKinnon, Marsali. Interview with Rodney Acraman, 9 March 1999. Audio 26–27, Transcripts. Pacific Manuscripts Bureau.

Manueli, Irene. 'Asylum can't cure morphine addict'. *Fiji Times,* 5 January 2002.

Mayhew, A.I. 'Report on education in Fiji'. *Legislative Council Paper* no. 3, 1937.

'Mental Health Decree 2010 (54/2010)', *Republic of Fiji Islands Government Gazette* 11, no. 119 (2010).

Methodist Church of Australasia. *Missionary review.* Sydney: Methodist Church of Australasia, 1891-1977.

Methodist Mission in Fiji. 'Minutes of the Fiji district for 1881'. F4 A. National Archives of Fiji, Suva.

Methodist Missionary Society of Australasia. *At the gateway of the day.* Suva: Methodist Missionary Society of Australasia, 1935.

Methodist Missionary Society of Australasia archives. National Archives of Fiji and Mitchell Library, Sydney.

Ministry of Overseas Development. *Report of the Higher Education Mission to the South Pacific: Appointed by agreement between the Governments of Britain and New Zealand with the co-operation of the Government of Australia.* London: H.M.S.O., 1966.

'Mob quelled as violence flares'. *Fiji Times,* 21 May 1987, 3.

Mokunitulevu Na Rai [Epeli Rokowaqa]. *Ai tukutuku kei Viti.* Suva: Methodist Church in Fiji, 1928.

Nacei, Luke. 'Health minister reveals plans to relocate St Giles Hospital to Ba'. *Fiji Times,* 15 October 2018.

Naisilisili, Seveci. *Tukutuku Raraba Bativudi.* Suva: Native Lands Commission, n.d. [1921?].

New Zealand Herald. Available at paperspast.natlib.govt.nz.

New Zealand Times. Available at paperspast.natlib.govt.nz.

Neyret, J. *Fijian dictionary.* MS, 1935. Fiji Government Archives.

Otago Daily Times. Available at paperspast.natlib.govt.nz.

'Passport applicants besiege Immigration Office in Suva'. *Fiji Times,* 30 May 1987, 10.

Perry, C.J. *Copy of a dispatch to the Right Honorable Earl of Carnarvon, Secretary of State for Colonies from the Polynesia Company, being a remonstrance against the unlawful withholding of the Company's lands at Fiji by his Excellency the Governor, Sir Arthur Hamilton Gordon.* Melbourne: Polynesia Company, 1877.

Pierce, Franklin. *Sloop of War 'John Adams' at the Feejee Islands: Message from the President of the United States communicating the report of Captain Boutwell, relative to the operations of the sloop of war 'John Adams' at the Fejee Islands.* [Washington]: House of Representatives Ex Doc No 115, 34th Congress, 1st Session, 1856.

Pritchard, WT. *Polynesian reminiscences, or life in the South Pacific islands*. London: Chapman & Hall, 1866.

'Proceedings of a native council or council of chiefs'. 1875–1917. National Archives of Fiji, Suva.

Ravulo, A. 'Finding homes for patients is a challenge: Dr Koroivuki'. *FBC News*, 8 October 2018. www.fbcnews.com.fj/news/finding-homes-for-patients-is-a-challenge-dr-koroivuki/.

Regulations of the Native Regulation Board: 1877–1882. London: Harrison and Sons, 1883.

Report of the commission appointed to inquire into the decrease of the native population. Suva: Government Printer, 1893.

Rogo, Kaminieli. *Tukutuku Raraba Nauluvatu*. Suva: Native Lands Commission, 1921.

Rokonadravu, Mary. 'Open Letter to Mr. Kris Prasad (Fiji)'. *Medium*, 30 October 2019.

'Rowdy gangs strike homes in Suva area'. *Fiji Times*, 22 May 1987, 3.

Samoa Times and South Sea Gazette. Available at paperspast.natlib.govt.nz.

Seemann, Berthold. *Viti: An account of a government mission to the Vitian or Fijian Islands*. London: Dawsons of Pall Mall, 1973.

Seemann, Berthold. *Viti: An account of a government mission to the Vitian or Fijian Islands in the years 1860–61*. Cambridge: Macmillan, 1862. doi.org/10.5962/bhl.title.54719.

Seni, Vetaia. *Tukutuku Raraba Nakurukuru*. Suva: Native Lands Commission, 1927.

Seniloli, A Savenaca. Letter to the Native Lands Commissioner. 30 January 1919. iTaukei Lands and Fisheries Commission. National Archives of Fiji, Suva.

Simmons, Matilda. 'First police station'. *Fiji Times*, 25 January 2020.

Singh, Thakur Ranjit. 'Fiji's failed military mutiny: The day Frank Bainimarama was supposed to die – a dark history of modern Fiji'. *Fiji Pundit* (blog), 1 November 2014, fijipundit.blogspot.com/2014/11/fijis-failed-military-mutiny-day-frank.html.

Spence, Frank and Central Archives of Fiji and the Western Pacific High Commission. *The claims and remonstrance of the Polynesia Company of Melbourne, examined and refuted*. Microform, National Library of Australia.

Stanmore, Lord (Sir Arthur Gordon). *Fiji: Records of private and of public life 1875–1880*. 4 vols. Edinburgh: self-published, 1897–1912.

Stephens, FB. 'Report on education in Fiji'. *Journal of the Fiji Legislative Council* no. 18 (1944).

St Giles Hospital Archives. St Giles Psychiatric Hospital, Suva.

'Suva lies silent'. *Fiji Times,* 22 May 1987, 2.

Suva Times. National Archives of Fiji.

Toge, Samu. *Tukutuku Raraba Navakavu*. Suva: Native Lands Commission, 1927.

Tokaduadua, Waisake. 'Tukutuku kī Vatuwaqa'. Transcript of 1984 interview in possession of Paul Geraghty.

UNISPAC [University of the South Pacific Student Association newspaper] 4, no. 4 (1971), USP Pacific Collection, USP Library.

Vakasukawaqa, Arieta. 'Father's death inspired sons to join RFMF'. *Fiji Sun*, 25 December 2016, fijisun.com.fj/2016/12/25/fathers-death-inspired-sons-to-join-rfmf/.

Vesikula, Kitione. *Tawavanua: Transcription of a series of talks on Radio Fiji One*. Suva: Fiji Broadcasting Commission, 1974.

Wallis, Mary. *Life in Feejee: Five years among the cannibals. By a lady.* Boston: William Heath, 1851.

Waqadau, Amenisitai. *Tukutuku Raraba Vatuwaqa*. Suva: Native Lands Commission, 1921.

Western Star (Australia). Available at trove.nla.gov.au.

Whonsbon-Aston, Charles W. *Pacific Irishman*. William Floyd memorial lecture, inaugural lecture. Stanmore: Australian Board of Missions, 1970.

'The woman who changed the lives of many Fijian women'. *Fiji Sun*, 19 September 2016. fijisun.com.fj/2016/09/19/the-woman-who-changed-the-lives-of-many-fijian-women/.

Wood, A Harold. *Overseas Missions of the Australian Methodist Church*. Vol. 2, *Fiji*. Melbourne: Aldersgate Press, 1978.

Wood, A Harold. *Overseas Missions of the Australian Methodist Church*. Vol. 3, *Fiji-Indian and Rotuma*. Melbourne: Aldersgate Press, 1978.

Secondary Sources

Adler, Antony. 'The capture and curation of the cannibal "Vendovi": Reality and representation of a Pacific frontier'. *Journal of Pacific History* 49, no. 3 (2014): 255–82. doi.org/10.1080/00223344.2014.914623.

Aikman, Colin M. 'Establishment: 1968–74'. In *Pacific universities: Achievements, problems and prospects*, edited by Ron Crocombe and Malama Meleisea, 35–52. Suva: Institute of Pacific Studies, University of the South Pacific, 1988.

Alefaio, Opeta. 'Archives connecting with the community'. Paper presented at the International Federation of Library Associations and Institutions, World Library and Information Congress, 'Connections. Collaboration. Community', Session 96, Asia and Oceania, Columbus, Ohio, 9–19 Aug. 2016.

Alexander, Gilchrist. *From the middle temple to the South Seas*. London: John Murray, Albemarle Street, 1927.

Ali, Ahmed. 'Girmit: The indenture experience in Fiji'. *Bulletin of the Fiji Museum* no. 5 (1979).

Bain, 'Atu. 'A protective labour policy? An alternative interpretation of early colonial labour policy in Fiji'. *Journal of Pacific History* 3, no. 2 (1988): 119–36. doi.org/10.1080/00223348808572584.

Bain, Kenneth. *Treason at ten: Fiji at the crossroads*. London: Hodder and Stoughton Ltd, 1989.

Bate, Weston. *A history of Brighton*. Carlton: Melbourne University Press, 1983.

Biersack, Aletta, ed. *Clio in Oceania: Towards a historical anthropology*. Washington: Smithsonian Institute Press, 1991.

Bossen, Claus. 'Festival mania, tourism and nation building in Fiji: The case of the Hibiscus festival, 1956–1970'. *The Contemporary Pacific* 12, no. 1 (2000): 123–54. doi.org/10.1353/cp.2000.0006.

Bourke, Joanna. *Rape: A history from 1860 to the present*. London: Virago, 2007.

Brereton, Bridget. *Law, justice, empire: The colonial career of John Gorrie, 1829–1892*. Barbados: University of the West Indies Press, 1997.

Britton, Henry. *The Suva land quest, by one of the party*. Melbourne, 1880.

Byrne, Paula. *Criminal law and colonial subject: New South Wales, 1810–1830*. Cambridge: Cambridge University Press, 1993. doi.org/10.1017/CBO9780511586101.

Calman, Donald. 'A history of Indians in Fiji'. MA thesis, University of Sydney, 1952.

Campbell, J.R. *Dealing with disaster: Hurricane response in Fiji*. Honolulu: Pacific Islands Development Program, East-West Center, 1984.

Cannon, Michael. *Land boom and bust*. Melbourne: Heritage Publications, 1972.

Carr, Edward Hallett. *What is history?* London: Macmillan, 1961.

Cato, A.C. 'Fijians and Indians: A cultural contact problem in the South Pacific'. *Oceania* 26, no. 1 (1955): 14–34. doi.org/10.1002/j.1834-4461.1955.tb00655.x.

Chambers, Ken. 'Ratu Epeli Kanakana versus A-G for Fiji (the Suvavou case): Blending equitable relief with judicial review'. *Journal of South Pacific Law* 12, no. 1 (2008): 111–19.

Citizens Constitutional Forum. *One nation diverse peoples: Building a just and democratic Fiji*. Suva: Citizens Constitutional Forum, September 1995.

Clark, Anna. *Women's silence, men's violence: Sexual assault in England, 1770–1845*. London and New York: Pandora Press, 1987.

Cleland, L, HE Maude, Robert Langdon, John Young, WN Gunson, and JS Craig. 'From the archives'. *Journal of Pacific History* 1, no. 1 (1966): 183–203. doi.org/10.1080/00223346608572089.

Clunie, Fergus. 'The Manila brig'. *Domodomo* 2, no. 2 (1984): 42–86.

Cooper, H.S. *The islands of the Pacific*. London: R. Bentley and Son, 1888.

Crocombe, Ron, Tupeni Baba and Malama Meleisea. 'The development of higher education in the Pacific Islands'. In *Pacific universities: Achievements, problems and prospects*, edited by Ron Crocombe and Malama Meleisea, 20–31. Suva: Institute of Pacific Studies, University of the South Pacific, 1988.

Daws, Gavan and Bennett Hymer, eds. *Honolulu stories: Voices of the town through the years; Two centuries of writing*. Honolulu: Mutual Pub., 2008.

Dawson, Bee. *Laucala Bay: The story of the RNZAF in Fiji 1939 to 1967*. Auckland: Penguin Random House, 2017.

Daya, Mary, ed. *Shedding silences: An anthology of writing from Fiji prisons*. Suva: University of the South Pacific, 2008.

de Bruce, Lucy. 'Histories of diversity: Kailoma testimonies and "part-European" tales from colonial Fiji (1920–1970)'. *Journal of Intercultural Studies* 28, no. 1 (2007): 113–28. doi.org/10.1080/07256860601082970.

Derrick, R.A. '1875: Fiji's darkest hour: An account of the measles epidemic of 1875'. *Transactions and Proceedings of the Fiji Society* 6, no. 1 (1955): 3–16.

Derrick, R.A. *A history of Fiji*. Vol. 1. Suva: Printing and Stationery Department, 1946.

Derrick, R.A. 'The removal of the capital to Suva'. *Transactions and Proceedings of the Fiji Society of Science and Industry* (1953): 203–9.

Duff, Peter. 'The evolution of trial by judge and assessors in Fiji'. *Journal of Pacific Studies* 21 (1997): 189–213.

Dumaru, Apete Rokotuiwai. 'Suva makawa'. Computer file in possession of Paul Geraghty, 1999.

Duncan, Margot. 'Autoethnography: Critical appreciation of an emerging art'. *International Journal of Qualitative Methods* 3, no. 4 (2004): 28–39. doi.org/10.1177/160940690400300403.

Eriksen, Thomas. *Common denominators: Ethnicity, nation-building, and compromise in Mauritius*. Oxford: Berg, 1998.

Ernst, Waltraud. *Work, psychiatry and society, c. 1750–2015*. Manchester: Manchester University Press, 2016. doi.org/10.7228/manchester/9780719097690.001.0001.

Estrich, Susan. 'Rape'. *Yale Law Journal* 95, no. 6 (1986): 1087–184. doi.org/10.2307/796522.

Etherington, Norman. 'The gendering of indirect rule: Criminal law and colonial Fiji, 1875–1900'. *Journal of Pacific History* 31, no. 1 (1996): 45–46. doi.org/10.1080/00223349608572805.

Etherington, Norman. 'Natal's black rape scare of the 1870s'. *Journal of Southern African Studies* 15, no. 1 (1988): 36–53. doi.org/10.1080/03057078808708190.

Fiji Corrections Service. '15 corrections centres', Fiji Corrections Service (2017). www.corrections.gov.fj/institutions.

Foucault, Michel. *Discipline and punish: The birth of the prison*. New York: Pantheon Books, 1977.

France, Peter. *The charter of the land: Custom and colonization in Fiji*. Melbourne: Oxford University Press, 1969.

Freeman, Susan. 'The centre-poled houses of western Vitilevu'. *Domodomo* 4, no. 1 (1986): 2–19.

Gatty, Ronald. *Fijian–English dictionary: With notes on Fijian culture and natural history*. Suva: Southeast Asia Program, Cornell University, 2010.

Geddes, William. 'Acceleration of social change in a Fijian community'. *Oceania* 16, no. 1 (1945): 1–14. doi.org/10.1002/j.1834-4461.1945.tb00428.x.

Geraghty, Paul A. *The history of the Fijian languages*. Oceanic Linguistics Special Publication 19. Honolulu: University of Hawai'i Press, 1983.

Geraghty, Paul A. 'Maps and the understanding of Fiji's toponymy 1643–1840'. *Globe* 88 (2020): 42–52.

Geraghty, Paul A. 'Suffixation as a place naming strategy in the Central Pacific and its implications for prehistory'. *Names* 65, no. 4 (2017): 235–44. doi.org/10.1080/00277738.2017.1370069.

Ghosh, Durba. 'Household crimes and domestic order: Keeping the peace in colonial Calcutta, c. 1770–c. 1840'. *Modern Asian Studies* 38 (2004): 599–623. doi.org/10.1017/S0026749X03001124,

Gillion, K.L. *Fiji's Indian migrants: A history to the end of indenture in 1920*. New York: Oxford University Press, 1962.

Goffman, Erving. *Asylums: Essays on the social situation of mental patients and other inmates*. New York: Doubleday Anchor, 1961.

Gonelevu, Shailin. 'From containment to correction and reformation: Exploring punishment and reform in the disciplinary system of Fiji women's prison'. MA thesis, University of the South Pacific, 2015.

Gravelle, Kim. *Fiji's heritage: A history of Fiji*. Nadi: Tiara Enterprises, 2000.

Gravelle, Kim. *Fiji's times: A history of Fiji*. 3 vols. Suva: Fiji Times, 1979.

Griffin, Chris and Michael Monsell-Davis. *Fijians in town*. Suva: Institute of Pacific Studies, University of the South Pacific, 1986.

Grimshaw, Beatrice. *From Fiji to the Cannibal Islands*. London: Eveleigh Nash, 1907.

Guthrie, Margaret W. *Misi Utu: Dr D. W. Hoodless and the development of medical education in the South Pacific*. Suva: Institute of Pacific Studies, University of the South Pacific with the South Pacific Social Sciences Association, 1979.

Halapua, Winston. *Living on the fringe: Melanesians in Fiji*. Suva: Institute of Pacific Studies, University of the South Pacific, 2001.

Halapua, Winston. 'A study of the evolution of marginalization: The case of the Solomoni community of Wailoku in Fiji'. PhD thesis, University of the South Pacific, 1993.

Halter, Nicholas. '"Cannibals and convicts": Australian travel writing about New Caledonia', in *The Palgrave Handbook of Prison Tourism*, edited by JZ Wilson, S Hodginkson, J Piché and K Walby, 867–84. New York: Springer Nature, 2017. doi.org/10.1057/978-1-137-56135-0_41.

Halter, Nicholas. 'Tourists fraternising in Fiji in the 1930s', *Journal of Tourism History* 12, no. 1 (2020): 27–47. doi.org/10.1080/1755182X.2019.1682688.

Halter, Nicholas and Max Quanchi. 'Boosting the frontier: Australian settler colonialism in the Pacific 1860s–1900s'. *Australian Historical Studies* (2022). doi.org/10.1080/1031461X.2021.2021961.

Hare, Eric B. *Fulton's footsteps in Fiji*. Washington DC: Review and Herald Publishing Association, 1969.

Heartfield, James. '"The dark races against the light"? Official reaction to the 1959 Fiji riots'. *Journal of Pacific History* 37, no. 1 (2002): 75–86. doi.org/10.1080/00223340120096242A.

Heartfield, James. '"You are not a white woman!"'. *Journal of Pacific History* 38, no. 1 (2003): 69–83. doi.org/10.1080/00223340306076.

Hempenstall, Peter and Noel Rutherford. *Protest and dissent in the colonial Pacific*. Suva: Institute of Pacific Studies, University of the South Pacific, 1984.

Howlett, Robert. *The history of the Fiji military forces 1939–1945*. London: Crown Agents for the Colonies on behalf of the Government of Fiji, 1948.

Hughes, Carl. 'Racial issues in Fiji'. DPhil thesis, Oxford University, 1965.

Inglis, Amirah. *Not a white woman safe: Sexual anxiety and politics in Port Moresby, 1920–1934*. Canberra: Australian National University Press, 1974.

Kaplan, Martha. *Neither cargo nor cult: Ritual politics and the colonial imagination in Fiji*. Durham: Duke University Press, 1995. doi.org/10.1215/9780822381914.

Kelly, John. '"Coolie" as labour commodity: Race, sex, and European dignity in colonial Fiji'. *Journal of Peasant Studies* 19, no. 3–4 (1992): 246–67. doi.org/10.1080/03066159208438495.

Knapman, Claudia. *White women in Fiji 1835–1930: The ruin of empire?* Sydney: Allen & Unwin, 1986.

Kolsky, Elizabeth. '"The body evidencing the crime": Rape on trial in colonial India, 1860–1947'. *Gender & History* 22, no. 1 (2010): 109–30. doi.org/10.1111/j.1468-0424.2009.01581.x.

Kolsky, Elizabeth. 'The rule of colonial indifference: Rape on trial in early colonial India, 1805–1857'. *Journal of Asian Studies* 69, no. 4 (2010): 1093–117. doi.org/10.1017/S0021911810002937.

Korovulavula, Manunivavalagi. *Gone ni Turaki*. Nasinu: Manu Korovulavula Publisher, 2011.

Korovulavula, Manunivavalagi Dalituicama. *Malayan campaign: 1st Battalion Fiji Infantry Regiment, 1952–1956*. Suva: Max Marketing and Publisher Limited, 2014.

Kuva, Aduru. *The Solomons community in Fiji*. Suva: South Pacific Social Sciences Association, 1974.

Laka, Levy M. *Solomon Islands descendants in Fiji: A case study of Wailoku*. Suva: University of the South Pacific, 1983.

Lal, Brij V. *Broken waves: A history of the Fiji Islands in the twentieth century*. Honolulu: University of Hawai'i Press, 1992.

Lal, Brij V. 'Bula Dredre'. In *Road from Mr Tulsi's store*, 139–60. Suva, University of the South Pacific Press, 2019.

Lal, Brij V. *Chalo Jahaji: On a journey through indenture in Fiji*. Canberra and Suva: Australian National University Press and Fiji Museum, 2000. doi.org/10.22459/CJ.12.2012.

Lal, Brij V. *In the eye of the storm*. Canberra: ANU E Press, 2010. doi.org/10.22459/ES.11.2010.

Lal, Brij V. 'Veil of dishonour'. In *Chalo Jahaji: On a journey through indenture in Fiji,* 215–38. Canberra and Suva: Australian National University Press and Fiji Museum, 2000. doi.org/10.22459/CJ.12.2012.

Lal, Brij V. 'Veil of dishonour: Sexual jealousy and suicide on Fiji plantations'. *Journal of Pacific History* 20, no. 3 (1985): 135–55. doi.org/10.1080/00223348508572516.

Lal, Brij V. *A vision for change: A. D. Patel and the politics of Fiji*. Canberra: Australian National University Press, 1997.

Leckie, Jacqueline. *Colonizing madness: Asylum and community in Fiji*. Honolulu: University of Hawai'i Press, 2019. doi.org/10.2307/j.ctvgs09bn.

Leckie, Jacqueline. *To labour with the state: The Fiji Public Service Association*. Dunedin: University of Otago Press, 1997.

Leckie, Jacqueline (with contributors). *A university for the Pacific: 50 years of USP*. Suva: University of the South Pacific, 2018.

Lee, Albert. *Historical notes on the city of Suva supplement*. Suva: National Archives of Fiji, 1984.

Lee, Albert. *Historical notes on the city of Suva with particular reference to the central business district*. Suva: National Archives of Fiji, 1974.

Lewis, Gordon. *The growth of the modern West Indies*. New York: Monthly Review Press, 1969.

Lukere, Victoria. 'The native mother'. In *The Cambridge History of the Pacific Islanders*, edited by Donald Denoon, 280–86. Cambridge: Cambridge University Press, 1997.

Mamak, Alexander. *Colour, culture & conflict: A study of pluralism in Fiji*. Rushcutters Bay: Pergamon Press, 1978.

Mander, Linden. *Some dependent peoples of the South Pacific*. New York: Macmillan, 1954.

Mann, Cecil W. *Education in Fiji*. Melbourne: Melbourne University Press, 1935.

Mara, Rātū Sir Kamisese. *The Pacific way: A memoir*. Honolulu: University of Hawai'i Press, 1997.

maskedman. 'Savage world'. Karate Resource forum, 10 December 2005, karateresource.proboards.com/thread/337.

Matahau, Anare and Associates. *Suva state land: 'Land of my fathers'*. Suva: Anare Matahau and Associates, 1991.

Mateiviti-Tulavu, Eseta. 'Connecting identities and relationships through Indigenous epistemology: The Solomoni of Fiji'. PhD thesis, University of Auckland, 2013.

McHugh, J.J. 'Recollections of early Suva'. *Fiji Society of Science and Industry* (19 July 1943): 210–14.

Meek, V Lynn and David R Jones. 'Particularism, universality, and the university'. In *Pacific universities. Achievements, problems and prospects*, edited by Ron Crocombe and Malama Meleisea. 13–17. Suva: Institute of Pacific Studies, University of the South Pacific, 1988.

Merry, Sally Engle. *Colonizing Hawai'i: The cultural power of law*. Princeton: Princeton University Press, 2000. doi.org/10.1515/9780691221984.

Miller, Willard. 'Taxation without representation'. *Fiji Times*, 14 November 2020. www.pressreader.com/fiji/the-fiji-times/20201114/281676847442554.

Milner, G.B., David George Arms and Paul Geraghty. 'Duivosavosa: Fiji's languages, their use and their future'. *Bulletin of the Fiji Museum* no. 8 (1984).

Mishra, Sudesh. '"Bending closer to the ground": Girmit as minor history'. *Australian Humanities Review* 52 (2012): n.p., australianhumanitiesreview.org/2012/05/01/bending-closer-to-the-ground-girmit-as-minor-history. doi.org/10.22459/AHR.52.2012.02.

Mitchell, John. '150th anniversary: Fiji's death penalty'. *Fiji Times,* 30 October 2019.

Miyazaki, Hirokazu. *The method of hope: Anthropology, philosophy, and Fijian knowledge*. Stanford: Stanford University Press, 2004.

Moses, Ruth. 'The Polynesia Company Limited of Melbourne and Fiji 1868–1883: A social history'. BA (Hons) thesis, University of Adelaide, 1971.

Naidu, Vijay. 'Coups in Fiji seesawing democratic multiracialism and ethno-nationalist extremism'. *Devforum* no. 26 (2007): 24–33.

Naidu, Vijay. *The Fiji Labour Party and the by-election of December 1985: A report*. SSED Working Paper no. 2. Suva: School of Economic and Social Development, University of the South Pacific, 1986.

Naidu, Vijay, Anawaite Matadradra, Josaia Osborne and Maria Sahib. 'Informal settlements and social inequality in Fiji: Evidence of serious policy gaps'. *Journal of Pacific Studies* 35, no. 1 (2015): 27–46.

Naidu, Vijay, Anawaite Matadradra, Maria Sahib and Josaia Osborne. *Fiji: The challenges and opportunities of diversity*. Suva: CCF & Minority Rights Group International, 2013.

Naidu, Vijay, Mahendra Reddy and Steven Ratuva. *Fiji prison reforms: From containment to correction and beyond*. Suva: Ecumenical Centre for Research, Education and Advocacy, 2009.

'Namena Tailevu – Noda Gauna'. YouTube, 16 July 2010, youtu.be/9KeZfVGY8IY (site discontinued).

Nayacakalou, R.R. 'The urban Fijians of Suva'. In *Pacific port towns and cities*, edited by Alexander Spoehr, 33–41. Honolulu: Bishop Museum Press, 1963.

Nicole, Robert. *Disturbing history: Resistance in early colonial Fiji.* Honolulu: University of Hawai'i Press, 2011. doi.org/10.1515/9780824860981.

Nicole, Robert. *Disturbing history: Resistance in early colonial Fiji.* Suva: University of the South Pacific Press, 2018.

Norton, Robert. 'Averting "irresponsible nationalism": Political origins of Ratu Sukuna's Fijian Administration'. *Journal of Pacific History* 48, no. 4 (2013): 409–28. doi.org/10.1080/00223344.2013.852706.

Norton, Robert. *Race and politics in Fiji.* 2nd ed. St. Lucia: University of Queensland Press, 1990.

O'Carroll, John. 'Multiple cities: Suva and the (post)colonial'. *Dreadlocks in Oceania* 1 (1997): 26–42.

Oram, N.D. *Colonial Town to Melanesian City: Port Moresby 1884–1974.* Canberra: Australian National University Press, 1976.

Page, Patricia. *Across the magic line: Growing up in Fiji.* Canberra: Pandanus Book, 2004.

Pape, John. 'Black and white: The "perils of sex" in colonial Zimbabwe'. *Journal of Southern African Studies* 16, no. 4 (1990): 699–720. doi.org/10.1080/03057079008708257.

Parke, Aubrey. *Degei's descendants: Spirits, place and people in pre-cession Fiji.* Edited by Matthew Spriggs and Deryck Scarr. Canberra: ANU Press, 2014. doi.org/10.22459/TA41.08.2014.

Parry, John T. 'Ring-ditch fortifications in the Rewa Delta, Fiji: air photo interpretation and analysis'. *Bulletin of the Fiji Museum* no. 3 (1977).

Penjueli, A. '220 squatter settlements across Fiji, majority in Suva'. *Newswire Focus,* 10 February 2016. newswire.internet.com.fj/community/220-squatter-settlements-across-fiji-majority-in-suva.

Premdas, Ralph R and Jeffrey S Stevens. *Electoral politics in a third world city: Port Moresby 1977.* Konedobu: University of Papua New Guinea, 1978.

Quanchi, Max. *This glorious company.* Suva: USP Press, 2020.

Quanchi, Max. 'This glorious company: The Polynesia Company in Melbourne and Fiji'. MA thesis, Monash University, 1977.

Quanchi, Max. *Glorious company: The Polynesia Company in Melbourne and Fiji.* Suva: Pacific Studies Press, 2022.

Quanchi, Max and Max Shekleton. *An ideal colony and epitome of progress: Colonial Fiji in picture postcards.* Suva: University of the South Pacific Press, 2019.

Reed, Adam. *Papua New Guinea's last place: Experiences of constraint in a postcolonial prison.* New York: Berghahn Books, 2003.

Riles, Annelise. 'Part-Europeans and Fijians'. In *Fiji in transition,* Vol. 1, edited by Brij V Lal and Tomasi Vakatora, 105–29. Suva: University of the South Pacific, 1997.

Robertson, Robbie. *The general's goose: Fiji's tale of contemporary misadventure.* Canberra: ANU Press, 2017. doi.org/10.22459/GG.08.2017.

Round, Sally. 'Motion for local elections defeated in Fiji parliament'. *Radio New Zealand,* 3 April 2019. www.rnz.co.nz/international/pacific-news/386256/motion-for-local-elections-defeated-in-fiji-parliament.

Routledge, David. *Matanitu: The struggle for power in early Fiji.* Suva: Institute of Pacific Studies, University of the South Pacific, 1985.

Routledge, David. 'Pre-Cession government in Fiji'. PhD thesis, Australian National University, 1965.

Saha, Jonathan. 'The male state: Colonialism, corruption and rape investigations in the Irrawaddy Delta c. 1900'. *Indian Economic and Social History Review* 48, no. 3 (2010): 343–76. doi.org/10.1177/001946461004700303.

Sahlins, Marshall. *The return of the event, again: With reflections on the beginnings of the great Fijian war of 1843 to 1855 between the kingdoms of Bau and Rewa.* Washington DC: Biersack, 1991.

Salesa, Damon. *Racial crossings: Race, intermarriage, and the Victorian British Empire.* Oxford: Oxford University Press, 2011. doi.org/10.1093/acprof:oso/9780199604159.001.0001.

Samson, Jane. *Imperial benevolence: Making British authority in the Pacific Islands.* Honolulu: University of Hawai'i Press, 1998. doi.org/10.1515/9780824862947.

Scarr, Deryck. *Fiji: A short history.* Sydney: Allen & Unwin, 1984.

Scarr, Deryck. *The majesty of colour: A life of Sir John Bates Thurston.* Vol. 1, *I, the very bayonet.* Canberra: ANU Press, 1973.

Schütz, Albert J, ed. *The diaries and correspondence of David Cargill, 1832–1843.* Canberra: Australian National University, 1977.

Schütz, Albert J. *Suva: a history and guide*. Sydney: Pacific Publications, 1978.

Scott, Henry. 'The Development of Suva'. *Transactions and Proceedings of the Fiji Society of Science and Industry* 2 no. 1 (1940): 15–20.

Scully, Pamela. 'Rape, race and colonial culture: The sexual politics of identity in the nineteenth-century Cape Colony, South Africa'. *American Historical Review* 100, no. 2 (1995): 335–59. doi.org/10.2307/2169002.

Sea Reel Productions. *A mariner's guide to Fiji shores & marinas 2019*. Suva: Sea Reel Productions Ltd., 2019.

Sellers, B.M. 'Development of Fiji prison service'. *Proceedings of the Fiji Society 1955–1963* 6 (1962).

Sharpham, J.R. *Rabuka of Fiji*. Rockhampton: Central Queensland University Press, 2000.

Sidal, Morven. *Hannah Dudley Hamari Maa: Honoured mother, educator and missioner to the indentured Indians of Fiji 1864–1931*. Suva: Pacific Theological College, 1997.

Simone, AbdouMaliq. *Jakarta: Drawing the city near*. Minnesota: University of Minnesota Press, 2014. doi.org/10.5749/minnesota/9780816693351.001.0001.

Smith, Abel. 'Community psychiatric nursing: The Fiji experience'. Presentation to Community Health Workshop, 15–19 April 1996, St Giles Hospital.

Steel, Frances. Oceania under steam: *Sea transport and the cultures of colonialism, c. 1870–1914*. Manchester: Manchester University Press, 2011.

Stepan, Nancy. *The idea of race in science: Great Britain 1800–1960*. London: Macmillan, 1982. doi.org/10.1007/978-1-349-05452-7.

Stephenson, Elsie. *Fiji's past on picture postcards*. Suva: Caines Jannif Group, 1997.

Stockdale, Eric. 'A short history of prison inspection in England'. *British Journal of Criminology* 23, no. 3 (1983): 209–28. doi.org/10.1093/oxfordjournals.bjc.a047376.

Stoler, Ann Laura. *Carnal knowledge and imperial power: Race and the intimate in colonial rule*. Berkeley, Los Angeles and London: University of California Press, 2003.

Strange, Carolyn. 'Masculinities, intimate femicide and the death penalty in Australia, 1890–1920'. *British Journal of Criminology* 43 (2003): 310–39. doi.org/10.1093/bjc/43.2.310.

Stuart, Ian. *Port Moresby: Yesterday and today*. Sydney: Pacific Publications, 1970.

Subramani, Anurag. 'The execution of Antonio Franks, Part 1 and 2'. *Fiji Times*, 17 and 24 November 2019.

Subramani, Anurag. *The Fiji Times at 150: Imagining the Fijian nation (or, a scrapbook of Fiji's history)*. Suva: Fiji Times, Forthcoming.

Sutherland, William. *Beyond the politics of race: An alternative history of Fiji to 1992*. Canberra: Australian National University, 1992.

Tavola, Kaliopate. *Kaidravuni* (blog). www.kaidravuni.com.

Thaman, Randolph R, Michael P Gregory and Shingo Takeda. *Trees of life. A guide to trees and shrubs of the University of the South Pacific*. Suva: The University of the South Pacific Press, 2012.

Thomas, Frank, Paul Geraghty and Elizabeth Matisoo-Smith. 'Lapita archaeology in the Southwest Pacific'. In *Encyclopedia of global archaeology*, edited by Claire Smith. New York: Springer, 2020. doi.org/10.1007/978-3-319-51726-1_3410-1.

Thomas, Nicholas. *Colonialism's culture: Anthropology, travel, and government*. Princeton: Princeton University Press, 1994.

Thompson, Basil. *The Fijians: A study of the decay of custom*. London: William Heinemann, 1908.

Thomson, Ian, Peter Thomson and Rob Wright. *Fiji in the forties and fifties*. Auckland: Thomson Pacific, 1994.

Thornley, Andrew. 'Fijian Methodism 1874–1945: The emergence of a national church'. PhD thesis, Australian National University, 1979.

Tippett, Alan R. *Aspects of Pacific ethnohistory*. South Pasadena: William Carey Library, 1973.

Tuimaleali'ifano, Morgan. *Samoans in Fiji: Migration, identity and communication*. Suva: Institute of Pacific Studies, Fiji, Tonga, and Western Samoa Extension Centres of the University of the South Pacific, 1990.

UN-Habitat. *Fiji: Greater Suva urban profile*. Nairobi: UN Habitat, 2012.

University of the South Pacific. *A garland of achievement. University of the South Pacific 1968–1993*. Suva: University of the South Pacific, 1993.

Usher, Len. *50 years in Fiji*. Suva: Shell, 1978.

Usher, Len. *Mainly about Fiji: A collection of writings, broadcasts and speeches*. Suva, Fiji Times, 1987.

Vakatora, Tomasi. *From the mangrove swamps*. Suva: Institute of Pacific Studies, University of the South Pacific, 1998.

van Aller, Bart. *Suva gaol*. Suva: National Trust of Fiji, 2015.

Vataiki, Tifa. 'Serious concerns raised as research shows microplastic in fish and other seafood sources in Fiji'. *Fijivillage*, 2 July 2020. www.fijivillage.com/news/Serious-concerns-raised-as-research-shows-microplastic-in-fish-and-other-seafood-sources-in-Fiji-58f4xr/.

Veramu, Joseph. *Growing up in Fiji*. Suva: Institute of Pacific Studies, 1984.

Vigarello, Georges. *A history of rape: Sexual violence in France from the 16th to 20th century*. Cambridge: Polity Press, 2000.

Vuataki, K. *Softly Fiji*. Bloomington: West Bow Press, 2013.

Vuetibau, I. K. 'Squatting and the California Highway settlement, Suva'. In *In search of a home*, edited by Leonard Mason and Patricia Hereniko, 145–54. Suva: Institute of Pacific Studies, University of the South Pacific, 1987.

Vunivalu, Ravuama and WL Verrier. *A social survey of Fijians in Suva*. Suva: 1959.

Wall, Colman. 'Historical notes on Suva', edited by Paul Geraghty. Domodomo 10, no. 2 (1996): 28–39.

Wall, Colman. 'Historical notes on Suva', edited by Paul Geraghty. *Domodomo* 11, no. 2 (1997): 15–37.

Wall, Colman. 'Historical notes on Suva', edited by Paul Geraghty. *Domodomo* 12, no. 2 (1999): 49–58.

Wall, Colman. 'Sketches in Fijian history'. *Transactions of the Fijian Society* (1919).

Ward, Albert E. 'Old land marks of Suva'. *Transactions and Proceedings of the Fiji Society of Science and Industry* Vol. 2: 215–17, 1953.

Weir, Christine. 'Methodist childhoods: The education and formation of the young Methodist in Australia and Fiji, 1900–1950'. In *Creating religious childhoods: Children, young people and Christianity in Anglo-World and British colonial contexts, 1800–1950*, edited by Hugh Morrison and Mary Clare Martin, 103–21. London: Ashgate, 2019.

West, Francis. 'Background to the Fijian riots'. *Australian Quarterly* 32 (1960): 46–53. doi.org/10.2307/20633592.

Whitehead, Clive. *Education in Fiji: Policy, problems and progress in primary and secondary education 1939–1973*. Canberra: Development Studies Centre, Australian National University, 1981.

Whitelaw, James Sutherland. 'People, land and government in Suva, Fiji'. PhD thesis, The Australian National University, 1966.

Wiener, Martin. *An empire on trial: Race, murder, and justice under British Rule, 1870–1935*. Cambridge: Cambridge University Press, 2009. doi.org/10.1017/CBO9780511800665.

Williams, Thomas and James Calvert. *Fiji and the Fijians*. New York: Alexander Heylin, 1860.

Young, Allison. 'World War II archaeology in Fiji: Assessing the material record'. *Nebraska Anthropologist* 170 (2012): 83–84.

Young, J.M.R. *Adventurous spirits: Australian migrant society in pre-cession Fiji*. St Lucia: University of Queensland Press, 1984.

Young, J.M.R., 'Australia's Pacific frontier'. *Australian Historical Studies* 12, no. 47 (1966): 373–88. doi.org/10.1080/10314616608595336.

Young, J.M.R., ed. *Australia's Pacific frontier: Economic and cultural expansion into the Pacific 1795–1885*. Melbourne: Cassell Australia, 1967.

Young, J.M.R. 'Evanescent ascendency: The planter community in Fiji'. In *Pacific Island portraits*, edited by James Wightman Davidson and Deryck Scarr. 147–75. Canberra: ANU Press, 1970.

Appendix 1. Recorded Population of Suva

The following table condenses census data from 1901 to 2017. In 1879 HS Cooper estimated Suva's population to be 200, and in 1888 the Colonial Report estimated the European population of Suva to be 700.[1] Since 1901, the census has changed the categories used to record ethnic data. It has also taken different approaches to distinguish between the town itself and the surrounding rural area.

---

1   HS Cooper, *The islands of the Pacific* (London: R. Bentley and Son, 1888) 206; Great Britain Colonial Office, *Fiji: Annual general report for the year 1888* (London: H.M.S.O., 1888).

Table A1.1: Recorded population of Suva over census years 1901 to 2017.

Census year	Fiji total population	Suva population	Ethnicity						
1901	120,124	4,695	Fijians 701	Indians 1,728	Whites 1,073	Half-castes 176	Polynesians 826	Others 191	
1911	139,541	7,788*	Fijian 1,246	Indian 3,320	European 1,376	Part-European 401	Polynesian 977	Chinese 73	Others 395
1921	157,266	12,982*	Fijian 1,981	Indian 7,246	European 1,753	Part-European 584	Polynesian 452	Chinese 343	Others 506
1936	198,379	15,522*	Fijian 3,471	Indian 7,821	European 1,863	Part-European 933	Polynesian 930	Chinese 494	Others 10
1946	259,638	25,409*	Fijian 6,406	Indian 12,729	European 2,299	Part-European 1,744	Polynesian 730	Chinese 871	Others 630
1956	345,737	37,371*	Fijian 9,758	Indian 19,321	European 3,394	Part-European 2,094	Other Pacific Islanders 731	Chinese 1,647	Rotuman 372	Others 54
1966	476,727	54,157	Fijian 16,305	Indian 27,710	European 3,020	Part-European 2,850	Other Pacific Islanders 878	Chinese 2,340	Rotuman 986	Others 68
1976	588,068	63,628	Fijian 23,031	Indian 29,758	European 2,416	Part-European 2,678	Other Pacific Islanders 1,209	Chinese 2,083	Rotuman 1,929	Others 524
1986	715,375	69,665 (71,608)**	Fijian 27,020 (31,115)	Indian 32,420 (35,467)	European 1,771 (367)	Part-European 2,455 (1,261)	Other Pacific Islanders 1,631 (1,171)	Chinese and part-Chinese 1,966 (622)	Rotuman 2,094 (1,529)	Others 308 (76)

APPENDIX 1

Census year	Fiji total population	Suva population	Ethnicity		
1996	775,077	77,366 (90,609)**	Fijian 38,656 (46,398)	Indian 26,587 (38,813)	Others## 12,123 (5,398)
2007	837,271	74,481 (11,210)#	iTaukei 39,714 (7,625)	Indian 22,478 (2,686)	Others## 12,289 (899)
2017	884,887	93,874	Ethnic data gathered in the 2017 census was not released.		

* Two populations were recorded in 1911, 1921 and 1936 – one for the Suva municipality and one for Suva suburbs. In 1946 an additional category of 'rural' was added. The figures listed here are a combined total. JS Whitelaw notes that there was no definition of what area the suburbs encompassed. In 1952 the boundaries of Suva were extended to include the area that had been called suburbs and rural in former censuses. This expanded the old town council area of one square mile to over eight square miles.[2]

** From 1986 the population of the peri-urban Suva area was counted separately (listed in this table in parentheses).

\# The Greater Suva Urban Area was reclassified and Nasinu was incorporated as a separate subdivision in the 2007 census. This explains the significant population decrease of the peri-urban population.

\#\# In the 1996 and 2007 censuses, ethnic data was collected but the general tables did not specify the ethnic data for Suva.

Source: Census data published by the British Colonial Government from 1901 to 1966 can be found in the National Archives of Fiji. Census data from 1970 onward was sourced from a number of archives, including the National Library of Australia, the University of the South Pacific Library's Pacific Collection and the Fiji Bureau of Statistics' website (www.statsfiji.gov.fj/).

---

2   JS Whitelaw, 'People, land and government in Suva, Fiji' (PhD thesis, The Australian National University, 1966), 63.

Appendix 2. Classification of Communal Units of Suvavou Recorded by Anthropologist Arthur Hocart, c. 1912

Larger group	*Mataqali*	Function	Envoy to	God	*Matabure*
Chief	Rokotuisuva	royal chief		Komaivatanitawake (Cagawalu)	
	Vunivalu	executive chief			
Qali vakavanua (land people)	Tuirara (Nadonumai)	*matanivanua*	Bau, Lami		
	Qiomila	*qasenivale*	Naitāsiri, Navakavu		Narewa
					Navusamata
					Uciwai
					Kanayala
	Nacokaika (Navumata)	*bati*	Vuna	Kuivisiga	
Qali vakawai (sea people)	Vuanimocelolo (Solia)		Burebasaga (Rewa)		
	Bautaci (Nauluvatuiwai)				
	Vatuwaqa			(vatu ni irevo)	
	Naceva			(marama rua)	
	Rasuwai	*mataisau*		Roko Dokidoki	Beranabuka
	Kaiwalu (extinct)	*Daunisuva*			

Source: Arthur Hocart, n.d., *The heart of Fiji*. MS. Turnbull Library, Wellington.

Appendix 3. Classification of Communal Units of Suvavou Recorded by the *Veitarogivanua* in 1902

Yavusa	Mataqali	Function	Matanibure
Nauluvatu	Rokotuisuva (Naicavunidraudrau)	Chief	Rokotuisuva
			Vunivalu
			Narikoso
	Tuirara	Matanivanua	Tamavua
			Vunikura
			Nadonumai
			Nalewenisau
	Qiomila		Nakanaiyala
			Nayavusamata
			Vunarewa
			Niukau
			Naqaiqai
Nayavumata	Nayavumata		Mataiqereqere
			Matasau
			Vuwai
			Naturu
			Burevani

Yavusa	Mataqali	Function	Matanibure
Vatuwaqa (qaliwai)	Vuanimocelolo		Solia
			Navusalevu
	Nasau	Matanivanua	Nasau
			Lomanikaya
	Bautaci		Bautaci
			Nauluvatuiwai
	Vatuwaqa		Bureiqio
			Namalaivo
			Namasira
	Naceva		Naitokoi
	Walu	Mataisau (carpenters)	Navuaniwi
			Tunidau
			Beranabuka
			Daunivuwai
			Daunicakau
			Narewa

Source: A Savenaca Seniloli, letter to the Native Lands Commissioner, 30 January 1919. iTaukei Lands and Fisheries Commission. National Archives of Fiji, Suva.

Note that the above is the 1902 listing, gathered by the Wilkinson Commission, the last native lands enquiry before the final one headed by Maxwell.[1] Seniloli (1919), who was the leading indigenous member of both commissions, comments that, contrary to this report, Nasau and Matasau are independent *mataqali* rather than *matanibure*, and that Beranabuka and Daunivuwai were *mataisau* of Nayavumata, and resided with them in Nairairainiwaqa (sic).[2]

---

1   Peter France, *The charter of the land: Custom and colonization in Fiji* (Melbourne: Oxford University Press, 1969), 139–48.
2   A Savenaca Seniloli, letter to the Native Lands Commissioner, 30 January 1919. iTaukei Lands and Fisheries Commission. National Archives of Fiji, Suva.

Appendix 4. Classification of Communal Units of Suvavou According to Testimony Recorded by the *Veitarogivanua* in 1921

Table A4.1: *Yavusa* Vatuwaqa, *yavutū* Vatuwaqa.

Mataqali	Function	Matanibure
Vuanimocelolo	Chief, 'Taukeinivanua'	Solia
		Navosalevu
		Lomanikaya
Boutaci	Bati (warriors)	Boutaci
		Nauluvatuiwai
Vatuwaqa	Bete (priest)*	Bureiqio
		Namalaivo
		Namasira
Naceva	Sauturaga	Naitokoi
		Valerere
		Vadracoka
Nasau	Matanivanua (herald)	Nasau

Note: * Deleted and altered to 'sauturaga' in a 1990 annotation.
Source: All tables from Amenisitai Waqadau, *Tukutuku Rāraba Vatuwaqa* (Suva: Native Lands Commission, 1921).

Table A4.2: *Yavusa* Nauluvatu, *yavutū* Nauluvatu.

Mataqali	Function	Matanibure
Naicavunidraudrau	Chief 'Vunivalu'	Naicavunidraudrau
Tuirara	Matanivanua (herald)	Tamavua
		Vunikura
		Nadonumai
Naqiōmila		Nakanaiyala
		Narewa
		Niukau
		Naqaiqai
Lenisau	Bete (priest)	Lenisau
Vuaniwī	Mataisau (*yavusa*)	Vuaniwī

Table A4.3: *Yavusa* Nayavumata, *yavutū* Nayavumata, Nacokaikā, Naitāsiri; moved to Tamavua then 'Narairainiwaqa'.

Mataqali	Function	Matanibure
Nayavumata	Chief 'Vunivalu'	Mataiqereqere
		Vuwai
		Vaturu
Matasau	Herald 'matanivanua'	Matasau
Salatu	Bete/priest	
Beranabuka	Mataisau	Beranabuka
Daunivuwa	Mataisau	Daunivuwa

Appendix 5. Classification of Communal Units of Suvavou According to the Final Report of the *Veitarogivanua*

Vanua of Suva. Head of *vanua*: Solomone Kinitavuki.

Table A5.1: *Yavusa* **Vatuwaqa,** *yavutū* **Vatuwaqa.**

Mataqali	Head	Tokatoka	Head
Vuanimocelolo	Solomone Kinitavuki	Solia	Solomone Kinitavuki
		Navusalevu	Liviana Tokalauvere
		Lomanikaya	Extinct
Boutaci	Ilaitia Sabareka	Boutaci	Ilaitia Sabareka
		Nauluvatuiwai	Setareki Cevaca
Vatuwaqa	Uraia Kerekerelevu	Namalaivo	Uraia Kerekerelevu
		Bureiqio	Ana Likuqanisici
		Namasira	Extinct
Naceva	Jone Boa	Naitokoi	Jone Boa
		Valerere	Extinct
		Vadracoka	Extinct
Nasau	Navitalai Navara	Nasau	Navitalai Navara
Daunicakau	Tutaisa Savunawa	Daunicakau	Tutaisa Savunawa
Narewa			Extinct

Source: All tables from Native Lands Commission, *Final report by chairman on the provinces of Tailevu (North), Rewa, Naitasiri and Colo East* (Suva: Native Lands Commission, 1959).

Table A5.2: *Yavusa* Nauluvatu, *yavutū* Nauluvatu.

Mataqali	Head	Tokatoka	Head
Naqiōmila	Samisoni Dakunivosa	Nakanaiyala	Samisoni Dakunivosa
		Nayavusamata	Livai Ratunigaloa
		Vunarewa	Extinct
Tuirara	Mosese Rokotakala	Tamavua	Mosese Rokotakala
		Nadonumai	Timaleti Serevoli
		Vunikura	Extinct
Naicavudraudrau			Extinct
Lewenisau			Extinct
Navuaniwi	Taito Delaivuna		
Tunidau	Maciu Gonevou		

Table A5.3: *Yavusa* Nayavumata, *yavutū* Nayavumata.

Mataqali	Head	Tokatoka	Head
Nayavumata	Seruveveli Dakai	Mataiqereqere	Seruveveli Dakai
		Vuai	Watisoni Rokoravarava
		Naturu	Samuele Ratulevu
		Matasau	Extinct
		Salatu	Extinct
		Beranabuka	Paula Roba
		Daunivuwai	Emori Savutini

Appendix 6. Nursery Rhymes of Fiji

English Version

We're going to Kentucky
We're going to the fair
To see the senorita with
Flowers in her hair;
So shake it shake it baby
Shake it up and down
Shake it like a milkshake
And shake it like a clown;
Roll it to the bottom
And roll it to the top
And turn around and turn around until you make an S-T-O-P
Stop!

Finglish Version

I wanna tucky tucky
A tucky tucky fair
I wanna Cinderella
To see a funny fella
Oh shaky shaky shaky
Shaky to me
Oh runner runner runner
Runner to me oh STOP

www.ingramcontent.com/pod-product-compliance
Lightning Source LLC
Chambersburg PA
CBHW040332300426

44113CB00021B/2732